Personality Psychology Meets Neuroscience

Personality Psychology Meets Neuroscience

Understanding Individual Differences

Compiled from:

Personality Psychology: Foundations and Findings
Marianne Miserandino

Perspectives on Personality Seventh Edition
Charles S. Carver and Michael F. Scheier

Personality, Individual Differences and Intelligence
John Maltby, Liz Day and Ann Macaskill

Theories of Personality: Understanding Persons Fifth Edition
Susan C. Cloninger

Development Through the Lifespan Third Edition
Laura E. Berk

Practical Skills in Biomolecular Sciences Third Edition
Rob Reed, David Holmes, Jonathan Weyers and Allan Jones

Concepts of Genetics Tenth Edition
William S. Klug, Michael R. Cummings, Charlotte A. Spencer and Michael A. Palladino

PEARSON

Harlow, England • London • New York • Boston • San Francisco • Toronto • Sydney • Auckland • Singapore • Hong Kong
Tokyo • Seoul • Taipei • New Delhi • Cape Town • Sao Paulo • Mexico City • Madrid • Amsterdam • Munich • Paris • Milan

Pearson Education Limited
Edinburgh Gate
Harlow
Essex CM20 2JE

And associated companies throughout the world

Visit us on the World Wide Web at:
www.pearson.com/uk

Compiled from:

Personality Psychology: Foundations and Findings
Marianne Miserandino
ISBN 978 0 205 73887 8
© 2012 by Pearson Education, Inc.

Perspectives on Personality Seventh Edition
Charles S. Carver and Michael F. Scheier
ISBN 978 0 205 21968 1
© 2012, 2010, 2008 by Pearson Education, Inc.

Personality, Individual Differences and Intelligence
John Maltby, Liz Day and Ann Macaskill
ISBN 978 0 13 129760 9
© Pearson Education Ltd 2007

Theories of Personality: Understanding Persons Fifth Edition
Susan C. Cloninger
ISBN 978 0 13 243409 6
© 2008, 2004, 2000, 1996 by Pearson Education, Inc., Upper Saddle River, New Jersey, 07458.

Development Through the Lifespan Third Edition
Laura E. Berk
ISBN 978 0 205 40376 9
© 2004, 2001, 1998 by Pearson Education, Inc.

Practical Skills in Biomolecular Sciences Third Edition
Rob Reed, David Holmes, Jonathan Weyers and Allan Jones
ISBN 978 0 13 239115 3
© Addison Wesley Longman Limited 1998
© Pearson Education Limited 2003, 2007

Concepts of Genetics Tenth Edition
William S. Klug, Michael R. Cummings, Charlotte A. Spencer and Michael A. Palladino
ISBN 978 0 321 72412 0
©2012, 2009, 2006 Pearson Education, Inc., publishing as Pearson Benjamin Cummings, 1301 Sansome Street, San Francisco, California 94111.

ISBN 978 1 78376 580 5

Printed by CPI UK

Contents

Winter Term

Summer Term

Winter Term

CHAPTER

1 WHO AM I? UNDERSTANDING THE BUILDING BLOCKS OF PERSONALITY

Read the Chapter on mysearchlab.com

> "Individual results may vary."
> *Advertising disclaimer*

The summer after my first year in high school, my mom and I spent a few weeks exploring the east end of Long Island. I had always loved the ocean growing up and I looked forward to the chance of spending every day at the beach. Until that summer, I thought I knew all about the ocean, having lived on Long Island my entire life—all 14 years of it—to that point. But that summer I learned that there was so much more to the ocean than I realized.

I was completely amazed at how different the ocean was each day. Some days the ocean would be very calm and we could walk out a long, long way before the water was over our heads. Other days, the ocean was too rough for small children to go into, with water over our heads and waves breaking just a few feet from shore. Some days the water would be very warm but then an overnight storm would churn up deep water delivering ice-cold water to the shore the next day. Even the color of the ocean varied from the light green of the sea foam to the dark forest green almost black of the deep water. I spent a lot of time thinking and daydreaming that summer while looking out to sea and it struck me that the ocean almost seemed to have a personality.

The ocean is a pretty good metaphor for personality. Think about it: The ocean is made up of water, but it is much more than that. There are tides, waves, inversions, salt, seaweed, and marine life; it is vast and deep; and it changes regularly. Could we understand the ocean only by studying water molecules? By exploring only its depths and ignoring the shore? Obviously, there are many different aspects of the ocean and scientists devote their lives to studying just a small part of what makes up the ocean. The ocean is all of these parts and yet it is also more than these parts. So it is with personality.

To understand personality, we need to understand what a person is like. Is she extroverted or introverted? Is he easygoing? Is she open to new ideas? Is he responsible? Would he make a good mate? Would she make a good lab partner? We also need to understand our genetics and physiology, which gives us our physical being and building blocks of neurons, hormones, and brain structures that take in and process information and direct our responses to the world. And we need to consider that there may be parts of the person hidden under the surface, much like how the ocean has tides and a myriad of creatures hidden in its depths. We also need to know how a person copes with the storms of life.

Even then, a person is more than these things, more than the sum of his or her parts. How does a person function in the world? How does a person think of himself or herself and interact with others? How do gender, sexual orientation, and other social identities and personal self-concepts affect a person? How does a person fit into the large social world, much like how the ocean is part of the larger ecosystem of the earth, including fish, birds, sky, and land? And finally, how does a person, like the ocean, change over time and yet remain fundamentally the same?

Two early personality psychologists mused that there are aspects of personality that are universal to all people, that are shared by similar people, and that are completely unique to a single individual (Kluckhohn & Murray, 1948).

Consider that all humans, regardless of culture, have a genetic makeup, a brain, a nervous system, and are born into a social group. To the extent that these forces affect human personality, there will be universals in human personality.

Of course, people do vary, but there is often a rhyme and a reason to their variance. At a basic level, there are people who are more likely to venture forth in the world to meet other people. We call such people extroverts. Other people, introverts, prefer to keep to themselves. We would expect people who behave similarly to share similar personality characteristics, whether it be extraversion or introversion, neuroticism or emotional stability, openness or concreteness, agreeableness or grumpiness, conscientiousness or impulsiveness, for example.

Finally, we could say that another human universal is the desire for actualization (i.e., to be who we are meant to be; to develop and express our individual identity). Though we may share the same mechanisms (genetics, physiology, neurology), some of the same characteristics (introversion-extraversion), and have some of the same experiences in the world (attachment to caregivers, sexual adjustment, trauma, happiness), the way these building blocks of personality come together forms a unique individual: you!

Knowing that people do vary, personality psychologists attempt to study both the ways people are similar and the ways people are different from each other.

The whole is greater than the sum of its parts: Just as the small pictures, like the ones on the left, combine to form the picture of the whole person on the right, personality is made up of building blocks.

In this book, I will share with you some of the building blocks of human personality at all levels, from the micro-level of genes on up to the macro- or meta-level of the social world. I hope to help you put these individual elements together and think across and beyond these individual levels to understand personality functioning.

What Is Personality Psychology?

Personality psychology is the scientific study of what makes us who we are. Using the scientific method of investigation, it is the study of individual differences: for identifying ways in which people are both similar and different, and for explaining how they became that way.

Part of personality is identifying and studying the building blocks or raw materials that make us think and act as we do. Consider the illustrations in the photos on the top of this page. Though the figure on the left is made up of smaller images, the figure as a whole is more than the mere sum of individual images. The same is true for personality. Although we can study the individual elements that make up the human personality, the elements come together to create a whole person in a way that is not reducible to its parts. And an individual's personality is more than the sum of his or her parts. Not only can the individual parts vary among people, but the way they fit together may vary as well.

"Whenever two people meet there are six present. There is the man as he sees himself, each as the other person sees him, and each man as he really is."

William James, the father of American psychology

The Building Blocks of Personality

What are these individual parts that come together to create a whole person? Most psychologists would agree that to understand human personality we need to understand traits, genetics, neuroscience, self and identity, intrapsychic aspects, regulation and motivation, and cognition. Missing from this list are social and environmental forces that impact human personality at all of these levels. For example, environmental forces—including culture, society, and socialization by parents and peers—have a huge impact on our personalities. The impact of the social environment is felt at multiple levels, from our sense of self and identity to the level of our genetics. Rather than viewing social influences as a separate building block, the impact of societal forces runs as a theme throughout all of the foundations. Let's take a closer look at the building blocks of personality.

SEE FOR YOURSELF

How would you describe yourself? The words that come most readily to mind are often trait terms.

Traits. How do we go about describing human personality and identifying important personality characteristics? The answer is **traits:** a person's typical way of thinking, feeling, and acting, in various situations, at different times. We may be born with a certain physiology that makes us more likely to develop certain characteristics, but there are many other characteristics that we can develop from our socialization (from parents, peers, teachers, society), and from our personal experiences. These traits will be consistent across our lives and will be expressed in all sorts of ways, as you will see in later chapters, from how we shake hands, to the kind of music we prefer, to even how we decorate our living spaces and the careers we choose.

THINK ABOUT IT

What does it mean to say we inherit "potentialities"?

Genetics. Personality starts with our genetic makeup that we have inherited from each of our birth parents. Over millennia, evolutionary forces have selected behaviors that improve the survival of the species or survival of an individual and an individual's close genetic relatives (Confer et al., 2010). **Genetics** is the study of how genes and environment affect personality and behavior. We know that even though many personality variables have a genetic component, *every one of them* has an environmental component as well. As we shall see in Chapter 6, nature and nurture work together to make us who we are. Whereas we may inherit specific personality characteristics, we also inherit potentialities that may be expressed in our personalities depending on the environment.

Neuroscience. Our genes encode our physical bodies, including our brain and nervous system. **Neuroscience** is the study of how our brain and nervous system affect personality and behavior through the study of bodily responses, brain structure, brain activity, and biochemical activity. Some of this research suggests that extroversion, neuroticism, and impulsivity are related to physiological and neurological differences which may be present at birth, or develop soon thereafter. Though the environment and our personal experiences can still impact how these characteristics develop, the current evidence suggests that part of who we are—at least in terms of these three characteristics—is built into us by our neurology.

THINK ABOUT IT

Are you born with a self or does a self develop?

Self and Identity. **Self and Identity** encompasses our own sense of who we are including our self-concept, self-esteem, and social identity. One of the hallmarks of being human is the ability to reflect on ourselves. We have a sense of who we are: our self-concept. And we have an opinion about that: our self-esteem. We may even try to present ourselves in a certain way to others, or we may embrace what others think about us, taking on a social identity. Where scientists once thought that self-reflection was unique to humans, we now know that a few other species share this capacity including dolphins and chimpanzees. Part of what makes up our personality, in addition to our traits, is our sense of self and social identity.

Intrapsychic Foundations of Personality. With this sense of self, we can look within ourselves (*intra*) to our own conscious and unconscious thoughts and feelings (*psychic*) that also make up our personality (**intrapsychic**). No doubt you've heard of Sigmund Freud, who established an entire theory about our unconscious motivations and the defenses we use to protect ourselves from threatening thoughts and desires.

"If a man has been his mother's undisputed darling he retains throughout life the triumphant feeling, the confidence in success, which not seldom brings actual success along with it."
Sigmund Freud

One of Freud's biggest contributions to psychology was the realization that physical disorders could have psychological causes, which were often unconscious. He also claimed that our early experiences left an indelible, but unconscious, imprint on our adult personalities. At the same time, Freud was one of the first to suggest that personality could be changed, and he originated a method of psychotherapy to do so. Since Freud's day, science has discounted some aspects of his theory, even as it has supported others (Westen, 1998a). Today, a complete understanding of personality must also take into account our unconscious motivations, including our defense mechanisms and important attachments, starting with our caregivers and continuing with our intimate relationships.

Regulation and Motivation: Self-Determination Theory. Although Freud believed that people were controlled by unconscious forces, a modern theory of motivation suggests that people can—and do!—regulate themselves consciously and unconsciously. According to self-determination theory (Deci & Ryan, 1985; Ryan & Deci, 2008), when people feel free to choose, are competent at what they do, and are connected to people around them, they will be motivated and self-directed for the task at hand. People differ in the extent to which they feel self-determined and regulate their own motivation. The building block of **regulation and motivation** is concerned with how people adjust their responses to the environment, both consciously and unconsciously.

Cognitive Foundations. Finally, people differ in how they process information, especially about the causes and impacts of events in their lives, and expectations for what may happen in the future. Specifically, there are individual differences in locus of control, learned helplessness, learned hopelessness, and optimism-pessimism. The **Cognitive foundation** describes how people perceive and think about information about themselves and the world.

Putting It All Together: Integration

Finally, in **Integration** we combine the building blocks of personality into a whole person. When it comes to personality, the whole is greater than the mere sum of the parts. Consider your own personality. You are equipped with a specific package of genes that have provided a certain type of physiological reactivity and brain function, which, along with life experiences have led you to develop a package of character traits. You are able to reflect on who you are, and who the world wants you to be. You may also be vaguely aware of hidden motives and desires, such as whom you feel emotional attachments to. You may also be enthusiastically engaged in certain activities and bored or disengaged from others. You may face the world with optimism (or pessimism), believing that you have an impact on what befalls you (or not!). Is knowing all of this about you enough to say that we really *know* you?

For the most part, all of these topics stand alone. That is, we can understand any one of them without thinking a whole lot about the others (indeed, your instructor might take these chapters in a different order or omit some of them altogether). However, some of the most interesting aspects of the human experience can be understood only by seeing how these blocks build on each other and interact.

THINK ABOUT IT

Do men and women have different personalities? Are these differences inborn or learned?

Take gender, for example. How much of our gender is genetic or physiological and how much of it is learned or socialized? Is gender identity grounded in our thoughts, beliefs, and cognitions? What impact do our society's beliefs about gender have on us? Do men and women have different personalities? To answer these questions, we need an understanding of genetics, physiology, self, and cognitions. The picture is even more complicated—and fascinating—when it comes to understanding whom we are attracted to. Genetics and neurology interact with cognitions, attachments, and motivations, to determine our sexual orientation.

Or, consider how people cope with stress. Are there differences in physiology that make some people hardier and more resilient to stress? Or is handling stress more an issue of mind over matter? Are some types of people better able to cope with stress and tragedy? To answer these questions, we need to build on our understanding of neurology, cognitions, and personality traits.

Who am I? Am I more than the sum of my genetics, neurology, traits, self and identity, intrapsychic motivations, attachments, and cognitions?

Organization of This Book

This book organizes these seven building blocks of personality into five parts, each revolving around a question, and includes a special section on putting it all together:

- *Part I: The Dispositional Foundations of Personality—Who Do You Say That I Am?* In this section, we consider the theories behind personality traits, the practical way traits are expressed in many aspects of our lives, and how best to measure personality. We also take a look at how people reflect on themselves. After reading this section, you will understand how psychologists describe human personality and also how people describe themselves as reflected in their own self-concepts, self-esteem, and social identities. This section includes four chapters: Chapter 2, Personality Traits: A Good Theory; Chapter 3, Personality Traits: Practical Matters; Chapter 4, Personality Assessment; and Chapter 5, Self and Identity.
- *Part II: The Biological Foundations of Personality—What Makes You* You*?* Here, we focus on how your unique genetic blueprint impacts your personality. In addition, we look at how your unique brain and physiology impact your personality. Together, these chapters describe the biological foundations of personality. The section includes Chapter 6, Genetics, and Chapter 7, The Neuroscience of Personality.
- *Part III: The Intrapsychic, Regulation, and Motivational Foundations of Personality—Who Do You Feel You Are?* Personality psychologists study aspects of our personality at a deep-down, almost gut level that we may not even be aware of. Sigmund Freud was the first, but by no means the last, to theorize that unconscious processes have a big impact on who we are. This section looks at Freudian theory as well as more modern theories of how unconscious processes such as our motivations, desires, and emotional attachments makes us who we are. This section includes two chapters: Chapter 8, Intrapsychic Foundations of Personality, and Chapter 9, Regulation and Motivation: Self-Determination Theory.
- *Part IV: The Cognitive Foundations of Personality—Who Do You Think You Are?* The philosopher René Descartes famously remarked, "I think therefore I am" and psychologists working in this area couldn't agree more. The specific thoughts we have—like the belief that we control what happens to us or whether we are helpless—make us who we are. Knowing what people think they are, like optimists or pessimists for example, tells us a lot, not just about their personalities, but also about their health and well-being and other important life outcomes. This section includes Chapter 10, Cognitive Foundations of Personality.
- *Part V: Integration Across the Building Blocks of Personality—Is the Whole Person Greater Than the Sum of His or Her Parts?* Finally, having a sense of what makes up the human personality, we need to consider how the individual foundations fit together to make a whole person. In the case of personality, the whole is definitely greater than the sum of its parts. That is, to understand the impact of gender and sexual orientation on personality, we need to consider multiple building blocks at the same time. In fact, if you want to know how an individual person functions in the world, adapting to both good times and bad, and in sickness and health, it would take a consideration of all of the building blocks to understand the resilience of the human spirit. This section includes Chapter 11, Gender and Personality; Chapter 12, Sexual Orientation: An Integrative Mini-Chapter; and Chapter 13, Resilience: An Integrative Mini-Chapter.

As we work our way through the building blocks of personality, you will see how personality psychology has attempted to answer these eternal questions using research. I should warn you right now: In the attempt to answer these questions researchers have discovered—more questions! Instead of definitive answers, think of this book as presenting more of the state-of-the-science on these questions.

How Do Psychologists Study Personality?

You might wonder what the difference is between personality psychologists and you sitting around with friends making guesses about the personality of people you see at a party. In a word: research. Research allows us to formulate and test questions about human behavior, to design accurate methods to answer these questions, and to test competing explanations against one another (Dunn, 1999). By conducting research using sound methods, scientists are able to generalize beyond their own findings and add to the collective knowledge about a given phenomenon and, in many cases, apply their results to make the world a better place for individuals and whole societies (Dunn, 1999).

SEE FOR YOURSELF

What do you think causes people to act the way they do? Where do you believe personality comes from?

The Scientific Method

Research rests on the philosophy of empiricism: using direct experience to draw conclusions about the world. Psychological research relies on the **scientific method** which describes how to make and test observations about the world in order to draw conclusions while minimizing error or bias (Dunn, 1999). The scientific method starts with the identification of basic facts about the world. Then, using this collection of facts, scientists build theories. For example, while people watching at a party we might recognize that there are similarities and differences in how people behave, such as how some people laugh more than others. Then, using these facts as a basis, we can reason what other ideas are likely to be true. We might start to notice that people who laugh a lot like to hang out with other people. Is this true? We could do some more controlled observations of people to test our theory. Theories help scientists ask new questions and suggest where to look for answers and what kinds of answers they might find.

THINK ABOUT IT

How do common sense, anecdotal evidence, personal experience, the opinion of experts, and research differ?

Then scientists make predictions and test predictions based on their theories using controlled methods. For example, you might devise an experiment for these laughing partygoers to see if people who laugh respond differently to the experiment than the nonlaughers, or you might administer a series of personality questionnaires to them and see if the laughers all share a common personality trait which is different from the nonlaughers.

Finally, scientists make their results public by publishing them in journals, on the Internet, or by presenting their results at conferences. They do this to seek out independent verification from other researchers. For example, after the party you might do some investigation using a psychological database such as PsycArticles and read about a study that was conducted by other researchers that also found that people behave differently at a party and identified two kinds of people: extroverts and introverts.

Personality hasn't always embraced the experimental method as much as other branches of psychology have (Cronbach, 1957; Eysenck, 1997), but over the last decade or so there has been a tremendous explosion in experimental personality psychology (John et al., 2008). Science progresses along a continuum from casual observations, which may inspire a hunch or guess about human behavior, to controlled experimentation, in which researchers attempt to prove a theory false (Eysenck, 1997; see Figure 1.1). As long as

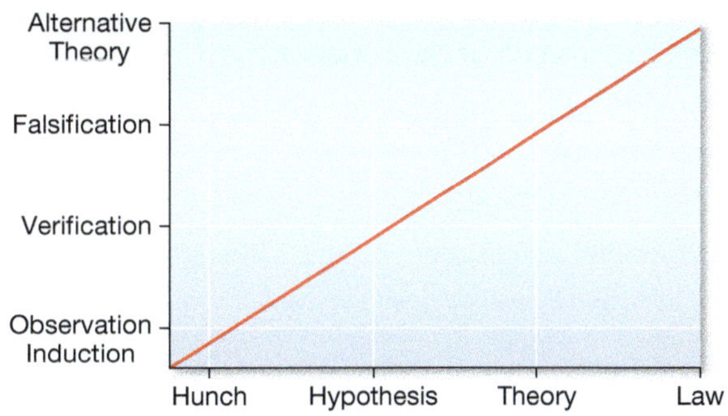

Figure 1.1 Science progresses along a continuum, with methods that become more sophisticated as hunches turn into theory and laws. *Source:* Eysenck (1997, Figure 1, p. 1225). Eysenck, H. J. (1997). Personality and experimental psychology. *Journal of Personality and Social Psychology, 73*(6), 1224–1237.

research evidence supports a theory, that theory will prevail and with more research will reach the status of a law until it is overthrown by an alternative theory that explains the evidence even better. For the most part, personality psychology has many theories, but unfortunately, very few (if any!) actual laws of human behavior.

Observational Studies and Personality Questionnaires

SEE FOR YOURSELF

Think about how extroverts may differ from introverts. How would you test your ideas to see if your hypotheses are correct?

Personality psychologists, like other researchers in psychology, draw on many kinds of methods to explore the human personality (Robins, Fraley, & Krueger, 2007; see Table 1.1). The methods researchers use depend on the kind of questions they are asking. For example, researchers might use an **observational study**, where they observe what people do, to understand a certain phenomenon such as: Do some people talk more than others at a party? Then, based on these observations researchers might make an educated guess or generate a **hypothesis** to explain their findings. Continuing our example, one researcher might hypothesize that extroverted people talk more than introverted people. He might give partygoers a self-report personality questionnaire to see if, indeed, extroverts are doing more of the talking at a party than the introverts are. **Personality questionnaires** are tests in which people answer questions about themselves that identify certain aspects of their personality, like how talkative, outgoing, and sociable they are, all typical traits of an extrovert. Another researcher might hypothesize that extroverts circulate more than introverts. She might give out a personality questionnaire and link people's answers to her observations of how many people each guest talks to and how long each interaction lasts.

Another researcher might present each person with an ambiguous picture and ask him or her to tell a story, administering a projective personality test. Yet another researcher

Table 1.1 Methods and Measures Used in Personality Research

Type of Measure	Mean Frequency	% Ever Used
Self-report scales and questionnaires	6.17	100%
Judgments of self and others	5.07	99
Informant reports	3.68	86
Behavioral observation	3.58	89
Structured interviews	3.15	76
Behavioral responses	3.11	81
Other judgments tasks (e.g., of stimuli)	3.10	79
Narrative/open-ended questionnaires	3.03	74
Reaction time	2.93	61
Experience sampling	2.89	65
Implicit measures	2.76	64
Memory tasks	2.52	62
Autonomic arousal	2.22	57
Judgments of groups/nations/cultures	2.19	43
Hormone levels	1.94	36
Neuroimaging (fMRI, etc.)	1.75	32
Molecular genetics/DNA testing	1.60	26

Note: Prominent personality psychologists ($N = 72$) were asked to rate how often they used each of 17 assessment methods using a scale ranging from 1 (*Not at all*) to 7 (*Very much*), with 4 (*Somewhat*) at the middle. The third column lists the percentage of researchers who have ever used the method in their work.

Source: Robins, Tracy, and Sherman (2007, Table 37.1, p. 676). From R. W. Robins, R. C. Fraley, & R. F. Krueger, eds., *Handbook of Research Methods in Personality Psychology.*

could ask guests about their past behavior or the behavior of their parents or siblings. Still another researcher might go so far as to compare the heart rate, hormone levels, or the brain activity of extroverts and introverts to see if differences in their behavior are due to underlying physiological or neurological differences between them. Another researcher might wonder if women are more talkative than men, and if so, how large, on average, is this difference?

Correlational and Experimental Designs

If researchers want to know more about *why* extroverts talk more, this will require different kinds of research. For example, one researcher may want to interview each person at the party or interview their friends, either using set structured questions for each person or by having each person merely tell his or her own story. Analyzing this kind of qualitative data requires different methods than rating scales or questionnaires (see Chapter 5 for more about these methods). Sigmund Freud, the founder of psychoanalysis, built much of his theory on case studies of his patients (we discuss how to conduct a case study when we discuss Freud in Chapter 8).

Still another researcher might investigate whether extroversion and introversion runs in families using a family study. She might even study twins who were separated at birth and adopted by different families to gauge the relative contribution of genetics and environment on extroversion-introversion. She might hypothesize that if extraversion runs in families, then people ought to resemble their birth parents more than their adoptive parents or their twins more than their nontwin siblings.

How do we gauge similarity between children and their parents or between twins? Enter the **correlation coefficient**, indicated by the symbol r. A correlation coefficient does just that: It measures the relationship, or *co-relation,* between two variables. Correlations can be positive or negative, depending on the type of relationship the two variables in question have. If two variables increase or decrease at the same time, then they are positively correlated. For example, softball skill and hits at bat are *positively correlated:* Better batters hit the ball more than weaker batters. However, if one variable increases as the other one decreases—or vice versa, decreasing as the other one increases—then the two variables are *negatively correlated.* Golf skill and golf scores are negatively correlated: Better players have *lower* scores.

By convention, correlations are considered high, medium, or low depending on how big they are (see Table 1.2). These numbers should be taken only as a rough guideline, as the size of a correlation doesn't tell us if the relationship is statistically significant, and not merely a fluke. For that, we need to know the sample size and some other information about the sample, so researchers generally report the significance level of any correlations they calculate.

When two variables are related, there are always at least three possible explanations for the findings. First, it's possible that the first variable causes the second. Second, it's possible that the second variable causes the first one. Finally, it's also possible that some third variable causes both of the variables. Because we can't be sure what is causing the relationship we see between two variables we must keep in mind that *correlation* is not the same as *causation.* Knowing that two variables are similar doesn't tell us about *why* they are similar.

Table 1.2 Interpreting Correlations

Negative Correlations	Size	Positive Correlations
.0 to −.3	Small	.0 to .3
−.3 to −.5	Medium	.3 to .5
−.5 to −.9	Large	.5 to .9

Source: From Cohen (1988).

Although a family study would yield some possible answers as to why extroverts talk more (e.g., "It's in their genes" or "They come from a very sociable family"), it wouldn't isolate a specific cause of the talkative behavior that we have observed. To test the theory that one variable *causes* another variable, scientists need to conduct a true experiment (described in the next section). When this is not possible either due to practical or ethical reasons, researchers use correlational studies. In **correlational studies** researchers generally don't manipulate variables, but instead measure two variables to see how they are related.

In personality psychology, in particular, when we want to study how a person with a certain personality behaves, we use a correlational study to measure both personality and behavior. For example, we might give people a personality questionnaire that measures their level of extroversion. Extroverts would score high on this questionnaire whereas introverts would score low. Later, we can see how introverts and extroverts interact with strangers, or differ in physiological arousal, or any other measure that we think would show a difference based on personality. Similarly, we could measure a person's typical level of anxiety and see how he or she reacts to a pop quiz. We would expect people high in anxiety to perform worse than people low in anxiety.

Many studies on the genetics or neuroscience of personality use correlational designs, such as twin or adoption studies. Indeed, when researchers can't manipulate the variable they want to study, they conduct their studies in the "real world" using field studies and natural manipulations, such as studying people coping with job loss, ill health, or natural tragedies, or war (see Chapter 10 for more on these methods). When correlational studies are well designed, replicated, and combined with other kinds of evidence, they are nearly as good as a true experiment in identifying the causes of outcomes (Aronson et al., 1990).

Research Methods Illustrated: A True Experiment

There are many different methods that psychologists use to study human personality and behavior (Revelle, 2007). Researchers could merely observe behavior or they might measure a personality characteristic or they might place people in a controlled situation and see how they react. This latter method, of placing people in a carefully controlled situation and measuring their responses, is called an *experiment*.

In a typical experiment, researchers decide what variable they wish to study. Researchers then design at least two conditions which differ in this variable. In one condition, called the **experimental condition**, participants experience one treatment. In the other, **control condition**, participants experience a different treatment or no treatment at all. Researchers will go to great lengths to ensure that the entire experimental procedure is exactly alike for all participants except for this one difference in the variable being studied.

Then, researchers must use **random assignment** to assign participants to one condition or the other. Random assignment means that every participant in the experiment has an equal chance of experiencing each of the conditions. In the case of two groups, the researcher might flip a coin to decide which treatment a participant will receive.

By having **experimental control**, where all aspects of the experiment are the same except for the variable being studied, and random assignment, where participants have an equal chance of being in any condition, researchers are able to conclude that a difference in reactions of participants must have been due to the variable that was manipulated. This is the logic of a **true experiment** which allows researchers to conclude that what they manipulated *caused* a difference in the outcome they measured (Aronson et al., 1990).

By manipulating one variable, researchers look to see if there was a difference in some response of the participants, which they measure. The variable that researchers manipulate is called the **independent variable** because it is independent of participants' responses. The variable that the researchers measure, the responses of the participants, is called the **dependent variable** because it depends on participants' responses. In fact, many experiments are aptly titled "The effect of _____ on _____" to help readers identify the independent variable (the first blank) and the dependent variable (the second blank) right away.

For example, suppose researchers wanted to see if some cognitive strategies for coping with failure were more effective than others. They might randomly assign participants to one of two treatment conditions: Effective Strategies or Ineffective Strategies. Then, after they learned and practiced these strategies, the researchers could measure how angry, anxious, disappointed, unhappy, and sad they felt afterward. In this experiment, the independent variable, what the researchers manipulated, is type of strategy. The dependent variable, what the researchers measured, is emotion.

If there is a difference in participants' emotions after the experimental treatment, and if the researchers successfully controlled *all other* differences between the groups, then we can conclude that the difference in emotions at the end of the experiment must be due to the treatment during the experiment.

When it comes to research in personality, there are a lot of variables that we cannot manipulate because it is impossible, impractical, or unethical to do so. For example, there is no way to randomly assign people to a certain personality type, like being an extrovert or an introvert. Similarly, it would be wrong to manipulate self-esteem in an experiment by making people in one condition feel bad about themselves. In these cases, researchers either use correlational designs or else researchers see if their manipulation has a different effect on people depending on their personality (Brewer, 2000; Revelle, 2007; Smith, 2000).

SEE FOR YOURSELF

Take a recent negative occurrence and see if you can think about it in a different way using ideas from the Effective Strategies condition. Does changing your thinking help you feel any better about the event?

This experiment on cognitive strategies for coping with failure was actually part of a more detailed experiment studying the effect of cognitive strategies and personality on emotions after failure (Ng & Diener, 2009). Participants imagined that they failed to get into any of the eight graduate programs to which they had supposedly applied. The researchers manipulated coping strategy, just as described, by randomly assigning all participants to an Effective Strategies condition or an Ineffective Strategies condition.

In the Effective Strategies condition, participants were instructed to reinterpret their failure to see it in a more positive light, to see if they could find something positive in the experience, and to reflect on how they might be able to grow as a person as a result of the event. They were also instructed to think about how they might do something to change or to improve the situation. Participants in the Ineffective Strategies condition were instructed to focus on how upset they were, to admit that they could not deal with what happened, and to think that they should just give up and stop trying to reach their goal of entering graduate school.

The researchers also took into account the personality of the participants by identifying them as being high or low in **Neuroticism**, a personality trait that describes how anxious and vulnerable to negative emotions a person is. Notice that the researchers are unable to randomly assign people to be high or low in Neuroticism, because it is a personality trait. Instead, they merely measured this variable and then assigned people high or low on Neuroticism to conditions, ensuring an equal number of people of both types in each condition.

"There are two possible outcomes: If the result confirms the hypothesis, then you've made a measurement. If the result is contrary to the hypothesis, then you've made a discovery."
Enrico Fermi

Finally, they measured how angry, anxious, disappointed, unhappy, and sad they felt afterward, combining these responses into one composite variable of negative emotion. The design of this experiment is a 2 (Coping Strategy) by 2 (Neuroticism) design. There are two **levels**, or groups, within each independent variable: Effective and Ineffective Coping Strategies and High and Low Neuroticism. Note that only one of these variables, Coping Strategy, was actually under experimental control, that is, actually manipulated by the experimenters.

The true experiment, where participants are randomly assigned to treatment conditions, is one of many methods personality psychologists use to study individuals.

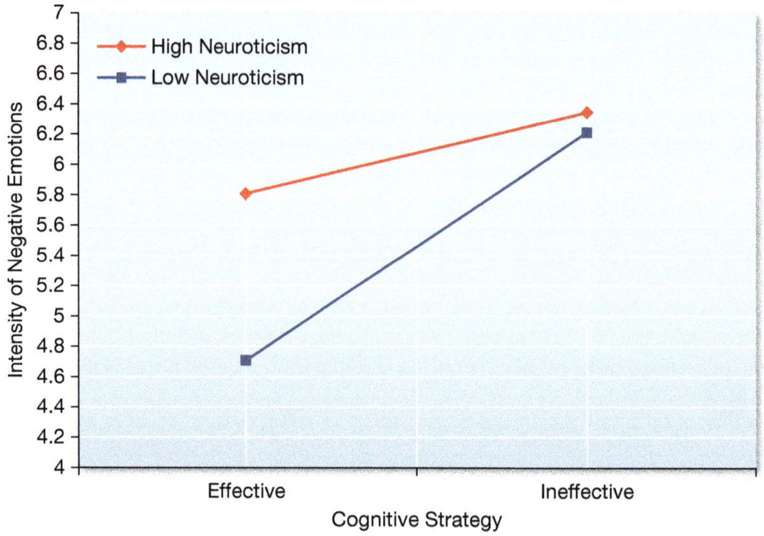

Figure 1.2 Negative emotions experienced by people high and low in Neuroticism who were instructed to use effective or ineffective cognitive strategies to cope with a hypothetical negative event. *Source*: Ng & Diener (2009, Figure 3, p. 459). Reprinted with permission from, "Feeling bad? The "power" of positive thinking may not apply to everyone," by Ng, W., & Diener, E. (2009), *Journal of Research in Personality*, 43, 455–463. Permission conveyed through the Copyright Clearance Center.

What did they discover? First, there was a main effect for condition, meaning that the condition that participants were in affected how much negative emotion they reported at the end of the experiment. Participants in the Ineffective Strategies condition reported more negative emotion than participants in the Effective Strategies condition. Second, there was also a main effect for personality, meaning that participants' levels of Neuroticism affected how much negative emotion they reported at the end of the experiment. People high in Neuroticism reported more negative emotion than people low in Neuroticism.

Finally, there was a significant *interaction* between condition and Neuroticism. Whenever we find a significant interaction, it means that one of the main effects is different depending on the level of the other variable. Interaction effects are easiest to see in a graph. Lines that are not parallel to each other suggest an interaction between variables (see Figure 1.2).

Here, the significant interaction between Coping Strategy and Neuroticism suggests that Effective Strategies were effective only for people low in Neuroticism. People low in Neuroticism who used Effective Strategies felt less negative emotions than people low in Neuroticism who used Ineffective Strategies. Essentially, using ineffective strategies made people low in Neuroticism feel like people high in Neuroticism. The conclusion from these results is that the effect of strategy depends on personality, or, as the researchers caution, the power of positive thinking may not work for everyone—it depends on your personality (Ng & Diener, 2009).

Why might be this be the case? Although this is a very good question, it was not the question the researchers sought to answer in this experiment. This question will have to wait for another experiment—or material we shall cover in the chapters ahead!

Types of Data and Personality Assessment

As you can see, there are many ways of answering the seemingly simple question of "Why do some people talk more at a party?" The most accurate answers come from using principles of good research design. As a general rule, we can put more faith in results that come from more than just one study or more than just one method. Even when studying just a single person—that cute, outgoing partygoer telling a joke to a small crowd of admirers—there are many kinds of data we can gather (John & Soto, 2007). We can collect **self-report data** (e.g., questionnaires, interviews), **observation data** from friends or trained observers, **test**

data (e.g., see how they behave in a controlled situation like the laboratory), or even **life data** (e.g., count how many times a person's photo appeared in his or her yearbook or how many campus organizations he or she belongs to). We explore these various kinds of data in more depth in Chapter 3.

Of course, a study is only as good as the instruments that a researcher uses. Even a seemingly straightforward personality test is backed by previous experimentation to assure that the questions are understandable and clear, that responders are giving sincere answers (as opposed to answering in bogus or unreliable ways), and that the results of such assessments are valid, reliable, and useful (Smith & Archer, 2008). How can a researcher be sure he or she is using the very best measurements in studies? This topic is so important to personality psychology that we spend an entire chapter discussing the common types of personality tests, the uses of personality tests, and what makes a good personality test, including reliability, validity, generalizability, and response sets.

"If the only tool you have is a hammer, you tend to see every problem as a nail."
Abraham Maslow

Scientists have a number of tools or methods at their disposal. And like a good carpenter, who chooses the right tool depending on the job at hand, personality psychologists use whatever tool is most appropriate for answering the question they wish to explore. As you learn about each of the building blocks of personality, you will also learn about one of the various methods personality psychologists have used to explore the human personality. Sometimes it is easier to understand a particular method when you can see how it is used by personality psychologists to answer a specific question or to test a specific theory.

The logic of the true experiment requires researchers to control all aspects of the laboratory environment even determining what participants in an experiment will be facing! As you can see, this is an awesome responsibility and one not to be taken lightly. Researchers must adhere to stringent ethical principles and guidelines set out by the American Psychological Association (American Psychological Association, 2002, 2010). These guidelines were put in place to ensure the safety, trust, and welfare of research participants. Let us now turn to a discussion of research ethics.

Then and Now: The Ethics of Research With People

One day in 2004, Paula's world suddenly changed forever. Though she knew she was adopted, the stranger on the other end of the phone gave her the news: You have an identical twin. Identical *strangers* is how Paula and Elyse came to refer to themselves (Schein & Bernstein, 2008). The women discovered that they were both interested in film, had lived in Paris, and were vulnerable to bouts of depression. But what truly disturbed them, is that they and their families, along with five other pairs of identical twins and one set of identical triplets, were unwitting participants in a strange study. The head psychiatrist at the adoption agency *purposely* separated identical twins. But not all identical twins were separated, only those who were born of mothers with a history of disorders like schizophrenia and bipolar disorder. He used the identical twins to conduct his own study of the impact of genetics and environment on

Identical twins Paula Bernstein and Elyse Schein didn't find out until they were adults that they had an identical twin and were unwitting participants in an unethical study in which identical twins who were put up for adoption were purposely separated at birth and adopted by separate families.

the development of mental illnesses, and did so without the knowledge and consent of the birth mothers and the adoptive families. Families thought that the kindly doctor who made regular visits was merely making sure that the children were adjusting well to their adoptive families.

Many adoptive parents said that they would have gladly adopted their child and their child's twin had they known. Many twins were understandably upset to discover—often well into their adult lives—that certain illnesses ran in their biological families, important information that was purposely kept from them and their adoptive families. Finally, although taken from their birth mothers right away, the twins were raised in foster care and not separated from each other until they were 6 to 9 months of age. Many twins reported growing up with a permanent sense of loss or the fantasy that they had a secret twin (Schein & Bernstein, 2008).

Elyse and Paula, like the other participants in this study, were outraged. Because of the pain the study caused and would continue to cause as participants discovered the true circumstances of their birth and adoption, a court order has sealed the documents describing the study and its results until 2066 (Schein & Bernstein, 2008). With horror, the more the facts of their birth came to light, the more their situation reminded Elyse and Paula of the experiments by the Nazi doctor Josef Mengele who conducted inhumane experiments on prisoners in the concentration camps (Lifton, 1986).

Sadly, this study is not the only incident in the history of unethical research that includes the Tuskegee Syphilis study (Reverby, 2009), in which impoverished African American sharecroppers were purposely given syphilis and prevented from obtaining treatment; the Nazi doctors (Lifton, 1986); and studies done on people in prisons, mental hospitals, and orphanages without their consent and often with coercion. Could this twin study be conducted today? The scientific community, including the American Psychological Association (American Psychological Association, 2002, 2010), along with many governments, including the United States (Department of Health and Human Services, 1979), have all agreed to standards of ethical conduct for research with human subjects that protect human participants and prevent studies like these from ever being conducted.

THINK ABOUT IT

Does your school have a requirement that students in introductory psychology classes participate in research studies? Is this ethical?

According to the Belmont Report (Department of Health and Human Services, 1979), research with humans must adhere to three principles: respect for persons, beneficence, and justice. The principle of **respect for persons** includes allowing people to choose for themselves whether they wish to participate or not, by giving their consent after they have been informed

Participants from the Tuskegee Study: From 1932 to public outcry in 1972, the U.S. government carried out an unethical study observing the natural progression of syphilis in humans. The study continued even after penicillin was discovered to be a cure for syphilis in the 1940s.

about the procedures and possible risks of the study. This is called **informed consent.** It also states that the researcher must give extra protection to people who have limited autonomy, or limited physical or mental capacity to give their informed consent.

For example, people who are in jail have limited autonomy and cannot be used for research without extra efforts to ensure that they understand that their participation will not impact their release in any way. Similarly, employees must be assured that their participation will not affect their employment status or their work evaluation. Also, students must be assured that their grades will not be affected by their willingness to participate in a research project or not. Children and people with certain disorders may lack the maturity or the cognitive capacity to evaluate the risks and benefits of participation for themselves, and so parents or legal guardians must give consent for them.

The principle of **beneficence** states that first, and foremost, researchers should do no harm to their participants. This includes using the best research methods and materials, having trained personnel interact with research participants, and minimizing possible harm and maximizing possible benefits of research participation.

Finally, the principle of **justice** suggests that the benefits and the burdens of research participants must be shared equitably among potential research populations. At a basic level, this means that researchers must treat all participants fairly and equally, avoiding samples of convenience, exploitation of vulnerable populations, and by not involving persons from groups unlikely to benefit from the research. For example, researchers should be sure to represent both genders and various ethnic groups in research that would potentially affect them. The principle of justice also states that if research supported by public funds leads to a therapeutic treatment, for example, that treatment must be available to all, not just to those who can afford it.

Justice also suggests that participants should receive some benefit or value for being in the study, either something direct and concrete (e.g., learning experience, monetary reward, treatment for an ailment under study) or more general for society (e.g., understanding personality or finding a cure for cancer).

The Belmont report also led to the **Common Rule** which was adopted by all federal agencies including the National Institutes of Health (NIH) and the National Institute of Mental Health (NIMH), and which is also the rule at all universities, schools, hospitals, and other places where research is conducted. The Common Rule mandates that institutions that conduct research must establish and maintain an **institutional review board (IRB)** to review all research to ensure that it upholds these standards. These boards must include researchers, an ethicist, and members of the community who discuss all research proposals, often making suggestions to ensure that participants' rights are protected. The Common Rule establishes procedures for obtaining informed consent from potential research participants and for explaining all experimental procedures (see Mills, 1976, for an example).

SEE FOR YOURSELF

Does your school have an IRB to review research conducted at your school?

If you have the opportunity to conduct research, you will need to submit a proposal to your school's IRB. Though the questions asked by the IRB on their forms may seem unrelated to research, you can readily see that the questions are all meant to ensure that the principles of respect for persons, beneficence, and justice have all been considered and protected (see Figure 1.3).

Researchers who violate ethical principles face censure from their institution's IRB, as well as from their professional societies, like the American Psychological Association, and from the federal government. Due to these principles and guidelines, it is unlikely that experiments like the twin study could be conducted today. Good researchers must always consider the rights and welfare of their participants in the design and planning of their research studies.

ARCADIA UNIVERSITY IRB Face Sheet

1. Administration of questionnaires, personality tests, quality of life assessments or other surveys? **IF YES,** ☐ Name and reference of questionnaire provided? ☐ Copy of questionnaire attached?	☐ Yes ☐ No
2. Are there any questions of a sensitive nature (e.g., drug/alcohol use/abuse, sexual behavior, sexual orientation)?	☐ Yes ☐ No
3. Does the research proposal involve the use and disclosure of research subject's medical record information for research purposes? 3a. **IF YES**, please check the box next to one of the following that is provided with this submission: ☐ Separate authorization for use and disclosure of identifiable health information. ☐ Modified research informed consent document that incorporates HIPAA requirements.	☐ Yes ☐ No
4. Are you performing a campus-wide survey of Arcadia faculty, staff and/or students? **IF YES,** attach copy of approval from Committee on Institutional Effectiveness	☐ Yes ☐ No
5. Do you or any member of your research group, spouses or any dependent children have any interest (i.e. any property of financial interest including stock in the sponsor company, patents, trademarks, copyrights or licensing, supplemental research grants or consulting arrangements) in the test drug/product, device or research procedure that is the subject of this study? **5a. IF YES, please complete a Conflict of Interest Disclosure Form available through the Arcadia University Grants Office.** Please discuss how these conflicts will be managed during the period of the trial. Include language disclosing such interest in the consent form for the use by research subjects. 5b. In addition, for industry-sponsored trials, please attach the documentation submitted to the sponsor as required by 21CFR54.1, if applicable.	☐ Yes ☐ No
6. Have the Principal Investigator, Co-PI(s) and faculty advisor taken the on-line CITI Course in the Protection of Human Research Subjects? • **IF YES,** attach copy(ies) of certification.	☐ Yes ☐ No
7. Human subjects or material involved in the proposed activity include any of the following vulnerable subjects ***(check all that apply, at least one box must be checked)*** ☐ Minors ☐ Pregnant Women ☐ Prisoners ☐ HIV positive subjects ☐ Patients ☐ Arcadia Employees, Staff, Students ☐ Mentally disabled or cognitively impaired subjects ☐ None of the Above ☐ **Other (specify):** ______________	
8. is this proposal currently under review, or has it been reviewed or approved by, another institution's IRB? • **IF YES,** include a copy of the proposal and if applicable, IRB approval from that institution. If the proposal has not yet been submitted to the other institution, please note an anticipated date of submission and a copy of the other institution's review guidelines.	☐ Yes ☐ No

Principal Investigator (PI) Signature ______ Date

Printed Name of PI ______

Co-Investigator's Signature ______ Date

Printed Name of Co-Investigator ______

Co-Investigator's Signature ______ Date

Printed Name of Co-Investigator ______

Co-Investigator's Signature ______ Date

Printed Name of Co-Investigator ______

** if require additional spaces for signatures please print another copy of this page and append to the first page #2 in the face sheet packet.*

Check all attachments that apply (see below for # of copies):

☐ Protocol Summary

☐ Informed Consent/Assent Form Document(s)

☐ Personality tests/inventories/questionnaires

☐ Human Subjects Oriented Training Research Certificate

☐ Conflict of Interest Disclosure Form (If Item #5 checked)

☐ Advertisement(s), recruitment flyers

☐ Copy of grant application (minus appendices) (if applicable)

☐ Copy of HIPAA if 3a is checked

☐ Copy of approval from Committee of Institutional Effectiveness if 4 is checked

☐ Copy of other institutions IRB approval if 8 is checked

February 2010

Figure 1.3 A copy of the form used by the Arcadia University IRB. Note that questions 3 and 7 ensure the principle of autonomy whereas questions 5 and 6 ensure the principle of beneficence. Researchers must address the principle of justice in their narrative describing the procedure of their study which they submit for review to the IRB along with this form. *Source:* Reprinted courtesy of Arcadia University.

Table 1.3 Science or Science Fiction?

1. Most experiments take place in a dark, dank laboratory with scary-looking equipment.
2. The English language contains 17,937 words to describe human personality.
3. Psychologists can judge what people are like based on their residence hall rooms, offices, web pages, and handshakes.
4. Employers can use personality tests to see if potential employees have what it takes to succeed on the job.
5. Dolphins, elephants, and chimpanzees know who they are.
6. Social experiences can change how our genes function.
7. Gamers can control their character in some video games simply by thinking about how they want the character to move.
8. Plastic baby carriers may make it more difficult for parents and children to bond.
9. People who feel competent and who are intrinsically motivated have less dental plaque.
10. College students today feel less in control of their lives than college students of earlier generations.
11. Men are just naturally better than women at certain mathematical tasks such as mental rotation, for example, and no amount of practice or experience can change this fundamental difference.
12. Women with a fluid sexual orientation are capable of experiencing a wider range of erotic experiences and feelings than captured by the labels of lesbian, bisexual, or heterosexual.
13. Experiencing positive emotions such as love, joy, playfulness, wonder, and love make people think more creatively than negative emotions such as sadness, disgust, or anxiety.

Note: All but two of these statements are based on science; the rest are science fiction. To find out which two, keep reading!

Science or Science Fiction? A Brief Introduction to Current Research Findings in Personality Psychology

Now that you know a bit about the methods psychologists use to study personality, it's time to explore their findings. But first, here's a chance for you to see for yourself just how exciting the field of personality psychology is. The field has changed so rapidly over the past decade or so that we might wonder if we are studying science or science fiction. Take a look at Table 1.3. Each of these statements draws on research you will learn about in the coming chapters. Can you tell which is science and which is science fiction?

Chapter Summary

This chapter introduced the topic of personality psychology—the scientific study of what makes us who we are. People vary and personality psychology studies both similarities and differences among people and how they became that way.

Though personality is made up of the building blocks of traits, genetics, neuroscience, self and identity, intrapsychic aspects, regulation and motivation, and cognitions, we are more than the mere sum of these parts. Especially when it comes to understanding gender, sexual orientation, and resilience, for example, these parts work together to make us who we are.

Personality psychologists use many methods to study personality. Using the scientific method, researchers make observations, build theories, and devise and test hypotheses. They may design true experiments, observational studies, correlational studies or administer personality questionnaires (both self-report and projective) to test their hypotheses and theories

Study and **Review** on **mysearchlab.com**
Go online for more resources to help you review.

> "Personality is essential. It is in every work of art. When someone walks on stage for a performance and has charisma, everyone is convinced that he has personality. I find that charisma is merely a form of showmanship. Movie stars usually have it. A politician has to have it."
> *Lukas Foss*

about human personality. They may also collect self-report data, observation data, test data, or life data on people. Like a carpenter with a toolbox full of specialized tools, researchers choose the best methods to answer their questions about human personality.

One method personality psychologists use to study people is the true experiment, where researchers have experimental control over the independent variable and randomly assign participants to conditions. If researchers succeeded in controlling all aspects of the experiment except for the one variable under study, then any difference in the dependent variable, or responses of the participants, must have been caused by the independent variable, what the experimenter manipulated. A true experiment is the only research design that allows researchers to draw conclusions about causality. However, there are times when it is impossible, impractical, or unethical to manipulate a variable—such as personality—so that researchers must use alternative methods like correlational designs.

The Belmont Report establishes guidelines researchers must follow for research with human participants. Researchers must apply the principles of respect for persons (including obtaining informed consent and protecting vulnerable populations), beneficence (minimize harm and maximize benefits), and justice (benefits and burdens of research must be shared equitably) while designing their experimental procedures. Researchers must then present their proposed study to an ethical review board, called an institutional review board (IRB), for approval. The IRB will review the proposal specifically making sure that the research upholds these standards. Institutions of the federal government all adhere to these principles, as outlined in the Common Rule, which includes the establishment and oversight of all IRBs throughout the United States.

Review Questions

1. What are some ways in which a single individual is like all others, like some others, and like no others?
2. What is personality psychology? What are the building blocks of personality?
3. How do psychologists study personality? What are some methods and measures used by personality psychologists?
4. What are the four different kinds of data a researcher can collect?
5. When researchers find a difference on some measure between two groups, is there a way to judge how large that difference is?
6. What is a correlation? When are correlational designs used? What is the difference between a correlational design and a true experiment?
7. What is so special about a true experiment? What two characteristics are present in a true experiment? What is an independent variable? What is a dependent variable?
8. According to the research by Ng and Diener (2009), are some coping strategies better than others? Why or why not? Where does personality fit in?
9. What are the three principles that researchers must adhere to in conducting research with human participants? What is an institutional review board?

Methods in the Study of Personality

Sam and Dave are taking a break from studying. Sam says, "My roommate's girl at home broke up with him. Chicks here better watch out, 'cause he's gonna be looking for some serious partying to help forget her."

"What makes you think so?"

"What kind of question is that? It's obvious. That's what *I'd* do."

"Huh. I know guys whose hometown girls dumped them, and *none* of them did that. It was exactly the opposite. They laid around moping. I think you're wrong about how people react to this kind of thing."

WHEN PEOPLE try to understand personality, where do they start? Where do theories come from? How are they tested? How do psychologists decide what to believe? These are all questions about the methods of science. They can be asked in all areas of science, from astronomy to zoology. They are particularly challenging, though, when applied to personality.

Gathering Information

Sources: Observe Yourself and Observe Others

One way to gather information about personality is to look to your own experience—a process called *introspection*. This technique (used by Sam in the opening example) is open to everyone. Try it. You have a personality. If you want to understand personality, take a look at yours. Sit back and think about events in your life. Think about what you did and how you felt, and pull from those recollections a thread of continuity. From this might come the start of a theory—a set of principles to explain your thoughts, feelings, and actions.

Examining your own experience is an easy beginning, but it has a problem. Specifically, your own consciousness has a special relationship to your memories because they're yours. It's hard to be sure this special relationship doesn't distort what you're seeing. For instance, you can misrecall something you experienced, yet feel sure your memory is correct.

This problem lessens when you look at someone else instead of yourself (Dave in the opening example). That's the second method of gathering information: observe someone else. This method also has a problem, though—the opposite of introspection's problem. Specifically, it's impossible to be "inside another person's head," to really know what that person is thinking and feeling. This difference in perspective can create vast differences in understanding. It can lead to misinterpretation.

Which starting point is better? Each has a place in the search for truth. Neither is perfect, but they sometimes can be used to complement one another.

Seeking Depth: Case Studies

These starting points lead in several directions. Personality psychologists sometimes seek explicitly to understand an entire person at once, rather than just part of the person. Henry Murray (1938), who emphasized the need to study the person as a coherent entity, coined the term **personology** to refer to that effort.

This view promotes a technique called the **case study.** A case study is in-depth study of one person. It usually entails a long period of observation and typically includes unstructured interviews. Sometimes, it involves spending a day or two being around the person to see how he or she interacts with others. Repeated observations let the observer confirm initial impressions or correct wrong impressions. Confirming or disconfirming an impression doesn't happen if you make only one observation. The depth of probing that's possible in a case study can reveal detail that otherwise wouldn't be apparent. This, in turn, can yield insights.

Case studies are rich in detail and can create vivid descriptions of the people under study. Particularly compelling incidents or examples may illustrate broader themes in the person's life. Because case studies examine the person in his or her life situation instead of settings created by the researcher, the information pertains to normal life. Because they're open ended, the observer can follow whatever leads seem interesting, not just ask questions chosen ahead of time.

Depth from Experience Sampling

Another kind of depth is provided by what are called **experience sampling** studies, or diary studies (Kamarck, Shiffman, & Wethington, 2011; Laurenceau & Bolger, 2005). These studies are also conducted across extended periods of time, like case studies. Instead of using an external observer, though, this procedure involves repeatedly prompting the person under study to stop and report on some aspect of his or her current experience. The prompt often is in the form of a signal from a pager. Sometimes these studies are very intensive, with reports made several times a day. Sometimes they are less intensive (e.g., morning and evening).

An important advantage of experience sampling methods is that they don't require the person to think back very far in time (maybe a half-day, maybe only an hour or so, maybe not at all). This allows less opportunity for distortion in recalling what the experiences actually were. Unfortunately, there is evidence that people don't do a very good job of remembering details of an event many hours later (Kamarck, Muldoon, Shiffman, & Sutton-Tyrrell, 2007; Stone, Kennedy-Moore, & Neale, 1995). Experience sampling methods let you get the events more "on line" than do other methods.

Experience sampling studies share with case studies the fact that a lot of information is obtained about each person being studied. In both cases, it's possible to search within this information for patterns of behavior within a given person across many situations. This is referred to an **idiographic** method (Conner, Tennen, Fleeson, & Barrett, 2009; Molenaar & Campbell, 2009), because the focus is on the individual. (The word *idiographic* has the same source as *idiosyncratic.*)

Seeking Generality: Studies of Many People

Case studies can provide insights into the human experience. They provide useful information for researchers and often serve as an important source of ideas. But single case studies aren't the main source of information about personality today. In large part, this is because a case study, no matter how good, is deficient in an important way: It deals with just one person. When you're forming theories or drawing conclusions from observations, you want them to apply to many people—if possible, to *all* people.

The generality of a conclusion can be established only by studying a mix of people from different backgrounds.

How widely a conclusion can be applied is called its **generality** or its **generalizability.** For a conclusion to be generalizable, it must be based on many people, not one or two. The more people examined, the more convinced you can be that what you see is true of people in general, instead of only a few people. In most research on personality, researchers look at tens—even hundreds—of people to increase the generality of their conclusions.

To truly ensure generality, researchers should study people of many ages and from all walks of life—indeed, from all cultures. For various reasons, this isn't always done, though it is becoming more common. As a matter of convenience, a lot of research on personality examines college students. Do college students provide a good picture of processes that are important in personality? Maybe yes, maybe no. College students differ from older people in several ways. For one, they have a less fully formulated sense of self. This may affect the research findings. How different college students are from everyone else is unclear. It does seem clear, though, that we should be cautious in assuming that conclusions drawn from research on college students always apply to "people in general."

Similarly, most observations on personality come from research done in the United States and western Europe. Most of the research has been done with middle- to upper-middle-class people. Some of it has used only one sex. We must be cautious in assuming that conclusions apply to people from other cultures, other socioeconomic groups, and (sometimes) both sexes.

Generalizability, then, is a kind of continuum. Rarely does any study range broadly enough to ensure total generalizability. Some are better than others. How broadly a conclusion can be generalized is an issue that must always be kept in mind in evaluating research results.

The desire for generality and the desire for in-depth understanding of a person are competing pressures. They force a trade-off. That is, given the same investment of time and energy, you can know a great deal about the life of one person (or a very few people), or you can know a little bit about the lives of a much larger number of people. It's nearly impossible to do both at once. As a result, researchers tend to choose one path or the other, according to which pressure they find more important.

Establishing Relationships among Variables

Insights from introspection or observation can suggest relationships between variables. A **variable** is a dimension along which variations exist. There must be at least two values or levels on that dimension, though some variables have an infinite number of values. For example, *sex* is a variable with values of *male* and *female*. *Self-esteem* is a variable that has a virtually limitless number of values (from *very low* to *very high*) as you make finer discriminations among people.

It's important to distinguish between a variable and its values, because conclusions about relationships involve the whole dimension, not just one end of it. Thus, researchers always study at least two levels of the variable they're interested in. For example, you can't understand the effects of low self-esteem by looking only at people with low self-esteem. If there's a relationship between self-esteem and academic performance, for example, the only way to find that out is to look at people with *different levels* of self-esteem (see Figure 2.1). If there is a relationship, people with low self-esteem should have poor grades and people with higher self-esteem should have better grades.

The last part of that statement is every bit as important as the first part. Knowing that people low in self-esteem have poor grades tells you nothing if people high

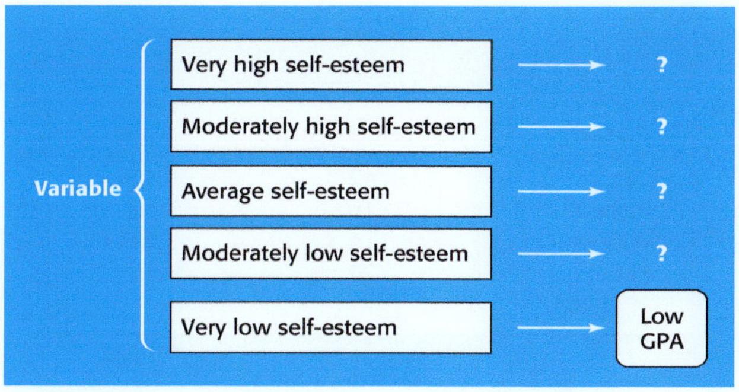

FIGURE 2.1
Whether a relationship exists between variables can be determined only by looking at more than one value on each variable. For instance, knowing that people low in self-esteem have poor academic performances leaves open the question of whether everyone else's performances are just as poor. This question is critically important in establishing a relationship between the two variables.

in self-esteem also have poor grades. It can be hard to keep this in mind. In fact, people often fail to realize how important this issue is. If you don't keep it in mind, though, you can draw seriously wrong conclusions (for illustrations, see Chapman, 1967; Crocker, 1981).

The need to examine people who represent a range of levels of a given variable is a second reason why it's important to go beyond case studies. (The issue of generality was the first one.) The need to examine a range of variability underlies several research methods.

CORRELATION BETWEEN VARIABLES

Two kinds of relationship can be established between variables. The first is called **correlation.** A correlation between two variables means that as you examine the variables across many people or instances, the values on the two tend to go together in a systematic way. There are two aspects of this relationship, which are separate from each other. They are the *direction* of the correlation and the *strength* of the correlation. To clarify what these terms mean, let's return to the example of self-esteem and academic performance.

A correlation between two variables means they covary in some systematic way. Here, there is a correlation between height and place in line.

A. Raw Data

Person	Self-Esteem Score	GPA
Tim	42	3.8
Susie	10	1.4
Warren	15	2.5
Ronald	22	3.1
. . . (etc.)		

B. Scatterplot

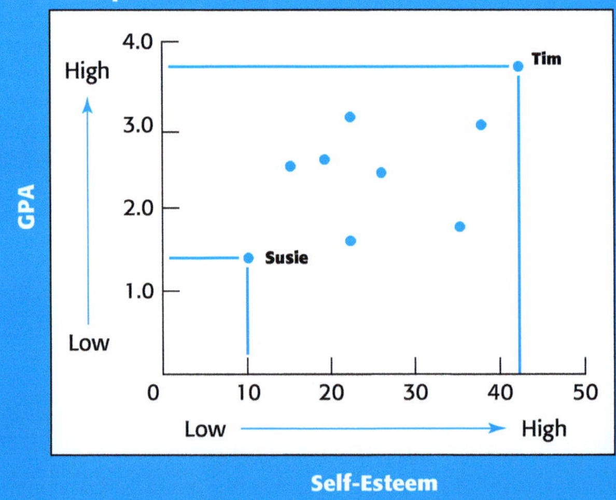

FIGURE 2.2
Thinking about the meaning of correlation (with hypothetical data): (A) For each person (subject), there are two pieces of information: a self-esteem score and a grade-point average (GPA). (B) The data can be arranged to form a scatterplot by plotting each person's self-esteem score along the horizontal dimension and his or her GPA along the vertical dimension, thereby locating the combination in a two-dimensional space.

Suppose you've decided to study whether these two variables go together. You've gone out and found 40 students. They've completed a measure of self-esteem and given you their current grade point average (GPA). You now have two pieces of information for each person (see Figure 2.2, A). One way to organize this information is called a *scatterplot* (see Figure 2.2, B). In a scatterplot, the variables are represented by lines at right angles (the axes of the graph). The point where the lines meet is zero for both variables. Being farther away from zero on each line means having a larger value on that variable. Because the lines are at right angles, the combination of any score on one variable and any score on the other variable can be portrayed as a point in two-dimensional space. For example, in Figure 2.2, Tim has a self-esteem score of 42 (and is toward the right side on the horizontal line) and a GPA of 3.8 (and is toward the top on the vertical line). The scatterplot for your study would be the points that represent the combinations of self-esteem scores and GPAs for all the people in the study.

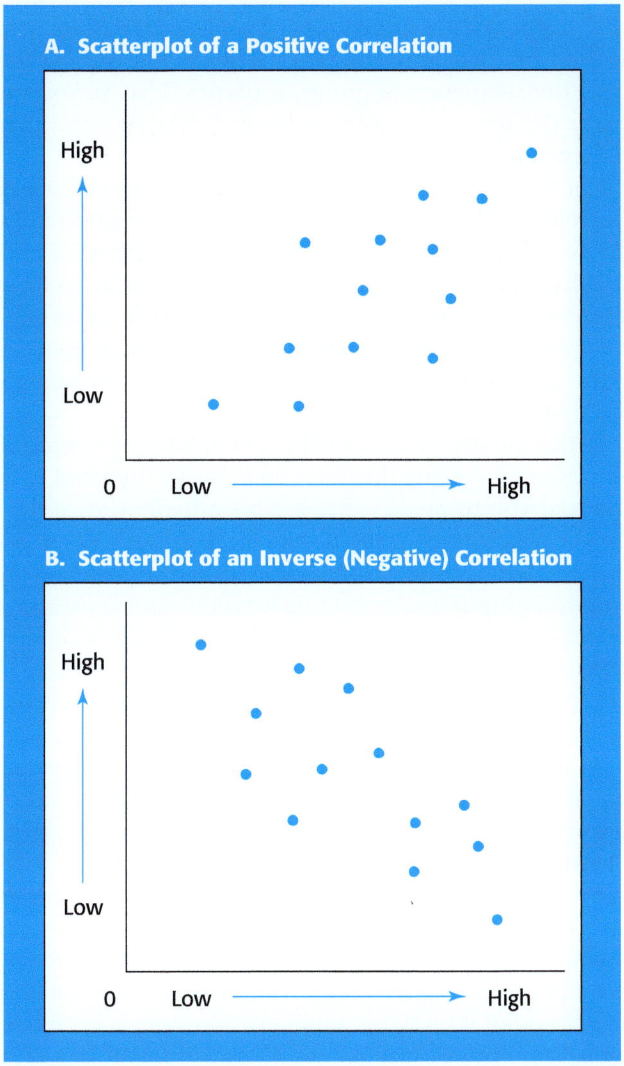

FIGURE 2.3
(A) If high numbers on one dimension tend to go with high numbers on the other dimension (and low with low), there is a positive correlation. (B) If high numbers on one dimension tend to go with low numbers on the other dimension, there is an inverse, or negative, correlation.

To ask whether the two variables are correlated means (essentially) asking the following question about the scatterplot: When you look at points that represent low versus high values on the *horizontal* dimension, do they differ in how they line up regarding the *vertical* dimension? If low values tend to go with low values and high values tend to go with high values (as in Figure 2.3, A), the variables are said to be *positively* correlated. If people low in self-esteem tend to have low GPAs and people high in self-esteem tend to have high GPAs, you would say that self-esteem correlates positively with GPA.

Sometimes, however, a different kind of pattern occurs. Sometimes, high values on one dimension tend to go with low values on the other dimension (and vice versa). When this happens (see Figure 2.3, B), the correlation is termed *inverse* or *negative*. This kind of correlation might emerge if you studied the relationship between GPA and the frequency of going to parties. That is, you might find that students who party the most tend to have lower GPAs, whereas those who party the least tend to have higher GPAs.

The *direction* of the association between variables (positive versus negative) is one aspect of correlation. The second aspect—entirely separate from the first—is the *strength* of the correlation. Think of strength as the "sloppiness" of the association between the variables. More formally, it refers to the degree of accuracy with which you can predict values on one dimension from values on the other one. For example, assume a positive correlation between self-esteem and GPA. Suppose that you know that Victoria has the second-highest score on self-esteem in your study. How accurate a guess could you make about her GPA?

The answer to this question is dictated by how strong the correlation is. Because the correlation is positive, knowing that Victoria is on the high end of the self-esteem dimension would lead you to predict that she has a high GPA. If the correlation is also *strong,* you're very likely to be right. If the correlation is weaker, you're less likely to be right. A perfect positive correlation—the strongest possible—means that the person who has the very highest value on one variable also has the very highest value on the other, the person next highest on one is also next highest on the other, and on so throughout the list (see Figure 2.4, A).

The strength of a correlation is expressed by a number called a **correlation coefficient** (often labeled with a lowercase *r*). An absolutely perfect positive correlation (as in Figure 2.4, A) is expressed by the number 1.0. This is the largest numerical value a correlation can take. It indicates a totally accurate prediction from one dimension to the other. If you know where the person is on one variable, you can tell with complete confidence where he or she is on the other.

The scatterplot of a somewhat weaker correlation is shown in Figure 2.4, B. As you can see, there's more "scatter" among the points than in the first case. There's still a noticeable tendency for higher values on one dimension to match up with higher ones on the other and for lows to match up with lows, but the tendency is less exact. As the correlation becomes weaker, the number expressing it becomes smaller (thus, virtually all correlations are decimal values). Correlations of 0.6 to 0.8 are strong. Correlations of 0.3 to 0.5 are moderately strong. Below 0.3 or 0.2, the prediction from one variable to the other is getting poorer. As you can see in Figure 2.4, C, weak correlations have even more scatter. The tendency toward a positive relation is there, but it definitely isn't strong. A correlation of 0.0 means the two variables aren't related at all. The scatterplot of a zero correlation is random dots.

As we said before, a correlation's strength is entirely separate from its direction. *Strength* refers only to degree of accuracy in prediction. Thus, it is eminently sensible to talk about a perfect negative correlation as well as a perfect positive correlation. A perfect negative correlation (see Figure 2.4, D) means that the person who had the highest value on one variable also had the very lowest value on the other variable, the person with the next-highest value on one had the next-to-lowest value on the other, and so on.

Negative correlations are expressed in numbers, just like positive correlations. But to show that the relationship is an inverse one, a minus sign is placed in front. Thus, an *r* value of −0.75 is precisely as strong as an *r* value of 0.75. The first expresses an inverse correlation, though, whereas the second expresses a positive correlation.

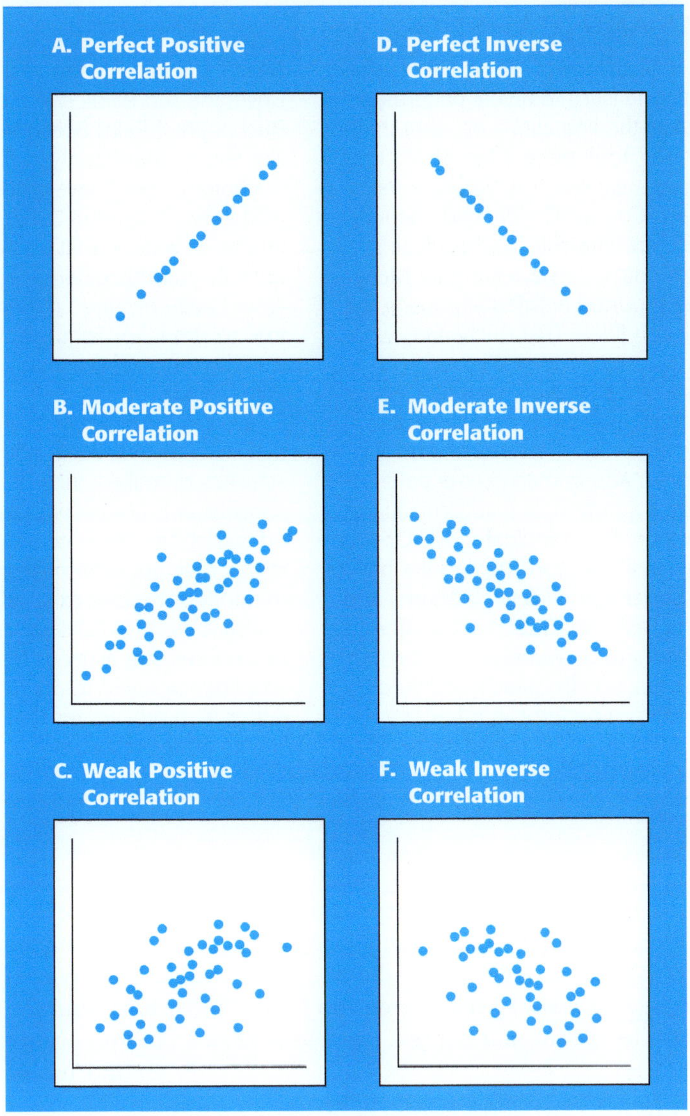

FIGURE 2.4
Six correlations: (A) Perfect positive correlation, (B) Moderate positive correlation, (C) Weak positive correlation, (D) Perfect inverse correlation, (E) Moderate inverse correlation, and (F) Weak inverse correlation. The weaker the correlation, the more "scatter" in the scatterplot.

Two Kinds of Significance

We've been describing the strength of correlations in terms of the size of the numbers that represent them. Although the size of the number gives information about its strength, the size of the number by itself doesn't tell you whether the correlation is believable or real. Maybe it's a fluke. This is a problem for all kinds of statistics. You can't tell just by looking at the number or looking at a graph whether the result is real. You need to know whether the result is **statistically significant**.

Box 2.1 Statistics and Statistics

Description versus Inference

When people think of *statistics,* they often think of the statistics that portray a set of events—for example, "The average American earns $37,000 a year" or "She averaged 21.6 points per game." These are called **descriptive statistics,** because their purpose is to give a description.

Psychologists also use different kinds of statistics, called **inferential statistics,** because they let the researcher make inferences. The information they provide guides the scientist in deciding whether to believe something is true. Interestingly enough, it isn't possible to *prove* something is true. What statistics do is show how likely the finding was, if there was no true relation. If it can be shown that the effect was very *unlikely* to have occurred, the researcher can infer that it's real.

An example of the ability of inferential statistics to reveal patterns, as well as the limitations on what they can say, took place after the 2000 U.S. presidential election. Voters in Palm Beach County, Florida, had encountered an unfamiliar and confusing ballot format on election day. Many later reported accidentally voting for one candidate (Pat Buchanan) while trying to vote for another one (Al Gore). The election, won by George W. Bush, was extremely close. Its outcome might have turned on the errors made in marking the ballot. Were these people just complaining because their candidate lost? Or was there really a problem with the ballot?

Social scientists Greg Adams and Chris Fastnow (2000) used inferential statistics to test whether the pattern of votes in Palm Beach County differed from patterns in other Florida counties. In every county but Palm Beach, the more votes cast for Bush, the more votes also cast for Buchanan. If Palm Beach had been like every other county in Florida, Buchanan would have gotten around 600 votes instead of 3,407. The inference was clear: It was extremely unlikely that this difference in pattern would have occurred if there were no true relation. Something apparently was throwing off the voting pattern in Palm Beach.

We say "apparently" to emphasize that whenever you use inferential statistics to make a judgment, the conclusion is always probabilistic. The odds that the inference was wrong in this case are *extremely* small. But the possibility does exist. Inferential statistics are thus best viewed as procedures that allow us to attach "confidence units" to our judgments, rather than procedures that lead infallibly to correct choices.

Significant in this context has a very specific meaning: It means that the correlation would have been that large or larger only rarely if no true relationship exists. When the probability is small enough (just under 5%), the correlation (or whatever statistic it is) is said to be *statistically significant* (see also Box 2.1). At that point, the researcher concludes that the relationship is a real one, rather than a random occurrence.

Random assignment is an important hallmark of the experimental method. The experimenter randomly assigns participants to a condition, much as a roulette wheel randomly catches the ball in a black or red slot.

A second use of the word *significant* is also common in psychology, which more closely resembles the use of the word in day-to-day language. An association is said to be **clinically significant** or **practically significant** if the effect is both statistically significant (so it's believable) and large enough to have some practical importance. How large is large enough to be practically important varies from case to case. It's possible, though, for an association to be statistically significant but to account for only a tiny fraction of the behavior. The practical significance of such an association usually isn't very great.

Causality and a Limitation on Inference

Correlations tell us whether two variables go together (and in what direction and how strongly). But they don't tell us *why* the variables go together. The *why* question takes us beyond the realm of correlation to a second kind of relationship. This one is called **causality**—the relationship between a cause and an effect. Correlational research isn't able to provide evidence on this second kind of relationship. A correlational study often gives people strong *intuitions* about causality, but no more.

Why? The answer is shown in Figure 2.5. Each arrow there represents a possible path of causality. What this figure shows is that there are always three ways to account for the results of a correlation. Consider the correlation between self-esteem and academic performance. What causes it? Your intuition may say the best explanation is that bad academic outcomes cause people to develop lower self-esteem, whereas having good outcomes causes people to feel good about themselves (arrow 1 in Figure 2.5). Or maybe you think the best explanation is that having low self-esteem causes people not to try as hard, resulting in poorer performance (arrow 2). Both of these explanations are plausible, though they go in the opposite directions.

It could also be, however, that a third variable—not measured, perhaps not even thought of—actually has a causal influence over both variables that were measured (the pair of arrows labeled 3). Perhaps having a high level of intelligence

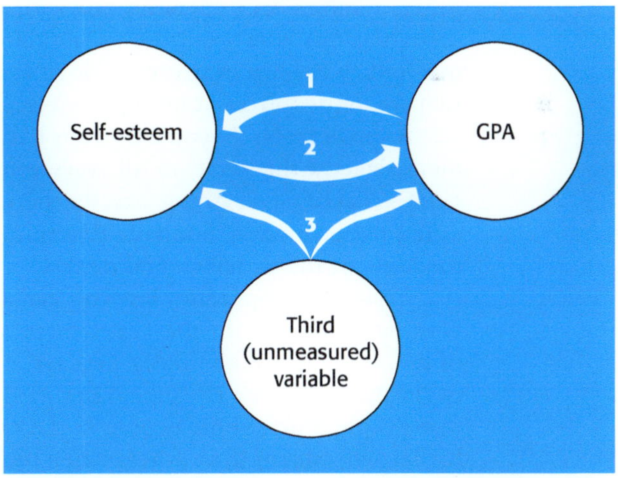

Figure 2.5
Correlation does not imply cause and effect, because there are always three possibilities: (1) variations in one variable (academic performance) may be causing variations in the second (self-esteem); (2) variations in the second may be causing variations in the first; or (3) a third variable may actually be causing both observed effects. Knowing only the single correlation between self-esteem and GPA doesn't allow you to distinguish among these possibilities.

causes a positive sense of self-esteem and also causes better academic performance. In this scenario, both self-esteem and academic performance are effects, and something else is the cause.

The possible involvement of another variable in a correlation is sometimes called the **third-variable problem.** It's a problem that can't be handled by correlational research. That method cannot tell which of the three possibilities in Figure 2.5 is actually correct.

Search for Causality: Experimental Research

There *is* a method that demonstrates cause and effect, however. It's called the **experimental method.** Think of it as having two defining characteristics. First, in an experiment, the researcher manipulates one variable—creates the existence of at least two levels of it. The one the researcher is manipulating is called the **independent variable.** It's the one the researcher is testing as the possible *cause* in a cause–effect relationship. When we say the researcher is "creating" two (or more) levels of this variable, we mean exactly that. There's some kind of event that *actively creates* a difference between the experience of some people and the experience of other people.

Sometimes researchers do experiments in order to better understand what they've seen in correlational studies. Let's illustrate the experimental method by doing just that. Let's pursue further the example we just discussed. Suppose you have a hunch that variations in academic performance have a causal effect on self-esteem. To study this possibility, you conduct an experiment, in which you hypothesize (predict) that academic outcomes cause effects on self-esteem.

You're not going to be able to manipulate GPA in this experiment, but it's fairly easy to manipulate other things with overtones of academic performance. For instance, you could arrange to have some people experience a success and others a failure on a cognitive task (using one rigged to be easy or impossible). By arranging this, you would *create* the difference between success and failure. You'd manipulate it—not measure it. You're sure that a difference now exists between the two sets of people in your experiment, because you *made* it exist.

As in all research, you'd do your best to treat every participant in your experiment exactly the same in all ways other than that one. Treating everyone the same—making everything exactly the same except for what you manipulate—is called **experimental control.** Exerting a high degree of control is important to the logic of the experimental method, as you'll see momentarily.

Control is important, but you can't control everything. It's rarely possible to have every person do the experiment at the same time of day or the same day of the week. More obviously, perhaps, it's impossible to be sure the people in the experiment are exactly alike. One of the main themes of this book, after all, is that people differ. Some people in the experiment are just naturally going to have higher self-esteem than others when they walk in the door. How can these differences be handled?

This question brings us to the second defining characteristic of the experimental method: Any variable that can't be controlled—such as an individual difference—is treated by **random assignment.** In your experiment, you would randomly assign each participant to either the success experience or the failure experience. Random assignment is often done by such means as tossing a coin or using a list of random numbers.

The use of random assignment rests on a specific assumption: that if you study enough people in the experiment, any important differences between people (and from other sources as well) will balance out between the groups. Each group is likely to have as many tall people, fat people, depressed people, and confident people as the other group—*if* you have a fairly large number of participants and use random assignment. Anything that matters should balance out.

So, you've brought people to your research laboratory one at a time, randomly assigned them to the two conditions, manipulated the independent variable, and exerted experimental control over everything else. At some point, you would then measure the variable you think is the effect in the cause-and-effect relationship. This one is termed the **dependent variable.**

In this experiment, your hypothesis was that differences in success and failure on academic tasks cause people to differ in self-esteem. Thus, the dependent measure would be a measure of self-esteem (for example, self-report items asking people how they feel about themselves). After getting this measure for each person in the experiment, you would compare the groups to each other (by statistical procedures that need not concern us here). If the difference between groups was statistically significant, you could conclude that the experience of success versus failure *causes* people to differ in self-esteem.

What would make you so confident in that cause-and-effect conclusion? The answer, despite all the detail, is really quite simple. The logic is displayed graphically in Figure 2.6 on page 26. At the start of the experiment, you separated people into two groups. (By the way, the reasoning applies even if the independent variable has more than two levels or groups.) If the assumption about the effect of random assignment is correct, then the two groups don't differ from each other at this point. Because you exercise experimental control, the groups still don't differ as the experiment unfolds.

At one point, however, a difference between groups is introduced—when you manipulate the independent variable. As we said before, you know there's a difference now, and you know *what* the difference is, because you created it yourself. For this reason, if you find the groups differ from each other on the dependent measure at the end, you know there's only one thing that could have caused the difference (see Figure 2.6). It *had* to come from the manipulation of the independent variable. That was the only place where a difference was introduced. It was the only thing that could have been responsible for causing the effect.

This reasoning is straightforward. We should note, however, that this method isn't entirely perfect. Its problem is this: When you do an experiment, you show that the *manipulation* causes the difference on the dependent measure—but you can't always be completely sure *what it was* about the manipulation that did the causing. Maybe it was the aspect of the manipulation that you were focused on, but maybe it was something else.

For example, in the experiment we've been considering, low self-esteem may have been caused by the failure and the self-doubt to which it led. But it *might* have been caused by other things about the manipulation. Maybe the people who failed were worried that they had spoiled your experiment by not solving the problems.

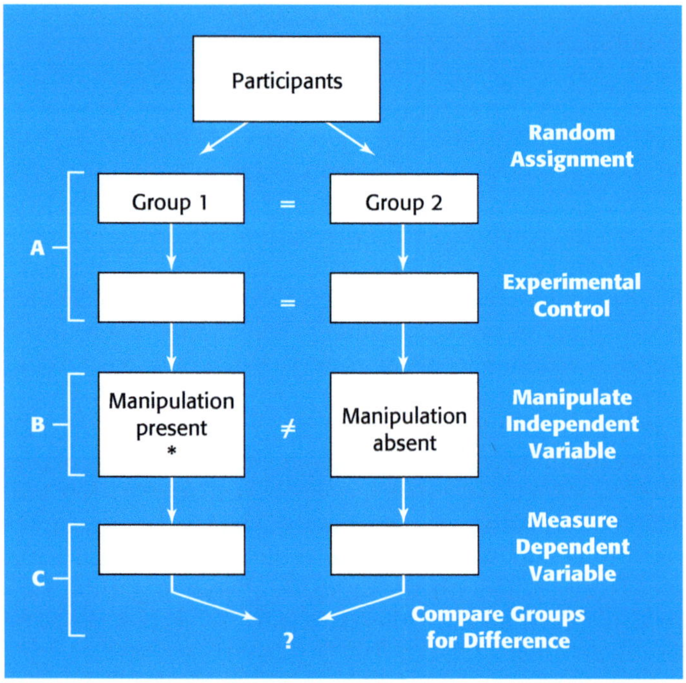

FIGURE 2.6
The logic of the experimental method: (A) Because of random assignment and experimental control, there is no systematic difference between groups at first; (B) The experimental manipulation creates—for the first time—a specific difference, (C) If the groups then are found to differ in another fashion, the manipulation must have caused this difference.

They didn't feel a sense of *failure* but were angry with themselves for creating a problem for you. This interpretation of the result wouldn't mean quite the same thing as your first interpretation of it. This issue requires us always to be a bit cautious in how we view results, even from experiments.

Recognizing Types of Study

When you read about correlational studies and experiments in this book, how easy is it going to be to tell them apart? At first glance, it seems simple. An *experiment* makes a comparison between groups, and a *correlational study* gives you a correlation, right? Well, no. Results of correlational studies aren't always reported as correlations. Sometimes the study compares two (or more) groups with each other on a dependent measure, and the word *correlation* is never even mentioned.

Suppose you studied some people who were 40% overweight and some who were 40% underweight. You interviewed them individually and judged how sociable they were, and you found that heavy people were more sociable than thin people. Would this be an experiment or a correlational study? Recall the two defining characteristics of the experiment: manipulation of the independent variable and random assignment of people to groups. You didn't randomly assign people to be heavy or thin (and you didn't *create* these differences). Therefore, this is a correlational study. The limitation on correlational research (the inability to conclude cause and effect) applies to it.

A good rule of thumb is that any time groupings reflect *naturally occurring differences* or are formed on the basis of some *characteristic that you measure*, the study is correlational. This means that all studies of personality differences are, by definition, correlational.

Why do personality researchers make their correlational studies look like experiments? Sometimes it's because they study people from categories, such as cultural groups or genders. It has the side effect, however, of making it hard to express the finding as a correlation. The result is correlational studies that look at first glance like experiments.

What Kind of Research Is Best?

Which kind of research is better: experiments or correlational studies? Both have advantages, and the advantage of one is the disadvantage of the other. The advantage of the experimental method, of course, is its ability to show cause and effect, which the correlational method cannot do.

But experiments also have drawbacks. One drawback (as noted) is that there's sometimes uncertainty about which aspect of the manipulation was important. Another drawback is that experiments on people usually involve events of relatively short duration, in carefully controlled conditions. The correlational method, in contrast, lets you examine events that take place over long periods (even decades) and events that are much more elaborate. Correlational studies also let you get information about events in which experimental manipulation would be unethical—for example, how being raised by divorced parents affects people's personality.

Personality psychologists sometimes also criticize experiments on the grounds that the kinds of relationships they obtain often have little to do with the central issues of personality. Even experiments that seem to bear on important issues in personality may tell less than they seem to. Consider the hypothetical experiment described earlier, in which you manipulated academic success and failure and measured self-esteem. Assume for the moment that those given a failure had lower self-esteem afterward than those given a success. You might be tempted to conclude from this that having poor academic outcomes over the course of one's life causes people to develop low self-esteem.

This conclusion, however, may not be justified. The experiment dealt with a brief task outcome, manipulated in a particular way. The broader conclusion you're tempted to reach deals with a basic, ingrained quality of personality. This latter quality may differ in many ways from the momentary state you manipulated. The "reasoning by analogy" that you're tempted to engage in can be misleading.

To many personality psychologists, the only way to really understand personality is to look at naturally occurring differences between people (Underwood, 1975). These researchers are willing to accept the limitation on causal inference that's inherent in correlations; they regard it as an acceptable price to pay. On the other hand, many of these psychologists are comfortable *combining* the correlational strategy with experimental techniques, as described next.

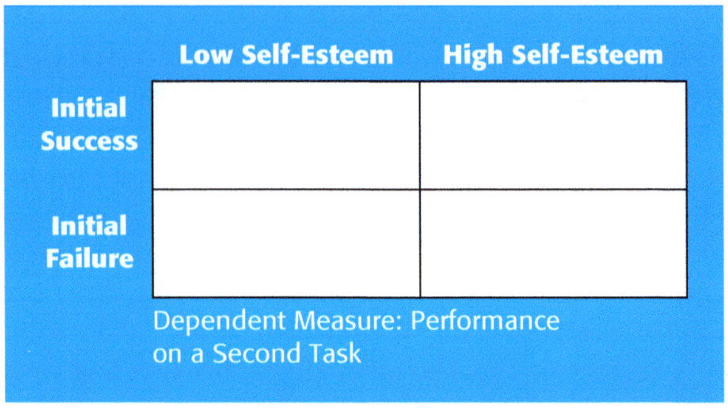

FIGURE 2.7
Diagram of a hypothetical two-factor study. Each square represents the combination of the value listed above it and the value listed to the left. In multifactor studies, all combinations of values of the predictor variables are created in this fashion.

MULTIFACTOR STUDIES

We've been describing studies as though they always involve predicting a dependent variable from a single predictor variable (an experimental manipulation or an individual difference). In reality, however, studies often look at several predictors at once by using multifactor designs. In a **multifactor study,** two (or more) variables are varied *separately*, which means creating all combinations of the various levels of the predictor variables. The study shown in Figure 2.7 has two factors, but more than two can be used. The more factors in a study, of course, the larger the resulting array of combinations, and the trickier it is to keep track of things.

Sometimes, the factors are all experimental manipulations. Sometimes, they're all personality variables. Often, though, experimental manipulations are crossed by individual-difference variables. The example shown in Figure 2.7 is such a design. The self-esteem factor is the level of self-esteem the people had when they came to the study. This is a personality dimension (thus correlational). The success–failure factor is an experimental manipulation, which takes place during the session. In this particular experiment, the dependent measure is performance on a second task, which the participants attempt after the success–failure manipulation.

These designs allow researchers to examine how different types of people respond to variations in situations. They thus offer a glimpse into the underlying dynamics of the individual-difference variable. Because this type of study combines experimental procedures and individual differences, it's often referred to as **experimental personality research.**

READING FIGURES FROM MULTIFACTOR RESEARCH

Because multifactor designs are more complex than single-factor studies, what they can tell you is also potentially more complex. Indeed, people who do experimental personality research use these designs precisely for this reason.

You don't *always* get a complex result from a multifactor study. Sometimes you find only the same outcomes you would have found if you had studied each predictor separately. When you find that a predictor variable is linked to the outcome in a systematic way, completely separate from the other predictor, the finding is called a **main effect.** For example, the study outlined in Figure 2.7 might find simply that people of both initial self-esteem levels perform worse after a failure than after a success.

The complexity occurs when a study finds what's termed an **interaction.** Figure 2.8 portrays two interactions, each a possible outcome of the hypothetical study of Figure 2.7. In each case, the vertical dimension portrays the dependent

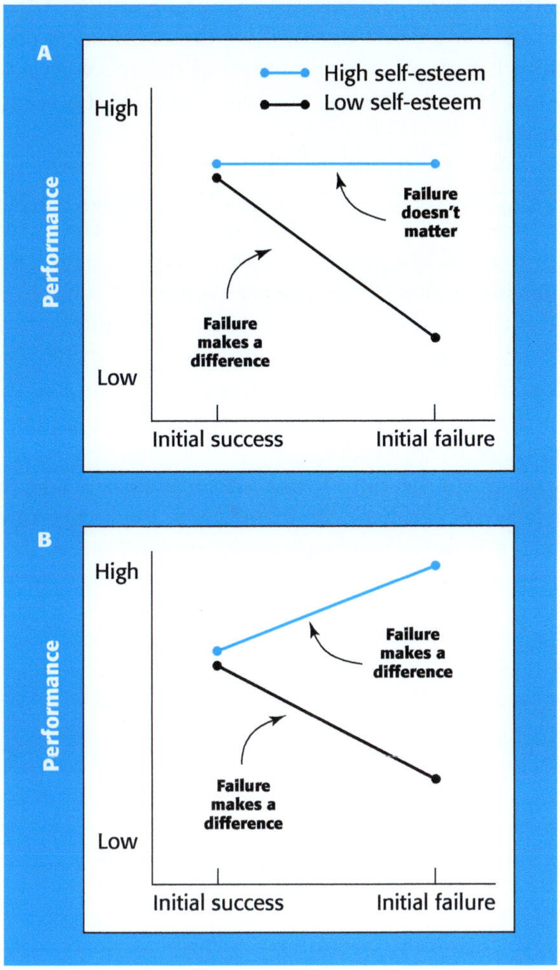

FIGURE 2.8
Two hypothetical outcomes of a two-factor study looking at self-esteem and an initial success-versus-failure experience as predictors of performance on a second task. (A) This graph indicates that experiencing a failure causes people low in self-esteem to perform worse later on than if they had experienced a success, but that experiencing a failure does not have any effect at all on people high in self-esteem. (B) This graph indicates that experiencing a failure causes people low in self-esteem to perform worse later on, but that experiencing a failure causes people high in self-esteem to perform better later on. Thus, the failure influences both kinds of people but does so in opposite ways.

measure: performance on the second task. The two marks on the horizontal line represent the two values of the manipulated variable: initial success versus failure. The color of the line depicts the other predictor variable: the color line represents people high in self-esteem, and the black line represents those low in self-esteem.

We emphasize that these graphs show *hypothetical* outcomes. They are intended only to give you a clearer understanding of what interactions mean. Figure 2.8, A, portrays a finding that people who are low in self-esteem perform worse after an initial failure than after a success. Among people high in self-esteem, however, this doesn't occur. Failure apparently has no effect on them. Thus, the effect of one variable (success versus failure) differs across the two levels of the other variable (degree of self-esteem). That is the meaning of the term *interaction.* In the case in Figure 2.8, A, a failure has an effect at one level of the second variable (in the low self-esteem group) but has no effect at the other level of the second variable (the high self-esteem group).

Two more points about interactions: First, to find an interaction, it's *absolutely necessary* to study more than one factor at a time. It's impossible to find an interaction unless both variables involved in it are studied at once. This is one reason researchers often use multifactor designs: They allow the possibility for interactions to emerge.

The second point is revealed by comparing Figure 2.8, A, with 2.8, B. This point is that interactions can take many forms. In contrast to the interaction just described, the graph in panel B says that failure has effects on both kinds of people—but opposite effects. People low in self-esteem perform worse after failure (as in the first graph), but people high in self-esteem actually perform better after a failure, perhaps because the failure motivates them to try harder.

These two graphs aren't the only forms interactions can take. Exactly what an interaction means always depends on its form. Thus, exploring interactions always requires checking to see in what way each group was influenced by the other variable under study.

• SUMMARY •

Research in personality relies on observations of both the self and others. The desire to understand a person as an integrated whole led to *case studies*: in-depth examinations of specific persons. The desire for *generalizability*—conclusions that would apply to many rather than to a few people—led to studies involving systematic examination of many people.

Gathering information is only the first step toward examining relationships between and among variables. Relationships among variables are examined in two ways, corresponding to two kinds of relationships. *Correlational research* determines the degree to which two variables tend to go together in a predictable way when measured at different levels along the dimensions. This technique determines two aspects of the relationship: its direction and its strength. The special relationship of cause and effect cannot be determined by this kind of study, however.

A second technique, called the *experimental method,* allows testing for cause and effect. In an experiment, an independent variable is manipulated, other variables are controlled (made constant), and anything that cannot be controlled is treated by random assignment. An effect caused by the manipulation is measured in the dependent variable. Experimental and correlational techniques are often combined in multifactor studies. When the study contains a personality variable and an experimental manipulation, it's termed *experimental personality research*. Multifactor studies permit the emergence of interactions.

• GLOSSARY •

Case study An in-depth study of one individual.

Causality (causal relationship) A relationship such that variation in one dimension produces variation in another.

Clinically significant An association large enough to have some practical importance.

Correlation A relationship in which two variables or dimensions covary when measured repeatedly.

Correlation coefficient A numeric index of the degree of correlation between two variables.

Dependent variable The variable measured as the outcome of an experiment; the effect in a cause–effect relationship.

Descriptive statistics Statistics used to describe or characterize some group.

Experience sampling A method in which people report repeatedly on their current experiences.

Experimental control The holding constant of variables that are not being manipulated.

Experimental method The method in which one variable is manipulated to test for causal influence on another variable.

Experimental personality research A study involving a personality factor and an experimental factor.

Generality (generalizability) The degree to which a conclusion applies to many people.

Idiographic Relating to an approach that focuses on a particular person across situations.

Independent variable The variable manipulated in an experiment and tested as the cause in a cause–effect relationship.

Inferential statistics Statistics used to judge whether a relationship exists between variables.

Interaction A finding in which the effect of one predictor variable differs depending on the level of another predictor variable.

Main effect A finding in which the effect of one predictor variable is independent of other variables.

Multifactor study A study with two (or more) predictor variables.

Personology The study of the whole person, as opposed to the study of only one aspect of the person.

Practical significance An association large enough to have practical importance.

Random assignment The process of putting people randomly into groups of an experiment so their characteristics balance out across groups.

Statistical significance The likelihood of an obtained effect occurring when there is no true effect.

Third-variable problem The possibility that an unmeasured variable caused variations in both of two correlated variables.

Variable A dimension along which two or more variations exist.

CHAPTER 3

Issues in Personality Assessment

THE MEASURING OF PERSONALITY is called **assessment.** It's something we all do informally all the time. We want to know what the people we interact with are like, so we know what to expect of them. For this reason, we develop various ways of gauging people, judging what they're like. You probably don't think of this as "assessment," but what you're doing informally is much the same—in principle—as what psychologists do more formally.

Forming impressions of what other people are like can be hard. It's easy to get misleading impressions. Personality assessment is also hard for psychologists. All the problems you have, they have. But personality psychologists work hard to deal with those problems.

Sources of Information

Informal assessment draws information from many sources, and so does formal assessment.

Observer Ratings

As suggested in Chapter 2, many measures of personality come from someone other than the person being assessed (Funder, 1991; Paunonen, 1989). The name for this approach is **observer ratings.**

There are many kinds of observer ratings. Some of them involve interviews. People being assessed talk about themselves, and the interviewer draws conclusions from what's said and how it's said. Sometimes people being interviewed talk about something *other than* themselves. In doing so, they reveal something indirectly to the interviewer about what they're like.

Other kinds of observer ratings don't require that kind of complexity. Observers may make judgments about a person based on watching his or her actions. Or observers may be people who already know the person being assessed well enough to say what he or she is like, and their ratings are simply those summary judgments. Observers can even observe a person's belongings and draw conclusions about what the person is like (see Box 3.1).

There are many different types of observer ratings. Here, an observer is directly rating a research participant's overt behavior.

Box 3.1 What Does Your Stuff Say about You?

Many people assume that the vast reach of the web and popular media has completely homogenized American culture. Everyone buys more or less the same stuff, and everyone's personal space therefore looks more or less the same. Not so. Not even close.

Sam Gosling and his colleagues have found that people "portray and betray" their personalities by the objects and mementos they surround themselves with (Gosling, 2008). Practicing a research technique they refer to as "snoopology" (the science of snooping), these researchers have extensively studied people's offices, bedrooms, and other personal domains. They've found evidence of three broad mechanisms that connect people to their spaces. They refer to these as identity claims, feeling regulators, and behavioral residue.

Identity claims are symbolic statements about who we are. Photos, awards, bumper stickers, and other objects that symbolize a past, current, or hoped-for identity (e.g., cheerleader pompoms) are identity claims. They are indicators of how we want to be regarded. They can be directed to other people who enter our space, or they can be directed to ourselves, reminders to ourselves of who we are (or want to be). Photos can be particularly revealing. They say, "Here I am being me" (Gosling, 2008, p. 16).

Feeling regulators aren't intended to send messages about our identities but to help us manage our emotions. Being in a particular desired emotional state can be important for a variety of life's activities, and emotions can be regulated in a wide variety of ways. You can improve your mood by looking at a picture that reminds you of a time when you were very happy. You can soothe yourself with pictures of tranquil nature scenes and with readily available music playing through a high-quality sound system. A bathtub surrounded by candles and scented oils can be eminently relaxing. And if you're the sort of person who thrives on excitement, there are plenty of things that can be included in your surroundings to stimulate those feelings, as well.

Behavioral residues are in some ways less interesting than either of these. Behavioral residues are physical traces left in our surroundings by everyday actions (trash is a special case of residue that is discarded repeatedly). What can these residues tell about you? A simple thing is how much residue you've accumulated. The more the residue, the less organized you probably are. A separate issue is what *kinds* of residue show up. As noted in Chapter 1, personality is displayed in consistencies. Similarly, behavioral residue tends to give an indication of what sorts of things take place repeatedly in your life space.

Self-Reports

Another category of assessment technique is **self-report.** In self-reports, people themselves indicate what they think they're like or how they feel or act. Self-reports thus resemble the process of introspection described in Chapter 2. Although self-reporting can be done in an unstructured descriptive way, it's usually not. Most self-reports ask people to respond to a specific set of items.

Self-report scales can be created in many formats. An example is the true–false format, where you read statements and decide whether each one is true or false for you. Another common one is a multipoint rating scale. Here, a wider range of response options is available—for example, along a 5-point response scale ranging from "strongly agree" to "strongly disagree."

Some self-reports focus on a single quality of personality. Often, though, people who develop assessment devices want to assess *several* aspects of personality in the same test (as separate scales). A measure that assesses several dimensions of personality is called an **inventory**. The process of developing an inventory is pretty much the same as that for developing a single scale. The difference is that for an inventory, you go through each step of development for *each scale of the inventory,* rather than just one.

Implicit Assessment

Also of increasing interest over the past decade (though they've been around for a long time) are techniques called **implicit assessment.** These techniques attempt to find out what a person is like from the person (like self-reports) but not by asking him or her directly. Rather, the person is given a task of some sort that involves making judgments about stimuli. The pattern of responses (e.g., reaction times) can inform the assessor about what the person is like.

An example of such a procedure is called the Implicit Association Test (IAT; for review, see Greenwald, McGhee, & Schwartz, 2008). It measures links among semantic properties in memory that are believed to be hard to detect by introspection (and thus are "implicit"). The IAT can be applied to virtually any kind of association. As applied to properties of personality, it would go like this. Your job is to categorize a long series of stimuli as quickly as you can. Each can be categorized according to either of two dichotomies: "me" versus "not me" or (for example) "plant" versus "mineral." You don't know which dichotomy makes sense until the item appears. Some items pertain to qualities of personality. If one of those items is strongly associated in your memory with you, your "me" response will be faster than if it isn't strongly associated with you. Thus, reaction times across a large number of stimuli can provide information about your implicit sense of self.

Implicit assessment techniques have been particularly important in the motive approach to personality. Accordingly, we will spend more time on that technique in Chapter 5.

As indicated by the preceding sections, the arsenal of assessment techniques is large. All require two things, though. First, in each case, the person being assessed produces a sample of "behavior." This may be an action, which someone observes; it may be internal behavior, such as a change in heart rate; it may be the behavior of answering questions; or it may be the accumulation of possessions over an extended period. Second, someone then uses the behavior sample as a guide to some aspect of the person's personality.

Subjective versus Objective Measures

One more distinction among measures is important. Some measures are termed **subjective**, and others are termed **objective.** In subjective measures, an interpretation is part of the measure. An example is an observer's judgment that the person he or she is watching looks nervous. The judgment makes the measure subjective, because it's an *interpretation* of the behavior. If the measure is of a concrete physical reality that requires no interpretation, then it's objective. For example, you could count the number of times a person stammers while talking. This would involve no interpretation. Although this count might then be used to infer nervousness, the measure itself is objective.

To some extent, this issue cuts across the distinction between observer ratings and self-reports. An observer can make objective counts of acts, or can develop a subjective impression of the person. Similarly, a person making a self-report can report objective events as they occur (as in experience sampling) or can report a subjective overall impression of what he or she is like. It should be apparent, though, that self-reports are particularly vulnerable to incorporating subjectivity. Even reports of specific events permit unintentional interpretations to creep in.

Reliability of Measurement

All techniques of assessment confront several kinds of problems or issues. One issue is termed **reliability** of measurement. The nature of this issue can be conveyed by putting it as a question: Once you've made an observation about someone, how confident can you be that if you looked again a second or third time you'd see about the same thing?

When an observation is reliable, it has a high degree of *consistency* or *repeatability*. Low reliability means that what's measured is less consistent. The measure isn't just reflecting the person being measured. It's also including a lot of randomness, termed **error.**

All measurement procedures have sources of error (error can be reduced, but not eliminated). When you use a telescope to look at the moon, a little dust on the lens, minor imperfections in the glass, flickering lights nearby, and swirling air currents all contribute error to what you see. When you use a rating scale to measure how self-reliant people think they are, the way you phrase the item can be a source of error, because it can lead to varying interpretations. When you have an observer watch a child's behavior, the observer is a source of error because of variations in how closely he or she is paying attention, thinking about what he or she is seeing, or being influenced by a thousand other things.

How do you deal with the issue of reliability in measurement? The general answer is to repeat the measurement—make the observation more than once. Usually, this means measuring the same quality from a slightly different angle or using a slightly different "measuring device." This lets the diverse sources of error in the different devices cancel each other out.

Reliability actually is a family of problems, not just a single problem, because it crops up in several different contexts. Each version of the problem has a separate name, and the tactic used to treat each version differs slightly from the tactics used for the others.

Internal Consistency

The simplest act of assessment is the single observation or measurement. How can you be sure it doesn't include too much error? Let's take an illustration from ability assessment. Think about what you'd do if you wanted to know how good someone was at a particular type of problem—math problems or word puzzles. You wouldn't give just a *single* problem to solve, because whether the person solved it easily or not might depend too much on some quirk of that particular problem. If you wanted to know (reliably) how well the person solves that kind of problem, you'd give *several* problems.

The same strategy applies to personality assessment. If you were using a self-report to ask people how self-reliant they think they are, you wouldn't ask just once. You'd ask several times, using different items that all reflect self-reliance, but in different words. In this example, *each item* is a "measuring device." When you go to a new item, you're shifting to a different measuring device, trying to measure the same quality. In effect,

Human judges are not infallible. They sometimes perceive things inaccurately.

Box 3.2 New Approaches to Assessment: Item Response Theory and Computer Adaptive Testing

The idea that having lots of items increases a scale's internal consistency comes from classical test theory, which guided scale construction for years. More recently, a different approach has emerged called *item response theory (IRT)*. IRT is an attempt to increase the efficiency of assessment (Reeve, Hays, Change, & Perfetto, 2007), while reducing the number of items

IRT focuses on determining the most useful items, and the most useful response choices, for the concept being measured. Determining which responses choices are most useful starts with creation of response curves. These show how frequently each response is used, and whether each choice is measuring something different from other choices (Streiner, 2010). For example, consider a scale where the response choices indicate the frequency of something: "always," "often," "sometimes," and "never." Analysis might find that "often" and "sometimes" are actually treated the same. If so, there's no point in offering these responses as separate alternatives.

IRT also determines the "difficulty" of an item (Streiner, 2010). For instance, on a scale assessing anxiety, the item "I worry" would be easier to endorse than the item "I get panicky." Why? Because the second item requires more anxiety. A more difficult item concerning anxiety will better distinguish people who have anxiety from those who do not.

One widely used application of IRT is *computerized adaptive testing (CAT;* Bjorner, Chang, Thissen, & Reeve, 2007; Cook, O'Malley, & Roddey, 2005). As a person completes a measure on a computer, the CAT program selects the best items for that person from a bank of questions. The items selected are based on the person's responses to prior items. For example, if someone endorses "I am always hopeful," it would not be useful to ask questions of less "difficulty," such as, "I am sometimes hopeful." CAT ensures that less difficult items are not given after an item of medium difficulty has been endorsed.

IRT and CAT have been applied to a diverse range of assessments including those for personality (e.g., Samuel, Simms, Clark, Livesly, & Widiger, 2010; Walton, Roberts, Krueger, Blonigen, & Hicks, 2008) and psychological disorders (e.g., Gelhorn et al., 2009; Purpura, Wilson, & Lonigon, 2010; Uebelacker, Strong, Weinstock, & Miller, 2009). One interesting finding from these analyses is that there is more overlap between measures of normal versus abnormal personality patterns than expected (Samuel et al., 2010; Walton et al., 2008).

---

you're putting down one telescope and picking up another. The reliability question is whether you see about the same thing through each of the different telescopes.

This kind of reliability is termed **internal reliability** or **internal consistency.** This is reliability within a set of observations of a single aspect of personality. Because different items have different sources of error, using many items should tend to balance out the error. The more observations, the more likely the random error will cancel out. Because people using self-report scales want good reliability, most scales contain many items (but see Box 3.2). If the items are reliable enough, they're then used together as a single index of the personality quality.

How do you find out whether the items you're using have good internal reliability? Just having a lot of items doesn't guarantee it. Reliability is a question about the correlations among people's responses to the items. Saying that the items are highly reliable means that people's responses to the items are highly correlated.

As a practical matter, there are several ways to investigate internal consistency. All of them examine correlations among people's responses across items. Perhaps the best way (although it's cumbersome) is to look at the average correlation between each pair of items taken separately. A simpler way is to separate the items into two subsets (often odd- versus even-numbered items), add up people's scores for each subset, and correlate the two subtotals with each other. This index is called **split-half reliability.** If the two halves of the item set measure the same quality, people who score high on one half should also score high on the other half, and people who score low on one half should also score low on the other half. Thus, a strong positive correlation between halves is evidence of internal consistency.

Inter-Rater Reliability

As noted, personality isn't always measured by self-reports. Some observations are *literally* observations, made by one person watching and assessing someone else. Use of observer ratings creates a slightly different reliability problem. In observer ratings, the *person making the rating* is a "measuring device." There are sources of error in this device, just as in other devices. How can you judge reliability in this case?

Conceptually, the answer is the same as it was in the other case. You need to put down one telescope and pick up another. In the case of observer ratings, you need to check this observer against another observer. To the extent that both see about the same thing when they look at the same event, reliability is high. This dual observation is logically the same as using two items on a questionnaire. Raters whose judgments correlate highly with each other across many ratings are said to have high **inter-rater reliability.**

In many cases, having high inter-rater reliability requires the judges to be thoroughly trained in how to observe what they're observing. Judges of Olympic diving, for example, have seen many thousands of dives and know precisely what to look for. As a result, their inter-rater reliability is high. Similarly, when observers assess personality, they often receive much instruction and practice before turning to the "real thing," so their reliability will be high.

Stability across Time

There's one more kind of reliability that's important in the measurement of personality. This type of reliability concerns repeatability across time. That is, assessment at one time should agree fairly well with assessment done at a different time.

Why is this important? Remember, personality is supposed to be stable. That's one reason people use the word—to convey a sense of stability. If personality is really *stable*—doesn't fluctuate from minute to minute or from day to day—then *measures* of personality should be reliable across time. People's scores should stay roughly the same when measured a week later, a month later, or four years later.

If all judges are seeing the same thing when they rate an event, then inter-rater reliability will be high.

Table 3.1 Three Kinds of Reliability. Each assesses the consistency or repeatability of an observation by looking a second time, either with the same measuring device or with a slightly different one.

Type of Reliability	Measuring Device	Type of Consistency
Internal reliability	Test item	Consistency within the test
Inter-rater reliability	Rater	Agreement between raters
Test–retest reliability	Entire test	Consistency across time

This kind of reliability is termed **test–retest reliability.** It's determined by giving the test to the same people at two different times. A scale with high test–retest reliability will yield scores the second time (the retest) that are fairly similar to those from the first time. People with high scores the first time will have high scores the second time, and people with lower scores at first will have lower scores later on. (For a summary of these three types of reliability, see Table 3.1.)

Validity of Measurement

Reliability is a starting point in measurement, but it's not the only issue that matters. It's possible for measures to be highly reliable but completely meaningless. Thus, another important issue is what's called **validity.** This issue concerns whether what you're measuring is what you *think* you're measuring (or what you're *trying* to measure). Earlier, we portrayed reliability in terms of random influences on the image in a telescope as you look through it at the moon. To extend the same analogy, the validity issue is whether what you're seeing is really the moon or just a streetlight (see also Figure 3.1).

How do you decide whether you're measuring what you want to measure? There are two ways to answer this question. One is an "in principle" answer, and the other is a set of tactics. The "in principle" answer is that people decide by comparing two kinds of "definitions" with each other. When you see the word *definition,* what probably comes to mind is a conceptual definition, which spells out the word's meaning in terms of conceptual qualities or attributes (as in a dictionary). It tells us what information a word conveys, by consensus among users of the language. Psychologists also talk about another kind of definition, however, called an **operational definition.** This is a description of a physical event.

The difference between the two kinds of definition is easy to illustrate. Consider the concept *love.* Its conceptual definition might be something like "a strong affection for another person." There are many ways, however, to define *love* operationally. For example, you might ask the person you're assessing to indicate on a rating scale how much she loves someone. You might measure how often she looks into that person's eyes when interacting with him. You might measure how willing she is to give up events she enjoys in order to be with him. These three measures differ considerably from one another. Yet each might be taken as an operational definition (or operationalization) of love.

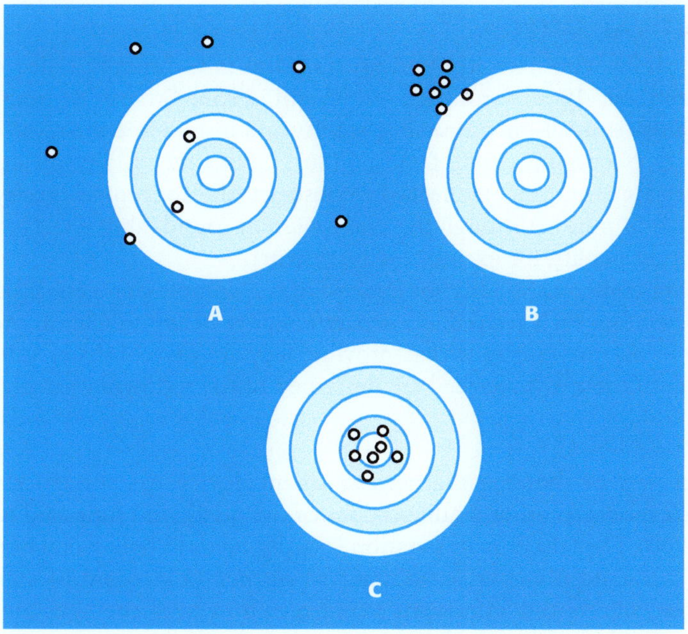

FIGURE 3.1
A simple way to think about the difference between reliability and validity, using the metaphor of target shooting. (A) Sometimes when people shoot at a target their shots go all over. This result corresponds to measurement that's neither reliable nor valid. (B) Reliability is higher as the shots are closer together. Shots that miss the mark, however, are not valid. (C) Good measurement means that the shots are close together (reliable) *and* near the bull's-eye (valid).

The essence of the validity issue in measurement can be summarized in this question: How well does the *operational* definition (the event) match the *conceptual* definition (the abstract quality you have in mind to measure)? If the two are close, the measure has high validity. If they aren't close, validity is low.

How do you decide whether the two are close? Usually, psychologists poke at the conceptual definition until they're sure what the critical elements are and then look to see whether the same elements are in the operationalization. If they aren't (at least by strong implication), the validity of the operationalization is questionable.

The validity issue is critically important. It's also extremely tricky. It's the subject of continual debate in psychology, as researchers try to think of better and better ways to look at human behavior (Borsboom, Mellenbergh, & van Heerden, 2004). The reason the issue is important is that researchers and assessors form conclusions about personality in terms of what *think* they're measuring. If what they're measuring isn't what they think they're measuring, they will draw wrong conclusions. Likewise, a clinician may draw the wrong conclusion about a person if the measure doesn't measure what the clinician thinks it measures.

Validity is important whenever anything is being observed. In personality assessment, the validity question has been examined closely for a long time. In trying to be sure that personality tests are valid, theorists have come to distinguish several aspects of validity from one another. These distinctions have also influenced the practical process of establishing validity.

Construct Validity

The idea of validity you have in mind at this point is technically called **construct validity** (Campbell, 1960; Cronbach & Meehl, 1955; Strauss & Smith, 2009). Construct validity is an all-encompassing validity, and is therefore the most important kind (Hogan & Nicholson, 1988; Landy, 1986). Construct validity means that the measure (the assessment device) reflects the construct (the conceptual quality) that the psychologist has in mind. Although the word *construct* sounds abstract, it just means a concept. Any trait quality, for example, is a construct.

Establishing construct validity for a measure is a complex process. It uses several kinds of information, each treated as a separate aspect of the validation process. For this reason, the various qualities that provide support for construct validity have separate names of their own. Several are described in the following paragraphs.

Criterion Validity

An important part of showing that an assessment device has construct validity is showing that it relates to other manifestations of the quality it's supposed to measure (Campbell, 1960). The "other manifestation" usually means a behavioral index, or the judgment of a trained observer, as an external *criterion* (a standard of comparison). The researcher collects this information and sees how well the assessment device correlates with it. This aspect of validity is sometimes referred to as **criterion validity** (because it uses an external criterion) or **predictive validity** (because it tests how well the measure predicts something else it's supposed to predict).

As an example, suppose you were interested in criterion validity for a measure of dominance you were developing. One way to approach this problem would be to select people who score high and low on your measure and bring them to a laboratory one at a time to work on a task with two other people. You could tape each group's discussion and score the tape for the number of times each person made suggestions, gave instructions, took charge of the situation, and so on. These would be viewed as behavioral criteria of dominance. If people who scored high on your measure did these things more than people who scored low, it would indicate a kind of criterion validity.

Another way to approach the problem would be to have a trained interviewer spend 20 minutes with each person who completed your scale and rate each person's dominance after the interview. The interviewer's ratings would be a different kind of criterion for dominance. If the ratings related to scores on your measure, it would indicate a different kind of criterion validity for the measure.

Criterion validity is regarded as the most important way to support construct validity. A controversy has arisen over the process of establishing it, however. Howard (1990; Howard, Maxwell, Weiner, Boynton, & Rooney, 1980) pointed out that people often assume the criterion that's used is a perfect reflection of the construct. In reality, though, this is almost never true. In fact, far too often, researchers choose criterion measures that are *poor* reflections of the construct.

We raise this point to emphasize how important it is to be careful in deciding what criterion to use. Unless the criterion is a good one, associations with it are meaningless. Despite this issue, criterion validity remains the keystone of construct validation.

Convergent Validity

Another kind of support for a measure's construct validity involves showing that the measure relates to characteristics that are similar to, but not the same as, what it's supposed to measure. How is this different from criterion validity? It's just a very small step away from it. In this case, though, you know the second measure aims to assess something a little different from what your measure assesses. Because this kind of information gathering often proceeds from several angles, it's termed **convergent validation** (Campbell & Fiske, 1959). That is, the evidence "converges" on the construct you're interested in, even though any single finding by itself won't clearly reflect the construct.

For example, a scale intended to measure dominance should relate at least a little to measures of qualities such as leadership (positively) or shyness (inversely). The correlations shouldn't be perfect because those aren't quite the same constructs, but they shouldn't be zero either. If you developed a measure to assess dominance and it didn't correlate at all with measures of leadership and shyness, you'd have to start wondering whether your measure really assesses dominance.

Discriminant Validity

It's important to show that an assessment device measures what it's intended to measure. But it's also important to show that it does *not* measure qualities it's *not* intended to measure—especially qualities that don't fit your conceptual definition of the construct (Campbell, 1960). This aspect of the construct validation process is termed **discriminant validation** (Campbell & Fiske, 1959).

The importance of discriminant validity can be easy to overlook. However, discriminant validation is a major line of defense against the third-variable problem in correlational research, discussed in Chapter 2. That is, you can't be sure why two correlated variables correlate. It may be that one influences the other. But it may be that a third variable, correlated with the two you've studied, is really responsible for their correlation. In principle, it's always possible to attribute the effect of a personality dimension on behavior to some other personality dimension. In practice, however, this can be made much harder by evidence of discriminant validity. That is, if research shows that the dimension you're interested in is unrelated to another variable, then that variable can't be invoked as an alternative explanation for any effect of the first.

To illustrate this, let's return to an example used in discussing the third-variable problem in Chapter 2: a correlation between self-esteem and academic performance. This association *might* reflect the effect of an unmeasured variable—for instance, IQ. Suppose, though, that we know this measure of self-esteem is unrelated to IQ, because someone checked that possibility during the process of its validation. This would make it hard to claim that IQ underlies the correlation between self-esteem and academic performance.

The process of discriminant validation is never ending, because new possibilities for third variables always suggest themselves. Ruling out alternative explanations is thus a challenging task, but it's also a necessary one. Earlier in the chapter (in Box 3.2), we discussed implications of item response theory for internal consistency. Item response theory also provides safeguards that help ensure that items measure only what they are intended to measure. This new method therefore offers a valuable tool to enhance discriminant validity and help reduce the third-variable problem.

Face Validity

One more kind of validity should be mentioned. It's much simpler and a little more intuitive, and most people think it's less important. It's called **face validity.** Face validity means that the assessment device appears, on its "face," to be measuring the construct it was intended to measure. It *looks* right. A test of sociability made up of items such as "I prefer to spend time with friends rather than alone" and "I would rather socialize than read books" would have high face validity. A test of sociability made up of items such as "Green is my favorite color" and "I prefer imported cars" would have low face validity.

Many researchers regard face validity as a convenience, for two reasons. First, some believe that face-valid measures are easier to respond to than measures with less face validity. Second, researchers sometimes focus on distinctions between qualities of personality that differ in subtle ways. It often seems impossible to separate these qualities from each other except by using measures that are high in face validity.

On the other hand, face validity can occasionally be a detriment. This is true when the assessment device is intended to measure something that the person being assessed would find threatening or embarrassing to admit. In such cases, the test developer usually tries to obscure the purpose of the test by reducing its face validity.

Whether face validity is good, bad, or neither, it should be clear that it does not substitute for other aspects of validity. If an assessment device is to be useful in the long run, it must undergo the laborious process of construct validation. The "bottom line" is always construct validity.

Culture and Validity

Another important issue in assessment concerns cultural differences. In a sense, this is a validity issue; in a sense, it's an issue of generalizability. Let's frame the issue as a question: Do the scores on a personality test have the same meaning for a person from an Asian culture, a Latino culture, or an African American culture as they do for a person from a middle-class European-American culture?

There are at least two aspects to this question. The first is whether the psychological construct *itself* has the same meaning from one culture to another. This is a fundamental question about the nature of personality. Are the elements of personality the same from one human group to another? Many people assume the basic elements of personality are universal. That may, in fact, be a dangerous assumption.

The second aspect of the question concerns how people from different cultures *interpret* the items of the measure. If an item has one meaning for middle-class Americans, but a different meaning in some other culture, responses to the item will also have different meanings in the two cultures. A similar issue arises when a measure is translated into a different language. This usually involves translating the measure into the new language and then translating it back into the original language by someone who's never seen the original items. This process sometimes reveals that items contain idiomatic or metaphorical meanings that are hard to translate. Adapting a measure from one culture for use in another culture is a complex process with many difficulties (Butcher, 1996). It must be done very carefully, if the measure is to be valid in the new culture.

Response Sets and Loss of Validity

Any discussion of validity must also note that there are problems in self-reports that can interfere with the validity of the information collected. We've already mentioned that biases in recall can distort the picture and render the information invalid. In the same way, people's motivational tendencies can also get in the way of accurate reporting.

The tendency to provide socially desirable responses can sometimes mask a person's true characteristics or feelings.

There are at least two biases in people's responses in assessment. These biases are called **response sets.** A response set is a psychological orientation, a readiness to answer in a particular way (Jackson & Messick, 1967). Response sets create distortions in what's assessed. Personality psychologists want their assessments to provide information that's free from contamination. Thus, response sets are problems.

Two response sets are particularly important in personality assessment. One of them emerges most clearly when the assessment device is a self-report instrument that, in one fashion or another, asks the person questions that require a "yes" or "no" response (or a response on a rating scale with "agree" and "disagree" as the opposite ends of the scale). This response set, called **acquiescence,** is the tendency to say "yes" (Couch & Keniston, 1960).

Everyone presumably has a bit of this tendency, but people vary greatly on it. That's the problem. If the set isn't counteracted somehow, the scores of people who are highly acquiescent become inflated. Their high scores reflect the response set, instead of their personalities. People who have extreme personalities but not much acquiescence will also have high scores. But you won't know whose high scores are from personality and whose are from acquiescence.

Many view acquiescence as an easy problem to combat. The way it's handled for self-reports is this: Write half the items so that "yes" means being at one end of the personality dimension. Write the other half of the items so that "no" means being at that end of the personality dimension. In the process of scoring the test, then, any bias that comes from the simple tendency to say "yes" is canceled out.

This procedure takes care of the problem of overagreement, but not everyone is convinced it's a good idea. Negatively worded items often are harder to understand or more complicated to answer than positively worded items. The result can be responses that are less accurate (Converse & Presser, 1986; Schriesheim & Hill, 1981). For this reason, some people feel it's better to live with the acquiescence problem than to introduce a different kind of error through complex wording.

A second response set is perhaps more important than acquiescence and also more troublesome. It's called **social desirability.** It reflects the fact that people tend to portray themselves in a good light (in socially desirable ways) whenever possible. Once again, this tendency is stronger among some people than others (Crowne & Marlowe, 1964; Edwards, 1957). As with acquiescence, if it isn't counteracted, people with strong concerns about social desirability will produce scores that reflect the response set, rather than their personalities.

For some personality dimensions, this isn't much of a problem. The reason is that there's really no social approval or disapproval at either end of the dimension. In other cases, though, there's a consensus that it's better to be one way (for example, honest or likable) than the other (dishonest or unlikable). In these cases, assessment becomes tricky.

In general, psychologists deal with this problem by trying to phrase items so that the issue of social desirability isn't salient. As much as anything else, this is a process of trying to avoid even bringing up the idea that one kind of person is approved of more than the other. Sometimes this means phrasing undesirable responses in ways that makes them more acceptable. Sometimes it means looking for ways to let people admit the undesirable quality indirectly. A different way to deal with the problem is to include items that assess the person's degree of concern about social desirability and use this information as a correction factor in evaluating the person's responses to other items. In any event, this is a problem that personality psychologists must constantly be aware of and constantly guarding against in trying to measure what people are like.

Two Rationales behind the Development of Assessment Devices

Thus far, this chapter has considered issues that arise when measuring any quality of personality. But how do people decide what qualities to measure in the first place? This question won't be answered fully here, because the answer depends partly on the theoretical perspective underlying the assessment. We will, however, address one general issue. In particular, development of personality measures usually follows one of two approaches or strategies, each of which has its own kind of logic.

Rational or Theoretical Approach

One strategy is termed a **rational** or **theoretical approach** to assessment. This strategy is based on theoretical considerations from the very start. The psychologist first develops a theoretical basis for believing that a particular aspect of personality is important. The next task is to create a test in which this dimension is reflected validly and reliably in people's answers. This approach to test development often leads to assessment devices that have a high degree of face validity.

It's important to realize that the work doesn't stop once a set of items has been developed. Instruments developed from this starting point must be shown to be reliable, to predict behavioral criteria, and to have good construct validity. Until these steps have been taken, the scale isn't considered a useful measure of anything.

It's probably safe to say that the majority of personality measurement devices that exist today were developed using this path. Some of these measures focus on a single construct, others are inventories with scales focusing on multiple constructs. Most of the measures discussed in later chapters were created by first deciding *what* to measure and then figuring out *how* to measure it.

Empirical Approaches

A second strategy is usually characterized as an **empirical**, or data-based, approach. Its basic characteristic is that it relies on data, rather than on theory, to decide what items go into the assessment device.

There are two important variations on this theme. In one of them, the person developing the measure uses the data to decide what qualities of personality even *exist* (e.g., Cattell, 1979). Because that line of thought is an important contributor to trait psychology, we're going to wait to discuss it until Chapter 4. We'll focus here on another empirical approach—one that reflects a very pragmatic orientation to the process of assessment. It's guided less by a desire to understand personality than by a practical aim: to sort people into categories. If a quick or inexpensive technique can be found to do this, the technique is useful.

Instead of developing the test first and then validating it against a criterion, this approach works in the opposite direction. The criterion is the groups into which people are to be sorted. To develop the test, you start with a huge number of possible items and find out which ones are answered differently by one criterion group than by other people. This is called the **criterion keying** approach. This label reflects the fact that the items retained are those that distinguish between the criterion group and other people. If an item set can be found for each group, then the test (all item sets together) can be used to tell who belongs to which group. In this view, it doesn't matter at all what the items look like. Items are chosen solely because members of a specific group (defined on some other basis) tend to answer them differently than other people.

This method underlies the Minnesota Multiphasic Personality Inventory, or MMPI (Hathaway & McKinley, 1943), revised in 1989 as the MMPI-2 (Butcher, Dahlstrom, Graham, Tellegen, & Kaemmer, 1989). This is a very long true–false inventory that was developed to assess abnormality. A large number of self-descriptive statements were given to a group of normal persons and to groups of psychiatric patients—people already judged by clinicians to have specific disorders. Thus, the criterion already existed. If people with one diagnosis either agreed or disagreed with an item more often than normal people and people with different diagnoses, that item was included in the scale for that diagnosis.

The MMPI-2 has become controversial in recent years, for several reasons. Most important for our purposes in this book, it is increasingly recognized that different diagnostic categories are not as distinct as they were formerly thought to be. As a result, scores on the MMPI tend to be elevated (if at all) on several scales, rather than just one. Once consequence of the recognition of this pattern is a broad (and intense) reconsideration of the nature of psychiatric diagnosis.

Better Assessment: A Never-Ending Search

No test is perfect, and no test is ever considered finished, just because it's widely used. Most personality scales in wide use today have been revised and restandardized periodically. The process of establishing construct validity requires not just a single study but many. It thus takes time. The process of establishing discriminant validity is virtually never ending. Tremendous effort is invested in creating and improving tests of personality. This investment of effort is necessary if people are to feel confident of knowing what the tests measure. Having that confidence is an important part of the assessment of personality.

The characteristics of personality tests discussed in this chapter distinguish these tests from those you see in newspapers and magazines, on TV, online, and so forth. Sometimes, the items in a magazine article were written specifically for that article. It's unlikely, though, that anyone checked on their reliability. It's even less likely that anyone checked on their validity. Unless the right steps have been taken to create an instrument, you should be careful about putting your faith in the results that come from it.

• SUMMARY •

Assessment (measurement of personality) is something that people constantly do informally. Psychologists formalize this process into several distinct techniques. Observer ratings are made by someone other than the person being rated—an interviewer, someone who watches, or someone who knows the people well enough to make ratings of what they are like. Observer ratings often are somewhat subjective, involving interpretations of the person's behavior. Self-reports are reports about themselves made by the people being assessed. Self-reports can be single scale or multiscale inventories. Implicit assessment is measuring patterns of associations within the self that are not open to introspection. Assessment devices can be subjective or objective. Objective techniques require no interpretation as the assessment is made. Subjective techniques involve some sort of interpretation as an intrinsic part of the measure.

One issue for all assessment is reliability (the reproducibility of the measurement). Reliability is determined by checking one measurement against another (or several others). Self-report scales usually have many items (each a measurement device), leading to indices of internal reliability or internal consistency. Observer judgments are checked by inter-rater reliability. Test–retest reliability assesses the reproducibility of the measure over time. In all cases, high correlation among measures means good reliability.

Another important issue is validity (whether what you're measuring is what you want to measure). The attempt to determine whether the operational definition (the assessment device) matches the concept you set out to measure is called *construct validation*. Contributors to construct validity are evidence of criterion, convergent, and discriminant validity. Face validity isn't usually taken as an important element of construct validity. Validity is threatened by the fact that people have response sets (acquiescence and social desirability) that bias their responses.

Development of assessment devices follows one of two strategies or approaches. The rational strategy uses a theory to decide what should be measured and then figures out the best way to measure it. Most assessment devices developed this way. The empirical strategy involves using data to determine what items should be in a scale. The MMPI was developed this way, using a technique called *criterion keying,* in which the test developers let people's responses tell them which items to use. Test items that members of a diagnostic category answered differently from other people were retained.

• GLOSSARY •

Acquiesence The response set of tending to say "yes" ("agree") in response to any question.

Assessment The measuring of personality.

Construct validity The accuracy with which a measure reflects the underlying concept.

Convergent validity The degree to which a measure relates to other characteristics that are conceptually similar to what it's supposed to assess.

Criterion keying The developing of a test by seeing which items distinguish between groups.

Criterion validity The degree to which the measure correlates with a separate criterion reflecting the same concept.

Discriminant validity The degree to which a scale does *not* measure unintended qualities.

Empirical approach (to scale development) The use of data instead of theory to decide what should go into the measure.

Error Random influences that are incorporated in measurements.

Face validity The scale "looks" as if it measures what it's supposed to measure.

Implicit assessment Measuring associations between the sense of self and aspects of personality that are implicit (hard to introspect about).

Internal reliability (internal consistency) Agreement among responses made to the items of a measure.

Inter-rater reliability The degree of agreement between observers of the same events.

Inventory A personality test measuring several aspects of personality on distinct subscales.

Objective measure A measure that incorporates no interpretation.

Observer ratings An assessment in which someone else produces information about the person being assessed.

Operational definition The defining of a concept by the concrete events through which it's measured (or manipulated).

Predictive validity The degree to which the measure predicts other variables it should predict.

Rational approach (to scale development) The use of a theory to decide what you want to measure and then deciding how to measure it.

Reliability Consistency across repeated measurements.

Response set A biased orientation to answering.

Self-report An assessment in which people make ratings pertaining to themselves.

Social desirability The response set of tending to portray oneself favorably.

Split-half reliability Assessing internal consistency among responses to items of a measure by splitting the items into halves and then correlating them.

Subjective measure A measure incorporating personal interpretation.

Test-retest reliability The stability of measurements across time.

Theoretical approach *See* **Rational approach.**

Validity The degree to which a measure actually measures what it's intended to measure.

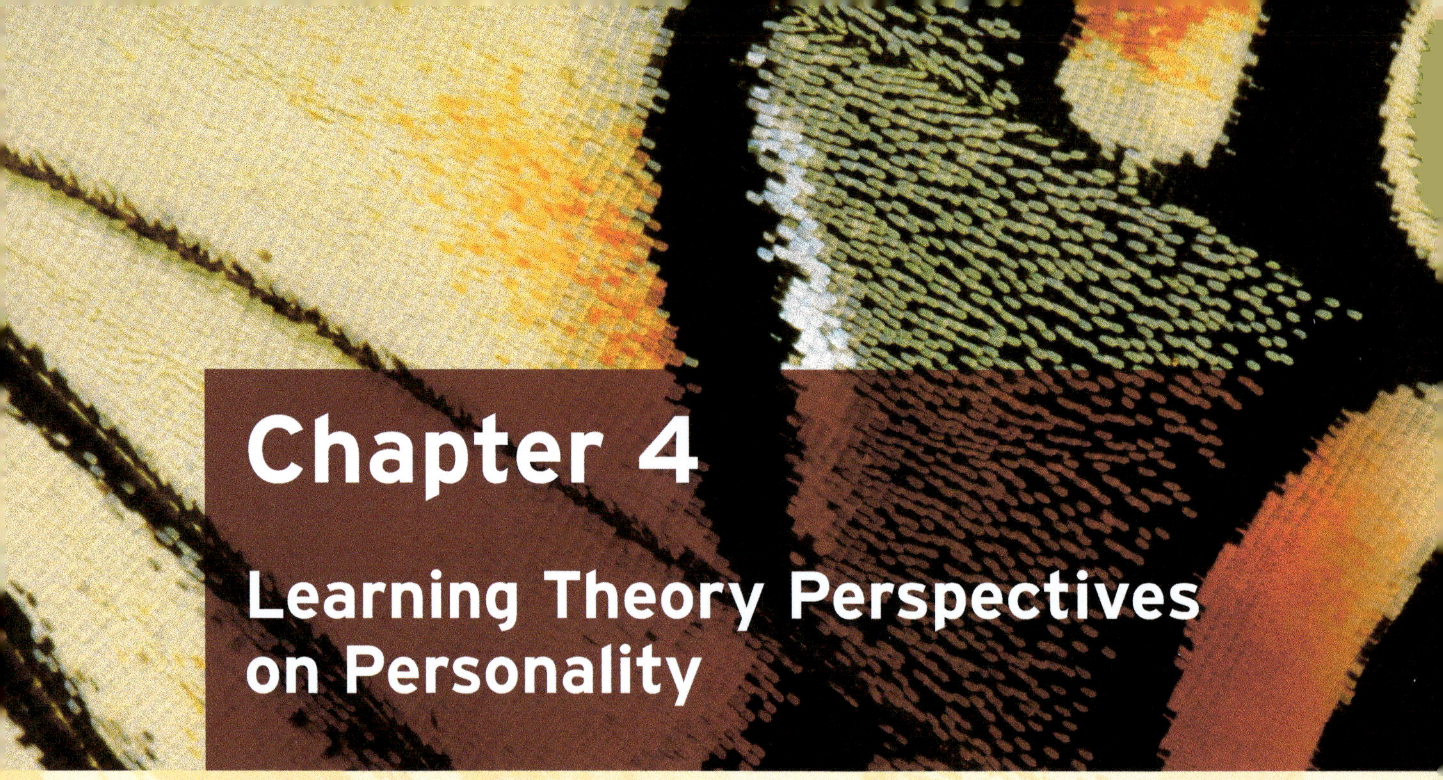

Chapter 4

Learning Theory Perspectives on Personality

Key Themes

- Historical learning theory approaches to personality
- Pavlov and classical conditioning
- Watson and behaviourism
- Skinner and operant conditioning
- Integrative personality theory of Dollard and Miller
- Social cognitive approaches of Bandura
- The concept of self-efficacy
- Rotter and the locus of control
- Mischel and social learning theory

Learning Outcomes

After studying this chapter you should:

- Understand the principles underlying the learning theory approach to personality
- Be aware of the opposing views about whether differences in behaviour are learnt or result from differences in personality
- Be able to identify the learning theorists that have contributed to personality theory
- Understand the principles of classical conditioning and some of its applications
- Appreciate Skinner's approach to psychology
- Understand the principles underlying operant conditioning
- Be aware of the work of Dollard and Miller, who attempted to integrate psychodynamic and behavioural concepts within a learning theory framework
- Understand Bandura's social learning approach to personality
- Appreciate the concept of self-efficacy
- Have developed an understanding of the concept of locus of control
- Understand the contribution that Mischel has made to personality research
- Appreciate the person-situation debate in personality
- Know how to critically evaluate learning theory approaches to explaining personality

Introduction

Source: Wonder Years/Brand X Pictures

Do you love parties and never miss one, or do parties make you anxious so that you avoid them if possible? What causes these differences? The concept of personality, as we have seen, is used to help explain such differences in behaviour between individuals. The theories we have previously examined suggest that differences in the personality structures that are said to exist within each individual interact to produce differences in behaviour. Our behaviour is driven by inner motives such as instincts, unconscious drives, feelings of inferiority and so on, that all shape our personality. Based on what we have read so far, we might well claim that the person who enjoys parties and interacting with others does so because they have an outgoing, sociable personality. They are driven by an inner need to be with other people and are not so comfortable in their own company. There are alternative explanations for personality, and this chapter is about a series of theoretical approaches that adopt a radically different view. These theories reject the idea of our behaviour being directed by inner motives, suggesting instead that all our behaviour is learned. Individual differences in behaviour are the result of the different learning experiences that people have had and the situations that they find themselves in. To understand why someone behaves in a particular way, you need to carefully examine the situation they are in and to explore their past experiences in similar situations, rather than explain differences in behaviour as resulting from differences in personality. No underlying personality structure like Jung's psyche is thought necessary; rather, individuals have learnt to behave in certain ways because in the past they have been rewarded or they have avoided discomfort or punishment by doing so.

These approaches to understanding the individual are based on theories of how we learn. The learning theory explanation of the happy partygoer would suggest that such individuals have learnt to enjoy parties. Their first experience of a party as a child was wonderful. They were given presents, everything went well and they had a good time. This initial positive party experience has been followed by others, so that the individual looks forward to parties as pleasant experiences because of their learning history of parties. By contrast, the individual who dreads parties will have had some initial bad experiences of parties. Perhaps they were made to share their special toys with other children, or the other children broke their presents, or they did not get what they wanted or they were punished for being rude and so on. Learning theory would suggest that this negative experience can lead the individual to dread parties, especially if the negative experience is repeated. These examples are somewhat simplified, but we hope they have got the point across. The contention is that your attitudes to events like socialising are dictated not by your personality but by the past experiences of parties and similar events that you have had. As we mentioned earlier, these approaches are based on learning theory, and they vary in terms of how radical they are. We shall begin by looking briefly at the history of learning theory and outlining the major concepts that you need to understand.

→

Early learning theory developed primarily in the United States. The roots of the psychoanalytic schools of personality were firmly based in the European tradition of psychology, as we have seen, although they later became established in North America. We shall examine some of the major approaches to learning theory in the United States, from the radical approach of B. F. Skinner to the more moderate views of John Dollard and Neal Miller. Next, we will examine the work of Albert Bandura. While still maintaining a learning theory approach, Bandura introduces cognitive and emotional variables as factors influencing behaviour. Next, we will look at two learning theory concepts that have stimulated enormous amounts of research. These are Bandura's concept of self-efficacy and Rotter's locus of control. Finally, we will examine the work of Walter Mischel. Mischel has not developed a full-blown theory of personality; but his critique of existing approaches has been enormously influential in personality psychology, as you will see.

The focus for much of this chapter is the question of whether you behave as you do because of an inner personality that drives your behaviour, or whether it is purely that you have learnt to behave in certain ways in particular situations.

Introduction to learning theory

We take a slight detour here and look at the history of learning theory, as many of the crucial concepts that underpin more current developments emerged early in the development of psychology as a discipline. You need to understand these core concepts as they have heavily influenced many later developments.

Although learning theory developed mainly in the United States, a major influence was the work of a Russian physiologist, Ivan Pavlov. At the beginning of the last century, Pavlov was exploring the digestive system in humans and other animals. While he was undertaking research examining the salivary response of dogs, he observed what appeared to him to be ways in which dogs learnt to respond to objects and people. When it is given food, a dog will automatically salivate. This is a naturally occurring response. In the terminology of learning theory, the food is called the **unconditioned stimulus** and the response of salivating is called the **unconditioned response**. Pavlov observed that if a light went on or a bell rang (**unconditioned stimuli**) before the dog received food, after a few trials the dog would salivate when the light went on or the bell rang. The dog had learnt to associate what had been a neutral unconditioned stimulus (bell or light) with the food and salivated at the neutral stimulus even in the absence of food. This is the basis of what is known as **classical conditioning**, and the basic process is summarised in Figure 4.1. Pavlov (1906, 1927, 1928) carried out extensive research on the learning associated with classical conditioning.

Classical conditioning also accounts for some learning in humans. For example, suppose a parental goal was to bring up their young child to enjoy books. One scenario for achieving this, according to classical conditioning, would be to start with the child being cuddled on a parent's lap – an experience that makes the child feel good. This is an unconditioned response (naturally occurring). Reading a book across a room to a young child will initially be a neutral stimulus. However, if the parent reads the book to the child while cuddling the child on their lap, after a few repeated sessions, being read to will produce pleasant feelings in the child even when they are not being cuddled by their parent. In this way, reading books has become a conditioned stimulus that produces pleasure in the child. Once reading the book has become a conditioned response, reading to the child across the room will induce the same pleasurable response in the child.

Pavlov demonstrated that the conditioned response could *generalise* to similar stimuli. In the dog example, it could be changes in brightness or colour or the light that would evoke the same response. Similarly with children, reading while on their parent's knee may generalise to being read to across a room and eventually to reading anywhere, even on their own, and finding it a pleasant experience. Pavlov showed that there are limits to generalisation. In the dog example, if the food is delivered to some sounds but not to others, the dog will learn to discriminate between the sounds and will only salivate to the 'food' sounds. Finally, Pavlov demonstrated that the conditioning process could be reversed. If the light is presented repeatedly with no food following, then the dog's salivary response gets weaker and weaker, till eventually what is termed **extinction** is achieved.

At this point, you may wonder what all of this has to do with personality, but Pavlov went on to show that classical conditioning could explain many of our emotional reactions. It could be that I am an anxious person because I have had experiences where I learnt to be anxious; it is not simply that I possess a neurotic personality. The crucial difference is that if you have learnt to be anxious, then you can unlearn; or, in learning theory terminology, the anxiety

1. Natural response (before conditioning occurs)

Stimulus	Response
Food presented to dog **[Food = Unconditioned stimulus]**	Dog salivates **[Salivation = Unconditioned response]**
Light is switched on **[Light = Neutral stimulus]**	**No response from the dog**

2. Conditioning procedure for several trials

Stimulus	Response
Light is switched on & **food** is presented to dog **Neutral stimulus + Unconditioned stimulus**	Dog **salivates** **Unconditioned response**

3. After the conditioning trials

Stimulus	Response
Light alone is presented to dog **Conditioned stimulus**	Dog **salivates** **Conditioned response**

Figure 4.1 Summary of classical conditioning.

response can be extinguished as it is not a part of your personality. We will return to this shortly with a detailed example once we have understood how Pavlov's work came to be so influential within psychology.

John B. Watson, an American psychologist, read the early work of Pavlov and was very impressed by it. He began to apply some of Pavlov's observational techniques in his own research and replicated some of his work in the United States. As he became established within psychology, Watson began to call for a change in the direction of American psychology so that it could become a true science. He wanted to reject the methods of introspection and interpretation of patients' reminiscences that Freud and the other psychoanalysts had employed. He saw these methods as unscientific and argued instead for a psychology that considered only observable aspects of behaviour. In practice, this means that no assumptions or hypotheses can be made about what is going on inside someone's mind. Stimuli and their effect on behaviour are the subject matter of the behavioural approach, and rigorous scientific methods, mainly based in laboratories, are used to collect data. Watson published his views in 1914 in a book entitled *Behaviour*. In 1919, he published *Psychology from the Standpoint of a Behaviourist*. This book was influential in American psychology. It included summaries of Pavlov's work on classical conditioning, thereby introducing Pavlov's work to a wider audience. Watson is generally credited as being the founding figure of the School of Behaviourism, but his career as a psychologist ended with his withdrawal from academia in 1920 to enter business. Behaviourism and the popularising of Pavlov's work had set the scene for developments in personality theorising and research. From this perspective variables are manipulated, ideally in a controlled laboratory setting, and then the effects of these manipulations on the subject of the research are carefully observed.

The clinical perspective within classical conditioning

If you recall in Chapter 1, a distinction was made between the *clinical* and *individual differences* approaches to the study of personality. Although the behavioural approach is a radical departure from the psychoanalytic approaches in previous chapters, it still maintained a heavy focus on behaviour change, particularly within a clinical context. Put simply, if your hypothesis is that behaviour is learnt, then it is necessary to show that it can be unlearnt. The behavioural approaches, like the psychoanalytic approaches, focussed on demonstrating

Stop and Think

Treating classically conditioned emotional responses

Systematic desensitisation

This can be used to treat phobias, for example, someone with a phobia of birds. The aim is to replace the old association between the feared stimulus (bird) and the feared response (panic symptoms) with a new association of relaxation. The client and therapist begin by ranking bird-related fears from most to the least feared. Holding a bird might be most feared; a picture of a bird might be least feared. Next, the client is taught how to relax. The response of relaxation is incompatible with the feared response. The client and therapist move through the list of fears, ensuring that at each level the feared response becomes conditioned to the relaxation response, till the client can comfortably face their worst fear of birds. Many phobias and other anxieties have been successfully treated with systematic desensitisation.

Alcoholism

Aversion therapy has been used to treat people with alcohol addictions. Here the image of a drink could be paired with images of being sick or other negative images. This therapy has also been used to assist individuals stop smoking.

that mental health problems (psychopathology) could be cured using behavioural interventions. A crucial difference between the psychoanalysts and the early learning theorists concerns how psychopathology arises. For the psychoanalysts, as we have seen, psychopathology arises because of inner causes such as unresolved developmental crises; or conflict between the structures within the personality such as the id, ego and superego; or problems in personality development of some other kind. The learning theorists rejected this as an explanation for the cause of mental problems, seeing it as unscientific to refer to what they saw as unobservable inner mental processes and/or structures to explain observed differences in behaviour. For these learning theorists, psychopathology was a learnt maladaptive response to a situation that may have generalised to other situations or similar stimuli, and as such, it could be unlearnt. Normal development was about learning adaptive responses in a variety of situations, while abnormal development resulted from acquiring maladaptive responses.

Pavlov (1927) began this line of research by inducing what he called **experimental neuroses** in one of his laboratory dogs. The dog was conditioned so that he would salivate to the shape of a circle. He then learnt to distinguish between circles and ellipses, only salivating to circles. However, when the distinctions between circles and ellipses became harder to distinguish, the dog became very distressed; his behaviour was disorganised, with a preponderance of neurotic symptoms. The dog barked when taken into the laboratory, shivered in his harness and tried to bite the restraining straps. Pavlov interpreted this as demonstrating that when the dog could no longer cope with what was being asked of him, he developed neurotic symptoms.

Watson and his colleague Rayner (1920) went on to demonstrate that human emotional responses could also be manipulated using classical conditioning. This is the famous classical conditioning experiment carried out on an 11-month-old infant called Albert. This has come to be known as the 'Little Albert' study and is still regarded as a classic in psychology. Albert initially did not display any fear of laboratory rats, but he did produce a startle and fear response to a loud noise made by banging a hammer on a metal bar. As Albert began to reach for a rat, the noise was made behind his head. After a few repetitions, he had been conditioned to fear the rat in the absence of any noise. This demonstrates how a child can learn an emotional response. This condtioned fear of white rats then generalised to other white, furry objects like a mask of Father Christmas and even Watson's own white hair. This work led to other psychologists exploring ways in which negative emotional reactions could be unlearned, and a great deal of work was carried out in this area from the 1920s until the 1980s. A summary of some of this work on classical conditioning is given above in Stop and Think: Treating classically conditioned emotional responses, for those of you with a clinical bent. The principles are still applied in some contexts; but our next theorist, Skinner, developed this work further.

The radical behaviourism of B. F. Skinner

Skinner had been influenced by the research of Pavlov and Watson, amongst others, and developed it further. (See the Profiles box on page 80.) He did not claim that unconscious

Stop and Think

Ethical reflection on the 'Little Albert' study

Do you consider it ethical to carry out experiments in which you make a young child fearful and upset to the point where the child cries? For most of us, this research is unethical, as modern codes of ethical conduct would make clear. The aim is to do distress in a very young child. Ethical issues are complex, however, and you may want to reflect on the following:

- Watson carried out much of his conditioning research on his own children. Does this make any difference?
- Was his research worthwhile? Have we gained useful knowledge from his work?

processes or inner states did not exist, but he strongly felt that it was unscientific and unnecessary to rely on these unobservable processes to explain behaviour. He did not deny that we had ideas and thoughts, but he strongly believed that these inner thoughts did not cause our behaviour. Suppose you do not turn up to do a seminar presentation; you may say that you were so anxious at the thought of doing it that you could not make yourself attend. For you, the explanation is that your anxiety prevented you from attending. You are claiming anxiety as the inner cause of your not attending behaviour. You may even go as far as to claim a neurotic personality. Skinner would not agree with this interpretation. This inner state of anxiety is not the cause of your non-attendance. He would argue that you experienced certain aversive behaviours when preparing to attend; you may have felt nauseous, had palpitations, sweated and so on, perhaps at the sight of your presentation or while packing your bag. This resulted in you altering your preparatory behaviour. The change in your behaviour and the change in your feelings have the same cause. Saying that you are an anxious person does not explain the cause of the anxiety. For Skinner the cause of your anxiety was located somewhere in your developmental learning history where you have learned maladaptive responses. Skinner felt that much of the time, we do not know the real causes of our behaviour, in terms of what stimuli in the environment trigger specific behaviour; and he rejected completely the notion of behaviour being motivated by inner states. So if you say you feel happy, something in the environment has triggered a response that you have previously learnt to label as happiness; it is not some internally generated feeling for Skinner, but is stimulated by something in the environment.

Skinner (1948) did not accept the concept of personality, seeing it as unnecessary and unscientific to postulate unobservable, inner psychological, personality-generating structures. He accepted that our genetic inheritance would have some influence on how we interacted with the environment, but he played it down, claiming instead that the situational determinants were crucial in explaining the cause of behaviour. He made reference to Charles Darwin's principles of natural selection, suggesting that over many generations human beings have evolved particular characteristics to meet the demands of their particular environment, and he believed this had led to some genetically based individual differences. Perhaps being agile had a survival value for a particular group of people; then these individuals would have opportunities to express their agility in their environment, and these responses would be reinforced. The more agile you were, the greater the reinforcement and so on. This then would explain observed individual differences in behaviour. Heredity would only impose limits on behaviour. For Skinner, it is not the kind of person you are, but the learning history you have had and the current demands of your environment that dictate how you behave.

Skinner accepted the principles of classical conditioning but felt that it applied to a limited range of learning situations. He argued that what happened after particular ways of behaving was a crucially important aspect of learning that applied to most situations where we learn. He suggested that the classical conditioning paradigm, consisting of a stimulus followed by a response, is too simplistic for most learning situations. He demonstrated that what happens after the response – the *consequences* of the response – is what is crucial, as it affects the probability of the response being repeated. If you are praised for your seminar presentation, then you are more likely to volunteer to do a seminar presentation in future; if you are heavily criticised, then you are more likely to want to avoid future presentations.

Skinner refers to this learning process as **operant conditioning**. If the consequence of a piece of behaviour is to encourage the repetition of that behaviour, this is termed **positive reinforcement**. Consequences that discourage repetition of the behaviour are termed **negative reinforcement**. Although Skinner's primary interest was in human behaviour, most of his research was on animals in laboratory situations in the now famous Skinner box. This is illustrated in the photo.

Profiles

Major figures in learning theory – Ivan Petrovich Pavlov, John Broadus Watson and Burrhus Frederic Skinner

Ivan Petrovich Pavlov

Pavlov was born in Ryazan, a small village in central Russia, in 1849. He was educated at a church school followed by a seminary and seemed destined to enter the priesthood. However, in 1870 he changed direction and studied chemistry and physiology followed by medicine at St Petersburg, becoming a skilful surgeon. After working for two years in Germany, he returned to St Petersburg and was made professor of physiology in 1890 at the Imperial Medical Academy. In 1904, he was awarded the Nobel Prize for his work on digestion. Pavlov was an independent, outspoken man; yet despite this, he managed to survive the Russian revolution and was allowed to continue his research although never becoming communist and openly criticising aspects of the regime. In 1922, at a time of famine in the Soviet Union, he asked Stalin for permission to take his laboratory overseas. This was denied as Stalin felt that the Soviet Union needed scientists like Pavlov. However Stalin did allowed Pavlov to visit America, first in 1923 and then in 1929. Although Pavlov was a physiologist, his research on learning and the methods associated with it have had, and continue to have, a major influence on the development of psychology.

John Broadus Watson

Watson was born in 1878, the first son of a poor family in Greenville, South Carolina. His father was a womaniser and abandoned his family when Watson was 13 years old. Watson found this difficult and rebelled against his mother and school. With the support of one of his teachers, he returned to study and eventually studied for a doctorate in psychology at the University of Chicago. In 1902, in the last year of his doctoral studies, he suffered an emotional breakdown. In his autobiography (Watson, 1936) he discusses how after his breakdown, he could accept the validity of much of Freud's work. This seems at odds with the individual who, as we have seen, founded the school of psychology known as **behaviourism**. In 1913 Watson lectured and published the seminal paper on behaviourism, *Psychology as the Behaviourists View It*. In 1915 while professor of psychology at John Hopkins University, he became president of the American Psychological Association and seemed set for a career as an eminent psychologist. However in his private life, like his father, he had a great number of affairs with women and in 1920, he was forced to resign from John Hopkins University over a sexual scandal involving his research assistant. His academic career was over, although he continued to publish for a few years. He went into the advertising business and became a successful businessman. However, his relationships with his family were poor; after his retirement from business in 1945 and the death of his second wife, he lived as a recluse on a farm in Connecticut until his death in 1958.

Burrhus Frederic Skinner

Skinner was born in Susquehanna, a small town in Pennsylvania, in 1904. He had a middle-class upbringing in a warm, supportive family. His initial interest was in literature, and he wanted to become a writer. While working in a bookstore to support himself, he read books by Pavlov and Watson. Wanting to know more about psychology, at age 24 he enrolled at Harvard for a research degree. This was supposedly jointly supervised by the physiology and psychology departments, but in reality, Skinner was allowed a great deal of freedom to develop his own research and experiment with equipment, developing the Skinner box illustrated on page 81. In 1936 he married and left Harvard for a lecturing post in Minnesota. During the Second World War, he was funded by the America government to carry out a project to train pigeons to guide bombs. The pigeons would keep pecking at a target that kept the missile on course. A parallel secret project was on the development of radar; and when that was successful, Skinner's research was discontinued. However, he had discovered that pigeons learnt more quickly than rats, and from this point onwards he used only pigeons in his research. In 1945, Skinner became professor of psychology at the University of Indiana; the following year, the Society for the Experimental Analysis of Behaviour was set up. This development reflected the growing influence of behaviourism in the United States. In 1948, Skinner was given a chair at Harvard. In the same year, he wrote his only novel, *Walden Two*. This describes a community governed by the principles of learning theory. It describes a utopian society, which provided a wealth of experience for individuals to fulfil their potential. Although the book was fictional, a group of young people set up a community based on the book in Virginia (Kinkade, 1973). Skinner continued to work until his death from leukaemia in 1990. He focussed on developing effective ways of teaching and learning, being an early proponent of programmed learning. In later life he became interested in philosophical issues, but he continued to be upset by the misrepresentation of his work by sections of psychology. However, the huge number of publications related to his work testify to his influence. Indeed the *Journal of Experimental Analysis of Behaviour*, set up in 1958, is still dedicated to research in the Skinnerian tradition.

Source: Nina Leen/Time Life Pictures/Getty Images

Skinner box.

There were slightly different versions of the box for different animals; but essentially, there is a lever of some sort that the animal in the course of exploring the box will press at some point. When this happens, the animal is rewarded with food. There is an electronic device attached to the lever to record the animal's rate of pressing. What Skinner demonstrated was that after the bar pressing had resulted in the animal's being reinforced with food, the rate at which the animal pressed the bar increased. The animal did not have to be reinforced every time for learning to occur, and Skinner studied the effects of different schedules of reinforcement. Much of the detail of this work is not particularly relevant in the context of personality theory, and we will cover only the relevant concepts.

Skinner demonstrated that **random or partial reinforcement schedules** produce behaviours that are very resistant to change, as an example will show. In one family, the teenage son was told that his weekend curfew was 11 p.m. However, every Friday night, Tim (the teenage son) would plead with his mother to be allowed to stay out later, and an argument would often ensue. The mother could not understand why Tim always had to argue and could not just accept that 11 p.m. was the curfew. She said he was stubborn and argumentative like his dad. In other words, it was down to his personality. When asked if she ever did allow Tim to stay out later than 11 p.m. on a Friday, she said that sometimes he just wore her down; or if she was in a good mood, she sometimes let him have another hour. In Skinnerian terms, Tim was on a random/partial reinforcement schedule. The rule was that his curfew was 11 p.m. However, Tim had learnt that it was always worth challenging this as sometimes his mother gave in and he was rewarded with a later curfew. So, for Skinner it was unnecessary and unscientific to refer to internal personality attributes to explain this behaviour, as learning theory provided an adequate explanation based on observable events. We are sure that if you reflect on some of the conflicts that you have experienced over family rules when you were growing up, you will find that operant conditioning provides a good explanation.

Another relevant Skinnerian concept is **shaping**. Skinner observed that when pigeons first entered a Skinner box, it might take them some time before they found the lever and pressed it. To speed up the process, he would deliver a food reward when they were facing in the direction of the lever, another reward when they came close to the lever and so on until the pigeon had actually achieved the desired response of pressing the lever. Shaping is applied to many aspects of behaviour where individuals are initially rewarded for behaviour that approximates the desired goal, and once that behaviour is established they are rewarded only for behaviour that comes closer to the goal and so on. Many of the current television programmes that help parents develop parenting skills areas are based on principles of operant conditioning where desired behaviours are gradually shaped. The children have a star chart. They are rewarded for 'good' behaviour with a star, and earning stars 'buys' treats. Gradually, as the initial good behaviour becomes established, the parents up the ante for the child to earn stars. Skinner's contention is that eventually the children's good behaviour will become self-reinforcing as their relationships will be better, and this is rewarding in itself.

As we have seen, one of the big questions for personality theory is the nature of human motivation. For Skinner (1971, 1972, 1976) the issue was straightforward. He believed that human beings aim to produce pleasant events and to avoid painful events, if possible. All our emotional states can be understood by analysing the behavioural events in the environment that preceded them. He does accept that some behaviour is private, but he refuses to accept that internal private behaviour causes our emotions. You don't get anxious because you have an anxious personality, but because something in your environment stimulates the anxious behaviour.

Skinner devoted a lot of his writing to examining Freudian concepts and dismissed most of them as unscientific, constructs for which there was no observable evidence. He agreed with Freud that the early experiences of the child had long-lasting effects, which could even continue into adulthood. However, he contended that it was the early conditioning experiences of the child that shaped their later behaviour, not the influence of inner conflicts between hypothesised personality structures. For Skinner, demanding individuals are not governed by their id impulses, as Freud would claim; rather, they have in the past been rewarded for displaying demanding behaviour by having their demands met and have therefore learnt to behave in a demanding way. Skinner (1953) agreed that personality trait names do convey useful information describing the individual, like how friendly or enthusiastic they are; but they do not explain, in any empirical way, how they came to be friendly or enthusiastic. For him the friendly person has been reinforced more for being friendly than has the unfriendly person and so on.

Skinner also denies that human beings are purposeful. He claims that what we label 'intentions' are really responses to internal stimuli. For example, when you say that you want to go for a picnic in the park, for Skinner, you are not setting some mental future goal; rather, you are responding to some observations – perhaps internal and external – that in the past were associated with you having a picnic. It could be that the sun is shining; you observe that you have nothing else to do, you catch sight of a thermos flask in your kitchen, or you drive past a park and perhaps a previous memory of a picnic is triggered. For Skinner these or variations of them are the stimuli that you are responding to when you make a statement of intent to have a picnic.

Attempts to apply learning theory approaches to personality

All learning theorists are not as radical as Skinner is, and the theorists that we will explore now all made serious attempts to apply concepts derived from learning theory to personality. John Dollard (1900–1980) and Neal Miller (1909–), two of the earliest of these theorists, both worked at Yale University. They are somewhat unique in that their aim was to try to integrate learning theory principles with Freud's psychoanalytic approach. Both Dollard and Miller had trained as Freudian analysts, Dollard at the Berlin Institute and Miller at the Vienna Institute. By background, Dollard was a social scientist, teaching anthropology, sociology and psychology and only specialising in psychology later in his career. Miller had trained as an academic psychologist before his analytic training. Both men were impressed with the work of the learning theorists while also influenced by Freud's theory. They sought to develop a synthesis of the two concepts to create a theory of personality.

Dollard and Miller collaborated on animal laboratory studies, mainly using rats, sharing Skinner's view that animal learning could be generalised to humans. However, unlike Skinner, they allowed for inner causation in behaviour. They believed that due to the higher mental processes of humans, our behaviour does not consist merely of responding to stimuli in our environment; instead, we can also respond to inner stimuli, and thoughts can be reinforcing for us. This is the first attempt to allow cognitive processing within a primarily learning theory model. The principles of learning demonstrated in lower species in the laboratory still applied to human learning, but because of their superior mental processes, humans were capable of more complexity. Thoughts and memories could cue behaviour within their model. This also allowed humans to plan ahead and anticipate events. There was even a role for the unconscious.

Dollard and Miller acknowledged the importance of unconscious processes in human behaviour, but their definition of the unconscious is different from Freud's; he saw the unconscious as comprising the sex and death instincts, which were inherited from birth. Dollard and Miller suggest that we are unaware of some processes because we acquired our drives and the cues before we learnt to talk and consequently they are not labelled. Examples might be some of our secondary drives for social contact, love and so on that we learnt as infants from our initial contacts with our parents. We have learnt to associate a particular smell, perhaps with the good feeling of being fed, but are unconscious of it. In future when we are exposed to the smell, it will affect our behaviour at an unconscious level. Other cues may be unconscious, as they are not labelled in our society. For example, in Japanese society to lose face (to be embarrassed or humiliated, especially publicly) is an important concept, and there is a richer vocabulary in Japanese for labelling the experience than is the case in English, where the concept is not so important. Whether labels are readily available also affects how we perceive cues. The well-known example always cited here is that of the Inuit people (people who live on the arctic coasts, including Siberia, Alaska and Greenland) and their wealth of labels for different types of snow. Consequently, they make discriminations between types of snow that English speakers would find difficult or even impossible to do. This then accounts for material being in the unconscious because it is **unlabelled**.

Cues may also be unconscious because they have been repressed. Dollard and Miller suggest that the defence mechanism of repression is a learned response, like the rest of our behaviour. When we discussed repression previously, as a Freudian defence mechanism, we saw that it involves suppressing inconvenient or disagreeable feelings or thoughts. If we cannot remember something, it cannot upset us. For Dollard and Miller, repression is about a failure to label the upsetting thoughts or memories so that they are not easy to recall and making a decision not to think about it. When you recall unpleasant events, this reinforces the negative experience you originally had. Repression avoids this, and not labelling the feelings makes it harder for them to be recalled to conscious thought. Dollard and Miller accepted the importance of the effects unconscious motivation and Freudian defence mechanism on behaviour, but they expressed defence mechanisms in learning theory terminology. The interested reader can find a very readable account in their book, *Personality and Psychotherapy*, published in 1950.

The stimulus-response model of personality of Dollard and Miller

As expected in a stimulus-response (S-R) theory, the emphasis was on how behaviour is learnt. From Hull, another early American learning theory researcher, Dollard and Miller borrowed the term **habit** to label the association between stimulus and response. Within their model, personality is composed largely of learned habits, and they go on to explain how these habits are acquired and maintained.

They agreed with Freud that the infant is born with some innate drives, which they termed **primary drives**, but disagreed with Freud about the nature of these drives. These innate primitive drives are physiological drives associated with ensuring survival for the individual. They include hunger, thirst, the need for sleep and the avoidance of pain. Reduction of these drives provides the most powerful reinforcement for the individual. Dollard and Miller (1950) claim that this reinforcement occurs automatically and unconsciously, and to be maximally effective, it should immediately follow the response. Like many other personality theorists with a clinical background, Dollard and Miller focus mainly on psychopathology in the development of their theory and then extrapolate this to normal development. For example, if an infant is left to become extremely hungry (primary drive), then it cries very loudly for attention (response). If the mother then feeds the infant, what the infant is said to have learnt is that making a fuss is rewarded. Such a child might then go on to make an excessive fuss every time they have a drive that requires satisfaction. In this terminology, making a fuss has become a habit. The baby whose primary drive of hunger was quickly met would not have this habit of overreacting and would develop normal levels of response, in this case distress. In most Western societies, primary drives are rarely directly observed, apart from in infant feeding, as societies have developed means of reducing them before they become pressing. The process for doing this involves the acquisition of what Dollard and Miller termed **secondary drives**. These secondary drives are learned mainly to help us cope with our primary drives. An example would be of setting regular mealtimes so that you are motivated to eat at particular times before the primary drive of hunger becomes overwhelming and therefore distressing. Associated with these primary and secondary drives are different types of reinforcement. For the innate primary drives, primary reinforcers are food, water, sleep and so on. Secondary drives similarly have **secondary reinforcers**. These secondary reinforcers are items or events that were originally neutral but have acquired a value as a reinforcer through being associated with primary drive reduction. A mother smiling at her child is a secondary reinforcer as it is associated with physical well-being. Money is also a secondary reinforcer as it is associated with being able to buy food, provide shelter and so on.

Dollard and Miller describe the learning of habits as being composed of four constituent parts: the initial drive, the cue to act, the response and reinforcement of the response. As discussed earlier, the drive stimulates the person to act. It does not guide them how to act but simply lets the person know that they want something. A drive might be hunger. Cues provide guidance about how to act or respond in S-R terminology. You notice a billboard advertising a new Chinese takeaway. This might be the cue for you to respond, by taking a detour past the takeaway, to get something to eat. If you then pick up a delicious meal that you enjoy hugely, you will no longer be hungry; your drive will have been satisfied. In this situation, the Chinese meal constitutes reinforcement. Reinforcement refers to the effect that a response has. As the meal was good, it reinforced your action of going to get it; and next time you are in a similar position, hungry when walking home, you may be tempted to repeat the experience. In S-R terms, a habit has been formed. If, on the other hand, the meal was disgusting and the portions were tiny, the experience of visiting the takeaway would not have been reinforcing and you are unlikely to visit it again. In S-R terms, if the response does not satisfy the drive, it will undergo extinction. It does not mean that you will never again visit the takeaway, but you are less likely to do so. Remember that habits can be both positive and negative. They are simply associations between stimuli and responses.

Dollard and Miller (1941, 1950) were particularly interested in what happened when we became frustrated in our attempts to satisfy our drives. They described four types of conflict situations that we could face. The conflict is caused by our tendencies to wish to obtain (termed 'approach') certain goals or objects. They developed a simple diagrammatic system to illustrate these conflicts, as they felt that this helped them understand exactly what was going on in any situation (see Figure 4.2).

- **Approach-approach conflict** – This describes the situation where there are two equally desirable goals, but they are incompatible. This could be when you are asked to choose between two equally desirable objects to have as a gift. You really want both but can only have one. Both goals are positive but incompatible.
- **Avoidance-avoidance conflict** – This is the situation where you are faced with what you perceive as two equally undesirable alternatives. You have a spare hour, and your partner asks you to go jogging, which you hate; or you could offer to do the ironing as an excuse not to go jogging, but you equally hate ironing. Here for you both goals are undesirable and incompatible in terms of not having a wish or time to do both.
- **Approach-avoidance conflict** – Here there is one goal, but while an element of it is attractive, an aspect of it is equally unattractive. For example, you are offered a place in what seems an ideal house; however, one of your housemates would be someone you really do not like.
- **Double approach-avoidance conflict** – Here there may be multiple goals, some desirable and some undesirable. This is more like most situations, where there are a variety of factors, positives and negatives to take into consideration before being able to make a decision.

Although we have used human examples to illustrate the analysis of conflict situations, Dollard and Miller used

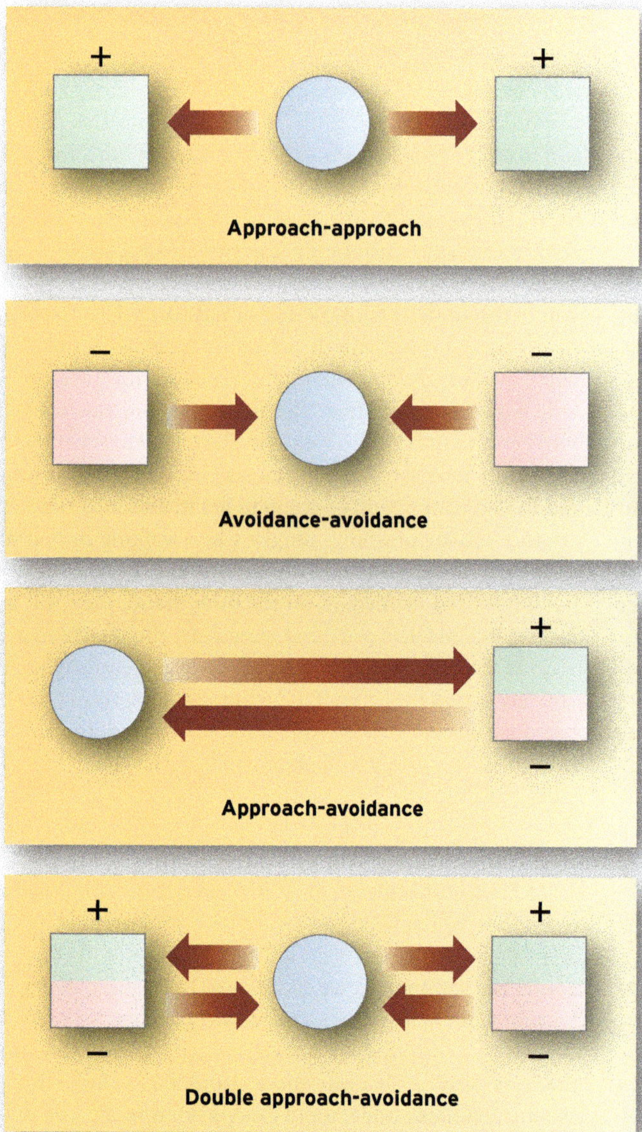

Figure 4.2 The Dollard and Miller system for analysing conflicts.

laboratory animals rather than humans to demonstrate that this system was accurate at predicting behaviour.

For Dollard and Miller, therefore, behaviour is motivated by the need to reduce our primary or secondary drives, and we learn new behaviours in the process. It is a deterministic account of human development. It is more complex than the early learning theory models as it allows for the inner influence of human cognitive processes, and in this, it is a forerunner of the cognitive models of personality that we will examine in the next chapter.

One aspect of Dollard and Miller's model that is subject to criticism from behaviourists as not being radical enough is their approach to the treatment of mental disorder. For them, as with the other learning theorists, psychopathology consists of learned, unproductive, unhelpful habits or responses. In their integrative approach, they suggested that some of these habits might be unconscious because of the reasons we have discussed earlier and that this factor added to the complexity. The aim of treatment is to remove these ineffective habits and replace them with new, more effective habits. Unlike the earlier behaviourists, Dollard and Miller did not adopt a purely deconditioning approach to treatment; they maintain significant elements of psychotherapy, the 'talking cure', in their approach. There are two phases to their treatment: first is a **talking phase**, where the problem habits are identified, explored and labelled. In the second phase, the patient is encouraged to learn more adaptive habits and apply them in their life. They call this phase the **performance phase**. They departed from their Freudian psychoanalytic training in not attending to the problems that patients had experienced in the past. They felt that past emotional issues do not have to be relived in therapy for them to be resolved. The past is only helpful sometimes in helping patients understand the source of their problems. Their focus was on current problems in living and future strategies. This predates the current treatment practice in cognitive therapy that we will examine in the next chapter.

One other significant contribution made by Dollard and Miller (1941) was to recognise and outline the process of observational learning. They demonstrated how performance on a novel task can be improved by seeing someone else perform the task. This increases the speed of the learning process. They suggested that observational learning is important in development as children learn from observing adults and other children in situations that are novel to them. They stressed that observational learning could explain how both adaptive and maladaptive habits are learned.

We will now examine the contributions of theorists Albert Bandura and Michael Rotter, who have further developed this concept of social and observational learning in ways that can be usefully applied within personality theorising.

Albert Bandura and social learning theory

One of the major questions in personality theorising is whether inner or outer forces control our behaviour. As we have seen, the psychoanalysts would have us believe that inner forces determine who we are and how we behave. The learning theorists we have examined so far conceptualise human beings as being at the mercy of outer forces. The environment determines your opportunities for learning new behaviour, the interests you are likely to develop and your history of learning. Dollard and Miller allowed for some inner influence from the higher cognitive functioning possessed by humans but said that principles of reinforcement external to the individual are thought to mainly control human behaviour. Bandura challenges this view, as we shall see. (For background on Bandura, see the Profile box.)

Profile Albert Bandura

Albert Bandura was born in 1925 in Mundare, a small Canadian town in the province of Alberta. He was an only son with five older sisters. His parents were farmers of Polish descent. Bandura went to a small school with a shortage of teachers. To combat this, the pupils formed groups to educate themselves in subjects where no teacher was available. This led to his interest in self-motivation and group effects in the process of learning and motivation. As a young man, he worked with a gang of labourers repairing the Alaskan highway. He met a diverse range of individuals, many escaping from the law and others on the fringes of society, and this is said to have sparked his interest in psychology and how it could address the real problems of living (Stokes, 1986). Bandura studied psychology at the University of British Colombia and the University of Lowa. Here he was introduced to researchers working on learning theory. He was appointed to a teaching post at Stanford University in 1954 and is still there. Bandura is one of the most distinguished living American psychologists. He received the American Psychological Association's award for Distinguished Scientific Contributions in 1980.

Bandura's work is grounded in the learning theory tradition, but his focus is on human problems in living. He moved from animal studies to focussing on purely human behaviour, although he kept the methodology of undertaking mainly laboratory-based research. His laboratory techniques are much more sophisticated, emphasising observation in situations designed to simulate real-life experiences. He is interested in developing theory and applying it to behavioural problems in order to facilitate positive change in individuals and groups.

The model of the individual in his approach is of an active player responding both to inner stimuli and the external environment and moving back and forward in a dynamic system. Individuals are seen to be influential in determining their own motivation, development and behaviour. Bandura (1978, 1989) uses the term **reciprocal determinism** to label the processes that drive behaviour. He sees an individual as being influenced by personal factors, behaviour and environmental factors. All three factors interact with one another to influence how individuals behave. The direction of these interactions is displayed in Figure 4.3.

Personal factors include the individual's cognitions, emotions and biological variables that contribute to their inner state. This is a major break from the traditional learning theory approaches we have examined previously. These personal factors can impact on both an individual's behaviour and on their environment. If you truly think you will fail at a task in a specific setting, Bandura (1995) has shown that this greatly increases the likelihood of failure as you approach the task differently. Your cognitions are affecting your behaviour. If you do not like opera, then you are unlikely to choose to go to an opera. Here your cognitions are influencing the environments you experience. Similarly, if you hate smoking, you may avoid bars that you know will be smoky. Here environmental factors and personal cognitions are impacting on your behaviour.

Bandura also suggests that **behavioural factors** can affect the individual's cognitions, feelings and emotions. Supposing you go skiing for the first time with some friends, and you prove to be good at it. You get your balance quickly, and the instructor is complementary. You now have the cognition that 'This is something I can do'. Your feelings may also change from apprehension about whether you could do it, to feeling positive about skiing. The converse might also be true if your initial experience of skiing was awful. Your behaviour with regard to the skiing experience has influenced your cognitions and your feelings, and both are likely to influence whether you choose to ski in future. If you take up skiing, you may even become an expert and your body will develop neurological networks reflecting your expertise. In this way, Bandura (2001) demonstrated how our behaviour affects our cognitions, feelings, emotions, and even our neurobiology in some instances.

With regard to the environment, we have seen from the earlier examples how **environmental factors** like polluted environments may affect our behavioural choices. The hole in the ozone layer is another good example that has resulted in us having to take more care to avoid burning when it is sunny. We may have to spend time and money buying sunscreens, or we may avoid sunbathing (behavioural factors). In addition, we may also worry about sunburn and plan ways to avoid it (personal factors). We hope that these examples give you an idea of Bandura's model of **reciprocal causation** in action. You surely can think of other examples. Doing this makes you aware of the complexity of learned behaviour that, unlike the earlier models, Bandura's model can handle.

Unlike Skinner, Bandura (1995, 1998) believes that individuals do possess free will and are not at the mercy of their drives and reinforcement schedules in their learning environment. For Bandura, our cognitive processes allow us some control in selecting the situations we operate in and in creating or transforming situations. We may have to work, but we can choose what we do in our leisure; or we may work towards changing a work situation to make it more amenable to us. We can start businesses or interest groups or throw parties to provide the experiences and environments that we need. Bandura has labelled this

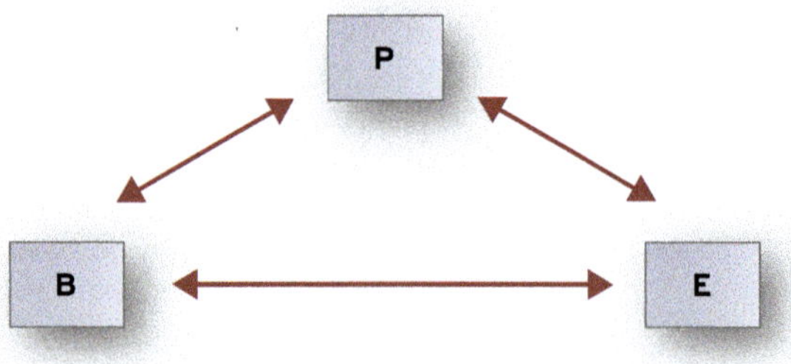

P = Person factors
B = Behavioural factors
E = Environmental factors

Figure 4.3 The interacting factors in reciprocal determinism.

personal agency: the belief that you can change things to make them better for yourself or others. Bandura (1999) has extended the concept to include **proxy agency**, where the individual enlists other people to help change some of the factors impacting on their life. They may ask a family member to look after their child so that they can get a job, or so that they can change their life in some other way. Bandura points out that there can be a downside to proxy agency in that people may in the process surrender their power to the other, who may not have their best interests at heart, and/or they may become subservient and give up control of their lives. He prefers the idea of **collective agency**, which is where a group of individuals come together believing that they can make a difference to their own and/or others' life circumstances. An example might be the recent emergence of farmers' markets. Here groups of like-minded people who want to be able to continue earning a living from farming by getting a fair price for their produce and who share a commitment to fresh local produce have joined together to sell their produce directly to the public for a fair price. There are many other examples of collective agency in community and national groups and charities.

Learning within Bandura's model

Within Bandura's model, personality development is about how we learn to become the person we are, and this then explains why we behave as we do. Bandura (1977) suggests that for learning to be effective, individuals have to be aware of the consequences of their behaviour. He demonstrated that people think about the consequences of their behaviour in learning situations. We think beyond the immediate situation and anticipate possible outcomes with an eye to the future. Being aware of the consequences of our behaviour also allows us **forethought**, in that we can anticipate what possible outcomes may follow our behaviour, and this knowledge can affect how we choose to behave and what we learn in the situation. Bandura (1995; 1999) sees awareness of the consequences of our behaviour and foresight as being human attributes as we possess language and symbolic thought which make it easier to record the consequences of our actions.

One of the most well-known aspects of Bandura's work is **observational learning**. He points out that more of our learning occurs by watching and following what other people do and imitating their behaviour than occurs by classical or operant conditioning. What happens is that an individual watches someone perform a novel behaviour, and when they are required to perform the same behaviour, they copy what they have previously seen. This is termed modelling by Bandura.

Bandura and Walters (1963) undertook a series of famous studies with a doll (Bobo); you may have covered these studies in your social psychology courses. To summarise, nursery school children were divided into two groups. One group, the experimental group, watched an adult playing aggressively with a plastic doll called 'Bobo'. The adult hit and kicked the doll, shouting things like 'Throw him in the air'. The second group of children, the control group, did not see the aggressive play. Later, both groups of children were allowed to play with the doll. Children in the experimental group displayed twice as much aggression towards the doll as did those in the control group.

From variations of this study, Bandura (1977) concluded that three factors are important in modelling. Firstly, the **characteristics of the model** influence how likely we are to imitate them. The more similar to ourselves the model is, the more likely we are to imitate them. Models undertaking simple behaviour are more likely to be copied than they are if the behaviour is complex. The type of behaviour being modelled also has an effect, with hostile and aggressive behaviour more likely to be modelled. Secondly, the **attributes of the observer** exert an influence. Less-confident individuals and those with low self-esteem or those who feel incompetent in the situation are more likely to imitate the model. Individuals with a learning history of being rewarded for conforming behaviour or who are highly dependent also imitate models more. Finally, Bandura showed that the **consequences of imitating a behaviour** are the most influential factor. If individuals believe that imitating a behaviour will bring positive results, then they are more likely to do so.

While we have talked about modelling using the term 'imitation', Bandura is insistent that modelling involves more than passive imitation. It is an active process of learning through observation, where the observer makes judgements and constructs symbolic representations of the behaviours observed. These symbolic representations may be verbal descriptions or visual images, and they are used to guide the individuals' future behaviour in similar situations. Bandura has studied the factors that may influence these processes in great detail; interested readers can refer to the further reading provided at the end of the chapter. Here we will restrict ourselves to a more aerial view of his theory as it relates to aspects of personality and its development. It is sufficient for us to be aware that modelling is not a passive process of observation, but an active process where the observer reviews what they have learnt and makes judgements about it and may decide to keep or discard parts of the behaviour. A distinction is also made between what we have learned (knowledge acquired) and what we can do (performance). Performance is seen to involve trial and error as we gradually shape our behaviour into the desired format. We also may acquire knowledge that we do not use, like learning about ways to murder someone from watching television; fortunately, few of us ever put this knowledge to use.

While reinforcement is crucial for learning in classical and operant conditioning, Bandura demonstrates that it is not always necessary in observational learning. You notice vivid billboard adverts, or loud noises, because they command your attention. You may not think about the information at the time; but when faced with an array of soap powder at the supermarket, you recognise the one from the billboard. Bandura also demonstrates that we can and frequently do reinforce our own behaviour. This **self-reinforcement** is where we evaluate our own behaviour; we may stop doing something we are getting no pleasure from, or that we judge as harming us in some way, while continuing to do things that bring positive reinforcement. The other crucial element for learning Bandura identifies is an **incentive** so that we are motivated to learn. Here **forethought** plays an important part, as well as the more traditional cues for learning. Forethought can allow us to anticipate reinforcements and thus motivate our behaviour. He suggests that motivation is crucial with observational learning, as it requires practice for the skills to be perfected. Motivation and reinforcement are much more dynamic complex processes in this model.

Bandura (2002) is keen to encourage the application of his social learning theory to address global problems such as the AIDS pandemic, population growth and gender inequalities. He sees social modelling and observational learning as being core components of behavioural change. The modelling principles in his famous Bobo study were incorporated into serial dramas and soap operas by a well-known writer (Sabido, 1981, 2002). These dramas incorporate positive role models demonstrating beneficial lifestyles, negative role models displaying detrimental lifestyles and individuals who are making the transition from negative to more positive life roles. Bandura (2002) reports that these dramas provide individuals with positive role models. They also provide the inspiration for viewers to make positive changes in their own lives. To assist in the change process, supporting resources on linked websites or in post-programme information slots are made available to the viewers. These dramas are tailored for different cultures and delivered in Africa, Asia and Latin America (Bandura, 2000; Brown & Cody, 1991; Singhal & Rogers, 1989; Vaughan, Rogers, & Swalehe, 1995). You see examples of post-programme information slots closer to home, with helpline details being provided after popular soap operas when particular social issues are included in the programme.

Personality development in social learning theory

It is this emphasis on observational learning that has led to the term 'social' being included in the theory, to stress that it is about how people learn from other individuals. In terms of how children develop their personalities, it is a learning process where parents, peers and others provide role models for children to learn from through observational learning mainly. The children learn to model their behaviour on successful models in their environment. This might be a sibling who manages to avoid trouble in one situation and a friend who gets on well in another and so on. Unfortunately, parents are others are not always consistent in their reinforcement, as we have seen, so the picture is more complicated than it might seem at first. Role models will be more or less effective, as will individual children's learning. Children will be exposed to different experiences, different environments and different cultures, and all of these influences help account for the observed diversity of human beings. The child is at the centre of these learning experiences and actively shaping the process. It is a truly dynamic, complex process.

Identifying goals to achieve is a crucial part of this process, and obtaining external feedback from relevant others on progress made towards achieving these goals plays an important part in maintaining motivation and ultimate success (Bandura, 1991). Bandura also demonstrated that goal achievement depends heavily on self-regulatory processes (Bandura, 1990, 1991, 1994, 1999, 2002). These **internal self-regulatory processes** include self-criticism; self-praise; valuation of own personal standards; re-evaluation of own personal standards if necessary; self-persuasion; evaluation of attainment and acceptance of challenges. Bandura (1990) describes these processes as being attempts at self-influence, and he has shown that the more of these factors involved in achieving a goal, the higher the levels of motivation to succeed. He identified self-efficacy as one of the most powerful of the self-regulatory processes, and we shall examine it next.

Self-efficacy as a self-regulatory process

Self-efficacy is defined as being your belief that if you perform some behaviour, it will get you a desired positive outcome (Bandura, 1989, 1994). It has become a really hot topic in psychology during the last 10 or so years and has stimulated a great deal of research especially in health. Individuals have been shown to vary greatly in their levels of self-efficacy related to specific tasks. If we take smokers who wish to stop smoking as an example, smokers will vary greatly in whether they believe that they can achieve their goal. It is a special kind of confidence in your ability to perform. In the smoking example, it might be that the smoker felt that not smoking at home and at work was achievable (high self-efficacy) but that not smoking when out with friends would be more difficult (low self-efficacy). Their overall judgement would depend on the relative amount of time they spent in each activity, and perhaps on their past experiences of similar success in a relevant area and so on. Bandura (1997) has shown that high self-efficacy significantly increases the likelihood of achieving success. Self-efficacy will influence whether a task will be attempted as well as the effort put into it and the persistence with which it is pursued in the face of difficulties or apparent lack of progress. For example, one recent study of the factors that affected the likelihood of relapse in a smoking cessation programme found that low levels of self-efficacy in individuals was a significant predictor (Segan, Borland & Greenwood, 2006). Another study looked at factors that predicted heavy drinking in anxiety-provoking social situations for a student population in the United States (Gilles, Turk & Fresco, 2006). The students most likely to drink heavily in these situations had low self-efficacy for avoiding heavy drinking in social situations and a correspondingly high belief that alcohol facilitated social interactions. Halkitis, Kutnick and Slater (2005) looked at adherence with HIV antiretroviral treatment in three hundred HIV-positive men. They found that poorer adherence was associated with low self-efficacy towards adherence, amongst other factors. Having confidence in your ability to succeed at something is consistently shown to be a significant factor in a wide range of scenarios (Bandura, 1997).

An example will help to clarify the application of self-efficacy. Let us compare two students, Dan and Stuart, who have to give assessed seminar presentations.

One student, Dan, is quite looking forward to his presentation. He knows that if he does well he will get a good mark, and he really wants to do well this year to get a good degree. He knows from experience that although he will be anxious initially, once he gets started he likes public speaking and will enjoy it. He is interested in the topic, and he is already quite well informed about it. He knows that he can organise his work effectively as he has received good marks previously when he has given himself sufficient time to undertake the preparatory work well. Not surprisingly then, his self-efficacy is high with regard to the seminar presentation; he feels confident about all the component parts that go into producing a good seminar presentation, and he has some positive experiences to reinforce this. The one proviso he has is about ensuring he has enough time to complete the task. As his motivation to succeed is high and his self-efficacy is high, he is more likely to devote the time to the work. The chances of Dan succeeding in delivering a good presentation are also correspondingly high.

Stuart dreads the event. He hates public speaking, and he has no confidence in his ability to master the constituent parts of the task. He knows that he has to do it, but his self-efficacy in relation to the task is low. As a result, thinking about it makes him anxious. He tries to put it out of his mind, and he avoids cues that remind him about it, like going to the library to prepare and so on. He indulges in ostrich-like behaviour and consequently, his chances of success are reduced. His initial low self-efficacy rating has resulted in him not being motivated to perform the task. Self-efficacy has been shown to be an important variable in predicting educational achievement. Lane and Lane (2001) showed that self-efficacy was a good predictor of British students' achievement on sports science courses. Hoy and Davis (2006) demonstrated that in school situations, teacher's ratings of their own self-efficacy in teaching are associated with the levels of achievement attained by their pupils.

Increasing self-efficacy ratings

The good news is that Bandura (1997) has demonstrated that self-efficacy can be modified by several different methods. Bandura (1999) has shown that the most straightforward way to improve self-efficacy is to get the person to 'perform the dreaded task'. If someone can be encouraged and supported to do something they fear, it has a dramatic effect on their self-efficacy. If the level of their performance is an issue, then further self-regulatory processes may be called into play so that the individual sees it as a gradual process. The first goal will be to perform, and subsequent goals may be about making improvements to their performance. **Vicarious experience** has also been shown to have an effect (Bandura, 1994). This is where the individual sees someone, whom they know shares the same fears as theirs, actually performing the task. Their cognitions become more positive, and they may say something like, 'If they can learn do it, then so can I'. This then changes their self-efficacy directly. The final method is termed **participant modelling**. In this method, the person with low self-efficacy shadows a person who is successfully completing the task. Even this imitative behaviour has been shown to lower anxiety.

Returning to the student seminar example discussed earlier, Bandura's model outlines three possible courses of action for the student low in self-efficacy. He would suggest that observing another anxious student perform successfully and discussing how they prepared for the seminar would be very helpful in raising self-efficacy. Taking this action allows the student to change their cognitions, to see that they can learn to deliver a good presentation as well. Another technique would be to pair up the anxious student

Source: David R. Frazier Photolibrary, Inc/Alamy

Children copy adults' behaviour in many different and subtle ways.

with someone less anxious. The anxious student would follow the confident student through the preparation and performance. Any possibility for feedback in the process would increase the chances of success by increasing the anxious student's confidence that they were progressing in the right direction. So obtaining feedback on the content is valuable, as is rehearsing the presentation with a friendly audience of family or friends. Once this rehearsal has been achieved, it again increases confidence. Any steps to improve confidence will improve the chances of a successful outcome.

Self-efficacy and the other self-regulatory processes help us to maintain our motivation and to be resilient even when faced with setbacks to our progress. Bandura (1990) quotes interesting examples of such resilience, including that displayed by the author James Joyce, whose book *Dubliners* was rejected by 22 publishers before becoming a successful book. Similarly, the artist Van Gogh died a pauper, having only ever sold one of his many paintings that are now worth a fortune. There are many more examples of amazing resilience shown by individuals in the face of rejection and apparent failure. Bandura sees the self-regulatory processes such as self-efficacy as being important in helping us to survive hard knocks and continue striving to achieve our goals. Benight and Bandura (2004) published an extensive review of research undertaken on the role of self-efficacy in helping individuals recover from traumatic experiences. They looked at natural disasters, war, terrorist attacks, loss of a spouse and other interpersonal traumas. They concluded that individuals who believe that they can overcome their difficulties (high in self-efficacy) are consistently shown in all the studies they examined to make a better recovery.

Measuring self-efficacy

Bandura is critical of attempts to measure self-efficacy with global scales. He points out that few people are confident about every aspect of their lives and the tasks they have to perform. Hence, self-efficacy is measured in relation to specific tasks. It demands confidence judgements to be made about the constituent skills or knowledge elements that make up a task. Researchers need to undertake this analysis systematically to ensure that all the relevant components are assessed. Bandura (2006) provides detailed guidance on measuring self-efficacy.

Julian Rotter and locus of control

We now want to introduce you to an important concept, **locus of control**, that has been and is still used extensively in research in personality and individual differences. This concept was first described by Julian Rotter (1916), another American learning theory researcher, who carried out most of his research at the University of Connecticut where he still works. We will begin by examining the theoretical background to the concept of locus of control before going on to explore how locus of control is measured. There is a wealth of research on locus of control, as it has been and continues to be as popular a research tool as are measures of self-efficacy. For this reason, we present only a brief taste of some of the research findings here, with an indication of the areas of research where it has been applied.

Like Bandura, Rotter felt that animal studies were too simplistic to address the complexity of human behaviour. Rotter was interested in how you might predict how individuals would respond in particular situations. Supposing someone makes a nasty remark about you in front of other people. You could respond angrily; you could mock them for doing it; you could get upset; you could go quiet; or you could walk away. There are a variety of possibilities. Rotter (1966) aimed to predict which option an individual might choose in a particular situation. He termed this the **behaviour potential**, that is, the likelihood of a specific behaviour occurring in a particular situation. The response that you choose will be the one with the strongest behaviour potential in that situation. However, the crucial question is, how is the strength of the behaviour potential determined? Rotter developed a formula to answer this question:

Behaviour potential = Reinforcement value × Expectancy

In this formula, **Expectancy** is our subjective estimate of the likely outcome of a course of behaviour. It is what we *expect* will happen. In learning theory terminology, it is our estimate of probability of our behaviour receiving a particular reinforcement in that situation. This is generally based on our experience of the same or similar situations. In the nasty insult example, it is your estimate of what you expect will happen if, for example, you mock the person. You may estimate that they will blush and feel ashamed of having made the nasty remark. Each option will have a different expectancy associated with it. This expectancy influences how you choose to behave in that situation. The final variable that contributes to predicting our behaviour is **Reinforcement value**. This refers to our preferences amongst the possible reinforcements available. You may be more inclined to help someone move some furniture if you know they will buy you a drink as a thank-you.

To summarise, Rotter suggests that to predict behaviour in a particular situation, we need to know what the options are and what the individual sees as being the possible outcomes for each option. The individual then assesses the likely outcome of each option (Expectancy). Next, they assess how much they value this outcome. The behaviour that is likely to occur (Behaviour potential) will be the behaviour that gets the highest rating. A summary of this decision-making process for our hypothetical example is shown in Table 4.1.

In novel situations, where by definition we have no experience to guide us, Rotter (1966) suggests that we rely on what he calls **generalised expectancies.** What he showed to be important about this concept is that individuals come to believe on the basis of their other learning experiences that either reinforcement is controlled by outside forces, or that their behaviour controls reinforcement (Rotter, 1966). The question he was interested in was whether it makes a difference if people believe that the reinforcement they receive is linked to how they perform, compared to individuals who believe that the reinforcement they receive is unrelated to their own behaviour. He labelled individuals who believe that reinforcement depends on external forces as **externals.** The external forces may include powerful others in the person's world, luck, God, fate, the State, and so on. What is crucial is that externals believe that the locus of control is external to them. What they do does not influence the outcomes. Individuals who believe that their behaviour does make a difference to the outcome are labelled **internals.** Rotter (1966) demonstrated that locus of control is a relatively stable personality

Table 4.1 Application of Rotter's equation for predicting behaviour to an insult.

Stimuli: Someone you know, Angela, makes a nasty remark about you in front of other people.

Behavioural option	Possible outcome	Rating of expectancy of outcome	Value of the outcome to the individual	Behaviour potential (probability that option will occur)
Angry reply	Argument	High	Low	Low
Mocking comment	Angela is embarrassed	High	High	High
Get upset	Angela feels remorse	Low	High	Low
Say nothing	Feel silly	High	Low	Low
Walk away	Feel silly	High	Low	Low

characteristic and developed a scale to assess it, the IE Scale. It is assessed via a 30-item forced-choice scale. Scores are on a continuum of I–E, and Rotter does not suggest a cut-off point to separate externals from internals. He has published normative scores for particular groups to allow comparisons to be made. Although other assessment tools to measure locus of control have been developed since Rotter's scale was published, his IE Scale is still the most widely used in research. Some sample items from the scale are shown in Figure 4.4.

The impact of locus of control on behaviour

Rotter (1982) demonstrated that people with an internal locus of control are more likely to feel in control of their lives, and to feel empowered to try to change things in their environment. Individuals with an external locus of control are more likely to feel powerless and helpless to change things and to be dependent on others. Research has shown that internality increases with age. Children become more internal as they develop into adulthood. Internality becomes stable in middle age and does not decrease in old age. Warm, supportive parents who encourage independence in their offspring have been shown to foster the development of internality in their children (de Mann, Leduc & Labrèche-Gauthier, 1992).

Locus of control scores tend to correlate with anxiety, and there tend be more externals than internals amongst people with mental health problems (Lefcourt, 1992). A major review of studies on depression and locus of control concluded that external scores correlate positively with higher levels of depression (Benassi, Sweeney & Dufour, 1988). This link with externality and depression is still reported currently, and it also links with suicidal behaviour. Cvengros, Christensen and Lawton (2005) examined relationships between locus of control and levels of depression in patients suffering chronic kidney disease. They compared patient scores on health, locus of control, depression and progression of the illness over a 22-month period. Results demonstrated that patients who experienced an increase in their locus of control scores, demonstrating that they felt that they had more control over aspects of their condition, were less likely to be depressed. Liu, Tein, Zhao and Sandler (2005) surveyed 1,362 adolescents in 5 schools in rural China and examined the relationships between locus of control, suicidal behaviours, life stressors, depression and family characteristics. They reported that high scores on the external locus of control were a risk factor for suicidal ideation and suicide attempts, along with high life stress, increasing age and depression.

A similar pattern is found for physical health, with internals becoming better informed about their illness and coping better with physical illness. Externals are more likely to adopt a passive patient role, while internals are more

Respondents are asked to circle either of the two statements to indicate which statement they agree with.

Item 2

- Many of the unhappy things in people's lives are partly due to bad luck. (external locus of control)
- People's misfortunes result from the mistakes they make. (internal locus of control)

Item 9

- I have often found that what is going to happen will happen. (external locus of control)
- Trusting to fate has never turned out as well for me as making a decision to take a definite course of action. (internal locus of control)

Item 29

- What happens to me is my own doing. (internal locus of control)
- Sometimes I feel that I don't have enough control over the direction my life is taking. (external locus of control)

Figure 4.4 Sample items from Rotter's Locus of Control Scale.

likely to get involved in their treatment by adopting healthier behaviour (Powell, 1992). Internal locus of control had been shown to be associated with improved quality of life in patients undergoing treatment for HIV (Préau and the APROCO study group, 2005). The study assessed quality of life, locus of control and demographic and health factors in 309 HIV-infected patients at the start of their treatment programme and then monitored the sample over 44 months of treatment. After 44 months of treatment, internal locus of control was a determinant of higher quality of both physical and mental health. Similar results, demonstrating better quality of life for internals, have been reported for individuals suffering from chronic illnesses such as epilepsy (Amir, Roziner, Knoll & Neufield, 1999), diabetes (Aalto, Uutela & Aro, 1997), and migraines (Allen, Haririfar, Cohen & Henderson, 2000).

Locus of control has also been shown to impact on behaviour in many other situations. Lerner, Kertes, and Zilber (2005) carried out a study examining risk and protective factors in psychological distress experienced by six thousand immigrants who had come to Israel from Russia. In a survey taken five years after the immigration, the researchers showed that psychological distress levels in the participants were linked with having an external locus of control as well as with other negative health and social factors. Locus of control is also applied in organisational research. For example, Allen, Weeks and Moffat (2005) looked at the role of locus of control among other variables in predicting whether employees acted on their intention to change jobs, or whether they simply talked about it. They found that individuals with an internal locus of control were more likely to translate their intention to change jobs into action and change their job.

Locus of control has also been applied in educational contexts. Martinez (1994) showed that internals tend to achieve greater academic success than externals do. It is suggested that when internals do well in examinations or essays, they tend to attribute their success to their own abilities or to having worked hard. Externals, on the other hand, are more likely to put their success down to luck or an easy test. These differences in causal attribution will affect the confidence with which internals and externals approach academic assessment. Bender (1995) has suggested that the experience of continued failure despite trying at school leads to the development of an external locus of control in schoolchildren. They see that trying hard brings no reward, so they give up and may come to see failure as their destiny. Anderman and Midgley (1997) suggest that in the circumstances of repeated failure, having an external locus of control protects the individual's self-esteem. It is then not their fault that they fail. Internals, on the other hand, will be more confident and have higher expectations of themselves, both of which increase their probability of success. With very few exceptions, it appears that internals are more successful than externals in most situations. However, remember that the IE Scale is a continuum, and scores tend to cluster around the middle of the scale with few very extreme scores.

Walter Mischel

We debated whether to place Mischel's theory in Chapter 5 on cognitive theories; however, we decided to include it in this chapter because of its focus on the importance of situations and as it is frequently described as a social-cognitive approach to personality. Mischel was also heavily influenced by Bandura's work on self-efficacy and Rotter's approach to personality measurement. Mischel's theory could equally well sit in Chapter 6 on cognitive theories.

In 1968 Walter Mischel published *Personality and Assessment*, a book that created enormous controversy in personality psychology. As outlined in the Profile box, Mischel's own research on the efficacy of global personality traits to predict performance led him to question the stability of personality traits across situations. This became known as the person-situation debate, or the 'personality paradox'. The question to be addressed was, do you behave as you do because of the situation you are in, or is it because of your personality? Mischel (1968) was concerned about the way psychologists interpreted personality test scores and then used them to make decisions about individuals. He pointed out that traits and other measures of personality are not good enough as predictive measures of how an individual will behave in different situations that they can be used to make important judgements about that individual, such as whether they are the right person for the job or if they are likely to violate the conditions of their parole. He pointed out that there was little evidence that individuals' behaviour is consistent in different situations. Mischel (1973, 1979, 1983a, 1983b) makes it clear that despite what some critics said, he was not questioning the existence of personality traits but simply the way they were interpreted.

Mischel (1968) claimed that the correlations between personality trait self-report measures and behaviour was between 0.2 and 0.3, meaning that the trait was accounting for under 10 per cent of the variance in behaviour. He termed this correlation between traits measures and behaviour the **personality coefficient**. Other researchers questioned the size he claimed for the personality coefficient, demonstrating that a more realistic figure is 0.4 (Nisbett & Ross, 1980) – which is still low.

Personality researchers tried to combat Mischel's argument by comparing how well situations and traits predict behaviour (Endler & Hunt, 1966, 1968). The conclusion was that knowing about both the situation and the personality

Profile Walter Mischel

Walter Mischel was born in Vienna in 1930, in a house that was a short walk away from where Freud lived. His family moved to New York when he was 10 years old to escape from the Nazis. He studied psychology but qualified as a social worker. He suggested that the early link with Freud led him to begin his career as an advocate of Freud and psychoanalysis. However, he found that the psychoanalytic approach was of little help in his work with inner-city aggressive youngsters. This led him to undertake a PhD in psychology at Ohio State University. Here he worked with George Kelly (Chapter 5) and Julian Rotter (this chapter). After graduation he worked at Harvard and then Stanford Universities before moving to his present post at Columbia University in 1984. While at Harvard he worked on a project assessing performance for the Peace Corps and found that global trait measures of personality were not good predictors of performance. This led him to question existing approaches to personality, as we shall see. He received the Distinguished Scientist Award from the Clinical Division of the American Psychological Association in 1978.

was better than knowing about either one on their own. However, this approach is impractical as there are so many possibilities, and researchers have to make decisions about which traits are likely to be relevant in particular situations. Mischel (2004) cites a study undertaken by Newcombe (1929) where 51 boys were measured on the personality characteristics of extraversion and introversion and then studied in 21 situations in a summer camp on a daily basis. Systematic recordings were made of the amount of time each boy talked at meals and of how much time he played alone or with others. Much to his dismay, Newcombe found that the average correlation of behaviour across situations based on these daily observations was 0.14. Mischel and others have continued to examine the consistency in behaviour that individuals display across situations and have concluded that there is substantial variation (Mischel, 1968, 1973; Mischel & Peake, 1982; Moskowitz, 1994; Ross & Nisbett, 1991).

Epstein (1979, 1980) argues that most personality researchers do not measure the relationships between personality traits and behaviour correctly. They take a personality score and then take one measure of behaviour, such as the likelihood of offering to donate blood rated on a Likert Scale. This violates the principles of good measurement (Epstein, 1980). You need multiple measures to ensure reliability. For example, if we wanted to compare the different amounts of time that introverts and extraverts spent studying, a reliable measure would not be obtained by asking then how long they studied the previous evening. We would have to measure their study habits over some more extended time to get a true picture. This is what researchers have done to address this issue of the variability across situations and the associated measurement error. Behaviour measures from individuals are aggregated. Using this approach, researchers have demonstrated that there are stable individual differences between individuals on almost every dimension studied (Epstein, 1979, 1980; Mischel & Peake, 1982; Pervin, 1994). Epstein (1979) compared extraversion–introversion scores in students with the number of social contacts they made, where the contacts were recorded in daily diaries over a two-week period. They found a personality coefficient of 0.52, which is a major improvement on previous figures. What aggregation does is to minimise the effect of the situation so that the stable underlying characteristics of the individual become apparent.

Mischel (2004) points out that the person versus situation debate caused real divisions between personality psychologists looking to show consistent differences in individuals that are independent of the situations they are in, while social psychologists stressed the importance of the situation (Nisbett & Ross, 1980; Ross & Nisbett, 1991). Some personality psychologists did examine the person-situation interaction in more detail (e.g., Fleeson, 2001; Moskowitz, 1994; Vansteelandt & Van Mechelen, 1998); but as Mischel (2004) points out, these were rare exceptions.

For Mischel, the way forward was to incorporate the findings from developments in cognitive psychology about how the mind works. Mischel (1973) outlined a set of social-cognitive person variables, as opposed to trait descriptors, to describe individual differences. These variables described processes that were important in describing how individuals construed situations (encoding and appraisal), variables relating to the situation (people and the self) and the beliefs, behavioural expectancies, goals and processes of self-regulation. The aim was to discover the psychological processes in order to determine how individuals characteristically interpreted the world and how particular situations produced characteristic behaviour in individuals. It is an interactional approach that still aims to uncover individual personality differences; but in Mischel's approach, these differences are not encapsulated in situation-free personality trait terms like 'optimistic', 'considerate', 'sociable', but in situation-related descriptions of how individuals characteristically behave. Examining some of the research undertaken by Mischel and his colleagues will make it clearer.

Mischel and Peake (1982) examined what they called 'college conscientiousness' and friendliness in college students. To begin with, the students themselves specified the behaviours and situational contexts that they considered relevant to the traits being examined. This ensured that the behaviours and situations being measured were personally meaningful for the college students' definitions of 'college conscientiousness' and friendliness. While the researchers found behavioural variability across different situations, so that one person might be very friendly in one situation but low in another, they also found temporal stability in individual's behaviour *within* similar situations. Mischel suggested that some situations were perceived as being highly similar, forming what he describes as a **functional equivalence class of situations.** Individuals perceived themselves as having the personality characteristic of friendliness, for example, based on how consistently they behaved within a particular situation rather than on how they behaved across situations. In other words, you might well see yourself as being high in the characteristic of friendliness even although you do not act in a friendly way in every situation. From this study, Mischel and Peake (1982) concluded that there was consistency in how individuals behaved within a situation, and there appeared to be consistent differences between types of situations that were worth exploring further.

While acknowledging that some of the differences between situations might be random noise, Mischel and his colleagues were convinced that there were also systematic differences in the perception of situations. They set out to look for some underlying structure that would help explain where these differences came from. An example may help your understanding here. Mischel (2004) compares two individuals who have the same score on a personality trait measure of aggressiveness. However, observation of their behaviour shows that they behave aggressively in very different situations and that these differences in their behaviour patterns are stable. One is aggressive to his junior colleagues at work but very friendly to his superiors, while the other is very friendly with colleagues but aggressive to his superiors. In this example, simply describing them as equally aggressive based on a trait measure does not give a real description of how they differ in terms of their personality characteristics.

Searching for invariance in an individual's behaviour across situations is a massive undertaking; but Mischel and his colleagues ran a replication of the Newcombe (1929) study, using a residential summer camp set up to treat children with behavioural problems, particularly aggression (Mischel, Shoda & Mendoza-Denton, 2002; Shoda Mischel & Wright, 1993, 1994). The children were filmed over many weeks and for many hours. Mischel et al. reported that aggressive behaviour observed in one type of situation was not a good predictor of how that individual would behave in another type of situation. This in itself is not surprising, but Mischel et al. demonstrated that an individual's rank-order position on aggression relative to others in the group changes predictably and dramatically in different situations. The conclusion was that individuals might have a similar mean level of aggression but there are predictable differences in terms of which situations they behave aggressively in, and these provide much more insight into the kind of person they are. It might be that one child is aggressive to his peers when asked for anything, but another child with the same aggression trait score might characteristically only be aggressive to adults when they are chastising him. Mischel and his colleagues helpfully characterise these stable situation-behaviour relationships with the phrase, 'if . . . then . . . ', and describes them as providing **a behavioural signature of personality** (Shoda, Mischel & Wright, 1993, 1994). These behavioural signatures represent our characteristic reactions to situations. Other researchers have confirmed the existence of behavioural signatures of personality that provide distinctive characterisations of individuals (Andersen & Chen, 2002, Cervone & Shoda, 1999; Morf & Rodewalt, 2001; Shoda & LeeTiernan, 2002). To summarise, Mischel and his colleagues have described the two types of behavioural consistencies. The first is behavioural consistency, called type 1 consistency, and it represents the trait ratings describing what individuals are generally like. Type 2 consistency represents the behavioural signatures of personality which show distinctive patterns of behaviour across similar situations, the if . . . then . . . propositions that encapsulate patterns of situational effects on personality.

Mischel argues the need for a dynamic personality system that will incorporate developments from cognitive science and genetics that are relevant to personality. He suggests that a dynamic personality system will go beyond mere descriptions of personality and give us more information about how the individual mind functions and personality is organised. He suggests that information about the individual's mental and emotional processes is an essential component of any model of personality. Mischel and Shoda (1995) outlined a model of a **cognitive-affective processing system (CAPS)** that fulfils some of these criteria. The aim was to demonstrate how the CAPS model can predict the type 1 and type 2 consistencies in personality that are described earlier. CAPS is composed of various mental representations, labelled **cognitive-affective units (CAUs)**. These CAUs include the individual's representations of self, others, situations, expectations, beliefs, long-term goals, values, emotional states, competencies, self-regulatory systems and memories of people and past events. Mischel and Shoda (1995) propose that the CAUs are organised in an interrelated system within the individual's stable networks of cognitions and emotions. A diagram showing how the CAPS model operates is shown in Figure 4.5. The yellow box contains developmental influences, and the green arrows indicate how these influences affect the system. All the other interactions, indicated by red lines and arrows, are envisaged to happen concurrently.

Higgins (1996) has demonstrated that within one individual, some representations are more accessible than others.

This differential accessibility of CAUs, and the differences in the ways that they are interrelated within each individual, both contribute to the observed differences in personality between individuals. Different CAUs will be activated in different situations and at different times, but the way that change occurs does not vary, reflecting the stability of structures within the individual's CAPS (Mischel & Shoda, 1995; Shoda & Mischel, 1998). The CAPS model has been shown to generate type 1 and type 2 behavioural consistencies in computer simulations (Mischel & Shoda, 1998; Shoda, LeeTiernan & Mischel, 2002).

The CAPS model produces descriptions of personality types based on how individuals organise their CAUs and how they process situational features. Downey, Feldman and Ayduk (2000) have provided an example describing the way that individuals who fear rejection respond to perceived uncaring behaviour in their partners, such as when their partner is paying attention to another person. Rejection-fearful individuals perceive, interpret and evaluate their partners' behaviour in terms of potential rejection. They ruminate about it, and these ruminations instigate the emotional responses of anger and fear as the individual becomes more fearful of being abandoned. They then respond to their partners by activating controlling, coercive behaviours and blaming their partner for this. This then creates a self-fulfilling prophecy as their partner in turn gets angry and may respond with threats of rejection. This response from the partner then reinforces the rejection-fearful individual's feeling that they are right to fear rejection – oblivious to the role that they themselves played in generating the rejection threat. From these observations, the personality signature of a rejection-fearing individual is apparent. When appraising interpersonal situations, they anxiously look for evidence of potential rejection, any evidence of rejection threat is magnified and they overreact to it with anger and blame (Downey et al., 2000).

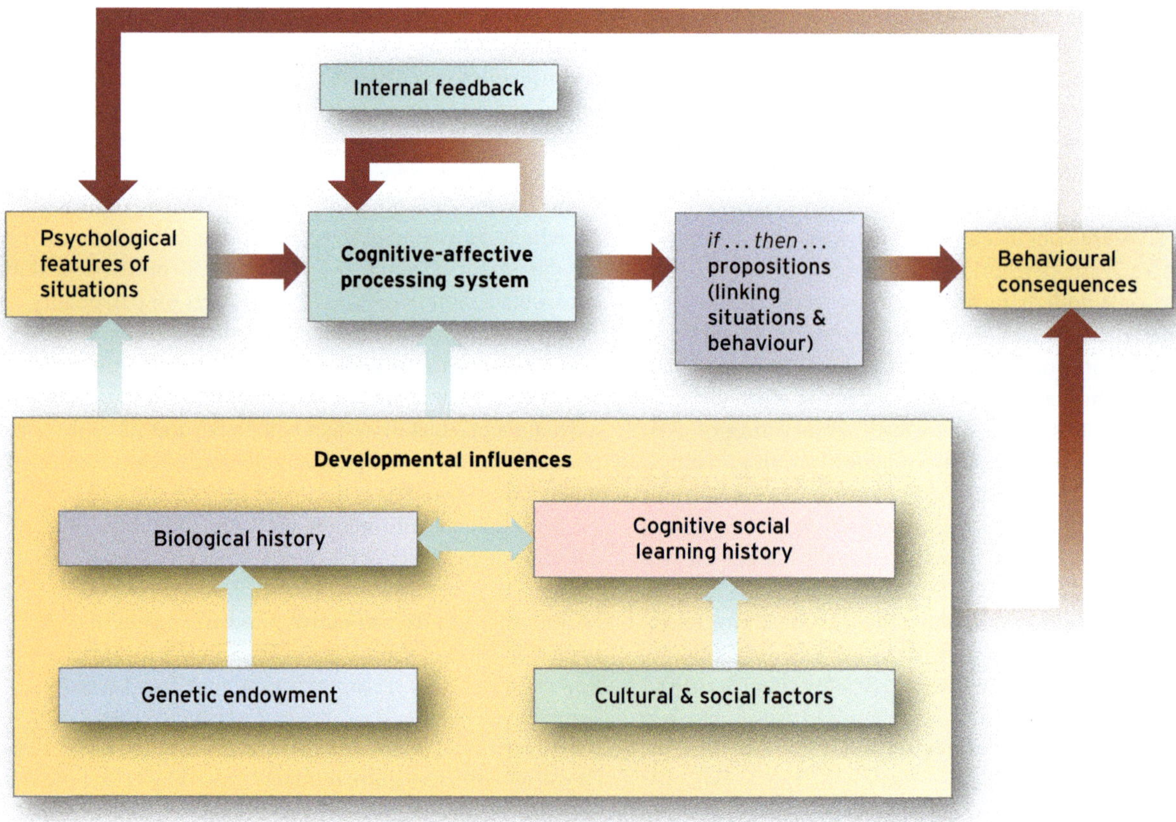

Figure 4.5 Mischel and Shoda's (1995) cognitive-affective processing system (CAPS).

This analysis demonstrates how personality signatures provide a more in-depth analysis of individual differences by incorporating situation-specific information or, in this instance, relation-specific information. Shoda et al. (2000) point out that in interpersonal situations, the 'situation' is another person, and they have demonstrated that the CAPS model deals equally well with this case. A great deal of work has already been accomplished on classifying different types of situations. Kelley et al. (2003) have published an *Atlas of Interpersonal Situations.* The aim was to go beyond a superficial description of situations and identify the psychologically important aspects of situations that play a functional role in generating behaviour. It is about the way that types of individuals characteristically perceive a situation, as demonstrated in the rejection-fearful example. More work is needed to develop a better understanding of how situation-behaviour signatures work and to link them with types of individuals.

What Mischel (2004) is arguing for is an approach to personality research that integrates research findings from other areas of psychology; he is arguing that cognitions, memories, emotions, perceptual processes, genetic influences, regulatory systems and memories all play a part in generating individual differences. As we have seen, Mischel and his colleagues have already demonstrated, with their CAPS model, that there is a complex interaction between situations and enduring individual personality differences. There are still debates about the details, and the effects of many variables still have to be examined. Carver and Scheier (2003) have been examining the self-regulatory process by looking at the relationships between behavioural goals and the effects of feedback on goals. It is a complex undertaking.

The impact of Mischel

Mischel (2004) relates an amusing incident where one of his students reports to him that, according to a multiple-choice question in a state licensing exam for psychologists, he does not believe in personality. After reflection, Mischel suggests that if personality is defined purely by trait and state measures (Chapter 7), the answer is true. However, he now believes that personality research is moving on; a new era is emerging as researchers are returning to the original aim of personality theorising, which was to understand the systems that produce individual differences in behaviour. Mischel's work has been a major stimulus in these developments, bringing closer the possibility of an overarching explanatory theory of personality.

Mischel's original paper in 1968 has had a major effect on personality research. Swann and Seyle (2005) conclude that initially it led to a decline in research in personality for about 10 years and that social psychologists began to focus on the impact of situations and de-emphasise any personality effects in their research. However, Mischel's paper did lead to significant improvements in personality research. There have been many rebuttals of Mischel's views that involved researchers looking very critically at their methodologies, admitting that measures were often weak and the selection of which traits to study was sometimes inappropriate (Baumeister & Tice, 1988; Bem & Allen, 1974; Funder, 1999, 2001).

The concern about the validity of personality tests led Cronbach and Meehl (1954) to develop a clear procedure for establishing the construct validity of psychological tests. There is now widespread adherence to these procedures in personality test construction, resulting in improved validity of tests, and more care is taken in the interpretation of test scores (Swann & Seyle, 2005). Meyer et al. (2001) have demonstrated that personality tests now share the same high levels of validity as seen in medical tests. More attention has also been paid to the design of studies, with variables being more carefully selected and operationalised (Block 1977; Funder, 1999, 2001, 2002).

The grand explanatory theory of personality that Mischel envisages has not yet emerged, but considerable progress has been made in resolving the person-situation debate and in developing our understanding of how the two interact to produce both consistency and change in behaviour. Situations affect individuals; but individuals also act to change situations, often in complex ways (Magnusson, 2001). Swann and Seyle (2005), in their review of the effects of Mischel's attack on traditional approaches to personality, conclude that while the new integrative approach is likely to be fruitful, there are still instances where it is helpful to make distinctions between personal and situational determinants of behaviour.

Evaluation of learning theory approaches

We will now evaluate learning theory approaches using the eight criteria we identified in Chapter 1: description, explanation, empirical validity, testable concepts, comprehensiveness, parsimony, heuristic value and applied value.

Description

Both classical and operant conditioning provide useful descriptions of relatively simple behaviour. However Pavlov, Skinner, and Dollard and Miller all based their research on observations of pigeons, rats and dogs; and the more developed and unique qualities of human beings, such as the effects of language on our behaviour, are largely ignored. Skinner (1963) did address this criticism by agreeing that human behaviour was very complex and therefore difficult to study. However, he strongly felt that the basic principles governing the way we learn behaviour are the same for humans and other animals. It was simpler to study animals in the laboratory, and as the testing conditions could be controlled very rigorously with animals, it was better science, as far as Skinner was concerned. These views of Skinner's were contentious and generated as much debate as Freud's theory. Opponents argued that people are capable of higher cognitive processing, resulting in more complex learning *than observed in rats and pigeons*, and that the principles of classical and operant conditioning do not really address that complexity (Bailey & Bailey, 1993; Garcia, 1993).

Bandura and Rotter addressed this issue by abandoning animal studies and by allowing for the effects of inner mental processes on human behaviour. In this way, they both provided a more comprehensive description of human behaviour although it was nothing like the complexity of Freud's work. By examining the importance of self-efficacy and locus of control, they have provided descriptions of valuable personality processes. Mischel's work follows in the tradition of Bandura and Rotter, but his ultimate aim is for an overarching, integrative theory of personality.

Explanation

The principles of learning theory do provide valid explanations of observed behaviour in specific situations. However, human beings have a rich mental life, which is ignored in the behavioural approaches. We are all capable of thinking and feeling, and these inner mental processes are ignored. As we have seen, many of the psychoanalytic theorists suggest that we are not always conscious of the reasons for our behaviour. Ruling out any idea of unconscious motivation as it cannot be directly observed seems absurd to such theorists. Dollard and Miller allowed for a concept of the unconscious, but they did not explain the role these processes play in determining behaviour.

These approaches can be criticised as being as deterministic as Freud's. The individual has no free will; our behaviour is determined by how others react to us. With the exception of the more recent work of Bandura, Rotter and Mischel, learning theory cannot explain intentional behaviour. We may have long-term goals that are unconnected with our prior learning history. An example will help illustrate this. Imagine that an individual grows up in a family where her mother and father were both doctors. The parents had a burning ambition for their daughter to follow in their footsteps, and she was certainly intelligent enough to achieve the necessary academic qualifications. According to the learning theorists, this example should result in the daughter becoming a doctor as she was brought up in an environment that fostered this, and her academic ability did not provide a bar. However, in this instance the daughter became a librarian. This is just one case history, but we are sure that if you ask around amongst your friends, you will come across other examples where children do not follow the paths that parents have wished for.

Sometimes we all do the unexpected in situations, and learning theory principles cannot easily explain this creativity in behaviour. Skinner (1972) rejected this criticism and said that it applies to classical conditioning with its emphasis purely on the stimulus and the response. In operant conditioning, we may behave in new and creative ways; but whether we repeat the behaviour is determined by its consequences. If we are rewarded in some way for the behaviour, then it should occur again, whereas if we are not rewarded, it should extinguish. I am sure you will agree that this is certainly not the case for much of human behaviour. Many would-be novelists continue to write, yet no one will publish their work; similarly, musicians continue to compose although no one plays their work, inventors continue to invent despite a lack of success and so on. We can still maintain goal-directed behaviour in the absence of positive consequences. Other personality theorists here might talk to inner drives that motivate us to behave in certain ways.

Bandura is the only learning theorist who addresses this issue with his concept of self-regulatory processes and self-reinforcement. These concepts allow for intentional behaviour and for behaviour to continue in the absence of any external reinforcement. The recognition of the role of cognitive processes and social factors in behaviour result in Bandura and Rotter's theories being very different from the earlier theories, although they still have the same emphasis on learning being a sufficient explanation for the development of personality. Mischel's position goes beyond that of Bandura and Rotter, although their approaches would be included as constituent components of an integrative theory as the effects of learning still need to be explained within such a theory. Rotter included the effects of memories of previous situations (prior learning) explicitly in the description of his theoretical approach.

For these learning theorists, any similarities in the way that people respond in different situations are down to environmental factors and prior learning. The environment that the person occupies is similar to a previous situation they had experienced; hence, they are responding in a similar fashion, rather than expressing a particular character trait that they possess. This rejection of the idea that people possess individual characteristics that influence how they behave in different situations flies in the face of all the empirical studies of stable measured individual differences in behaviour that are evidenced in chapters of this book. Again, Bandura, Rotter and Mischel are exceptions in that they have each identified individual personality characteristics. Both Bandura and Rotter see these differences resulting from learning experiences. At no point do Bandura and Rotter acknowledge a role for any possible genetic inheritance of personality traits – unlike Mischel, who is clear that biological factors have a part to play.

Empirical validity

One strength of the learning theorists is that their work is based on empirical data collected under controlled laboratory conditions. However, researchers such as Black (1973) have suggested that these theorists sometimes go beyond the data they have collected and make assumptions. This is especially the case with regard to complex human behaviour. Much of the empirical data is about animal behaviour, but the assumption is that the principles uncovered with animals will apply to human beings. They have examined very simple learning situations in animals and then go on to assume that somehow, some combination of the same learning principles can be used to explain much more complex behaviour in human beings (Skinner, 1973). There is no empirical evidence for these claims. Bandura and Rotter do not use animal studies; but even in their human studies, they too are sometimes guilty of making assumptions that go beyond their data. The same cannot be said about Mischel, although the early critiques of his position claimed that he did. He successfully refuted these claims, as overviews by Snyder and Ickes (1985) and Swann and Seyle (2005) make clear.

Certainly the concepts of classical and operant conditioning can be, and have been, tested quite exhaustively. The argument is not that we cannot demonstrate the occurrence of both classical and operant conditioning; rather, that the concepts are not sufficient in themselves as an explanation of human behaviour. The animal explanation applies here also. The concepts may have been adequately tested in regard to rats, pigeons and dogs; but this is not the case for much of human behaviour, especially the more complex human behaviour.

Testable concepts

With regard to Bandura, Rotter and Mischel's work, the concepts they have developed have been extensively tested in a variety of psychological disciplines, and there is a great deal of supporting evidence. They have provided useful conceptualisations of elements of the process of acquiring personality. Mischel has gone further and caused personality psychologists to improve their methodologies and measurement tools.

Comprehensiveness

Skinner rejected the idea of personality and did not see himself as creating any theory; rather, he tackled specific problems in learning and behaviour. Taken at this level, he has provided a sound explanation of some aspects of learning and some specific behaviour, although most of the emphasis has been on lower animals, not humans. Within his research, Skinner focussed on simple behaviours as they were easy to control, but this has resulted in his work failing to adequately address the complexity of human behaviour. This was also true of Pavlov, who was purely interested in learning mechanisms.

Dollard and Miller, Bandura and Rotter were interested in personality and in developing relevant theories. Dollard and Miller's attempts were not very comprehensive. They did provide learning theory descriptions for how some Freudian defence mechanisms could be acquired. However, they fell short of developing a comprehensive theory of personality. Bandura's theory is probably the most comprehensive, but the lack of any discussion of genetic influences on personality development is a weakness in all the learning theory approaches. While Rotter has not yet produced a detailed comprehensive theory of personality, he has outlined the major components of such a theory.

Parsimony

From what we have discussed so far, it is apparent that learning theories can be criticised for being too parsimonious to adequately explain all of human behaviour and human motivation. The approaches are very parsimonious; they assume a small number of principles will apply to all situations, sometimes without empirical evidence. Towards the end of his life, Skinner did accept that additional concepts might be necessary to explain the more complex learning that occurs in humans. This criticism cannot be applied to Rotter's work as it aims to incorporate relevant explanatory and organisational concepts from all areas of psychology relevant to personality.

Heuristic value

As we have seen, both classical and operant conditioning have had an enormous impact on the discipline of psychology. Firstly, by emphasising the importance of empirical research evidence in theory development and hypothesis testing, the learning theorists played a major role in shaping psychology as an empirical science. They also demonstrated the importance of attending to situational and environmental variables that may affect behaviour in any situation and led to an early emphasis on laboratory studies where such variables can be more readily controlled. This early work has generated and continues to stimulate research within psychology, as evidenced by the continuation of the *Journal of Experimental Analysis of Behaviour*, which is devoted to learning theory approaches to research. Skinner himself has been a controversial figure, and his work has created great debates within psychology, psychiatry, education, philosophy, politics and the general public.

Bandura and Rotter, with their concepts of self-efficacy and locus of control in particular, have stimulated a huge amount of research. Mischel has also stimulated a great deal of controversy and research in both personality and social psychology, and it may well be that Rotter's work has created major changes in the discipline, some of which are yet to become apparent.

Applied value

In terms of applications of psychology, all the learning theorists have advocated the adoption of very pragmatic approaches to disturbed behaviour, and this has led to many new treatments for mental illness. By focussing on the detail of the ill person's behaviour, they have provided unique understanding of how such behaviour may have arisen in the individual's previous learning. The concept of disturbed behaviour as a maladaptive response that has previously been reinforced immediately opens up the possibility of that behaviour being extinguished and new responses being acquired. This concept also helps to demystify mental illness and consequently, it can be presented as a positive approach to mental illness.

The concepts of self-efficacy and locus of control have both been valuable additional factors to consider in behavioural change programmes. Programmes have been developed to improve self-efficacy in treatment programmes ranging from smoking cessation to safe sex campaigns. Similarly, locus of control has proved a useful tool in understanding treatment compliance issues in a variety of areas. Mischel too has always been interested in clinical aspects of psychology, and his work has led to better understanding of how personality attributes interact in situations to amplify disturbed behaviour, as in our example of the rejection-fearful individual.

This very idea of changing behaviour also leads to concerns about the potential to apply learning theory in unethical ways to mould both individual behaviour and that of societies. One example that we have already examined is the development of experimental neuroses in the Little Albert case study. As we have seen in his novel *Walden Two*, Skinner also acknowledged this concern. Behavioural approaches need to be applied ethically, as with all attempts to change behaviour – hence the importance of research ethics. Ethical issues in relation to personality research are discussed further in Chapter 25.

Summary

- The early learning theories reject the idea of our behaviour being directed by inner motives. All our behaviour is learned. Individual differences in behaviour are the result of the different learning experiences that people have had and the situations that they have experienced rather than being due to differences in personality.
- Pavlov demonstrated how behaviour is learnt via classical conditioning. The process begins with an unconditioned stimulus (e.g., food), which is something that automatically produces the response you are interested in, called unconditioned response (salivating).
- Pavlov demonstrated that the acquisition of many of our emotional responses can be explained by classical conditioning.
- Watson, influenced by Pavlov's work, called for the adoption of rigorous scientific method in psychology and for theory building to be based on empirical evidence rather than the introspection, reflection and anecdotal case study methodologies of the psychoanalytic school.
- For the learning theorists, psychopathology is due to faulty learning. Normal development is about learning responses that are adaptive in the individual's environment. Abnormal development occurs when maladaptive responses are learned.
- Skinner was a radical behaviourist, and he did not allow for inner experiences in his account of learning. As inner experiences could not be observed, he therefore considered them unscientific. Only behaviour that could be observed was included in his

model of learning. For the same reason, he rejected the concept of personality as being produced by the interaction of inner forces. All behaviour was learnt. He demonstrated three key concepts important for learning: operant conditioning, positive reinforcement and negative reinforcement.

- Skinner's theory is deterministic. He rejects the concept of free will and the idea of intention or creativity in human behaviour. We merely respond to stimuli in our environment, and the consequences of our responding determine our learning.
- A strength of all the learning theory approaches is their emphasis on the application of rigorous methodologies to collect data and the underpinning of all theory with empirical data. Criticisms are that they fail to address the complexity of human behaviour. They are too heavily grounded in animal studies and have a very limited conceptual basis.
- Dollard and Miller made the first attempt to allow for cognitive processing in learning theory. They allow for unconscious influences on motivation but strictly define what they mean by the unconscious.
- Dollard and Miller outlined a stimulus-response (S-R) theory of learning. This includes the consideration of primary drives and secondary drives.
- Dollard and Miller demonstrated that observational learning played an important in role in learning. Role models are observed, and their performance is imitated.
- Bandura was the first learning theorist to allocate a significant role in learning to inner cognitive processes. Bandura uses the term reciprocal determinism to label the processes that drive behaviour. He sees an individual as being influenced by three interacting factors: personal factors, behaviour and environmental factors.
- Bandura further develops Dollard and Miller's concept of observational learning and has demonstrated its importance in the acquisition of aggressive behaviour in particular with the Bobo doll study. He demonstrated that the characteristics of the model, attributes of the observer and the consequences of imitating behaviour are all influential factors in the learning process.
- For Bandura, modelling behaviour was an active process of learning through observation where the observer makes judgements and constructs symbolic representations.
- Bandura demonstrated that we humans use self-reinforcement to control our behaviour via internal self-regulatory processes.
- Self-efficacy is identified as one of the most powerful of the self-regulatory processes.
- Rotter demonstrated that the likelihood of a behaviour occurring, termed behaviour potential, is predicted by our expectancy and reinforcement value.
- Rotter termed our generalised expectancies in new situations as locus of control.
- Mischel began his major work by criticising traditional trait and state approaches to measuring personality, claiming that not enough attention was paid to situational factors.
- Mischel and his colleagues carried out extensive research to examine the interactions between personality dispositions and situations. This work produced behavioural signatures of personality.
- Mischel and Shoda (1995) outlined and tested a model of the Cognitive-Affective Processing System (CAPS). Individual differences in this system result from differential accessibility of CAUs and differences in their interrelationships.
- Evaluative criteria are applied to all the theories covered in this chapter.

Connecting Up

In this chapter we started to introduce some cognitive ideas that overlapped with learning theories. You will learn more on cognitive ideas of personality in the next chapter in this book.

In this chapter we emphasised how behaviours are learnt. Chapter 17 demonstrates a further consideration of learning theories when we outline the theory of learned optimism.

Critical Thinking

Discussion questions

- Skinner argues that humans do not have free will. Critically discuss.
- How necessary is external reinforcement for behaviour? Can you think of examples where either positive or negative reinforcement is ineffectual?
- Discuss the contribution that learning theories have made to the treatment of mental illness.
- 'Behavioural treatments need to be applied within an ethical framework'. Critically discuss.
- Discuss whether the concept of personality is necessary.
- Has the person-situation debate been adequately resolved?
- Earlier in this chapter, we asked you to make some ethical reflections on the Little Albert study. Nowadays carrying out such research on your own children would be likely to bring you into conflict with social services. It could be construed as child abuse. While we have gained useful knowledge from this study, it would be very unlikely to get ethical approval currently. Would this be a loss to psychology? You may want to reflect on current ethical codes and consider whether we have become too stringent to the detriment of scientific knowledge (for more, see Chapter 25). The situation may be straightforward when children are involved, but how about if it were adults old enough to freely consent?
- How adequately do learning theorists explain human motivation?
- Are learning theories only about forms of reward and punishment?

Essay questions

- Compare the differences between classical and operant conditioning.
- Discuss how learning theorists have contributed to personality theory
- 'Personality is no more than the sum of our learning experiences.' Discuss in reference to learning theories.
- How adequately does learning theory explain the development of personality?
- Discuss the concept of reward and punishment within learning theory.
- Critically compare two of the following three theorists:
  - Skinner
  - Bandura
  - Mischel.

Going Further

Books

- Skinner, B. F. (1971). *Beyond freedom and dignity.* London: Prentice Hall. This is a controversial book that sparks debate. Skinner argues in this book that human beings do not have free will, so there is no real concept of choice in human behaviour.
- Nye, R. (1992). *The legacy of B. F. Skinner. Concepts and perspectives, controversies and misunderstandings.* Belmont, CA: Brooks/Cole. This book provides an excellent, fair evaluation of Skinner's work.
- Skinner, B. F. (1978). *Reflections on behaviourism and society.* Englewood Cliffs, NJ: Prentice Hall. In this book, Skinner discusses the development of his ideas and their application in the real world.
- The classic source for Dollard and Miller is *Personality and psychotherapy: An analysis in terms of learning, thinking, and culture* (1950, McGraw-Hill).
- Bandura, A. (1996). *Self-efficacy: The exercise of control.* New York: Freeman. This is the most recent publication by Bandura specifically on self-efficacy.
- Rotter, J. B., Chance, J., & Phares, E. J. (Eds.) (1972). *Application of a social learning theory of personality.* New York: Holt, Rinehart, & Winston. This is the book where Rotter, in collaboration with Chance and Phares, described a general theory of social learning.
- Lefcourt, H. M. (1981, 1983, 1984) has edited three volumes of the early work on locus of control. These volumes are titled *Research with the locus of control construct* (New York: Academic Press).

Journals

- Bandura, A. (1974). Behaviour theory and models of man. *American Psychologist, 29*, 859–869. In this article, Bandura discusses his concept of personality. Published by the American Psychological Association and available online via PsycARTICLES.
- Bandura, A. (1977). Self-efficacy: Toward a unifying theory of behavioural change. *Psychological Review, 84*, 191–215. This is the classic account of self-efficacy. Published by the American Psychological Association and available online via PsycARTICLES.
- Bandura, A. (2002). Swimming against the mainstream: The early years from chilly tributary to transformative mainstream. *Behaviour Research & Therapy, 42*, 613–630. This is Bandura's account of the development of his ideas and their application in therapeutic contexts. *Behaviour Research and Therapy*, an international multidisciplinary journal, is published by Oxford Elsevier and is available online via Science Direct.
- If you are interested in examining applications of locus of control in health, *Journal of Health Psychology* (2005), Vol. 10, No. 5, is a special edition devoted to the measure, including a short version, and to its new applications in health.
- Mischel, W. (2004). Toward an integrative science of the person. *Annual Review of Psychology, 55*, 1–22. This article by Mischel gives an excellent overview of his current position and the progress that personality theory has made in addressing the person-situation controversy. *Annual Review of Psychology* is published by Annual Reviews of Palo Alto, California, and is available online via Business Source Premier.
- If you want to look through some journals related to Behavioural Analysis, there are these:
  - **Journal of Applied Behavior Analysis.** A journal primarily for the original publication of experimental research involving applications of the experimental analysis of behavior to problems of social importance.
  - **Journal of the Experimental Analysis of Behavior.** A journal primarily for the original publication of experiments relevant to the behavior of individual organisms; also publish review articles and theoretical contributions.

Web links

- **The Cambridge Center for Behavioral Studies** is a resource for those interested in behaviour analysis and its role in education, health and the workplace. Also provides a comprehensive list of links to other behavior analysis resources **(http://www.behavior.org/).**
- This site has a wealth of material on self-efficacy, including contributions from Bandura himself. It also has an extensive reference list of research on self-efficacy **(http://www.des.emory.edu/mfp/self-efficacy.html).**
- This is the link to Walter Mischel's website. Here you will get an idea of the work he is currently undertaking and a list of his most recent publications **(http://www.columbia.edu/cu/psychology/indiv_pages/mischel.html).**

Film and Literature

- **Nineteen Eighty Four** (George Orwell, 1949, Penguin). Primarily concerned with the prospect of state control by behaviourist means. In *Nineteen Eighty Four*, rats are used as a means of shaping Winston's behaviour to produce the required response. *Nineteen Eighty Four* is also available online **(http://www.online-literature.com/orwell/1984/)** and was made into a film in 1984 (directed by Michael Radford).
- **Brave New World** (Aldous Huxley, 1932, Penguin). Also a book primarily concerned with the prospect of state control by behaviourist means.
- **Token Economy: Behaviourism Applied** (Educational Resource Film; McGraw-Hill, 1972). Outlines B. F. Skinner's ideas on behaviourism and rewards. Concord Video and Film Council.
- **Classical and Operant Conditioning** (Educational Resource Film, 1996). The work of Ivan Pavlov and B. F. Skinner is outlined. The two types of conditioning are illustrated, including examples of historical laboratory work and Skinner boxes. Uniview WorldWide.
- **Discovering Psychology video** (Educational Resource Film, 1990). The theory of self-efficacy. WGBH/Annenberg-PCB-Project/CS.

CHAPTER

12

Mischel and Bandura

Cognitive Social Learning Theory

Chapter Overview

ILLUSTRATIVE BIOGRAPHY

Frida Kahlo

The cognitive social learning perspective, exemplified in this chapter by Albert Bandura and Walter Mischel, focuses on the cognitions that people have learned in their life experience. These cognitions, which may be quite nuanced in taking aspects of the environment into account, determine life choices and striving (or, for others, giving up). One woman whose life could have taken many directions but whose cognitions propelled her to an original and creative artistic life, is Mexican painter Frida Kahlo.

Frida Kahlo was born on July 6, 1907, in an old residential area on the outskirts of Mexico City. Her childhood was a time of war. The Mexican Revolution broke out in 1910 when Frida was only 3 years old, and guerrilla armies led by Pascual Orozco, Pancho Villa, and Emiliano Zapata began an uprising that continued for a decade, finally leading to the inauguration of revolutionary president Alvaro Obregón.

When Frida was 6, she contracted the crippling disease polio, and her right leg remained very weak for the rest of her life. Self-conscious of the deformity, she wore layers of socks and later long skirts to hide it. On the advice of doctors, she remained physically active. When Frida was 18 years old, an accident further damaged her body and changed her life. Riding in a bus home from school in Mexico City, a collision with a streetcar impaled her on a metal bar, fracturing her spine, crushing her pelvis, and breaking one foot. During her forced bed rest, she began to paint to relieve the boredom. For the rest of her life, she endured at least 32 surgeries, pain, and fear of infection. The accident left her unable to carry children to term successfully.

Frida left her small village in 1922 to attend the National Preparatory School in Mexico City, where she was offered an excellent education and the companionship of Mexico's intellectual elite. She was not intimidated, but actively participated, was somewhat of a prankster, and fell passionately in love with an artist commissioned to paint murals in the auditorium. She and Diego Rivera, more than 20 years older than Frida, later married (1929) and became internationally

Frida Kahlo (1907–1954), "Self Portrait with Monkey", 1938. Oil on Masonite, overall: 16″ × 12″ (40.64 × 30.48 cm). ©Banco de Mexico Diego Rivera & Frida Kahlo Museums Trust. Av. Cinco de Mayo No. 2, Col. Centro, Del. Cuauhtemoc 06059, Mexico, D.F. Reproduction authorized by the Instituto Nacional de Bellas Artes and Literature. Courtesy of Albright-Knox Art Gallery, Buffalo, New York, Bequest of A. Conger Goodyear, 1966.

known as an artist couple. Frida painted colorful and symbolic images of herself and her family. Many self-portraits portrayed her physical deformities (crippled leg, injured spine) and contained symbols, including images of herself as a fetus in her mother's body and as a cactus flower being pollinated by the wind. She also painted cultural themes of native and colonial people in Mexico.

Frida's artistic fame was second to that of her husband, whose career took him to the United States, where he was commissioned to paint murals for Henry Ford and others. And their physical appearance, petite Frida and immense Diego, conveys this discrepancy—except that Frida's behavior was outgoing and often outrageous, enlarging her in a metaphorical sense. She also wore unusual clothes for her circle: traditional Mexican long colorful dresses.

Her one art exhibition in Mexico came in 1953. In ill health, she was brought by ambulance on a stretcher to the gallery. Her typical good humor kept her joking and drinking with the crowd, who loved Frida and her art. Soon her health declined even further. Her right leg was amputated because of infection, and she became depressed. She died at home in bed at age 47, writing in her diary, "I hope the leaving is joyful and I hope never to return."

Development

Personality develops by learning. We learn behaviors, and we learn what to expect when we behave in particular ways. One important source of learning, in Bandura's theory, is by observing models of behavior. We also learn because of other people's reactions to our behavior.

Obviously Frida Kahlo learned the technical craft of her painting, but she also learned what themes to paint. For Frida Kahlo, her father was an important model. She was his favorite child, and they were bonded not only by temperament but by physical problems (he was epileptic). Her father was a photographer, and from his pictures she saw images of Mexican indigenous culture, undoubtedly inspiring her own great interest, which influenced her painting and also her choice of clothing. The long skirts also hid her legs, helping avoid embarrassment from her physical deformity. Her interest in self-portraiture likely stems from the many months of bedrest, when she could see little except her own reflection in a mirror that was hung over her bed. Whatever the origins of her nonconformist and extraverted social behavior, perhaps in part from the civil unrest that prevails during a revolution, her lively pranks earned attention, reinforcing her for nonconformity.

Description

Instead of listing traits, Bandura and Mischel describe the cognitive constructs of a person, using detailed categories that are further explained in this chapter. These include beliefs about what he or she is capable of doing and expectations about what would be reinforcing.

Despite her physical suffering, Frida did not take on the role of a victim. Quite the contrary; behaviorally, she was assertive to the point of being abrasive. This strength derived in part from a feeling of connection with strong Mexican peasants and a rejection of the European-based influence. The personal construct she had of nurturance is beautifully portrayed in her 1949 pointing, *The Love Embrace of the Universe, the Earth (Mexico), Diego, Me and Señor Xolotl.* While she is being embraced by the Mexican earth mother, she in turn is embracing her husband, who seems more like an adult child. If a person does not think of herself as a victim, she is not, whatever misfortune has come to her.

Mischel's theory describes behaviors as situationally variable because of the different constructs that people apply in various situations. Frida's affectionate behavior toward close friends and audiences, contrasted with her abrasive incivility toward those she construed as overly ambitious and shallow, illustrates this situational specificity.

Cognition

As mentioned earlier, cognition is the central focus in these theories. A person's *competencies* describe what he or she is able to do. Mischel and Bandura use the term *self-efficacy* to refer to a person's confidence in being able to do something, asserting that without self-efficacy in a particular domain of behavior, performance will be limited. Knowing that one can do a behavior does not, in itself, ensure the behavior will occur. It also must be expected to lead to some desired outcome.

Frida Kahlo's competencies include her artistic ability, learned undoubtedly from observing her father's photographs and practiced in her long period of forced bedrest as she recovered from the streetcar accident that nearly took her life. The persistence of Frida's artistic effort attests to her sense of self-efficacy for painting. Experience taught Frida that she would earn approval from those in her artistic circle and from those who admired it without themselves being artists, and it was especially the opinion of the artistic elite whose opinion she valued. Without the approval of these, including her husband Diego Rivera, her art might have languished.

Because there is such a gap between the tastes of the vanguard of artists and that of most of the population, it is no surprise that artists like Frida and Diego were particularly drawn to a bohemian circle of friends. Was it, perhaps, uncertainty about the less predictable reactions of those who did not really understand art but simply consumed it, as part of their lifestyle, that led Frida to be verbally aggressive toward them? That, at least, would lead to predictable outcomes of attention and awe.

Adjustment

Through elaborate learning, people develop self-systems that permit them to pursue goals effectively. Bandura calls these self-regulatory systems and plans.

The self-regulatory system that organized Frida Kahlo's striving was uniquely hers (as a cognitive social learning perspective would predict). Her sexual promiscuity reflected her own values and those of her bohemian friends. Her artistic goals and self-judgments were obviously unique, as even casual examination of her paintings reveals. For despite similarities to surrealistic painters, she was obviously not trying to imitate someone else's style but rather exploring vividly colorful and symbolically haunting images of ancestors and political celebrities, deformed bodies and fetuses, and herself in many poses and costumes. (Cognitive social learning theorists do not engage in symbolic interpretation of artistic images, unlike psychoanalysts, but some of these are obvious, such as the portrayal of her damaged spine with the architectural image described in the title of her 1944 painting, *The Broken Column*.)

Society

Personality is learned in a cultural context, so naturally the expectations and values of the society influence the individual. It is probably a reflection of American cultural values that so much research inspired by these theories focuses on what a person can accomplish—for example, self-efficacy expectations. When people join together to pursue goals that they can achieve as a group but not alone, they exhibit what Bandura calls *collective efficacy*.

Frida Kahlo bore close allegiance to the indigenous culture of Mexico, and when she was in the United States, she rejected the ambitious values that she observed, even in the art community. What of her political convictions? A child during the time of the Mexican revolution, she witnessed models of revolutionary rejection of established authority that neglected the interests of the people. Powerful established authority did not have legitimacy in these childhood lessons, and her communist and socialist sympathies later echoed this message of rebellion and the moral authority of the people at large, not the elite at the top. Participation in this circle must have provided predictable social rewards and a sense of fellowship, not to mention lovers. It also reflected a sense of collective efficacy, that they could together overcome those who would exploit the common people.

Culture brings odd combinations of people: Frida and her husband Diego were politically active, supporting communism and liberal causes. As successful artists, they were invited to social functions by well-to-do society people, where she acted outrageously, used obscene language, spoke disrespectfully of religion in the home of Catholics, and praised communism in the home of capitalist Henry Ford's sister (Herrera, 1983, p. 135). Frida did not share the cultural values she saw in the United States, especially the rampant ambitiousness. She did not think of her painting from the perspective of a business, even when she became financially successful. She seemed content to have her husband Diego be the publicly more esteemed artist, although it is not clear how much of this was a gender role restriction and how much a simple expression of her personal values.

She tolerated his many sexual infidelities (and responded with her own, with both men—including Trotsky—and women). Their relationship was stormy, and they even divorced for a year but reunited.

Bandura's concept of reciprocal determinism reminds psychologists that not only are people shaped by their environment, but they also have an impact on it, as this artist did on the art world.

Biology

No theory can deny the impact of biology on personality, and cognitive social behaviorists have found some positive associations between high efficacy expectations and health.

Perhaps Frida's efficacy expectations helped her endure her physical pain and infections better than she could have done if she had adopted a victim mentality instead. With a single case, one can never be sure.

Final Thoughts

This theory makes a general point that is easy to grasp: Our beliefs are powerful determinants of our behavior. The elaborate details that follow are more at home in research journals than in life narratives. However, without knowing what a person, in this case Frida Kahlo, believes about herself and expects as a result of her behavior, we cannot truly grasp her personality.

Preview: Overview of Mischel's and Bandura's Theories

Walter Mischel and Albert Bandura analyze personality in the tradition of learning theory, but focus particularly on cognitive variables because the human capacity to think is central to personality. Although Mischel and Bandura have many similar theoretical orientations, have cited one another's work, and have collaborated (Bandura & Mischel, 1965), most of their formal theoretical developments and research have been published independently. Mischel's social cognitive alternative to trait explanations takes the particular context into account. Bandura emphasizes how behavior is impacted by cognition, especially thoughts about one's goals and abilities.

Mischel's and Bandura's theories have implications for major theoretical questions, as presented in Table 12.1. Their theories are evolving statements within an ongoing, active research perspective shared by many researchers. Its basic tenets—the processes of learning and the relevance of cognition for behavior—are well established. Unlike some of the more historical theories, these ideas are not so much being validated as they are being used to generate refined hypotheses and to organize research in studies of many populations, ranging from young children to old people. The theory is comprehensive in covering various life stages and both normal and problematic behavior, although only a few relationships with biological variables have been reported. The applied value of the perspective includes its suggestions for therapy and for businesses and for understanding more effective strategies for education and child development.

Traits in Cognitive Social Learning Theory: Mischel

Behaviorism emphasizes the importance of situations as determinants of behavior. This poses a challenge to traditional psychoanalytic and trait approaches, and Walter Mischel took on the challenge. It was not easily resolved. A heated theoretical controversy about the relative importance of personality traits and situations in predicting behavior stimulated personality researchers to ask how personality and situations both contribute to behavior.

TABLE 12.1 Preview of Mischel's and Bandura's Theories

Individual Differences	Individuals differ in behaviors and in cognitive processes because of learning.
Adaptation and Adjustment	New therapies using modeling and other techniques to treat phobias and other disorders have been found effective. Techniques to increase self-efficacy are effective.
Cognitive Processes	Cognitive processes (including expectancies and self-efficacy) are central to personality.
Society	Modeling has major implications for society, including TV violence, which promotes aggression.
Biological Influences	Although the theory does not focus on biological phenomena, Bandura found that self-efficacy improves immune functioning among phobic subjects.
Development	Children learn much through modeling, as demonstrated in research using children as subjects. Learning can occur throughout life. Expectancies and other cognitive learning variables can change as a result of experience.

BIOGRAPHY OF WALTER MISCHEL

WALTER MISCHEL

Walter Mischel was born in 1930 in Vienna, Austria. His family fled Europe to avoid the Nazi persecutions at the beginning of World War II, when he was a young boy. Like many Europeans, they immigrated to New York City, where Mischel later studied at the City College of New York. He became a social worker, focusing on juvenile delinquents.

Mischel's graduate work at Ohio State University in the 1950s had an effect on his developing cognitive emphasis. In particular, he was influenced by the work of his mentors, George Kelly and Julian Rotter (Mischel, 1984b). He used in his own theory the concept of personal construct, an idea developed by George Kelly (presented in Chapter 13). After several brief faculty positions, Mischel moved to Stanford University, where he taught and did research from 1962 to 1983. Since 1983, he has been on the faculty of Columbia University.

The Trait Controversy: Mischel's Challenge

Traditional personality theories, including trait and psychodynamic approaches, assumed that individual differences consist of global characteristics affecting a wide variety of behaviors (Mischel, 1973). Walter Mischel (1968) startled the field by questioning this fundamental assumption, contributing to a paradigm crisis in personality theory (Epstein & O'Brien,

1985; Mischel, 1973, p. 254). He stated, after examining the research literature, "With the possible exception of intelligence, highly generalized behavioral consistencies have not been demonstrated, and the concept of personality traits as broad predispositions is thus untenable" (p. 140). The average relationship between self-report personality measures and behavior was only $r = 0.30$, which Mischel termed the **personality coefficient**. It is low, accounting for less than 10% of the variability in behavior.

personality coefficient the average relationship between self-report personality measures and behavior, estimated by Mischel at $r = 0.30$

Personality psychologists commonly believe that "people are characterized by broad dispositions resulting in extensive cross-situational consistency, [but] the research in the area has persistently failed to support that intuition" (Mischel, 1984a, p. 357). In a much-cited study, Walter Mischel and Philip Peake (1982) examined the consistency of college students on two characteristics, conscientiousness and friendliness. Although common sense would seem to predict that each student would behave consistently across situations, depending on their traits of friendliness and conscientiousness, the results indicated there was virtually no tendency for intersituational consistency ($r = 0.13$). Critics objected that this result could be related to methodological faults, but Mischel believed that the lack of consistent behavior across situations required revision of the theory of traits.

THE CONSISTENCY PARADOX

This discrepancy between the intuition that people are consistent and empirical findings that they are not poses a **consistency paradox**. People who are honest in the classroom may cheat on taxes; children who wait patiently in the presence of a parent may act impulsively when the situation changes. That is, behavior is not determined by general personality traits, but is situation specific. Even the religious beliefs and worldviews of elderly people, studied in longitudinal research, vary considerably from one testing to another (Kim, Nesselroade, & Featherman, 1996).

consistency paradox the mismatch between intuition, which says that people are consistent, and research findings, which say they are not

A social learning approach does not predict that behavior will be consistent across situations. Behavior depends on the consequences (rewards and punishments) it produces. If the same behavior in different situations produces different consequences (e.g., talking in a restaurant or talking in a library), adaptive responses will vary from situation to situation. Consistency is expected only when the same behavior is reinforced in a variety of situations or if a person is unable to discriminate among situations. For example, a child who is rewarded at play by friends, at school by teachers, and at home by parents for speaking will learn to speak in a great variety of situations. A child who cannot tell when speaking will result in punishment and when it will not may learn to be quiet all the time. When such consistency is found, social learning theory explains it as a consequence of a particular learning history, without resorting to a concept of traits, like extraversion or introversion.

That does not mean, though, that we must discard the concept of traits, provided we are aware of its limitations. Mischel pointed out that laypeople have always made trait attributions. Traits constitute summaries of multiple behavioral observations and may have some descriptive usefulness for salient characteristics, although they exaggerate consistency and make inferences about unobserved behavior (Carlson & Mulaik, 1993; Hayden & Mischel, 1976; Mischel, 1973). For Mischel, traits are not causes but merely summary labels. They describe, but do not explain, personality.

Mischel's challenge to an overgeneralized conceptualization of traits was not intended to displace traits entirely from personality theory. Rather, he advocated replacing overgeneralized trait concepts with more refined analyses and to understand when people behave consistently and when they discriminate among situations (Mischel, 1983a, 1984b;

Mischel & Peake, 1983; Peake & Mischel, 1984). Perhaps it will not surprise those who view the field from a distance that the consistency question has bothered personality theorists more than the average person. When people are given personality information in laboratory tasks, they can often reconcile inconsistent information readily. Told that a particular individual is both "generous" and "thrifty," observers do not find these traits inconsistent but reason that the individual is generous in situations that call for that, and thrifty when other circumstances make thrift sensible (Hampson, 1998).

THE SITUATIONAL CONTEXT OF BEHAVIOR

Consider the following research that Mischel and colleagues conducted with college students. You are asked to vividly imagine yourself having gotten a poor grade on an important paper. Next, you fill in the blanks on a questionnaire, with items like: "I am _____ when._____" This procedure, the researchers assume, will put you in the frame of mind of imagining that your characteristics vary from one situation to another. Compared to other subjects, who go through the same imaginary exercise but have fill-in-the-blank questions that do not refer to situations ("I am_____ ."), you will be less extreme in thinking that one failure means you are overall a failure; the imaginary exercise will have a less devastating effect on your self-concept. That is what Mischel and his colleagues predicted, and found (Mendoza-Denton et al., 2001). Keeping the situational context in mind helps prevent people from making overgeneralized conclusions about their failure—or, for that matter, success, or stereotypes about people.

Knowing that traits are oversimplified explanations unless they take situations into account, Mischel and his colleagues have developed sophisticated models of how traits affect behavior in situations (e.g., Mischel & Shoda, 1995; Wright & Mischel, 1987). For example, even aggressive people do not hit and yell all the time, and helpful people may act no different from others unless they see someone in need. The relationship between traits and behavior takes situations into account (see Figure 12.1). A given trait, such as aggressiveness, influences behavior only under certain conditions. For example, the trait of aggressiveness will influence behavior (hitting, yelling, etc.) only under certain conditions: when a person feels angry or frustrated and when people threaten or criticize.

This situational context for behavior makes a great deal of sense, if we think of traits as learned ways of adapting to situations. Situations activate thoughts and emotions that were developed as a result of prior experience with that situation (Mischel, 1973; Mischel & Shoda, 1995). Moods, fantasies, plans, goals, and other internal reactions are triggered by specific situations. The psychological situation that a person is in is therefore not simply the objective situation but the subjective amalgam of that plus internal reactions to it. In fact, by ruminating about situations, people activate these dynamics themselves. In so doing, one individual may be particularly sensitive to rejection, responding to the slightest hint of abandonment with an exaggerated, even aggressive, response. Another may exaggerate the romantic possibilities of encounters (Mischel & Shoda, 1995).

The situational approach is consistent with people's everyday descriptions of behavior. When individuals describe other people's behavior, they hedge their statements with pronouncements about the conditions under which traits will be manifested (Wright & Mischel, 1988). For example, they may say, "Johnny will hit back [aggressive behavior] when he is teased [conditional modifier, or hedge]." Conditional statements about the expression of dispositionally relevant behaviors take the form "Person does *x* when *y*." When people describe behavior, they do not use trait terms (e.g., aggressive) in a global, overly simplified manner that ignores the situation.

Figure 12.1 Illustration of a Dispositional Construct (Aggressive) as an If-Then Linkage between a Category of Conditions and a Category of Behaviors

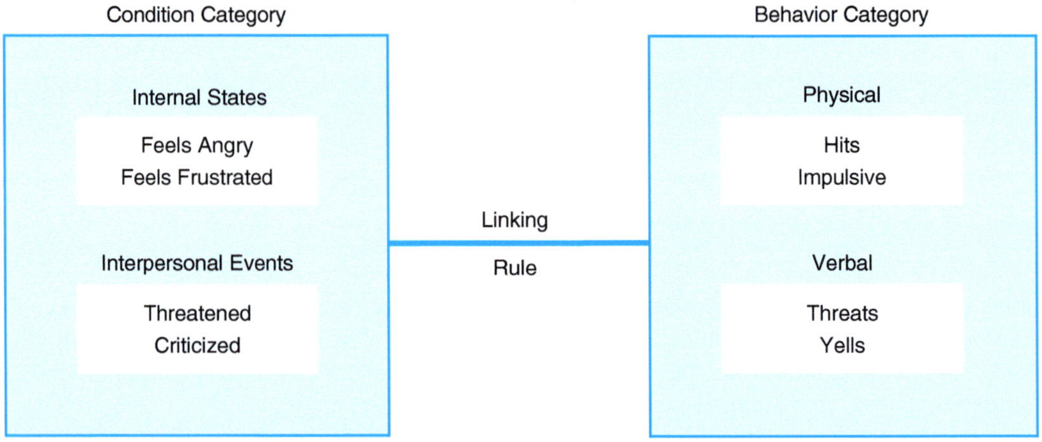

Behavior results from a set of conditions, rather than from a trait alone. Only under certain conditions does a trait of "aggressiveness" influence behavior.

(From J. C. Wright & W. Mischel (1987). A conditional approach to dispositional constructs: The local predictability of social behavior. *Journal of Personality and Social Psychology, 53,* 1159–1177. Copyright 1987 by the American Psychological Association. Reprinted by permission.)

What happens when people are presented with information about behavior that occurs in situations in which it is unlikely to occur naturally? Data from such a study strengthen Mischel's argument that situations are always relevant to trait judgments. Accurate situational descriptions of children's behavior (e.g., "child hits when provoked") were perceived meaningfully. However, descriptions that distorted the situational context of behavior in unnatural ways (e.g., "child hits when praised") yielded descriptions of children as odd, withdrawn, or psychotic (Shoda, Mischel, & Wright, 1989). Judges labeled the children as aggressive or as odd depending on the situations that provoked the hitting. People have distinctive patterns of situation–behavior relationships. In a study of perceptions of children at a summer camp, extensive records were kept of each child's behavior and of situations as they changed hour by hour over the 6-week camp session. These were analyzed idiographically, in the behavioral tradition, to show the behavior of each individual child separately for various kinds of situations. Individual differences emerged. One child, for example, was verbally aggressive when punished by an adult. Another child was verbally aggressive when warned by an adult but less so when actually punished. A third child was verbally aggressive when approached by another child. Thus there are consistent individual differences in situation–behavior relationships. Furthermore, these consistent patterns were independent of the average level of the behavior (verbal aggression) across all situations, strengthening Mischel's contention that it is situation–behavior relationships, rather than overall behavior, that defines traits (Shoda, Mischel, & Wright, 1994).

Situational variation should not be considered a problem for personality theory. In fact, the ability to discriminate among situations is characteristic of people who are well adapted (Mischel, 1968, 1973, 1984a). The assumption of global personality traits was an oversimplified theory that did not even include the wisdom of everyday people, who implicitly know that situations matter. One intriguing finding comes from an unlikely source: a genetic study of temperament in twin toddlers. The children were observed in standard laboratory situations to see how they responded to toys, to adults, and so on. Emotional reactions, activity, and other behaviors were observed—not simply for overall traits of temperament but to find situation-specific reactions. For example, sometimes during the cognitive tests one twin became more sociable toward the experimenter, and the other became less sociable but more fussy. These individual differences were consistent with parents' reports of how the twins responded at home. Statistical analyses suggest that reactions to specific situations are influenced by both genetics and experience (Phillips & Matheny, 1997).

Another theoretical development suggests that people are best described by a distribution of trait-related behavior not by simply their typical behavior. Consider conscientiousness behavior, for example: An individual may be very conscientious sometimes (carefully proofreading a term paper), moderately conscientious at other times, and not at all careful at others. The situational context influences this variability. An overly simplified concept of a trait score does not convey this variability; thinking, instead, of traits as distributions of behaviors, with a central or typical score for an individual plus a distribution around that middle, is a newer suggestion (Fleeson, 2001).

Cognitive Person Variables

Instead of global traits, Mischel (1973) proposes that personality psychologists consider several psychological processes within a person that determine how a particular situation will influence a person's behavior. These aspects of personality enable adaptation to the environment, in the unique style of an individual. He calls these concepts *cognitive social learning person variables* because they are derived from cognition and from social learning. More briefly, we may call them **cognitive person variables**.

cognitive person variables cognitive factors within a person, less global than traits, which influence how an individual adapts to the environment

ENCODING STRATEGIES AND PERSONAL CONSTRUCTS

Trait terms, which people use to describe themselves and other people, are called **personal constructs**. They are personal both in the sense that they describe individuals and in the sense that they vary from one person to another. Personal constructs that people use to describe themselves may be termed a *self-system*. They are unique to each person.

personal constructs trait terms that people use to describe themselves and other people

Besides personal constructs, people also have other kinds of **encoding strategies**, including concepts for describing situations and events. Because of their different learning histories, the meaning of situations varies from person to person. Behavior is influenced by environmental stimuli, but it is a person's unique interpretation of these stimuli, rather than objective aspects, that matters. Mischel (1968) suggests, "Assessing the acquired meaning of stimuli is the core of social behavior assessment" (p. 190). For this purpose, it is necessary to rely on subjects' reports because only they have access to their cognitions (Mischel, 1973).

encoding strategies person variables concerned with how a person construes reality

Personal constructs are different from the traits of personality theories. Rather than judging personality consistency based on similar behavior across many situations (as a researcher might), the average person looks for consistency across time in a small number of behaviors that are seen as particularly characteristic (prototypical) of a given trait (Mischel, 1984b). In formal logic and in the simplified environment of a Skinner box, events either do or do not belong to a particular category. Logical reasoning demands that we are able to say that something either is A or not A, and it seems the two choices cover all options. In a Skinner box, a discriminative stimulus may consist of a signal light, which is either on or off. But what if the light is flickering? What if the thing we are judging as A or not A is an ostrich, and A is the category bird? Suddenly, things are not so easy, and we turn from logical categories to prototypes, which permit us to convey that some birds (robins and canaries) are more birdlike than others (ostriches and turkeys). A **prototype** is a typical example of a category.

prototype a typical example of an object or type of person; a "fuzzy concept" typical of the categories people use in perceiving others

We also have "personality prototypes—abstract representations of particular personality types" (Cantor & Mischel, 1979b, p. 188)—such as introverts and extraverts. We judge whether a particular individual is an introvert or an extravert based on similarity to the prototype. Some people are difficult to classify, just as the ostrich is difficult to categorize as a bird or not a bird (Cantor & Mischel, 1979a). Prototypes include social stereotypes, such as redneck, and do-gooder, although researchers generally use more value-neutral labels, such as comedian type or pet-owner type (Andersen & Klatzky, 1987). We also have prototypes of various kinds of love: romantic love, maternal love, self-love, and so on (Aron & Westbay, 1996; Fehr & Russell, 1991).

Prototypes range from very broad categories (e.g., extravert) to narrow ones (e.g., door-to-door salesperson). Broader categories are distinctive, with little overlap among categories, and they correspond to broad personality types (cf. Chapter 1). Narrower categories are more vivid and concrete, conjuring up clearer visual images and trait descriptions (Cantor & Mischel, 1979a). It is more difficult to recall information about people who do not consistently fit a prototype (Cantor & Mischel, 1979b).

COMPETENCIES

competencies person variables concerned with what a person is able to do

What can a person do? What can a person think? These are the person's cognitive and behavioral construction **competencies**. These competencies "to construct (generate) diverse behaviors under appropriate conditions" (Mischel, 1973, p. 265) vary widely from person to person, "as becomes obvious from even casual comparison of the different competencies, for example, of a professional weight lifter, a distinguished chemist, a retardate, an opera star, or a convicted forger" (Mischel, 1977, p. 342). Leaders of neighborhood block organizations have higher construction competencies for skills relevant to leadership, including talking in front of a group and being able to get others to follow one's ideas (Florin, Mednick, & Wandersman, 1986).

Construction competencies include many learned behaviors and concepts (see Table 12.2). They refer to what a person knows or is able to do (not what the person actually does). Therefore, assessing competencies requires providing incentives for the performance of the behavior. Competencies have better stability across time and situations than do many of the personality traits that Mischel (1973, p. 267) criticizes because they are free of the variable factors that determine whether a person will do what he or she can do. Such factors include various expectancies about the situation.

EXPECTANCIES

expectancies subjective beliefs about what will happen in a particular situation (including behavior outcomes, stimulus outcomes, and self-efficacies)

Whether people will behave in a particular way depends not only on whether they know how (their competencies) but also on their **expectancies**. Mischel said that internal subjective expectancies determine performance. Several kinds of expectancies can be distinguished: behavior-outcome expectancies, stimulus-outcome expectancies, and self-efficacy expectancies.

Will racing to the corner in 11 seconds result in catching the bus, or will the driver ignore me and not stop? Will opening a door for a woman result in a "thank you" or a

TABLE 12.2 Examples of Cognitive and Behavioral Construction Competencies

Sexual gender identity
Knowing the structure of the physical world
Social rules and conventions
Personal constructs about self and others
Rehearsal strategies for learning

(Adapted from Mischel, 1973, p. 266.)

reprimand for sexist assumptions? A **behavior-outcome expectancy** is an expectation about what will happen if a person behaves in a particular way. Such expectancies are already evident in preschool children (Hegland & Galejs, 1983; Mischel, Zeiss, & Zeiss, 1974), although of course they can change with experience.

behavior-outcome expectancy expectancy about what will happen if a person behaves in a particular way

People also develop expectancies about how events will develop in the world, aside from their own actions. These are termed **stimulus-outcome expectancies**. "If the number 10 bus has just left, the number 23 must be coming soon." "If Jerry is shouting, he may soon hit someone." Although not always directly connected with immediate behavior, these expectancies are important in maintaining a person's ongoing awareness of the environment. Sometimes they may motivate an individual to change environments.

stimulus-outcome expectancies expectancies about how events will develop in the world, i.e., what events will follow other environmental stimuli

"Can I even make it to the bus stop in 11 seconds, or will I fall flat on my face trying?" Expectancies about whether one actually can do the behavior are termed **self-efficacy expectancies**. They are different from behavior-outcome expectancies, as any student knows who believes that 12 hours of straight study would result in an A on an exam (high behavior-outcome expectancy) but who also believes that such a feat would not be possible (low self-efficacy expectancy). Self-efficacy expectancies are central to the cognitive social learning approach and have been discussed by both Walter Mischel (e.g., 1981b, p. 349) and Albert Bandura (as we see later in this chapter). An idea this important has, not surprisingly, been expressed in other theories as well, although not always by the same name and not always identical in meaning: Julian Rotter (1966, 1990) describes internal-external locus of control; Martin Seligman (1992) describes helplessness (which corresponds closely to low self-efficacy); Carol Dweck describes mastery orientation (Dweck & Leggett, 1988). All of these theoretical concepts share the idea that people's beliefs about what they can accomplish influence behavior in important ways.

self-efficacy expectancies (or self-efficacy) subjective beliefs about what a person will be able to do

These various types of expectancies that Mischel described, behavior-outcome, stimulus-outcome, and self-efficacy, develop from experience in various situations. When a person is in a new situation, his or her expectancies are derived from past experience in similar situations (Mischel & Staub, 1965). Such generalized expectancies are replaced by specific situational expectancies when experience permits. A child will expect that a new baby-sitter will ignore obscene language if past baby-sitters have done so, but with experience the child may learn that she punishes such utterances.

SUBJECTIVE STIMULUS VALUES

Not all people value the same outcomes. The term **subjective stimulus value** refers to the extent to which a person regards an outcome as desirable or undesirable—that is, a person's goals or values. In learning terms, it is the value of the reward. Mischel (1981a)

subjective stimulus value how much an outcome is valued by an individual

offers the example of a teacher's praise. This outcome may have high subjective stimulus value for a student trying to get good grades but would have quite a different value for a rebellious adolescent who rejects school.

SELF-REGULATORY SYSTEMS AND PLANS

self-regulatory systems and plans ways that a person works on complicated behavior (e.g., by setting goals and by self-criticism)

Among the most important cognitive person variables are **self-regulatory systems and plans**. These are internal mechanisms that have powerful implications for behavior. People set performance goals for themselves (whether it is running a 4-minute mile, skiing an advanced slope, or graduating with honors); they reward themselves; they criticize themselves; they pass by immediate pleasure for long-term goals (delay of gratification). All these are self-regulatory systems "through which we can influence our environment substantially, overcoming 'stimulus control' (the power of the situation)" (Mischel, 1981b, p. 350). One important self-regulatory system is the ability to delay gratification.

Delay of Gratification

delay of gratification the ability to give up immediate gratifications for larger, more distant rewards

Modern culture offers instant gratification of many needs and tempts consumers with a barrage of advertisements for immediate happiness (Goldman, 1996). Our own impulses, too, beg for immediate gratification. In the face of these temptations, **delay of gratification**, the ability to defer present gratification for larger future goals, is an important adaptational skill that develops in childhood. Mischel and his colleagues explored this self-regulatory system in several studies (e.g., Mischel, 1966, 1974). They gave young children the choice of receiving a small reward (e.g., one marshmallow) immediately or a larger reward (two marshmallows) later. Some children were tested with pretzels instead of marshmallows. By manipulating aspects of the situation and by teaching the children strategies for waiting, Mischel and his colleagues learned what facilitates delay of gratification and what prevents it.

Delay is more difficult if the rewards are visible (Mischel & Ebbesen, 1970) and if the child is thinking about how wonderful the marshmallow will taste (Mischel & Baker, 1975). If the marshmallows are out of sight (Mischel & Ebbesen, 1970) and if the child is thinking about something else (Mischel, Ebbesen, & Zeiss, 1972), delay of gratification is easier. Paying attention to pictures of the rewards (that is, symbolically presented rewards) instead of the actual rewards increases delay of gratification (Mischel & Moore, 1973). By age 5, children develop effective strategies that enable them to wait for rewards: covering the rewards (marshmallows) and thinking about something else (H. N. Mischel & Mischel, 1983). Children can be taught to think about other things, which improves their ability to delay gratification (Mischel et al., 1972). Adolescents who have difficulty controlling aggression can be taught to use imagery as a technique for increasing self-control (Lennings, 1996). The ability to delay gratification can also be improved by exposure to models who delay their own gratification (Bandura & Mischel, 1965; Mischel & Liebert, 1966).

Research on delay of gratification adds wisdom beyond that known intuitively by parents. When mothers of preschool children were asked to predict which techniques would be most effective, they underestimated the value of distraction in producing delay of gratification. They predicted that tasting a desired marshmallow would help children wait longer for it—when in fact that technique had the opposite effect (Hom & Knight, 1996).

Fortunately, children can be taught to delay gratification. When mothers are more authoritative, providing direction, their children develop more ability to delay gratification, compared to those whose mothers are more permissive (Mauro & Harris, 2000). Children diagnosed with attention-deficit/hyperactivity disorder are prime candidates because of their impulsive behavior. An intervention with three children, ages 3 to 5, was successful in teaching them to forgo immediate rewards (such as a chocolate chip cookie) in favor of delayed but larger rewards (Binder, Dixon, & Ghezzi, 2000).

The delay of gratification research seems to be tapping a core ego strength (as it would be called in psychoanalytic language). When children learn to delay gratification, they are mastering a skill with important consequences for their future. Preschool children who waited longer for marshmallows or pretzels were rated higher by parents on cognitive and social competence years later when they were juniors and seniors in high school (Mischel, 1983b, 1984a; Mischel, Shoda, & Peake, 1988; Mischel, Shoda, & Rodriguez, 1989) (see Table 12.3). Preschoolers who delayed gratification longer had higher SAT verbal and math scores in high school. They were described by their parents as better able to concentrate and to cope with frustration and stress (Shoda et al., 1990). In contrast, children who are impulsive, who have temper tantrums more often than other children in late childhood (age 8 to 10), have poorer life outcomes later, with more frequent divorce and less successful occupational lives than their better controlled peers (Caspi, Elder, & Bem, 1987). Even among adults, some continue to choose small immediate reinforcers (such as briefly playing a video game) in favor of larger, delayed reinforcers (having a longer play time) (Navarick, 1998).

Longitudinal studies find that young children's ability to control their impulses, called *ego control*, is stable over time (J. Block, 1993). A related construct, *ego resiliency*, is the ability to modify one's behavior according to the demands of the situation (J. H. Block & J. Block, 1980). This ability helps people learn from experience, further developing their personality in healthy directions. For example, ego resiliency measured at age 7 predicts which children will have more advanced understanding of friendship and higher moral judgment 8 years later (Hart et al., 1998).

Personality is adaptational, and the personality characteristics proposed by Mischel prepare an individual to cope with situations. Mischel's research inspires intervention programs for children who do not develop normal abilities to delay gratification, such as those who are aggressive or hyperactive (Mischel, Shoda, & Rodriguez, 1989; Rodriguez, Mischel, & Shoda, 1989). Inhibition of behaviors, although a valuable ego skill, sometimes comes at a price, resulting in emotional distress and even ill health (Polivy, 1998). Such

TABLE 12.3 Examples of High School Behavior Ratings Predicted from Preschool Delay of Gratification

Is attentive and able to concentrate.
Is verbally fluent, can express ideas well.
Uses and responds to reason.
Tends to go to pieces under stress, becomes rattled. (disagree)
Reverts to more immature behavior under stress. (disagree)

(From W. Mischel (1984a). Convergences and challenges in the search for consistency. *American Psychologist, 39,* 351–364. Copyright 1984 by the American Psychological Association. Adapted by permission.)

costs underscore the importance of learning more about both healthy and inadequate development of people's capacity to seek gratifications in the long term as well as the short term.

The mature resolution of the conflict over delay of gratification within the individual is still being explored. It has been theorized as essentially a battle for cognition over emotion, with a hot "go" emotional system that urges the person to go for the immediate pleasure and a cool "know" cognitive system that inspires restraint (Metcalfe & Mischel, 1999). A tempting stimulus activates the "go" emotional system, so delay of gratification constitutes overcoming stimulus control. Young children, because of their immaturity, have not yet developed the "cool" system sufficiently to be able to delay gratification. Metcalfe and Mischel speculate that this may be because the hippocampus and frontal lobes of the brain are not yet developed enough to take over this function, leaving the "hot" amygdala less controlled; but they do not commit to particular neural structures in their model. They also suggest that at very high levels of stress, the "cool" function becomes less effective, leaving more impulsive behavior. This model is exciting, not only because of the possibility of integrating with neuroscience, but also because it treats delay of gratification as a process and not simply a developmental level. That is, in addition to the many studies of individual differences in delay of gratification that have been reported, the model helps us understand why the same person will sometimes be able to delay gratification and other times (e.g., under high stress), will not.

Mischel's model of personality offers a way of integrating two competing approaches in personality: the approach that seeks to identify personality traits or dispositions as stable determinants of behavior and the approach that minimizes individual differences and focuses instead on personality dynamics, the processes by which all of us are influenced in similar ways by situations (Mischel & Shoda, 1998). Mischel's focus on competencies and other cognitive person variables emphasizes the adaptational function of personality. His research on the delay of gratification shows how individual children learn to overcome the power of situations to gain self-control (e.g., Mischel, 1984a, p. 353). Mischel has offered an exciting and practical theory, rich with implications for research and intervention.

Performance in Cognitive Social Learning Theory: Bandura

Albert Bandura, like Walter Mischel, recognizes the importance of the social context for personality and presents a detailed description of cognitive variables that can be used instead of traits to describe personality and to predict behavior in various situations. Bandura's theoretical contributions permit personality theory to resolve a difficult dilemma: whether to treat people as pawns, whose behavior and experience are determined from the outside, or whether to treat them as the causes of their own behavior. Much is at stake. As Bandura puts it (2001b, p. 1), "The capacity to exercise control over the nature and quality of one's life is the essence of humanness."

BIOGRAPHY OF ALBERT BANDURA

Albert Bandura was born on December 4, 1925, in northern Alberta, Canada. Elementary and high school were combined in one school in the small town of Mundare. Bandura worked on the Alaska highway before entering the University of

ALBERT BANDURA

British Columbia, graduating in 3 years. He did his graduate work at the University of Iowa, finishing his doctorate in clinical psychology in 1952. There he met his future wife, Virginia Varns, who taught in the School of Nursing. After a postdoctoral internship at the Wichita Guidance Center, he went to Stanford University in California, where he has been on the faculty his entire career, becoming a full professor in 1964 and holder of an endowed chair from 1974. He headed the Department of Psychology from 1976 to 1977.

His interests have been broad, including not only the therapeutic concerns that might have been anticipated from his clinical training but also broad issues in child development and social problems. He was president of the American Psychological Association in 1974 and has received many professional honors for his scholarly work, including the American Psychological Association's Award for Distinguished Scientific Contributions in 1980 (American Psychological Association, 1981).

Bandura has two daughters. In addition to research, he enjoys hiking in the mountains and attending the opera.

Reciprocal Determinism

Many psychological approaches deal with only some aspects of the complex network of interacting causes, describing how situations influence behavior (as behaviorism does) or how personality traits influence behavior (as trait approaches do). Bandura (1978, 1984b) expanded these more limited cause-and-effect models with his concept of **reciprocal determinism**. This concept recognizes that the person, the environment, and behavior all influence one another, as illustrated in Figure 12.2.

reciprocal determinism the interacting mutual influences of the person, the environment, and the behavior

The concept of reciprocal determinism recognizes that the environment influences behavior, as behaviorism has always suggested. (Libraries are conducive to studying; the student lounge is not.) It also recognizes that characteristics within a person influence behavior, as trait approaches have traditionally emphasized. (Conscientious students study more.) Reciprocal determinism goes beyond these approaches, pointing out that behavior also causes changes in the environment (studying instead of spending time with friends reduces social pressures or invitations to go out) and in the individual (studying increases academic self-confidence). The environment is not only a cause of behavior but also an effect of behavior. One way in which personality influences situations is that people choose situations differently, depending on their personalities (Emmons, Diener, & Larsen, 1985).

A complete understanding of personality requires the recognition of all of these mutual influences among personality, situation, and behavior. In addition, fortuitous chance also plays a role in determining the paths that we take through life—as in the example of a professional who by chance took an empty chair at a conference presentation, whereupon he met, in the adjacent chair, the woman who was to become his wife (Bandura, 1998). Determinist science must be salted with a few grains of unpredictability.

Figure 12.2 Reciprocal Determinism

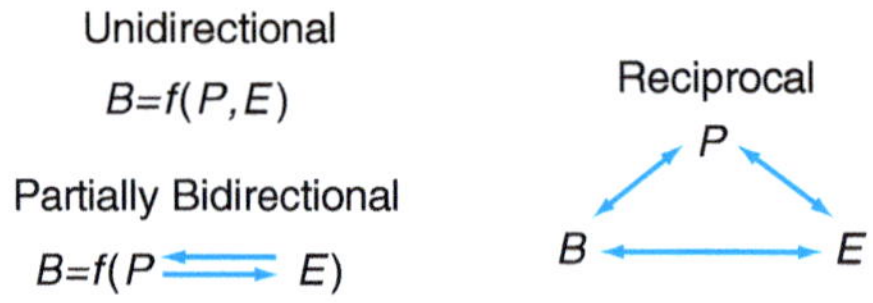

Schematic representation of three alternative conceptions of interaction. *B* signifies behavior, *P* the cognitive and other internal events than can affect perceptions and actions, and *E* the external environment.

(From A. Bandura (1978). The self system in reciprocal determinism. *American Psychologist, 33,* 344–358. Copyright 1978 by the American Psychological Association. Reprinted by permission.)

Self-Regulation of Behavior: The Self-System

People have considerable control over their own behavior. They vary, of course, in how effectively they exert this control. Sometimes they procrastinate, putting off projects rather than working on them; sometimes people engage in self-handicapping, doing work in ways that make it difficult to succeed, such as trying to study in a place that has too many distractions (Lay, Knish, & Zanatta, 1992). In contrast, other people make the most of their potential. A study of gifted students reports that they are more likely than other students to take responsibility for their own learning. Thomas Edison, for example, read almost all the books in the local library, if his own report is accurate (Risemberg & Zimmerman, 1992). By teaching us about the processes by which people regulate their own behavior, Bandura's theory promises to give people more control over their own lives.

To contrast with the old behavioral model of a person who simply responds to the environment, or even a complicated information-processing system, Bandura speaks of *human agency.* In this mode, people act with intention, forethought, self-reactiveness, and self-reflectiveness (Bandura, 2001b). Humans are conscious beings, and we act intentionally, with a desire to achieve some end (although sometimes our intentional acts do not work out as we plan). By anticipating the future and adopting goals, people become, in essence, self-directed. As they progress toward these goals, they monitor their progress, evaluate how they are doing, and correct their course. Personal values and identity come into play here.

self-system personal constructs that people use to describe themselves; cognitive structures and subfunctions for perceiving, evaluating, and regulating behavior (not a psychic agent that controls action)

The processes are cognitive, and they are collectively called the **self-system**. "A self-system within the framework of social learning theory comprises cognitive structures and subfunctions for perceiving, evaluating, and regulating behavior, not a psychic agent that controls action" (Bandura, 1978, p. 344). These cognitive processes are outlined in Figure 12.3. Notice that self-regulation is more than simply giving oneself reinforcements, which alone does not work very well (Sohn & Lamal, 1982).

Choosing goals is an important step in self-regulation. Higher goals generally produce higher performance. In the applied psychology research literature, one of the most replicated findings is that people who are given higher goals perform at a higher level than those given lower goals (Phillips & Gully, 1997). In many instances, people set their own goals. Setting subgoals generally enhances performance, especially if there is some flexibility about immediate tasks as we work toward longer-term goals (Kirschenbaum, 1985).

People can self-regulate their emotions as well as their behavior. Life's events surely contribute to our happiness or sadness, and other emotions, but we also can feel differently by internal processes of self-regulation. People in laboratory situations were shown unpleasant videotapes about mass destruction caused by an atomic bomb. Naturally, they

Figure 12.3 Self-Regulation Processes

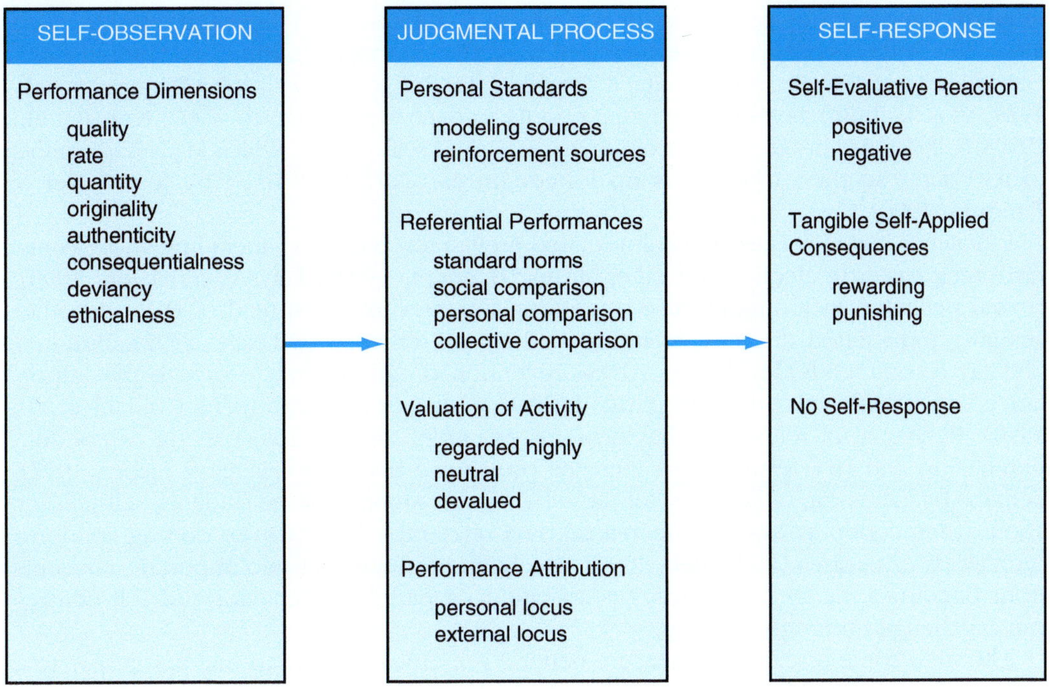

Component processes in the self-regulation of behavior by self-prescribed contingencies.

(From A. Bandura (1978). The self system in reciprocal determinism. *American Psychologist, 33,* 344–358. Copyright 1978 by the American Psychological Association. Reprinted by permission.)

experienced unpleasant emotions, but some of them defended against this unpleasantness by conjuring up pleasant memories (Boden & Baumeister, 1997). The ability to avoid thinking about unpleasant things can be adaptive; for example, it helps bereaved adults cope with the death of their spouse (Bonanno et al., 1995). At other times, putting a positive spin on events may prevent us from dealing with unpleasantries that need attention.

Self-Efficacy

Self-efficacy means believing "that one can organize and execute given courses of action required to deal with prospective situations" (Bandura, 1980). A person who has a high self-efficacy expectation in a particular situation is confident of mastery. For example, a tennis player who believes his or her serve is reliably excellent has a high self-efficacy expectation. A person who doubts that he or she can do the required behavior has a low self-efficacy expectation. A stage-frightened performer, who believes the first lines will be spoken with a squeaky voice, suffers from low self-efficacy. High self-efficacy leads to effort and persistence at a task and setting higher goals, whereas low self-efficacy produces discouragement and giving up (Bandura, 1989b; Phillips & Gully, 1997). Homeless people higher in self-efficacy are more persistent in seeking housing and employment; those with lower scores give up sooner (Epel, Bandura, & Zimbardo, 1999). Parents with high self-efficacy for parenting do a better job of it (Jones & Prinz, 2005).

Health depends considerably on lifestyle, and the lifestyle choices that people make are matters of self-regulation, largely determined by efficacy (Bandura, 2001b). Health interventions, such as programs for weight loss, exercise, and stopping smoking, are more likely to succeed if self-efficacy is high (Desharnais, Bouillon, & Godin, 1986; Dzewaltowski, 1989; Garcia, Schmitz, & Doerfler, 1990; O'Leary, 1985, 1992; Weinberg et al., 1984; Wojcik, 1988). Self-efficacy helps people to control pain (Dolce, 1987; Kores et al., 1990). Self-defense programs for women increase their self-efficacy, which leads participants to feel safer so their mobility is no longer unreasonably restricted by fear (Ozer & Bandura, 1990).

Efficacy is key to successful health-related prevention programs, including adolescents' resistance to using alcohol and other drugs (Bandura, 1999b; Hays & Ellickson, 1990). Sexual behavior, including the use of condoms to prevent the spread of HIV and other sexually transmitted diseases, is influenced by self-efficacy (O'Leary, 1992). Bandura (1990a) recommends developing AIDS-prevention programs that recognize the importance of self-efficacy, which is particularly low among runaway teens (Kaliski et al., 1990). Rehearsal of relevant behaviors—for example, through role playing of condom purchasing and HIV testing—can increase preventive behavior (Fisher & Fisher, 1992), perhaps by increasing self-efficacy for these behaviors. Among college students, self-efficacy about using condoms has been increased by a relay race that involved putting condoms on models of penises (J. Hayden, 1993), surely an illustration of two important concepts from Bandura's theory: Self-efficacy is specific to a particular behavior and self-efficacy can be changed through learning.

Although some researchers measure general self-efficacy, a broad trait applicable to a variety of behaviors (Shelton, 1990), Bandura recommends using measures self-efficacy specifically for a particular domain of behavior (e.g., Wells-Parker, Miller, & Topping, 1990). A public health survey confirms that health self-efficacy comprises several specific dimensions (nutrition, medical care, and exercise), as Bandura predicted, rather than one global dimension (Hofstetter, Sallis, & Hovell, 1990). Measures of efficacy that refer to a particular situation predict better than global measures (Wollman & Stouder, 1991). If intervention programs, such as programs to reduce tobacco use in youth, are to succeed, they should target their teaching toward the specific problem—for example, teaching adolescents the cognitive and behavioral skills needed to resist pressure to smoke (J. A. Epstein, Botvin, & Diaz, 1999).

outcome expectations the belief about what desirable or undesirable things will occur if a behavior is successfully performed

Bandura (like Mischel) distinguishes between self-efficacy (the belief that one has the ability to perform the behavior) and **outcome expectations** (see Figure 12.4). The latter refers to the belief that if the behavior is successfully done, it will lead to desirable outcomes. If I am confident that I can put my coins in a soda machine but doubt the machine will deliver my chosen soda, I have low outcome expectations despite high efficacy expectations. Obviously, both types of expectations must be high for a person to attempt a specific behavior.

The concept of efficacy has been applied to many areas of life. Mothers who are higher in self-efficacy for specific problems in caring for their infants were rated higher in maternal competence by observers who watched them interact with their children (Teti & Gelfand, 1991). Low self-efficacy is associated with negative emotions, including depression (Bandura, 1989a; Davis-Berman, 1990). Politically active citizens scored higher on a measure of political efficacy (Zimmerman, 1989). People with high-efficacy expectations about computers are less anxious and use them more (Compeau, Higgins, & Huff, 1999). In organizations, where theories are evaluated by their practical contribution to corporate profitability, self-efficacy and other social cognitive concepts help predict career aspirations and job performance (Lent & Hackett, 1987; Stajkovic & Luthans, 1998).

Figure 12.4 Diagrammatic Representation of the Difference between Efficacy Expectations and Outcome Expectations

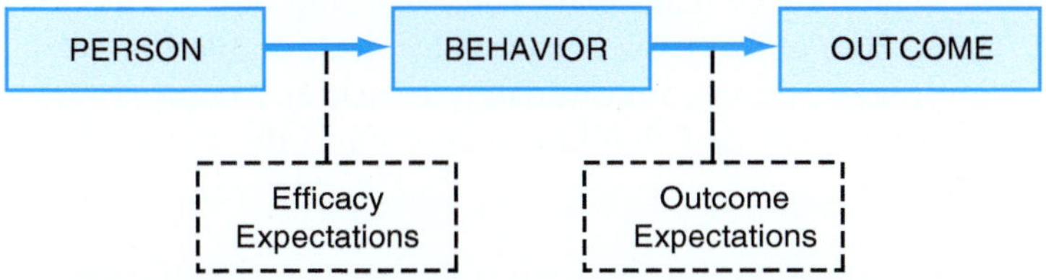

(From A. Bandura (1977). Self-efficacy: Toward a unifying theory of behavioral change. *Psychological Review, 84,* 191–215. Copyright 1977 by the American Psychological Association. Reprinted by permission.)

EFFICACY AND STRIVING TOWARD GOALS

People vary in the goals that they value, whether health, wealth, a college degree, and so on; but striving toward goals is characteristically human and a major concern in personality, with implications for our emotional well-being (Austin & Vancouver, 1996; Brunstein, Schultheiss, & Grässmann, 1998; Emmons, 1997). Self-efficacy promotes striving toward goals. Students who have higher self-efficacy beliefs are more persistent in their academic work and achieve higher levels of academic performance (Multon, Brown, & Lent, 1991). Occupational choice is influenced by efficacy. In a study of high school equivalency students, those who had a broader generality of self-efficacy considered a wider possible range of occupations; they also had a greater range of interests (Bores-Rangel et al., 1990).

Athletes who are more confident perform better, and elite coaches use a variety of techniques to build such a sense of efficacy, including enhancing performance through drilling, modeling of confidence, and encouraging positive talk (Gould et al., 1989). Self-efficacy promotes good performance among graduate students in business in simulated managerial decision making (Bandura & Wood, 1989; Wood, Bandura, & Bailey, 1990). A sense of self-efficacy leads to persistence in the face of setbacks. Persistence, in turn, ultimately leads to greater success (Wood & Bandura, 1989b). Leading subjects in a managerial task to believe that performance is a skill that can be learned, rather than a stable ability trait, makes them more persistent, so early failures do not lead to giving up (Wood & Bandura, 1989a).

Efficacy is increased if subjects gradually improve their performance on a task. This efficacy, in turn, improves later decision making (Bandura & Jourden, 1991). At least under some circumstances, breaking a large task into smaller subgoals beneficially affects performance because it increases a sense of efficacy. Stock and Cervone (1990) found that subjects who worked toward proximal subgoals on complex problems had increased self-efficacy and persisted longer than those who worked only toward more remote goals. Students with low self-efficacy are especially likely to perform better if they are instructed to set goals for each day's work (Tuckman, 1990). Sexton and Tuckman (1991) studied female college students on a series of mathematics tasks. Based on changes over time, they proposed that self-efficacy beliefs are especially important at the beginning of a task. Thereafter, the behaviors themselves become more important than cognitive variables.

Considerable evidence exists that efficacy expectations and similar positive expectations (such as optimism) contribute to effective functioning in a variety of ways. Before signing up for a motivational "think positive" seminar, though, we should keep some cautions in mind. First, Bandura warns that efficacy expectations should be grounded in experience, or they may not last. Second, it is possible to have unrealistically high efficacy expectations that are harmful, for example, when we expect to be able to stop a bad habit cold and are therefore unprepared to deal with a relapse (Litt, 1988). Or unrealistically high efficacy expectations may cause us to commit to actions that are beyond our ability and therefore harmful or dangerous, such as skiing down a mountain beyond our competence. Third, high efficacy expectations for undesirable behavior (such as aggression) will facilitate those actions, unfortunately (Crick & Dodge, 1994). High efficacy expectancies are helpful, provided they are realistic and the behavior is desirable.

PHYSIOLOGICAL CORRELATES OF EFFICACY

When a person has low self-efficacy, the body, as well as the mind, responds. The autonomic nervous system is aroused (Bandura, Reese, & Adams, 1982). In one study, women phobically afraid of spiders confronted spiders in the laboratory. Sometimes the task was one that the subjects felt they had high efficacy to accomplish (e.g., seeing a spider at a distance); other tasks were more difficult. The women's level of efficacy predicted changes in plasma catecholamine secretion (epinephrine, norepinephrine, and DOPAC). When therapy increased their efficacy expectations, the physiological indicators also changed (Bandura et al., 1985).

Stressors can enhance or suppress immune system functioning. When subjects in a laboratory had low self-efficacy about performing the tasks they were given, their endogenous opioid systems were activated (Bandura et al., 1988; Bandura et al., 1987), which can interfere with the immune system. When subjects who had snake phobias developed self-efficacy to control phobic stressors (because of an experimental manipulation), immune functioning was enhanced (Wiedenfeld et al., 1990).

Although the relationship of efficacy and goal striving more generally to biological variables is only scant, this seems a direction for potential further developments. Self-directed motivated behavior, according to brain development research, plays a role in shaping the brain itself (Bandura, 2001b). Bandura clearly states, though, that psychological analysis cannot be reduced to biological explanation. Changes in such major characteristics as gender roles and a country's peaceful or warlike nature can occur rapidly, as a result of cultural change, not biological or evolutionary mechanisms (Bandura, 2001a; Bussey & Bandura, 1999). As part of an increasingly multilevel approach to theory in personality, the control beliefs described by Bandura (and others) serve an important bridge because they connect to both biological level variables and societal level outcomes (Haidt & Rodin, 1999).

Processes Influencing Learning

Bandura considered in some detail how cognitive person variables such as efficacy are developed. Much more occurs in learning than an automatic "stamping in" of preceding responses, based on reinforcement. His early studies, described here, showed that children could learn aggressive behaviors simply by observing models perform them, without reinforcement. Learning without reinforcement required a new theoretical explanation, which Bandura (1986b) offers: a set of theoretical concepts for understanding the complex events within people that must occur for observed models to produce changes in performance. Briefly, the learner must observe the behavior, remember it, be able to do it, and be motivated to do it. Let's examine these processes in more detail (see Table 12.4).

TABLE 12.4 Processes in Observational Learning

1. ATTENTIONAL PROCESSES: Noticing the Model's Behavior.	
The Model:	Distinctive
	Affective Valence
	Complexity
	Prevalence
	Functional Value
The Observer:	Sensory Capacities
	Arousal Level
	Motivation
	Perceptual Set
	Past Reinforcement
2. RETENTION PROCESSES: Putting the Behavior into Memory.	
	Symbolic Coding
	Cognitive Organization
	Symbolic Rehearsal
	Motor Rehearsal
3. MOTOR REPRODUCTION PROCESSES: Being Able to Do It.	
	Physical Capabilities
	Availability of Component Responses
	Self-Observation of Reproductions
	Accuracy Feedback
4. MOTIVATIONAL PROCESSES: Deciding It Is Worth Doing.	
	External Reinforcement
	Vicarious Reinforcement
	Self-Reinforcement

(Albert Bandura, *Social Foundations of Thought & Action: A Social Cognitive Theory*. © 1986, p. 2. Reprinted by permission of Prentice Hall, Englewood Cliffs, New Jersey.)

ATTENTIONAL PROCESSES: OBSERVING THE BEHAVIOR

Nothing will be learned that is not observed. People who have difficulty remembering names, for example, often simply do not pay attention to them in the first place. Several characteristics of the model and of the observer influence modeling. Models catch our attention more when they look distinctive because of their clothes or other aspects of their physical appearance, when they are liked or disliked, and when they are seen repeatedly, as advertisers well know. All these are examples of **attentional processes**. Characteristics of the observer, too, influence attention, including sensory capacities, arousal level, motivation, perceptual set, and past reinforcement.

attentional processes noticing the model's behavior (a prerequisite for learning by modeling)

RETENTION PROCESSES: REMEMBERING IT

retention process remembering what a model has done

As any student knows who has paid attention to a classroom lecture or film, not all that is observed is retained. The **retention process** occurs through imaginational representations (such as images of places or people that are familiar) and through verbal coding, which can be much more efficient. Symbolic coding facilitates retention, as cognitive psychology suggests it should. In academic settings, pedagogues teach students to work actively with material to remember it. The same advice applies in other settings as well (e.g., Bandura, Grusec, & Menlove, 1966). Additional factors influencing retention include cognitive organization, symbolic rehearsal, and motor rehearsal.

MOTOR REPRODUCTION PROCESSES: DOING IT

motor reproduction process being able to do what one has seen a model do

The behavior being modeled must then be reproduced from its remembered encoding **(motor reproduction process)**. No response can be emitted that is beyond the physical capacity of the individual. Complex behaviors can be reproduced by combining their component response elements, if they are known. Feedback about our performance, such as an athletic trainer's comments or videotaped images of our own play, improve this motor reproduction phase of learning.

MOTIVATIONAL PROCESSES: WANTING IT

motivational process deciding whether it is worthwhile to behave as a model has behaved

Coaches also give pep talks, recognizing the importance of **motivational processes** to learning. Bandura clearly distinguishes between learning and performance. Unless motivated, a person will not produce learned behavior. This motivation can come from external reinforcement, such as the experimenter's promise of reward in some of Bandura's studies, or the bribe of a parent. Or it can come from vicarious reinforcement, based on the observation that models are rewarded. High-status models can affect performance through motivation. For example, girls age 11 to 14 performed better on a motor performance task when they thought it was demonstrated by a high-status cheerleader than by a low-status model (McCullagh, 1986).

Observational Learning and Modeling

We are so aware today of the importance of good models that it is easy to overlook the theoretical advance that occurred when modeling was introduced to the learning-theory paradigm within personality. Radical learning theory, in the Skinnerian tradition, required that responses must occur and be reinforced to be strengthened. Even Neal Miller and John Dollard (1941), for all their theoretical innovation, assumed that responses must be reinforced to be learned. Laboratory rats and pigeons in Skinner boxes were subjected to exhausting shaping interventions to bring about those necessary conditions for learning. If elaborate procedures were necessary to trigger relatively simple motor responses, how could learning theory possibly explain the much more extensive developments that occur in human personality formation?

Humans learn by observing. This is the simple answer that Bandura proposed. Intuitively, it is obvious. However, observational learning violates a traditional assumption of learning theory—that learning can occur only if there is reinforcement. Bandura asserted that learning and performance could be distinguished. Reinforcement provides incentives necessary for performance, but it is not necessary for learning.

modeling learning by observing others; also called vicarious learning

vicarious learning learning by observing others, without being directly rewarded oneself

Behavioral changes that result from exposure to models are variously called **modeling**, imitative learning, observational learning, or vicarious learning. These terms are interchangeable in Bandura's usage. He defines **vicarious learning** as learning in which

> new responses are acquired or the characteristics of existing response repertoires are modified as a function of observing the behavior of others and its reinforcing consequences, without the modeled responses being overtly performed by the viewer during the exposure period. (Bandura, 1965c, p. 3)

In everyday experience, a child may see a friend grab a ball away from a classmate and learn to grab as a result. Or a TV viewer may see a mass murder on television and later imitate the crime. More positively, exposure to competent and socialized adults teaches children desirable behaviors. Bandura's laboratory investigations show that exposure to adult models can lead to diverse effects, including the elevation of the level of moral reasoning (Bandura, 1969; Bandura & McDonald, 1963) or, conversely, an increase in aggressive behavior.

Bandura's interest in modeling had roots in other theoretical traditions. Psychoanalytic approaches emphasize identification with parents as the basis for much personality development. Previous researchers reasoned that children may identify with parents because of their power (as controllers of rewards) or because of their status (as recipients of rewards). Bandura designed a laboratory experiment to test these proposed causes of identification. Preschool children observed various kinds of models, some powerful, called *controller models* (because they controlled access to highly desirable toys) and some high status, called *consumer models* (because they received rewards). The children observed the models engaging in playful behavior with several distinctive components, such as putting on a hat backward or walking and saying, "Left, right, left, right."

Then the children played with the same toys, and observers counted the number of responses patterned after each model. Children modeled their behavior more after the controller models, not the consumer models. In a traditional family, with a working father and a homemaker mother, this would produce greater identification with the father, as much psychoanalytically derived research has suggested. Other family power structures exist, of course, and were explored in this study. Whether the controller model was male or female and whether the subjects were boys or girls, the controller model was imitated more than the consumer model. Overall, the research indicates that power leads to identification (Bandura, Ross, & Ross, 1963a). Other research has confirmed that models that dispense rewards to children have more effect on children's learning than nonrewarding models do (Grusec & Mischel, 1966).

Models also can influence children's development of standards for behavior (cf. Mischel, 1966). How good does a performance have to be before self-congratulations are deserved? Bandura and Whalen (1966) exposed 8- to 11-year-olds to models who rewarded themselves for their scores on a bowling task, giving themselves praise and candy according to a performance criterion that varied for different groups of subjects. Some models rewarded themselves only for superior performance; others demanded of themselves moderately good performance; and lenient models rewarded themselves for all but the very worst scores. When the children later played the game themselves, they demanded very high performance before rewarding themselves only if their models had set high standards. Even the most permissive models, however, produced self-reward standards higher than a control group of children who had not observed any model. Later research (Bandura, Grusec, & Menlove, 1967a) found that children were influenced by peer models who set high standards, as well as adult models.

Aggression, too, is learned by modeling (Bandura, 1965a, 1965b, 1973). Boys and girls, age 3 to 5, watched a film in which adults played with a variety of toys, including a large inflated Bobo doll. The adult models engaged in distinctive aggressive behaviors that the children would not have seen before to provide an opportunity to learn new responses.

> First, the model laid the Bobo doll on its side, sat on it, and punched it in the nose while remarking, "Pow, right in the nose, boom, boom." The model then raised the doll and pommeled it on the head with a mallet. Each response was accompanied by the verbalization, "Sockeroo . . . stay down." Following the mallet aggression, the model kicked the doll about the room, and these responses were interspersed with the comment, "Fly away." Finally, the model threw rubber balls at the Bobo doll, each strike punctuated with a "Bang." This sequence of physically and verbally aggressive behavior was repeated twice. (Bandura, 1965b, pp. 590–591)

For some children, this was the end of the film (no consequences condition). Other children saw the film continue, ending with the model being punished by another adult for his aggression (model punished condition) or with another adult praising the aggressive model for being a "strong champion" and rewarding him with food (model rewarded condition).

To test for modeling, the children were brought to a playroom similar to the one they had seen on the film. Observers counted the number of aggressive responses the children imitated from the film. As predicted, there was less imitation in the model-punished condition than in the other two conditions. There was no difference between the model-rewarded condition and the no-consequences condition. These modeling effects were similar for boys and for girls, although the girls behaved less aggressively overall (see Figure 12.5), consistent with other studies finding greater aggression in boys. Whether these sex differences were caused by different learning experiences for boys and girls or from the influence of biological differences such as hormones (Collaer & Hines, 1995) could not be answered from this study.

It is tempting to conclude that aggressive television is no danger as long as the villain is punished in the end. Although observing a model who is punished can sometimes inhibit aggression (Bandura, Ross, & Ross, 1963b), such a conclusion is not always warranted. Bandura included another feature in this study, which discredits this erroneous conclusion. For some children in each condition Bandura offered incentives (stickers and juice) if they could behave like the model they had seen. These children showed high levels of learning of the aggressive behaviors in all conditions. Thus punishing the villain may temporarily suppress the performance of imitative aggression, but the behaviors have been learned and may emerge later when incentive conditions change.

Ever since Bandura's early research, hundreds of studies using a variety of research methods have examined the relationship between TV violence and behavior. The overwhelming finding is that in the real world, as well as in the laboratory, models do teach aggression. Fortunately, as other studies show, models can also teach high standards and other positive social behaviors.

Modeling is not limited to childhood. Industrial psychologists use principles of learning through modeling to train workers (Decker & Nathan, 1985). In a field experiment, female college students who were in a car were more likely to use a seat belt if the driver did so (Howell, Owen, & Nocks, 1990). Even the Philadelphia Zoo has increased the attention of visitors to its exhibits, causing them to linger instead of moving quickly on to the next by placing strategic models who expressed interest in various exhibits (Koran & Camp, 1998). Modeling is a powerful determinant of the sorts of behaviors that have traditionally interested personality theorists. Bandura's clear theoretical specification of the processes involved in modeling and other forms of learning makes a precise, verifiable theory.

Figure 12.5 Modeling of Aggression

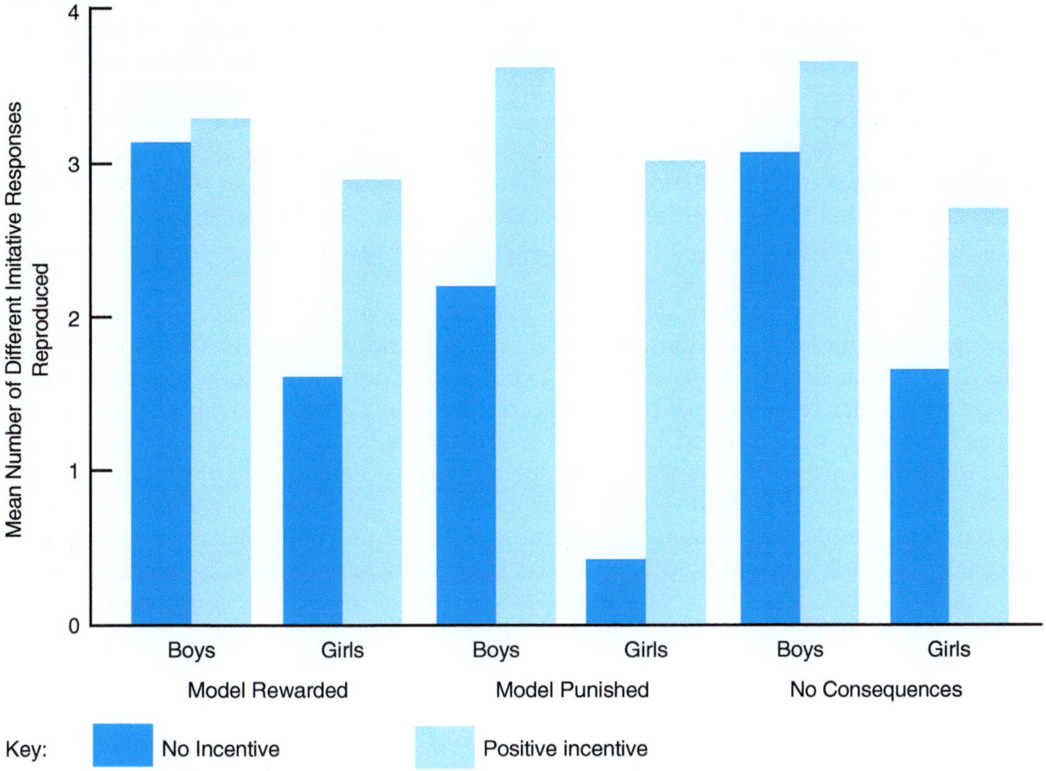

Mean number of different matching responses reproduced by children as a function of positive incentives and the model's reinforcement contingencies.

(From A. Bandura (1965). Influences of models' reinforcement contingencies on the acquisition of imitative responses. *Journal of Personality and Social Psychology, 1*, 589–595. Copyright 1965 by the American Psychological Association. Reprinted by permission.)

Therapy

Bandura (1961) criticizes therapy based only on talking, when known learning principles could improve outcomes. This evaluation is widely shared; cognitive behavioral approaches in therapy have been the most rapidly growing citations in recent years (Killgore, 2000), and cognitive behavioral therapy has demonstrated success in treating a variety of problems, including depression, eating disorders, and several kinds of anxiety disorders, and it even has value in treating sexual offenders and those who suffer from schizophrenia (Butler et al., 2004). Programs to increase clients' ability to avoid relapse after giving up alcohol have been devised, using social learning principles to individualize treatment for each alcoholic's high-risk situations (Annis, 1990). Efficacy expectations help people stop using marijuana (Stephens, Wertz, & Roffman, 1995).

Therapy that uses social learning principles such as modeling can successfully treat adults and children who suffer from phobias, including excessive fear of snakes, without any need for symbolic interpretation of the snake phobia (Bandura, Adams, & Beyer, 1977; Bandura & Barab, 1973; Bandura, Blanchard, & Ritter, 1969; Bandura, Grusec, & Menlove,

1967b; Bandura, Jeffery, & Wright, 1974; Bandura & Menlove, 1968). Other studies confirm that therapies based on learning principles are effective for various phobias, including agoraphobia, a fear of public places (Bandura et al., 1980). These findings contradict the prediction of psychoanalytic theory that only resolution of deep-seated unconscious conflicts could bring about a cure. They are consistent, though, with a study of the thoughts of agoraphobic people as they faced enclosed places, which they feared. These patients thought much more about their ability or inability to manage their anxiety than they did about any danger in the situation (Williams et al., 1997). Bandura (1961) argues that psychotherapy should be regarded as a learning process. More systematic application of learning principles (including reward, extinction, and discrimination learning, among others) can improve therapeutic outcomes.

In Bandura's view, changing self-efficacy expectations are key to successful therapy for fears and avoidant behavior (Bandura, 1977, 1984a; Bandura et al., 1980). Bandura suggests that phobias result from low efficacy expectations, not low outcome expectations. A person with a fear of flying may be convinced that, if only it were possible to get on the plane, life would be improved by desirable recreational and business outcomes (high outcome expectation). But as long as it seems impossible to board the plane and sit calmly in a seat during a flight (low efficacy expectation), that person will not be able to fly. Bandura stated, "treatments that are most effective are built on an empowerment model. If you really want to help people, you provide them with the competencies, build a strong self-belief, and create opportunities for them to exercise those competencies"

Figure 12.6 Changing Efficacy Expectations Through Therapy

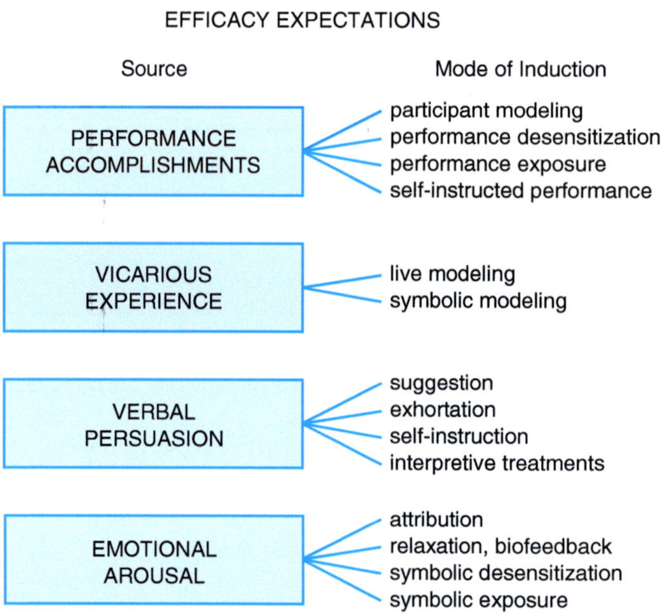

Major sources of efficacy information and the principal sources through which different modes of treatment operate.

(From A. Bandura (1977). Self-efficacy: Toward a unifying theory of behavioral change. *Psychological Review, 84,* 191–215. Copyright 1977 by the American Psychological Association. Reprinted by permission.)

(R. I. Evans, 1989, p. 16). Therapy will succeed if it increases self-efficacy. Bandura suggests that various therapy techniques, including talk therapy, are effective for a common reason: They change dysfunctional expectancies. People avoid actions that they do not expect they are able to do (Bandura, 1986a, 1989a, 1991a). Behavioral therapies, according to Bandura, are the most efficient and effective ways to raise efficacy expectations and therefore are the treatment of choice for phobias. Other techniques may be effective but only to the extent that efficacy expectations are raised. Even depth psychoanalysis can change dysfunctional expectancies but slowly. After many months or years, a patient may come to expect that adult life will be improved because problems are seen as stemming from childhood conflicts that are considered resolved. Figure 12.6 lists some of the therapeutic alternatives for increasing efficacy expectations.

Sometimes increasing efficacy is simple but nonetheless effective. Naval cadets who were simply told that they would probably not become seasick, and that if they did, it would probably not interfere with their work, in fact experienced less seasickness as a result (Eden & Zuk, 1995). Usually, though, more extensive therapeutic intervention is required to modify efficacy expectations. Knowing its importance, researchers who evaluate the effectiveness of therapies, such as interventions to help people with disabilities, now include measures of empowerment as one desirable outcome of their interventions (Zimmerman & Warschausky, 1998). We can think of increased empowerment or efficacy as a *nonspecific* outcome of therapy, in contrast to *specific* outcomes, such as a reduction in fear (Frank, 1982; Keijsers, Schaap, & Hoogduin, 2000).

The Person in the Social Environment

Many of the terms we have been using—*self* and *goals*, for example—conjure up images of the individual pursuing selfish goals with no thought of others, but that misperception probably comes from the overwhelming individualism of the culture in which most of us were raised. In fact, the environment in Bandura's three-part reciprocal determinism does more than simply provide an arena for individual accomplishments. It is a place of community, with goals and values that we share with others; of social responsibility, where our efficacy and ability can be put to work on behalf of others.

In addition to individual efficacy, Bandura suggests that a sense of **collective efficacy** occurs when groups believe that they, as a group, can do what needs to be done (R. I. Evans, 1989). Working together, they exert collective agency, in contrast to individual agency (Bandura, 2001b). As expected, the higher the sense of collective efficacy, the more groups mobilize toward their goals and resist obstacles, and the more they accomplish (Bandura, 2000).

collective efficacy the sense that a group can do what is to be done

Bandura (1990b, 1991b) warns that individuals often fail to regulate their own behavior in ways that live up to high moral standards. They exploit others, commit aggressive acts, pollute the atmosphere, and engage in many other behaviors that violate moral standards. This is a problem of **moral disengagement** (Bandura, 1978, 2001b; R. I. Evans, 1989). People can turn off, or disengage, their moral standards by a variety of techniques: convincing themselves that the ends justify the means, using euphemistic language that does not convey the immorality of the action, comparing with far worse behavior, displacing responsibility onto others, dehumanizing the victims, and so on (Bandura, 2001b). Like defense mechanisms described by psychoanalysts, these maneuvers protect from guilt. What is more, though, the social sensitivity of this theory makes a point that intrapsychic psychoanalytic theory does not: The moral disengagement mechanisms

moral disengagement failure to regulate one's behavior to live up to high moral standards

facilitate immoral behavior against others. Measures of moral disengagement (e.g., agreeing with the statement "If people are careless where they leave things, it is their own fault if they get stolen") predict that people will commit more transgressions (Bandura et al., 2001). Bandura (1999a) argues that societies must exert social control to supplement individuals' undependable moral self-control.

Fortunately, there is not a conflict between individual efficacy and moral responsibility. In fact, Bandura (2001b) reports that children who are high in efficacy are more cooperative and helpful to others, not less.

Summary

- Mischel challenged the assumption of *global personality traits* that led to consistent behavior across many situations, finding inconsistency instead. Behavior is much more situationally variable than trait theory had assumed.
- Instead of traits, Mischel proposed *cognitive person variables*, including *competencies, encoding strategies*, and *personal constructs*.
- Mischel has investigated children's development of a capacity to *delay gratification*. Cognitive variables are important in this development. Children learn such strategies as thinking about something else to avoid impulsive behavior.
- Bandura's concept of *reciprocal determinism* describes the mutual influences among the person, the environment, and behavior.
- Bandura has divided learning into four processes, allowing more precise prediction of when learning will occur. These are *attentional, retention, motor reproduction*, and *motivational processes*.
- Bandura demonstrated that children are influenced by *models* of desirable and undesirable behavior. They can learn to delay gratification or to be aggressive by watching adults in real life and on television.
- *Self-efficacy* refers to the belief that one can perform a particular behavior.
- Extensive research shows that *efficacy beliefs* affect the choice and persistence of behavior.
- Efficacy beliefs can be increased in *therapy*, and this is the mechanism by which therapy is effective, according to Bandura.

Thinking about Mischel's and Bandura's Theories

1. Do you think that cognitive social learning theory is capable of describing the most important human personality characteristics, or is it too focused on cognition?
2. Do you believe that people are consistent or not consistent? Explain.
3. How would you determine whether competencies and expectancies are the causes of behavior or the effects?
4. Compare delay of gratification to what psychoanalysts meant by the ego; compare modeling with identification.
5. Do you believe that media violence contributes to aggression in society? If so, what should be done about it?
6. How do schools and/or parents influence children's sense of self-efficacy? What advice would you give?

Study Questions

1. Summarize the trait controversy and Mischel's role in it.
2. Explain the term *personality coefficient*. Why does it present a problem for traditional personality theory that this number is low?
3. Explain Mischel's concept of situational hedges. How is this concept relevant to the trait versus situation controversy?
4. Explain what Mischel meant by cognitive person variables as alternatives to traits. Give examples.
5. Explain what is meant by competencies. How are they different from expectancies?
6. Define self-efficacy. Why are self-efficacy expectancies important?
7. Explain how expectancies can be influenced by experience.
8. What is the function of self-regulatory systems and plans in personality? Give an example.
9. Summarize research on delay of gratification. What evidence shows the importance of developing this capacity in early life?
10. Diagram and explain Bandura's concept of reciprocal determinism. Discuss how this concept is different from Skinner's concept of environmental determinism.
11. What is a self-system, in Bandura's theory?
12. What is self-efficacy? How is it related to behavior?
13. What evidence has Bandura presented to indicate that self-efficacy affects the body?
14. List and explain Bandura's four processes that influence learning. Give an example of each process as it might influence a person who is learning to act like a famous athlete.
15. Summarize Bandura's research on modeling. Explain the relevance of this research for personality development.
16. Describe the evidence Bandura presented that indicates a relationship between seeing aggressive models and behaving aggressively. Why can aggression still result, even if the aggressive model is punished?
17. What has cognitive social learning theory contributed to psychotherapy?
18. How does self-efficacy change during therapy?
19. What is collective efficacy? Give an example from your own observation.
20. Explain what Bandura meant by moral disengagement. How does this process raise problems that must be solved by society, and not simply by changing individuals?

CHAPTER 5

The Motive Perspective

"I'm in the pre-med program, and I really want to get into a good medical school. The courses aren't that easy for me, so I have to study more than some people. I can't even take time off on weekends, because I'm taking an extra-heavy load. I don't mind, though, because when I do well, I feel really satisfied."

Most college students spend at least part of their time planning what they will do after college. Some have ambitions they're already pursuing full speed (like the pre-med student, above). Most college students also devoted part of their energies to close relationships. Some are already thinking about being married in the years to come and building a life together with someone.

These two concerns are probably familiar to you. Work and love are issues in everyone's life. But people vary quite a lot in how central each of these issues is. And not even these issues are everything, of course. Some people have a deep desire to influence others—maybe in politics, or in show business, or by running a successful company. Some people want to find order and meaning in life. Some seek truth, some seek beauty.

There's a lot of diversity in the concerns people focus their lives around. Yet despite the diversity, all have something in common: They imply the existence of needs and motives behind people's thoughts and actions. How do people describe their preoccupations? "I *need* to find a soul mate. I *need* to accomplish things in my life. I *want* to do well in school. I *need* to feel in control." There are also individual differences here. For any aspect of life you might imagine, some people feel a deep need within it; others don't.

If needs and motives influence people's thoughts and actions this way, they're important. It can even be argued that a person's needs define who the person is. This idea forms the basis for the viewpoint on personality that's examined in this chapter.

Basic Theoretical Elements

Needs

The fundamental principle of this approach is that behavior is best understood as a reflection of the strength of the person's needs. A **need** is an internal state that's less than satisfactory, a lack of something necessary for well-being. Henry Murray (1938), who began this approach to personality, defined a *need* as an internal directional force that determines how people seek out or respond to objects or situations in the environment.

Some needs are biological (needs for food, water, air, sex, and pain avoidance). Others—such as the needs for power, achievement, and intimacy—either derive from biological needs or are inherent in our *psychological* makeup. It's easiest to start with biological needs, because biology is a good model for how needs work. Biological needs must be satisfied repeatedly over time. As time passes, the needs gradually become more intense, and the person acts to cause the needs to be satisfied. For example, over time, your body starts to need food. When the need gets strong enough, you'll do something to get some food. That reduces the need.

The strength of a need influences the intensity of the related behavior. The stronger the need, the more intense the action. Intensity can be reflected in several ways, such as vigor, enthusiasm, and thoroughness. But intensity can also be expressed in less obvious ways. For example, need strength can help set priorities—which action you do first versus put off until later. The stronger the need, the sooner it's reflected in action. Figure 5.1 shows how this prioritizing can create a continually changing stream of actions, as need strengths build and subside. The need that's greatest at any given point is the one that shows up in behavior.

Every need has associated with it some category of *goal objects.* When you're thirsty, you need water, not food.

Needs are directive: They help determine which of many possible actions occurs at a given time. They are directive in two senses. First, when you have a need, it concerns something in particular. When you need water, you don't just *need*; you need *water*. Needs thus pertain to classes of goal objects or events. Needs are also directive in that they create movement either *toward* the object or *away* from it. A need aims to get something or to avoid something. Thirst reflects a water-related need, but it's more than just water *related*. Fear of going swimming also reflects a water-related need. Thirst reflects a need to *get* water. Moving toward versus moving away is part of the directionality of all needs.

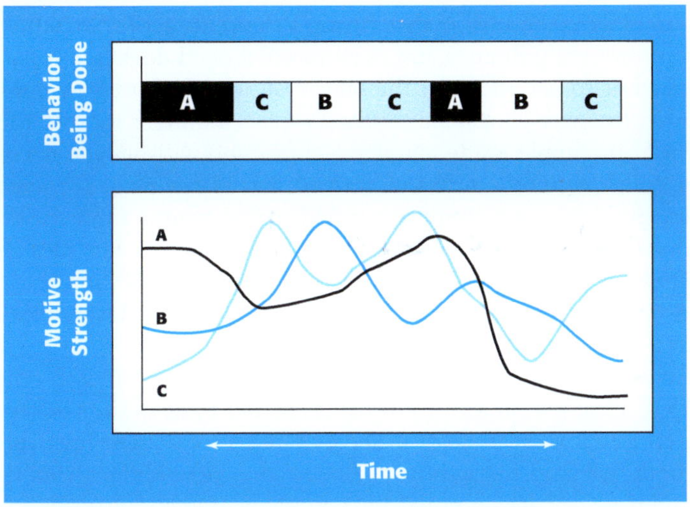

FIGURE 5.1
A graphic display of how changes in behavior over time can be explained by variations in the relative strengths of several motives over the same time. The letters at the top of the diagram indicate which of three activities the person is engaged in at any given time (shifting from one to the other). The three lines indicate the levels of the three motives related to these three activities. As one motive rises above the other two, the behavior changes.

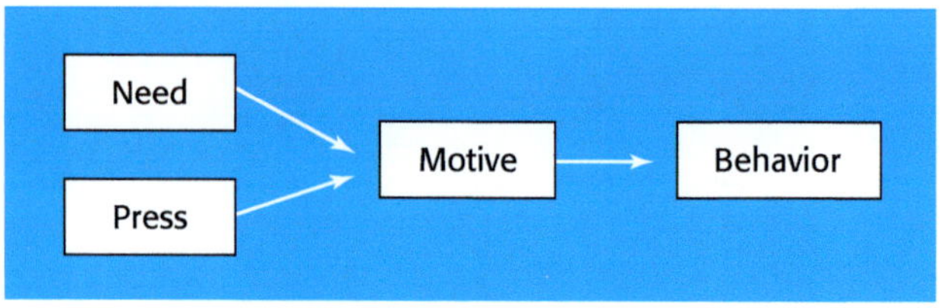

FIGURE 5.2
Internal need states and external press can both influence motives to engage in particular kinds of action, which in turn become realized in overt behavior.

MOTIVES

Needs work through **motives**. Motives are a step closer to behavior. David McClelland (1984), an important contributor to this view of personality, said motives are clusters of *cognitions with affective overtones, organized around preferred experiences and goals*. Motives appear in your thoughts and preoccupations. The thoughts pertain to goals that are either desired or undesired. Thus, they are emotionally toned. Motives eventually produce actions.

To illustrate the relationship between need and motive, the need for food occurs in the tissues of the body. But the need results in a motive state called *hunger*. Unlike the need for food, hunger is experienced directly. It creates mental preoccupation and leads to behavior that will reduce the hunger (and the need for food). Thus, we distinguish needs from motives partly by the existence of a subjective experience. A need is a physical condition you don't sense directly. It creates a motivational state that you *do* experience.

PRESS

Motives are influenced by needs, but they're also influenced by external events. Murray (1938) used the term **press** to refer to such external influences. A press (plural is also *press*) is an external condition that creates a desire to get (or avoid) something. It thus has a motivational influence, just as an internal need does (see Figure 5.2).

It may be easiest to get a feel for the effects of need and press by considering a biological motive. Imagine your need for food creates a hunger motive. You respond by eating lunch. Your simple sandwich, dry and crumbly, satisfies the need for food. But just as you finish, someone walks in with an extra-large pizza (or whatever you find irresistible). Suddenly you aren't as satisfied as you were a moment before. The motive to eat has been rekindled—not by a need but by a press. The idea also applies to purely psychological motives. Seeing someone else receive an honor can increase your motive for recognition. Being around someone who's engaged may increase your motive to be in a close relationship.

Although needs and motives clearly *can* be distinguished from each other, people don't always do so. One reason for this is that it's harder to keep the concepts distinct for psychological needs than biological needs. A need for achievement involves no deficit in the body. It's hard to say how the need to achieve differs from the motive to achieve. For this reason, it's common for people writing about needs and motives in personality to use the two terms interchangeably.

Needs, Motives, and Personality

When motives are strong, they influence behavior. Motives vary across time and situations. But people also vary in *dispositional* motives. That is, some people naturally

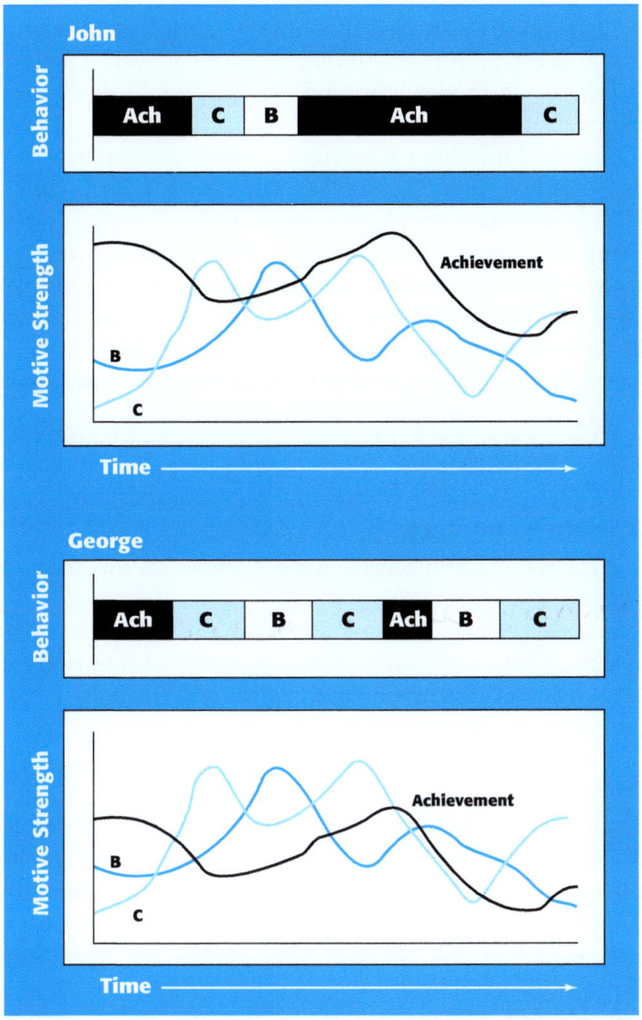

FIGURE 5.3
John has a high dispositional need for achievement; George's is lower. Assume this need fluctuates for both of them in the same pattern across time. John's and George's levels of two other needs are identical (and also fluctuate). The difference in the dispositional need for achievement creates a great difference in the overt actions John and George display (the bars above the lines).

have more of a given motive much of the time than other people do. Such **motive dispositions** begin to form a picture of the person's personality.

Motive States and Motive Dispositions

We've already shown how to think about temporary fluctuations (see Figure 5.1, earlier). People shift from doing one thing to doing something else, as one need is satisfied and others build up. Ongoing behavior reflects whichever need is now greatest. That model provides a sense of how people shift from one action to another over time.

Now let's add the idea that people vary in their dispositional levels of needs. This can be portrayed as differences in the overall heights of the lines. Such differences can have large effects on moment-to-moment behavior. For example, John has a high dispositional need for achievement, whereas George's dispositional need for achievement is lower. Assume that this motive goes up and down in the same pattern for both across time. Assume also that they have identical patterns in all their other needs. As Figure 5.3 shows, John and George would display quite different patterns of behavior over time. Why? Because even when John's other needs are also elevated, his need for achievement is so high it tends to remain above the others. As a result, he tends to do achievement-related things a lot of the time. For George, the achievement motive rarely gets high enough to be the strongest motive. Thus, George doesn't engage in achievement-related behavior very often.

Henry Murray (1938) was the first to develop a view of personality organized in terms of needs and motives. He and his colleagues generated a list of needs that they believed underlie personality. Murray believed that all people have the same basic needs, but that everyone has a dispositional tendency toward *some particular level* of each need.

Measuring Motives: The Thematic Apperception Test or Picture Story Exercise

To develop the motive approach to personality, researchers had to measure motives. For several reasons, they began not by asking people about their motives but by using another strategy. This was a fortuitous decision. *Why* it was fortuitous gets us ahead of our story, however.

What was this alternative strategy? Morgan and Murray (1935) suggested that needs are *projected* into a person's fantasy, just as a movie is projected onto a screen. (This idea derives from psychoanalytic theory, the subject of Chapter 8.) Murray called this process **apperception**. The idea that people do this easily and often led to the **Thematic Apperception Test (TAT)** (Morgan & Murray, 1935; Murray, 1938; Smith, 1992).

When your motives are being assessed by TAT, you view a set of pictures and are asked to create a story about each one. The pictures are ambiguous. Your story is supposed to describe what's happening, the characters' thoughts and feelings, the relationship among characters (if there's more than one), and the outcome of the situation. The key assumption is this: Through apperception, the themes in your stories will reflect your implicit motives.

Do fantasy stories really reflect people's needs? Early studies tested the procedure by creating situational needs. One such study looked at the need for food. People were deprived of food for varying lengths of time, so they would have different needs for food. They subsequently differed in their food-related TAT imagery (Atkinson & McClelland, 1948).

Another early study manipulated the achievement motive, by giving some people a success and others a failure. A failure should temporarily increase the achievement need by creating an achievement deficit. As expected, the failure caused greater achievement imagery than occurred in a group that had not experienced the failure (McClelland, Atkinson, Clark, & Lowell, 1953). Unexpectedly, though, achievement imagery was also elevated in a group that had experienced a success. This finding led McClelland to conclude that deprivation isn't necessary to arouse a motive (Winter, 1998). The motive can be aroused by any circumstances that point to the motive's relevance.

Studies of Specific Dispositional Motives

Once tested in studies of situational motives, the apperception procedure was used to measure motive *dispositions*. The TAT pictures were used in some of this work, but variations on the TAT with other pictures were also developed. The procedure in its various forms is now often referred to as the **picture story exercise (PSE)**. Researchers have used this procedure to study several motive dispositions in detail, as outlined in the next sections.

Persons high in achievement motivation have a strong need to succeed.

Need for Achievement

Of the various needs identified by Murray, the first to receive research attention was the **need for achievement**. This motive was studied for decades by David McClelland, John Atkinson, and many others (e.g., Atkinson & Birch, 1970; Atkinson & Raynor, 1974; Heckhausen, 1967; Heckhausen, Schmalt, & Schneider, 1985; McClelland et al., 1953).

Achievement motivation is *the desire to do things well, to feel pleasure in overcoming obstacles*. Need for achievement is reflected in PSE responses that mention performing well at something, reaching goals or overcoming obstacles to goal attainment, having positive feelings about success, or negative feelings about failure.

People who differ in achievement motivation differ in several ways in achievement-related situations. Consider the very act of choosing a task. Tasks (or problems within a task) can be easy, hard, or somewhere in between. Given a choice, which would you prefer? (When you plan your course schedule for next semester, do you choose easy courses and professors, hard ones, or ones in between?)

People low in need for achievement prefer tasks that are either very easy or very hard (Atkinson, 1957). It's easy to understand the easy ones. There isn't much achievement pressure in an easy task, and it's nice to get something right, even if everyone else gets it right too. Why, though, would people with a low achievement need choose a hard task? Clearly, it's not for the challenge. It seems to be more that doing poorly on a hard problem doesn't reflect badly on them. And there's always the possibility (however remote) that they will get lucky and succeed. In contrast, people high in need for achievement tend to prefer tasks of moderate difficulty. They also work harder on moderately difficult tasks than on very hard or very easy ones (Clark & McClelland, 1956; French, 1955).

Why do people high in achievement motivation prefer tasks of middle difficulty? Maybe it's because these tasks give the most information about ability (Trope, 1975, 1979). If you do well at an easy task, you don't learn much about your ability, because everyone does well. If you *fail* at a *hard* task, you don't learn much about your ability, because almost *no one* does well. In the middle, though, you can find out a lot. Perhaps people high in achievement motivation want to find out about their abilities. Trope (1975, 1980) tested this by having people choose test items. He figured out a way to manipulate (separately) the items' difficulty and their **diagnosticity** (how much they tell about ability). People with a high achievement need had a strong preference for

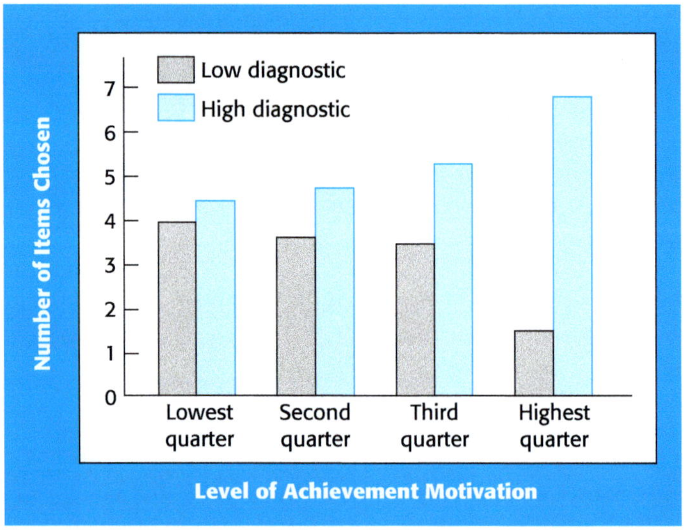

FIGURE 5.4

Participants in this study chose items to work on that they expected to be either highly diagnostic of their abilities or not diagnostic. This figure divides participants into four levels of achievement motive, ranging from very low to very high. There is an increasingly strong preference for highly diagnostic items among those with higher levels of achievement motivation. *Source:* Based on Trope, 1975.

diagnostic items (see Figure 5.4), whereas difficulty in itself turned out not to be important.

Effects of achievement motivation have been studied in lots of domains over the years. The need for achievement relates to greater persistence in the face of failure (e.g., Feather, 1961), better task performances (e.g., Lowell, 1952), higher grades (Schultz & Pomerantz, 1976), and greater educational achievement among 20,000 students in Holland (Hustinx, Kuyper, van der Werf, & Dijkstra, 2009). Indeed, it's even been suggested that the need for achievement plays a role in the economic rise and decline of entire cultures.

This idea led to studies of literature from several civilizations, at several distinct points in their history. The literature is interpreted for its themes, in much the same way as PSE responses are interpreted. The economic growth and decline of that civilization are then plotted over the same period. One impressive study of this sort (Bradburn & Berlew, 1961) examined the history of England from 1500 to just after 1800. The researchers divided this period into 50-year segments and coded achievement imagery and economic development in each. Achievement imagery was stable for 100 years, fell off, and then rose sharply. The index of economic development followed a nearly identical pattern of falling then rising—but 50 years later. This suggests that shifts in achievement motives had economic consequences.

Another even more complex study of this sort was done by McClelland (1961). This study focused on a much narrower period—1925 to 1950—but looked at 23 cultures across the world. McClelland coded achievement imagery from children's schoolbooks at both points in history. He developed two measures of economic growth over the intervening period and compared the achievement imagery to economic growth. A moderately strong association emerged between achievement imagery in 1925 and economic growth from 1925 to 1950. As in the earlier study, there was virtually no relation between economic growth and later achievement imagery. This pattern suggests that motivation (reflected in the imagery) produced the economic achievement, instead of vice versa.

Achievement motivation predicted economic success in these studies, but in some situations a need for achievement is less helpful. For example, people in high-level politics have the task of mobilizing others (which draws on a different need), and they often have little personal control over outcomes (Winter, 2010). As a result, the need for achievement is frustrated, rather than producing good outcomes. Indeed, the achievement motive has been linked to lower effectiveness among U.S. presidents (Spangler & House, 1991). Winter (2010) has also found that need for achievement is valuable in the business world only when control is relatively high.

An interesting aspect of the literature on the achievement motive is that, at first, far more was known about its effects among men than among women, because most early studies looked only at men. Moreover, even when studies did address achievement motivation across gender, they typically focused on stereotypically masculine pursuits (e.g., work income), rather than look at a variety of areas for achievement (e.g., family roles; Duncan & Peterson, 2010). Eventually, however, researchers looked at achievement needs among women. Some of this work suggests that achievement needs are expressed in varying ways among women, depending on the direction they take in their lives.

Elder and MacInnis (1983) recruited two sets of 17- to 18-year-old girls. One group was family oriented, the other group had a mix of family and career interests. Achievement motives, assessed at the same time, predicted different outcomes in the two groups as they moved into adulthood. Among family-oriented women, those with a high achievement need invested energy in activities leading to marriage and family. In effect, they expressed achievement by creating and sustaining a family. Among career-minded women, having a high achievement need led to putting off marriage and families. Presumably, this was because they were focusing on their careers. Thus, what women value as a goal determines what behaviors follow from their achievement needs.

Another way of putting this is to say that women with achievement needs pursue achievement in ways that fit their views of themselves and the world they live in. It seems reasonable that this principle should also influence what careers women consider. Jenkins (1987) looked at career choices made by women who were college seniors in 1967. Those high in the need for achievement were likely to become teachers but not to go into business. Why? Teaching gave them an outlet for their achievement needs but didn't conflict with traditional women's roles. Business careers didn't fit those roles as well. Thus, the achievement needs of these women were channeled by other aspects of their social environments.

Need for Power

Another motive that's been studied extensively by David Winter (1973) and others is the **need for power**. Need for power is *the motive to have impact on others, to have prestige, to feel strong* compared to others. PSE responses that reflect the need for power have images of forceful, vigorous action—especially action that evokes strong emotional responses in others. Responses showing concern about status or position also reflect the need for power.

What kinds of behavior reflect the power motive? Not surprisingly, people high in need for power seek out positions of authority and influence and surround themselves with symbols of power (Winter, 1972, 1973). For example, students high in the power motive are likely to be office holders in student organizations (Greene & Winter, 1971). The power motive also predicts the likelihood of holding execu-

The need for power is often expressed in the tendency to acquire high-status positions and to surround oneself with symbols of power.

tive positions in organizations (Harms, Roberts, & Wood, 2007). People high in the need for power are concerned about controlling the images they present to others (McAdams, 1984). They want to enhance their reputations. They want others to view them as authoritative and influential. Not surprisingly, they tend to be somewhat narcissistic, absorbed in their importance (Carroll, 1987). They also are more sexually active than persons lower in this motive (Schultheiss, Dargel, & Rohde, 2003).

The power motive can be helpful in many contexts. People high in the power motive are less likely to make concessions in diplomatic negotiations than those lower in this motive (Langner & Winter, 2001); this can yield better outcomes in the negotiations. When power-motivated people win, they learn implicitly (outside their awareness) to continue what they had been doing. When they lose, they learn implicitly not to continue what they had been doing (Schultheiss, Wirth, Torges, Pang, Villacorta, & Welsh, 2005).

There's evidence that the power motive also enhances effectiveness in managing others. For example, U.S. presidents high in the power motive were more effective than those who were lower (Spangler & House, 1991). Winter (2010) has argued that what makes the power motive effective in politics (where the achievement motive is ineffective) is that people high in the power motive aren't bothered by the lack of control in political situations. They just keep adjusting their behavior in a continuing effort to have influence.

In their personal lives, men with high power needs are inclined to say that the ideal wife is a woman who's dependent (Winter, 1973). An independent woman is a potential threat. A dependent woman allows the man to feel superior. A later study found that the wives of men high in the need for power were indeed less likely to have a career outside the home (Winter, Stewart, & McClelland, 1977).

This isn't to say that the need for power is something that matters only among men. Women vary in this need, as well, and studies have proven that it predicts important outcomes among women. One study (Jenkins, 1994) found that women high in the need for power have more power-related job satisfactions than women lower in this need but also more *dis*satisfactions. These women also made greater strides in career development over a 14-year period—but only if they were in power-relevant jobs.

The level of a person's need for power can also influence the manner in which he or she relates to others. The need for power relates to taking an active, assertive, controlling orientation in peer interactions (McAdams, Healy, & Krause, 1984). People

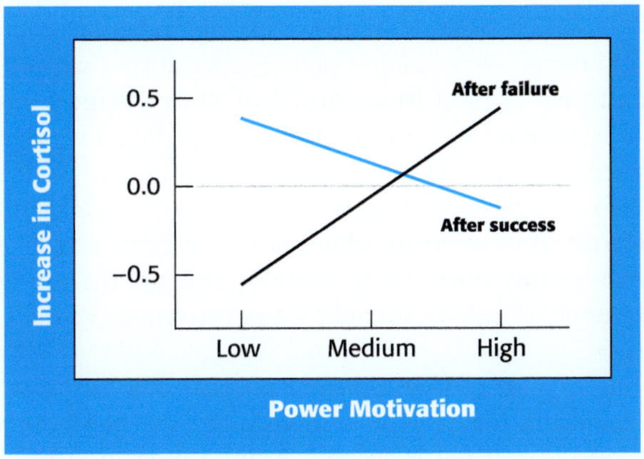

FIGURE 5.5
Increase in the stress hormone cortisol after a failure was greater among persons higher in the need for power; increase in cortisol after a success was greater among persons lower in the need for power. *Source:* Based on Wirth et al., 2006.

high in the need for power are rewarded by low-dominance expressions from others (indeed, are especially attentive to them; Schultheiss & Hale, 2007), and they're disrupted by high-dominance expressions from others (Schultheiss, Pang, Torges, Wirth, & Treynor, 2005). These people are also more angered when others don't respond well to their efforts to exert influence (Fodor & Wick, 2009). The dominating style of interacting that characterizes the need for power can also have more ominous overtones: Men high in power needs are more likely than men with lower power needs to physically abuse their female partners during arguments (Mason & Blankenship, 1987).

The desire for dominance often leads to success, but sometimes it's frustrated by failure. People with a high need for power have an increase in the stress hormone cortisol after a failure (Wirth, Welsh, & Schultheiss, 2006). Interestingly, people with a low need for power have an increase in cortisol after a success! Apparently, what constitutes a stressor differs between these two sorts of people (see Figure 5.5). Both success and failure can be stressful but they're stressful for different people. Stress seems to follow when the outcome *isn't* the one you are motivated for or accustomed to.

Oliver Schultheiss and his colleagues have found that the need for power also relates to the sex hormone testosterone (we say more about this hormone's influence on personality in Chapter 7). There's a slight link between power needs and baseline testosterone (Schultheiss et al., 2005). More interesting, however, is what happens to testosterone after success and failure. Among men, a high need for power relates to both a larger increase in testosterone after a success and a greater reduction in testosterone after failure. Among women, however, the associations were much more complex.

On the other hand, there's also evidence that the sex hormone estradiol (which is closely related to testosterone chemically) plays a role in women similar to that played by testosterone in men (Stanton & Schultheiss, 2007). First, high power motivation was related to a higher level of estradiol at baseline. More striking, after a competition, the changes in estradiol were very similar to those shown in testosterone by the men in the earlier study. Among winners, estradiol increased most among those who were highly power motivated. Among losers, estradiol decreased most among those who were highly power motivated. A similar pattern emerged in a later study by Stanton and Edelstein (2009), showing that women not taking oral contraceptives had an even higher correlation between estradiol and power motivation than other women.

Is the power motive a good thing or a bad thing? Winter has suggested that the power motive is manifested in two paths, depending on whether or not the person acquires a sense of responsibility during socialization (Winter, 1988; Winter & Barenbaum, 1985). For those high in the sense of responsibility, the motive yields a conscientious pursuit of prestige, in which power is expressed in socially accepted ways. For those without this sense of responsibility, though, the motive leads to problematic ways of influencing others, including aggressiveness, sexual exploitation, and alcohol and drug use.

Winter and Barenbaum (1985) reported considerable support for this reasoning. In one sample, among men low in responsibility, the need for power related to drinking, fighting, and sexual possessiveness. Among men high in responsibility, the need for power related inversely to all these tendencies. Similarly, Magee and Langner (2008) found that the two forms of the power motive resulted in antisocial and prosocial decisions, respectively. Men with a high need for power without the sense of responsibility also displayed a notable rise in testosterone when imagining and experiencing a power-related success (Schultheiss, Campbell, & McClelland, 1999; Schultheiss & Rohde, 2002).

All of this suggests that the power motive can be "tamed" by proper socialization. There's an important qualifier to this conclusion, however: Prosocial decisions promote the good of one's group. But sometimes, larger issues intrude. Winter (2007) analyzed communications of various sorts that occurred during a set of crises that developed into wars and a matched set that were peacefully resolved. Results showed that the war crises involved higher displays of the power motive but also—paradoxically—higher levels of responsibility. Winter noted that in many circumstances, going to war seems to be the responsible thing to do. Thus, the carefully socialized sense of responsibility may tame the power motive, but only up to a point.

Need for Affiliation

Another motive that received a good deal of attention early in the development of the motive perspective is the motive to affiliate. The **need for affiliation** is *the motive to spend time with others and form friendly social ties*. This isn't a need to dominate others but to be in social relationships, to interact with others (for a review, see Sokolowski, 2008). In this need, social interactions aren't a means to an end; they're a goal in their own right. In PSE responses, the need for affiliation is reflected in concern over acceptance by others and by active attempts to establish or maintain positive relations with others.

Studies have uncovered several manifestations of this motive. For example, people who want to affiliate want to be seen as agreeable. If a group exerts pressure on them, they're more likely to go along than people with lower affiliation needs (Hardy, 1957). These people get nervous if they think others are judging their interpersonal skills (Byrne, McDonald, & Mikawa, 1963). They prefer interaction partners who are warm, compared to those who are reserved (Hill, 1991). They're more likely to make concessions in negotiations (Langner & Winter, 2001), and they're more likely to initiate contacts and try to establish friendships (Crouse & Mehrabian, 1977). They're especially sensitive to angry expressions from others (Schultheiss et al., 2005).

The active initiation of social contact suggests that affiliative needs go beyond worrying about acceptance from others. These needs can also lead to active participation in social events. For example, Sorrentino and Field (1986) studied the emergence

Need for intimacy is the desire to experience warm, close, and meaningful relationships with others.

of leadership in discussion groups that met in five weekly sessions. At the end, group members were asked to indicate whom they viewed as group leaders. People high in the need for affiliation were nominated more often than people lower in the need for affiliation.

As suggested by Sorrentino and Field's research, people with a strong affiliation motive spend more time engaged in social activities than people lower in this motive. These people make more phone calls (Lansing & Heyns, 1959), and when they're paged they're more likely to be engaged in some social activity—conversing or letter writing, for example (Constantian, 1981; McAdams & Constantian, 1983). When they're alone, they're more likely to express the wish to be interacting with others (McAdams & Constantian, 1983; Wong & Csikszentmihalyi, 1991).

Links between the affiliation motive and relationship satisfaction are complex (Meyer & Pepper, 1977). Happiness depends partly on the balance of affiliation needs between partners. That is, well-adjusted husbands and wives have affiliation needs that *correlate* with each other. To put it concretely, if you have a low affiliation need, you're best off with someone who has a similarly low affiliation need. If your affiliation need is high, you're best off with someone whose affiliation need is also high.

Need for Intimacy

Another motive that has emerged as a research focus is the **need for intimacy**. It's been studied intensively by Dan McAdams (1982, 1985, 1989) and his collaborators. Intimacy motivation is *the desire to experience warm, close, and communicative exchanges with another person, to feel close to another person*. Intimacy motivation shares with affiliation motivation a wish to be with others as an end, rather than a means. It goes beyond the need for affiliation, though, in its emphasis on closeness and open sharing with another person.

McAdams proposed this need partly because he felt the need for affiliation didn't focus enough on the positive, affirmative aspects of relationships. Additionally, the need for affiliation is an active, striving, "doing" orientation, whereas the need for intimacy, as McAdams views it, is more of a "being" orientation (McAdams & Powers, 1981). The two aren't fully distinct, of course. McAdams and Constantian (1983) reported a correlation of 0.58 between them.

What kinds of behaviors reflect the intimacy motive? In one study, people higher in the need for intimacy reported having more one-to-one exchanges with other people, though not more large-group interactions (McAdams et al., 1984). The interactions reported by intimacy-motivated people involved more self-disclosure, as well.

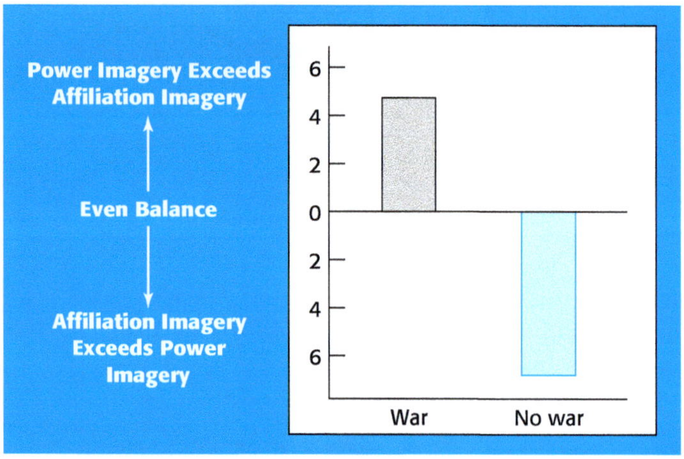

FIGURE 5.6
Balance of power motive imagery versus affiliation motive imagery in sovereign's speeches during the year before Great Britain entered a war (18 cases) compared to the year before Britain did *not* enter a war (36 cases). *Source:* Based on Winter, 1993, Table 3.

To put it differently, people with a high intimacy need are more likely to share with friends their hopes, fears, and fantasies. The sharing goes both ways: People with a high intimacy need report doing more *listening* than people with a low intimacy need, perhaps because they are more concerned about their friends' well-being. Indeed, intimacy seems to entail both self-disclosure and partner disclosure (Laurenceau, Barrett, & Pietromonaco, 1998).

Because having close interactions is important to people with high intimacy needs, it should be no surprise that these people define their lives partly in terms of such interactions. McAdams (1982) collected autobiographical recollections among students high and low in intimacy needs. They were asked to report a particularly joyful or transcendent experience from their past and then an important learning experience. Content was coded several ways. For instance, some events involved considerable psychological or physical intimacy with another person; others did not. Analysis revealed that intimacy motivation was strongly correlated with memory content that also implied intimacy.

How do people high in the intimacy motive act when they're with others? They laugh, smile, and make more eye contact when conversing than do people with lower intimacy needs (McAdams, Jackson, & Kirshnit, 1984). They don't try to dominate the social scene (which is what people with the need for power do). Instead, they seem to view group activities as chances for group members to be involved in a communal way (McAdams & Powers, 1981).

The desire for intimacy is good for people, based on evidence from a study in which men wrote narrative fantasies at age 30 and were assessed 17 years later (McAdams & Vaillant, 1982). Men with higher intimacy motives at 30 had higher marital and job satisfaction at 47 than did those with lower intimacy motives. Another study found that women high in the intimacy motive reported more happiness and gratification in their lives than those low in the intimacy motive—unless they were living alone (McAdams & Bryant, 1987).

Interestingly, intimacy needs (needing to be close) don't seem to coexist well with power needs (needing to influence or dominate others). Persons who are high in both needs are often poorly adjusted (Zeldow, Daugherty, & McAdams, 1988).

Patterned Needs: Inhibited Power Motive

Thus far, we've discussed needs individually. Indeed, for many years, that's how they were examined—one at a time. However, some studies have examined patterns involving several needs at once—sometimes, in combination with other characteristics. One well-known pattern combines a low need for affiliation with a high need for power, in conjunction with the tendency to inhibit the expression of the latter. This pattern is called **inhibited power motivation** (McClelland, 1979). The reason for interest in this pattern depends on the context in which it's examined.

One context is leadership. The line of reasoning goes as follows: A person high in need for power wants to influence people. Being low in need for affiliation lets the person make tough decisions without worrying about being disliked. Being high in self-control (inhibiting the use of power) means the person will want to follow orderly procedures and stay within the framework of the organization. Such a person should do very well in the structure of a business.

This pattern does, in fact, relate to managerial success. In one study that spanned a 16-year period, people with the inhibited power pattern moved to higher levels of management than others, but only those who were nontechnical managers (McClelland & Boyatzis, 1982). Among managers whose jobs rested on engineering skills, personality didn't matter. This is understandable, because the managerial value of these people depends heavily on their particular skills.

There's also evidence that people with this pattern are especially effective at persuasion (Schultheiss & Brunstein, 2002). Their persuasiveness stems both from greater verbal fluency and from an effective use of nonverbal cues, such as gesturing. Presumably, being more persuasive helps these people be effective in mobilizing others.

The pattern of high power motivation and low affiliation motivation may be good for getting others mobilized, but even this may be a mixed blessing. Winter (1993) argued that this pattern is conducive to starting wars. Historical data show that high levels of power imagery and low levels of affiliation imagery in the statements of politicians predicted going to war. For example, speeches by the rulers of Great Britain contained more power imagery than affiliation imagery in the year before the country entered a war, whereas the reverse was true during years before a no-war year (see Figure 5.6). In another case involving U.S. leaders—the Cuban missile crisis of 1962—greater affiliation than power imagery occurred before the successful avoidance of a war.

Implicit and Self-Attributed Motives

As noted earlier in the chapter, the motivational view is that personality is a system of multiple motives. Each motive exists in every person. Behavior, at any given time, depends partly on how intense the various motives are, which is determined partly by personality and partly by context.

Incentive Value

This analysis sounds reasonable, but it's missing something. It predicts that if your need for affiliation is more intense than your other needs, you'll engage in an affiliative act. But *what* act? Additional concepts are needed to address this question (McClelland, 1985).

One such concept is **incentive**: the degree to which a given action can satisfy a need for you. It's sort of a personalized weighting of how relevant an act is to the need. Incentive values determine how a motive is expressed behaviorally. For example, a person with a high need for affiliation who loves music will go to clubs and concerts with friends. A person with a high need for affiliation who loves sports will go to football and basketball games with friends. But people don't engage in all conceivable need-related behaviors. They choose ways to satisfy their needs, based on the incentive values that various activities have for them.

We didn't introduce the concept of incentives earlier in the chapter along with the concept of need. Clearly, though, something like it is needed to account for the diversity of behavior. People differ in the activities they engage in, even when satisfying the same need. As noted earlier, some women satisfy the need for achievement through careers, others by achieving strong family lives. These activities differ greatly, yet both can satisfy the need to achieve.

This principle relates to a point made in Chapter 4 regarding interactionism: We said there that people choose for themselves which situations to enter and which to avoid, thus creating an interaction between person and situation. We didn't say *why* different people choose different situations. One answer is that various situations have different *incentive* values to different people, even if the situations fulfill the same need.

Needs and incentives both influence behavior, but in different ways. McClelland (1985) said that need strength relates to long-term *frequencies of need-relevant actions of any type*. Incentive values, on the other hand, should relate to *choices within a domain of action*. In McClelland's view, needs influence behavior primarily at a nonconscious level, whereas values influence the more conscious process of choice.

Implicit Motives Are Different from Self-Attributed Motives

The last paragraph was deceptively simple, but it has a great many implications. Earlier in the chapter, we described development of the TAT or PSE to assess motives. We said there that the decision to use that strategy, instead of asking people about their motives, was fortuitous. Why? Because it allowed the discovery of something that today seems very important indeed.

The PSE procedure was used in the vast majority of the work described thus far. And from the wide range of findings, we feel relatively confident that it does assess people's motives. Given the large effort required to score the PSE, however, other researchers created self-report scales to assess motives, which were far simpler. They intended those self-reports to measure the same motives as the PSE. But the self-reports turned out to correlate poorly with PSE assessment (McClelland, Koestner, & Weinberger, 1989; Pang & Schultheiss, 2005; Schultheiss & Brunstein, 2001). Why? What's going on?

McClelland and his colleagues argued that the two kinds of assessments are, in fact, measuring different things (McClelland et al., 1989). They used the term **implicit motive** to refer to what the PSE measures (Schultheiss & Brunstein, 2010). They called the motives *implicit* because the person may or may not be aware of them. They used the term **self-attributed motive** to refer to what's measured by self-reports (also now termed *explicit motive*). An increasing body of evidence indicates that implicit motives and self-attributed motives are different. *Implicit motives* are what we have been calling *motives*. *Self-attributed motives* are closer to what was described in the preceding section as *incentives*.

McClelland et al. (1989) held that implicit motives are more basic. They are the recurrent preferences for classes of affective experiences that McClelland believed lie at the heart of motives (the feeling of "doing better" for the achievement motive, the feeling of "being strong" for the power motive, the feeling of "being close" for the intimacy motive). Implicit motives are seen as primitive and automatic (Schultheiss, 2002; Schultheiss & Brunstein, 2010). Because they are basic, they are good predictors of broad behavioral tendencies over time. In contrast, self-attributed motives relate to specific action goals. They tell how a person will act in a particular situation. For this reason, they're better at predicting responses in structured settings.

This distinction has been pursued further in several projects. Brunstein and Maier (2005) expanded on the idea that both implicit and self-attributed achievement motives play important but distinct roles in achievement behavior. They found evidence that the implicit achievement motive acts primarily as an energizer, boosting effort when the person falls behind. The self-attributed achievement motive, in contrast, acts primarily as an influence on decision making, influencing how people seek information about their skills compared to other people (for example, by choosing to continue a task or not).

Evidence that these qualities are distinct also comes from research in which people completed PSE and self-report measures and then kept records of memorable experiences over 60 days (Woike, 1995). The records were coded for motive relevance and for feelings. Strength of implicit motives (PSE) related to the frequency of reporting feelings that relate to that motive. Strength of self-attributed motives did not. Self-attributed motives related instead to the frequency of reporting motive-related events with no feelings (but PSE scores did not).

It seems, then, that the two aspects of motivation link to different aspects of memory. Further evidence that they link to different aspects of memory comes from studies showing that self-attributed motives predict recall of general memories related to the self-concept, whereas implicit motives predict recall of specific events (Woike, Mcleod, & Goggin, 2003).

Another example of the value of distinguishing between implicit and self-attributed motives comes from a set of studies by Baumann, Kaschel, and Kuhl (2005). They argued that people sometimes have motive-related intentions (explicit) that fit poorly with their implicit motive dispositions. When this happens, the person is stressed, which has adverse effects on his or her well-being. They argued further that this tendency is particularly pronounced among persons who are also poor at regulating negative emotions. Evidence from three studies fits that picture.

The idea that incongruence between one's implicit and explicit motives can be problematic has been studied in several other contexts. As in Baumann et al.'s (2005) work, the idea is that the motive discrepancies create stress by having conflicting influences on behavior. There's evidence, for example, that motive discrepancy of this sort can lead to unhealthy eating (Job, Oertig, Brandstätter, & Allemand, 2010). More generally, it's been proposed that optimal well-being follows from having explicit motives that are congruent with one's implicit motives and acting in way that satisfies both motives (Schüler, Job, Fröhlich, & Brandstätter, 2008).

McClelland believed that both the implicit motive and the self-attributed motive are important, but that they should be viewed separately. The evidence appears to support that belief. Sometimes it makes sense to expect an implicit motive to predict an outcome but not a self-attributed motive. Sometimes the opposite is true. For this reason, it's important to be sure which one you want to measure and to measure it

Table 5.1 Sample Hypothesis about the Interaction between the Affiliation–Intimacy Motive and the Trait of Introversion–Extraversion.

	Affiliation–Intimacy Motive	
	Low	High
Extravert	Intimate relationship not salient as a desire	Desire for intimate relationship leads to single stable relationship
Introvert	Intimate relationship not salient as a desire	Desire for intimate relationships but difficulty maintaining them, because having a high focus on one's inner world is disruptive of a connection to the other person

Source: Based on Winter et al., 1998.

correctly (McClelland, 1989). The distinction between implicit and self-attributed motives is one aspect of the motive view on personality that is receiving increasingly close attention.

Approach and Avoidance Motives

Another distinction that's also increasingly important is the distinction between approach and avoidance. As noted early in the chapter, a motive is either a readiness to approach something or a readiness to avoid something. Thus far, we've written only about approach. For example, people motivated to achieve try to approach success. But any achievement task also holds a possibility of failure. It seems likely that the desire to avoid failure also plays a role here. Just as Atkinson (1957) tied the need for achievement to the capacity to feel pride in success, the need to avoid failure relates to a tendency to feel shame after failure (McGregor & Elliot, 2005).

A simple way to avoid failure is to avoid achievement situations altogether. *Never trying* keeps you from failing. Another way to avoid failing is *the very act of succeeding*. It may be that some people who struggle to achieve don't care so much about gaining success as they care about the fact that gaining success lets them avoid failure.

Much of the early research on achievement actually measured both of these motives. A lot of it derived from Atkinson's (1957) theory of achievement behavior. That theory makes its clearest predictions for people whose only motivation is to approach success and people whose only motivation is to avoid failure. Predictions are less clear for people high in both motives and people low in both motives. For that reason, studies often included only the two groups who were high in one motive and low in the other.

That strategy was guided by theory, but it has a bad side effect: It completely confounds the two motives. This causes ambiguity in interpretation (Chapter 2). If the groups act differently, is it because of the difference in the motive to approach success or because of the difference in the motive to avoid failure? There's no way to know, although interpretations tend to focus on the motive to approach success.

In recent years, the distinction between approach and avoidance motivation has re-emerged as a focus for research on achievement, much of it by Andrew Elliot and his colleagues (e.g., Elliot, 2005; Elliot & Harackiewicz, 1996; Elliot & McGregor, 2001). Part of their theory is that achievement can reflect either of these motives. Which motive is central, however, will influence many aspects of the person's experience.

Elliot and McGregor (2001) found that the motive to succeed in mastering course material (approach) related to study strategies that involve thoughtfully elaborating on the material. The avoidance motive related to memorization. Avoidance motivation also related to having trouble organizing study time effectively. Elliot and Sheldon (1997) found that the motive tendencies also have different effects on subjective experiences. People who focus their effort on trying to avoid failure report less emotional well-being and less satisfaction with their performance than people who are trying to approach success.

Though it might generally be better to approach than to avoid, there's also evidence that people do better when they're doing what's familiar to them. Specifically, people with a high fear of failure are made uneasy and upset by imagining success (Langens & Schmalt, 2002). As suggested in the context of the power motive, it may be that what's stressful to you is what you're unfamiliar with.

Approach and Avoidance in Other Motives

Once you grasp the idea of separate approach and avoidance motives, you realize that the idea has implications for every motive you can think of (see also Carver, Lawrence, & Scheier, 1999; Higgins, 1997; Ogilvie, 1987). Try it out. Pick a motive. Identify a behavior that reflects that motive. Then see if you can spot the opposing motive that might create the same behavior. For example, acts of affiliation can come from the desire to be with others (need for affiliation) but they can also come from the desire to avoid being alone (Boyatzis, 1973; Pollak & Gilligan, 1982). These aren't the same. One is a motive to approach; the other is a motive to avoid. The same issue can be raised for any motive you can think of.

Box 5.1 The Process Underlying the TAT or the PSE

Take a good look at the picture on the right. Something's happening, but what? Decide for yourself. Make up a story that fits the picture. Include the following information (and whatever else you want to include):

- What's just happened to these people?
- What's the relationship between them?
- What are their present thoughts and feelings?
- What will be the outcome of the situation?

Take your time, and make your story as long and detailed as you wish.

What you've just done is similar to what people do when completing the Thematic Apperception Test (TAT; Morgan & Murray, 1935) or picture story exercise (PSE; McClelland et al., 1989). The idea is that people's motives show up in what comes from their minds when they try to make sense of an ambiguous picture. The ambiguity makes it less likely that press will dictate your story's content and more likely that your motives will influence what you write.

When people complete a PSE, they write stories for several pictures. Different pictures tend to elicit stories with different themes. Some pictures naturally elicit achievement-related stories; others are more amenable to stories with affiliation themes. Over the course of several pictures, however, dispositional tendencies emerge in people's narratives. Presumably, these storytelling tendencies reflect the motives that underlie the person's personality.

If you're interested in the motives that dominate your own personality, look at the story you wrote to see if there's evidence of any of the motives discussed in this chapter.

Illustration by Stephen P. Scheier. Reproduced by permission.

Just as with achievement behavior, evidence is beginning to accumulate that approach and avoidance motives have different consequences in other domains. A powerful example is a study of commitment between romantic partners (Frank & Brandstätter, 2002). This study found that commitment based in approach predicted more relationship satisfaction 6 and 13 months later. However, commitment based in avoidance (i.e., avoiding the process of breaking up) predicted lower relationship satisfaction at the follow-ups.

The idea that a given behavior can be based on either an approach motive or an avoidance motive (or some combination of the two) raises very broad questions about why people do the things they do. Are people generally moving toward goals, or are they trying to avoid or escape from things? Do actions differ depending on which motive is more prominent? Do the feelings that go with the actions differ?

The general idea that any approach motive has a corresponding avoidance motive has very broad implications. It complicates the picture of human behavior enormously. We will put this idea aside for the rest of this chapter, but you should keep in mind that it's always in the background.

Motives and the Five-Factor Trait Model

When thinking about motive dispositions as the core of personality, a question that naturally arises concerns the relation between the motive view and the trait view described in Chapter 4. Does the five-factor model absorb the qualities that motive theorists see as important?

One way this question can be approached is to analyze measures of self-attributed motives. Stumpf (1993) used one such measure, the Personality Research Form (PRF; Jackson, 1984), and concluded that it captured all of the "big five" except neuroticism. Costa and McCrae (1988a) also found that many PRF scales reflect underlying qualities of the five-factor model. On the other hand, several PRF scales loaded on two or more of the five factors rather than one, suggesting that those motives relate to several traits. This general pattern was also found by Paunonen et al. (1992). In contrast, somewhat better support for a fit to the five-factor model has been found in a different measure of needs (Piedmont, McCrae, & Costa, 1992).

Traits and Motives as Distinct and Complementary

The attempt to fit motives to the five-factor model can be seen as an effort to integrate across theoretical boundaries. However, many believe that the effort is misguided and that traits and motives are fundamentally different (Winter, John, Stewart, Klohnen, & Duncan, 1998). Note that the evidence reviewed just above involved self-attributed motives, not implicit motives. The fact that self-attributed and implicit motives are not strongly related is reason enough to be wary about concluding that traits and motives are the same. There's also separate evidence that implicit motives relate poorly to the five-factor model (Schultheiss & Brunstein, 2001).

Winter et al. (1998) proposed an integration but of a different sort: They proposed that motives are fundamental desires and that traits channel how those desires are expressed. Thus, they argued, motives and traits interact to produce behavior. In some respects, this resembles the argument described earlier in the chapter about implicit motives and incentive values. In the view taken by Winter et al., traits may represent patterns of incentive preferences.

In support of their argument, Winter et al. presented two studies of extraversion and (PSE-derived) motives. The studies examined women's lives across many decades. Winter et al. argued that intimacy needs would have different effects among introverts and extraverts (see Table 5.1). For women with low intimacy needs, it shouldn't matter much whether they are introverts or extraverts. Intimacy isn't a big need for them. The complicated situation occurs among those with high intimacy needs. An extravert with high intimacy needs should do fine in relationships, because extraverts are comfortable with, and good at, various kinds of social interaction. In contrast, introverts with high intimacy needs should have problems. Their highly inner-directed orientation should interfere with relationships. Their partners may see them as remote or withholding. The result should be a greater likelihood of marital problems. That's exactly what was found.

The bottom line here appears to be that implicit motives exist at a different level of abstraction than traits. Exactly how these constructs relate to each other doubtlessly will be a subject for continued research.

Personology and the Study of Narratives

Research on the effects of motive dispositions tends to take one of two approaches. Some studies examine how people respond to particular events, in the laboratory or in the field. Other studies collect evidence of a dispositional motive (or set of motives) at one time and relate the motive to some outcome that occurs considerably later.

Both of these approaches differ greatly from the one favored by Murray, the father of this viewpoint. Murray believed that the way to understand personality is to study the *whole person* and to do so over an extended period. The work on which he based his theory was an intensive study of 51 college men (Murray, 1938). Each was tested in many ways and interviewed by a staff of professionals, who came to know each man's personality quite thoroughly.

This approach was idiographic. It focused on the pattern of qualities that made each person unique. Murray disliked nomothetic methods. He thought their focus on comparison keeps them from probing deeply into a person's life. To Murray, the nomothetic approach yields only a superficial understanding. Murray's concerns led him to coin the term **personology** to refer to the approach he preferred. He defined *personology* as the study of individual lives and the factors that influence their course. He believed that personology was more meaningful than other approaches because of its emphasis on the person's life history. According to Murray (1938), "the history of a personality *is* the personality" (p. 604).

Recent years have seen a resurgence of interest in this way of thinking about personality. For example, Dan McAdams, whose work on intimacy motivation was described earlier, has written extensively on the idea that identity takes the form of an extended narrative—a life story that each of us writes and lives out over time (McAdams, 1985; McAdams & Pals, 2006). This narrative has chapters, heroes, and thematic threads that recur and permeate the story line (see also Rabin, Zucker, Emmons, & Frank, 1990).

Here's an example of how narratives can differ from person to person. Some themes emphasize growth ("I found out how to make our relationship better"), others emphasize safety ("I hope that never happens again") (Bauer, McAdams, &

Sakaeda, 2005). As another example of a narrative focus, McAdams (2006) identified a constellation of themes focused on personal redemption—a transition from a state of suffering to a better psychological state—which characterizes the lives of some middle-aged Americans.

From this point of view, the person's identity lies in keeping a coherent narrative going across time (McAdams & Pals, 2006; Singer, 2004). This way of thinking speaks directly to the uniqueness of each person, because every life story is unique (Singer, 2005). Whether this approach will become more prominent in personality psychology in the future remains to be seen, but it's surely a development that Murray would have applauded.

Assessment

Assessment of personality from the motive viewpoint is a matter of determining the levels of a person's motive dispositions. The assessment technique most associated with assessment of these dispositions is the PSE (Smith, 1992; Winter, 1996).

Earlier in the chapter, we described the essence of the procedure by which the PSE is administered (see also Box 5.1). People who are completing it view a set of ambiguous pictures, in which it isn't clear what's happening. They're asked to create a story about each picture. The story should describe what's happening, the characters' thoughts and feelings, their relationship to each other (if there's more than one character), and the outcome of the situation. Through apperception, the themes that are manifested in the stories reflect implicit motives.

Scoring people's responses can be complex (Winter, 1994), but here's a simplified version. Look to see what kinds of events take place in the story and what themes and images are in it. Events that involve overcoming obstacles, attaining goals, and having positive feelings about those activities reflect the achievement motive. Events in which people choose to be with other people and stories that emphasize relationships among people reflect the affiliation motive. Stories with images of one person controlling another reflect the power motive. More than one theme can occur in a given story. These can be scored separately, so the stories can be used to assess several different motives at the same time.

The use of stories written about ambiguous pictures is the core method for assessing motives in research deriving from this theoretical viewpoint. It's not just stories that can be scored for motive imagery, of course. Anything that's written—speeches, diaries, letters—can be scored in the same way (Winter, 1994). However, variations on the PSE remain the most popular method of assessing implicit motives.

The PSE is widely used to measure motives, but it has had its share of criticism. Questions have been raised about its relatively low internal consistency and test–retest reliability (Entwisle, 1972; Lilienfeld, Wood, & Garb, 2000). Defenders of the technique reply that there are good reasons for both of these to be low. The pictures in any PSE vary considerably in content, so it's not surprising that they bring out different kinds of stories. That reduces internal consistency. It also may be that being told to tell several stories in the same session creates implicit pressure to avoid repetition. This can reduce both internal consistency and test–retest reliability (Atkinson & Raynor, 1974). There's evidence, though, that the reliability of the PSE need not be as low as was once believed (Lundy, 1985; Schultheiss, Liening, & Shad, 2008; Schultheiss & Pang, 2007).

Another criticism of the PSE is far more pragmatic: It takes a lot of time and effort to give and score it. This is a key reason why people wanted to develop self-report measures of motives. As noted earlier in the chapter, however, there's now substantial evidence that self-attributed motives (assessed by self-report scales) and implicit motives (assessed by story imagery) are not the same. Each captures something about human motivational experience, but what is being captured differs from one to the other.

Other Implicit Assessments

People working within the motive tradition in personality have relied heavily on the PSE as the primary tool of implicit assessment. In recent years, however, other ways of assessing implicit constructs have been developed (which were discussed in Chapter 3). The reasoning behind them doesn't rely on the concept of projection, but rather on the idea that a good deal of people's knowledge is associative in nature (largely due to processes of conditioning, discussed in Chapter 10). If you ask people to introspect about that knowledge, they won't be able to give you accurate answers, because the knowledge isn't explicit (able to be verbalized). Instead, it's in the pattern of associations. It may well represent different sources of information than create explicit knowledge (Rudman, Phelan, & Heppen, 2007).

An example of a procedure derived from this reasoning is the implicit association test (IAT; Greenwald, McGhee, & Schwartz, 2008). It measures links among semantic properties in memory that are believed to be hard to detect by introspection. As noted in Chapter 3, the IAT can be applied to virtually any kind of association. When it's applied to properties of personality, reaction times for various associations can be informative about the implicit sense of self. Just as explicit and implicit motives predict different aspects of behavior, explicit and implicit (IAT) measures of self-concept contribute separately to predicting behavior (Back, Schmukle, & Egloff, 2009).

Some research has compared the TAT and IAT (Sheldon, King, Houser-Marko, Osbaldiston, & Gunz, 2007). The two measures were correlated and had similar patterns of correlations with other scales. This suggests that they may be measuring similar things.

Problems in Behavior, and Behavior Change

People working within the motive approach to personality have been interested in specific domains of human activity (e.g., achievement, affiliation, power, intimacy) and in the more general idea of motivation as a concept. They haven't spent nearly as much effort analyzing problems in behavior. Nevertheless, the literature has at least tentative links to some problems.

The Need for Power and Alcohol Abuse

It's been suggested that the need for power can play a role in developing a drinking problem (McClelland, Davis, Kalin, & Wanner, 1972). This idea stems partly from the finding that drinking alcohol leads to feelings of power. Thus, a person with a need for power can satisfy that need, at least somewhat, by drinking. This doesn't satisfy the need for long, of course, because the feeling of power is illusory. It goes away when the person sobers up.

The idea that alcohol abuse may reflect a need for power leads to some recommendations for treatment. In particular, it suggests that people who are using alcohol this way aren't aware of doing so. They would probably benefit from realizing what

Motivation seminars are often used to enhance achievement motivation among people in business.

they're doing. By encouraging other ways to satisfy the power motive, therapists can treat the issue productively, rather than simply treating a symptom. One study (Cutter, Boyatzis, & Clancy, 1977) found that this approach can be more effective than traditional therapies, yielding nearly twice the rate of rehabilitation at one-year follow-up.

Focusing On and Changing Motivation

Psychologists contributing to the motive approach to personality have also had relatively little to say about therapeutic behavior change. Murray, the father of this approach, was a therapist, but he didn't develop new techniques. In general, he applied the currently existing psychodynamic techniques to people's problems.

It would seem, however, that the study just discussed makes some suggestions about behavior change. As noted, some people appear to use alcohol as a way of temporarily satisfying a desire for power. A treatment program developed for these people focused on two things: It made them more aware that this motive was behind their drinking, and it helped them find other ways to satisfy the need for power, thus making drinking unnecessary.

A broader implication of this discussion is that people may *often* be unaware of the motives behind their problem behaviors. Many problem behaviors may reflect needs that are being poorly channeled or reactions to conflicts between implicit motives and self-attributed motives. If so, taking a close look at the person's motive tendencies might reveal something about the source of the problem. Knowing the source may make it easier to make changes.

Another program of study, conducted by McClelland and his colleagues (McClelland, 1965; McClelland & Winter, 1969), has also had indirect implications for therapy. It was a training program developed to raise achievement motivation among businesspeople (see also Lemann, 1994). The program was rooted in the idea that thinking a lot about achievement-related ideas increases your motive to achieve.

The program began by describing the nature of the achievement motive and instructing people on how to score TAT protocols for achievement imagery. People were then taught to use achievement imagery in their thoughts as much as possible. By teaching themselves to think in terms of achievement, they increased the likelihood of using an achieving orientation in whatever activity they undertook.

Achievement-related thinking is important, but it isn't enough by itself. A second goal of the training was to link these thoughts to specific, concrete patterns of action. It was also important to be sure the patterns worked outside the training program. The people were encouraged to think in achievement terms everywhere—not just in the training sessions—and to put the action patterns into motion. People in the course wrote down their plans for the next two years. They were taught to plan realistically and to set goals that were challenging but not out of reach. This planning provided a way of turning the achievement orientation they learned into a self-prescription for a course of activity. This prescription then could be used in guiding actual achievement later on.

Was the course effective? The answer seems to be yes. In a two-year follow-up, participants had higher business achievements, were more likely to have started new business ventures, and were more likely to be employing more people than before, compared to control participants (McClelland & Winter, 1969).

This program showed that it's possible to change people's achievement-related behavior, but a question remains about whether it changes their underlying needs. It also remains uncertain how much these effects can be generalized to the domain of therapy. Nonetheless, the studies do seem to provide intriguing suggestions about behavior change.

Motive Theories: Problems and Prospects

The theorists represented in this chapter look to motivational processes and the pressures they place on people as a way to specify how dispositions influence actions. By providing a way to think about how dispositions create behavior—by specifying a type of intrapersonal functioning—this approach to dispositions evades one of the criticisms of trait theories.

A criticism that's harder to evade is that decisions about what qualities to study have been arbitrary. Murray developed his list of needs from his own intuition (and other people's lists). Others working in this tradition have tended to go along uncritically. Yet McAdams noted one omission from that list—the need for intimacy—that's strikingly obvious as a human motive. This suggests that Murray's intuitive list was incomplete. A response to this criticism is that the motives that have been examined most closely are those that fit with ideas appearing elsewhere in psychology, as well. This convergence suggests that the needs really are fundamental.

Another criticism bears less on the theory than on its implementation. Murray was explicit in saying that the dynamics of personality can be understood only by considering multiple needs at once. However, research from the motive approach to personality has rarely done that. More often, people study one motive at a time to examine its dynamics. Occasionally, researchers have stretched to the point of looking at particular clusters of two or three needs, but even that has been rare.

Despite these limitations, work on personality from the viewpoint of motive dispositions has continued into the present. Indeed, this area of work has enjoyed a resurgence in the past decade or so. The idea that people vary in what motivates them has a good deal of intuitive appeal. Further appeal derives from the idea that motive states wax and wane across time and circumstances. These ideas provide a way to incorporate both situational influences and dispositional influences in an integrated way. Given these "pluses" and a growing interest in understanding how implicit motives and self-attributed motives work together, the future of this approach seems strong.

• SUMMARY •

The motive approach to personality assumes that behavior reflects a set of underlying needs. As a need becomes more intense, it's more likely to influence behavior. Behavior is also affected by press: external stimuli that elicit motivational tendencies. Needs (and press) vary in strength from moment to moment, but people also differ in patterns of chronic need strength. According to this viewpoint, this difference is the source of individual differences in personality.

Murray catalogued human motives, several of which later received systematic study by others. One (studied by McClelland, Atkinson, and others) was the need for achievement: the motive to overcome obstacles and to attain goals. People with high levels of the achievement motive behave differently from those with lower levels in several ways: the kinds of tasks they prefer, the level of task difficulty they prefer, their persistence, and their performance levels. Early research on achievement tended to disregard how approach and avoidance motives might separately influence behavior. More recent work has begun to examine those distinct influences.

The need for power—the motive to be strong, compared to other people—has also been studied extensively. People who score high in this need tend to seek out positions of influence, to surround themselves with the trappings of power, and to become energized when the groups they're guiding have difficulties. People with high levels of the power motive tend to choose as friends people who aren't influential or popular, thereby protecting themselves from undesired competition. The power motive can lead to unpleasant forms of social influence, unless it's tempered by a sense of responsibility.

The need for affiliation is the desire to spend time with other people—to develop and maintain relationships. People who score high in this need are responsive to social influence, spend a large proportion of their time communicating with other people, and when alone, often think about being with others. A related motive that isn't represented in Murray's list but has received attention in recent years is the need for intimacy. People high in this need want warm, close, and communicative relationships with others. People with strong intimacy needs tend to spend more time in one-to-one interaction and less time in groups. They tend to engage in interactions that involve a lot of self-disclosure and are concerned about their friends' well-being.

Research has also investigated patterns of motives, such as inhibited power motive. This pattern is defined by having more of a need for power than a need for affiliation and by restraining the power need. People with this pattern do well in managerial careers, but the pattern has also been linked to political stances that preceded wars.

Theorists of this view use other concepts besides motives in talking about behavior. Incentive value—the extent to which a given action will satisfy a given need for a person—helps to explain why people with the same motive express it in different ways. Indeed, the concept of incentive provides an opening into a broader issue. Specifically, assessment of motives by the picture story exercise (PSE) technique does not relate well to assessment by self-report. What's assessed by the PSE has come to be called implicit motives, and what's assessed by self-report has come to be called self-attributed or explicit motives. Implicit motives are thought to function mostly unconsciously, and self-attributed motives are thought to function mostly consciously. One active area of interest is how these two aspects of motives function and relate to one another.

Murray emphasized the study of individual lives in depth over extended periods of time. He coined the term *personology* to refer to the study of the whole person, and personology was his goal. This emphasis has not been strong in the work of most others, but it has re-emerged more recently in the work of McAdams and his colleagues.

The contribution to assessment that's most identified with the motive approach is the PSE. It's based on the idea that people's motives are reflected in the imagery they "apperceive"—that is, read into ambiguous stimuli, such as a set of pictures depicting people in ambiguous situations. There are also self-report measures of motives, but they appear to measure something different from what the PSE measures.

The motivational approach to personality has largely ignored the issue of analyzing problems in behavior, although at least some evidence links the need for power to the misuse of alcohol. It's possible to infer from this evidence, however, that many problems in behavior stem from inappropriate channeling of motives. It's also reasonable that people can be helped by increasing their awareness of the motive that underlies the problem and then channeling the motive in alternative ways. Research on increasing the need for achievement suggests that it may be possible to alter people's dispositional levels of the motives that make up personality.

• GLOSSARY •

Apperception The projecting of a motive onto an ambiguous external stimulus via imagery.

Diagnosticity The extent to which a task provides information about something.

Implicit motive A motive assessed indirectly because it's relatively inaccessible to consciousness.

Incentive The degree to which an action can satisfy a particular need for a person.

Inhibited power motivation The condition of having more need for power than for affiliation but restraining its use.

Motive Cognitive–affective clusters organized around readiness for a particular kind of experience.

Motive disposition The dispositional tendency toward a high or low level of some motive.

Need An unsatisfactory internal condition that motivates behavior.

Need for achievement The need to overcome obstacles and attain goals.

Need for affiliation The need to form and maintain relationships and to be with people.

Need for intimacy The need for close communication and sharing with someone else.

Need for power The need to have influence over other people.

Personology Study of the entire person.

Picture story exercise (PSE) Any one of a family of tests that uses stories written about pictures to assess motive strength through narrative fantasy.

Press An external stimulus that increases the level of a motive.

Self-attributed motive A motive that's consciously reported.

Thematic Apperception Test (TAT) A particular method of assessing the strength of a motive through narrative fantasy.

CHAPTER

2 PERSONALITY TRAITS: A GOOD THEORY

Read the Chapter on mysearchlab.com

"There is nothing so practical as a good theory."
Kurt Lewin

Have you ever tried to judge someone's personality from his or her living space? When I was a brand-new college student, my roommate Kathy was a cheerleader, daughter of the head football coach and little sister of their star quarterback. She was tall, blonde, charming, sociable, flirty, attractive, outgoing, conservative, and slightly daring. We quickly unpacked and set up our room. Then we had the idea of walking down the hallway and introducing ourselves to our new hall-mates. This would both satisfy our curiosity—who were these people we would be living with?—and give us decorating ideas. After all, there's not much one can do with a stark, square, concrete-block room of a dull-pastel color.

We were amazed at the ingenuity with which our peers had transformed these "cell blocks" into cozy and often inviting living spaces: cutesy posters and classic rock album covers on the walls, seashells, massive stereo systems, a snowboard, an open violin case, dressers with elaborate makeup holders and perfume bottles, golden posters for far-away places (Vienna! Venice!), color-coded filing systems, and photos of cool boyfriends. We were amazed at what we could tell about these strangers from their rooms!

As the astute psychology majors that we were, we wondered how much we really learned about our hall-mates. Certainly people decorate their rooms to impress others or to create certain images—and there was a lot of that going around our first year—but at the heart of it all, to what extent does an individual's personality manifest itself in the design and content of a dorm room?

Gosling, Ko, Mannarelli, and Morris (2002) asked this very question in a systematic way. They reasoned that when people live in an environment they leave **behavioral residue** behind. Such physical traces left behind by everyday actions are hints or cues to the personality of the occupant (Gosling et al., 2002). For example, specific items may be left behind either carelessly, like a snowboard that wasn't put away properly, or on purpose to convey a certain image (e.g., "Hey, I'm cool, I'm edgy, I'm a snowboarder!"). Similarly, people may keep mementos from a summer vacation, like seashells, in a prominent place because such items have personal meaning to them or reinforce their own self-views (e.g., "I'm a nature lover"). People may have tidy rooms and organized bookshelves so they can find what they need quickly. All of these are ways we express personalities and leave, perhaps inadvertently, cues for observers (Gosling, 2008).

In this study, anywhere from 1 to 6 observers, ordinary folk with no particular training, visited actual rooms of 83 college student volunteers. These volunteers lived in private houses, apartments, residence halls, co-ops, and Greek-system housing either on or just off campus. The researchers covered names and any photos in the rooms so that observers would not know

What can you tell about the personality of the occupant of this room?

for sure the race or gender of the occupant. The observers then glanced around the rooms and made ratings on a 7-point scale of the extent to which they thought each of 44 descriptions applied to the occupant of the room. Some of the descriptions included:

Anxious, easily upset
Extraverted, enthusiastic
Conventional, uncreative
Critical, quarrelsome
Disorganized, careless

Amazingly enough, there was a great amount of consensus. That is, observers readily agreed on what they thought an occupant was like. Even more amazing, observers were often very accurate in guessing the personality of the occupants. What cues were they using? Sometimes the neatness of a room indicated how conscientious the occupant was. Other times the distinctive look of a space, the presence of unique items, or the variety of books and magazines indicated a creative, open personality. And still other times the researchers couldn't be sure what cues observers used to accurately judge an occupant's extraversion, emotional stability, and agreeableness (see Table 2.1). You can see where you fall on these five factors by taking a short personality test similar to the one used in the study shown in Table 2.2.

Gosling and his colleagues repeated the study looking at people's office spaces and got pretty much the same results. In which space do you think people's personalities shone through the most? If you thought that it would be easier for people to truly express themselves in their bedrooms you'd be right (Gosling et al., 2002). Workplaces tend to constrain how much decoration and personal expression workers can show.

So, my roommate Kathy and I were indeed able to get to know our hall-mates a bit and to identify interesting people on our hallway that we wanted to get to know better. However, we also discovered that our tastes in friends and room decorations were quite different . . . as befitting two very different personalities!

THINK ABOUT IT

Besides living spaces, where else might we see people express their personalities?

As the opening research study illustrates, there are many ways of describing human personality: charming, sociable, flirty, outgoing, conservative, daring, conventional, uncreative, disorganized, careless, extraverted, enthusiastic, critical, quarrelsome, anxious, easily upset, and some 17,937 others (Allport & Odbert, 1936)! Such descriptors of personality are called traits. In this first chapter on traits, as Kurt Lewin suggested, we start with understanding the theories behind personality traits—including two approaches to studying traits—and the kinds and numbers of traits, and discuss whether there are universal traits that can describe *any* personality. In the next chapter we will study some of the practical applications of trait psychology and, in particular, how traits are expressed in many aspects of our lives, from our handshakes

Table 2.1 Cues Observers Use to Determine Personality of Room Occupants

Trait	Consensus	Accuracy	Valid Cues
Neuroticism	.08	.36**	(none)
Extraversion	.31*	.22*	(none)
Openness	.58**	.65**	Distinctiveness of the space, level of decoration, variety of magazines and books
Agreeableness	.20	.20*	(none)
Conscientiousness	.47**	.33**	Organized, neat, uncluttered

Note: Numbers in the table are correlations among observers' ratings. Recall that correlations can be positive or negative. Higher numbers mean that there is a stronger relationship between the variables. Significant effects are noted by asterisks.

* $= p < .05$, ** $= p < .01$.

Source: From Gosling et al. (2002, Tables 4 and 5) Gosling, S. D., Ko, S. J., Mannarelli, T., & Morris, M. E. (2002). A room with a cue: Personality judgments based on offices and bedrooms. *Journal of Personality and Social Psychology*, 82(3), 379–398. Copyright American Psychological Association. Adapted with permission.

Table 2.2 Test Your Own Personality: The Ten-Item Personality Inventory (TIPI)
Here are a number of personality traits that may or may not apply to you. Please write a number next to each statement to indicate the extent to which *you agree or disagree with that statement.* You should rate the extent to which the pair of traits applies to you, even if one characteristic applies more strongly than the other.

Disagree Strongly	Disagree Moderately	Disagree a Little	Neither Agree Nor Disagree	Agree a Little	Agree Moderately	Agree Strongly
1	2	3	4	5	6	7
1.____	Extraverted, enthusiastic					
2.____	Critical, quarrelsome					
3.____	Dependable, self-disciplined					
4.____	Anxious, easily upset					
5.____	Open to new experiences, complex					
6.____	Reserved, quiet					
7.____	Sympathetic, warm					
8.____	Disorganized, careless					
9.____	Calm, emotionally stable					
10.____	Conventional, uncreative					

Note: To score, take the average of your score on the two items listed for each factor. Items marked with an *R* are reversed scored. Extraversion: 1, 6R; Agreeableness: 2R, 7; Conscientiousness: 3, 8R; Emotional Stability: 4R, 9; Openness to experience: 5, 10R. To reverse score, 1 = 7, 2 = 6, 3 = 5, 4 = 4, 5 = 3, 6 = 2, 7 = 1.

Source: Gosling, Rentfrow, and Swann (2003, Appendix A, p. 525). From Gosling, S. D., Rentfrow, P. J., & Swann, W. B. (2003), "A very brief measure of the big-five personality domains," *Journal of Research in Personality*, 37, 504–528. Copyright © 2003 by Academic Press. Reprinted with permission.

to the kind of music we like, to the kind of careers we choose, including how our personality stays consistent, changes, or shows coherence over time.

What Is a Personality Trait?

"Nobody seems to know what a trait is, so it appears to us better to use 'characteristic.'"
Healy, Bronner, and Bowers (1931, p. 311)

SEE FOR YOURSELF

What kind of person are you? List the traits that best describe yourself.

Traits describe a person's typical style of thinking, feeling, and acting in different kinds of situations and at different times (McCrae & Costa, 1997b). Although we might act differently in specific situations (e.g., a job interview compared to hanging out with a close friend), or at different times (e.g., think of what you were like in high school compared to now), if someone were to follow you around for a while to witness your behavior in many situations and at different times in your life he or she would see some commonalities and consistencies in your reactions (Allport, 1927). These generally persistent ways of acting and reacting are captured by the concept of traits. In contrast, temporary states (such as emotions), attitudes (liberal, conservative), and physical attributes (short, muscular) are not considered personality traits.

Traits are measured over a continuum—that is, in a continuous stretch, from low to high. This means that people who score high on a particular trait, say talkativeness, are more likely to strike up a conversation with a stranger than a person who is low on talkativeness (or high on the trait of "quiet," its opposite). If we were to ask several people from different walks of life "How talkative are you?" we would probably find a normal distribution of responses: Some people would be extremely high or low whereas others would fall somewhere in the middle (see Figure 2.1) on this continuum of talkativeness.

Because traits cannot be directly measured in the same way that, say, height and weight can, psychologists think of traits as hypothetical concepts. That is, psychologists assume traits exist even though we can't see them. For this reason, some psychologists view traits as purely descriptive summaries of behavior without thinking about where they came from or why a person acts that way ("Mario is very sociable; just look at how well he's getting along with everybody").

Other psychologists see traits as internal, causal properties ("Well, of course Mario is getting along with everybody; he's a sociable person") and view a trait as a capacity that is present even when the trait is not being directly expressed. Just because you sit quietly in your personality class doesn't mean that you are a quiet person. Just wait until the professor's back is turned and see how many people start to express their talkative natures!

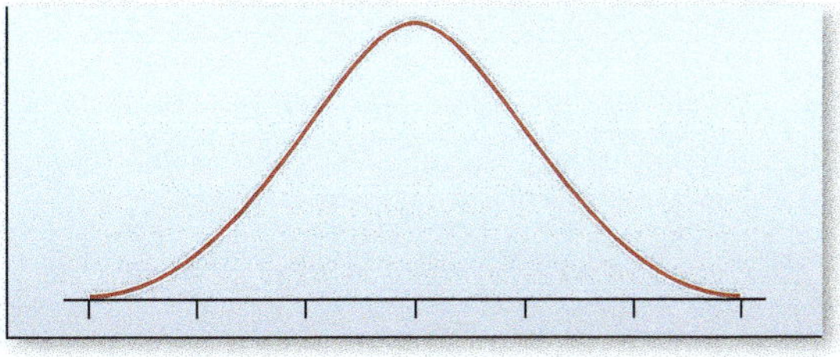

Figure 2.1 Normal Distribution of the Trait of Talkativeness.

Psychologists have long debated the exact number and kinds of traits. In fact, psychologists have even debated how best to study traits. The next section examines two main ways that psychologists have approached the study of traits: through the detailed study of a single individual and through the combined study of numerous people. These approaches have been called idiographic and nomothetic, respectively (Allport, 1937; Allport, 1937/1961). However, because science, by definition, searches for generalized truths, there is an inherent tension between these two approaches to personality that even Allport struggled with (Allport, 1937).

Two Approaches to the Study of Personality Traits

In the **idiographic approach**, the goal is to understand the personality of a single individual with all of his or her quirks or idiosyncrasies and characteristics that make them unique. The psychologist starts with what a single individual thinks is important to know about him or her and seeks to answer the question, "What unique combination of traits best describes this person?" Think about the insights into humankind that we glean from a study of history, the contemplation of a great painting, the power of a moving dramatic performance or a compelling biography. These are examples of idiographic ways of understanding.

"A description of one individual without reference to others may be a piece of literature, a biography or a novel. But science? No."
Meyer (1926, p. 217)

By using techniques of good science such as striving for objectivity and minimizing biases, psychologists are able to use case studies and other idiographic methods to study individual personalities (for example, see the Swann, Pelham, & Krull, 1989, and Pelham, 1993, experiments on self-concept).

In the **nomothetic approach**, the goal is to discover universals—concepts that can apply to everyone—by identifying traits that can describe all people or that can be applied to any person. Think about this: According to current estimates the number of people inhabiting planet Earth is over 6.7 billion. Does this mean that we need more than 6.7 billion traits to be able to describe each person? Of course not, but what exactly is the "right" number of traits, and how best should we organize them? This philosophical question started what I like to call The Great Nomothetic Search for Human Universals. The right number of trait terms is a source of some debate, as we will soon see.

"Although the endless variety and colorfulness of human personality intrigue the artist . . . many psychometrists have nevertheless fled from this richness of human nature as from some fearsome [demon]. They have left reality to the novelist."
Cattell (1946, p. 1)

Although Allport is often blamed for starting the battle between the idiographic and nomothetic approaches, he is seldom given credit for his brilliant resolution of the conflict. Just as the practice of medicine is essentially idiographic—doctors must diagnose and treat their individual patients—their methods of diagnosis and standards for treatment are based on solid nomothetic sciences of biochemistry,

The idiographic approach uses many variables to describe the personality of a single individual in great detail.

The nomothetic approach identifies the few key variables that can describe the personality of many people.

bacteriology, and so on. That is, the idiographic and nomothetic overlap and both contribute to a complete understanding of human personality (Allport, 1937).

Allport cautioned that "individuality cannot be studied by science" (Allport, 1937/1961, p. 8), yet he recognized a place for the study of the individual within psychology:

> *Why should we not start with individual behavior as a source of hunches (as we have in the past), and then seek our generalizations (also as we have in the past), but finally come back to the individual—not for the mechanical application of laws (as we do now), but for a fuller, supplementary, and more accurate assessment than we are now able to give? I suspect that the reason our present assessments are now so often feeble and sometimes even ridiculous, is because we do not take this final step. We stop with our wobbly laws of personality and seldom confront them with the concrete person.* (Allport, 1962, p. 407)

SEE FOR YOURSELF

Can you see which habits and responses make up each of your traits?

Hans Eysenck took up Allport's challenge and found a way of reconciling these two seemingly different approaches to the study of human personality. He realized that one could study both the general (nomothetic) and the specific (idiographic) within a single person and develop a theory of personality from there (Eysenck, 1998). He hypothesized that the human personality is organized into a hierarchy, which we can think of as a pyramid (see Figure 2.2). This pyramid

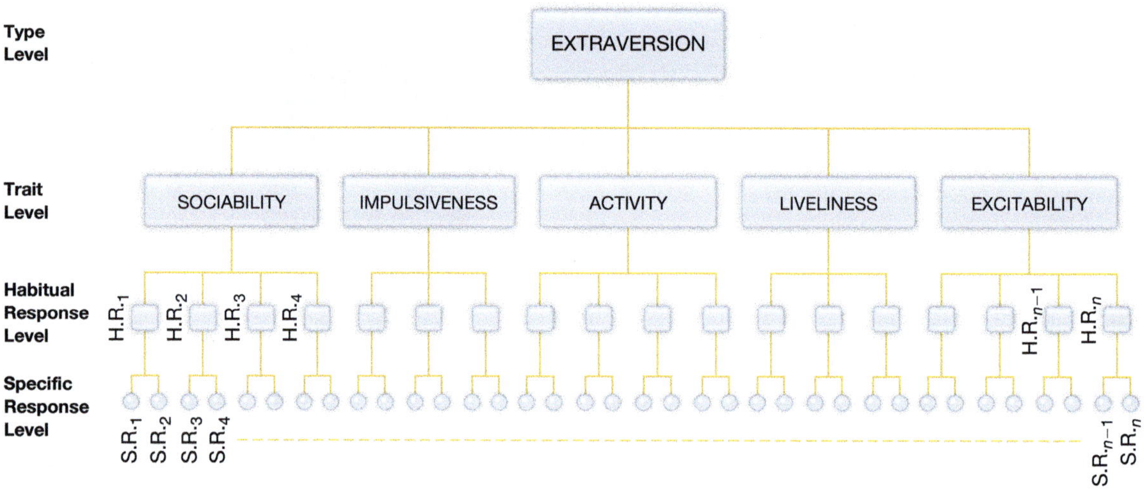

Figure 2.2 The Personality Pyramid: The Hierarchical Organization of Human Personality.
Source: Reprinted with permission from Eysenck, H. J. (1967), The Biological Basis of Personality, (Springfield, IL: Charles C. Thomas). Permission conveyed through the Copyright Clearance Center.

categorizes human personality from the most general level at the top to the most specific level at the bottom. General means a trait is universal or applicable to other people, whereas specific means a trait is more unique to a single individual.

At the very bottom level of the pyramid are specific behaviors including responses, acts, cognitions, or reactions to everyday life (Eysenck, 1990). Because these reactions are observed only once, they may or may not be related to one's personality. However, if the same reaction occurs many times then we might say that the response has become a habit or a typical way of responding. Further, if certain habits occur over time and across situations, then we might say the person is exhibiting a personality trait. Further, if we notice that certain traits tend to occur together in people then we can say that we've identified a personality type, a syndrome (Cattell, 1946), a superfactor, or an "observed constellation of traits" to use Eysenck's words (Eysenck, 1998, p. 36).

According to Eysenck, the lower we go on the pyramid the more idiosyncratic our reactions are. Similarly, the higher we go on the pyramid, the more similar we become to people who may be of a similar personality type. To illustrate how this works, let's imagine a junior engineering major we'll call Lakeisha. Suppose Lakeisha spent Thursday night with her hall-mates watching TV in the lounge. Does this make Lakeisha an extrovert? From one specific *response* we can't draw any conclusions about Lakeisha's personality. After all, there could have been a special show on TV. Now suppose that Lakeisha regularly says "Hi!" to people she passes on campus and often meets up with friends for lunch. We might judge that she has the *habit* of being friendly toward others or seeking the company of others. If she exhibited these habits over time (e.g., during her sophomore year or junior year) and across different situations (e.g., at home, school, a summer internship), then we might say that Lakeisha shows the trait of sociability. If she also demonstrated the traits of impulsiveness, activity, liveliness, and excitability, then we might say that she is an extroverted type and is similar to other extroverted people. Although this example started by studying a single individual—Lakeisha—and ended by drawing conclusions about groups of people, Eysenck cautions that our conclusions must be based experimentally to build a valid scientific theory.

What Do We Know About Personality From the Idiographic Approach?

Studying Individual Personalities: The Idiographic Approach

Imagine a person who describes herself as stubborn, critical, curious, intelligent, funny, and sarcastic. Now compare her to a person who describes herself as caring, quiet, creative, loyal, funny, and loving. Both of these are actual students who responded to the question "What kind of person are you? List the traits that best describe yourself." Such a description, where the psychologist focuses on understanding a specific person and where that person chooses which traits are important to him or her, is an example of the idiographic approach to personality.

> "The personality of each man is a unique integration, and as such is a datum for psychology, and for psychology only."
> *Gordon Allport*

Using this approach, Allport identified three different kinds of traits: central traits, secondary traits, and cardinal traits (Allport, 1937). **Central traits** are traits that are of major importance in understanding the person. They are the 5 or 10 traits that people who know you might mention in your letter of recommendation or to someone who doesn't know you when describing you. **Secondary traits** are traits of lesser importance, less consistently displayed or seldom displayed or only slightly revealed so that only a very close friend might notice them (e.g., "shy with new people," "leader like at times").

THINK ABOUT IT

Why is it that cardinal traits seem to occur more often among fictional characters?

Finally, an unusual person may have one and only one trait that describes him or her. Such single traits that completely dominate a personality are called **cardinal traits**. These traits are so pervasive and extremely influential that practically every aspect of a person's life is touched by this "ruling passion" or "master sentiment" (Allport, 1937, p. 338). Do you know somebody like this? Even though it is highly unusual in real life to find a one-trait personality, it may not be so rare in the world of fictional characters. Just think of Don Juan, Don Quixote, Oscar the Grouch, or any of Snow White's seven little friends! Allport himself noted that the occurrence of a cardinal trait is so unusual in the population that when it does occur we name individual traits after the "celebrity." Notice how the names of actual people like Beau Brummell (the fashionista of early 1800s England), Machiavelli (the manipulative Florentine diplomat), and the Marquis de Sade (don't ask) have entered the English language as trait terms (Allport, 1937, p. 338).

The Idiographic Approach Applied: The Case of Jenny

"[I]nstead of studying a thousand rats for one hour each or a hundred rats for ten hours each the investigator is more likely to study one rat for a thousand hours. The procedure is . . . appropriate to an enterprise which recognizes individuality."
B. F. Skinner

Around 1946 Allport had the unique opportunity to apply the idiographic approach to a real person: "Jenny" (Allport, 1965; Anonymous, 1946). Jenny Gove Masterson was a pseudonym for a woman who wrote a detailed correspondence to two friends over a period of 10 years. Allport edited and published these letters with psychological commentary (Allport, 1965).

Jenny was born in Ireland in 1868 and as a young woman moved to the United States with her husband. Soon, they had a baby and, tragically, her husband passed away leaving Jenny a single mother to fend for herself and baby Ross far away from her native country. To say that Ross became the center of his mother's life was an understatement, and this led to tension between mother and son when Ross was an adult. Jenny wrote to Ross's college roommate, Glenn, and his wife, Isabel, some 10 years after Ross's college years, about the time when their relationship was the most strained. Consider this excerpt from the second letter she wrote to Glenn and Isabel in 1926:

> *All during those years and years that I have lived as a hermit socially in order to pay the bills of that contemptible dog, I have never formed any social connection. I never had proper clothes—never had money to spare to entertain, even in a small way. And I would not be a sponge. My whole life has been wasted.* (Allport, 1965, p. 11)

The following month, when Jenny was planning on visiting Glenn and Isabel, she sent the following letter:

> *My dear Glenn: I enclose a check for fifty ($50) dollars, payable to you. If anything happens to me on my trip East please cash the cheque, and use it for my cremation. If I arrive OK you can let me have the money then. In case of accident, or death, insist on getting my heavy coat—I shall wear it on the trip East. Sewed in the lining of the coat at the bottom hem, left side, is fifty dollars. Five tens. Keep it. I shall have 8 or 10 in my purse, and a $10 bill in a pocket sewed on my corset.* (Allport, 1965, p. 17)

As you can see, Jenny was an interesting and articulate woman who wrote with great sincerity and candor. No wonder Allport found these letters a treasure-trove for understanding personality traits. Jenny's personality came out naturally in the letters she wrote. By analyzing her letters, might we be able to identify the traits that made Jenny a unique person? Allport thought so. After editing, Allport enlisted the aid of 36 people who read the letters and described Jenny's traits. They used 198 trait terms, which Allport then arranged in clusters of related words: quarrelsome-suspicious, self-centered, independent-autonomous, dramatic-intense, aesthetic-artistic, aggressive, cynical-morbid, sentimental, and some 13 that remained unclassified.

THINK ABOUT IT

Would you enjoy having Jenny as a friend?

Allport and others have gone on to analyze Jenny by applying various personality theories, including those of Sigmund Freud and Carl Rogers (Allport, 1965; Baldwin, 1942). Indeed, there are many such cases that illustrate personality functioning through the idiographic method (cf. Barenbaum, 1997; Barry, 2007; Nasby & Read, 1997; Rosenberg, 1989; Simonton, 1999; Swede & Tetlock, 1986; Winter & Carlson, 1988). In fact, others have analyzed *Allport's* personality in his treatment of Jenny: As it turns out, Jenny was writing the letters to him and his wife Ada (Winter, 1997)!

Using the idiographic method, Gordon Allport analyzed the letters of "Jenny" and identified sentimental, suspicious, and quarrelsome, among her central traits.

What Do We Know About Personality From the Nomothetic Approach?

Finding Universals: The Nomothetic Approach

Do you remember the two students from my personality class? Between the two of them they used 11 different trait terms to describe themselves. In fact, my whole class of 46 people used 116 different terms to describe themselves. I noted earlier that psychologists who follow the nomothetic approach seek to identify the basic traits that make up the human personality.

"The idiographic pattern is best illuminated by the nomothetic trend."
Saucier and Goldberg (1996, p. 35)

Deciding on the right number of traits, or factors, to account for human personality is like figuring out how many playlists and what labels you need to keep your MP3 collection organized. Some people might organize their individual tracks into playlists by artist, album, genre (e.g., rock, blues, classical), purpose (e.g., working out, driving, studying, relaxing, partying), mood (e.g., angry, melancholy, happy), or even a combination of these. The best way to keep your collection organized depends on your purpose. The same logic applies to traits.

There are at least three different ways to identify the most meaningful and applicable words to describe personality. Researchers typically use a combination of the theoretical approach, the lexical approach, and the measurement approach (sometimes called the questionnaire or assessment tradition; John, Naumann, & Soto, 2008). Once the basic traits have been identified by one of these methods, psychologists use statistical techniques, such as factor analysis, to verify and validate that they have indeed found important traits. These traits can then be applied, or generalized, to other people or populations.

The Theoretical Approach. Sometimes personality psychologists start with a theory or even common wisdom about human personality (Barenbaum & Winter, 2008), referred to as a **theoretical approach** (Barenbaum & Winter, 2008). For example, do you remember Niccolò Machiavelli? Two researchers were so taken by his book of advice to the prince of Florence, *The Prince* (Machiavelli, 1532/1940), that they devised a personality scale to measure Machiavellianism, or manipulativeness (Christie & Geis, 1970; an excerpt from the scale is presented in the chapter on personality assessment). This is how common wisdom can inspire the study of personality traits.

Other times, psychologists start with a theory. Carl Jung hypothesized that people differ in how they evaluate information: either rationally, what he called the thinking function, or through emotions. Jung (1921) spoke of at least two types of personality, *feeling types* and *thinking types.* Sigmund Freud (1915/2000) had a theory that if a child had problems with weaning or toilet training this would affect later adult personality. Perhaps you've heard of an oral personality who is overly dependent or anal personality who is incredibly organized and uptight. These are examples of how psychologists use theory to identify meaningful traits.

The Lexical Approach. The **lexical approach** to personality traits explores a particular language and identifies the number of synonyms that describe personality. The reasoning is that if a concept is important to speakers of a language, then that concept will be encoded in their language in multiple ways. People invent terms for salient or useful ideas and these new terms spread and become commonplace in the language. At the same time, useless words drop out. Presumably describing what your loved ones and neighbors are like is very relevant and useful, so crucial individual differences have become encoded in language (Allport, 1937). Now if the same personality trait is found across many different languages, such a trait may qualify as a human universal. In this way an analysis of language, specifically looking for many synonyms and commonalities across languages, may help personality psychologists identify key terms for describing human personality (Goldberg, 1981), whether they be adjectives (Allport & Odbert, 1936) or nouns (Saucier, 2003).

The Measurement Approach. For the last 60 years or so personality psychologists have been working separately on discovering important aspects of personality and trying to measure personality (Hogan, 1996), called the **measurement approach**. Some psychologists worked within a theoretical tradition, some operationalized their own observations, whereas still others focused on developing the best questionnaires and measurement techniques apart from a theoretical context. For a while it seemed that each researcher devised an original questionnaire to measure what he or she deemed were the most important personality traits (John et al., 2008). The field almost seemed to care more about how accurate their measurements were than about what they were actually measuring (Hogan, 1996)! It needed a taxonomy, or some systematic method of identifying and classifying trait terms that unified them into a coherent body. After all, "the astronomer classifies stars, the chemist elements, the zoologist animals, the botanist plants" (Eysenck, 1991, p. 774).

One way of doing this is to use mathematical and statistical techniques such as *factor analysis* to see if the various trait terms cluster together in some way. For example, Raymond Cattell started with the 4,504 trait terms identified by Allport and Odbert (1936). He reduced these terms to 160 by eliminating similarities in the list. Then he added all traits that had been identified by other psychologists in previous research. Finally, he used an early and crude form of factor analysis—as this was done way before the day of computers—and discovered 16 factors (Cattell, 1946) that formed the basis of his questionnaire: The 16 Personality Factors (16PF; Cattell, Eber, & Tatsuoka, 1970). Ironically, due to some misguided statistical practices of the time, Cattell didn't realize that the 5 factors that are so widely accepted today were staring him right in the face in his own data (Digman, 1996). The Research Methods Illustrated feature explains more about this technique.

Since that time and with the advent of powerful and accessible computers, researchers have been using a combination of these three approaches—theoretical, lexical, and measurement—to identify and organize personality traits. How successful have they been? Read on to find out.

Research Methods Illustrated: Factor Analysis

Imagine that we give a group of participants a questionnaire that lists many different types of music, from soul and funk to heavy metal to country. Participants rate how much they liked each of these genres on a 7-point scale from 1 (*Not at all*) to 7 (*A great deal*).

If people have consistent feelings about any of these types of music then we would expect them to answer the pertinent questions in roughly the same way. For example, say one group of people really enjoy blues and jazz and that their answers to these particular questions are more similar than to questions on how much they like country and religious music. Are there dimensions or aspects of music that are common to blues and jazz but that distinguish this kind of music from country and religious music? From hip-hop? More generally, is there some underlying structure to the answers of our participants? If there is, then do we really need all the separate questions or will fewer questions work just as well?

These are the questions that psychologists try to answer by using factor analysis (Lee & Ashton, 2007). **Factor analysis** is a statistical technique that mathematically identifies a meaningful underlying structure among a set of variables. Suppose some questions are related to each other—but not to other questions; then we can say that we have identified a unique factor in participants' responses to these questions. Depending on what we're studying—say personality or intelligence—it's possible to identify a number of factors that underlie participants' responses.

How do we know that some questions go together? We look at the correlations among all of the questions in our data. Recall that correlations (symbolized by *r*) represent the strength of a relationship between two variables, with larger numbers indicating that the two variables are highly related. The sign of the *r* tells us that the two variables are either directly related (positive) or inversely related (negative). The pattern of correlations will tell us which variables go together or correlate with each other and which variables don't seem to fit. Then the computer uses complex matrix algebra to try to re-create this pattern of correlations from a combination of one or more mathematical equations. The result of all this combining and weighting of participants' responses is the formation of factors. A small number of these factors are usually able to re-create the variation among responses in our data set almost as well as all of the original answers themselves.

Each factor can explain a certain amount of variation, called variance, in answers between participants. This is called the **eigenvalue** of the factor. From the eigenvalues, we calculate **factor loadings**, which is an estimate of how strongly each question fits into a given factor. We can interpret factor loadings much like correlations, with higher numbers indicating a stronger correlation between the item and the factor and the positive or negative sign indicating the direction of the relationship. Each factor is defined by the questions with the highest factor loadings. Researchers look at the questions and try to identify what underlying concept the questions are all getting at.

When we do a factor analysis, the first factor that emerges generally accounts for the greatest amount of variation in the data. But because this is mathematically derived rather than inspired by our actual questions, there is no guarantee that the factor makes any sense. At this stage a researcher might move around the factors to find which questions go together the best. This is called rotating the factors and allows us to understand the factors better (kind of like rotating a map to match the direction you are facing to better see where you're going). This doesn't change the number of factors, nor does it change the relationship among the factors, but it does change which questions cluster together. By rotating the factors—and there are a number of mathematical ways of doing this—the combining and weighting of questions that make up that factor shift slightly so that the researcher is better able to see what the underlying factor is.

How do we know how many factors best explain the data? This is where factor analysis is more "art" than "science." Much debate exists on the pros and cons of the various ways of deciding on the right number of factors. Researchers may stop when a new factor doesn't add much, often determined mathematically (e.g., by accepting all eigenvalues greater than 1) or graphically. Often, researchers take a pragmatic approach and keep only the few factors that are actually interpretable. Later factors may capture only measurement error or response bias instead of a meaningful underlying concept.

Once the right numbers have been identified, the researcher must then name the factors. The way to do this is to look at the items that fall together on each factor and see what concept they all appear to be getting at. Take our music taste example from the beginning of this section which was based on an actual experiment. Rentfrow and Gosling (2003) designed the Short Test of Musical Preferences, called the STOMP, in which participants rated how much they liked each of 14 musical genres. The researchers then used factor analysis to see if there was some underlying construct that could explain similarities and differences in participants' musical tastes. The results are shown in Table 2.3. Can you think of an adequate name for each of the factors?

This is how factor analysis is a useful tool for exploring the number and kind of traits contained in the human personality. But note that it does not give the definitive answer to this question (Darlington, 2009). Keep in mind that factor analysis is a useful, but limited statistical method and is only as good as the researcher behind it. At nearly every step of the way, researchers make choices and their choices impact the results. From choosing which questions to ask (and submit to factor analysis), to determining the right number of factors, to interpreting the factors, factor analysis has its shortcomings (Fabrigar, Wegener, MacCallum, & Strahan, 1999). Whereas factor analysis gives *an* answer, it is up to the researchers to make a solid case for their conclusions and to replicate their findings before we can believe it is *the* answer.

Table 2.3 Factor Loadings of the 14 Music Genres on Four Factors

Genre	Factor 1	Factor 2	Factor 3	Factor 4
Blues	**.85**	.01	−.09	.12
Jazz	**.83**	.04	.07	.15
Classical	**.66**	.14	.02	−.13
Folk	**.64**	.09	.15	−.16
Rock	.17	**.85**	−.04	−.07
Alternative	.02	**.80**	.13	.04
Heavy metal	.07	**.75**	−.11	.04
Country	−.06	.05	**.72**	−.03
Soundtracks	.01	.04	**.70**	.17
Religious	.23	−.21	**.64**	−.01
Pop	−.20	.06	**.59**	.45
Rap/hip-hop	−.19	−.12	.17	**.79**
Soul/funk	.39	−.11	.11	**.69**
Electronica/dance	−.02	.15	−.01	**.60**

Note: $N = 1{,}704$. The highest factor loadings for each dimension are listed in boldface type. The researchers named the factors Reflective and Complex; Intense and Rebellious; Upbeat and Conventional; and Energetic and Rhythmic.

Source: Rentfrow and Gosling, 2003, Table 1, p. 1242 Rentfrow, P. J., & Gosling, S. D. (2003). The do re mi's of everyday life: The structure and personality correlates of music preferences. *Journal of Personality and Social Psychology*, 84(6), 1236–1256. Copyright American Psychological Association. Adapted with permission.

The Great Nomothetic Search for Universal Principles of Personality

How did these three traditions—theoretical, lexical, and measurement—lead to this "most celebrated empirical accomplishment" (McCrae & Costa, 1996, p. 53)? First, recall that Allport and Odbert conducted a lexical analysis and uncovered 4,504 trait terms. From this list of trait terms, Cattell, using factor analysis, identified 16 factors—not realizing the import of only 5 of his factors (Cattell, 1946; Cattell et al., 1970). Others, building on Cattell's statistical work, identified a solution of 5 remarkably similar factors (e.g., Fiske, 1949; Norman, 1963) known as the **Big Five** (Loehlin, 1992). This moniker was not to extol their greatness so much as to emphasize that they are broad factors (John et al., 2008). Each of the Big Five factors describes personality at a high level of abstraction (remember Eysenck's pyramid?) summarizing a large number of more distinct lower level traits.

At the same time, working in the questionnaire approach, researchers found that popular personality tests at the time including the Personality Research Form (Jackson, 1984), the California Q-set (Block, 1961), and even the Myers-Briggs Type Indicator (Myers & McCauley, 1985) all contained 5 factors (Digman, 1996), as do numerous other questionnaires from widely different theoretical traditions (McCrae, 1989).

SEE FOR YOURSELF

How many factors did you use to describe your personality?

Finally, others have theorized that for personality traits to be universal they must be rooted in biology (Eysenck, 1990; McCrae & Costa, 1996) or solve evolutionary problems, which these 5 factors appear to do (Buss, 1996).

The remarkable convergence of theory, research, and measurement makes this a particularly exciting time for personality psychologists as the evidence for a **five-factor model** of personality mounts. But there are still plenty of researchers who are not convinced that five is the right number of trait factors and who have proposed their own dimensions or who have identified important traits left out from the five-factor model. However, to fully appreciate the significance of the current five-factor taxonomy—not to mention these alternative models and critiques—we will need to understand earlier models of personality traits.

Three Superfactors: Eysenck

Psychologist Hans Eysenck spent his lifetime conducting experiments to identify and describe key differences between people. So convinced was he that there were fundamental constitutional differences between people that he first described these personality types in terms of physiological or biological differences between people (Eysenck, 1998). More recent research has proved that Eysenck had the general principle right: His early twin studies support his claim for genetic differences in the three factors, even as the exact physiological mechanisms were unknown to scientists at the time (Eysenck & Eysenck, 1985). He identified three broad dimensions of personality: Psychoticism, Extraversion, and Neuroticism. Eysenck also identified more specific, what he called **narrow traits**, associated with each of these factors (see Table 2.4). Together, these three superfactors form the basis of Eysenck's PEN model of personality (Eysenck, 1952).

The first factor, **Psychoticism**, describes how tough-minded or antisocial people are. We can also think about this as impulsivity or disinhibition versus constraint or as undercontrolled versus overcontrolled (Clark & Watson, 2008). People who are high in Psychoticism tend to be selfish and antisocial (Eysenck, 1990; Eysenck & Eysenck, 1985). The narrow traits associated with Psychoticism are aggressive, cold, egocentric, impersonal, impulsive, antisocial, lacking empathy, creative, and tough-minded (Eysenck, 1990; Eysenck & Eysenck, 1985). One writer describes Psychoticism as low agreeableness and low conscientiousness (from the five factors) "with a few other very bad things thrown in" (McAdams, 2009, p. 199). According to Eysenck, a person high in Psychoticism

> *may be cruel and inhumane, lacking in feeling and empathy, and altogether insensitive. . . . He has a liking for odd and unusual things, and a disregard for danger. He likes to make fools of other people and to upset them.* (Eysenck & Eysenck, 1975, pp. 5–6)

Table 2.4 Eysenck's PEN Model: Factors and Narrow Traits

Factors	Narrow Traits
Psychoticism	Aggressive Cold Egocentric Impersonal Impulsive Antisocial Unempathetic Creative Tough-minded
Extraversion	Sociable Lively Active Assertive Sensation-seeking Carefree Dominant Surgent Venturesome
Neuroticism	Anxious Depressed Guilt feelings Low self-esteem Tense Irrational Shy Moody Emotional

Source: From Eysenck (1990, p. 246).

The second factor is **Extraversion** (Eysenck, 1990). Extraversion describes how outgoing people are, both to the social and the physical environments. The narrow traits associated with extraversion are sociable, lively, active, assertive, sensation-seeking, carefree, dominant, surgent, and venturesome (Eysenck, 1990; Eysenck & Eysenck, 1985). In contrast to introverts, extraverts tend to be outgoing and experience many positive feelings such as happiness and joy.

According to Hans Eysenck and Sybil Eysenck in their *Manual of the Eysenck Personality Inventory:*

> *The typical extravert is sociable, likes parties, has many friends, needs to have people to talk to, and does not like reading or studying by himself. He craves excitement, takes chances, often sticks his neck out, acts on the spur of the moment, and is generally an impulsive individual. . . . [H]e is carefree, easy-going, optimistic, and likes to "laugh and be merry". . . . [A]ltogether his feelings are not kept under tight control, and he is not always a reliable person.* (Eysenck & Eysenck, 1975, p. 5)

In contrast, the typical introvert is

> *a quiet, retiring sort of person, introspective, fond of books rather than people. . . . [H]e does not like excitement, takes matters of every day life with proper seriousness. . . . He tends to plan ahead, "looks before he leaps" and distrusts the impulse of the moment. . . . He keeps his feelings under close control . . . [H]e is reliable [and] somewhat pessimistic.* (Eysenck & Eysenck, 1975, p. 5)

SEE FOR YOURSELF

Where do your personality traits fall on these three factors?

The third factor, **Neuroticism**, refers to negative emotionality and emotional reactivity. The narrow traits associated with Neuroticism are anxious, depressed, guilt feelings, low self-esteem, tense, irrational, shy, moody, and emotional (Eysenck, 1990; Eysenck & Eysenck, 1985). People high in Neuroticism tend to be easily upset and vulnerable to negative emotions. In contrast, those low in this trait are even-tempered, calm, relaxed, carefree, unworried, somewhat unemotional, and recover quickly after an upsetting experience.

You can see sample questions from the Eysenck Personality Questionnaire (Eysenck & Eysenck, 1976) used to measure Psychoticism, Extraversion, and Neuroticism in Table 2.5. Eysenck and his colleagues conducted extensive research to demonstrate differences among people high and low in these fundamental factors. Much of his research focused on the physiological differences and genetic evidence for his theory, which we will briefly cover in those chapters.

Table 2.5 Sample Items From an Early Version of the Eysenck Personality Questionnaire

Psychoticism Questions
1. Do you enjoy practical jokes that can sometimes really hurt people? 2. Are there several people who keep trying to avoid you? 3. Do you think people spend too much time safeguarding their future with savings and insurances?
Extraversion Questions
1. Do you have many different hobbies? 2. Do you often take on more activities than you have time for? 3. Would you call yourself happy-go-lucky?
Neuroticism Questions
1. Does your mood often go up and down? 2. Do you ever feel "just miserable" for no reason? 3. Do you worry too long after an embarrassing experience?

Note: Respondents answered *Yes* or *No* to each question.

Source: From Eysenck and Eysenck (1976, pp. 65–68).

For many years Eysenck's theory held an important place in trait theory and inspired numerous experiments. Alas, the prominence of his theory has been eclipsed by the explosion of research on the five-factor model (John et al., 2008). One problem with Eysenck's theory is that many personality psychologists feel that important traits are missing. Eysenck totally disagreed, and claimed that they were looking at different levels in the hierarchy.

Specifically, he believed that other conceptualizations of traits are invalid because they include traits from multiple levels of the hierarchy. For example, Eysenck claimed that Cattell's 16 personality factors are at the third level (the level of traits) and when factor analyzed reduce to Eysenck's three superfactors (Eysenck, 1990). Further, Eysenck was talking about factors at the very top of the hierarchy (the type or superfactor level), but some measures of the five-factor model claim to have identified traits yet instead have mixed habits and responses. When you factor analyze these terms, you get the three superfactors of Psychoticism, Extraversion, and Neuroticism (Eysenck, 1990). Indeed, although Eysenck acknowledged that aspects of the five-factor model overlapped with his theory (e.g., Extraversion and Neuroticism), he countered that the factors of Agreeableness and Conscientiousness were at the level of habits, and therefore not comparable. Finally, he claimed that Openness is more of a cognitive factor and should not be considered a dimension of personality (Eysenck, 1990).

"Personality psychologists who continue to employ their preferred measure without locating it within the five-factor model can only be likened to geographers who issue reports of new lands but refuse to locate them on a map for others to find."
Ozer and Reise (1994, p. 361)

Five Factors: The Big Five and the Five-Factor Model

The five factors that appear to be our best candidates for universal traits are Neuroticism, Extraversion, Openness, Agreeableness and Conscientiousness (John, 1990; John et al., 2008). Because many researchers use slightly different terminology to summarize "their" five factors, even using Roman numerals to identify the factors rather than words, Oliver John and his colleagues (John, 1990, p. 96; John et al., 2008, p. 139) suggested that we think of the five factors using multiple words:

N: Neuroticism, Negative Affectivity, Nervousness (Factor IV)

E: Extraversion, Energy, Enthusiasm (Factor I)

O: Openness, Originality, Open-mindedness (Factor V)

A: Agreeableness, Altruism, Affection (Factor II)

C: Conscientiousness, Control, Constraint (Factor III)

Neuroticism, in contrast to Emotional Stability, refers to how well a person adjusts to the "slings and arrows of daily life." It refers to emotionality, psychological distress, and reactivity. For example, does George worry a lot about what people think of him? Does Ally fall apart under stress? George and Ally would be considered high in Neuroticism. Does Yang stay calm, cool, and collected under pressure? Does James keep his feelings under control? Yang and James are low in Neuroticism, and would be considered high in Emotional Stability. People who are low in Neuroticism are not necessarily high in overall mental health (McCrae & John, 1992)—that would depend on the other factors and perhaps some aspects of personality not captured by a trait model at all. People low in Neuroticism are even-tempered, calm, relaxed, and unruffled (McCrae & John, 1992). One of the best indicators for Neuroticism is agreement with the item "I often feel tense and jittery" from the NEO Personality Inventory—Revised (NEO-PI-R; McCrae, 2007).

According to the NEO-PI-R, each of the five factors are made up of six subscales called **facets**. If we think of Neuroticism as the superfactor, then the facets or narrow traits that make up Neuroticism are anxiety, angry hostility, depression, self-consciousness, impulsiveness (immoderation), and vulnerability to stress (Costa & McCrae, 1992; see Table 2.6).

People who are high in Neuroticism show poorer coping skills in stressful situations, poorer health, and are likely to experience burnout and job changes (John et al., 2008). They are also prone to negative emotions such as fear, sadness, embarrassment, anger, guilt, and disgust (Costa & McCrae, 1992). Emotionally stable people show more commitment to work and great satisfaction with their personal relationships (John et al., 2008). Among undergraduate students at one Swiss university, those who were high on impulsivity—an important facet of Neuroticism—spent more time on the phone, made more cell phone calls in a day, and reported

THINK ABOUT IT

Why are people high in Neuroticism more vulnerable to stress and poor health?

Table 2.6 Facets of Neuroticism

Anxiety
Angry hostility
Depression
Self-consciousness
Impulsiveness
Vulnerability to stress

Source: From Costa and McCrae (1992).

Table 2.7 Facets of Extraversion

Warmth
Gregariousness
Assertiveness
Activity
Excitement-seeking
Positive emotions

Source: From Costa and McCrae (1992).

being more dependent on their cell phones than people who were low in impulsiveness (Billieux, Linden, D'Acremont, Ceschi, & Zermatten, 2006).

Is Dominick full of life and fun to be around? Does Christine enjoy parties with lots of people? Is April more reserved and quiet? Dominick and Christine are more extroverted, whereas April is more introverted. The second factor listed, Extraversion, is contrasted with Introversion and describes how one "surges" or energetically engages with the social world. Extraverted people just *like* other people. They are assertive, active, talkative, and cheerful, enjoy large groups and gatherings, and enjoy excitement (Costa & McCrae, 1992).

The factor of Extraversion is made up of the facets of warmth (friendliness), gregariousness, assertiveness, activity, excitement-seeking, and positive emotions (cheerfulness; Costa & McCrae, 1992; see Table 2.7). Extraversion also refers to energetically seeking out and interacting with others (John & Robins, 1993; McCrae & John, 1992). One of the best indicators of Extraversion is agreement with the item "I am a cheerful, high spirited person" from the NEO-PI-R (McCrae, 2007).

Keep in mind that an energetic, optimistic person who shows enthusiasm and cheerfulness is not necessarily low in anxiety or depression. Anxiety and depression are related to Neuroticism (McCrae & John, 1992). Extraverts are likely to hold leadership positions in groups, have many friends and a greater number of sexual partners, and are more likely to be selected as foreperson of a jury than are Introverts. In contrast, introverts are more likely to experience poorer relationships with parents and peers (John et al., 2008).

The third factor is **Openness** or "Inquiring Intellect" (Digman, 1996; Fiske, 1949). Openness includes the facets of fantasy (imagination), aesthetics (artistic interests), feelings (emotionality), actions (adventurousness), ideas (intellect), and values (psychological liberalism; see Table 2.8). Does Jim have a very active imagination? Does Ellen get completely absorbed in music she is listening to? Jim and Ellen are high in openness. Is Rick pretty well set in his ways? Is Catherine against controversial campus speakers? People high in Openness tend to be imaginative and creative, whereas people low in openness tend to be more conventional, practical, and down-to-earth. People high in Openness tend to go further with their education, to succeed in creative jobs, and to create distinctive work and home environments (John et al., 2008). One of the best indicators of Openness is the experience of chills or goosebumps in response to an aesthetic experience (McCrae, 2007). In sum, a person high in Openness is seen as

> *interested in experience for its own sake, eager for variety, tolerant of uncertainty, leading a richer, more complex, less conventional life. By contrast, the closed person is seen as being impoverished in fantasy, insensitive to art and beauty, restricted in affect, behaviorally rigid, bored by ideas, and ideologically dogmatic.* (McCrae, 1990, p. 123)

Table 2.8 Facets of Openness

Fantasy
Aesthetics
Feelings
Actions
Ideas
Values

Source: From Costa and McCrae (1992).

Openness refers to an appreciation of the life of the mind in such things as ideas, thoughts, fantasies, art, and beauty, and is not the same as intelligence. People can score high in Openness without having a high IQ (McCrae & John, 1992). Similarly, artistic interests are not the same as artistic ability, which is not a personality trait. Openness includes an appreciation of a wide range of feelings in contrast to touchiness or defensiveness, which is part of Neuroticism (McCrae, 1990). Openness refers to an openness to ideas and new things

People high in Openness tend to enjoy the adventurousness of traveling abroad.

rather than an openness to people, which is part of Extraversion. Openness is not the same as excitement-seeking, which is part of Extraversion. People high in Openness like new experiences, not necessarily dangerous or exciting ones.

Having high Openness may sound better or more fun than being low in Openness, but there's no particular psychological benefit to being high or low on this factor (and the same can be said for Extraversion). Rather, the value of creativity or conventionalism depends on the situation, with people at either end found in everyday walks of life (Costa & McCrae, 1992).

Agreeableness refers to the quality of interpersonal relations—that is, how much a person feels for and gets along with others; whether he or she seeks out such enjoyment, as would an extravert, or does not, as would an introvert. Agreeableness can also be thought of as a prosocial or communal orientation to others and is contrasted with antagonism or competitiveness (Costa & McCrae, 1992; Graziano & Eisenberg, 1997; John et al., 2008). People low in Agreeableness show hostility, self-centeredness, spitefulness, indifference, and even jealousy toward others (Digman, 1990). Agreeableness includes the facets of trust (of others), straightforwardness (honesty or morality as opposed to manipulativeness), altruism, compliance (cooperation), modesty, and tender-mindedness (sympathy; see Table 2.9).

Does Ramiro believe that most people are basically well intentioned? Does Betty have great empathy for people in need? Ramiro and Betty would be high in Agreeableness, showing trust in and sympathy for other people, a concern for social harmony, and getting along with others. In contrast, people low in Agreeableness distrust the motives of others and are on the lookout for others who might be trying to take advantage of them. For example, does Jasmine bully or flatter people into getting them to do what she wants? Does Darnell believe that most people will take advantage of you if you let them? Jasmine and Darnell are low in Agreeableness. Some measure of Disagreeableness might be useful in situations requiring tough judgments or "tough love." Some of the most successful U.S. presidents have been low in Agreeableness (Rubenzer, Faschingbauer, & Ones, 2000). Generally, people high in Agreeableness show better performance in work groups than do those low in Agreeableness (John et al., 2008). People low in Agreeableness are often at risk for cardiovascular disease, juvenile delinquency, and interpersonal problems (John et al., 2008). However, Costa and McCrae (1992) noted that the "readiness to fight" is often an advantage in life, and good science demands the skepticism and critical thinking of the person low in Agreeableness.

Finally, **Conscientiousness** refers to an individual's degree of organization, both physical organization, such as the organization of one's office, or mental organization, as in planning ahead and having goals to be achieved. Conscientiousness also includes how we regulate our own impulses such as thinking before acting, delaying gratification, or following norms and rules (John et al., 2008). For example, does Brittany have separate files for each of her

Table 2.9 Facets of Agreeableness

Trust
Straightforwardness
Altruism
Compliance
Modesty
Tender-mindedness

Source: From Costa and McCrae (1992).

Table 2.10 Facets of Conscientiousness

Competence
Order
Dutifulness
Achievement-striving
Self-discipline
Deliberation

Source: From Costa and McCrae (1992).

THINK ABOUT IT

Can people change how agreeable they are?

SEE FOR YOURSELF

Where do your personality traits fall on these five factors?

classes? Does Dimitri put away his video games after he plays with them? If so, Brittany and Dimitri are displaying aspects of Conscientiousness. But consider a person like Charlie who is not dependable and who even cheats at solitaire! Or Lonette, who often does things on the spur of the moment without thinking of the consequences. Both of these people are low in Conscientiousness and might be expected to place short-term pleasures ahead of long-term accomplishments.

Conscientiousness includes the facets of competence (self-efficacy), order, dutifulness, achievement-striving, self-discipline, and deliberation (cautiousness; see Table 2.10). Interestingly, people high in Conscientiousness are rated by their peers and even their spouses as well organized, neat, thorough, and diligent (McCrae & Costa, 1987). They also have higher grade point averages and better on-the-job performance (John et al., 2008). People low in Conscientiousness are more likely to smoke, abuse alcohol and other drugs, show attention deficit disorder, have a poor diet, and not exercise enough. In contrast, people high in Conscientiousness are more likely to adhere to doctor's orders, and—when compared to those low in Conscientiousness—live longer (John et al., 2008)! But don't be so smug if you are high in Conscientiousness; high levels of this trait may also lead to annoying habits such as fastidiousness, compulsive neatness, or workaholic behavior (Costa & McCrae, 1985).

If some of these factors sound familiar, they should: These five are very similar to Eysenck's three factors. That is, both the five-factor model and Eysenck's model identify Neuroticism and Extraversion as two important dimensions of human personality. Further, Eysenck's Psychoticism factor is a combination of Agreeableness and Conscientiousness (Digman, 1996).

People high in conscientiousness have higher grade point averages than people low in this trait.

A Rose by Any Other Name? Two Models of the Five Factors. Part of the confusion for the names of the factors is that the factors, especially Openness, look slightly different depending on the method used to identify them. When researchers start with the lexical approach, they get the Big Five of Surgency (Extraversion), Agreeableness, Conscientiousness, Emotional Stability, and Culture (Goldberg, 1990; Norman, 1963). Generally, the phrase the *Big Five* refers to this lexical solution. The Big Five factors are identified by Roman numerals that signify the frequency of the factor words in the lexicon. For example, words that refer to lexical factor I, Extraversion, are more common than words of lexical factor V, Openness. Roman numerals also have the advantage of being neutral from a theoretical standpoint (McCrae & John, 1992). However, numbers are less memorable than mnemonics and so the OCEAN labeling has caught on more, especially among students of personality psychology (McCrae & Costa, 1985).

At roughly the same time, Costa and McCrae (1976), using factor analysis, discovered three factors: Anxiety-Adjustment (now called Neuroticism), Introversion-Extraversion, and Openness to experience. They devised an inventory to measure these three factors (the NEO; McCrae & Costa, 1983, 1985), and then persuaded by the strength of the lexical findings, they added scales to measure the factors of Agreeableness and Conscientiousness in 1990 and called their solution the five-factor model (FFM; Costa & McCrae, 1992; Costa, McCrae, & Dye, 1991; Digman, 1996). Indeed, comparing the lexical model with their five-factor model, McCrae and Costa (1985) noted that "the similarities are far more remarkable than the differences" (p. 720). Today, the five factors of the five-factor model—Neuroticism, Extraversion, Openness, Agreeableness, and Conscientiousness—are measured using the revised version of the NEO Personality Inventory (NEO-PI-R; Costa & McCrae, 1992). This ordering of the factors, incidentally, reflects the amount of variance, from largest to smallest, accounted for by each of the five factors.

"Factor analysis has improved the situation, as has clearer theorizing, but the problem of naming factors is of course still with us."
Hans Eysenck

So, what's the difference between the two models? After all, they seem pretty similar. The major similarity is, of course, a five-factor solution, which is no small feat given all the controversy! Also, the two solutions identify virtually identical factors. One difference is the name of the individual factors. What the Big Five calls Emotional Stability the FFM calls Neuroticism. Both terms refer to the same dimension; the only difference is in direction, or which end of the pole researchers wish to emphasize. Second, the Big Five Culture factor is a narrower view of the FFM factor Openness, which refers to openness to aesthetic or cultural tastes, a wide range of emotions, and a need for variety, and is not limited to creativity and intellectual interests. Yet, both the Big Five and FFM solutions agree that creativity, imagination, and originality are aspects of this factor (Saucier, 1992). Recall that there are fewer words in the English language that describe Openness of personality, so it's no wonder there are disagreements about what this factor represents. Maybe there are some aspects of personality we need questionnaires to measure such as sensitivity to art and beauty (McCrae, 1990).

THINK ABOUT IT

Can you think of traits to describe a person who appreciates art and beauty?

Other differences are more philosophical and deal with the history behind the two traditions and the empirical usefulness of the models. For example, the Big Five describes personality without attempting to explain where these attributes come from (i.e., they are in our language so they must be important). In contrast, the FFM theorizes, much in the tradition of Eysenck, that the five factors are biological traits (Saucier & Goldberg, 1996). That is, these traits are causal entities that correspond to neuropsychic structures that are in the process of being identified (John & Robins, 1993). Second, because the Big Five is grounded in adjectives, it has been replicated cross-culturally in many different languages. The NEO-PI-R, because it uses sentences, may be more dependent on language and culture and may lose something in the translation (Saucier & Goldberg, 1996). We'll examine cross-cultural evidence for the five-factor solution in the next chapter on traits. For now, we'll use the term *Big Five* when referring to lexically derived factors, *five-factor model* or *FFM* when referring to the questionnaire factors, and *five-factor taxonomy* or *the five factors* when the specific model doesn't matter.

Research on both the Big Five (using adjectival measures) and the FFM (using the NEO-PI-R questionnaire) yield similar results (John & Robins, 1993), giving us even greater faith in a five-factor solution of Neuroticism, Extraversion, Openness, Agreeableness, and Conscientiousness.

Is Five Really the Ultimate Answer to Life, the Universe, and Everything? Although that sounds like a simple question, the answer is quite complicated. Remember Cattell's claim that 16 was the right number of factors to describe human personality? Eysenck critiqued Cattell's model and noted that direct factor analysis of the 16PF questionnaire recovers 3 factors, remarkably similar to Psychoticism, Extraversion, and Neuroticism (Eysenck, 1991). Interestingly, though similar, this factor analysis failed to find the extreme antisocial aspects of Eysenck's Psychoticism factor. This suggests, according to Eysenck, that the Cattell scales are missing key aspects of personality (Eysenck, 1991). Further, even though one study recovered five factors from the responses on the 16PF questionnaire from more than 17,000 people (Krug & Johns, 1986), Eysenck claimed that "it would need a lot of interpretive ingenuity" to make these resemble the Big Five factors of Norman (1963; Eysenck, 1991, p. 778). Instead, the three factors of Psychoticism, Extraversion, and Neuroticism fit the data better (Eysenck, 1991). And on top of it all, Eysenck claims, the 16 factors of Cattell are not even replicable!

Statistically, 16 factors explain more of the variance in personality than 3 factors do, but is the difference theoretically, socially, or practically important (Eysenck, 1991)? It all depends on what your goals are or on what you are trying to predict. We might think of the whole debate as a trade-off of fidelity versus bandwidth (John, 1989). Would you rather have a radio that picks up few stations with fantastic quality of sound or many stations with decent sound? Well, it depends on why you are listening to the radio. When I was a kid, it was incredibly exciting to discover that we could pick up far-away radio stations on our AM transistor radios—one of my classmates claimed that he could hear people talking in French!—never mind that we had to turn up the volume all the way and use a bit of our imaginations. On the other hand, you may be an opera fan who wants to tune in to the Metropolitan Opera Saturday afternoon broadcast to hear your favorite soprano in HD. So, if you are an explorer of personality, like Cattell and the early researchers, then a higher number of factors suits your purpose. If you're trying to find out how people act differently depending on their traits, then a smaller number may be better.

Another way to think of this dilemma of identifying the right number for a taxonomy of personality traits is to consider what happens in a field such as biology with a well-established taxonomy for animals. We can classify the new creature lapping our face at the pound as an animal or as a dog or as a poodle or even as Mr. Bowser, the newest member of your family! The "broadest level of the hierarchy," says John (1989), is to "personality what the categories 'plant' and 'animal' are to the world of natural objects—extremely useful for some initial rough distinctions but of less value for predicting specific behaviors of a particular object" (p. 268).

Researchers have championed anywhere from 1 to 16 factors. We'll consider some of these conceptualizations in turn.

A One-Factor Solution

The smallest number of factors that can account for human personality is, of course, one. Researchers have called this the **general personality factor** or **GPF** (Musek, 2007; Rushton & Irwing, 2008; van der Linden, te Nijenhuis, & Bakker, 2010). The GPF is hypothesized to explain all of human personality in much the same way that *g* represents a general factor of intelligence underlying all mental abilities (Musek, 2007). This GPF lies at the very top of a hierarchy of personality traits (see Figure 2.3).

What exactly is the GPF? According to Musek (2007) this factor includes all the positive aspects of the five factors: Emotional Stability, Agreeableness, Extraversion, Conscientiousness, and Intellect. Further, the GPF encompasses the two factors of *Alpha* (the emotional stability to get along with others) and *Beta* (the flexibility to deal with change, challenges, and demands) (Musek, 2007). People who are high in GPF are altruistic, sociable, able to handle stress, relaxed, open to experience, dependable, and task-focused (Rushton & Irwing, 2008). Rushton and his colleagues argued that these aspects of personality have been evolutionarily hard-wired as they are necessary for survival (e.g., Rushton, Bons, & Hur, 2008; Rushton & Irwing, 2008).

In one study, participants answered three different measures of the five-factor model and other personality questionnaires (Musek, 2007). When their responses were factor analyzed it turned out that the first factor, the GPF, accounted for 40 to 50% of the variance in participants' responses. The second factor accounted for 17 to 26%. Further, this GPF correlated with measures of well-being and self-esteem. Other researchers found similar evidence for the same GPF using different trait measures (Rushton et al., 2008; Rushton & Irwing, 2008, 2009).

Although this GPF sounds an awful lot like a general "social desirability" factor or a "conformity" factor, Musek (2007) argued that the pattern of results—how this GPF correlates with other personality measures—rules out both of these alternative explanations. However, other researchers believe that a two-factor solution is merely an artifact of the way we measure traits

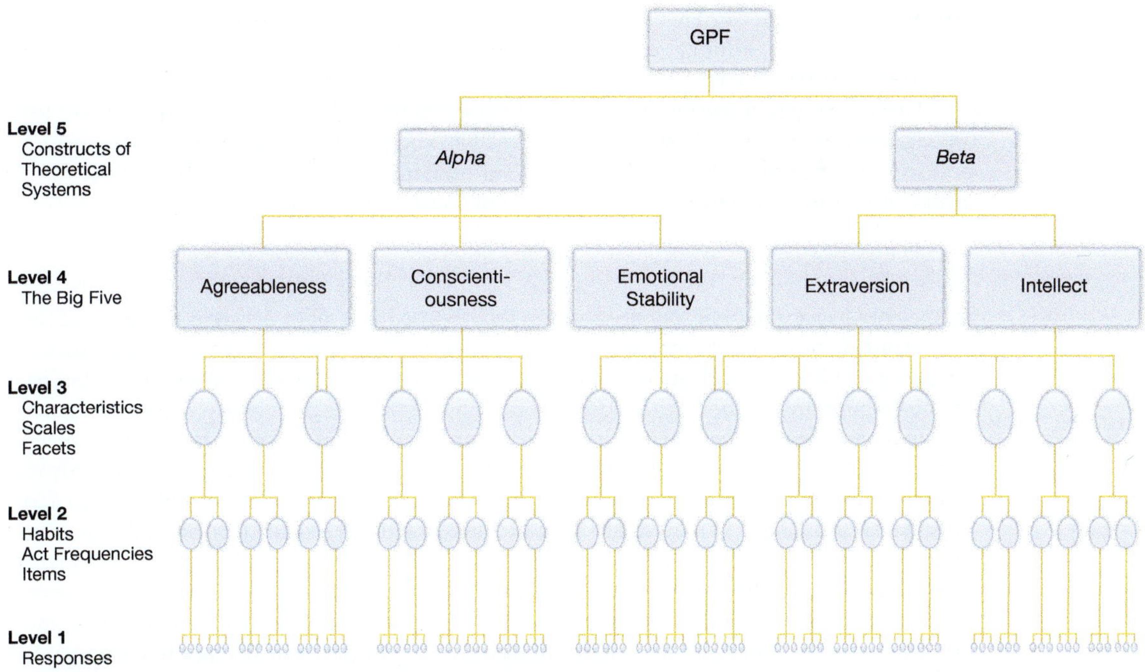

Figure 2.3 The Current Hierarchical Model of Human Personality. *Source:* Adapted from Musek (2007, Figure 2, p. 1225) and Digman (1997, Figure 1, p. 1252). Musek, J. (2007), "A general factor of personality: Evidence for the Big One in the five-factor model," *Journal of Research in Personality,* 41, 1213–1233. Reprinted by permission of Academic Press.

and have evidence that a five- or six-factor solution is superior to a two-factor solution (Ashton, Lee, Goldberg, & de Vries, 2009).

Six- and Seven-Factor Solutions . . . and Beyond!

An alternative to the five-factor taxonomy is the **HEXACO** (or six-factor) **model** (Ashton & Lee, 2005, 2007; Lee & Ashton, 2004). The six factors are Honesty-Humility, Emotionality, Extraversion, Agreeableness, Conscientiousness and Openness to Experience. Five of the factors are very similar to their five-factor counterparts; the major difference is the addition of Honesty-Humility as a separate factor (Ashton & Lee, 2005). This factor emerged out of research in other cultures and languages (e.g., Ashton, Lee, Perugini, et al., 2004; Fung & Ng, 2006) and might be best thought of as a genuineness or trustworthiness factor in English (Ashton, Lee, & Goldberg, 2004). Honesty-Humility includes the facets of sincerity, fairness, greed avoidance, and modesty as contrasted with arrogance and egotism (Lee & Ashton, 2004). Although this sounds similar to Agreeableness, the difference has to do with manipulation and power. For example, a person high in Agreeableness is willing to help another person even when it might be against his or her own self-interest (i.e., altruism). Someone high in Honesty-Humility would not take advantage of another person, especially if that person is disadvantaged in some way (Lee & Ashton, 2004).

However, the HEXACO is not without its critics. For example, McCrae and Costa (2008) suggested that this sixth factor is just a variation of Agreeableness tapping more introverted aspects of Agreeableness, whereas the standard facets of Agreeableness (trust, straightforwardness, altruism, cooperation, modesty, sympathy) tap the more extroverted aspects of getting along with others. They believed that the six-factor model is redundant with the five-factor model and not an improvement on it.

One criticism of five-factor solutions (cf. Saucier, 1997) is that many of them can be traced back to Allport and Odbert (1936), who omitted adjectives that represented temporary states (such as moods) or evaluations (i.e., judgments of character, such as *insignificant, worthy*). When such terms are added back in, the result is a seven-factor solution (Almagor, Tellegen, & Waller, 1995; Benet & Waller, 1995; Benet-Martínez & Waller, 2002). These "Big Seven" factors are very similar to the Big Five, with the two additional factors of Negative Valence and Positive Valence. These additional evaluative dimensions are especially useful for understanding pathology (Durrett & Trull, 2005).

This is one area of current research and debate as researchers try to garner evidence for and against their theories. In sum, John et al. (2008) suggested that five factors is our current best working hypothesis for the organization of human traits. There is much evidence from cross-cultural studies to support this view as well, as we will soon see.

Then and Now: The Four Temperaments and the Five Factors

In ancient Greece, the philosopher Empedocles proposed that all of nature is made up of the four elements of air, earth, fire, and water. Hippocrates, building on this early work, further proposed that humans contained elements of the cosmos, therefore we have within our bodies the corresponding "humors" that affected our temperament or personality. A predominance of blood and one was cheerful and happy; too much yellow bile and one was quick to anger. But it was the Roman physician Galen, around AD 150, who linked these temperaments to diseases and is credited with being the first to recognize a relationship between physiology and personality (see Table 2.11). We might dismiss these ancient personality theories today in favor of empirically based theories, but the wisdom of the ancients is remarkably in line with many modern personality theories.

Because our personality is expressed in our facial expressions, body movements, and gestures, Gordon Allport showed illustrations of these four personality types to participants and found that most people were able to correctly guess which temperament went with each picture (you can try this yourself in Figure 2.4). Allport noted that the four temperaments fit easily into two-factor theories of personality, whether the two factors be speed and intensity of emotional arousal or activity level and a tendency to approach or withdraw from situations (Allport, 1937/1961). Similarly, Hans Eysenck noticed that the four temperaments matched the dimensions of emotional/nonemotional and changeable/unchangeable, two important personality factors identified by the founder of modern experimental psychology, Wilhelm Wundt in the 19th century (Eysenck, 1967). Perhaps you recognized that these dimensions correspond to Neuroticism and Extraversion of both Eysenck and the current five-factor taxonomy (see Figure 2.5).

Today, while researchers have pretty much decided that the five factors—Neuroticism, Extraversion, Openness, Agreeableness, and Conscientiousness—are the major dimensions of human personality; others have suggested that these five are aspects of a two-factor solution, *alpha* and *beta* (Digman, 1997).

Factor ***alpha*** consists of Emotional Stability, Agreeableness, and Conscientiousness whereas Extraversion and Openness to Experience make up ***beta*** (Digman, 1997). Digman (1997) suggested that these two factors represent the major tasks of personality development: socialization and actualization (although he didn't use these labels). By socialization he meant developing according to "society's blueprint" (p. 1250), including learning how to regulate one's own emotions and impulses, living up to expectations, and not being too defensive when interacting with others. By actualization he meant personality growth, or going out into the world being open to new experiences (recall that Surgency is another name for Extraversion) and adapt to them

Table 2.11 The Four Temperaments

Element	Property	Humor	Temperament	Characteristic
Air	Warm and moist	Blood	Sanguine	Hopeful
Earth	Cold and dry	Black bile	Melancholic	Sad
Fire	Warm and dry	Yellow bile	Choleric	Irascible
Water	Cold and moist	Phlegm	Phlegmatic	Apathetic

Source: Adapted from Allport (1937/1961, p. 37). Allport, G. W. (1937/1961). Pattern and growth in personality. New York: Holt, Rinehart and Winston.

(Digman, 1997). Similarly, others have suggested that all humans, regardless of culture, may seek to categorize people as benign versus harmful (socialized) and stimulating versus boring (actualized). They have found evidence for this two-factor solution in Greek samples using Greek trait terms (Saucier, Georgiades, Tsaousis, & Goldberg, 2005).

These two aspects of personality—socialization and actualization—are common themes in many theories of personality. In fact, Wiggins (1968, p. 309) called Extraversion and Anxiety the "Big Two" because they appear in numerous observations, theories, tests, and experimental results of personality psychologists. Although these two factors were replicated by some researchers using various methods (Blackburn, Renwick, Donnelly, & Logan, 2004; DeYoung, 2006; DeYoung, Peterson, & Higgins, 2002; Markon, Krueger, & Watson, 2005), other researchers question these findings (McCrae et al., 2008; Mutch, 2005).

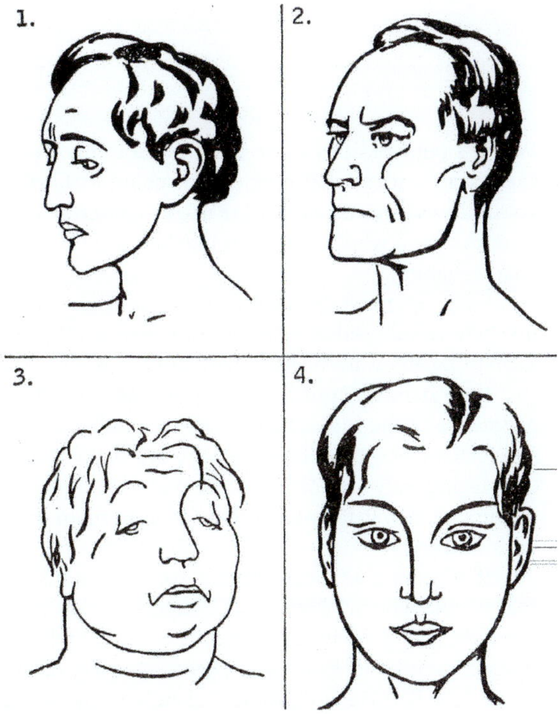

Figure 2.4 Physiognomic Representation of the Four Temperaments: Melancholic, Choleric, Phlegmatic, and Sanguine. *Source:* Allport, G. W. (1937/1961). Pattern and growth in personality. New York: Holt, Rinehart and Winston.

The two factors *alpha* and *beta* are very similar to the dimensions of emotional/nonemotional and changeable/unchangeable first identified as part of the four temperaments of personality over two millennia ago. As Eysenck pointed out, the ancients were not so much trying to devise theories about human personality as they were describing what their "friends, Romans, countrymen" were like. Time—and research—have proven their hunches remarkably accurate. Now if we could only see how they decorated their ancient living spaces!

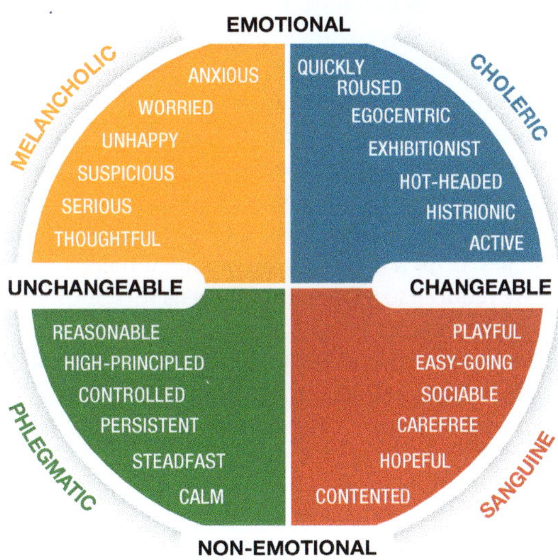

Figure 2.5 Eysenck's Representation of the Four Temperaments in Two Dimensions. *Source:* From Eysenck (1967, p. 35). Reprinted with permission from Eysenck, H. J. (1967), The Biological Basis of Personality, (Springfield, IL: Charles C. Thomas). Permission conveyed through the Copyright Clearance Center.

The Personality of Everyday Life

What can you tell about someone from his or her living space?

People's personalities shine through in many aspects of their daily lives, as we saw in the research study that opened this chapter (Gosling et al., 2002). Now that you know about the various traits that are used to describe personality, you can use this knowledge to understand what people are like based on the physical cues of their surroundings or "native habitat."

First, you must decide if the item or decoration was put there on purpose or if it was just behavioral residue from everyday living. Of course, the person's carelessness tells you something about his or her personality as well!

If an item was put there on purpose, consider the following questions: Is the item expressive of the individual's true personality or was it put there to convey a particular image? One way of telling this is to see if the item is in public view (e.g., a photo on a desk facing outward) or in a place that only the occupant can see (e.g., a photo on a desk facing inward). If it was put there to convey an image, what impression does the owner wish to convey?

If an item is a true expression of the owner's personality, what does it tell us? Recall that people who are high in Conscientiousness tend to have rooms that are more organized, neat, and uncluttered. People who are high in Openness tend to have more decorations in their living space and a greater variety of magazines and books.

As for Extraversion, Neuroticism, and Agreeableness, there are no specific cues you can look for, but perhaps you may be able to take a guess. Recall that for these traits observers were pretty good at guessing the occupants' personality, even though there was little agreement on the specific cues they used to make their judgments.

By applying these findings from the Gosling et al. (2002) study you can be your own Sherlock Holmes!

Chapter Summary

Study and **Review** on **mysearchlab.com**

Go online for more resources to help you review.

In this chapter we defined traits as a person's typical style of thinking, feeling, and acting. Traits can be organized into a hierarchy, moving up from specific responses to habitual responses to traits to a psychological type. Psychologists have studied traits through the idiographic approach, describing a single individual with all of his or her idiosyncrasies, or through the nomothetic approach, describing *any* personality using a set number of key traits.

Within the idiographic approach, individuals may have central and secondary traits or, rarely, a cardinal trait. Allport's analysis of Jenny illustrates the idiographic approach.

Within the nomothetic approach, psychologists might start with a theory to which traits are most useful for describing personality or conduct an analysis of the lexicon to see which descriptions of personality have been coded into language, by statistical and mathematical techniques, or by a combination of any of these approaches. Factor analysis, where numerous traits are reduced to a few meaningful factors, is often used to identify the underlying structure among a set of traits.

Psychologists have debated the right number of factors claiming that 1 to 7 or 16 factors best account for personality. For example, Eysenck identified the three factors of Psychoticism, Extraversion, and Neuroticism. Others have claimed that a single general personality factor explains all of personality, whereas still others identify just two factors of socialization (*alpha*) and actualization (*beta*). Today there is tremendous consensus that the five factors of Neuroticism, Extraversion, Openness, Agreeableness, and Conscientiousness best account for human personality. Some overlap occurs between the theories of Eysenck and the five factors, which, amazingly enough, is similar to ancient conceptualizations of the four temperaments (air, earth, fire, and water).

We opened this chapter with a study that found that observers are able to guess the personality of individuals by observing their living spaces. We saw that people express their personalities by the way they decorate their residence hall rooms, apartment bedrooms, and even offices. In the next chapter, we will consider other ways people express their personalities including music preferences, web pages, and careers and to what extent people change or remain the same—or at least consistent in their personalities—across the life span.

Review Questions

1. What is a trait? Explain how traits are organized into a hierarchy.
2. What is the idiographic approach to the study of traits? Describe Allport's case of "Jenny." How is this an example of the idiographic approach?
3. What is the nomothetic approach? What are the three main ways of identifying the most meaningful and applicable words for describing human personality? What is factor analysis and how is it used in the nomothetic approach?
4. What three factors best account for human personality, according to Eysenck?
5. What are the five factors? What facets make up each factor? What are some important correlates of people high and low in each of the five factors?
6. Is human personality reducible to one factor? Two factors? Six or seven factors? Explain.
7. How is today's view of personality similar to the view of the ancients?
8. What can you tell about a person from their living space?

Key Terms

Behavioral residue
Trait
Idiographic approach
Nomothetic approach
Central traits
Secondary traits
Cardinal traits
Theoretical approach
Lexical approach
Measurement approach
Factor analysis
Eigenvalue
Factor loadings
Big Five
Five-factor model
Narrow traits
Psychoticism
Extraversion
Neuroticism
Facets
Openness
Agreeableness
Conscientiousness
General Personality Factor (GPF)
HEXACO model
Alpha
Beta

CHAPTER

7 THE NEUROSCIENCE OF PERSONALITY

Read the Chapter on mysearchlab.com

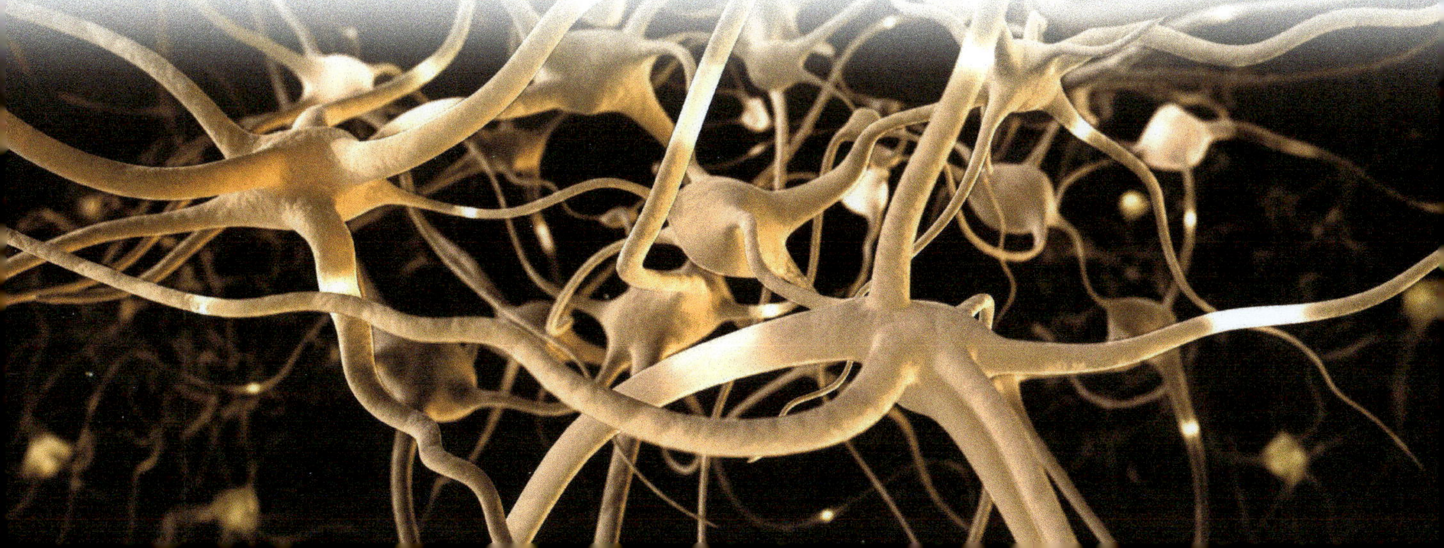

"As physicists had to learn that they were dealing with a space-time continuum, psychologists will have to learn that they have to deal with a mind-body continuum—not with Cartesian entities entirely separate from each other."

Eysenck (1997, p. 1224)

SEE FOR YOURSELF

Take a few minutes to close your eyes, sit still, clear your mind, and focus on your breathing. Were you able to do this? Did you start to feel more relaxed?

What if I told you there was a way that you could be healthier and happier? It's not a drug, it doesn't involve massive psychotherapy, it's not painful, and it's totally free. What is this miracle cure? Believe it or not, it's meditation!

Although some religious and cultural traditions embrace meditation as a powerful spiritual practice, modern medical research has traditionally scoffed at alternative treatments. However, Dr. Jon Kabat-Zinn, professor of medicine emeritus at the University of Massachusetts Medical School, has changed all this with his brand of Westernized stress reduction using Eastern principles of meditation. And he and his colleagues have been doing controlled experiments to test the effectiveness of these techniques.

In one study, participants who wanted to learn about meditation as a form of stress reduction were randomly assigned to either a meditation group or a control group (Davidson et al., 2003). The meditation group went through an extensive 8-week training in mindfulness-based stress reduction meditation, whereas people in the control group were put on a wait list for the 8 weeks to receive the training at a later time. In this way, both groups were essentially equivalent except for participation in the meditation training.

During the training, participants practiced being in the moment instead of planning, worrying, thinking, or fantasizing about the future, the way most of us do when given a few moments to sit still. The meditation group members tuned in to their breathing and practiced regulating their attention to *not* think about these things—to think about nothing, in fact (Kabat-Zinn, 1990).

At the end of the training session the two groups were compared on a number of measures. The researchers found that the group that had learned meditation showed less anxiety. This would be exciting enough—that people who meditate have less anxiety—but the real news is that they also showed differences in how their brains responded to emotional stimuli (Davidson et al., 2003). People who meditated showed greater brain activation on the left prefrontal cortex of their brains both at rest and in response to positive and negative emotional events. As a special bonus, participants in the meditation group also showed better immune functioning than participants in the control group.

THINK ABOUT IT

Does physiology determine personality or does personality determine physiology? Can it be both?

Overall, the data suggest that regular meditation fundamentally changes how our brains work and that this activation is related both to the emotions we feel and to how we respond to stressful events. The researchers surmised that meditation makes people more open to experiencing positive emotions and less reactive to negative emotions with the overall effect of decreasing their anxiety and improving immune functioning (Davidson et al., 2003)—all of this without drugs!

When it comes to understanding our biological functioning and personality, it's like the question of which came first, the chicken or the egg: Does our physiology determine our personality, or does our personality determine our physiology? We may be born with a certain

Evidence suggests that the regular practice of mindfulness meditation makes people more receptive to positive emotions, decreases anxiety, and bolsters the immune system.

physiology that may cause us to develop certain traits, but the environment can modify aspects of our personality. Perhaps the best way to think of our physiology is as a package of potentialities for personality traits that may be developed, discouraged, or even modified by our experiences. However, at the same time research such as the meditation study suggests that our behavior also affects our physiology. How much so and for which specific aspects of our personality are still open questions.

In this chapter we briefly review the major physiological systems and discuss two personality theories that hypothesize that neurological differences cause differences in personality traits. Then we consider the physiology and neurology behind some common personality characteristics.

What Is Neuroscience and How Do We Study It?

Researchers who explore the neuroscience behind personality focus on the brain and the nervous system. A brief overview of the parts of the nervous system will help us better understand some of the recent findings in this area.

"It is unlikely that you would define your personality in terms of molecular and cellular brain processes. . . . Yet personality is the product of the brain."
Corr (2006, p. 519)

The nervous system is made up of the **central nervous system** and the **peripheral nervous system**. The central nervous system includes the brain and the spinal cord whereas the peripheral nervous system includes the **somatic nervous system**, which controls movements of the muscles, and the **autonomic nervous system**, which regulates smooth muscle (e.g., inner organs), cardiac muscle, and glands. The autonomic nervous system is further divided into the **sympathetic division** and the **parasympathetic division**. The sympathetic division mobilizes energy (e.g., for fight or flight), whereas the parasympathetic division supports systems that replenish the body's energy stores (e.g., salivation, digestion, etc.; Carlson, 2010).

The brain is protected by a bath of *cerebrospinal fluid (CSF)* that cushions the delicate brain and also flows through spaces in the brain called *ventricles*. CSF is similar to blood plasma, and is continually produced, circulated, and reabsorbed through the brain and the ventricles (Carlson, 2010).

The brain contains a number of structures and systems that control everything from thinking, reasoning, learning, and memory, to breathing, sleeping, and eating, to movement and the processing of sensory information, to the experience of emotions. Because all of these parts are crucial for basic functioning, we should not expect to see large differences among people. However, individuals can vary in all kinds of ways, from how they may respond to stress (e.g., heart palpitations, sweating) to what they think is happy or sad, to how they respond to hormones and drugs. Researchers hypothesize that differences in *bodily responses, brain structure, brain activity,* and *biochemical activity* are all related to individual differences in personality (Zuckerman, 2005). All of the research that has been done on exploring physiological and neurological differences in personality fits into one of these four categories. These categories and the common physiological measures of each are summarized in Table 7.1.

Bodily Responses

When our body responds to arousing events in the environment it is the autonomic nervous system that responds. When aroused, the sympathetic division responds by increasing heart rate, blood pressure, blood flow to the extremities, respiration, sweating, and muscle activity. Essentially the body curtails some of its regular maintenance functions to mobilize an immediate response.

Sweating is measured by **galvanic skin response (GSR)** which is a measure of skin conductance or how quickly a slight electrical current passes through two points on the skin. The faster the conductance of the current, the more moisture is present that indicates greater arousal.

Muscle activity is measured by **electromyography (EMG)** or myoelectric activity, which estimates the electrical impulses of the muscles during contraction and relaxation. EMG is often used in biofeedback to train people to perceive muscle contractions so that they can learn to relax their muscles.

Table 7.1 Common Markers of Neurological and Physiological Differences in Personality

Bodily Responses	Brain Structure	Brain Activity	Biochemical Activity
Cardiovascular	Dissection	Cortical stimulation	Neurotransmitters:
Heart rate	Cytology	EEG	Dopamine,
Blood pressure	CT scan	Evoked potential	Serotonin,
Blood flow	MRI	PET scan	GABA
Respiratory function		fMRI	Enzymes:
Galvanic skin response		Transcranial magnetic stimulation	MAO
Electromyography			Hormones:
			Epinephrine,
			Norepinephrine,
			Cortisol
			Drug responses

Note: See the chapter text for descriptions and explanations of abbreviations.

SEE FOR YOURSELF

Have you ever had a CT scan, CAT scan, or an MRI? What information was your doctor hoping to find that couldn't be found through other methods?

THINK ABOUT IT

Which of these four markers of neurological and physiological activity do you think are most promising for understanding personality: bodily responses, brain structure, brain activity, or biochemical activity? Why?

Brain Structure

Another place that researchers have looked for differences among people is in the relative size and weight of specific parts of the brain, or even in the kinds and number of cells found in various parts of the nervous system. In the past, the only way of studying differences in brain structure and cells was through dissecting the brain after death. During an autopsy the brain may be removed and sections of tissues preserved for cytological (cell) study.

Today, through the advent of more sophisticated techniques we can study the structure of a living human brain through noninvasive procedures. For example, **computerized tomography** (**CT**), called a CT scan, takes a high-resolution x-ray picture of the brain. By looking at thin cross sections of the brain—often less than a millimeter!—we can detect abnormalities or differences in brain tissue. (This same technique was once called **computer axial tomography** [**CAT**], or CAT scan.)

A similar technique involves **magnetic resonance imaging** (**MRI**). Here radio frequency waves are used instead of x-rays. First, a strong magnetic field causes the nuclei of some atoms to resonate. Then radio frequency waves are used to detect the activity of these atoms. Because

Paper-thin slices of human brain mounted on slides for study.

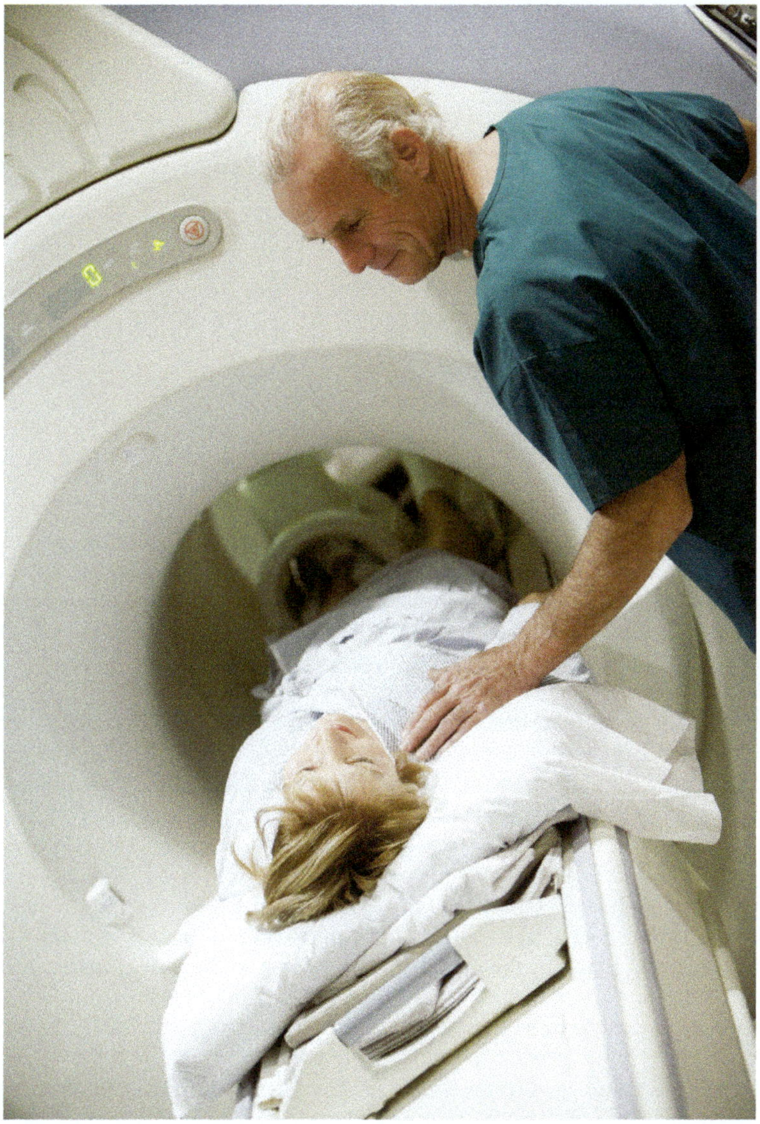

Non-invasive procedures, like the CT scan shown here, allow researchers to study brain structures.

hydrogen atoms are present in all tissues but in varying concentrations, the pattern of resonance formed by the hydrogen atoms forms a multidimensional picture of the brain.

Brain Activity

Both CT scans and MRIs can detect only static pictures of the brain—that is, pictures of brain structure at one moment in time. Measures of brain activity are ways of looking for differences in brain structures while the brain is stimulated. Often, participants are given a mental task to work on or other stimuli to react to while measures of brain activity are taken.

One early technique of studying brain activity is cortical stimulation. Using either electrodes implanted in the brain or direct electrical stimulation of parts of the brain, the patient is awake and can report on sensations as various parts of the brain are being stimulated. Today, we are able to use less invasive procedures. For instance, in an **electroencephalogram (EEG)** electrodes are placed on the scalp to monitor electrical activity of the brain. When electrical activity of the brain or other part of the nervous system is measured in response to a specific stimulus, this is called an **evoked potential (EP)**. Both EEGs and EPs indicate amount of brain activity in response to a stimulus. However, newer techniques identify the exact location of brain activity.

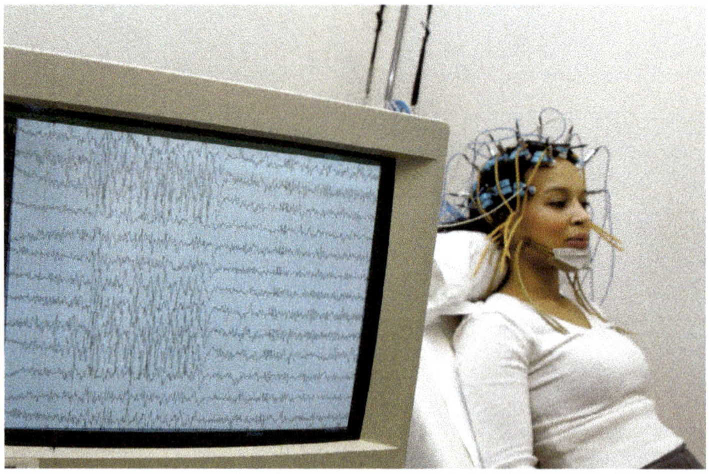

Electrodes are attached to this woman's head to measure brain activity.

In **positron emission tomography (PET)**, called a PET scan, a slightly radioactive glucose-like substance with a very short half-life (rate of breakdown) is injected into the brain and the person is placed in a scanner similar to a CT scanner. Active regions of the brain use up more glucose than inactive regions and, with the aid of computer enhancement, scans of these regions appear in different colors related to their activity level.

The most detailed view of brain activity at a cellular level comes from **functional magnetic resonance imaging (fMRI)**. This works the same as the traditional MRI except that brain activity levels are monitored over time by tracing blood oxygen levels in the brain. The more active areas use up more oxygen and this activity is translated into different color scans of the brain. Often images are taken while the participant is engaged in some cognitive activity or viewing stimuli, so that the researcher takes a series of these functional images over time.

Though the use of fMRI for personality research is on the rise, there are some notable problems with fMRI research. One problem is timing of response. When viewing a stimulus, our thoughts react within milliseconds whereas blood flow takes about 2 seconds. This makes it difficult to pinpoint the precise area that fired at the exact moment of a thought or reaction. Another problem is that the procedure is time-intensive and the equipment expensive so that often experiments use only a small number of participants. Small sample sizes make it difficult to find a reliable and significant effect (Yarkoni, 2009). A third problem, called the **nonindependence error**, is that researchers may unintentionally bias their results by not independently selecting which brain areas to correlate with, say, personality characteristics or other variables (Vul, Harris, Winkielman, & Pashler, 2009a). We'll talk more about this error and the controversy surrounding fMRI studies in the Research Methods Illustrated section.

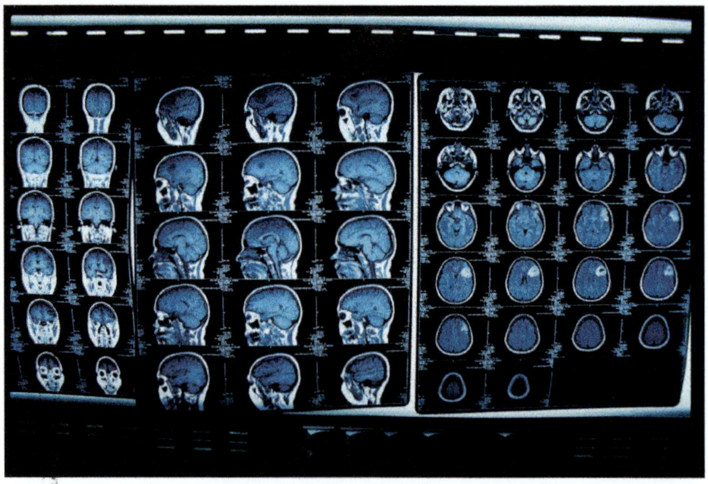

These fMRI images of a woman's brain show areas of her brain that are active while she is engaged in a cognitive task.

Finally, confounds such as time of day and nervousness of participants can also affect the results of neuroimaging studies (Dumit, 2004; Uttal, 2001).

One of the newest techniques for studying brain activity is **transcranial magnetic stimulation (TMS)**. With TMS a brief electrical current passes through a coil placed on the head. The magnetic field disrupts the regular activity of the neurons, sometimes impairing and sometimes enhancing function (Schutter, 2009). By carefully mapping parts of the brain that are stimulated and noting what kind of functioning is disrupted, researchers are able to pinpoint with greater accuracy than cortical stimulation or EP the exact area affected. Essentially TMS mimics a brain lesion, which allows researchers to draw inferences about cause and effect. This is a huge improvement over earlier techniques that only suggested a correlational relationship between brain activity and behavior (Walsh & Cowey, 2000). Although this technique has been used to treat various disorders including depression and anxiety (George & Bellmaker, 2000) and the pain of fibromyalgia (Sampson, 2006), we do not know yet how useful TMS will be for the study of personality.

This imaging research is very exciting, but there is one major problem with interpreting the results of brain scan research: What exactly does it mean when an area reacts in response to certain stimuli? According to critics of brain localization techniques, it could mean a number of things (Dumit, 2004; Uttal, 2001; Wade, 2006). First, it could mean that the area in question is indeed the center for that characteristic or response. But there could also be other areas that are less active but of equal or even greater importance that may have disinhibited the more active area. Also, when an area responds to stimulation we know that the area is necessary, but we don't know if it is a sufficient cause of the characteristic or response that we have observed. Maybe it's sufficient only if other parts of the brain are also involved. Finally, when a PET scan finds an area of increased glucose use, it may indicate activity or it may also indicate a neuron that is working less efficiently needing more glucose. However, by using fMRI, PET scans, and other neuroimaging techniques in the context of a controlled experiment we can figure out what brain activity really means.

Biochemical Activity

Finally, physiological differences may appear as differences in how the brain and body process various chemicals including neurotransmitters, hormones, and drugs. Depending on how and where these chemicals function, we might analyze cerebrospinal fluid, saliva, blood, or urine to monitor levels of these chemical substances.

Neurotransmitters are chemicals released by neurons to inhibit or excite the next neuron into action. In this way, neurotransmitters do just that: help transmit signals through the nervous system. Some important neurotransmitters are *norepinephrine, epinephrine, dopamine,* and *serotonin.* These all have a similar molecular structure, so that drugs that affect one tend to affect all of them. Norepinephrine (noradrenaline) and epinephrine (adrenaline) are also considered stress hormones. They help the body deal with threat by increasing blood flow to the muscles which increases heart rate and blood pressure. Dopamine is related to feelings of pleasure, and helps regulate movement, learning, attention, and rewards. Serotonin is involved with mood regulation, arousal, the control of sleeping and eating, and pain regulation. Depression, anxiety, and other mood disorders are related to how the body processes serotonin. The enzyme *monoamine oxidase (MAO)* regulates, to some degree, the availability of dopamine, norepinephrine, and epinephrine in the system.

Norepinephrine and serotonin may also be related to symptoms of depression (Thorn & Lokken, 2006). Some antidepressants, for example, work by blocking the reuptake of norepinephrine, serotonin or both, so that they stay in the spaces between the neurons a bit longer (Thorn & Lokken, 2006). Antianxiety drugs work by mimicking another neurotransmitter, *gamma-aminobutyric acid (GABA),* an inhibitory neurotransmitter (Thorn & Lokken, 2006).

Researchers may study neurotransmitters and the systems that process them by having participants engage in a task or activity and monitor the fluctuations in these chemicals. When it is impossible to directly measure the level of neurotransmitters—as with norepinephrine, for example—researchers indirectly monitor how the neurotransmitter is being used by measuring known byproducts of neurotransmitter metabolism. Another way is through a **challenge test** in which researchers administer a drug that is known to either increase or decrease a neurotransmitter's functioning and monitor the impact of this new substance on reactions presumed to be related to the neurotransmitter.

Research Methods Illustrated: Correlational Designs II: Scatterplots, Correlations, and the Alleged "Voodoo Science" of fMRI Studies

Are fMRI studies "voodoo science"? Are pretty scatterplots misleading? Oh, say it isn't so! In March 2009 the journal *Perspectives on Psychological Science* published a series of invited papers and made overt a debate that had been brewing on the Internet for some time (Diener, 2009). It seems that a small group of researchers noted that some fMRI studies of emotion, social cognition, and personality reported, in the words of one overzealous researcher, "insanely strong" correlations (Vul, Harris, Winkielman, & Pashler, 2009b, p. 320). The group suspected that these correlations were too good to be true. What they found set off a whole controversy (Vul et al., 2009a; see also Diener, 2010).

To understand all the fuss, we need to start with the concept of correlation. Recall that correlation is a measure of the relationship between two variables. If two variables increase or decrease at the same time—such as age and height—they are positively correlated. If one variable decreases (or increases) while the second variable increases (or decreases)—such as practice and typing errors—then the variables are negatively correlated. You can vividly see the relationship between two variables by graphing them against each other on the same graph.

Consider the graphs in Figure 7.1. The graph on the left shows Neuroticism scores on the *x*-axis plotted against thickness of a section of the orbital frontal cortex (OFC) on the *y*-axis. The graph on the right shows a similar graph for Extraversion scores. These are called **scatterplots or scattergrams** because they show the scatter, or spread, of the data. Many brain-imaging studies will use scatterplots to illustrate their results. Each point represents a participant in the study. In this graph, the blue circles represent females and the red squares represent males (ignore for a moment the diagonal lines drawn through the dots).

Notice how the cloud of data points on the left graph seems to slope downward. That tells us that as Neuroticism scores increase, thickness of this region of the OFC decreases. That suggests a negative correlation. Now look at the width of the cloud. Is it thinner or thicker? The thinner a cloud, the more closely related the two variables are and the stronger the correlation will be. The scatterplot on the left shows us that there is a moderately negative correlation between Neuroticism and thickness of the OFC. Indeed, the correlation of these data is −.65 (Wright et al., 2006). The line through the cloud of points is called a *linear regression line* and it estimates our best guess of how we can predict *y*-values from *x*-values.

What do you think about the correlation between Extraversion and thickness of the OFC as illustrated in the graph on the right? Here, the dots seem to be more scattered, making more of a circle than an oval. This tells us that there is not much of a correlation between the two variables, .18 in fact (Wright et al., 2006).

As you can see, a scatterplot is a very useful graphic. It can tell us at least three things about a set of data. First, it can alert us to outliers, or participants who score extremely high or low in one or

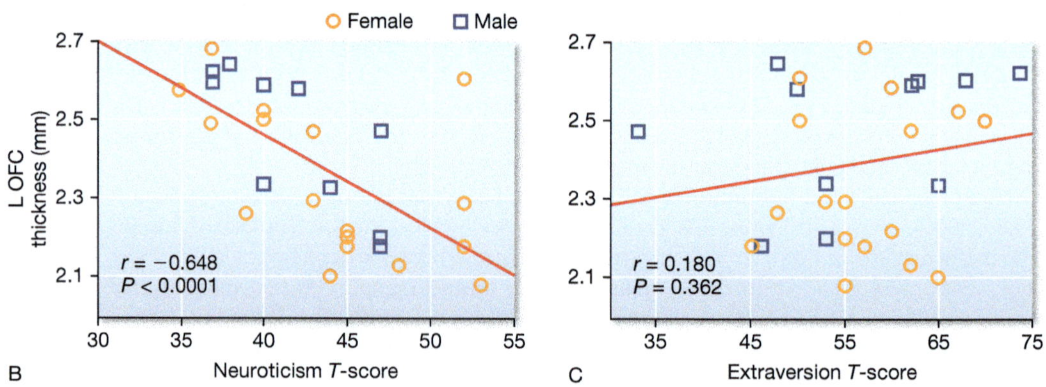

Figure 7.1 Scatterplots showing the relationship between cortical thickness and Neuroticism (left) and Extraversion (right) in the orbitofrontal cortex. *Source:* Adapted from Wright et al. (2006, Figure 3, p. 1814). From Wright, C. I., Williams, D., Feczko, E., Barrett, L. F., Dickerson, B. C., Schwartz, C. E., et al. (2006), "Neuroanatomical correlates of extraversion and neuroticism," Cerebral Cortex, 16(12), 1809–1819. Reprinted by permission of Oxford University Press.

both of our variables. There doesn't seem to be any outliers in the Wright et al. (2006) data, except for maybe the male who is very low in Extraversion in the graph on the right. Second, a scatterplot can tell us the direction of the correlation: whether it's positive (the cloud of dots points upward) or negative (the cloud points downward). Third, the thickness of the cloud or scatter of the dots tells us the strength of the correlation. The more the scatterplot looks like a circle, the less the two variables are related. The more the scatterplot looks like an oval, the more strongly the two variables are related. A perfect correlation will look like a straight line, whereas a zero correlation will look like random dots spread out around the graph. Check out the graphs in Figure 7.2 and try to guess whether the correlations are positive or negative, and high, medium, or close to zero.

Wright et al. (2006) also correlated cortical thickness in key areas with participants' scores on Extraversion, Neuroticism, Openness, Conscientiousness, and Agreeableness. Can you think of why they did this? They wanted to show specifically that Neuroticism was related to the thickness in some areas of the brain whereas Extraversion (and the other personality traits) was not. Because Neuroticism and Extraversion correlate with thickness in some areas and not in others, and only these two traits and not all five factors correlate with these areas of the brain, we have more confidence that the researchers have found a true result and not a significant result by chance alone.

Notice that Wright et al. (2006) cross-checked an area of the cortex that they thought was related to positive and negative emotions (Extraversion and Neuroticism, respectively) but was not related to other traits (Openness, Agreeableness, Conscientiousness). Other researchers are not so careful to cross-validate their findings. Instead, they selected which areas to study based on how well signals from that area correlated with their dependent variable (e.g., personality) and then calculated correlations based on this narrower range of values. That is, the same sample was used to decide what ought to be correlated and for the calculation of the actual correlation itself.

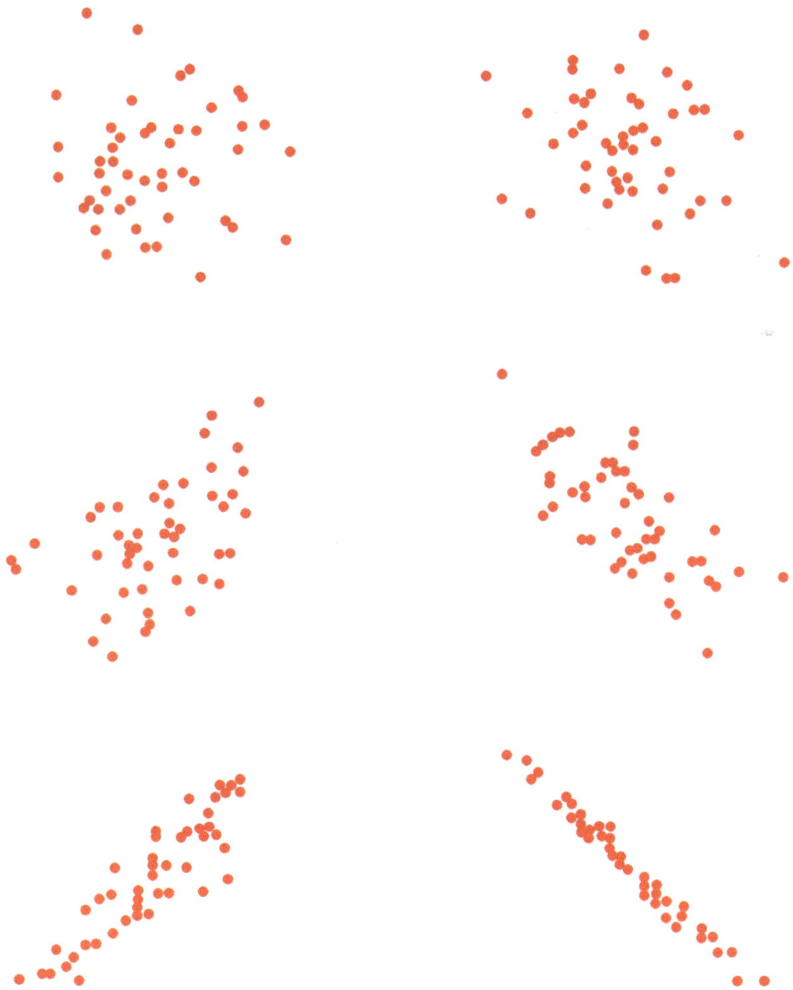

Figure 7.2 Scatterplots illustrating various correlations in hypothetical data. The correlations are (left to right): 0, −.3, .5, −.7, .90, −.99.

Technically, these two decisions should be made based on separate samples. It would be like deciding to have a state championship by choosing the best athletes in a specific sport—the sport you know your school excels in—instead of choosing a sport at random. Because the criterion and the outcome were determined within the same sample and not independent samples, the researchers made the nonindependence error (Vul et al., 2009a). This error caused artificially large correlations that made it seem like all kinds of social behaviors could be located in the brain. These "puzzlingly" large correlations led to accusations of fraudulence and claims that the researchers were conducting "voodoo science" and inflating their correlations on purpose (Vul et al., 2009b). Many of the researchers so accused defended the logic of their studies and claimed that Vul et al. (2009a) were exaggerating and that, in fact, the methods used by the authors to judge the studies in question were themselves flawed (Lazar, 2009; Lieberman, Berkman, & Wager, 2009; Lindquist & Gelman, 2009; Nichols & Poline, 2009).

The good news is that both sides agree that the methodology of fMRI studies correlating blood oxygen level dependent (BOLD) effect to personality are not perfect and can be improved. The problems that Vul et al. (2009a) identified, though not unique to fMRI studies, can be readily fixed, sometimes without collecting new data (Barrett, 2009; Vul et al., 2009a, 2009b; Yarkoni, 2009). The whole scientific community is now committed to understanding the debate—ceasing with the name-calling—and coming to a thoughtful resolution that will no doubt improve both our methods and our findings in behavioral neuroscience.

This brings us to a familiar caution: Our results are only as good as our measures. Think of it this way: Imagine beachcombing. You walk along a beach looking for interesting things that people may have lost. Part of your success comes from knowing where to look, like going to popular beaches or searching under the boardwalk where people may have dropped change from the food stands above. But part of your success comes from having the right equipment: your eyes versus a rake versus a metal detector. With a metal detector—especially a very powerful one—you are more likely to find coins, jewelry, watches, and other valuables buried inches under the sand. However, you may also find things such as old bottle caps, broken toys, and rusty nails. As researchers, we want to find good, significant effects, but we also want to minimize the "junk" we find along the way.

Neurological Theories of Personality

"Biological differences are innate and form the foundation upon which mature personality develops."
Clark and Watson (2008, p. 266)

In the 1998 revision to his 1947 classic book *Dimensions of Personality*, Hans Eysenck noted that even as we recognize that a substantial portion of our personality is inherited "there must be biological intermediaries between DNA and personality, and these intermediaries should be specified by theory and investigated" (Eysenck, 1998, p. xii). These biological intermediaries, what Eysenck's technology was not sufficiently advanced in 1947 to detect, are physiological differences.

Although Eysenck and others would like to be able to identify specific aspects of our physiology—be it bodily responses, brain structures, brain activity, or biochemical activity—that can account for differences in personality, this "holy grail" of personality research eludes us. Despite bigger and better and less invasive techniques and even with the ability to decode the smallest gene, protein, and neurotransmitter, scientists are not able to find consistent physiological differences that relate in a clear way to differences in personality characteristics (e.g., Eysenck, 1990). It may be that our techniques are not up to the task or it may be that aspects of the human nervous system interact in complicated ways that we have yet to untangle. Even when we are able to identify such differences, we still have a long way to go to prove that these differences actually cause us to develop the personalities that we have considering that our personalities have developed over a lifetime of interactions with other people.

THINK ABOUT IT

Are infants a blank slate at birth or are they born with a personality?

We can't be sure that differences in physiology cause us to develop different full-blown personalities, but perhaps we are expecting too much. Maybe biology has the biggest impact at a broader, more general level of personality, called **temperament**. What is temperament? Temperament is a set of personality characteristics that are (Zuckerman, 2005)

1. Relatively stable across the life span
2. Expressed through general energy level
3. Present from early childhood
4. Similar in other species of animals

Eysenck believed that temperament, determined by genes and passed on from parents to children, is the intermediary between DNA and personality.

5. Present at birth, at least in a general way
6. Determined by genetic factors
7. Changeable with maturation and experience

In their search for the biological basis of personality nearly all major personality typologies converge on three primary temperaments (Zuckerman, 2005), or clusters of related personality traits:

- *Extraversion:* Positive emotion, reward sensitivity, social rewards, sociability, approach.
- *Neuroticism:* Negative emotion, anxiety, punishment sensitivity, withdrawal.
- *Impulsivity:* Psychoticism, lack of constraint, sensation seeking, novelty seeking, lack of conscientiousness, lack of agreeableness.

Indeed, there has been striking similarity in the various models that researchers have proposed. For example, Eysenck's Psychoticism, Extraversion, and Neuroticism model (PEN model; Eysenck, 1990), the five-factor model (FFM; Costa & McCrae, 1992; John, 1990; John et al., 2008), the Big Five (Goldberg, 1990; Norman, 1963), Gray's RST (Corr, 2008b), and Cloninger (1998) all posit at least two of these three dimensions as part of their theories. However, both the FFM and the Big Five split Eysenck's Psychoticism factor into Agreeableness and Conscientiousness (Digman, 1996). Other researchers write about an approach temperament (i.e., Extraversion) and an avoidance temperament (Neuroticism; Elliot & Thrash, 2008) or positive emotionality (Extraversion) and negative emotionality (Neuroticism; Depue, Luciano, Arbisi, Collins, & Leon, 1994).

Table 7.2 summarizes some of these relationships. Despite various names for the factors—and great debate about the "right" number of factors, something we investigated more closely in Chapter 2 on traits—when it comes to identifying basic *physiological* temperaments, the evidence from many theoretical backgrounds and different kinds of research methods converges on these three.

Table 7.2 Correspondences Among Three Personality Clusters and Major Trait Theories

	Cluster		
Theory	Extraversion	Neuroticism	Impulsivity
Eysenck	Extraversion	Neuroticism	Psychoticism
Gray	Behavioral Approach System	Behavioral Inhibition System	
Five Factors	Extraversion	Neuroticism	Low Conscientiousness
Cloninger	Reward Dependence	Harm Avoidance	Novelty Seeking

Note: The Openness factor of the five-factor model, the Intellect factor of the Big Five, and Gray's fight-flight-freeze system do not appear to correspond to any of the three primary traits identified by Zuckerman (2005).

To understand both the logic and the evidence supporting this assertion, let's take a close look at two important biological theories of personality: Hans Eysenck's PEN model and Jeffrey Gray's reinforcement sensitivity theory. Afterward, we'll look at the biological basis of the three temperaments of positive emotion, negative emotion, and impulsivity.

Eysenck's PEN Model

When Eysenck first started working in the 1940s, he was unusual in his desire to build a personality theory based on experimental findings (Eysenck, 1998). Further, he believed that a comprehensive theory should explain *how* people developed their personalities as well as predict consequences and outcomes of various personalities. While studying normal and psychiatric patients he developed his theory and identified two factors of personality, Extraversion and Neuroticism (Eysenck, 1998), and later he added Psychoticism, the third dimension. Together these three dimensions—Psychoticism, Extraversion, and Neuroticism—form the PEN model (Eysenck, 1952). This model is used to describe personality. People can be high or low on each of the three factors.

Overview of Eysenck's Three Dimensions. The first of Eysenck's factors is **Extraversion**. People who are high in this factor, extroverts, tend to be sociable, popular, optimistic, and somewhat unreliable. Those low in Extraversion—introverts—tend to be quiet, introspective, reserved, and reliable, and to have a few close friends. Essentially, Extraversion refers to how outgoing people are, to both the social and the physical environments.

Eysenck's second factor is **Neuroticism**, which we might contrast with emotional stability. People high in this factor tend to be distressed, insecure, and upset in many areas of life. They are chronically worried, nervous, and moody, hold a low opinion of themselves, and find it difficult to get back on an even keel after an upsetting experience. In contrast, emotionally stable people are even-tempered, calm, relaxed, carefree, unworried, and somewhat unemotional, and return to their natural state quickly after an emotional experience (Eysenck & Eysenck, 1975).

SEE FOR YOURSELF

Can you think of people you know or characters from movies, books, or TV who exemplify Eysenck's three factors?

Eysenck called the third factor **Psychoticism**. We might think of Psychoticism as being antisocial and contrast it with ego control. People high in Psychoticism tend to be loners, egocentric, troublesome, manipulative, impulsive, uncooperative, hostile, and withdrawn, and do not fit in anywhere (Eysenck, 1990; Eysenck & Eysenck, 1985).

In contrast, people low in Psychoticism tend to be altruistic, socialized, empathetic, and conventional. They care about others and are able to control their impulses to a greater extent than those high in Psychoticism.

Eysenck and Eysenck suggested that the pathological labels of Psychoticism and Neuroticism be dropped in favor of tough-mindedness and emotionality to emphasize that this is a theory of normal, nonpathological behavior and to eliminate the negative connotations of these labels (Eysenck & Eysenck, 1975, p. 3).

Eysenck drew on at least three pieces of evidence to support his view that these differences in personality are genetic and biological. First, cross-cultural universality in traits implies a strong biological component (Eysenck, 1990). After all, we would expect that large differences in culture and environment would produce different kinds of personality factors. However, this is not the case, as one study of personality in 25 diverse countries including Uganda, Nigeria, Japan, Mainland China, the United States, the Soviet Union, Hungary, Bulgaria, and the former Yugoslavia suggested (Barrett & Eysenck, 1984). The fact that three factors of Psychoticism, Extraversion, and Neuroticism occur in such diverse cultures suggests a biological, rather than cultural, explanation.

Second, people show tremendous consistency in these three traits over time, despite changing environments. Responses and habits might change over time and situations, but traits do not. This consistency suggests a strong biological component to these traits (Eysenck, 1990).

The third piece of evidence is the robust finding that Extraversion, Neuroticism, and Psychoticism each have moderate heritability (Eaves, Eysenck, & Martin, 1989). As Eysenck (1990) stated, "Genetic factors cannot directly influence behavior or cognitions, of course, and the intervening variables must inevitably be physiological, neurological, biochemical, or hormonal in nature" (p. 247).

Although Eysenck suspected that arousal and attention were involved with all three of his factors, he admitted that the research evidence did not suggest a clear hypothesis for a biological explanation of psychoticism (Eysenck, 1990; Eysenck & Eysenck, 1976). We now turn to a discussion of the physiological explanations Eysenck proposed for Extraversion and Neuroticism.

Neurology of Extraversion. Eysenck thought that the main difference between introverts and extraverts had to do with arousal, and on that score he was right (Eysenck, 1990). He considered two possibilities: that introverts and extraverts differed in arousal level or in arousability (Eysenck, 1967).

Eysenck thought that introverts had greater cortical arousal than extraverts, particularly in the **ascending reticular activating system (ARAS)**, a pathway transmitting signals from the limbic system and hypothalamus to the cortex (Eysenck, 1967; Eysenck & Eysenck, 1985). The ARAS processes the more cerebral aspects of arousal or emotion (e.g., thinking about a difficult calculus problem). Activation in the ARAS can make a person alert and mentally sharp or sluggish and mentally dull.

SEE FOR YOURSELF

Think of people you know who are extraverted and introverted. Is there a difference in where they prefer to study? Why might this be?

Because of their hypothesized overaroused baseline condition, introverts act more restrained and inhibited. That is, they avoid conditions that would aggravate their already overstimulated condition, preferring to stay to themselves and engaging in more quiet activities. In contrast, the system of extraverts, Eysenck reasoned, lets in too little stimulation so that their underaroused condition leads them toward more stimulating and unrestrained behaviors. Basically, extraverts are more outgoing and engaged with the world to raise their naturally low level of arousal. In this way, both extraverts and introverts attempt to regulate their own arousal striving to find their comfort zone: an optimal level of arousal (e.g., Hebb, 1955).

This sounds like a nice hypothesis, but is this true? Consider this: If there is a natural difference in arousal level between introverts and extraverts then we ought to see a difference between them even if they are sleeping or resting. Turns out we can readily test this hypothesis because arousal produced by the ARAS can be seen using EEG, whereas the arousal in the limbic system can be seen in the GSR and EMG (Eysenck, 1967).

Alas, using these traditional measures of arousal and even the newer methods (e.g., PET scans, cortical EPs) this is not the case. Indeed, over 1,000 studies have been conducted testing Eysenck's theory of arousal with no success (Geen, 1997). There is only a tiny, if any, difference in arousal level between extraverts and intraverts at rest. However, there is a significant difference in how extraverts and introverts respond to moderate stimulation, suggesting that the key difference between them is in their **arousability** or sensory reactivity (De Pascalis, 2004; Stelmack & Rammsayer, 2008; Zuckerman, 2005).

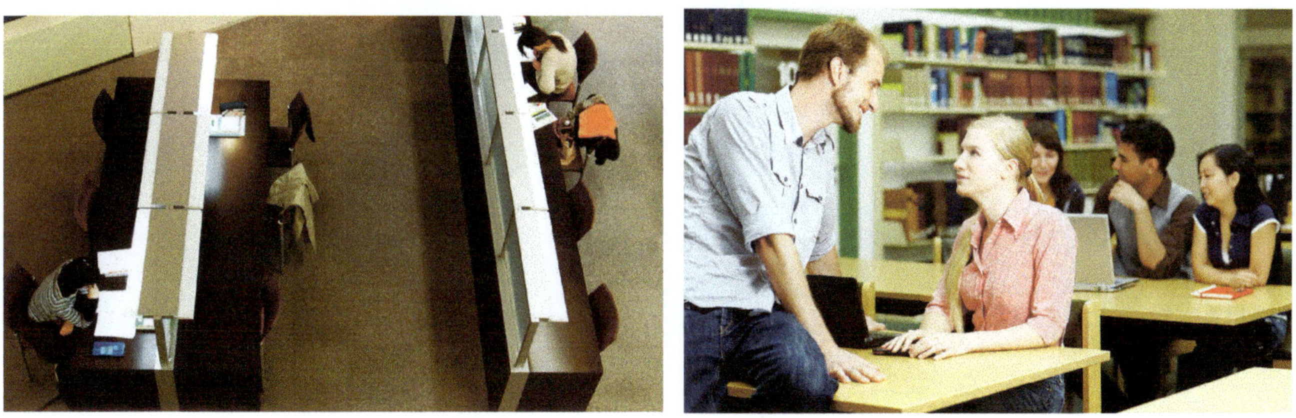

Is choice of study area related to personality? Which kind of study area do you think introverts and extraverts would prefer?

Given these differences in arousability, we would expect introverts and extraverts to differ in their choice of situations: noisy versus quiet. One study found that people studying in the quiet study spaces of their college library—spaces with individual carrels, small tables—tended to be introverted. Where did the extraverts prefer to study? In the noisy but highly sociable areas of the library: big rooms with open spaces and large tables (Campbell & Hawley, 1982).

THINK ABOUT IT

How else might extraverts and introverts regulate their arousability? Might they differ in preferences for caffeinated beverages for example? Favorite kinds of music?

But here's a question: Who performed better on their exams? Does noise level really matter when it comes to learning and performance? It sure does! Introverts and extraverts volunteered for a study in which they had to perform a moderately difficult cognitive reasoning task (Geen, 1984). Participants were given two words, one that fit a rule and the other that didn't. By observing a number of such pairs, participants had to figure out the rule. For example, the rule might be animal words or words that start with vowels.

While participants were viewing the words and trying to figure out the rule, they were bombarded with random bursts of white noise. Participants were randomly assigned to one of three conditions. In the choice condition, they were told that although they couldn't turn off the noise, they could select the volume that was "Just right for you." In the second and third conditions, participants were unable to control the volume. Instead, they were assigned the level of volume that matched what a participant in the first condition chose. In the assigned-same condition their volume was matched to the volume chosen by a personality just like them, either introverted or extraverted. However, in the assigned-different condition they were subjected to the volume chosen by a person different from them: an introvert, if they themselves were extraverted, or an extravert if they were introverted.

Who do you think chose the lower volume? Introverts in the choice condition chose a lower volume than extraverts in the choice condition. The difference was about that between a private office and a noisy group office. Second, who do you think experienced greater arousal as measured by heart rate and skin conductance? Well, it depended on which level of noise they were faced with. Both extraverts and introverts with noise levels at their optimum level of arousal—in either the choice condition or the assigned same condition—had similar levels of arousal as measured by heart rate and skin conductance. However, when faced with a level of noise not to their liking, introverts showed greater arousal and extraverts showed lower arousal. Essentially, introverts were overaroused by the loud "extraverted" level of noise whereas extraverts were underaroused by the soft, boring "introverted" level of noise.

SEE FOR YOURSELF

Based on these results, where should you study for optimum performance?

Finally, how well did participants perform? By now you get the drill: It depended on if they were working at their optimum level of noise. Introverts assigned to the extravert's noise level performed the worst, needing more trials to learn the rule. Next came extraverts assigned to the introvert's noise level. The choice and assigned-same conditions performed best, learning the rule in the fewest number of trials. As you can see in Figure 7.3, what's just right for introverts—leading to their optimum performance—is too little for extraverts

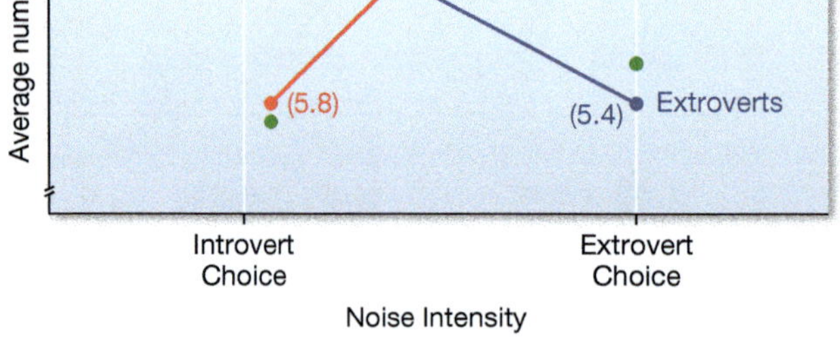

Figure 7.3 Performance as function of noise intensity condition and personality. Higher numbers indicate more trials were needed to learn the rule. Note: Red line = Introverts, Blue line = Extraverts, Green dots = Assigned same condition. *Source:* From Geen (1984).

and what's just right for extraverts is too much for introverts. People's noise preferences and performance outcomes depend on their optimal level of arousal as determined by their personality (Geen, 1984). Keep this study in mind the next time you are trying to decide where to study!

Neurology of Neuroticism. Eysenck hypothesized that physiological arousal could also account for individual differences in Neuroticism. In contrast to Extraversion, which was related to activation of the ARAS, he thought that Neuroticism had to do with stability or instability of the sympathetic nervous system (i.e., those parts of the brain that are involved in emotional regulation such as the hippocampus, amygdala, cingulum, septum and hypothalamus; Eysenck, 1967, 1990). Basically, the vulnerability of people high in Neuroticism to negative emotions such as fear and anxiety was due to an extrasensitive emotional or drive system (Eysenck, 1967, 1990). Whereas postulating separate physiological processes to account for Extraversion and Neuroticism, Eysenck acknowledged that the cortical and sympathetic systems were interconnected (Eysenck, 1967, 1990).

THINK ABOUT IT

If extraverts are more sensitive to positive emotions are they more vulnerable to happiness?

A vivid metaphor for how this might work is to think of Neuroticism as a smoke detector (Nettle, 2007). A good smoke detector alerts a building's occupants to a fire, but it doesn't go off for harmless events like someone burning the toast one morning. For the person high in Neuroticism, it's as if they are living in a house with an overly sensitive smoke detector that sends out a warning under the kinds of conditions that people low in Neuroticism would readily dismiss as safe. (If you're still thinking about how safe toast-burning is, then you are probably high in Neuroticism!) Extraversion and Neuroticism are similar in that both involve arousal; however, the big difference is in the valence or quality of that arousal. Extraversion is marked by positive arousal such as excitement and energy, whereas Neuroticism is marked by negative arousal such as fear and anxiety (Knutson & Bhanji, 2006; Zuckerman, 2005).

How did Eysenck's theory about Neuroticism fare in the face of research evidence? Well, it appears that Eysenck was on the right track. Simple measures of sympathetic nervous system activation (e.g., heart rate, skin conductance), both at rest and during stressful situations do not show any relationship with Neuroticism, but people who are high in Neuroticism do show an increase in heart rate in response to an intense stimulus (Zuckerman, 2005). So do introverts! However, people high in Neuroticism, but not introverts, show greater startle response to fearful pictures (Zuckerman, 2005). Together, these findings suggest that people high in Neuroticism may be more sensitive to negative emotions in particular, and not to arousing situations in general, the way that introverts are.

THINK ABOUT IT

If people high in Neuroticism are more sensitive to negative emotions, are they more vulnerable to depression?

If it is true that the defining feature of Neuroticism is sensitivity to negative emotions, then it would be particularly difficult for researchers to identify specific physiological differences between people high and low in Neuroticism. This is because people vary greatly in their sympathetic responses (e.g., heart rate, skin conductance, breathing, blood flow, etc.; Eysenck, 1990). All in all, there is no support for Eysenck's hypothesis that Neuroticism is related to activation in the sympathetic nervous system (Strelau, 1998).

Reinforcement Sensitivity Theory (RST)

An alternative theory was proposed by Jeffrey Gray. For Gray, personality *is* the variation in the functioning of brain systems. Indeed, the very essence of what makes people unique is differences in their responses to stimuli in the world (Corr, 2008b). Gray's idea was to (1) identify brain-behavior systems that accounted for important differences among individuals and (2) link these systems to standard measures of personality (Corr, 2008b). At first, he hypothesized two behavioral systems and linked these behavioral systems to Extraversion and Neuroticism in Eysenck's PEN theory (Gray, 1970, 1976, 1982). But now, after some 40 years of research and refinement, evidence suggests that there are three important behavioral systems that do not exactly map onto any existing measure of personality (Corr, 2004, 2008b; Gray & McNaughton, 2000; McNaughton & Corr, 2004, 2008; Pickering & Corr, 2008).

Overview of Three Neurological Systems. According to **reinforcement sensitivity theory (RST)** there are three hypothetical brain-behavior systems. These systems are presumed to exist based on evidence from neurology, physiology, behavior, and personality. Together they form a framework through which we can infer neural activity. Rather than identify isolated parts of the brain working separately, we can look for interconnected areas that function similarly and work together in accord with one of these hypothesized systems. Gray's great contribution was in recognizing that *everything* in the brain is interconnected. The conception of these three systems is his way of studying these interconnections. We may think of these systems as a kind of shorthand for a whole set of neural networks.

The first is called the **fight-flight-freeze system (FFFS)**. This system is associated with the emotion of fear and is responsible for orchestrating our reactions to aversive stimuli. We may opt to confront or fight the stimulus, avoid or escape it, or to remain frozen in place hoping the danger passes (Corr, 2004). The personality factor that matches this biological system is fearfulness and avoidance, which, if extreme, may lead to phobias and panic disorders (Corr, 2008b).

The second system, the **behavioral approach system (BAS)** organizes reactions to "appetitive stimuli," that is, stimuli that are enticing, pleasurable, and rewarding (Corr, 2004, p. 324). BAS makes a person more sensitive to reward. The related personality factor is optimism, impulsiveness, and the emotion of "anticipatory pleasure" (Corr, 2008b, p. 10). In the extreme, this system may lead to addictive behaviors, high-risk impulsive behaviors, and mania.

The third system, the **behavioral inhibition system (BIS)**, once thought to control the inhibition of behavior, is now hypothesized to resolve conflicts (Corr, 2004). These may be conflicts between two really good things, like deciding which movie to watch with friends, or between two distasteful things, like deciding which to open first, the electricity bill or the phone bill. Or between two options that have both upsides and downsides to them, such as whether or not to go to a party where you will see people you like as well as a few people whom you'd rather not hang out with. BIS also is activated when there is a conflict within one of the other systems (e.g., FFFS–FFFS or BAS–BAS conflicts; Corr, 2008b). Until the conflict is resolved, we

The fight-flight-freeze system (FFFS) regulates our reactions to aversive stimuli including fears, phobias, and panic disorders.

may experience anxiety, worry, rumination, risk assessment, vigilance for bad things, or a sense of possible danger or loss. Clinically, this system may lead to obsessive-compulsive disorder or generalized anxiety disorder (Corr, 2008b).

People may feel anxiety from BIS to a greater or a lesser degree depending on the specific rewards or punishments that are potentially in conflict. When BIS is activated, people become more sensitive to punishment (Corr, 2004) and often more cautious (Corr, 2008b). Further, there is an optimal level of BIS arousal. Too little leads to risk proneness, similar to Eysenck's notion of Psychoticism. Too much leads to risk aversion and generalized anxiety disorder (Corr, 2008b). RST suggests that choice—even between two rewarding options—has a negative component. Corr (2008b) wondered if having too many good things to choose from (e.g., Caribbean? Europe? Sports car? SUV?) may be a cause of discontent and depression in our affluent society.

BAS is very similar to Extraversion and BIS is very similar to Neuroticism. Current evidence suggests that they are quite similar but not identical (Smits & Boeck, 2006). The dimensions of FFFS/BIS and BAS are about 30 degrees off from Eysenck's dimensions of Neuroticism and Extraversion. Think of BAS as "2 parts Extraversion to 1 part Neuroticism" and BIS as "2 parts Neuroticism to 1 part Extraversion" (Smillie, Pickering, & Jackson, 2006, p. 323). Specifically, punishment sensitivity is manifested as neurotic-introversion and reward sensitivity is manifested as neurotic-extraversion. Sensitivity to punishment and sensitivity to rewards are the biological systems that together are hypothesized to develop into the traits of Extraversion and Neuroticism (Corr, 2004). Table 7.3 lists sample items from an early measure of BIS and BAS based on the original version of RST (Carver & White, 1994).

Think of it like this: Extraversion reflects the trade-off of rewards and punishments, whereas Neuroticism reflects the combination of rewards and punishments. For example, punishment makes a person less willing to take action—unless of course that action is to flee the situation—whereas the possibility of a reward increases the action. If the situation is clearly punishing or rewarding, then *everybody* will go for the reward or avoid the punishment.

However, the situations that define and challenge us are ones that are not clearly rewarding or punishing. That is, the real question of character is: What will you choose when rewards and punishments are both present? Because these situations involve some degree of conflict, BIS will

SEE FOR YOURSELF

Are you more willing to risk a punishment to gain a reward or to forego a reward to avoid a punishment?

Table 7.3 Sample Items From the BIS/BAS Scale

BAS Drive
1. When I want something I usually go all-out to get it.
2. If I see a chance to get something I want I move on it right away.
BAS Fun Seeking
1. I'm always willing to try something new if I think it will be fun.
2. I crave excitement and new sensations.
BAS Reward Responsiveness
1. When I'm doing well at something I love to keep at it.
2. When I get something I want, I feel excited and energized.
BIS
1. Criticism or scolding hurts me quite a bit.
2. If I think something unpleasant is going to happen I usually get pretty "worked up."

Note: Responses are indicated on a 4-point scale labeled *Very true for me, Somewhat true for me, Somewhat false for me,* and *Very false for me.*

Source: Adapted from C.S. Carver and White (1994, Table 1, p. 323). Carver, C.S., & White, T.L. (1994). Behavioral inhibition, behavioral activation, and affective respones to impending reward and punishment: The BIS/BAS scales. *Journal of Personality and Social Psychology,* 67(2), 319–333. Copyright American Psychological Association. Adapted with permission.

be activated and this will become manifested as Neuroticism. If rewards are more salient than punishments, then we will get a person who is willing to venture out into the world: a neurotic extravert. But if the punishment is more salient than the reward, or if the conflict is more salient than either the reward or the punishment, then we will get a person who would rather stay to himself or herself: a neurotic introvert. Who gets to decide if the rewards and punishments are in conflict? That's where Neuroticism comes in. Somebody who is low in Neuroticism would not experience conflict over the same situation that might cause consternation in somebody who was high in Neuroticism.

You can see that Gray suggested two things: our inherent behavioral systems—FFFS, BAS, and BIS—predispose us to respond to punishments, rewards, and conflicts in a certain way. Then, a lifetime of experiences refine our personalities (neurotic, emotionally stable, extraverted, introverted). In addition, RST suggests that the difference between healthy personality and psychopathology is one of degree: The underlying biological systems are essentially the same, differing only in their strength (See Table 7.4 for a summary of these three systems).

If we could look through the skull into the brain of a consciously thinking person, and if the place of optimal excitability were luminous, then we should see playing over the cerebral surface, a bright spot with fantastic, waving borders constantly fluctuating in size and form, surrounded by a darkness more or less deep, covering the rest of the hemisphere.
Ivan Petrovich Pavlov (1928, p. 222)

Neurology of FFFS, BAS, and BIS. What evidence is there for these three systems? The short answer: Quite a lot! Although much of the research has been done on animals, RST appears to be a good general theory of emotion, motivation, and learning in humans too (Pickering & Corr, 2008; Smillie, 2008; Smillie et al., 2006). However, the long answer is that researchers are struggling with how to operationalize and test some of the propositions of RST (see Corr, 2001; Pickering et al., 1997; Smillie, 2008; Smillie et al., 2006; Torrubia, Ávila, Moltó, & Caseras, 2001 for reviews), especially the implications of RST for trait theory (Smillie et al., 2006). The biggest issue is that we cannot tell if there is a problem with Gray's theory or a problem with the scales designed to measure the personality traits exhibited by these brain systems. As a sign of just how lively the debate is, recently *The European Journal of Personality*

Table 7.4 Summary of Reinforcement Sensitivity Theory Systems

	FFFS	BAS	BIS
Input:	Punishment	Reward	Conflict Punishment (?)*
Response:	Avoidance Freezing Defensive attack	Approach Exploration Active avoidance	Passive avoidance Risk assessment Information processing Arousal
Emotion:	Panic Phobia Rage Fearfulness	Anticipatory pleasure Hope	Rumination
Trait:	Psychoticism Neurotic-introversion	Extraversion Neurotic-extraversion	Neuroticism Anxiety
Pathology:	Phobias Panic disorders	Addictive behaviors Mania	Obsessive-compulsive disorder Generalized anxiety disorder
Motto:	"Escape!"	"Go for it!"	"Be careful!"

*There is disagreement among researchers about whether some kinds of punishments (e.g., conditioned) are still under BIS control in the revised RST (cf. Corr, 2002).

Note: See the chapter text for descriptions and explanations of abbreviations.

Sources: Adapted from Corr and McNaughton (2008, Table 5.2, p. 182) and Smillie (2008, p. 362). Corr, P. J., & McNaughton, N. (2008). Reinforcement sensitivity theory and personality. In P. J. Corr (Ed.), The reinforcement sensitivity theory of personality (p. 155–187). Cambridge, UK: Cambridge.

The behavioral approach system (BAS) regulates our reaction to things that are enticing, pleasurable, and rewarding.

dedicated an entire special issue to personality and RST (Ávila & Torrubia, 2008; Carver, 2008; Chavanon, Stemmler, & Wacker, 2008; Cloninger, 2008; Corr, 2008a; Johnson & Deary, 2008; Matthews, 2008; McNaughton, 2008; Reuter & Montag, 2008; Revelle & Wilt, 2008; Smillie, 2008).

The theory does, however, suggest a number of important and intriguing hypotheses for understanding human personality. To give you a sense of the evidence that led to the formulation of RST and the biology behind it, let's review research on two key predictions of RST: individual differences in reward sensitivity and learning.

Consider one very important class of rewards for most people: Food. Given that BAS is related to how sensitive people are to rewards, we might wonder if people high and low in strength of BAS would have different reactions to images of food. But we're not talking about *taste* for food. RST suggests that the *brains* of people high and low in BAS will respond differently to food.

There are at least five parts of the brain that are related to responding to visual food cues: the ventral (underside) part of the striatum, the amygdala, the orbitofrontal cortex, the ventral (underside) part of the pallidum and the midbrain regions that are associated with increased dopamine activity (Beaver et al., 2006). Participants looked at color photos of appetizing food (e.g., chocolate cake, an ice cream sundae), disgusting food (rotten meat, moldy bread), bland food (e.g., uncooked rice, potatoes), and nonfood items (e.g., an iron, a videocassette). While viewing these photos, their brains were scanned using fMRI.

Researchers found that BAS drive significantly accounted for differences in signals to appetizing food and disgusting food compared to bland foods in all five of these regions related to reward. Further, these responses were not related to a BAS measure of fun seeking so that they were unique to BAS drive. Participants with a strong appetitive drive as measured by BAS scores showed stronger reactions to photos of appetizing and disgusting foods in these parts of the brain that are known to be related to food regulation (Beaver et al., 2006). This is an example of how neural differences may be related to BAS, BIS, and FFFS functioning.

SEE FOR YOURSELF

Which statement do you agree with more: "Nothing ventured, nothing gained" or "Better safe than sorry"?

An important individual difference, according to RST, is how quickly people learn from rewards and punishments. This reinforcement sensitivity is the whole premise on which the theory rests. People with a strong BAS are more sensitive to reward, meaning that they will condition—or learn responses—more quickly by responding than by withholding a response. However, people with a strong BIS are more sensitive to punishment, meaning that they will condition more quickly by withholding a response than by responding (Gray, 1970, 1976). Think about it: Would you learn better by concentrating on not doing things wrong and avoiding a punishment, or by doing things right and gaining a reward?

This question was explored in an experiment in which participants had to learn the right response to a computer task—either press the "3" key or do nothing—when presented with random two-digit numbers (Zinbarg & Mohlman, 1998). The participants had to learn which numbers required a response and which numbers required that they withhold a response. Every trial was different, so that participants had to figure out all over again which numbers to respond to (e.g., hit the "3" key) or to withhold a response from (e.g., do nothing).

The behavioral inhibition system (BIS) regulates our reactions to conflicts between the fight-flight-freeze system and the behavioral approach system such as worry, rumination, vigilance, and obsessive-compulsiveness.

To let participants know whether they were correct or not, they received rewards and punishments depending on their responses. But instead of being rewarded *every time* they were correct ("You won 25 cents") or punished *every time* they were wrong ("You lost 25 cents"), there was a twist. On some trials taking action was associated with gaining a reward. On other trials, *not* taking action would avoid a punishment (see Figure 7.4). This pattern of feedback gave participants enough information to master the task. However, there is a big difference between learning by doing and learning by not doing. The question is, do some people learn better by taking actions or by withholding actions?

As it turned out, just as RST predicts, people with a reactive BAS learned the correct responses faster from reacting than from withholding their responses. However, people with high scores on a mixed FFFS/BIS scale learned faster from withholding than from reacting. In addition, people who scored high on an anxiety scale also learned faster from withholding than from reacting (Zinbarg & Mohlman, 1998). This experiment shows differences in learning from rewards and punishments in humans as a function of BAS and BIS/FFFS (See The Personality of Everyday Life for an application of RST theory to test-taking). This study is the human equivalent of the many studies of rats and other animals that led to the original statement of RST.

Figure 7.4 Schematic of participant feedback in the Zinbarg and Mohlman (1998) study.

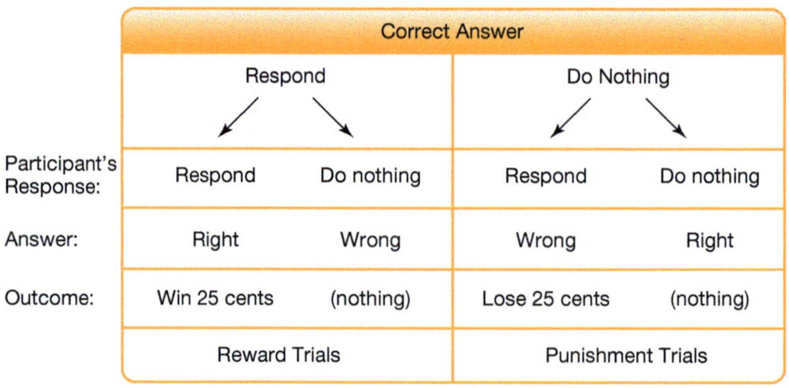

The Personality of Everyday Life

Personality and the guessing penalty

Have you ever taken a test where you were faced with the dilemma of guessing or leaving a question blank? Some standardized tests such as the SAT or the ACT have what is commonly called a *guessing penalty.* Test takers get one point for a correct answer, but lose one-fourth point for a wrong answer. This scoring is meant to discourage a person from randomly guessing on a multiple-choice test with four choices. Is there an effective way to deal with these exams?

That depends on the relative strength of your BAS and BIS (Ávila & Torrubia, 2004). The participants in this study regularly faced exams in which they not only needed to know the material, but they had to decide whether they should respond to a question they were unsure of or to leave the question blank because there was a guessing penalty built into the exam.

How did participants deal with this conflict? Participants who scored high in sensitivity to reward made more incorrect responses and left fewer questions blank than participants who scored low in sensitivity to reward (see Table 7.5). Essentially, people who are sensitive to reward are more likely to go for it, but then they are also more likely to pay for it, compared to people who are less sensitive to reward (see Figure 7.5).

However, participants who scored high in sensitivity to punishment left more questions blank but gave more correct answers than participants who scored low in sensitivity to punishment. Participants who were sensitive to punishment seemed to go by the rule "when in doubt, leave it out."

Alas, Ávila and Torrubia (2004) did not report if there was a difference in grades as a function of high and low sensitivity to reward or punishment. However, an earlier study did (Torrubia, Ávila, Moltó, & Grande, 1995). Despite these differences in incorrect responses and omissions, there was no difference in overall exam scores between participants who were high in sensitivity to punishment or sensitivity to reward. This suggests that the contrasting strategies work equally well.

People who are more sensitive to reward—such as extraverts—seem to go though life with the philosophy "Nothing ventured, nothing gained." In contrast, people who are more sensitive to punishment—such as people high in anxiety and/or fear—would rather be safe than sorry. The good news is, both strategies can be effective.

Table 7.5 Sample Items From the Sensitivity to Punishment and Sensitivity to Reward Questionnaire (SPSRQ)

Sensitivity to Punishment Questions
1. Are you often afraid of new or unexpected situations?
2. Is it difficult for you to telephone someone you do not know?
3. As a child, were you troubled by punishments at home or in school?
Sensitivity to Reward Questions
1. Do you often do things to be praised?
2. Do you like being the center of attention at a party or a social meeting?
3. Do you spend a lot of your time on obtaining a good image?

Source: Adapted from Torrubia et al. (2001, Table 2, p. 846). Reprinted with permission from Torrubia, R., Ávila, C., Moltó, J., & Caseras, X. (2001), "The sensitivity to punishment and sensitivity to reward questionnaire (SPSRQ) as a measure of Gray's anxiety and impulsivity dimensions," Personality and Individual Differences, 29, 837–862. Permission conveyed through the Copyright Clearance Center.

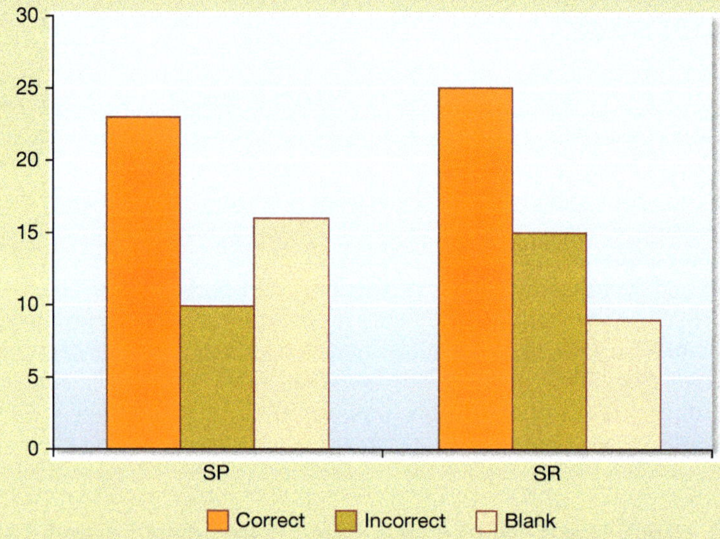

Figure 7.5 A schematic showing differences in number of questions correct, incorrect, and left blank as a function of sensitivity to punishment (SP) and sensitivity to reward (SR). *Source:* Based on data from Torrubia, et al. (1995).

"There is not the slightest resemblance between the phrenologist's localization of function that we find in physiological psychology."
Review of Charles H. Olin's 1910 book Phrenology *as cited in Seashore (1912, p. 227)*

Then and Now: Phrenology, the New Phrenology, and the Future of Neuroimaging for Personality and Beyond

Ever since ancient times, we humans have wondered, what makes us who we are? The ancient Greek philosopher Aristotle debated whether the heart or the brain was the seat of the soul or psyche, what we think of today as personality (Cowey, 2001). Since that time, others have wondered about the relationship between specific parts of the brain and personality. But it was the physician and anatomist Franz Joseph Gall in the 1790s who turned it into a science: **phrenology**. Gall reasoned—well ahead of his time—that certain functions of the brain were localized in parts of the cerebral cortex. That much, he had right. However, he also believed that the size of the cortex, as indicated by the size, shape, and in particular the location and size of bumps on the scalp, was related to particular mental or personality characteristics.

We know today that this system is completely without merit, "absolutely absurd," and "preposterous nonsense" according to the reviewer of a 1910 book on phrenology (Seashore, 1912, p. 227). However, Gall inspired a later phrenologist, George Combe, who made two interesting observations in 1836. Combe discovered that by pressing his thumb on parts of the exposed cortex of patients who had serious head injuries, he was able to change their behavior. He also noticed that some areas of brain tissue became filled with blood when the patient was thinking, dreaming, or talking (Cowey, 2001). The detection of blood-flow fluctuation eventually led to the development of fMRI, which one researcher viewed as the greatest single influence in neurological research in over 2,000 years (Cowey, 2001).

Then in 1884 William Wundt, a doctor, psychologist, and physiologist, viewed by many as the founder of experimental psychology, gave a lecture with the provocative title "Old and New Phrenology" (1894). In it he was critical of both phrenology and brain localization. Ironically, brain localization turned out to be the beginning of an important branch of psychology, as Combe's observations attested to, but at the same time Wundt was eerily on target when he cautioned that the "hypothesis of [localization] gives no account of the manifold forms of ideational and sensational connexion." (Wundt, 1894, p. 447). Indeed, his critique of brain localization was echoed 90 years later by a neuropsychologist who called neuropsychology "the currently fashionable name for phrenology" (Marshall, 1984, p. 210). The problem is that theories of localization fail to account for the connectivity of ideas in the mind, according to Wundt (1894), and the complex interaction of brain systems, according to Marshall (1984).

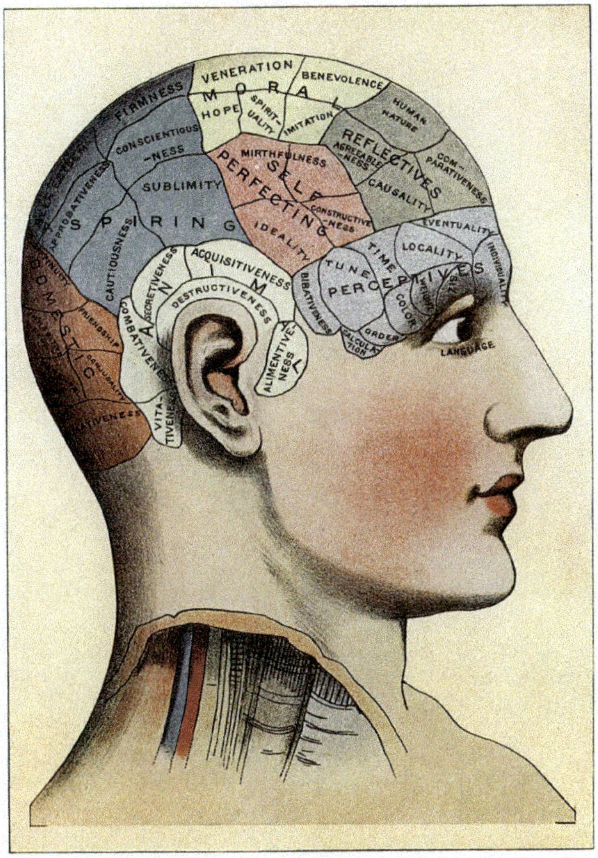

Are theories linking parts of the brain with differences in personality as simplistic and outdated as phrenology?

In the last decade or so, researchers came to realize that the various parts and systems of the brain, especially in humans, work in concert to impact behavior (Knight, 2007). Especially when it comes to understanding something as complicated as personality, we need to look at how systems within the brain work together (Uttal, 2001). Today, diffusion tensor imaging (DTI), a special type of fMRI that traces the diffusion of water in cells, is giving even more detailed pictures of the brain. But more importantly, DTI can highlight connections between cortical and subcortical regions (Cowey, 2001). DTI moves beyond localization and has the potential to enable researchers to study systems and functions as a whole rather than piecemeal.

What might this new technology reveal? For one, we may be able to locate and study Gray's hypothetical BAS, BIS, and FFFS. For example, Whittle, Allen, Lubman, and Yücel (2006) suggested that the prefrontal cortex and limbic structures (including the amygdala) are associated with the three temperaments we have been discussing in this chapter: Extraversion, Neuroticism, and Impulsivity. Their model (see Figure 7.6) is based on neural circuitry that past research has suggested may be related to personality and psychopathology. Direct evidence for their model comes from imaging studies using fMRI, DTI, and even newer and more powerful technology still being

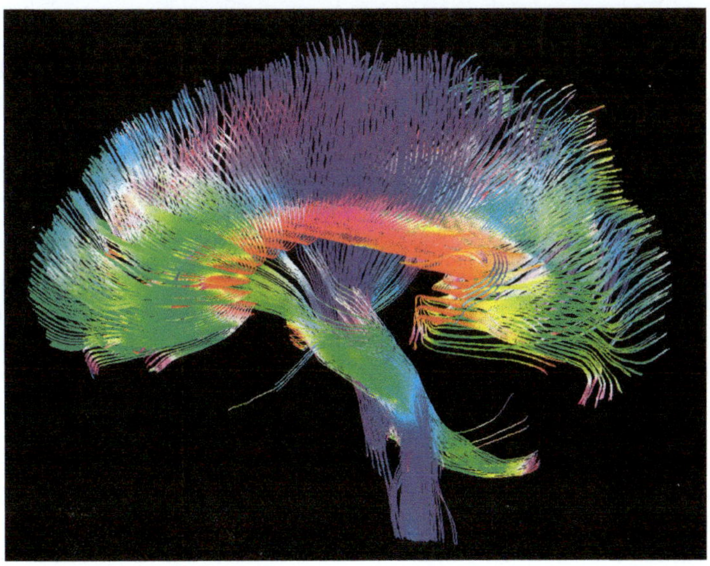

Visualization of a DTI measurement of a human brain. Coloured 3-dimensional magnetic resonance imaging (MRI) scan of the white matter pathways of the brain, side view. White matter is composed of myelin-coated nerve cell fibres that carry information between nerve cells in the cerebrum of the brain (top half of image) and the brain stem (bottom centre). This image was created by an MRI scanner sensitised to the movement of water around the brain. Blue represents neural pathways from the top to the bottom of the brain, green represents pathways from the front (left) to the back (right), and red shows pathways between the right and left hemispheres of the brain.

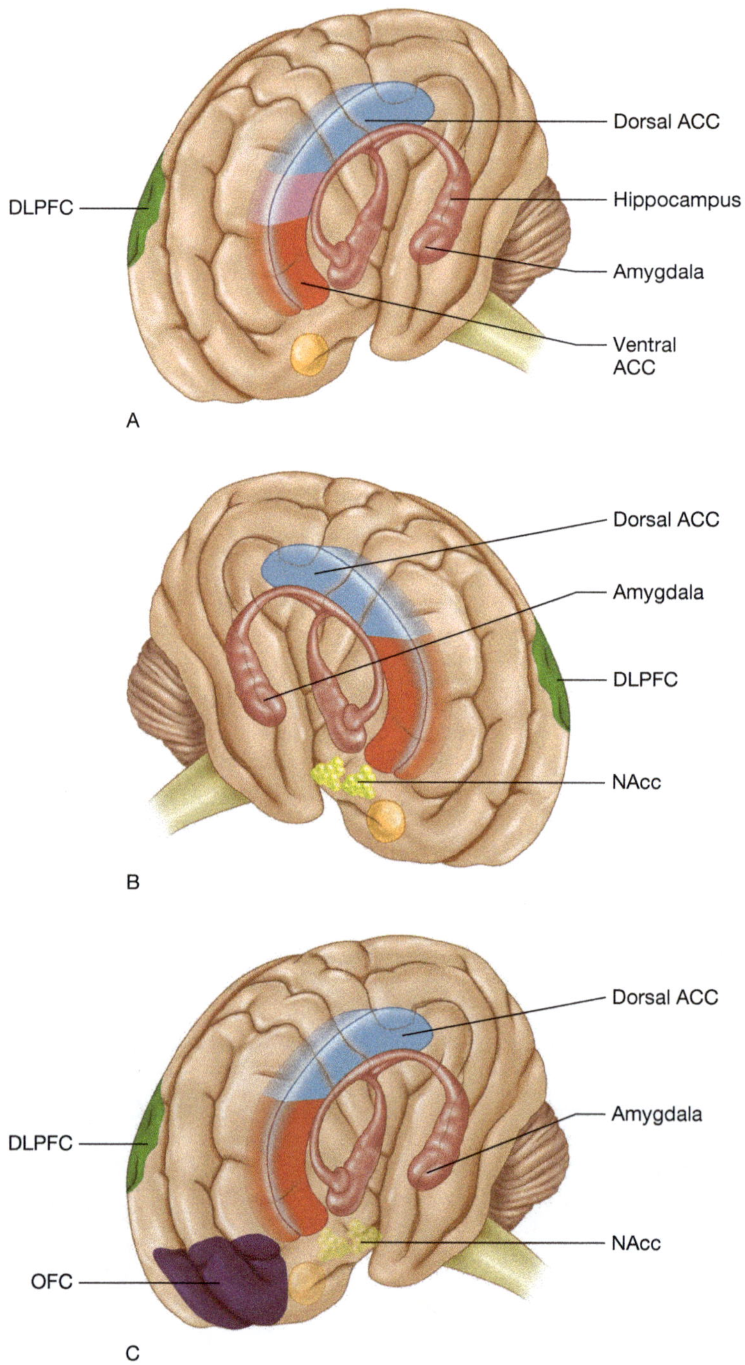

Figure 7.6 Structures proposed to comprise the neural circuits underlying the three temperaments: (a) Neuroticism (negative affect) (b) Extraversion (positive affect) and (3) low Impulsivity (high constraint). *Note:* NAcc = nucleus accumbens; OFC= orbitofrontal cortex; ACC = anterior cingulate cortex; DLPFC = dorsolateral prefrontal cortex. Solid colors indicate structures, shaded colors indicate resting state activity, red indicates positive correlation (more activity), blue indicates negative correlation (less activity). *Source:* From Whittle et al. (2006, Figure 1, p. 520). Whittle, S., Allen, N. B., Lubman, D. I., & Yücel, M. (2006), "The neurobiological basis of temperament: Towards a better understanding of psychopathology," Neuroscience and the Biobehavioral Reviews, 30, 511–525. Permission conveyed through the Copyright Clearance Center.

developed. Whittle et al. (2006) proposed to use these techniques to study the neural networks of young people who may be at risk for depression, anxiety disorders, or delinquency based on their temperament. By studying preteens whose brains are still growing and forming connections even as they are developing their own unique personalities, Whittle et al. (2006) hoped to relate changes in neural networks with behavior and psychopathology over time (Whittle et al., 2008).

Researchers in the Digital Media program at Drexel University have used Combe's observation of the change in cerebral blood flow caused by mental activity to design video games in which the gamer controls the character's actions *just by thinking!* There is no remote, joy stick, mouse, or other control in this game. Instead, infrared sensors, placed on a specially designed headband worn by the player, measure changes in blood oxygen levels in the frontal cortex.

Blood flow, as Combe discovered, increases with concentration. The computer monitors these fluctuations and allows the gamer to interact in a virtual world (CBS3 News, 2008). In a joint endeavor between video game designers and medical scientists, the research team has designed a game that is fun, engaging, and that studies brain function at the same time (*Drexel University Replay Lab,* 2009). Researchers hope that the game and associated technology can one day be used to help people with ADHD focus better or to enable people with severe disabilities to communicate through their computer (CBS3 News, 2008).

Neurological Correlates of Personality

If RST and Eysenck's PEN theory are beginning to blur in your mind, take heart: there's a good reason for that. Both theories make predictions for the three personality clusters, or temperaments, we identified earlier: Extraversion, Neuroticism, and Impulsivity.

A consistent finding is that a key difference between Extraversion and Neuroticism is in how emotions are experienced. Both extraverts and people high in Neuroticism have more positive emotions and negative emotions, respectively, and they also react more strongly to their positive or negative emotions than do introverts or emotionally stable people (Gross, Sutton, & Ketelaar, 1998; Larsen & Ketelaar, 1989, 1991). That is, extraverts experience more positive emotions and react to them more strongly than introverts, whereas people high in Neuroticism experience more negative emotions and react to them more strongly compared to people low in Neuroticism. In addition, extraverts experience more positive emotions but less negative emotions than people high in Neuroticism. Indeed, much of the day-to-day anxiety and moodiness experienced by people high in Neuroticism is due to their reactivity compared to people low in Neuroticism (Bolger & Schilling, 1991).

"When we deal with brain science, we are dealing with the organ that makes us unique individuals, that gives us our personality, memories, emotions, dreams, creative abilities, and at times our sinister selves."

Ruth Fischbach and Gerald Fischbach as cited in Ackerman (2006)

Keep in mind that positive emotions (a marker of Extraversion) and negative emotions (a marker of Neuroticism) are not opposites but rather two separate dimensions (Diener & Emmons, 1984). That is, people can have a lot of both kinds of emotions or a little of both. Being high in one does not imply being low in the other. Indeed, the lack of positive emotion is not negative emotion, but a state called **anhedonia**, which is the loss of or inability to experience pleasure that may or may not be accompanied by the presence of negative emotions. In fact, extraverts report experiencing more happiness, positive emotions, and life satisfaction than introverts, whereas people who are high in Neuroticism experience more negative emotions, unhappiness, and dissatisfaction with life compared to more emotionally stable individuals (Costa & McCrae, 1980).

THINK ABOUT IT

How would impulsive behavior such as gambling relate to BAS and BIS functioning?

Impulsivity, the third temperament, involves a lack of constraint or a state of being undercontrolled (Clark & Watson, 2008). Although this sounds very similar to Eysenck's third factor of Psychoticism, they are not the same. Eysenck maintained that his concept of psychoticism was a "more general higher-order concept" involving antisocial aspects of behavior than just impulsivity (Eysenck, 1990, p. 269). Impulsivity is related to a broader cluster of characteristics including sensation seeking, novelty seeking, or venturesomeness (Pickering & Gray, 1999).

The early work on RST proposed that Impulsivity was controlled by BAS. With the revised RST, there is consensus among researchers that BAS sensitivity is related to Extraversion (i.e., surgency: seeking incentives in the world) where impulsivity is

People high in extraversion show increased activity in parts of the brain to positive photos like these compared to when they viewed negative pictures.

caused by the failure of BIS to inhibit behavior, especially around novel or exciting stimuli (Smillie et al., 2006). As a result, there may be two very different motivations behind a seemingly impulsive behavior such as excessive alcohol use. People may drink frequently or excessively as a means of gaining a reward (strong BAS) or because they are incapable of inhibiting a response (weak BIS; Pardo, Aguilar, Molinuevo, & Torrubia, 2007).

At some level, all of these terms are related and define a temperament of a person who seeks novelty and excitement and who sometimes acts without thinking about the consequences. There are similar physiological processes involved in Extraversion and Neuroticism, but Impulsivity seems to have a very different underlying physiology. Let us take a closer look at the neurological correlates behind Extraversion, Neuroticism, and Impulsivity.

Extraversion and Neuroticism

Because people who are high in Extraversion or high in Neuroticism differ in their experience of emotions, it should come as no surprise that they also differ in the neurological structures and systems that are involved in the experience and regulation of emotion. We experience emotions as a result of complex systems that coordinate form and function across brain structures, brain activity, and biochemical processes. These differences in sensitivity to positive or negative emotion, although not reflected in heightened bodily responses, are reflected in differences in brain structures that control emotion, brain activity in response to emotional stimuli, and biochemical activity that regulates emotions. We'll review some of this evidence, focusing on this general picture of personality differences more so than the neuroscience of emotional regulation.

Brain Structure Differences in the Cortex and the Amygdala. Two main areas of the brain show differences in size depending on personality differences in Extraversion and Neuroticism: the cortex and the amygdala.

The Cortex. One area that is important for the experience of emotion is the prefrontal cortex; and introverts and extraverts show differences in the size of their cortexes. In one study, the brains of normal, healthy volunteers were scanned using MRI while at rest (Wright et al., 2006). Introversion was correlated with thickness of three sections of the right, but not the left, cortex. That is, introverts appeared to have more gray matter in these right hemisphere areas than extraverts (see Figures 7.7 and 7.8; Wright et al., 2006).

Wright et al. (2006) suggested that the relative thinning of these areas may be a neurological symptom of the lessened social inhibition found in extraverts. However, they also cautioned that smaller size doesn't necessarily indicate diminished function. We know that one way the nervous system works is to start out with a lot of neurons and connections that gradually get abandoned or cut back as connections become more refined. It's possible that neurons in these areas may have been pruned back during development, leading to greater efficiency in the system rather than reduced function.

In contrast, Neuroticism scores were negatively correlated with parts of the left, but not the right, cortex (Wright et al., 2006). That is, people high in Neuroticism had less gray matter in these left hemisphere areas compared to people low in Neuroticism (see Figure 7.9). This effect

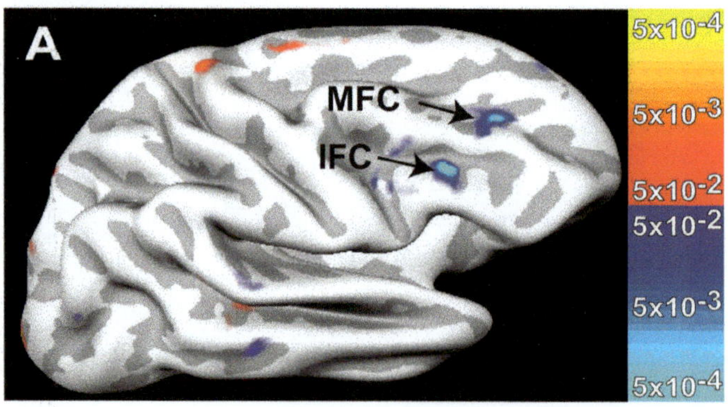

Figure 7.7 Significant correlations of cortical thickness and Extraversion in the lateral prefrontal cortex. The areas highlighted in red-yellow are thicker in extroverts. The areas highlighted in blue-green are thicker in introverts. *Source:* From Wright et al. (2006, Figure 1, p. 1812).

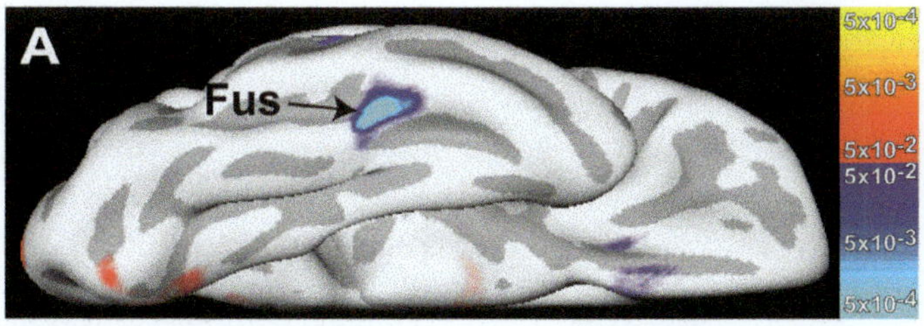

Figure 7.8 Significant correlations of cortical thickness and Extraversion in the right fusiform cortex. The areas highlighted in red-yellow are thicker in extroverts. The areas highlighted in blue-green are thicker in introverts. *Source:* From Wright et al. (2006, Figure 2, p. 1813).

was stronger in males than in females. These results confirm an earlier study that found that people high in Neuroticism, especially in anxiety and self-consciousness, had lower brain volume and that brain volume was not related to Extraversion nor to other traits (Knutson, Momenan, Rawlings, Fong, & Hommer, 2001).

The Amygdala. Extraversion and Neuroticism are also related to structural differences in the amygdala. Extraverts had a higher concentration of gray matter in the left amygdala as measured by MRI than introverts, and people high in Neuroticism had a lower concentration of gray matter in the right amygdala than people scoring low in Neuroticism (Omura, Constable, & Canli, 2005). Other studies have found that depressed people also have less gray matter in the amygdala. Because of its association with Neuroticism, Omura et al. (2005) stated that this reduction in the mass of the amygdala is not a result of depression, but instead, occurs before the depression hits.

Brain Activity Differences in the Cortex, Left–Right Asymmetry, and the Amygdala. In addition to differences in brain structures, there are differences in how the brains of people high in Extraversion or high in Neuroticism function. These are reflected in brain activity differences in the cortex, including left–right asymmetry, and in the amygdala.

The Cortex. Extraversion and Neuroticism are each correlated with activity in the temporal and frontal parts of the cortex, areas that control consciousness (frontal) and emotions (both temporal and frontal), but in different ways: Extraversion is correlated with activity for positive emotions and Neuroticism is correlated with activity for negative emotions (Canli et al., 2001).

THINK ABOUT IT

Why would individual differences in positive but not negative emotions evolve?

To illustrate, consider the following experiment. Women participants saw 20 positive and 20 negative pictures while their brains were being scanned using fMRI (Canli et al., 2001). The positive pictures included a happy couple, sunsets, and pictures of appetizing foods such as ice

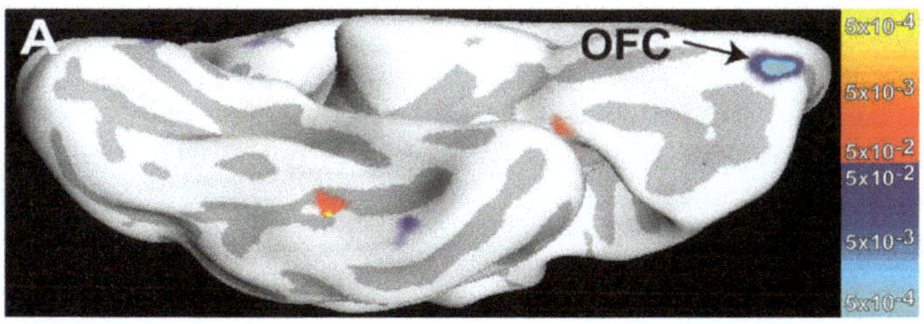

Figure 7.9 Significant correlations of cortical thickness and Neuroticism in the orbitofrontal cortex. The areas highlighted in red-yellow are thicker in people who are high in Neuroticism. The areas highlighted in blue-green are thicker in people low in Neuroticism. *Source:* From Wright et al. (2006, Figure 3, p. 1814).

People high in Neuroticism show increased activity in parts of the brain to negative photos like these compared to when they viewed positive pictures.

cream and brownies. The negative pictures included images of people crying, spiders, and a cemetery. While looking at the positive pictures, extraverts showed more activity in the temporal and frontal parts of the cortex compared to when they saw the negative pictures. However, people high in Neuroticism showed greater activity in the temporal and frontal parts of the cortex when looking at negative pictures than when looking at positive pictures. Further, one study identified an amazing 15 different cortical and subcortical regions of the brain where extraverts responded with greater brain activation to positive stimuli compared to negative stimuli (Canli et al., 2001).

Left–Right Asymmetry. Although the two hemispheres of the brain are specialized for different processes (e.g., linguistic processes in the left hemisphere among right-handers), there are individual differences in how the cortex of the brain reacts to specific emotional stimuli as shown by EEG brain wave response or fMRI. Specifically, the right frontal and prefrontal cortexes are more active than the left during negative emotions, whereas the left portion of these regions are more active than the right portion during positive emotions (Davidson, 1992, 2004). But more importantly, people differ in how large these relative differences are in responding to positive and negative emotions. Further, these differences are present as early as the first year of life. We call these differences **left–right asymmetries.**

Some people show more left asymmetry: their left cortex responds to positive emotion more than their right cortex responds to negative emotion. Other people show more right asymmetry: their right cortex responds to negative emotions more than their left cortex responds to positive emotion. People with greater left asymmetry report more positive emotion to film clips than people with right asymmetry; people with greater right asymmetry report more negative emotion to film clips than people with left asymmetry (Davidson, 1992).

THINK ABOUT IT

If meditation changes left–right asymmetry and if left–right asymmetry shows consistent differences among people, does meditation change personality?

What kind of people are likely to show left or right asymmetry? Shy, inhibited children and depressed adults show greater right asymmetry, as do people who are high in Neuroticism, both at rest and in response to emotional stimuli (Davidson, 1992). People who experience positive emotion, like those high in extraversion, show greater left asymmetry both at rest and in response to positive emotion (Tomarken, Davidson, Wheeler, & Doss, 1992).

Do you recall the meditation study that opened this chapter? One of the results was that people in the meditation condition showed greater left brain asymmetry both at rest and in response to positive and negative emotional events (Davidson et al., 2003). Psychologist Richard Davidson actually conducted an fMRI of a Tibetan monk with over 10,000 hours of training in meditation (Savory, 2004). This monk turned out to have the most extreme left asymmetry that Davidson had ever seen! We can see now that meditation reduces reactions in the right brain to stress and increases reactions in the left brain to positive emotions. The net result is that little stressors don't bother people as much and they get more joy out of the small pleasures in life.

Of course we must be cautious, as these results may hold for only the kind of people who seek out and voluntarily invest the time and energy to learn and practice meditation. We can't be sure if there is something special about these people, compared to people who are uninterested in meditation, or if it is the meditation per se that causes these changes. It is possible that yoga, spirituality, or any form of relaxation can lead to similar results.

Richard J. Davidson meeting the Dalai Lama, the supreme leader of Tibetan Buddhism. The Dalai Lama visited Davidson's lab at the University of Wisconsin–Madison in May 2001 to discuss ways science could study meditation to promote human happiness.

The Amygdala. Extraversion is also related to activity in the amygdala, a brain region involved in the processing and memory of emotions (Canli, Sievers, Whitfield, Gotlib, & Gabrieli, 2002). While viewing happy faces, extraverts showed more activity in the amygdala than did introverts (see Figure 7.10). Other research confirms these results (see Gross, 2008, for a review).

However, there was no relationship between Extraversion and amygdala response to negative faces nor was there any relationship between amygdala activation and Neuroticism in response to any of the other emotional faces used (e.g., angry, fearful, happy, sad, or neutral). The researchers believed that response to threatening faces—at least at this gut emotional level—is an important survival mechanism and so is unrelated to individual differences in personality (Canli et al., 2002).

Biochemical Activity. Given that Extraversion and Neuroticism are associated with differences in brain structure and brain activity, it follows that there are biochemical differences as well. For Extraversion, these differences involve the dopamine system, whereas for people high in Neuroticism, serotonin seems to be key.

Dopamine and Extraversion. You know how introverts have greater sensitivity to sensory stimulation—that is, arousability—than extraverts? It turns out that introverts are also more sensitive to fluctuations in the neurotransmitter dopamine in the brain as a result of sensory

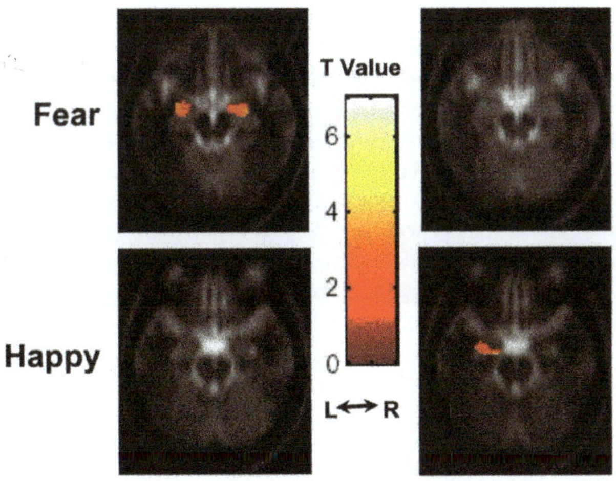

Figure 7.10 Response of the amygdala to emotional faces. The left fMRI images show significant activation to fearful (top) but not happy faces (bottom) across all participants. The right images show areas where greater activation to emotional images was significantly correlated with higher scores in Extraversion for happy (bottom) but not for fearful faces (top). Redder areas show greater activation. *Source:* From Canli et al. (2002, Figure 1, p. 2191).

input. This may explain their preference for quiet and solitude (Stelmack & Rammsayer, 2008). However, extraverts have greater dopamine activity than introverts in general. This may be due to either more extensive dopamine pathways in the brains of extraverts or a greater responsiveness to dopamine in general (Depue & Collins, 1999; Depue et al., 1994). This makes sense because the dopamine system connects with the amygdala, which is more responsive in extraverts, as we just saw (Gross, 2008; Knutson & Bhanji, 2006).

Serotonin and Neuroticism. For people high in Neuroticism, the neurotransmitter serotonin and the serotonin receptors in the brain may be more important than dopamine and the dopamine system. Serotonin and parts of the brain sensitive to serotonin such as the cortex and amygdala but also the hippocampus, septum, and hypothalamus are involved with mood regulation, depression, and anxiety disorders (Canli, 2006). Therefore it's likely for these to be related to Neuroticism as well.

There is evidence that extreme levels of anxiety and depression, as found in clinical depression, posttraumatic stress disorder, chronic anxiety, and other kinds of pathology, may be related to low serotonin levels (Stelmack & Rammsayer, 2008; Zuckerman, 2005). Given that anxiety and depression are aspects of Neuroticism, this suggests that serotonin may also be related to individual differences in Neuroticism.

SEE FOR YOURSELF

Do you learn better through rewards or punishments? Is this related to how extraverted or neurotic you are?

We know from the previous chapter on genetics that Neuroticism has a strong genetic component. People high in Neuroticism are more likely than emotionally stable people to have the short allele of a serotonin transporter that people low in Neuroticism lack (Lesch et al., 1996). People with this variation of the gene have less serotonin in their system and are therefore at increased risk for mood and anxiety disorders (Canli & Lesch, 2007; Lesch, 2007).

Recall that Neuroticism is associated with increased neural activity, as measured by fMRI, in the amygdala especially during negative emotions such as fear (Hooker, Verosky, Miyakawa, Knight, & D'Esposito, 2008). Additional research finds that people with a genetic variation in a serotonin transporter, which causes lower levels of serotonin in the system, showed greater amygdala reactivity to fearful faces, especially for people who were higher in BIS threat sensitivity (Cools et al., 2005). These studies suggest that people high in Neuroticism may have stronger and longer-lasting learned associations, especially to punishment (Hooker et al., 2008). This would account for the earlier findings from reinforcement sensitivity theory that extroverts are more sensitive to reward whereas people high in Neuroticism are more sensitive to punishment.

"To me, one of the deepest motivations in the human spirit is to lead an interesting, exciting and thrilling life. It's not for everybody, but I think it's a powerful force."
Frank Farley as cited in Munsey (2009, p. 40)

Impulsivity and Sensation Seeking

Sensation seeking is the "seeking of varied novel, complex, and intense sensations and experiences, and the willingness to take physical, social, legal, and financial risks for the sake of such experiences" (Zuckerman, 1994, p. 27). Sensation seekers are not so much into the danger of such behaviors—like risking all their money on a big bet; they are more into the fun part—like spending an entire evening at a casino.

Marvin Zuckerman first identified this personality trait while he was engaged in sensory-deprivation and social isolation research in the 1960s (e.g., Zuckerman, Persky, Link, & Basu, 1968). He and his colleagues found that many of their volunteers—people who were willing to go into physical isolation, alone in a dark, sound-proofed room, with heavy gloves covering their hands—were high in sensation seeking. Paradoxically, these high sensation seeking volunteers sought sensory deprivation in the hopes of having unusual sensory experiences like hallucinations as a result of the extreme deprivation in the experiments (Zuckerman, 2008). Low sensation seekers found such experiments particularly anxiety-provoking (Zuckerman et al., 1968). This led Zuckerman and his colleagues to realize that sensation seeking involved a desire for novel mental, internal sensations as well as exciting activities (Zuckerman, 2008). Sensation seekers were more likely to volunteer for studies involving unusual experiences such as hypnosis, ESP, meditation, encounter groups, or viewing pornography, but nor for more run-of-the-mill experiments in learning or social psychology (Zuckerman, 2008).

Sensation seeking is typically measured by the Sensation Seeking Scale which is divided into four subscales, each measuring a different aspect of sensation seeking (Zuckerman, 1971). **Experience seeking** measures the desire for moderate arousal through different kinds of experiences involving both the mind and the senses, perhaps through music, travel, or an unconventional lifestyle (Zuckerman, 1971, 2008). It is very similar to the concept of Openness from the five-factor model (McCrae & Costa, 1997a). **Boredom susceptibility** taps the need for change and variety and an aversion to routine and sameness (Zuckerman, 1971). **Thrill and adventure seeking** measures arousal seeking through physical sensations produced by speed, height, falling, danger, and unique experiences such as exploring an underwater world by scuba-diving (Zuckerman, 1971, 2008). Many extreme sports athletes are no doubt high in thrill and adventure seeking! **Disinhibition** is the extent to which people have lowered social inhibitions and enjoy letting loose in the company of others, without a thought about decorum, proper behavior, or social norms. Disinhibition often takes the form of alcohol use, partying, and sex (Zuckerman, 2008). Table 7.6 contains sample items of the Brief Sensation Seeking Scale (Hoyle, Stephenson, Palmgreen, Lorch, & Donohew, 2002) so you can see for yourself what these four dimensions look like.

Sensation seeking shows a consistent gender difference and an age difference, with men scoring higher than women and young people scoring higher than older people, on average (Zuckerman & Neeb, 1980). Sensation seeking peaks in the late teens and early 20s.

High sensation seekers differ from low sensation seekers in some interesting ways. High sensation seekers are more likely to be younger at the age of first intercourse, and to have more sexual partners, more varied sexual experiences, and risky sex, defined as sex with strangers or under the influence of alcohol or other drugs (Hoyle, Fejfar, & Miller, 2000; Zuckerman, 2007).

"Bones heal, chicks dig scars, pain is temporary, glory is forever."

Evel Knievel, American daredevil and entertainer

High sensation seekers are also more likely to smoke cigarettes than low sensation seekers, a finding that has remained consistent over some 30-plus years of research and across many countries including Switzerland, Norway, the Netherlands, Israel, and the United States (Zuckerman, 2008). Sensation seeking also correlates with drug and alcohol use including stimulants such as cocaine, amphetamine, marijuana and LSD, and depressants such as heroin (Zuckerman, 1979). Among people who use drugs, high sensation seeking is associated with the range of different kinds of drugs used, more so than with any one drug (Kaestner, Rosen, & Apel, 1977).

From the discussion so far, you might think that "sex, drugs, and rock 'n' roll" somehow go together. Well, at least when it comes to the tastes of the high sensation seeker, they do! These are new and, to some extent depending on the generation, unusual and antisocial experiences. High sensation seekers prefer rock, heavy metal, and punk music over movie soundtracks and religious music (Litle & Zuckerman, 1986). They also enjoy alternative, rap, and electronic dance music more so than people low in sensation seeking (McNamara & Ballard, 1999).

SEE FOR YOURSELF

How much of a sensation seeker are you? Why do you say this?

Table 7.6 The Brief Sensation Seeking Scale

Experience Seeking

1. I would like to explore strange places.
5. I would like to take off on a trip with no preplanned routes or timetables.

Boredom Susceptibility

2. I get restless when I spend too much time at home.
6. I prefer friends who are excitingly unpredictable.

Thrill and Adventure Seeking

3. I like to do frightening things.
7. I would like to try bungee jumping.

Disinhibition

4. I like wild parties.
8. I would love to have new and exciting experiences, even if they are illegal.

Note: To what extent do you agree or disagree? Answer using a 5-point scale from *Strongly disagree (1), Disagree (2), Neither disagree nor agree (3), Agree (4),* and *Strongly agree (5).* In a sample of 8th to 11th graders, females averaged 3.68 and males 3.54.

Source: Adapted from Hoyle et al. (2002, p. 405). Reprinted with permission from Hoyle, R. H., Stephenson, M. T., Palmgreen, P., Lorch, E. P., & Donohew, R. L. (2002), "Reliability and validity of a brief measure of sensation reliability and validity of a brief measure of sensation seeking," Personality and Individual Differences, 32, pg. 401–414. Permission conveyed through the Copyright Clearance Center.

Ice climbing is an example of an extreme sport that involves inherent danger.

High and low sensation seekers also differ in the kinds of careers they enjoy. Whereas sensation seekers are not drawn more to the military or to law enforcement than low sensation seekers, they are more likely to volunteer for riskier assignments in both careers (Zuckerman, 2008). Speeders and reckless drivers—and the officers who engage in high-speed criminal chases—are more likely to be high sensation seekers (Zuckerman, 2008). People who deal with risk on a daily basis such as air traffic controllers and rape counselors, or physicians, nurses, psychologists, and paraprofessionals who voluntarily work in an emergency room are all higher in sensation seeking than people working in more traditional settings (Zuckerman, 2008).

What might it be like to be in a close relationship with a high sensation seeker? It depends: People have greater marital satisfaction when their partners are similar to them on this trait (Schroth, 1991). However, couples are less likely to divorce if both partners are low in sensation seeking (Zuckerman & Neeb, 1980).

It isn't all fun and games for a high sensation seeker. Tragically, sometimes high sensation seekers behave a little too riskily or impulsively for their own good. Casual observations in the past had noted that spinal cord injuries often happen due to poor judgment and impulsivity (Mawson, Jacobs, Winchester, & Biundo, 1988). Might personality (i.e., sensation seeking) be related to type of injury? An interesting study was conducted in which 140 men with spinal cord injuries were matched with control subjects who were of the same age, gender, educational attainment, and lived in the same zip code (Mawson et al., 1988). Through phone interviews, both injured and control participants filled out the Sensation Seeking Scale (Zuckerman, 1971) and answered questions about their lives.

Sure enough, the spinal cord injured participants scored higher than the matched control participants on boredom susceptibility and disinhibition. Even more interesting, when the researchers selected the injured participants who scored in the top and bottom 10% of the Sensation Seeking Scale (i.e., the highest and lowest sensation seekers, respectively) the highest sensation seekers were significantly more likely than the lowest sensation seekers to have an arrest record, be younger at the time of their injury (26.1 vs. 41.5 years of age), and to have been using alcohol or taking drugs at the time of their injury (Mawson et al., 1988).

Recently, Zuckerman has refined the concept of sensation seeking to the more specific impulsive sensation seeking (Zuckerman, 1993a, 2002). Impulsive sensation seeking is very close to Eysenck's concept of Psychoticism. In contrast to high scorers, low scorers show restraint, responsibility, and inhibition (Zuckerman, 2008). Impulsive Sensation seeking is part of an alternative five-factor measure of personality that includes Impulsive Sensation Seeking, Neuroticism-Anxiety, Aggression-Hostility, Sociability, and Activity (Zuckerman, 1993a, 2005).

SEE FOR YOURSELF

When you hear a strange noise or see something unusual, are you more likely to show a startle reflex or an orienting reflex?

Bodily Responses. Why are some people high in sensation seeking and impulsiveness and others not? Zuckerman once thought that high sensation seekers were merely trying to increase their arousal to some optimum level of arousal, much like Eysenck thought extraverts and introverts do (Zuckerman, 1969). However, experimental tests failed to support this idea (Geen, 1997). More recently, evidence suggests that the key difference may be in orienting—or how people react to a novel stimuli—which may involve the reactivity of the nervous system, which is regulated by neurotransmitters (Geen, 1997).

Physiological reactions to novel stimuli, as measured by GSR, heart rate, and cortical activity (e.g., EPs), suggest that what is viewed as a potential threat by the low sensation seeker may be of keen interest to the high sensation seeker. That is, high and low sensation seekers differ in how they react to a novel stimulus. High sensation seekers are more likely to react with a physiological pattern of responses that are more similar to an orientating reflex, indicative of interest and a desire to approach. In contrast, low sensation seekers are more likely to react with a defensive startle reflex, indicative of danger and a readiness for action (Geen, 1997; Zuckerman, 2005, 2008). For example, at the onset of a moderate noise, both high and low sensation seekers react with a spike in heart rate. As the noise continues, high sensation seekers will quickly habituate to the noise and their heart rate will rapidly decrease. In contrast, the heart rate of low sensation seekers will continue to increase, indicating a readiness to fight, flight, or freeze. Eventually, they too will habituate to the noise, but at a rate slower than high sensation seekers (Zuckerman, Simons, & Como, 1988).

Other evidence suggests that high sensation seekers have greater pain tolerance, higher Extraversion, less hypochondriasis, and higher sensory thresholds compared to low sensation seekers (Goldman, Kohn, & Hunt, 1983; Kohn, Hunt, & Hoffman, 1982). This suggests that high sensation seekers are not trying to maintain an optimal level of arousal, but that they are able to handle and even enjoy more intense sensory stimulation (Stelmack & Rammsayer, 2008).

Brain Activity. There are remarkably few studies done looking at brain imaging and sensation seeking. One of these few compared fMRI scans of high and low sensation seekers while they viewed positive and negative emotional images (Joseph, Liu, Jiang, Lynam, & Kelly, 2009). Some of the images were highly arousing, depicting things such as violence, extreme sports, and erotica. Other images, such as pictures of objects, people, or food, were not as arousing. High sensation seekers, compared to low sensation seekers, had stronger reactions in parts of the brain related to arousal and reinforcement while viewing the highly arousing pictures, regardless of whether they were positive or negative (Joseph et al., 2009). In contrast, low sensation seekers showed faster and stronger activation in regions related to emotional regulation and decision making. Overall, high sensation seekers were more reactive to the arousal level of the pictures and were less sensitive to their positive or negative content compared to low sensation seekers.

THINK ABOUT IT

Why were high sensation seekers more sensitive to the arousal than to the content in this study?

Biochemical Activity. Do you recall the important neurotransmitters dopamine, norepinephrine and epinephrine, and how they are all broken down by the enzyme MAO? All of these—dopamine, norepinephrine, epinephrine, MAO—show correlations with sensation seeking and impulsivity (Carver, 2005; Rawlings & Dawe, 2008; Ruchkin, Koposov, af Klinteberg, Oreland, & Grigorenko, 2005; Zuckerman, 1984, 1994, 1995, 2007, 2008). Zuckerman's (2008) latest model suggests that high sensation seeking comes from an interaction of these three systems: dopamine reactivity (which increases exploration of novel stimuli), low serotonin (which fails to inhibit behavior) and low norepinephrine/noradrenaline (which lessens the stress response to novel stimuli and the threat of punishment).

Much evidence suggests that high sensation seekers either have higher levels of dopamine or a more reactive dopamine system than low sensation seekers (Pickering & Gray, 1999; Stelmack & Rammsayer, 2008; Zuckerman, 1993b, 2008). And, indeed, high sensation seekers have lower levels of serotonin than low sensation seekers (Rawlings & Dawe, 2008; Zuckerman, 2007). Because MAO regulates dopamine and norepinephrine we would expect differences in MAO between high and low sensation seekers (Geen, 1997). Some have compared the action of MAO to the braking system of a car: less braking power (e.g., less MAO) means more forward motion (e.g., more dopamine, serotonin, or norepinephrine). Though researchers have hypothesized that high sensation seekers have lower levels of MAO (e.g., Zuckerman, 1995), until recently, the results have been inconsistent (Geen, 1997).

Conclusion: What Have We Learned From the Neuroscience of Personality?

> *Putting together a [physiological approach] to personality is like assembling the pieces of a jigsaw puzzle or fitting words into a crossword puzzle. In the crossword puzzle, horizontal words (relationships between traits and behaviors) require vertical words (between traits and behaviors and underlying biological traits) to confirm them. The puzzle . . . is beginning to form some semblance of a theoretical model, although many pieces are missing and many words are disconnected.*(Zuckerman, 2006, p. 51)

Although Zuckerman wrote these words referring to sensation seeking, this statement could apply to any personality characteristic. We know that about 40% of the variance in a personality trait is due to genetics (Krueger & Johnson, 2008; Turkheimer, 2000) and, as Eysenck suggested, genetics must work through physiology and neurology. There are a few theoretical models, notably Eysenck's PEN model and Gray's RST, that try to account for personality in terms of genetics and neurological differences. But even this equation leaves us with the question of where the other 60% of the variance in personality traits comes from. Generally we say the environment, but really the answer is more complicated, as we know that experiences, including thoughts and behaviors, can affect our physiology. Think about the experiment that opened this chapter showing that meditation caused changes in brain functioning (Davidson et al., 2003).

Ultimately, even if we were to find a "Neuroticism" area of the brain, does this mean that neurology *causes* us to develop a certain personality? Does it mean that a lifetime of acting anxious *causes* our brains to develop a certain way? Maybe having a rough life filled with many unfortunate events makes one neurotic *and* changes our brains. No matter how good our imaging techniques are, we are unable to determine the answer to this fundamental causal question without conducting a true experiment.

What might such an experiment look like? Right now, a standard treatment for patients with severe tremors in their hands or other limbs is to implant a tiny electrode. When switched on, a slight electrical current inhibits the tremor and the person is able to function without shaking. Could you imagine such a device implanted in an area of the brain that is related to Extraversion? Would turning on the electrode make a person want to be with other people? Would turning off the electrode make a person want to sit quietly and read a book?

"As the Dalai Lama himself said in his book *The Art of Happiness*, we have the capacity to change ourselves because of the very nature, of the very structure and function of our brain."
Richard J. Davidson as cited in Savory (2004)

Or, what if we randomly gave some people a drug that artificially lowers their levels of serotonin? Would they become more anxious? It is this *random assignment* to condition or a treatment that is the only way of determining causality. This serotonin study was actually conducted. What did they find? The result depended on the level of the participant's BIS. Participants with high BIS were more sensitive to negative stimuli as measured by BOLD levels in the amygdala (Cools et al., 2005). That is, serotonin level alone is not enough to *cause* a difference in brain functioning. This study highlights two important lessons from this chapter. First, we need to think of personality in terms of brain systems and not just localized areas of the brain. Second, we need to move beyond correlational methods if we hope to figure out how much of our personalities is due to our physiology and neurology.

Chapter Summary

Study and **Review** on **mysearchlab.com**

Go online for more resources to help you review.

How does our neurology and physiology make us who we are? The answer to this chicken-and-egg question is still a bit murky. Let's start with what we do know:

1. The field of neuropersonality studies the relationship between neurology and personality by studying bodily responses, brain structure, brain activity, and biochemical activity related to personality and personality functioning.

2. There appear to be broad, inborn, biological differences among individuals, called temperaments, that develop into personality characteristics over a lifetime of interacting with the social environment.
3. Three broad temperaments or clusters of personality traits are Extraversion, Neuroticism, and Impulsivity (e.g., sensation seeking).
4. These three traits are related to physiological and neurological differences in dopamine and dopaminergic systems, emotion systems, and serotonin and serotonergic systems.
5. Just as phrenology, the science of determining personality from bumps on the head, is outdated, looking for correlates of personality in specific areas of the brain is outdated as well. Neuroscientists now think in terms of brain systems.

We learned how Hans Eysenck's Psychoticism–Extraversion–Neuroticism model and Jeffrey Gray's reinforcement sensitivity theory are models of personality grounded in physiological and neurological differences and refined and revised in light of research evidence. These two theories are good examples of the questions—and answers—pursued by personality psychologists.

We discovered that high sensation seekers are driven toward excitement and novelty. Evidence suggests that they have different reflexes or gut-level reactions to unusual stimuli. Sensation seekers appear to thrive on levels of excitement that would make low sensation seekers' heads spin. This is a personality trait with a strong physiological correlate.

Now for what we don't know. When it comes to neurology and personality, researchers often rely on correlational designs using neuroimaging techniques such as fMRI. These techniques and designs, though imperfect, can tell us which part of the brain is active in which kinds of people on which kinds of tasks. Although it might be tempting to conclude that the brains of extraverts are this way whereas the brains of introverts are that way, we ultimately don't know *why* the brains and physiologies of people differ. The techniques used by neurologists cannot tell us the ultimate answer, of whether our physiology causes us to develop certain personalities or whether certain personalities develop certain neurology or whether certain experiences alter both our brains and our personalities. The answer will have to wait for more sophisticated methods and methodologies.

Review Questions

1. What are the four types of common markers of neurological and physiological differences in personality? What are some examples of each?
2. What is a correlational design? How does it compare to a true experiment? What are scatterplots? Why are some fMRI studies suspect?
3. What is Eysenck's PEN model? What is the main physiological difference between introverts and extraverts?
4. What are the three main systems of Gray's reinforcement sensitivity theory? What kind of people learn better from rewards? What kind of people learn better from punishments?
5. What is phrenology? What is brain localization? In contrast to these methods, what do researchers today focus on? What are some preliminary findings from these cutting-edge methods in personality neuroscience?
6. How do extraverts and people high in Neuroticism respond to emotion? What differences in brain structure, brain activity, and biochemical activity are related to Extraversion and Neuroticism?
7. What is sensation seeking? How do high and low sensation seekers differ from one another? What three systems appear to be related to sensation seeking?

Summer Term

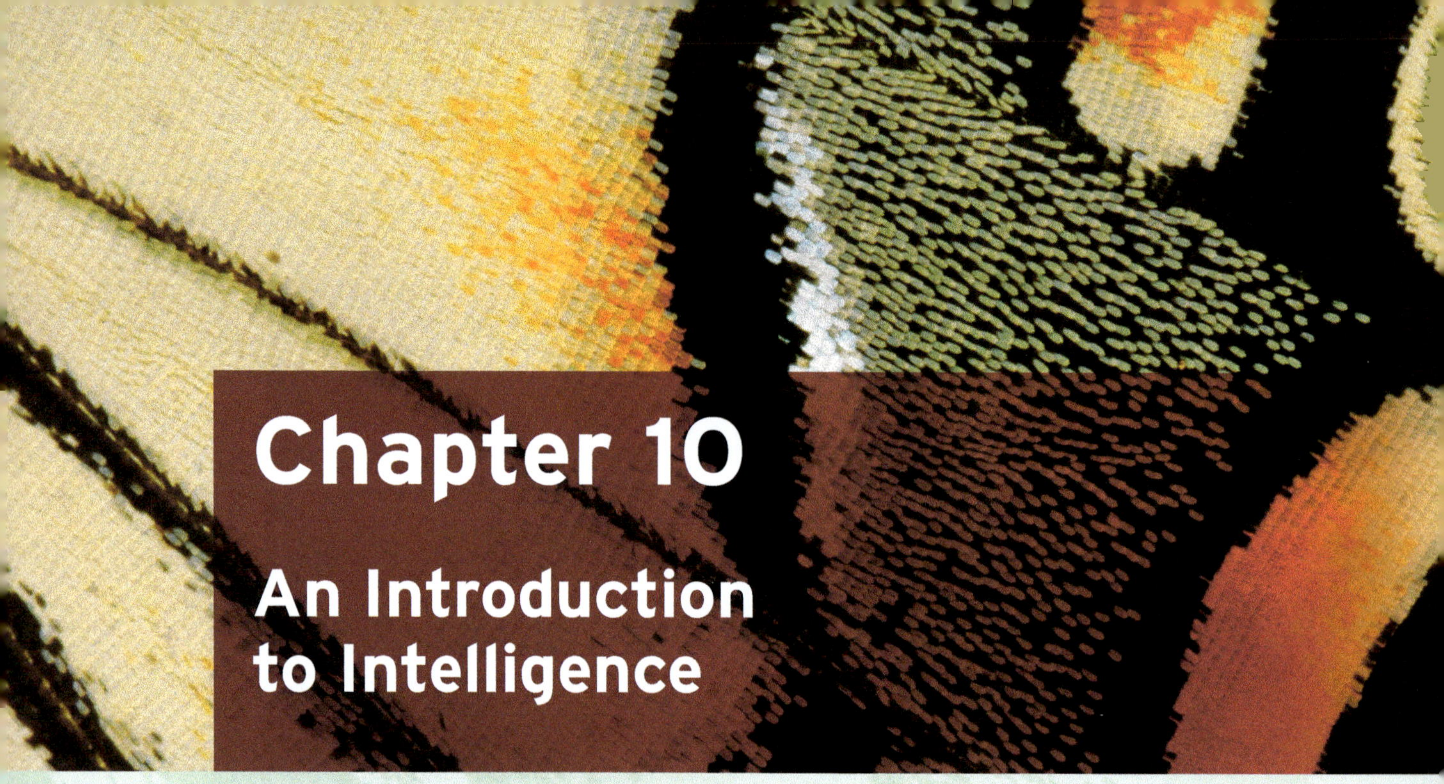

Chapter 10

An Introduction to Intelligence

Key Themes

- Implicit theories of intelligence
- Expert and non-expert (laypersons) theories of intelligence
- Implicit theories of intelligence across the life span
- Implicit theories of intelligence across cultures
- The American Psychological Association Task Force on Intelligence

Learning Outcomes

After studying this chapter you should:

- Be aware of laypersons' implicit theories of intelligence
- Understand how implicit theories of intelligence change across the life span
- Be familiar with how implicit theories of intelligence change across cultures
- Be aware of experts' implicit theories of intelligence

Introduction

Intelligence is part of our society. Each year, over 10,000 people take the Mensa Intelligence Test. Mensa is an organisation for people with high intelligence. Mensa was founded in England in 1946 by Roland Berrill, a barrister, and Dr. Lance Ware, a scientist and lawyer. They had the idea of forming a society for bright people; the only qualification for membership was a high intelligence. The society's sole requirement for entry is that potential members must score within the top 2 per cent in any approved standardised intelligence test. Of the 10,000 people who take the Mensa Intelligence Test each year, around 2,500 pass to become members. Those who become members are now part of a forum for intellectual exchange, via lectures, journals and interest groups. In the summer of 2002, nine million people in the United Kingdom – to find out how intelligent they, and the rest of the country, were – took part in a national intelligence test broadcast via television. This programme is now repeated in the United Kingdom every year. In 2003 a report from researchers in Russia expressed concern that lead poisoning can affect children's intelligence. Scientists at the Ural Regional Centre for Environmental Epidemiology at Ekaterinburg in Russia have found that lead is found naturally in soil and dust, and children who don't wash and who chew their nails are at greater risk of lead poisoning. These Russian scientists have suggested that lead poisoning is a concern because apart from raising health concerns, it can affect children's intelligence.

These are examples. However, in this chapter we will show you how intelligence and conceptions of intelligence matter to humans. We will introduce you to the importance of everyday conceptions of

intelligence and how conceptions of intelligence change over lifetimes, across cultures and around the world. We will also tell you why, in 1996, the American Psychological Association, the most powerful psychological association in the world, decided to gather 11 leading psychological experts in intelligence together to write a defining paper on intelligence. This chapter will provide you with a basic understanding of some of the issues and debates underlying the psychological study of intelligence.

Why does intelligence matter?

Why does intelligence matter? Professor Robert J. Sternberg, who is a Professor of Psychology and Education at Yale University and a world authority on intelligence, suggests that our theories of intelligence are an important aspect of our everyday life. Our ideas of intelligence, and the way in which we perceive and evaluate our own and other people's intelligence, are at the heart of some of our everyday decisions as well as long-term decisions with regard to ourselves, our loved ones and even our children.

If you imagine your education so far, aside from your formal exam results, you and others have offered opinions about your and your friends' intelligence. For example, regardless of your previous examination results, you have some idea about how intelligent you *really* are. Your intelligence might be greater than your exam results suggest, or it might be less. Similarly, your parents have probably at some stage made comments about how intelligent you are. You also have some perception of your friends' intelligences. You will also have evaluated how you compare in terms of your friends' intelligence. You will know which of your friends are most intelligent, and which are less intelligent. You may even find that some of your conversations within the group focus or are orientated around each other's intelligence.

You can see, then, that even at this simple level among friends, intelligence is important. For Sternberg (1985b, 2001a) it is this perception and evaluation of intelligence that drives so many things in society. From birth, parents are concerned with their children's intelligence. Ideas of what intelligence is will drive parents to make decisions about when to correct children if they make an error in their speech. In love, intelligence matters. Most people want their long-term partners to be intelligent, so they can be with someone who will make proper and accurate decisions and act intelligently throughout the partnership (though for some short-term relationships, intelligence might be actively discouraged). In work, perceptions of intelligence are crucial. A candidate perceived as intelligent in a job interview situation will always be more likely to get the job than a candidate who is perceived as unintelligent. Throughout life your intelligence, and that of others, forms a crucial aspect of the decisions you make. It is this recognition, by academics such as Sternberg, of the importance of intelligence to everyone in everyday life that leads us to our first area of study in introducing the topic of intelligence: implicit theories of intelligence.

Implicit theories of intelligence

Implicit theories are people's everyday ideas that surround a particular topic area. Therefore, implicit theories of intelligence are our everyday ideas that surround intelligence. Sternberg (2001a) suggests four reasons that implicit theories of intelligence are important.

First, implicit theories of intelligence are important for the reasons just discussed above: they are important to everyday life. Implicit theories of intelligence drive the way in which people perceive and evaluate their own intelligence and that of others. Subsequently, people use such perceptions and evaluations to draw conclusions about themselves and others and make judgements about everyday life. It is easy to imagine how perceptions and evaluations of intelligence would inform job selection, parenting styles and approaches to friends and partners.

Secondly, implicit theories of intelligence can give rise to more formal theories of intelligence that researchers can investigate. Imagine an academic wants to understand intelligence in a particular area of the world; let us say, for example, Europe. Then one method this academic might consider is to go out into the world and discover what folk, lay, everyday theories exist in Europe. The academic then can condense all these theories into one big descriptive work, which provides a framework for researchers in the field to understand intelligence.

Thirdly, implicit theories are useful because they may provide useful avenues to research when an investigator thinks explicit theories are wrong. Again, let us use our example of the academic who wants to understand intelligence in Europe and has gathered together a number of implicit theories about intelligence. The researcher might then set about testing which implicit theories are supported with evidence and which are not.

Fourthly, and finally, implicit theories of intelligence can inform theories around psychological constructs, such

Profile Robert J. Sternberg

Robert J, Sternberg was born in December 1949 in Newark, and grew up in Maplewood, New Jersey, USA. Sternberg is a leading expert in a number of areas of psychology, but his foremost expertise is in intelligence, where his academic works and research dominate the literature.

There seems to be a huge amount of irony surrounding Sternberg's early academic career and his latest achievements. Sternberg says he first became interested in psychology because as a child he performed badly in an intelligence test and was put back an academic year. It was only later at school, thanks to a teacher who believed he was capable of doing better, that he started doing very well at school. Sternberg went on to study psychology at Yale University. At university, he was initially put off studying psychology because a course lecturer suggested, when Sternberg got a C grade in an Introductory Psychology course, that there was already a famous psychologist of the same name in psychology - and it was obvious from his work that there would not be another famous psychologist called Sternberg. Despite this discouragement, Sternberg eventually graduated with honours with exceptional distinction in psychology. Sternberg studied for his PhD at Stanford University and has since received four honorary doctorates from universities in Spain, France, Belgium and Cyprus.

Professor Sternberg is presently an IBM Professor of Psychology and Education at Yale University. He has had a distinguished career. He has published nearly one thousand academic papers and books and has attracted nearly $7 million in academic research grants. He is highly cited in academic journal and Introductory Psychology textbooks, and during his career he has been the editor of *Contemporary Psychology* and *Psychological Bulletin*. He has received a number of awards from prestigious psychological associations and societies, including an early career award from the American Psychological Association and the Cattell award from the American Psychological Society.

Not content with being a world-leading expert in intelligence, Sternberg has done extensive research work and made significant contributions to the understanding of creativity, wisdom, thinking styles, and love and hate.

as the development of intelligence and cross-cultural aspects of intelligence. For example, researchers may have a good understanding of intelligence in their own country or their own part of the world. However, when it comes to studying other cultures, they may feel less confident. Consequently, collecting information on implicit theories of intelligence in a number of countries might help researchers understand how the perception and evaluation of intelligence changes across cultures.

So what work has been done to explore implicit theories of intelligence?

Research into implicit theories of intelligence

In this section we are going to explore some of the research that has been conducted regarding implicit theories of intelligence. We are also going to show how research into implicit theories of intelligence has shown that changes in implicit theories of intelligence depend on the sample or population examined, and particularly how these changes in implicit theories of intelligence inform cultural and developmental aspects of intelligence.

Laypersons' implicit theories of intelligence

A **layperson** is a non-professional or non-expert in an area. As we shall see, researchers have found it useful to look at laypersons' theories of intelligence. We will give you two examples of studies among US individuals so you can see how such studies are conducted as well as see some of the results. Robert J. Sternberg and three colleagues (Sternberg, Conway, Ketron & Bernstein, 1981) investigated individuals' conceptions of intelligence in a series of experiments. In the first experiment, 61 people studying in a college library, 63 people entering a supermarket, and 62 people waiting for a train in a railway station were asked to list behaviours that were characteristic of 'intelligence', 'academic intelligence', 'everyday intelligence', or 'unintelligence'. Then 122 other people were asked to rate how well each of behaviours listed in the first experiment reflected aspects of intelligence. Using findings from both of these studies, Sternberg and his colleagues found three dimensions of intelligence among this sample:

- **Practical problem solving** – Practical problem solving is the ability to be practical and logical with regard to the problems we all face in various situations and relationships. Specifically, when someone has a problem, they may feel overwhelmed and cannot see a way out. People who are good at practical problem solving show the ability to analyse situations well and engage in a decision-making process that involves reasons. They are able to think around a situation, creating viewpoints and possible solutions to the problem. They are then able to effectively address the problem. For example, a student may have a problem with a particular essay. Good practical problem-solving skills would be to explore the essay topic, perhaps by seeking advice from the lecturer, revisiting the lecture notes, spending some time researching key papers and brainstorming several different answers to the essay question. Evidence of poor practical problem-solving skills here would be to complain about the essay to one's housemates and then head out for a consolatory drink.

- **Verbal ability** – This is the ability to express yourself and converse with others confidently and with some eloquence. Someone with high verbal ability understands the correct meaning for a word, is able to use language confidently, would be able to show comprehension when reading written text, would be able to identify what a missing word in a sentence is and can talk to others in a way that others understand. Verbal ability includes things like the use of antonyms and analogies. An **antonym** is a word that has a meaning opposite to that of another word. So for example, 'unhappy' is an antonym of 'happy'. The ability to use **analogies** is the ability to see similarity between two things that are otherwise dissimilar. So for example, we might ask you to complete the phrase 'Cat is to MEOW as dog is to __________'. If you answered BARK or WOOF, you would be completing the analogy. Your lecturers will often use analogies. When explaining a complicated topic, they might use an everyday example to explain the concept to you. Or (and you understand this is an analogy), you may use an analogy when describing an argument with someone to your friend, 'Sometimes, it's like talking to a brick wall!'
- **Social competence** – This ability refers to the skills necessary to be accepted and fulfilled socially. Someone who has high social competence demonstrates high levels of knowledge, understanding, competency, motivation and confidence in terms of themselves and others. Someone who has a high level of self-awareness, shows good interpersonal skills and a good balance between independence and interdependence (relying on relationships with others) would be socially competent. He or she would have good life skills, be able to cooperate with others and see other people as important, as well as themselves. Someone with good social competence would display personal responsibility and show a positive regard for others. For example, if someone made an accusation, and then found out they were mistaken, a socially competent person would admit their mistake and would apologise to the person involved. A person who is not socially competent would refuse to apologise.

Another classic experiment into layperson's theories of intelligence was carried out by Robert J. Sternberg (Sternberg, 1985b). In a series of experiments (though we will concentrate on just two of the studies here), Sternberg asked a total of 47 adults to think of behaviours that were characteristic of an ideally intelligent person. From this sample Sternberg was able to provide 40 *descriptors* of intelligent behaviours. Sternberg then got 40 Yale college students to sort these descriptors into those that were 'likely to be found together' in a person. From this sorting task Sternberg reported similar findings to his 1981 study, but this time he found six aspects to intelligence:

- **Practical problem-solving ability** – Descriptors in the study that fell within this aspect included 'tends to see attainable goals and accomplish them' and 'is good at distinguishing between correct and incorrect answers'.
- **Verbal ability** – Descriptors included 'can converse on almost any topic' and 'has demonstrated a good vocabulary'.
- **Intellectual balance and integration** – Descriptors included 'has the ability to recognise similarities and differences' and 'makes connections and distinctions between ideas and things'.
- **Goal orientation and attainment** – Descriptors included 'tends to obtain and use information for specific purposes' and 'possesses ability for high achievement'.
- **Contextual intelligence** – Descriptors included 'learns and remembers and gains information from past mistakes or successes' and 'has the ability to understand and interpret his or her environment'.
- **Fluid thought** – Descriptors included 'thinks quickly' and 'has a thorough grasp of mathematics'.

We're not looking for any particular cohesion here in the results across the studies, though there are similarities. We have purposely gone into some detail about each of the aspects, so you can see the sort of language that is used around intelligence constructs in intelligence theory and research. What we will show you next is how implicit theories of intelligence change, particularly when considered (1) across cultures, (2) by experts and (3) across the life span.

Laypersons' implicit theories across cultures

It is clear to intelligence researchers (for example, Sternberg, 2001a: Berry, 1984) that conceptions of intelligence change depending on what area of the world you are in.

In Western cultures researchers suggest there is an emphasis on the speed of mental processing and the ability to gather, assimilate and sort information quickly and efficiently (Sternberg et al., 1981). As we can see in Western cultures, speed is of the essence. Someone who can see answers to problems quickly and then act on them, or who comes up with the solution first, is seen as highly intelligent. Someone who articulates these ideas verbally, clearly, fluently and in a precise manner is also seen as intelligent. Someone who ponders the answers to questions, and perhaps suggests there are many answers and takes time to answer a question, is seen as less intelligent.

However, in studies that have tried to compare Western and non-Western ideas of intelligence, researchers have found similarities and differences relating to this Western idea of an intelligent person.

The main emphasis in these cultural differences in intelligence is on how intelligence is related to the self and the social world. For example, Cypriot psychologists Andreas Demetriou and Timothy Papadpoulous (2004) draw attention to the fact that in Western views of intelligence, good cognitive skills and good memory refer only to the individual; in Eastern cultures, these ideas additionally extend to social, historical and spiritual aspects of everyday interactions, knowledge and problem solving. For example, in non-Western cultures the ability to show skills in problem solving includes not only the individual's own ability to solve the problem but also consideration of their

- family and friends (perhaps through seeking advice);
- knowledge of history (knowing how wise people have approached this problem in the past);
- own spiritual needs (What consequences does the actions around the problem have for the human soul?).

For example, Shih-Ying Yang and Robert Sternberg (1997a) looked at Chinese philosophical (enlightened and wise) ideas of intelligence through two main traditions in China, the Confucian and the Taoist tradition. The Confucian tradition in China comes from the teachings of Confucius (551–479 BC), a Chinese philosopher, whose moral and political teachings included instruction to love others, to honour one's parents and to do what is right instead of what is of advantage. Taoism is China's only indigenous higher religion. The classical roots of Taoism lie in the writings and practices of unknown men and

Source: Workin' Man Films/FilmFour/The Kobal Collection

Fingers on the buzzer: In Western cultures, researchers suggest there is an emphasis on the speed of mental processing.

women who tried to refine and transform themselves to attain full integration with life's deepest realities. In terms of intelligence, Yang and Sternberg suggest that Confucian philosophy emphasises intelligence through benevolence (an inclination to perform kind, charitable acts) and doing the right thing, while the Taoist tradition emphasises humility, freedom from more traditional or conventional dimensions of judgement, the ability to be perceptive and responsive to changes in circumstances and the ability to show full knowledge and understanding, not only of oneself but of the world around oneself.

Similarly, US psychologists Bibhu Baral and J. P. Das looked at Indian culture and examined how perceptions of intelligence in India differ from perception in Western cultures (Baral & Das, 2004). In Indian culture high levels of thinking, judgement and decision making are all important in intelligence. However, it is the way in which these different aspects of intelligence *gel* that is seen as crucial in defining intelligence. This gelling is achieved through a harmony of thought resulting from self-awareness and consciousness. Furthermore, intelligence in India is also thought to show an appreciation of others, politeness, interest in others and modesty.

Specific research examples allow us to examine some of these speculations. Yang and Sternberg (1997b) followed up their analysis of Chinese philosophy. In a methodology similar to that employed in Sternberg's earlier work, Yang and Sternberg looked for descriptors of intelligence among 68 Taiwanese Chinese people (government administrators, French-major college students, preschool teachers, soldiers, factory workers, businesspeople and high school teachers). The researchers then asked 434 individuals (about half were undergraduate students; about half were non-student adults) to rate each of these descriptors based on their importance in showing intelligent behaviour. You will remember that Sternberg's previous research had found practical problem solving, verbal ability and social competence (as well as goals, context and fluidity of thought) to be important. Among Taiwanese Chinese people, five factors of intelligence emerged:

- **A general cognitive factor of intelligence**, which is like the Western idea of practical problem solving and understanding. In this study this included descriptors such as 'makes quick responses', 'has strong learning responses; learns things faster than others' and 'has strong intellectual ability, especially for some abstract disciplines like maths and physics'.
- **Interpersonal intelligence** refers to relating with others harmoniously and efficiently. Descriptors included 'is good at understanding and empathising with others' feelings', 'is kind and compassionate: treats others with politeness, warmth and understanding' and 'knows the appropriate ways to treat others and deal with daily matters'.
- **Intrapersonal intelligence** refers to knowledge about the self and the ability to view oneself objectively. Descriptors included 'knows the meaning and purpose of his/her life and has his/her own philosophy of life', 'has good self-control over the desire to show off: is a high achiever but does not flaunt achievements' and 'accepts different opinions and does not insist on his/her own ideas'.
- **Intellectual self-assertion** refers to a process for individuals who are confident and aware of their intellect and derive self-worth from it. Descriptors included 'puts his/her interests first', 'thinks him/herself very intelligent and is arrogant and proud', 'occasionally draws excessive attention to self' and 'claims others' affection easily and is well-liked'.
- **Intellectual self-effacement** refers to modesty or humility surrounding the person's intellect. Descriptors included 'is lonesome', 'is sensitive', 'likes to think quietly, day-dream, or be lost in thinking' and 'is often quiet in conversation, but talks at length about the topics which interest him/her'.

As we can see from Yang and Sternberg's results, these factors reflect some of the emphasis within the Chinese philosophy of humility, the ability to be perceptive and show full knowledge and understanding of not only oneself but also the world that surrounds the individual.

Other authors looking at implicit theories of intelligence (including historical views) suggest that though constructs such as good thinking skills always appear in Western and non-Western cultures, there are some stark differences between conceptions of intelligence across the world. We have collected a list of findings from studies of implicit theories of intelligence around the world (see Figure 10.1).

As you can see, the map largely supports the view that intelligence in the West is thought to comprise good individual cognitive skills, while in Eastern cultures these ideas extend to social, historical and spiritual aspects of everyday interactions, knowledge and problem solving.

However, one interesting study to note on the map is the study in Korea by US psychologists Woong Lim and Jonathan A. Plucker and Korean psychologist Kyuhyeok Im (Lim, Plucker & Im, 2002). Interestingly, findings in Korea are not very far from Western ideas of intelligence. In their study, which employed a methodology very similar to the methodology used by Sternberg in his studies, Lim et al. found 5 factors among 384 Korean adults:

- **Social competence** – Descriptors in this study included 'befriends people easily', 'is modest and sets an example to others' and 'has a quick wit'.

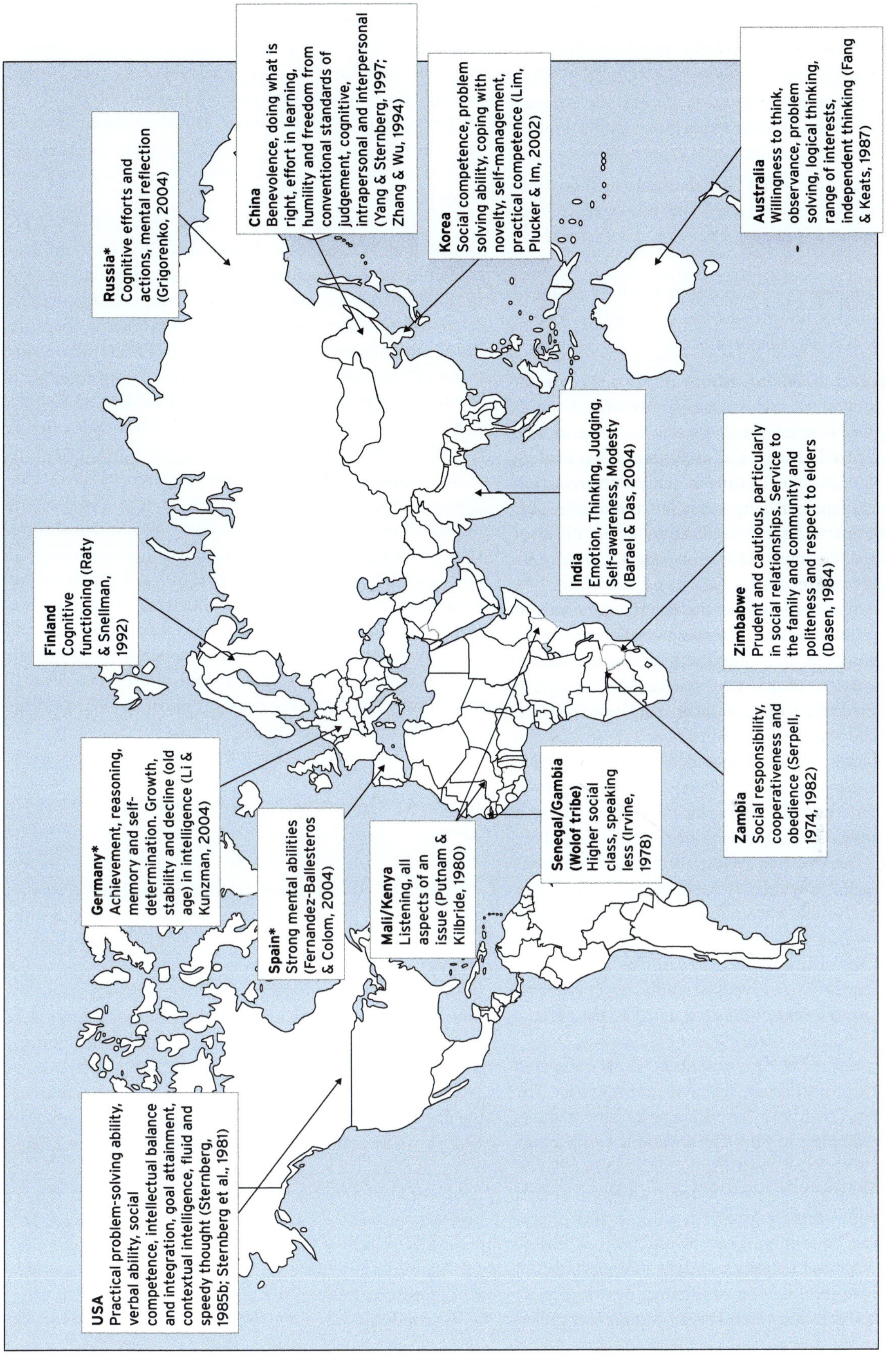

Figure 10.1 Implicit theories of intelligence by countries around the world.

- **Problem-solving ability** – Descriptors included 'has an ability to connect and generalise different academic themes', 'talks logically' and 'comes up with new ideas'.
- **Coping with novelty** – Statements in this study included 'solves puzzles well', 'is good at computer games' and ' is sensitive to new information'.
- **Self-management ability** – Statements in this study included 'thinks before acting', 'controls one's feelings well' and 'keeps his personal life and professional life separate'.
- **Practical competence** – Statements in this study included 'makes a record of things in a systematic way' and 'carries out the plan and is confident about it'.

On the face of it, Korean adults' implicit theories of intelligence look similar to studies of Western samples by including problem solving and social competence and intelligence centred around the individual. This finding might point to similarities in Korean and Western conceptions of intelligence, suggesting that the differences between Western and Eastern cultures are not as different as first thought. However, Lim et al. suggest that there might be a different reason for this. Lim et al. asked their respondents which aspects of intelligence they valued most. They found that Koreans value social competence and responsibility the most, and the other aspects less so. Lim et al. have described how the presence of other aspects may influence implicit theories of intelligence. Western intelligence tests have been used in Korea and other Asian countries and have had the unintended effect of reshaping cultural definitions and introducing different aspects of intelligence. The researchers present no evidence for this finding, but suggest an important aspect for us to consider. That is, in the modern age, Western and Eastern conceptions of intelligence might be converging.

Finally, clearly one way of comparing Western and Eastern conceptions of intelligence is to directly compare implicit theories of intelligence in samples at the same time. Two examples of these types of studies have suggested there is a crossover between Western and Eastern perceptions of intelligence, and there are some differences.

Research conducted by Fang and Keats (1987) compared the conceptions of intelligence in China and Australia. The researchers found that both Australian and Chinese adults believe that willingness to think, observation, a wide range of interests, and independent thinking are indicators of intelligence. However, the two samples differed in that Australian adults thought problem solving and logical reasoning were also important to intelligence, while Chinese adults thought ability to learn, analytical ability, sharp thinking and displaying confidence were indicative of intelligence. Chen and Chen (1988) compared implicit theories of intelligence among students from Chinese-language schools as opposed to English-language schools. Both sets of students found non-verbal reasoning, verbal reasoning, social skills, numeracy and memory to be important descriptors of intelligence. However, students from the Chinese-language schools rated verbal skills as less important than did students from the English-language schools.

The various research studies show cross-cultural similarities and differences in intelligence. It is important to remember that differences between Western and Eastern implicit theories of intelligence do not suggest distinct differences, but rather emphasis in cultures. That is, there are many similarities between Western and Eastern conceptions of intelligence, but the emphasis is different with Western cultures emphasising the individual and Eastern cultures emphasising the individual and how this extends to others, history and spiritual needs. Furthermore, Lim et al.'s research into Korean implicit theories of intelligence, in which they suggest that Western and Eastern conceptions of intelligence might be converging over time, clearly highlights the role that both culture and year of study play in everyday conceptions of intelligence. In our map of the world of implicit theories of intelligence (Figure 10.1), you can see that the studies are spread over 20 years. We must ask what might happen if we compared these countries today – would we find different results? Would we begin to see the convergence of implicit theories of intelligence across cultures?

Implicit theories of intelligence across the life span

We have looked at how perceptions of intelligence change across cultures. But perceptions of intelligence change within cultures. This is particularly true for how perceptions of intelligence change across the life span. The strongest findings in this area have been among children, as we are now living in a time when individuals' perceptions and knowledge of the world change dramatically, and researchers can easily compare implicit theories among different age groups. We will begin by looking at implicit theories of intelligence among children. We will look at the theories in two ways. The first is to consider how people perceive intelligence at different stages of the life span. For example, do people expect intelligent behaviour in a 15-year-old to be the same as intelligent behaviour in a 35-year-old? The second is to look at how individuals at different ages perceive intelligent behaviour. For example, do 15-year-olds report different perceptions of what intelligence is than 35-year-olds do?

Stop and Think

Different concepts of intelligence in different countries

Here is a table of studies or papers that have emphasised different concepts of intelligence in different countries. Rate on a scale of 0 (very uncharacteristic) to 10 (very characteristic) how relevant each dimension of intelligence is to the ideal intelligent person in your country.

Country	Dimension of intelligence	Out of 10
United States (Sternberg, 1985; Sternberg et al., 1981)	Practical problem-solving ability Verbal ability Social competence Intellectual balance and integration Goal attainment Contextual intelligence Fluid and speedy thought	
China (Yang & Sternberg, 1997)	Benevolence (an inclination to perform kind, charitable acts) Wanting to do what is right Spends much effort in learning Humility (the quality or condition of being humble) Freedom from conventional standards of judgement Full knowledge of oneself and external conditions	
Africa (Irvine, 1978; Putnam & Kilbride, 1980)	Higher social class Someone who speaks less Listening, all aspects of an issue	
India (Baral & Das, 2004)	Emotion Thinking Judging Self-awareness Modesty	

Do people perceive intelligence differently for different stages of the life span?
(Do people expect intelligent behaviour in a 15-year-old to be the same as intelligent behaviour in a 35-year-old?)

There is clear evidence that conceptions of intelligence differ for different ages. A clear example of how conceptions of intelligence change is in early child development. US psychologists Robert S. Siegler and D. Richards (1982) compared implicit theories of intelligence among US adults for four different stages of the life span. Siegler and Richard asked respondents to describe ideal intelligent persons at 6 months of age, 2 years of age, 10 years of age and as adults. At 6 months old, the ideal intelligent baby was thought to be able to recognise people and objects, show signs of motor co-ordination, show levels of awareness and make some verbalisation. Intelligence at 2 years was thought to comprise verbal ability, evidence of an ability to learn, awareness of people and the environment, motor co-ordination and curiosity. At 10 years, intelligence is thought to consist of verbal ability, learning, problem solving, reasoning and creativity; while among adults, these familiar concepts of implicit theories of intelligence emerge: problem solving, verbal ability, reasoning, learning and creativity.

Canadian psychologist Prem Fry (Fry, 1984) compared implicit theories of intelligence at three stages of educational development: primary school (5- to 11-year-olds), secondary school (11- to 18-year-olds), and tertiary (college and university) levels (18+-year-olds). In this study, Fry asked teachers to rate the ideal intelligent person. At primary levels, social variables such as popularity, friendliness, respect for rules and order and an interest in the environment were seen as important. At secondary levels, energy and verbal fluency were seen as most important, while at tertiary levels of education (e.g., college and university), logical thinking, broad knowledge, reasoning and the ability to deal maturely and effectively with problems were seen as evidence of intelligence.

Cynthia Berg and Robert Sternberg (1992) examined whether young (30 years), middle-aged (50 years) and older (70 years) adults view the concept of an intelligent person as similar or different during adulthood. In a similar methodology to that used in Sternberg's other studies, where a number of descriptors were generated by one sample and then rated by another sample, 140 adults (aged between 22 and 85 years) were used to characterise both 'average' and 'exceptional' intelligent behaviour of 30-, 50- and 70-year-olds. Average intelligence was defined in all three age groups as interest and ability to deal with novelty, everyday competence and verbal competence. However, when it came to exceptional intelligence, the trait of interest and ability to deal with novelty was emphasised as important for describing the exceptionally intelligent 30-year-old. Everyday competence and verbal competence were emphasised as important for describing exceptionally intelligent 50- and 70-year-olds.

Do individuals perceive intelligent behaviour differently at different ages? *(Do 15-year-olds report different perceptions of what intelligence is than 35-year-olds do?)*

The question of whether individuals at different ages perceive intelligent behaviour differently has been examined in the intelligence literature. Children do hold different concepts about intelligence at different ages. US psychologists Steven R. Yussen and Paul Kane (1985) interviewed 71 high school children of differing ages (11 to 16 years) regarding their beliefs about intelligence. The researchers asked the children about their different views of intelligence (the sort of personal qualities and attributes that accompany intelligent behaviour), the nature of intelligence (i.e., how it comes about with the individual) and how it develops through life.

One of Yuseen and Kane's first findings applied to how children view intelligence. The researchers found that older students categorise intelligence into different aspects – academic intelligence, social intelligence and physical intelligence – whereas younger students do not differentiate between these aspects and generally think of intelligence as one-dimensional. Therefore, among older students, a person can be academically intelligent but not socially intelligent; whilst younger students do not make these distinctions and tend to see people as either intelligent or not. Yussen and Kane, though, found all the students consider knowledge to be central to intelligence; but older students report that academic skills are much more important to intelligence than social skills are. Another important finding from this study was in response to questions about the nature of intelligence. Younger children held a stronger belief that intelligence is the result of nature, that it is inborn (i.e., either individuals are intelligent or not). However, older children believe more strongly in the joint effect of nature and nurture on intelligence.

So why is there this change in young people's perceptions of intelligence? Two Hong Kong researchers, Zi-juan Cheng and Kit-Tai Hau (2003) have suggested there are two reasons for this shift. The first reason for the differences between younger and older students is that older students are thought to have matured cognitively. That is, as children go through school they have a number of cumulative experiences regarding their own intelligence. They may succeed at certain things (e.g., they may pass an examination), and they may fail (they may do badly or struggle in a particular subject). Consequently their experience and understanding of what constitutes intelligence will become more and more complex as they understand that several different factors determine intelligence.

The second reason for the differences between younger and older students is that older students have undergone a process of socialisation. While students have been schooled, they have also been socialised by teachers, friends and family. Teachers, friends and family will influence students' ideas of what intelligence is. Teachers will indicate in class what is expected from an intelligent individual (working hard, showing good problem-solving skills), while friends will emphasise that different elements of intelligence (communication, coming up with ideas) are important to the friendship group. Meanwhile, parents may spend time extending children's education out of school by encouraging them to work harder and expecting their children to demonstrate other aspects of intelligence (respecting one's elders, being interested in out-of-school activities such as sports or social clubs).

To summarise the last two sections, we can see from the various studies that our views of intelligence, and the emphasis we give to certain behaviours as characterising intelligence, change throughout the life span. Evidence suggests this occurs from very young to very old, both in terms of how we perceive intelligence as being different for

Source: Photodisc/Getty Images

Do our perceptions of intelligence differ for different generations?

different stages of the life span, and how at different stages of the life span we perceive intelligence differently.

Expert conceptions of intelligence

So far we have concentrated on research that has used non-experts for its definitions of intelligence. However, what do the experts of intelligence say about what comprises intelligence? Attempts to do this research started in 1921, when the editors of the *Journal of Educational Psychology* convened a special issue of the journal in which prominent psychological theorists of the day were asked to describe what they imagined intelligence to be. These experts included Edward L. Thorndike (a major figure in several fields of psychology: learning theory, applied psychology and mental measurement), Lewis M. Terman (a pioneer in mental measurement) and Louis Leon Thurstone (an intelligence theorist and psychometrician). Their definitions of intelligence were diverse:

- the power of good responses from the viewpoint of truth or facts (E. L. Thorndike);
- the ability to carry on abstract thinking (L. M. Terman);
- the capacity to inhibit an instinctive adjustment, the capacity to redefine the inhibited instinctive adjustment in the light of imaginably experienced trial and error and the capacity to realise the modified instinctive adjustment in overt behaviour to the advantage of the individual as a social animal (L. L. Thurstone).

In all, 14 different opinions were offered. Some of the opinions referred to perceived intelligent behaviours like those just listed; some referred to the measurement of intelligence. Sixty-five years later, in the form of a book entitled *What Is Intelligence?* (1986), Robert Sternberg and Douglas Detterman repeated the 1921 exercise by asking 24 experts (some of whom we will mention in this book) for their definition of intelligence. The researchers received many different definitions, including adaptability to new problems in life, ability in abstract thinking, adjustment to the environment and capacity for knowledge, independence and originality.

Opinion differs in how much these publications told us about the nature of intelligence. Some authors interpret these findings as showing there was no consensus as to the meaning, definition or measurement of intelligence (e.g., Jensen, 1998), with 38 different experts in intelligence emphasising 38 different types of intelligence. However, an analysis by Sternberg (2000) suggests that the two publications (Jensen, 1998; Sternberg & Detterman, 1986) told us two things. First, certain themes and consensus did emerge between experts. Intelligence qualities such as adaptation to the environment, basic mental processes and aspects of higher-order thinking such as reasoning, problem solving and decision making are evident in both listings. Second, these differences between experts emphasise an argument about whether intelligence represents just one thing, or a multitude of different abilities and behaviours.

One study emphasises this last point that intelligence represents a multitude of different abilities and behaviours.

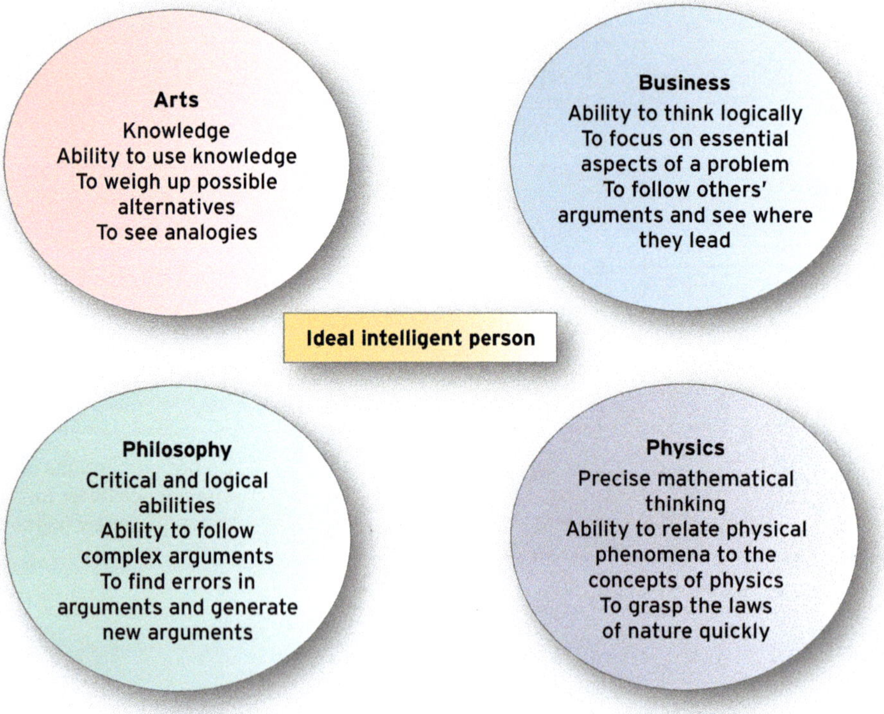

Figure 10.2 Similarities and differences between expert implicit theories of intelligence across academic disciplines.

Source: Sternberg (1985).

Sternberg (1985b), using the same methodology as in his other studies, asked 25 art, 26 business, 20 philosophy and 26 physics professors at US universities to list descriptors of an ideally intelligent person in their respective academic fields. Then, Sternberg asked 200 professors in the academic areas of art, business, philosophy and physics to rate the descriptors obtained from the first study for an ideally intelligent person in their area of study. Perhaps not unexpectedly, Sternberg found that professors from the different disciplines differed in their perceptions of the ideal intelligent person (see Figure 10.2):

- Art professors emphasised knowledge, the ability to use that knowledge to weigh up possible alternatives and the ability to see analogies.
- Business professors emphasised the ability to think logically, to focus on essential aspects of a problem and to follow others' arguments and see where they lead.
- Philosophy professors emphasised critical and logical abilities, the ability to follow complex arguments and the ability to find errors in arguments and generate new arguments.
- Physics professors emphasised precise mathematical thinking, ability to relate physical phenomena to the concepts of physics and the ability to grasp the laws of nature quickly.

These findings suggest that there is diversity among experts on what constitutes intelligence. As in studies of implicit theories of intelligence among general populations, though there is sometimes agreement on some constructs, there can be a huge diversity of conceptions of intelligence.

A task force in intelligence

However, the need for an expert view on intelligence was never more obvious than in 1994 when two US intelligence authors, Richard J. Herrnstein and Charles Murray, published a book called *The Bell Curve: Intelligence and Class Structure in American Life* (1994). The book caused

Stop and Think

Experts and lecturers

1. Nicholas Butler (1862–1947), an American educationalist, said of experts that 'an expert is one who knows more and more about less and less'. It is well accepted in academic circles that the more a person knows, the more they know they don't know. How appropriate are these sayings to attempts made by experts within the last hundred years to define intelligence?
2. Sternberg's research among art, business, philosophy and physics professors suggests there are different conceptions of intelligence across different subjects at university. Think about the Psychology discipline. What characteristics do you think your lecturers would say an ideal intelligent person in psychology has?

huge debate. It reported many things about intelligence, including the extent to which intelligence is genetically inherited. The authors claimed the rise of a 'cognitive elite' – a social group of persons with high intelligence, with an increasingly high chance of succeeding in life. They noted a number of cultural differences in intelligence, but also made some suggestions regarding the intellectual inferiority of certain cultural groups. Such work was perceived by many as difficult for US society because such findings were seen as having implications for social and public policy. For example, if academics presented evidence for one cultural group as intellectually inferior due to their genes, that might affect how government treated that group, particularly in terms of funding educational and social enhancement. An unkind government might withdraw support for that group because they felt no amount of support would help its members because they were just naturally intellectually inferior. Such concerns were raised by this book, with the authors presenting data from US society on a number of aspects of intelligence and readers of the book debating the implications for US society.

We will go into some of the findings of and responses to *The Bell Curve* in Chapter 13. But what is important about this book is that it caused a very public reaction and debate, particularly over its claims regarding intelligence and race. The book received a great deal of positive publicity, including cover stories in *Newsweek* and articles in *Time*, the *New York Times* and the *Wall Street Journal*. However, there was a large amount of negative response, particularly in the scientific community, suggesting the book was oversimplified and contained flawed analysis. This controversy surrounding *The Bell Curve* prompted the American Psychological Association (the largest and most influential psychological society in the world) to establish a special task force to publish an investigative report on the research presented in the book and to include an analysis of what is known and unknown about intelligence.

This task force was headed by Ulric Neisser (see Profile box, page 252) then at Emory University in the United States. After an extended consultative process, Neisser chose a range of academics representing a broad range of expertise and opinion in the literature on intelligence: Gwyneth Boodoo, Thomas J. Bouchard Jr, A. Wade Boykin, Nathan Brody, Stephen J. Ceci, Diane F. Halpern, John C. Loehlin, Robert Perloff, Robert J. Sternberg and Susana Urbina (some of whose work we outline in this book). The task force then set out to discuss a number of issues relating to intelligence and met twice in 1995. Between and after these meetings, sections of a report were circulated and revised and disputes were resolved by discussion. As a result, the task force presented a report that had the unanimous support of its members.

Formally, the task force set out to ask what is known and not known about intelligence and what questions need to be answered in the area of intelligence:

- major theories and concepts of intelligence;
- the role of intelligence tests and their scores;
- the relative importance and role of genes and the environment in determining intelligence.

However, what is also important for you to note is that though the task force was able to agree on a number of knowns about intelligence, it also outlined a number of unknowns about intelligence. The challenges set out by the task force included understanding

- the exact nature of the influence of genetics on intelligence;
- the exact nature of the influence of the environment on intelligence;
- how nutrition (the nourishment from food) affects intelligence;
- why there are differences in scores of intelligence tests between various groups.

Profile Ulric Neisser

Ulric Neisser was born in Kiel, North Germany, in 1928; he went, with his parents, to the United States at the age of 3. He studied at Harvard for both his bachelors' degree and PhD. He switched from physics to psychology and received his bachelors' degree in 1950. He studied behaviourism for his PhD, which he received in 1956. He then taught at Brandeis University, where he had the opportunity to pursue his interest in cognitive psychology. He has also taught at Cornell and Emory universities in the United States.

Neisser is thought to be one of the forefathers of cognitive psychology, and the modern growth of cognitive psychology was thought to be led by the publication of his book, *Cognitive Psychology*, in 1967. His publications are in cognitive psychology, and his main research interests include memory (especially recall of life events) and intelligence (especially IQ tests and their social significance). In his later writings, he became critical of the methodology of much cognitive psychology, faulting it for being 'ecologically invalid'. Neisser emphasized the study of memory in natural surroundings. He argued that laboratory experiments on memory did not reveal how a person's memory worked in everyday life. Gradually, people began trying to develop methods of improving memory in everyday life in these real-world settings. In 1995, Neisser headed an American Psychological Association task force that reviewed controversial issues in the study of intelligence.

He is best known for his books *Cognitive Psychology* (Appeton-Century-Crofts), *Cognition and Reality* (Freeman), *Memory Observed* (Freeman), *The School Achievement of Minority Children* (Erlbaum) and *The Perceived Self* (Cambridge University Press), as well as for his studies of memory in natural settings.

The focus of this part of the book

The theory and research we have described shows you that everyone has an idea about what constitutes intelligence. More important, you now know that many people have many different ideas about intelligence and that these ideas change as we get older and as we move from culture to culture. However, you will have also noticed how similar themes and ideas do occur throughout these differing research studies.

So what has psychology formally contributed to our understanding of intelligence? Well, in the rest of Part 2 (Chapters 10 to 15), we are looking at how psychology has formally measured intelligence and how intelligence is related to a number of variables, ranging from the sex and genetic makeup of a person, through culture, to numerous variables such as nutrition, education, child-rearing practices and work.

The focus for Part 2 of the book takes its lead from the 1995 task force report. The following chapters will deal with these topics:

- theories of Intelligence (Chapters 11 and 12);
- measurement of intelligence (Chapters 11 and 12);
- problems, methodological issues and alternative approaches surrounding the measurement of intelligence (Chapter 12);
- how nutrition (the nourishment from food) affects intelligence (Chapter 12);
- intelligence and the nature-nuture debate: the exact nature of the influence of genetic and the environment on intelligence (Chapter 12; mostly Chapters 13 and 14);
- group differences (sex and race) in intelligence (Chapters 13 and 14).

We of course elaborate on some of these issues discussed by the task force and cover some of these areas in greater depth. Furthermore, we dedicate large sections to concepts that were not covered at the time of the task force, notably emotional intelligence (Chapter 14) and how intelligence and personality ideas extend to education and workplace (Chapter 15).

We have deliberately spread some of this material over two chapters. This is because many of the central issues relating to intelligence are considered in different contexts. We also hope you remember that this is a controversial but well-researched area. There is some challenging material, and you may do well to look over the supplementary material given at the end of this book, especially regarding academic argument (particularly fallacies in Chapter 22), statistics (particularly factor analysis and meta-analysis in Chapter 23) and psychometric testing (particularly notions of reliability and validity in Chapter 24).

One last point – often you will find intelligence referred in the literature as either *intelligence* or *cognitive ability*. Don't let this put you off. Throughout this book, we will use the term 'intelligence'. However, in your further reading you may come across papers or studies that use the term 'cognitive ability'. Much more often than not, the authors will be referring to what we know as intelligence.

Final comments

We have used this chapter to introduce you to some of the ideas that you will come across in the next five chapters on intelligence. We have covered implicit theories of intelligence and shown you how implicit theories of intelligence change across the life span, between experts and non-experts and around the world.

Summary

- Intelligence is seen as central to human life in the present day.
- Implicit theories are folk theories, layperson, everyday ideas that surround a particular topic area.
- Implicit theories of intelligence drive the way in which people perceive and evaluate their own intelligence and that of others. Implicit theories of intelligence can give rise to more formal theories of intelligence that researchers can investigate. Implicit theories are useful when an investigator thinks existing explicit theories are wrong and may provide useful avenues for research. Implicit theories of intelligence can elucidate theories around psychological constructs, such as the development of intelligence and cross-cultural aspects of intelligence.
- Sternberg and his colleagues found three dimensions of intelligence: practical problem solving, verbal ability and social competence.
- In Western cultures, researchers suggest, there is an emphasis on the speed of mental processing and the ability to gather, assimilate and sort information quickly and efficiently. In Eastern cultures these ideas extend to social, historical and spiritual aspects of everyday interactions, knowledge and problem solving. In non-Western cultures the ability to show skills in problem solving, verbal ability and social competence would not just extend to the individual, but rather to their ability to solve a problem within the context of their family and friends.
- There is evidence from Korea to suggest that Western and Eastern conceptions of intelligence might be converging.
- One way of comparing Eastern and Western conceptions of intelligence is to compare implicit theories of intelligence in samples at the same time.
- Perceptions of intelligence change across the life span. There are two ways of looking at this: (1) to look at how people perceive intelligence at different stages of life and (2) to examine how individuals at different ages perceive intelligent behaviour.
- Other research has asked intelligence experts for their definition of intelligence. Intelligence qualities such as adaptation to the environment, basic mental processes and aspects of higher-order thinking like reasoning, problem solving and decision making emerge from such research. However, professors in different academic disciplines differed in their conceptions of intelligence.
- The American Psychological Association (the largest and most influential psychological society in the world) established a special task force to publish an investigative report on the research presented in the book *The Bell Curve* and to conduct an analysis of what is known and not known about intelligence.

Connecting Up

This is an introductory chapter to Chapters 11 through 15.

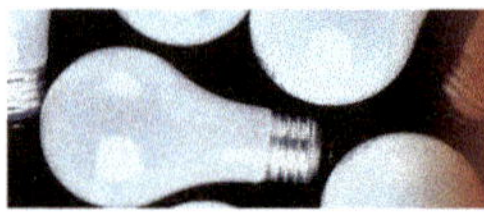

Critical Thinking

Discussion questions

- Do you think there are differences between Western and Eastern conceptions of intelligence?
- Studies on implicit theories of intelligence give us a wealth of characteristics that define intelligence around the world. Which characteristics best describe the ideal intelligent person in your country?
- Pick another country in the world (i.e., from another continent). Which characteristics best describe the ideal intelligent person in that country?
- What are characteristics of the ideal intelligent person in your country at 20 years of age, 40 years of age, and 60 years of age?

Essay questions

- Critically compare Western and Eastern conceptions of intelligence.
- Critically discuss laypersons' versus experts' implicit theories of intelligence.
- Critically discuss how culture, between and within countries, influences implicit theories of intelligence.
- Critically examine what implicit theories of intelligence tell us about intelligence.

Going Further

Books

- Sternberg, R. J. (Ed.). (2000). *Handbook of intelligence*. Cambridge: Cambridge University Press.
- Deary, I. J. (2001). *Intelligence: A very short introduction*. Oxford: Oxford University Press.
- Mackintosh, N. J. (1998). *IQ and human intelligence*. Oxford: Oxford University Press.
- Sternberg, R. J. (Ed.) (2004). *International handbook of intelligence*. Cambridge: Cambridge University Press.

Journals

- One article that will help you with a good overview of intelligence theory and research not just for this, but for later chapters is Sternberg, R. J., & Kaufman, J. C. (1998). Human abilities. *Annual Review of Psychology, 49*, 479–502. *Annual Review of Psychology* is published by Annual Reviews, Palo Alto, California. Available online via Business Source Premier.
- **Intelligence: A Multidisciplinary Journal.** This is one journal that you should start using. This psychology journal is devoted to publishing original research and theoretical studies and review papers that substantially contribute to the understanding of intelligence. It provides a new source of significant papers in psychometrics, tests and measurement as well as all other empirical and theoretical studies in intelligence and mental retardation. Published by Elsevier Science. Available online via Science Direct.
- **American Psychologist**. This is another journal that might be worth checking whether you have access to at your university. This journal also contains regular debates about intelligence. Published by American Psychological Association. Available online via PsycARTICLES.

Web resources

- A copy of the report prepared by the 1995 American Psychological Association Task Force on Intelligence is available at all these sites:
  - **http://www.lrainc.com/swtaboo/taboos/apa_01.html**
  - **http://www.mugu.com/cgi-bin/Upstream/Issues/psychology/IQ/apa.html**
  - **http://www.ship.edu/~cgboeree/iku.html**
- A full intelligence resource overseen by J. A. Plucker. This website covers historical influences, current controversies, teaching resources, debates and research in intelligence **(http://www.indiana.edu/~intell).**

Film and Literature

- **Being John Malcovich** (1999; directed by Spike Jonze). A puppeteer (John Cusack) discovers a door in his office that allows him to enter the mind and life of John Malkovich (playing himself), though only for 15 minutes. The puppeteer then tries to turn the portal into a small business. This film explores the themes of what it is like to be inside someone else's head (albeit a famous actor). Would such experiences change our understanding and knowledge of the world around us?
- **Q.I.** (Television series; hosted by Stephen Fry with Alan Davies). A comedy panel game in which being Quite Interesting is more important than being right. Stephen Fry is joined each week by four comedians to share anecdotes and trivia and maybe answer some questions as well. It is important to see this series because it tries to address the importance and unimportance of intelligence. Stephen Fry is clearly an extremely intelligent man. Alan Davies clearly is as well, but in a different way. The interaction between Stephen Fry and Alan Davies in acknowledging and appreciating each others' intelligence makes great viewing.

Chapter 11

Theories and Measurement of Intelligence

Key Themes

- Early theorists in intelligence: Galton, Binet, Terman and Yerkes
- General intelligence and its measurement: Spearman's 'g', the Wechsler and Raven's Matrices IQ tests
- Multifactor theorists: Thurstone, Cattell and Guilford
- Hierarchal theorists: Vernon and Carroll
- Gardner's multiple intelligences and Sternberg's triarchic model of intelligence

Learning Outcomes

After studying this chapter you should:

- Be able to describe the birth of intelligence and IQ testing
- Be able to describe the theory of 'g' and some alternative models
- Be aware of some well-known measures of intelligence
- Know about multifactor and hierarchical theories of intelligence
- Be familiar with the theories of multiple intelligences and the triarchic model of intelligence

Introduction

In the last chapter we introduced you to the concept of intelligence, particularly through implicit theories of intelligence. In this chapter we will introduce you to explicit, more formal theories of intelligence. Furthermore, we will see how the development of theories of intelligence in psychology is intertwined from the very beginning, from the first attempts to conceptualise and measure intelligence. We will take you through the theories and measurement of intelligence from a historical perspective. Though the history of intelligence research in psychology goes back more than two hundred years, throughout history the nature of intelligence has fascinated thinkers and scholars. Plato (428/427–348/347 BCE), a Greek philosopher, wrote that knowledge was not 'given' by the senses but acquired through them, and it was intelligence through reason that organised and made sense out of what was perceived. Aristotle (384–323 BCE), also a Greek philosopher and by some credited as the first psychologist, wrote about intelligence. He suggested that intellect takes the form of the psyche, that it is essential to man, it is part of nature (and therefore biological) but it is what separates man from the animals. He suggested that intellect comprises two parts: passive intellect and active intellect. Similarly to Plato, Aristotle suggested that active intellect, the psyche, takes information that is gained through the senses (passive intellect) and organises it, makes sense of it and uses it. Therefore, for Plato and Aristotle, the active intellect explained intellectual activities such as thinking and intuition.

In this chapter we will show you how theories of intelligence and its measurement in psychology started and how they developed. We will show you why in the late 1990s a leading intelligence test developer, the leading proponent of intelligence theory and one of the pre-eminent educational psychologists and scholars sat in meeting and finally were able to combine much that had been thought and learnt about intelligence into a single theory.

The birth of the psychology of intelligence: Galton and Binet

The modern foundations of intelligence theory and tests were formed just before the end of the nineteenth century through the work of two men: an Englishman, Francis Galton, and a Frenchman, Alfred Binet.

Galton

In 1865 Sir Francis Galton began to study heredity, after reading his cousin's (Charles Darwin) publication, *Origin of Species*. You may remember from Chapter 9 that Charles Darwin was the British naturalist who became famous for his theories of evolution and natural selection, which emphasised variations across species in nature. Following this work, Galton became interested in studying variations in human ability, and particularly intelligence. In particular, in his book *Hereditary Genius* (1869), Galton was convinced that higher intelligence was due to superior qualities passed down to children through heredity. Much of this work was concerned with the hereditary nature of intelligence, and we will return to this topic in Chapter 13. What is important to theories and measurement of intelligence is that Galton was the first to be interested in showing that human beings did differ in intelligence.

Galton is the forefather of intelligence tests. His central hypothesis was that there were differences in intelligence, and he set out to explore this hypothesis. Galton maintained that it is possible to measure intelligence directly, and he used a variety of methods to provide such measures. His choices of measurements are based clearly on a biological background and on the thoughts of some of the early philosophers we previously mentioned. Galton felt that intelligent people show the ability to respond to the large range of information experienced through the senses. However, he said that 'idiotic' people demonstrate problems dealing with information gained through the senses. Galton felt that people of low intelligence will show less response to sensory information, such as being unable to distinguish between heat and cold and being unable to recognise pain. Galton suggested several methods such as reaction time, keenness of sight and hearing, the ability to distinguish between colours, eye judgement and strength as a way to determine intelligence through responsiveness to stimuli. Therefore, he claimed that someone who shows a low reaction time, has poor sight and hearing, is unable to distinguish between colours and shows poor eye judgement can be considered unintelligent. Galton tested people at his Anthropometric Laboratory that was set up in the International Health Exhibition in 1884, where visitors to the exhibition could take the tests.

Perhaps it is easy to scoff at the reliability and validity of some of these measures. Clearly, poor eyesight does not determine poor intelligence, but is the result of a problem with the eyes. However, some of the measures Galton developed, such as reaction time, are still used today. Galton's work presented the first attempt to measure intelligence directly.

Binet

Alfred Binet created the first intelligence test. In 1904, the French Ministry of Public Instruction commissioned him to provide techniques for identifying children at a primary age whose lack of success or ability might lead them to require special education. In 1905, with Theodore Simon, Binet produced the Binet-Simon scale, the first intelligence test, which Simon later described as 'practical, convenient, and rapid', that went on to be used with around 50 children.

To develop their test, Binet and Simon choose a series of 30 short tasks related to everyday life. This intelligence test included these tasks:

- following a lighted match with your eyes;
- shaking hands;
- naming parts of the body;
- counting coins;
- naming objects in a picture;
- recalling a number of digits after being shown a long list;
- word definitions;
- filling in missing words in a sentence.

The test questions were arranged in an increasing degree of difficulty to indicate levels of intelligence. The easiest of the tasks were tasks such as whether a child could follow a lighted match with their eyes, these tasks were expected to be completed by all children. Slightly harder tasks included asking children to name certain body parts or repeat simple sentences. More difficult tasks involved asking children to reproduce a drawing or construct a sentence that included certain words. The hardest tasks required children to repeat seven random digits and to find rhymes for difficult words. Each level of test was designed to match a specific developmental level for children based on age ranging from 3 to 10 years old. The Binet-Simon test could be used to determine a child's 'mental age' and whether a child was advanced or backward for their age. A child of 7 who passed the tests designed for a 7-year-old but failed the tests for an 8-year-old would be assigned a mental age of 7.

This use of age in psychological testing is one of Binet's lasting contributions to psychology. Within Binet's system, age among children could be used as a criteria of intelligence.

Profiles Francis Galton and Alfred Binet

Francis Galton

Francis Galton was born in 1822. At university he started out to study medicine but took time out to travel abroad. When he returned, he took a degree in Mathematics from Trinity College in Cambridge. Outside his research and writing in psychology and intelligence, Galton was an explorer in Africa and the Middle East and created the first weather maps. He discovered that fingerprints were an index of personal identity and persuaded Scotland Yard to adopt a finger-printing system.

During his later career, Galton coined the term 'nature versus nature', developed statistical concepts of correlation and regression to the mean and was first to utilize the survey as a method for data collection.

Galton produced over three hundred papers and books throughout his lifetime; they included *Hereditary Genius: An Inquiry into Its Laws and Consequences* (1869) and *Inquiries into Human Faculty and Its Development* (1883). He was knighted in 1909.

Alfred Binet

Alfred Binet received his law degree in 1878 and later studied natural sciences at the prestigious Sorbonne University, Paris. Binet began to teach himself in psychology and became interested in the ideas of British philosopher John Stuart Mill, who believed that intelligence could be explained by the laws of associationism, a theory that suggests consciousness results from the combination of information derived from sense experiences.

Between 1883 and 1889, Binet worked as a researcher in a neurological clinic at the Salpêtrière Hospital, Paris. In 1891, Binet worked at the Sorbonne's Laboratory of Experimental Psychology and was appointed Director of the laboratory in 1894. That year he co-founded the *L'Annee Psychologique*, a major psychology journal. In 1904 Binet was called upon by the French government to appoint a commission on the education of retarded children; its purpose was to identify students in need of alternative education.

Binet published more than two hundred books and articles in experimental, developmental, educational, social and differential psychology; but today he is most widely known for his contributions to intelligence, particularly his 1905 work *New Methods for the Diagnosis of the Intellectual Level of Subnormals* and (with T. Simon) *The Development of Intelligence in Children* (1916).

That is, Binet-Simon could determine what level in an intelligence test children should be attaining at any given age. You will certainly have come across this idea at school with the idea of reading age, in which children are judged on their ability in reading in relation to where they should be at a certain age (this is applied to the sales of books; for example, the Harry Potter series is determined as having a reading age of 9–11 years).

Early IQ tests involved elementary tasks.

Binet and Simon's intelligence test was a turning point in psychology. Not only did they devise a test, but they devised a test in which the performance of the child was compared to the performance of children of the same age. The final publication of tests was in 1911 (Binet & Simon, 1911), with not only tests for 3- to 10-year-olds, but some further tests for 12- and 15-year-olds and adults.

The search for measurement continues: the birth of 'IQ' and standardised testing

The search for the measurement of intelligence then shifted to the United States. It is here we see the growth of the measurement of intelligence, the birth of the intelligence quotient (IQ), standardised testing, cultural considerations and time limits on taking an intelligence test.

Terman

The first notable development was made when Lewis Terman of Stanford University in the United States decided to use the Binet-Simon test among California schoolchildren. He found that the age norms that Binet and Simon had devised for children in France didn't work very well for schoolchildren in California. So Terman revised the test, adapting some of the items and writing 40 new items. In 1916 Terman introduced the Stanford-Binet test, which was applicable for use with children aged from 4 to 14 years.

Items on the test were similar to Binet and Simon's test. At 4 years, children would be asked to do things such as (1) compare two horizontal lines and say which is longer, (2) copy a square and (3) find a shape that matches a target shape. At 9 years, a child would be asked to do things such as (1) show awareness of dates, including what day of the week it is and what year; (2) arrange weights from highest to lowest; and (3) be able to do some mental arithmetic.

Terman went on to use the test with over 1,000 children aged from 4 to 14, which was a much larger group than the 50 children used by Binet. Terman was able to gain far more accurate information on how children typically scored on intelligence tasks because he had a much more representative sample of children. This issue of researchers using representative samples to determine accurate and representative scores was the beginning of recognising the need for 'standardised testing'. That is, in order to assess one child by comparing them with other children, researchers need to ensure that data they have on other children is representative so the assessment of the one child is fair.

One of the main advances towards standardised testing was made at this time. In 1912 a German psychologist, William Stern, developed the idea of the intelligence quotient, or as it is more popularly known today, IQ. Stern had been using Binet's intelligence test in Germany. While studying scores on Binet's test, Stern noticed that 'mental' age varied among children proportionally to their real age. So, for example, if a child who at the age of 6 years scores 1 year below their age on the test and has a mental age of 5, then when they are 10 years of age, they will have a mental age of 8 – two years below their real age. Stern discovered that if the mental age were divided by the chronological age, the ratio was fairly constant (as shown in the following example). He named the ratio of the mental age divided by the chronological age the intelligence quotient (IQ).

In its fullest sense, the definition of **IQ** is (mental age ÷ chronological age) × 100.

This calculation set an IQ of 100 as an average intelligence. That is, if a child of 8 takes an intelligence test and receives a score that indicates a mental age of 8, they would have an IQ of 100 (8 divided by 8 = 1, and 1 multiplied by 100 = 100). An IQ score of 100 indicates that a child is performing at the expected age, and 100 sets the standard by which children are then compared. This allows children to be compared not only across a particular age group but also across ages. A child who is 8 and has the mental age of a child of 10 will have an IQ of 125 (10 divided by 8 = 1.25; 1.25 multiplied by 100 = 125). A child who is 10 years old and has a mental age of 6 will have an IQ of 60 (6 divided by 10 = 0.60; 0.60 multiplied by 100 = 60).

Let us use the imaginary scores given in Table 11.1 to show how IQ is calculated. As we can see from our example table, the child who scored the mental age scores at the following ages based on Stern's findings (mental age of 5 at 6 years, mental age of 8 at 10 years and mental age of 11 at 14 years) would score an IQ of around 80 over their childhood (between 79 and 83).

Terman adopted this procedure for calculating IQ based on his test. Using this procedure, together with the items of the Standford-Binet test and the need to get a large and representative samples to develop age "norms" for the test, Stanford-Binet had developed an intelligence test against which all other tests were compared.

Yerkes

The demand for intelligence tests quickly increased. In 1917 the United States entered World War I, and a committee was appointed by the American Psychological Association to

Table 11.1 Example of Stern's ratio of real age to mental age, used to develop his concept of intelligence quotient (IQ).

Mental age	Chronological age	Ratio (mental age ÷ chronological age)
5	6	0.83
8	10	0.80
11	14	0.79

consider ways in which psychology could help the war effort. Head of this committee was Robert Yerkes, then President of the American Psychological Association (though committee members included Terman) and also a U.S. Army major. The committee was quick to realise that psychology could help the Army because assessing the intelligence of recruits would enable the Army to classify and assign soldiers to suitable tasks. However, it was also realised that such an exercise would involve a huge number of people and that the sorts of tests developed by Binet and Terman were not suitable as they were time intensive. That is, an experimenter had to sit down with the subject and take them through 5 or 6 tasks. The committee decided that what was needed was a test that could be completed simultaneously by a number of people, administered by one examiner. Yerkes' aim was to develop group intelligence testing.

Yerkes, alongside a staff of 40 psychologists (including Terman) developed two group intelligence tests, known as the Army Alpha and Army Beta tests. The Army Alpha was designed for literate groups, and the Army Beta was designed for illiterates, low literates or non-English-speaking groups.

The Army Alpha Test

The Alpha Test battery for literates included the testing of a wide variety of cognitive abilities by addressing the person's knowledge base in both oral language and written language. The Alpha Test included eight tests of an individual's ability to:

- follow oral directions, involving the comprehension of simple and complex oral language directions;
- solve arithmetical problems, showing knowledge of arithmetic and the ability to perform simple computations;
- show practical judgement, involving the ability to make the 'correct' choice on a scenario presented to the individual;
- use synonyms and antonyms, knowledge of the 'same' and 'opposite' of words;
- rearrange disarranged sentences, such as 'I back it and door ran to the opened';
- complete an uncompleted series of numbers (1, 2, 4, 8, 16, . . .);
- see analogies, which require the ability to see similarity between two things that are otherwise dissimilar;
- demonstrate information, an examination of the person's everyday knowledge base.

The administration of each of the eight subtests was designed to be completed within a certain time.

The Army Beta Test

The Beta Test was an intelligence test comparable to the Alpha but freed of the influences of literacy and the English language. People who were non-English speakers or poor at speaking English, or those who typically had less than six years of experience in speaking the English language, were sent to Beta testing. Furthermore, those who had tried the Alpha Test but were later judged to be poor readers, were retested using the Beta Test.

The Beta Test instructions were given by the testor and their aides by making hand signals. The examiners recorded responses. The Beta Test included seven tests of ability in which the participants had to:

- complete a maze task, by finding the best route to be taken on a picture of a maze;
- complete a cube analysis, by counting cubes in a graphic representation;
- read an X-O series of graphic displays in left-to-right sequences;
- complete a test using digit symbols, requiring scanning and matching of numbers to symbols;
- complete a test using number symbols, requiring scanning and matching of symbols to numbers;
- complete a picture by looking at an uncompleted picture and using given objects to complete the picture (a little like a jigsaw);
- undertake geometrical construction, which involved working with graphics information and mentally rearranging it to construct a figure.

Again, like the Alpha Test, the administration of each Beta subtest was completed within a certain time.

For each test, to determine each person's intelligence level, scores for all subtests were combined into one total score. Based on the total score, each individual was assigned a category based on a letter grade. A letter grade of A suggested superior intelligence; B, C+, C meant average intelligence, and C−, D, D− were considered as signifying inferior intelligence. The letter grade indicated the person's mental intelligence and was taken as a general indicator of the person's native intelligence.

In the end, Yerkes and his colleagues tested over 1.75 million people. This work was not completed until late in the war, and the work actually had little effect on the war effort; but it did a lot to raise the status of psychology and the profile and potential usefulness of intelligence testing. For example, after the war, Yerkes received requests from the general public, business, industry and education for the intelligence test. In 1919 the National Intelligence Test was published and sold over half a million copies in its first year.

You can see that a growth in intelligence tests occurred from the work of Terman and Yerkes. Growth occurred not only in terms of what is measured and who can be measured but also (1) in the number of people who can be measured at one time, (2) in developing an official way of scoring intelligence through IQ and (3) in the consideration of culture and time limits on taking an intelligence test. These elements remain central to modern intelligence tests.

General intelligence (g): the theory and the measurement

Up to this point in the history of intelligence testing, approaches to intelligence had been very practical. Tests were developed for particular needs, that is, in response to French or American government demands. However, between 1904 and 1927, an English psychologist, Charles Spearman, introduced another way of conceptualising intelligence. He based his approach on the factor analysis of data (a technique for simplifying the relationships between a number of variables; see Chapter 23) that had already been collected. We will outline Spearman's research and theory of general intelligence and then introduce you to two measures of intelligence: the Wechsler and Raven's intelligence tests, which are designed to measure 'g'.

'g'

Charles Spearman (1904, 1927), over the course of two publications – '"General Intelligence": Objectively determined and measured' and 'The abilities of man', introduced one of the most influential ideas in psychology, **general intelligence** or **'g'**.

In 1904 Spearman set out to estimate the intelligence of 24 children in the village school. Initially, Spearman used intelligence tests of memory, light, weight and sound in which participants were asked to identify changes in illumination, weight and pitch of Spearman's instruments and perform memory tasks.

Spearman's first 24 participants were the oldest pupils of a village school in Berkshire. Spearman claimed that this sample was most favourable as it was within 100 yards of his own house, and all the families of the children resided in the immediate neighborhood (perhaps the most convenient sample of what is known these days as 'convenience' sampling). Like other intelligence tests, the test was done on a one-to-one basis.

After this first experiment Spearman moved onto the next 36 oldest children in the school, and then to a local school which sent a lot of its pupils to Harrow (a well-known public school in the United Kingdom). Over a period of time, further data collections were taken among individuals who lived further from Spearman's home. Between 1904 and 1921, Spearman analysed the relationships between the data collected using a variety of intelligence tests and subjected them to factor analysis.

He found that his data indicated a trend towards positive correlations between intelligence tests. That is, a person who does well on one intelligence test will perform equally well on a variety of *intellectual* tests, be they tests concerned with vocabulary, mathematical or spatial (awareness of space and movement around oneself) abilities. Equally, if a person did poorly on one intelligence test, then they will also tend to perform poorly on other intellectual tasks. He called this positive correlation between tests the 'positive manifold'. Spearman used this idea of a positive manifold between intelligence tests to propose a 2-factor theory of intelligence.

The first factor of intelligence was **specific abilities**, or **'s'**. This was the name given to each type of intelligence needed for performing well on each different intelligence task that Spearman had observed. Therefore, vocabulary intelligence is a specific ability, mathematical intelligence is a specific ability and spatial intelligence is a specific ability.

The second factor was what Spearman thought was underlying all the positive correlations, and this was perhaps his most important and notable contribution to psychology: general intelligence, or 'g'. He argued that 'g' was underlying all the positive correlations. 'g' was the intelligence required for performance of intelligence tests of all types. Spearman envisaged 'g' as a kind of mental energy that underlies specific factors of intelligence. He saw it as a deeper fundamental mechanism which informed a number of intelligence abilities but was an intelligence also able to see relationships between objects, events and information and draw inferences from those relationships.

Spearman saw a person's ability in one specific ability test – for example, mathematical ability – not only as affected by one's specific ability to perform mathematical tasks but also as largely determined by that person's general intelligence. The main point of Spearman's findings was the idea of 'g', and this became a major theory that informs many subsequent approaches to intelligence. Proponents of general intelligence, or 'g', still exist amongst prominent psychologists.

Measuring 'g': the Wechsler and Raven's matrices

After Charles Spearman's introduction of his theory of intelligence, a central interest to intelligence developers was to develop a good measure of general intelligence, particularly among adults. Spearman's theory and research,

Profile Charles Edward Spearman

Charles Edward Spearman was born in London to eminent parents in 1863. He joined the British Army and became an officer, serving in the Burmese and Boer Wars. After 15 years, he resigned his army post to study psychology. At the time, British psychology was more a branch of philosophy; and so in 1897, Spearman chose to study in Leipzig, Germany. Spearman was accepted, at University, though he had no conventional qualifications, partly due to his officer and army training. There he studied under Wilhelm Max Wundt (a German physiologist and psychologist who is generally acknowledged as one of the founders of experimental psychology and cognitive psychology). After some interruption - he was recalled to the army during the South African War - Spearman gained his PhD in 1906 when he was 41, though he had already published his paper on the factor analysis of intelligence in 1904.

Spearman then took a position in Psychology at University College, London. Spearman had impressed the psychologist William McDougall, an English psychologist who studied the theory of instinct and of social psychology. McDougall arranged for Spearman to replace him when he left his position at the university. Initially, Spearman was head of the small psychological laboratory, but in 1911 he was promoted to a professorship of the Philosophy of Mind and Logic. He was elected to the Royal Society (the oldest learned society concerned with the improvement of natural knowledge) in 1924. His title changed to Professor of Psychology in 1928, when a separate Department of Psychology was created at University College, London. Spearman stayed at University College until he retired in 1931. During his time at the university, Spearman and a colleague, Karl Pearson, developed separately the two most well-known correlation techniques in psychology. Above all, Spearman is renowned for (1) determining the concept of general intelligence and (2) his work on factor analysis.

Spearman's most famous works are 'General Intelligence: Objectivity Determined and Measured' (1904) and 'Proof and Measurement of Association between Two Things', which were both published in the *American Journal of Psychology*, and his book, *The Abilities of Man: Their Nature and Measurement* (Macmillan, 1927).

together with the work of Terman and Yerkes, led to the development of more rigorous intelligence tests that could be used across the population to assess intelligence. However, there was some further work to be done. Both the Binet tests were primarily concerned with testing among children, and any testing done with adult samples involved relatively small samples. The Yerkes test was subject to a similar criticism. Though this test had been tested used with nearly one and a half million adults, they were all people who had applied to join the U.S. Army. It was left for psychologists to devise intelligence tests that could be used to determine intelligence among the general populations, and be used to accurately assess a person's intelligence in comparison to other people.

Two intelligence tests stand out in present psychology that show a historical move to standardised intelligence testing: the Wechsler test of intelligence and the Raven Matrices.

The Wechsler tests

David Wechsler was a US psychologist at Columbia University. In 1917 he had originally worked under the American Psychological Association/Yerkes' Army initiative and administered and interpreted intelligence tests that were used to assign army recruits to military jobs. During that time, the Army sent Wechsler to England and the University of London to work with Charles Spearman and Karl Pearson.

The history of what has now become known as the Wechsler tests spans the period from 1939 to the present day. Although Wechsler did not always agree with Spearman's view of intelligence, Wechsler's first tests were modelled on Spearman's 2-factor model and Spearman's central position that intelligence covers a huge range of specific abilities that correlate within one another to form an overall measure of general intelligence (or 'g').

In 1939 Wechsler published the first of the Wechsler tests, the Wechsler-Bellevue Scale. The Wechsler-Bellevue Scale, unlike some former intelligence tests, was designed and standardised among a sample of 1,500 adults. However, in 1955 Wechsler introduced two tests:

- the Wechsler Adult Intelligence Scale (WAIS), that had been standardised among 2000 adults aged between 16 and 75;
- the Wechsler Scale for Children (WISC) for children aged between 5 and 16 years.

As with the Binet tests, the Wechsler tests were administered on a one-to-one basis. Both Wechsler scales contained a number of subtests to measure several different aspects of intelligence, including verbal and performance tests such as:

- **Arithmetic (verbal)** – This subtest involves solving problems using mental arithmetic.

(a)

(b)

(c)

Item	Response
Q-3	3-Q
T-9-1	1-9-T
M-3-P-6	3-6-M-P
F-7-K-2-8	2-7-8-F-K
5-J-4-A-1-S	1-4-5-A-J-S
C-6-4-W-O-7-D	4-6-7-C-D-O-W

(d)

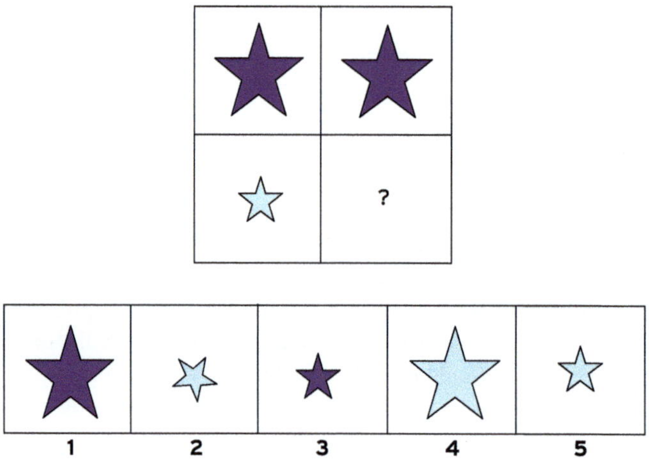

(e)

(f)

Paraphrased Wechsler-like Questions

Information

1. How many wings does a bird have?
2. How many nickels make a dime?
3. What is steam made of?
4. Who wrote "Tom Sawyer"?
5. What is pepper?

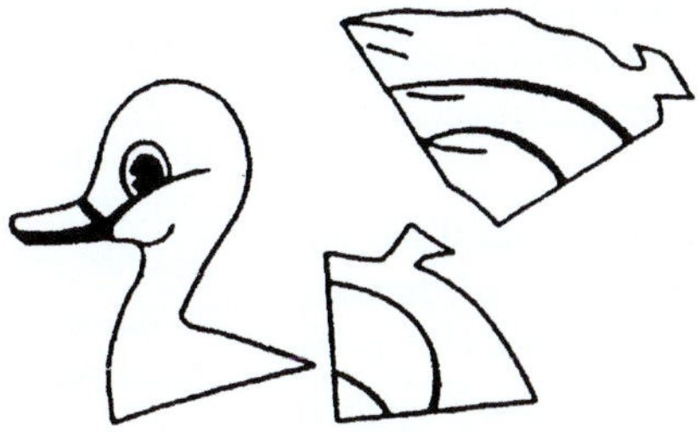

Comprehension

1. What should you do if you see someone forget his book when he leaves a restaurant?
2. What is the advantage of keeping money in a bank?
3. Why is copper often used in electrical wires?

Arithmetic

1. Sam had three pieces of candy and Joe gave him four more. How many pieces of candy did Sam have altogether?
2. Three women divided eighteen golf balls equally among themselves. How many golf balls did each person receive?
3. If two buttons cost $.15, what will be the cost of a dozen buttons?

Similarities

1. In what way are a lion and a tiger alike?
2. In what way are a saw and a hammer alike?
3. In what way are an hour and a week alike?
4. In what way are a circle and a triangle alike?

Vocabulary

This test consists simply of asking, "What is a ____________?" or "What does ____________ mean?" The words cover a wide range of difficulty.

Figure 11.1 Simulated items similar to those in the *Wechsler Adult Intelligence Scale*: picture arrangement (a), block design (b), letter-number sequencing (c), matrix reasoning (d), picture completion (e) and object assembly and Wechsler-like questions (f).

Source: Simulated items similar to those from *Wechsler Adult Intelligence Scale*, Third Edition.

- **Block design (performance)** – In this subtest, the participant is presented with 9 coloured blocks, each with 2 red, 2 white, and 2 diagonally red and white sides. In this task the participant is asked to arrange the blocks to form certain patterns.
- **Comprehension (verbal)** – This subtest involves the participant demonstrating an understanding of the meaning of words and sayings, and the appropriate response to a number of scenarios (e.g., 2 trains are travelling in opposite directions 100 miles apart; 1 train is travelling at 40 miles an hour while the other is travelling at 60 miles an hour. How long before the 2 trains meet?).
- **Digit span (verbal)** – In this subtest the participant is asked to repeat a series of digits in exact or reverse order.
- **Digit symbol (performance)** – This subtest requires the participant to symbols to numbers.
- **Information (verbal)** – This subtest requires the participant to show general knowledge of areas such as science, politics, geography, literature and history.

- **Object assembly (performance)** – This subtest requires a number of simple jigsaws to be completed within a particular time limit.
- **Picture arrangement (performance)** – In this subtest, participants are presented with a series of cards with a number of pictures. They must arrange the cards to tell a simple story.
- **Picture completion (performance)** – In this subtest, the participant has to complete line drawings of objects or scenes in which one or two lines are missing.
- **Similarities (verbal)** – This subtest involves the participant comparing two things that are alike.
- **Vocabulary (verbal)** – This subtest involves asking the participant for definitions of words.

Some examples from the Wechsler Adult Intelligence Scale are given in Figure 11.1.

These scales are well-known tests which are still used today, though they have been revised. The Wechsler tests departed from previous intelligence tests in two important ways. First, the Wechsler scales were different from previous tests in that they were designed so all people of all ages could take them. This was unlike Binet's test, which primarily required a 7-year-old to take tests designed for 7-year-olds, and 10-year-olds to take tests designed for 10-year-olds. Clearly, it would not have been useful or productive to design intelligence tests for all the years from early childhood to late adulthood. The Wechsler intelligence test includes a number of subtests for different aspects of intelligence, and within each subtest there are a variety of items with a wide range of difficulty. However, all participants are tested on the same items.

The second way in which the Wechsler tests differed from previous tests was the introduction of the concept of 'deviation IQ'. You will remember that Terman used the concept of IQ based on the mental age and the real age of the participant [(mental age ÷ chronological age) × 100]. However, Wechsler was primarily concerned with applying intelligence testing to adults, and the calculation that Terman used was not wholly applicable to adults. For example, let us apply Terman's method for calculating an average intelligence test score to adults. A 20-year-old and a 40-year-old take the same intelligence test and score in a way that indicates they are of the same mental age, thus the 40-year-old would appear to be half as intelligent as the 20-year-old (solely based on age). This problem stems from the fact that there is a huge range of years in adulthood as compared to childhood and that intelligence increases rapidly in childhood yet starts to level out in adulthood. Therefore, the challenge faced by Wechsler was to arrive at a fairer system of assessing IQ.

Wechsler's solution was not to define and score IQ based on mental and chronological age, but in terms of an individual's actual score on the intelligence test relative to the average scores obtained by others of the same age on the same intelligence test. The new formula for interpreting test scores in terms of deviation IQ was (actual test score ÷ expected score for that age) × 100.

However, this calculation involved two further steps to allow the standardisation in using the Wechsler IQ test: (1) Determining the expected score for any particular age so all people could be compared and (2) transforming the wide range of scores and variations among the population to a standardised form.

1. Determining the expected score for a particular age. Wechsler had to determine the average score on the intelligence test for all possible ages, so that it could be used effectively as a basis of comparison. To ensure he had a reliable comparison, Wechsler collected data through stratified sampling, whereby sampling is based on randomly sampling individuals from mutually exclusive subgroups or strata of population (e.g., a certain amount of 20-year-olds, 30-year-olds and so on). Wechsler ensured that he sampled people from various demographics, including social class, sex and region of the country. From this sampling Wechsler was able to establish intelligence norms for all ages.

2. Transforming the wide range of scores and variations among the population to a standardised form. You will remember that the original calculation of IQ was based on an observation by German intelligence tester William Stern that 'mental' age varies among children proportionally with their real age. It was this growth of mental age against chronological age that allowed Stern to make certain assumptions in calculating IQ. However, Wechsler could not make these assumptions. First, Wechsler was not surprised to find that mental age and chronological age do not grow or change proportionally. Rather, he found that mental age fluctuates (goes up, goes down, stays stable) compared with chronological age. He could not assume the proportional growth that Stern used in calculations.

Wechsler developed a measure that used a comparison of the person scores to means, rather than age. To do this, he still used the idea of average IQ as being 100. The choice of 100 was fairly arbitrary, but was based on the original IQ calculations suggested by Stern and used by Terman. Therefore, all ranges of intelligence tests score for all ages were transformed so they had a middle score of 100. If 35-year-olds had a mean score of 80.1 IQ points on the intelligence test, then their average would be transformed to 100, and all scores would be shifted around this average. Final IQ scores for each individual were based on how much they deviate from the average. **Deviation IQ** was calculated as how much someone deviates from the average IQ of 100.

If you want to read more on how IQ scores are calculated, go to Stop and Think: IQ scores and the normal distribution.

Stop and Think

IQ scores and the normal distribution

The introduction of mean scores to calculating IQ led to complication of how to calculate IQ. Overall, researchers found that they were dealing with much more information by introducing numerous mean scores across a huge age range on an intelligence test (for example, 103.2 average IQ test score for 32-year-olds, 102.2 average IQ test scores for 33-year-olds and so on), rather than equally increasing absolute age over a limited time period (5 to 16 years). This result led to issues for allowing comparisons.

For example, if a company was interested in obtaining IQ scores in recruiting for jobs, then the present scoring system would be complicated. Suppose, for example, a recruiter has two candidates:

- Person A, aged 20 years, who scored 105 on the intelligence test; this was 10 points below the average for 20-year-olds (115 being the average intelligence test score among 20-year-olds).
- Person B, aged 25 years, who scored 100 on the intelligence test; this was 5 points below the average for 25-year-olds (105 being the average intelligence test score among 25-year-olds).

Who should the recruiter hire - the person with the highest IQ (Person A), or the person who scores nearest to the average for their age (Person B)?

Wechsler realised that he had to standardise the scoring of IQ. He had to find a way of comparing all these different scores and still provide a standardized scoring system. To do this, Wechsler used the normal distribution curve. You may remember from your statistics classes that a normal distribution curve (see Figure 11.2) is the symmetrical distribution of scores in a curve, with most of the scores situated in the centre and then spreading out, showing progressively lower frequency of scores for the higher and lower values.

What is particularly notable about this approach is that researchers have found that many of the variables measuring human attitudes and behaviour follow a normal distribution curve. This finding is one of statistics' more interesting elements. Statisticians and researchers are often not certain why many variables fall into a normal distribution; they have just found that many attitudes and behaviours do, including intelligence.

However, statisticians have noted that if scores on a variable show a normal distribution, this is potentially a powerful statistical tool because we can then begin to be certain about how scores will be distributed in a variable (i.e., that many people's scores will be concentrated in the middle and few will be concentrated at either end). This certainty has given statisticians the impetus to develop ideas about statistical testing, including most notably probability and significance testing, but also intelligence.

Normal distribution and the certainty that surrounds the ability to calculate where people fall under different points of the curve allow the calculation of how much people deviate from the IQ score. Because of what we know about a normal distribution, and because Wechsler decided to use 100 as an average IQ (based on the original IQ calculations), we know that

- 68 per cent of scores lie within 1 standard deviation of the mean (plus/minus), so 68 per cent of the population will score between 85 and 115.

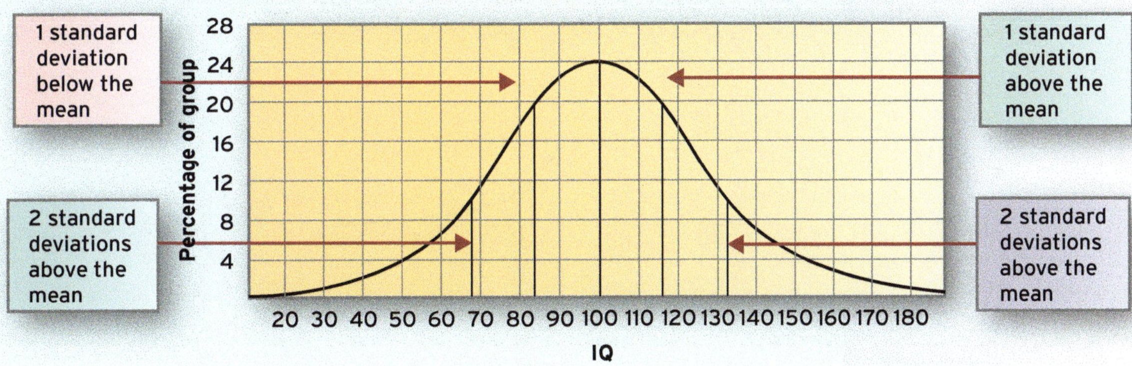

Figure 11.2 A normal distribution curve of intelligence scores.

- 95 per cent of scores will fall within 2 standard deviations of the mean, therefore 95 per cent of the population will score between 70 and 130. The average IQ score is 100. The standard deviation of IQ scores is 15.

It is then, within these aspects, that these scores are interpreted and classified. A score that is no more than 1 standard deviation (85-115) away from 100 can be interpreted as a normal score. A score that is between 1 and 2 standard deviations away from 100 can be interpreted as low (70-85) or high (115-130). A score that is more than 2 standard deviations away from 100 (lower than 70 or higher than 130) can be interpreted as very low (lower than 70) or very high (higher than 130). Therefore, Wechsler had provided a benchmark by which all people of all ages could be compared in IQ by using standard deviations.

IQ scores have been traditionally categorised to provide some understanding of level of intelligence. Some labels that have been used to describe low, high and average scores are provide in Figure 11.3.

Raven's Progressive Matrices

Scottish psychologist John Carlyle Raven first published his Progressive Matrices in 1938. In comparison to the Wechsler tests, the Raven Progressive Matrices seem dramatically different. However, like the Wechsler test, their rationale is based on the theory of Spearman.

In his writing, Spearman had emphasised 'g' as the abstract ability (theoretical thought, not applied or practical) to see relationships between objects, events and information and draw inferences from those relationships. Raven thought the best way to test this abstract ability was to develop a test that was free of cultural influences, particularly language. As you have seen with the Wechsler tests, there was some reliance on culture and language (e.g., tests of general knowledge and vocabulary). Though this reliance on language is not always true of the Wechsler tests (e.g., block design, object assembly), Raven's Progressive Matrices were designed to minimise the influence of culture and language by relying on non-verbal problems that require abstract reasoning and do not require knowledge of a particular culture.

Examples of the items in Raven's Progressive Matrices are given in Figure 11.4. The participant is shown a matrix of patterns in which one pattern is missing. The aim of each item is to test a person's ability to form perceptual relations and to reason by analogy independent of language. Put simply, the patterns within the matrix form certain rules, and the participant shows higher intelligence by being able to work out the rules that govern the patterns and then use these rules to select an item that best fits the missing pattern.

Raven's Progressive Matrices can be used with persons ranging from 6 years to adult. The overall test comprises 60 items, arranged into 5 sets of items, with each set of items arranged in increasing order of difficulty. Typically,

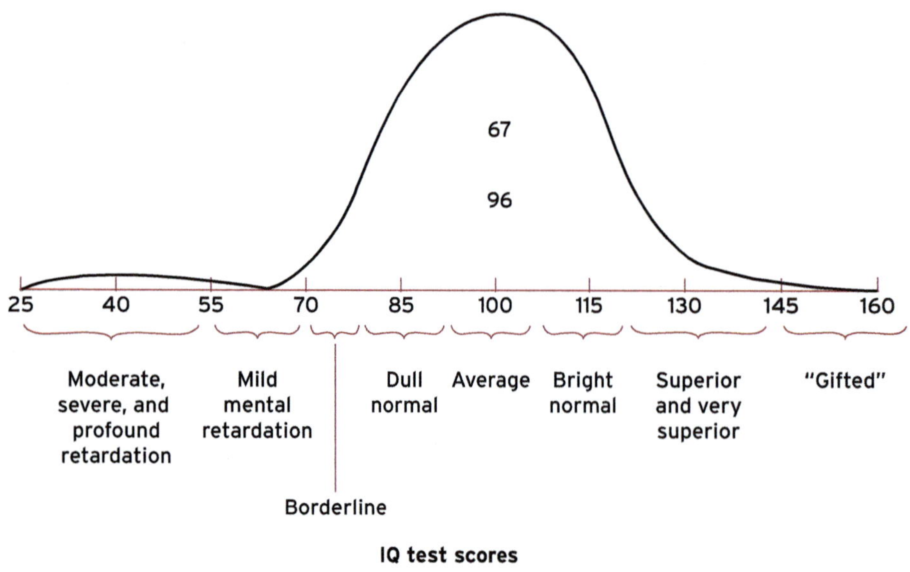

Figure 11.3 Labels traditionally given to IQ scores.

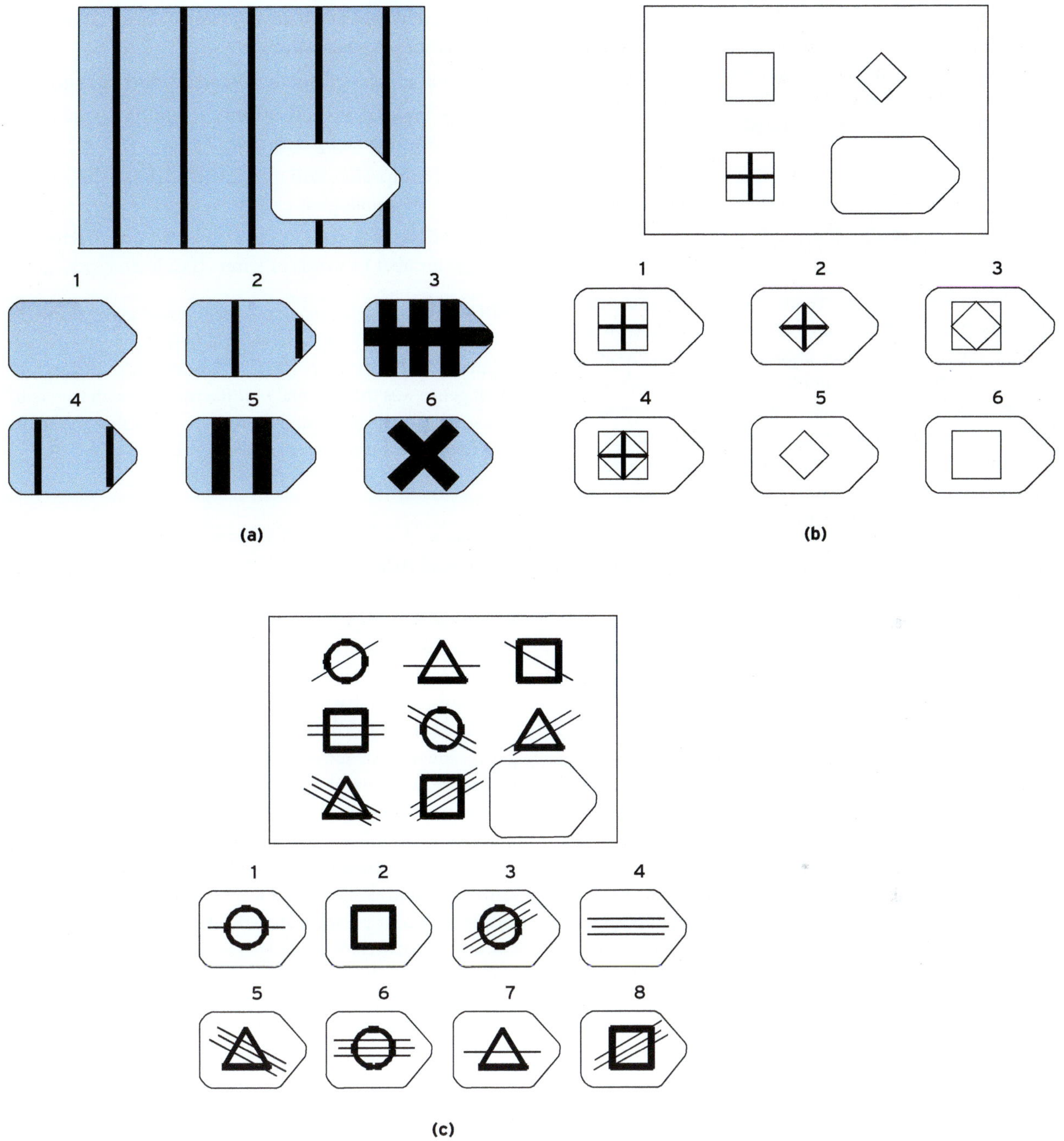

Figure 11.4 **Simulated items similar to those in the *Raven's Progressive Matrices*: Raven's Colored Progressive Matrices (CPM) (a), Raven's Standard Progressive Matrices (b) and Raven's Advanced Progressive Matrices (APM) (c).**

Source: Simulated items similar those from *Raven's Progressive Matrices*. Copyright © 1998 by Harcourt Assessment, Inc. Reproduced with permission. All rights reserved.

like Wechsler's test and Spearman's theory of 'g', for the Progressive Matrices respondents are given an overall score. As in the Wechsler test, the overall IQ score is based on an individual's deviation from standardised norms. With the Matrices' emphasis on abstract (theoretical thought, not applied or practical) ability to see relationships among objects, events and information and draw inferences from those relationships and its non-dependence on language, the Matrices are often favoured as a good measure of 'g'. Arthur Jensen, a prominent IQ researcher, wrote that when compared to other measures of general intelligence, Raven's Progressive Matrices is probably the best measure of a general intelligence factor (Jensen, 1998).

Multifactor theorists: Thurstone, Cattell and Guilford

Both Wechsler's and Raven's intelligence tests were developments in the history of intelligence based on Spearman's theory, and these tests are used in present-day research. However, other developments from Spearman's theory sought to develop its theoretical elements. Our next section outlines three such developments via the research of three academics: Louis L. Thurstone, Raymond B. Cattell and J. P. Guilford. A common thread running through all these academics' work was that they used the factor analysis approach, which Spearman developed, to understand intelligence. However, you will see that each of these academics produced rather different perspectives on the nature of 'g'.

Thurstone: 'g' results from seven primary mental abilities

L. L. Thurstone was a US psychologist and psychometrician who originally studied engineering at Cornell University under Thomas Edison (one of the most prolific inventors of the late nineteenth century). Thurstone completed a PhD at the University of Chicago.

Thurstone used factor analysis to inform his findings. That is, he explored the relationships between a number of intelligences and looked for underlying patterns and structures. Thurstone agreed with Spearman's hypothesis of a general factor of intelligence; however, he viewed 'g' differently from Spearman. Spearman defined 'g' as a central factor of intelligence, underlying and informing all aspects of intelligence, including specific abilities. Thurstone disagreed. He couldn't see how, from Spearman's studies, he had shown that a general factor of intelligence was influencing all single aspects of intelligence. Thurstone argued that all Spearman had shown was that intelligence tests correlate positively, and he maintained that there was no evidence for Spearman's description of 'g'. Thurstone agued that 'g' results from, rather than lies behind, these seven primary mental abilities:

- **associative memory** – ability for rote (learning through routine or repetition) memory;
- **number** – ability to accurately carry out mathematical operations;
- **perceptual speed** – ability to perceive details, anomalies, similarities in visual stimuli;
- **reasoning** – ability in inductive and deductive reasoning
- **space (spatial visualisations)** – ability to mentally transform spatial figures;
- **verbal comprehension** – ability in reading, comprehension, verbal analogies;
- **word fluency** – ability to generate and use effectively a large number of words or letters (i.e., in anagrams).

Within Thurstone's theory of intelligence, general intelligence was the result of these seven different aspects of intelligence, which formed parts of 'g'. Thurstone's approach to intelligence was the first real *multi*factor approach to intelligence. That is, he suggested there were a number of factors to intelligence, rather than just one or two.

Cattell: fluid and crystallised intelligence

Raymond B. Cattell was born, studied and lectured in the United Kingdom. He later moved to the United States, where he become a Research Associate of E. L. Thorndike at Columbia University in New York.

Cattell also used factor analysis in his studies of intelligence. He acknowledged Spearman's work in accepting that there was general intelligence, but he suggested that 'g' comprises two related but distinct components: crystallised intelligence and fluid intelligence.

Cattell described **crystallised intelligence** as acquired knowledge and skills, such as factual knowledge. It is generally related to a person's stored information and to their cultural influences. Knowledge of vocabulary, comprehension and general knowledge would all be tests of an individual's crystallized intelligence. Following Spearman's lead (who termed general intelligence 'g'), Cattell abbreviated this component as 'Gc' (the *c* standing for crystallised).

Cattell described **fluid intelligence** ability as a primary reasoning ability; the ability to solve abstract relational problems, free of cultural influences. This component is defined by intelligence abilities such as acquisition of new information, understanding new relationships, patterns and analogies in stimuli. Cattell abbreviated this component as 'Gf' (the *f* standing for fluid).

Cattell saw a dynamic relationship between these two intelligence components. Crystallised intelligence (for example, knowledge) is intelligence that increases throughout life and is a reflection of one's cumulative learning experience. Fluid intelligence is thought to be present from birth and then is meant to stabilise in adulthood. An example of how crystallised and fluid intelligence may work in society is seen in the way these different components inform certain types of thinking. It is often found that the great mathematicians do some of their best work when they are in younger adulthood. This is because mathematics is based on abstract thinking, and achievement in this area reflects fluid intelligence. However, in other disciplines, such as history and literature, some of the best work is produced by academics in later adulthood as they have accumulated more knowledge; achievement in this area reflects crystallised intelligence.

One interesting aspect of Cattell's work is the distinction between fluid and crystallised intelligence in relation to developments in IQ testing. The Wechsler tests are, to some extent, measuring crystallised intelligence, containing measures such as comprehension, knowledge and vocabulary. Raven's Progressive Matrices, which reflect abstract thinking, are often used as a measure of general fluid intelligence.

Guilford: many different intelligences and many different combinations

J. P. Guilford was a US psychologist who studied at the University of Nebraska and Cornell University. He also conducted research at the University of Southern California and Santa Ana Army Air Base.

Guilford disagreed with the stance of Spearman and to some extent with Thurstone and Cattell. He didn't acknowledge the existence of 'g'; instead, Guilford (1977) eventually proposed that intelligence was the result of 150 independent abilities (though originally he suggested 120 independent abilities [Guilford, 1959]). His theory was named the Structure of Intellect (SI) theory.

Guilford argued that these elementary abilities fall into three groups: operations, contents and products.

Operations are types of mental processing, for example, what a person does. There are five types of operations:

- **evaluation** – ability to examine and judge carefully and appraise;
- **convergent production** – ability to bring together information into a single theme (e.g., a list comprising 'cats, dogs, mice' would be converged into 'type of animals');
- **divergent production** – ability to produce ideas from a common point (e.g., if a person was asked to list animals, divergent production would be to list 'cats', 'dogs', 'mice' etc.);
- **memory** – mental faculty of retaining and recalling past experience and information;
- **cognition** – mental process of knowing, including aspects such as awareness, perception, reasoning and judgement.

Contents comprise the mental material we possess *on* which operations are performed. There are five types of contents:

- **visual** – material relating to or gained by the sense of sight;
- **auditory** – material relating to or gained by the sense of hearing;
- **symbolic** – material relating to or expressed by means of symbols or a symbol;
- **semantic** – material relating to meaning, especially meaning in language;
- **behavioural** – material relating to our own behaviour.

Products consist of the form in which the information is stored, processed and used by the person to make associations or connections. There are six types of products:

- **units** – comprises the ability to use information relating to something being classed as a unit. It may be an individual, group, structure or other entity regarded as part of a whole (e.g., a 1-euro note [€1] is a *unit* of money);
- **classes** – comprises the ability to use information relating to a set, collection, group or configuration containing members regarded as having certain attributes or traits in common (e.g., the monetary units of euros – €2, €1, 50 cent, 20 cent, 10 cent, 5 cent, 2 cent and 1 cent – are a *class* of money);
- **relations** – comprises the ability to use information relating to seeing a logical or natural association between two or more things (e.g., there are 100 cents to €1; the association between these two units is a *relation*);
- **systems** – comprises the ability to use information relating to seeing a group of interacting, interrelated, or interdependent elements forming a complex whole (e.g., the euro, sterling, US dollars, Chinese yen and all the other currencies in the world form a *system*);
- **transformation** – comprises the ability to understand the changing nature, function or condition of any information (e.g., exchange rates between currencies);
- **implication** – comprises the ability to use a variety of information and apply logic to it or further understand suggestions, meaning and significance relating to that information (i.e., If I had all the money in the world, that would mean I would be rich).

A popular way of illustrating Guilford's Structure of Intellect (SI) theory is given in Figure 11.5.

Guilford argued that theoretically, 150 different components of intelligence emerge from the combinations of these

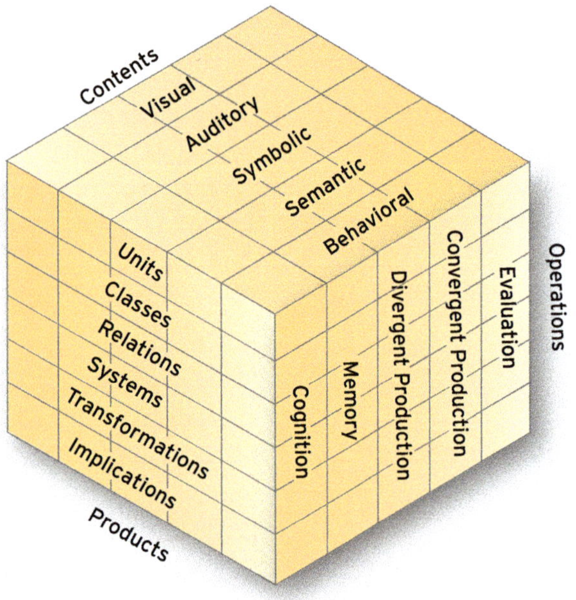

Figure 11.5 **Guilford's Structure of Intellect (SI) theory.**

Source: From Guilford, J.P. (1967). *Nature of human intelligence.* New York: McGraw-Hill Companies, Inc. Copyright © The McGraw-Hill Companies, Inc. Reprinted with permission.

different skills. So, for example, the ability to remember seeing a dog would use all of the following components:

- visual (content; the act of visualing the dog – remember *seeing* the dog);
- unit (product; the object itself – the dog – remember seeing the *dog*);
- memory (operation; the remembering part – *remember* seeing the dog).

Guilford suggested that the model could be simplified and that further groups of intelligence could be recognised by taking each of the five intelligence operations and applying them to the products and contents aspects (see Figure 11.5). Guilford recognised a further set of abilities:

- Reasoning and problem-solving intelligence could be fully understood by taking convergent and divergent operations and subdividing them into the 30 distinct abilities for the 6 products and 5 contents.
- Memory intelligence could be fully understood by subdividing the memory into the 30 distinct abilities for the 6 products and 5 contents.
- Decision-making skills could be fully understood by subdividing evaluation into the 30 distinct abilities for the 6 products and 5 contents.
- Language-related skills could be fully understood by subdividing cognition into the 30 distinct abilities for the 6 products and 5 contents.

Guilford's model of intelligence really opens up the possibilities of intelligence. It clearly broadens the view of intelligence, whilst detailing how different aspects of intelligence intertwine to form specific abilities. However, it may be too complex to provide a definitive theory. Guilford researched and developed a wide variety of psychometric tests to measure the specific abilities predicted by SI theory. He largely based this work on groups of intelligence that could be found among the 150 different components. Although these tests may be useful on their own, when research has conducted factor analysis to examine whether these intelligences gather together in the way Guilford suggests, there has been little support for his overall theory (Guilford & Hoepfner, 1971).

Intelligence and factor analysis – a third way: the hierarchal approach

So far we have considered theories of intelligence where 'g' is central (Spearman), apparent but not the most important (Thurstone and Cattell) or rejected (Guilford). Figure 11.6a shows how the theorists tend to be split between general theories of intelligence and specific abilities. However, there is a set of factor analysis theorists whose work fills the gap between the work of Spearman and Thurstone (see Figure 11.6b). These theorists developed hierarchical theories of intelligence; and we will now outline the work of Philip E. Vernon, John B. Carroll and John Horn.

Vernon

Philip E. Vernon was an English psychologist educated at Cambridge University. He was a Professor of Psychology and Educational Psychology at the Institute of Education, University of London.

Vernon (1950) described several different levels of intelligence. Vernon proposed that neither Spearman nor Thurstone had considered the existence of group factors that linked 'g' to specific intelligence abilities. Vernon argued that intelligence comprises various sets of abilities that can be described at various levels (i.e., from specific to grouped to general). Vernon's theory was the elaboration of 'g' to a series of group factors *in between* 'g' and 's' factors (see Figure 11.7).

Within Vernon's hierarchal theory, the highest intelligence level is 'g'. Like Spearman, Vernon thought 'g' was the most important factor underlying intelligence in human beings. The next level in Vernon's hierarchy comprises

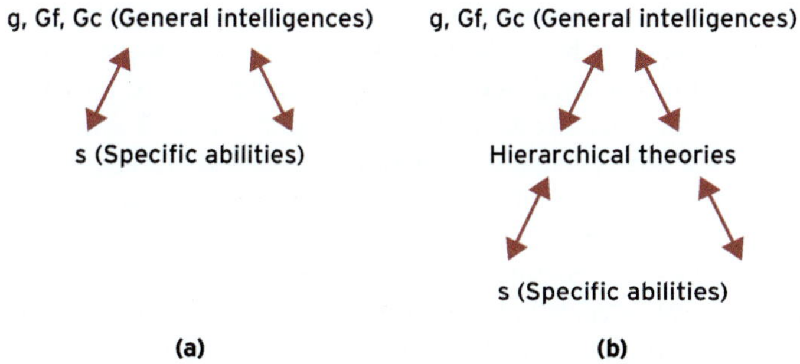

Figure 11.6 (a) Overview of theories by general intelligences and specific abilities. (b) How the hierarchical theories fit into this overview.

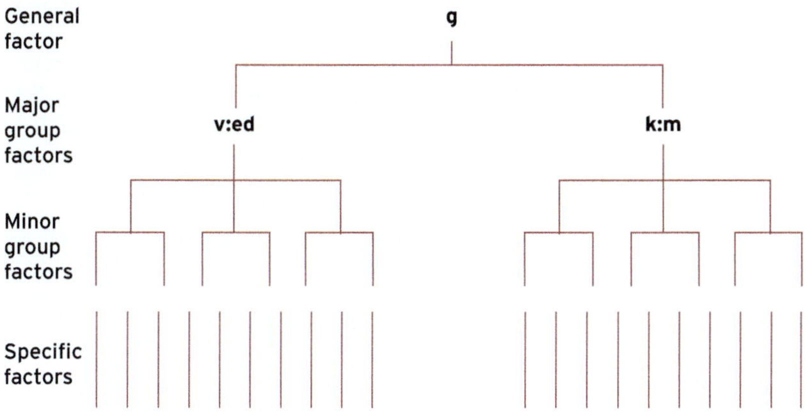

Figure 11.7 Vernon's hierarchal theory of intelligence.

two *major group factors*, verbal/educational (v:ed) and spatial/mechanical abilities (k:m).

- The 'v:ed' factor represents largely verbal/educational intelligence, including verbal-numerical-educational abilities.
- The 'k:m' factor comprises spatial/mechanical intelligence, including practical-mechanical-spatial-physical abilities.

The next level of Vernon's hierarchy contains *minor group factors*, divided from the major group factors. That is, from the major group factor, 'v:ed', verbal, numerical and educational abilities are minor group factors. Similarly, from the major group factor, 'k:m', practical, mechanical, spatial, and physical abilities are minor group factors.

At the bottom of the hierarchy are the specific intelligence factors. These are divided from the minor group factors. That is, from the 'v:ed' major group factor family, and the educational abilities minor group factors, there would be specific abilities such as reading, spelling, use of grammar and punctuation. Similarly, from the 'k:m' major group factor family, and the spatial abilities minor group factors, there would be specific spatial abilities such as recognising an object when it is seen from different locations, the ability to imagine movement of an object and ability to think about spatial relations when the body of the observer is central.

Carroll: from the Three-Stratum Model of Human Cognitive Abilities to CHC

John B. Carroll, an American Educational Psychologist, proposed a hierarchical model of intelligence officially named the Three-Stratum Model of Human Cognitive Abilities.

Carroll (1993) proposed this hierarchical model of intelligence based on the factor analysis of 461 data sets obtained between 1927 and 1987. These data sets were important because they included a number of intelligence data sets from class intelligence studies reported during the past 50 to 60 years. Based on this analysis, Carroll proposed three hierarchical levels to intelligence, which he termed stratums:

- Stratum I comprises specific levels of intelligence. Overall, Carroll identified 69 different cognitive abilities/intelligences.
- Stratum II is made up of eight broad factors arising from these specific abilities:
    - fluid intelligence, abbreviated to (in a similar way to Cattell) Gf;
    - crystallised intelligence, abbreviated to Gc;
    - general memory and learning, abbreviated to Gy;
    - broad visual perception, abbreviated to Gv;

- broad auditory perception, abbreviated to Gu;
- broad retrieval ability, abbreviated to Gr;
- broad cognitive speediness, abbreviated to Gs;
- processing speed, abbreviated to Gt.

- Stratum III is the general level of intelligence representing general intellectual ability, similar to 'g'.

Carroll's work perhaps provided a much-needed systematic organisation and integration of over fifty years of research on the structure of human cognitive abilities. As you can see, it brings together a number of themes including Spearman's 'g' and specific factors, Cattell's 'gc' and 'gf', Thurstone's specific factors and Vernon's hierarchical approach.

Cattell, Horn and Carroll (CHC): theory, research and practice together

Our story of factor-analytic studies and theories would be expected to stop with Carroll's 1993 work. However, it continues with recent convergence between Cattell's original work and Carroll's factor-analytic work.

US psychologist John Leonard Horn (Department of Psychology at the University of South Carolina), along with his advisor, Raymond B. Cattell, had been developing Cattell's original theory of intelligence that specifies two broad factors, fluid and crystallised intelligence. The main thrust of Horn's work had been to look for numerous specific factors that support the general ones. However, by the middle 1980s, John Horn had begun to conclude that the available research supported the presence of seven additional broad 'g' abilities beyond that of Gf and Gc and had abandoned the notion of a general 'g' factor. Though Horn retained the title 'Gf–Gc' (known as Cattell-Horn 'Gf–Gc') to describe the theory, there were actually nine dimensions to the intelligence theory, with an abbreviation accompanying each intelligence:

- fluid reasoning (Gf);
- acculturation knowledge intelligence (Gc);
- short-term apprehension and retrieval abilities (SAR);
- visual processing (Gv);
- auditory processing (Ga);
- tertiary storage and retrieval (TSR/Glm);
- processing speed (Gs);
- correct decision speed (CDS);
- quantitative knowledge (Gq).

Together, Carroll's and Cattell and Horn's work had dramatically informed people who were developing and using psychometric tests. One such person was Richard W. Woodcock (a US psychologist who has a wide background in education and psychology). With his colleague M. B. Johnson, Woodcock developed a series of intelligence tests called the Woodcock-Johnson Psychoeducational Battery, of which the latest, Woodcock-Johnson Psychoeducational Battery-Revised: Tests of Cognitive Ability, is used for measuring cognitive ability for people age 2 years and older. The test battery contains 21 different subtests and measures seven broad intellectual abilities, including visual process, processing speed, long-term retrieval, short-term memory, auditory processing, comprehension knowledge, and fluid reasoning.

Woodcock had noticed that researchers and testers in the educational and applied psychometric testing field have struggled with the subtle differences between Horn's and Carroll's theories. Woodcock felt, as you may have noticed, that some amalgamation could be made between the two theories.

For example, though Cattell-Horn's model of intelligence didn't acknowledge a general 'g' factor, Carroll's did. Cattell-Horn's model emphasised a factor of quantitative knowledge that was not matched by Carroll, and both recognised similar factors such as

- fluid intelligence (be it reasoning [Cattell-Horn, CH] or intelligence [Cattell, C]);
- crystallised intelligence (be it acculturation knowledge [CH] or crystallised intelligence [C]);
- general memory and learning abilities (be it short-term apprehension and retrieval abilities [CH] or general memory and learning [C]);
- visual perception (be it visual processing [CH] or broad visual perception [C]);
- auditory perception (be it auditory processing [CH] or broad auditory perception [C]).

So in 1999, Woodcock met with Horn and Carroll at Chapel Hill, North Carolina, to seek a more comprehensive model that would incorporate the similarities between their respective theoretical models, yet also acknowledge and incorporate their differences. Woodcock engaged Horn and Carroll in a sequence of conversations and private communications, and as a result of those meetings, the Cattell-Horn-Carroll (CHC) theory of cognitive abilities was developed.

The CHC theory represents both the Cattell-Horn and Carroll models of intelligence and was first described in the psychological literature by Flanagan, McGrew and Ortiz (2000) and Lohman (2001).

There are two main strata in the Cattell-Horn-Carroll (CHC) theory of cognitive abilities: a broad stratum (stratum II) and a narrow stratum (stratum I), with the abandonment of a general intelligence factor. Overall there are 16 intelligences in the broad stratum, with each of these being divided into a number of abilities that make up the narrow stratum (see Table 11.2).

The CHC model of intelligence shows an attempt to build a synthesis of several intelligence theories and

Table 11.2 Cattell-Horn-Carroll (CHC) theory of cognitive abilities: A broad stratum (stratum II) and narrow stratum (stratum I).

Broad stratum (stratum II)	Narrow stratum (stratum I)
Fluid intelligence/Reasoning (Gf) - The use of mental operations to solve novel and abstract problems	General sequential (deductive) reasoning Induction, quantitative reasoning, logical thinking and speed of reasoning
Crystallized intelligence/Knowledge (Gc) - Intelligence that is incorporated by individuals through a process of culture	Language development, lexical knowledge, listening ability, general (verbal) information, information about culture, communication ability, oral production and fluency, grammatical sensitivity, foreign language proficiency and foreign language aptitude
General (domain-specific) knowledge (Gkn) - Breadth and depth of acquired knowledge in specialized (not general) domains	Knowledge of English as a second language, knowledge of singing, skill in lip-reading, geography achievement, general science information, mechanical knowledge and knowledge of behavioural content
Visual-spatial abilities (Gv) - The ability to invent, remember, retrieve and transform visual images	Visualization, spatial relations, closure speed, flexibility of closure, visual memory, spatial scanning, serial perceptual integration, length estimation, perceptual illusions, perceptual alternations and imagery
Auditory processing (Ga) - Abilities around hearing	Phonetic coding, speech sound discrimination, resistance to auditory stimulus, distortion memory for sound patterns, general sound discrimination, temporal tracking, musical discrimination and judgement, maintaining and judging rhythm, sound-intensity/duration discrimination, sound-frequency discrimination, hearing and speech threshold factors, absolute pitch and sound localization
Short-term memory (Gsm) - The ability to encode, be aware of information in the short-term memory.	Memory span and working memory
Long-term storage and retrieval (Glr) - The ability to store information in long-term memory	Associative memory, meaningful memory, free recall memory, ideational fluency, associational fluency, expressional fluency, naming facility, word fluency, figural fluency, figural flexibility, sensitivity to problems, originality/creativity and learning abilities
Cognitive processing speed (Gs) - The ability to perform cognitive tasks automatically and fluently	Perceptual speed, rate of test-taking, number facility, speed of reasoning, reading speed and writing speed
Decision/Reaction time or speed (Gt) - The ability to react and make decisions quickly in response to simple stimuli	Simple reaction time, choice reaction time, semantic processing speed, mental comparison speed and inspection time
Psychomotor speed (Gps) - The ability to perform body motor movements rapidly and fluently	Speed of limb movement, writing speed, speed of articulation and movement time
Quantitative knowledge (Gq) - A personal breadth and depth of other abilities gained primarily during formal educational experiences of mathematics	Mathematical knowledge and mathematical achievement
Reading/Writing (Grw) - Abilities relating to reading and writing skills and knowledge	Reading decoding, reading comprehension, printed language comprehension, cloze ability, spelling ability, writing ability, English usage knowledge, reading speed and writing speed

(Continued)

Table 11.2 *(Continued)*

Broad stratum (stratum II)	Narrow stratum (stratum I)
Psychomotor abilities (Gp) - Ability to perform body motor movements with precision and coordination	Static strength, multilimb coordination, finger dexterity, manual dexterity, arm-hand steadiness, control precision, aiming and gross body equilibrium
Olfactory abilities (Go) - Abilities relating to the sense of smell	Olfactory memory and olfactory sensitivity
Tactile abilities (Gh) - Abilities that depend on the sense of touch	Tactile sensitivity
Kinesthetic abilities (Gk) - Abilities that depend on the sense that detects bodily position, weight or movement of the muscles, tendons and joints	Kinesthetic sensitivity

measurements. However, we might here see some of the difficulties in combining the theoretical approach to intelligence with the practical use of intelligence tests. Clearly, the expectations of individual factor-analysis academics working in a research setting and of those working in the applied setting might differ slightly. While individual factor-analysis academic researchers might be ultimately looking for a definitive model of intelligence, those individuals working in the psychometric test area might be looking not only for a definitive model of intelligence but also to develop an intelligence test that measures many aspects of intelligence (even those that are less popular) so they can produce a strong product that is of most use.

We can see that with the transfer of Carroll's work into applied test situations, his model of intelligence does not come through as strongly as it once seemed. Carroll's work seems to have led intelligence testing to a pinnacle by providing all sorts of definitive answers from his work, with over 460 data sets on intelligence. However, following the meeting with educational test publishers, there seems to be a deviation from Carroll's concise 8-factor model to a more convoluted 15-factor model, which seems to satisfy the need of covering a number of possible dimensions in applied testing, but leaves us with the finding that some aspects of intelligence in this model (e.g., fluid intelligence and crystallised intelligence) are valid, comprehensive and more developed and understood than other aspects are (e.g., olfactory and tactile abilities).

Other theories of intelligence: Gardner and Sternberg

The CHC model shows a development of theory and measurement right up to the present day. However, there are two more theorists whose theories of intelligence are crucial in modern-day psychology: Howard Gardner and his theory of multiple intelligences and Robert Sternberg and his triarchic theory of human intelligence.

Howard Gardner: multiple intelligences

Howard Gardner is a Professor in Cognition and Education at the Harvard Graduate School of Education. Howard Gardner's first concern is educational psychology. A lot of his work in this area favours and informs educational theory and practice, and to some extent is wary of the crossover between scientific study and educational practice (Gardner, 1983).

Gardner feels that there are difficulties with transferring scientific findings in intelligence to educational settings. He suggests that any findings in science may not be compatible with educational settings, as science demands objectivity, quantifiable data and direct measurement, while in education, researchers are dealing with children and applied settings and need more versatile methods. You can see how the more scientific aspects of intelligence testing do not translate easily into the classroom, where teachers are wrestling with improving the intelligence of children within all sorts of constraints, including the child's interest, their interactions with other children and their family background.

Gardner feels there are some myths in traditional intelligence theory. One is that many intelligence theorists see intelligence as a sensory system. Gardner's view is that intelligence does not depend on an individual's sensory system; rather, intelligence is the sum of the processes that can take place, no matter what the sensory system. So, for example, linguistic intelligence can be demonstrated with all the senses, via being able to express oneself intelligently about what one sees, hears, tastes, touches and smells. Similarly, Gardner disagrees with theories of intelligence that suggest intelligence is the same as a learning mechanism, or a way of working. Rather, he describes intelligence as a computer that works more or less well.

Gardner's background is to challenge some of the assumptions of intelligence theory and IQ testing, particularly in education. He says that Western educational systems tend to tailor their system of teaching around the logical-mathematical and the linguistic intelligences rather than other intelligences, such as interpersonal intelligences. He argues that this approach leads to bias in the education system, as teaching favours those children who are strong in specific intelligences (logical-mathematical and linguistic intelligences) over those who are not strong in those intelligences but strong in other intelligences (such as interpersonal skills). In all, Gardner identifies nine intelligences (Gardner, 1983, 1998; Gardner, Kornhaber & Wake, 1996).

In 1983 Gardner first suggested there were seven distinct intelligences. The first three are recognisable from conventional intelligence theory and IQ tests:

- linguistic (language skills);
- logical-mathematical (numerical skills);
- spatial (understanding relationships in space).

However, Gardner also included these four intelligences:

- musical (skills such as playing an instrument);
- bodily kinaesthetic (using the body);
- interpersonal (understanding and relating to others);
- intrapersonal (understanding oneself).

After 1996, Gardner suggested there are two other intelligences:

- **naturalist** – ability to interact with nature; people who are high in this intelligence might also excel at meteorology and biology.
- **existentialist** – ability to understand one's surroundings and place in the grand scheme of things. This intelligence might be linked to spiritual thinking.

Gardner explained that within his theory, each intelligence resides in separate sections of the brain; they are independent of each other and exist as single entities without control from any other intelligence or central function of the brain. However, Gardner felt that they do interact and work together when needed. For example, being able to dance and sing at the same time requires the interaction of musical and bodily kinaesthetic intelligences; solving a mathematical puzzle with a group may require logical-mathematical and interpersonal intelligence. He also argued that each individual has a separate set of intelligences, unlike those of others. Two people might have musical intelligence, but one might be able to sing while another can play the piano. Similarly, two people might have logical-mathematical intelligence, but one might be good with theoretical mathematics while another might be good with the real world of mathematics and applied statistics.

Gardner's theory of multiple intelligences challenges the entire IQ theory – that intelligence can be summed in one

Source: BananaStock/Alamy

Is this a form of intelligence?

Profile Howard Gardner

Howard Gardner was born in Philadelphia, Pennsylvania, in 1943. His parents were refuges from Germany in the war. His favourite childhood pastime was playing the piano, and he cites music as being important in his life. He studied at Harvard University, originally as a developmental psychologist and then later as a neuropsychologist.

Howard Gardner is now the Professor of Cognition and Education at the Harvard Graduate School of Education. He also holds positions at Harvard University and is Senior Director of Harvard Project Zero, a research group in human cognition that has a focus on the arts to achieve more personalized curriculum, instruction and assessment in educational settings.

Gardner is the author of over twenty books, the best known being *Frames of Minds* (1983), *The Art and Science of Changing Our Own and Other People's Minds* (Harvard Business School Press, 2004), and *Making Good; How Young People Cope with Moral Dilemmas at Work* (Harvard University Press, 2004).

Gardner has received numerous prizes for his work. He also has received honorary degrees from twenty colleges and universities, including institutions in Ireland, Italy and Israel.

number, the intelligence quotient. He says that each intelligence has a separate index that is independent of the others. For example, whether someone has a high level of musical intelligence has no bearing on his linguistic intelligence. Theoretically, Gardner says each intelligence can be measured, but not through traditional IQ tests. Rather, it should be assessed through the activities engaged in by children at school (Gardner, Kornhaber & Wake, 1996). He also suggests that a precise measurement would require an extremely long test.

Though some authors (Sternberg, 2000) have suggested that Gardner's theory needs wider examination and testing before it can be accepted as a valid theory, Gardner's theory represents an interesting approach. It attempts to explore a number of intelligences not commonly identified in intelligence testing.

Robert Sternberg

You were already introduced in the last chapter to Robert Sternberg and his work on implicit theories of intelligence. However, Sternberg (Sternberg, 1985b, 1988) himself has developed a theory called the triarchic theory of intelligence. In this theory Sternberg identifies three different types of intelligence in terms of subtheories (however, these theories sometimes go by different names, depending on the audience):

- **Componential subtheory** – This subtheory refers to the mental mechanisms that underlie intelligent behaviour.
- **Contextual subtheory** – This subtheory describes how mental mechanisms interact with the external world to demonstrate intelligent behaviour.
- **Experiential subtheory** – This subtheory describes how experience interacts with internal and the external world to form intelligence behaviours.

The componential subtheory

This subtheory of intelligence is sometimes referred to as *internal* aspects of intelligence and was described as *analytic* intelligence by the APA Task Force (see last chapter). The componential subtheory refers to the internal mechanisms that underlie intelligent behaviour. Sternberg described three sets of components (hence the name 'componential') that reflect these internal mechanisms of intelligent functioning:

- **Metacomponents** – These are mental mechanisms used by the individual to recognise a problem, to determine the exact nature of the problem and to develop strategies to solve the problem, allocating mental resources for solving the problem, monitoring the success of the strategy and evaluating the success of the efforts to solve the problem.
- **Performance components** – These are the processes actually involved in solving the problem. While the metacomponents form a type of executor that oversees the processing, the performance components are the processes that operate according to the plans laid down by the metacomponents. So performance components are the processes involved in perceiving the problem, mentally generating a number of available solutions and comparing them.
- **Knowledge-acquisition components** – These include processes involved in acquiring and learning new material and using processes such as sifting out relevant from irrelevant information (Sternberg called this selective encoding), putting together new information into a whole (Sternberg called this selective combination) and comparing the new information with old information (Sternberg called this selective comparison).

These components are perhaps the hardest part of the triarchic theory of intelligence to distinguish between. So, we will give you a simplified example to illustrate how the componential subtheory might work. In this example, we are stepping a little outside of the model because much of it is to do with internal working of the mind. However, imagine doing an essay for one of your academic modules. You have started, but you are beginning to wonder whether you are getting it right:

Your metacomponents would do these things:

- start you to think about whether you are getting the essay right;
- start you to assess to what extent you are sure you are getting the essay right;
- suggest the development of strategies to ensure (reassure yourself) that you're getting the essay right;
- suggest that you check that any strategy adopted is successful.

Your **performance components** would do these things:

- determine whether you think you need any extra help with the essay;
- identify the possible different sources of help, that is, seeking advice from a lecturer, seeking advice from other students on the course, doing more reading or doing some more planning;
- determine which might be more effective strategies to be employed first, for example, talking to a lecturer;
- determine whether talking to the lecturer has been a successful strategy. (Did the lecturer tell you what you had already written, or did they give you more ideas?)

Your **knowledge-acquisition components** would (after you had spoken to the lecturer) do these things:

- sift out the information that is important to your essay (new ideas and new theories), separating it from irrelevant information (material that the lecturer may have used to illustrate an example but that shouldn't be used in an academic essay);
- combine the different pieces of information that were given to you by the lecturer so it all fits together and can be added to your essay;
- determine how this material can be integrated into the current content of your essay.

Remember that all these actions would have occurred in your mind when working through the problem of determining whether you were on the right lines in your essay. As such, this is all intelligence behaviour. The componential subtheory represents a mental analysis of a potential problem through general strategic thinking processes (metacomponents), specific problem-solving thinking processes (performance components) and information-processing processes (knowledge-acquisition components).

As we indicated earlier, Sternberg described the metacomponents as comprising higher-level processes, while the performance and knowledge-acquisition components are lower-level processes. For Sternberg, it is the metacomponents that represent what we know as 'g' (general intelligence), which is measured by the more traditional intelligence tests.

The contextual subtheory

This subtheory of intelligence is sometimes referred to as *external* aspects of intelligence and was described as *practical* by the APA Task Force. The second part of the triarchic theory involves the application of the componential subtheory (metacomponents, performance components and knowledge-acquisition components) in the real world, that is, their practical application.

Whereas the componential subtheory addresses internal mechanisms, the contextual subtheory sees what drives these components in the real world. That is, our internal dimensions of intelligence are forever interacting with the external world, and the context of the external world also determines our intelligence behaviour. Sternberg sees intelligence as forming within the context of three external dimensions: adaptation, shaping and selection.

- **Adaptation** – This dimension sees the individual's intelligence behaviour as adapting to the world around the individual. So for example, people at university have learnt (adapted to) what constitutes intelligent behaviour in writing essays, performing well in exams, solving problems, presenting and talking to others.

The other two external world contexts arise when the individual is not satisfied with their ability to adapt their present and existing external world:

- **Shaping** – This dimension involves the individual adapting the environment to the individual, rather than the other way round. Sternberg thought this an important aspect of intelligence thought and behaviour, because it explained original thought and behaviour such as that of the great scientists who identified scientific theories and models rather than simply following them.
- **Selection** – This dimension involves choosing one environment over another. Often individuals have choices about the external world in which they exist. For example, you may have a choice of doing two psychology projects: one involves developing questionnaires, collecting quantitative data and using statistical analysis techniques; the other involves collecting interview data by talking to people and assessing their responses. You may feel that your intelligence abilities are best based around using quantitative data and mathematical techniques, and consequently you would select the first project.

Unlike some aspects of componential subtheory that were measurable via traditional IQ tests, Sternberg needed to measure contextual subtheory (practical intelligence). To do so, he used a concept called tacit knowledge.

Sternberg, Wagner, Williams and Horvath (1995) defined tacit knowledge as 'action-oriented knowledge', usually learned without the help of others, or as direct instruction that allows people to achieve goals they personally value. Tacit knowledge is based on understanding procedures rather than facts, that is, knowledge about how to do something rather than knowledge about it. Largely, measures of tacit knowledge have been used in applied settings, particularly in a business setting to assess job performance. However, an example more suited to you involves the findings of research carried out by Nancy Leonard and Gary Insch (Leonard & Insch, 2005). This study looked at students' use of tacit knowledge in higher education, that is, procedures and processes (tacit knowledge) that led to success as a student rather than simple knowledge of facts. Leonard and Insch found, among 428 undergraduate students, that the following six aspects of tacit knowledge were important in education:

- cognitive self-motivation skills (e.g., attending class regularly and making time to study);
- cognitive self-organisation skills (e.g., showing self-control and staying on task);
- individual technical skills (e.g., speaking with lecturer after class and asking the lecturer questions);
- institutional technical skills (e.g., setting regular study times and meeting regularly with lecturers and advisers);
- task-related interaction skills (e.g., participating in student-organised study groups and getting to know other students in a class);
- social interaction skills (e.g., participating actively in different activities on campus and getting involved in campus clubs and societies).

The tests that measure tacit knowledge are domain-specific tests. That is, they are designed for particular areas of intelligence such as intelligence in business and intelligence in the army rather than as a measure of general intelligence across the population, which is the case with more traditional IQ tests.

Stop and Think

Applying for a job

Imagine you are applying for the following job. This was a real job advertised in 2004.

Title: Part-time Research Assistant (.3 for 6 months)

Grade: R & AIA (Grade 6)

Department: Psychology

Main purpose of post

The appointee will take a role in an evaluation study, funded by the Learning and Teaching Support Network in Psychology, examining the usefulness of using mathematical puzzles to aid the learning of statistical concepts. The evaluation work is taking part on two university sites.

The main role of the appointee is to collect and analyse interview data with undergraduate students to enable evaluation of the usefulness of mathematical puzzles in aiding the learning of statistical concepts. The appointee will be expected to collect data on both of the aforementioned university sites. The post is a .3 post, which comprises 1 and a half days a week. There is a small travel budget available for traveling between the Leicester and Sheffield university sites.

Duties and responsibilities

- To assist the main researcher in undertaking the work supported by the Learning and Teaching Support Network in Psychology
- To interview 1st-year undergraduate students regarding learning experiences
- To provide a preliminary analysis of interview data

Personal specifications

Essential criteria:

- Have a relevant first degree.
- Some experience of collecting data, particularly within University settings.
- The ability to communicate effectively with research participants.
- Some experience of computers, mainly word processing.

Desirable criteria:

- Some experience of introductory statistics

Consider the Cattell-Horn-Carroll and Gardner's and Sternberg's theories of intelligence. Think about how, if you were to apply for the job, you might use each theory and the terms of the theory to show the prospective interview panel that you were an intelligent individual suitable for the job.

The experiential subtheory

This subtheory of intelligence relates to aspects of experience and was referred to as *creative* intelligence by the APA Task Force. The experiential subtheory examines how experience interacts with intelligence in terms of the individual's internal world and the external world. Sternberg recognised that information-processing components are always applied to tasks and situations where the person has some level of previous experience. Sternberg identified two aspects of the experiential subtheory.

- **Novelty** – The ability to deal with relative novelty is a good way of assessing intelligence. People who are good at managing a novel situation can often solve it, and most people would not notice. For example, you may be given an exam in a particular topic, and though you may not have taken an exam in that academic area before, you may use your experience of other exams (how to revise, plan and how to present ideas) to do well at this new exam. Consequently, intelligent thinking and behaviour can emerge from an individual taking advantage or learning from one's experiences to solve new problems.
- **Automisation** – The ability to automise information is a key aspect of intelligence. Automatisation is an ability that has been performed many times and can now be done with little or no extra thought. Once a process is automatised, it can be run in parallel with the same or other processes. An example of this is reading. Remember your development from reading out loud in a deliberate fashion, concentrating on every syllable (and . . . the . . . stu . . . dent . . . said . . . to . . . the . . . lec . . . tu . . . rer) to reading silently and quickly. Now you can read the subtitles of a foreign film without it spoiling your appreciation of the visuals of the film.

Sternberg's theory is very influential in psychology, and we will see more of his work in Chapter 15 when discussing giftedness, wisdom and creativity. However, a lot of Sternberg's work remains relatively unexamined empirically. For example, though he has developed the Sternberg Triarchic Abilities Test, it is still an unpublished research instrument.

Final comments

Overall, in this chapter we have taken you from the earliest conceptions of intelligence in psychology (Galton, Binet), through many of the major theorists (Spearman, Cattell, Carroll), major measures of intelligence and its estimation (the Wechsler and Raven's Matrices IQ tests, IQ and deviation IQ), multifactoral and hierarchical model (Guilford and Carroll) and modern-day theorists (Gardner and Sternberg). Taken together, you should now have an understanding of how intelligence, both the concept and its measurement, has developed for over a century. In the next three chapters we aim to develop some of the ideas, and look at many of the debates and controversies that surround intelligence.

Summary

- Galton is the forefather of intelligence tests. His central hypothesis was that there are differences in intelligence, and he set out to explore this hypothesis.
- Alfred Binet created the first intelligence test. In 1905, with Theodore Simon, Binet produced the Binet-Simon scale, the first intelligence test, which Simon later described as 'practical, convenient, and rapid'.
- Terman began to recognise the need for 'standardised testing'.
- William Stern developed the idea of the intelligence quotient, or as it is more popularly known today, IQ.
- Yerkes developed a group intelligence test, resulting in the Army Alpha and Army Beta tests.
- Charles Spearman introduced a 2-factor theory of intelligence. The first factor of intelligence was specific abilities, 's'. The second factor was what Spearman thought was underlying all the positive correlations between intelligence tests, general ability, 'g'.
- In 1939 Wechsler published the first of the Wechsler tests, the Wechsler-Bellevue Scale. Later he introduced two tests that are still used today; the Wechsler Adult Intelligence Scale (WAIS) and the Wechsler Intelligence Scale for Children (WISC). Alongside these tests, he published a new way of calculating IQ through the use of standard deviations.
- Scottish psychologist John Carlyle Raven first published his Progressive Matrices in 1938. His test was a non-verbal measure of 'g'.

- **Thurstone agreed with Spearman's hypothesis of a general factor of intelligence. However, he viewed 'g' differently from Spearman. Thurstone argued that 'g' results from, rather than lies behind, seven primary mental abilities.**
- **Cattell acknowledged Spearman's work in accepting that there was general intelligence, but he suggested that 'g' comprises two related but distinct components: crystallised intelligence and fluid intelligence.**
- **Guilford disagreed with the stance of Spearman, and to some extent with Thurstone and Cattell; he did not acknowledge the existence of 'g'. Instead, Guilford (1977) eventually proposed that intelligence was the result of 150 independent abilities. His theory was named the Structure of Intellect (SI) theory.**
- **Vernon described intelligence as a hierarchy. Vernon thought that 'g' accounts for the largest amount of variability among humans. The next level in Vernon's hierarchy comprises two major group factors, then minor group factors and then specific factors.**
- **Carroll (1993) proposed a hierarchical model of intelligence, the Three-stratum Model of Human Cognitive Abilities. Stratum I comprises specific levels of intelligence, Stratum II is made up of eight broad factors arising from these specific abilities. Stratum III is the general level of intelligence representing general intellectual ability, similar to 'g'.**
- **Gardner suggested there are nine distinct intelligences, resulting in his multiple intelligence theory.**
- **Sternberg developed the triarchic theory of intelligence, with intelligence comprising componential, contextual and experiential subtheories.**

Connecting Up

- This chapter is a forerunner for Chapters 12 and 13 in this section. You may need to access Chapter 23 of this book, which explains statistical techniques and particularly factor analysis.
- We saw in this chapter the issues that occur between theory and research and practice in trying to arrive at a good theoretical definition and measurement of intelligence. We will see these issues repeated when we explore emotional intelligence (Chapter 14) and the difficulties of applying personality and intelligence constructs to education and the workplace (Chapter 15).

Critical Thinking

Discussion questions

When discussing intelligence, you really need to think about how all these different intelligence theories fit together. Should you reject 'g' as a valid theory as some theorists have done, or is it a simple and influential idea of intelligence that has helped researchers define and refine ideas about intelligence?

- What are your views on whether 'g' exists?
- Which of the theories of intelligence do you think are strongest?
- Should the measurement of intelligence combine verbal and non-verbal problems?
- Gardner identified musical skills as a form of intelligence. Why do you think Gardner chose music and not other arts like painting or acting?
- Can we consider particular forms of body movement (such as gymnastics, sport and dance) as forms of intelligence?
- Without intelligence tests, there would be no intelligence theory. Without intelligence theory, there would be no intelligence tests. Discuss.

Essay questions

- Critically discuss the theory of 'g'.
- Critically discuss Gardner's theory of intelligence.
- Critically examine how many intelligences there are.
- Critically discuss the role that factor analysis has had in informing theories of intelligence.
- Critically discuss how hierarchal theories of intelligence inform the debate about the nature of intelligence.
- Discuss the role of intelligence tests in the development of intelligence theory.

Going Further

Books

- Robert J. Sternberg (Ed.). (2000). *Handbook of intelligence*. Cambridge: Cambridge University Press.
- N. J. Mackintosh (1998). *IQ and human intelligence*. Oxford: Oxford University Press.
- Gardner, H. (1983). *Frames of mind: The theory of multiple intelligences*. New York: Basic Books.

Journals

- Sternberg, R. J., & Kaufman, J. C. (1998). Human abilities. *Annual Review of Psychology, 49*, 479–502. *Annual Review of Psychology* is published by Annual Reviews, Palo Alto, California. Available online via Business Source Premier.
- Gottfredson, L. S. (1997). Why g matters: The complexity of everyday life. *Intelligence, 24*, 79–132. Published by Elsevier Science. Available online via Science Direct.
- Intelligence: A Multidisciplinary Journal. This journal in psychology is devoted to publishing original research and theoretical studies and review papers that substantially contribute to the understanding of intelligence. It provides a new source of significant papers in psychometrics, tests and measurement as well as all other empirical and theoretical studies in intelligence and mental retardation. Published by Elsevier Science. Available online via Science Direct.

Web resources

There are some classic intelligence papers that you can access on the web including Spearman, Binet and Terman.

- Spearman, C. (1904). 'General intelligence', objectively determined and measured. *American Journal of Psychology, 15*, 201–293 (at **http://psychclassics.yorku.ca/Spearman/**).
- Binet, A. (1905/1916). New methods for the diagnosis of the intellectual level of subnormals. In E. S. Kite (Trans.), *The development of intelligence in children*. Vineland, NJ: Publications of the Training School at Vineland. (Originally published 1905 in *L'Année Psychologique, 12*, 191–244.) Available online **(http://psychclassics.yorku.ca/Binet/binet1.htm).**
- Terman, L. M. (1916). The uses of intelligence tests. From *The measurement of intelligence* (chapter 1). Boston: Houghton Mifflin. Available online **(http://psychclassics.yorku.ca/Terman/terman1.htm).**

You can find out more about Cattell, Horn and Carroll's integration of work here on IQ Tests; available online **(http://www.2h.com/Tests/iqtrad.phtml).**

Film and Literature

- If you are looking for an example of someone who shows a great deal of intelligence by his reasoning ability, then the complete series of Sherlock Holmes by Arthur Conan Doyle (containing 4 novels and 56 short stories) is an excellent example. However, you may feel that these stories, like the portrayal of intelligence, are dated. In that case the Morse series by Colin Dexter, the Rebus series by Ian Rankin and the Banks series by Peter Robinson are excellent alternatives. They also display more modern examples of reasoning ability.
- **A Beautiful Mind** (2001; directed by Ron Howard). If you would like to see a film about someone with a great intelligence, see this film about the life of John Forbes Nash Jr, a math prodigy able to solve problems that baffled the greatest of minds.
- We outline Gardner's theory of multiple intelligences, one of which is bodily kinaesthetic – using the body. You may not be convinced that using the body constitutes intelligence. However, consider this view in light of Asian films such as *Hero* (2002; directed Yimou Zhang) and *Crouching Tiger, Hidden Dragon* (2000; directed by Ang Lee), which emphasise intelligence as part of the movement of the body.

Chapter 12

Intelligence Tests:

What Do Scores on Intelligence Tests Reflect?

Key Themes

- Psychometric intelligence tests
- Cognitive, biological and physiological measures of intelligence
- Uses of intelligence tests
- Criticism of intelligence tests
- Flynn effect
- Cognitive stimulation
- Nutrition

Learning Outcomes

After studying this chapter you should:

- Be familiar with modern themes in intelligence tests
- Understand the features and uses of popularly used intelligence tests
- Know about the general criticisms of or concerns with intelligence tests
- Be able to discuss advantages from the continued use of intelligence tests
- Understand what the Flynn effect is and the discussions that emerge from this phenomena
- Be able to outline the cognitive stimulation and nutritional hypotheses of intelligence

Introduction

Intelligence matters in the modern world. In 1999 the UK government gathered together a group of education experts to (1) advise education ministers on how best to make sure that children fulfil their potential and (2) to tackle what they saw as an ethos of underachievement in schools. As part of this effort, the government set up the Excellence in Cities scheme, aimed to help children living in the inner cities break out of poverty. Furthermore, in 2002 a National Academy for Gifted and Talented Youth was set up to provide special provision for those children thought to be in the top 5 per cent of intelligence. The European Union has introduced initiatives like REACH (which involves the proper Registration, Evaluation and Authorisation of Chemicals) because of the effect chemicals can have on, among other things, our intelligence. Intelligence tests are used in government departments, in selecting for the civil service and in the Armed Forces. You can see from examples like these that even at the highest levels of society, with those who govern us, intelligence matters.

Source: The Photolibrary Wales/Alamy

What we are going to do in this chapter is to begin to examine the role that intelligence and the measurement of intelligence plays in society. We have in the last chapter discussed several ways that intelligence has been conceptualised and measured over much of the twentieth century. In this chapter we are going to start looking at intelligence tests in modern use and outlining the uses and the criticisms of these intelligence tests. We are going to expand our consideration of intelligence tests to include measures that emphasise cognitive, physiological and biological processes. We are also going to examine a particular finding in the intelligence literature, the Flynn effect, and its relationship to two hypotheses in intelligence, the cognitive stimulation hypothesis and the nutrition hypothesis.

Types of intelligence tests

In the last chapter we outlined the theory and gave you examples of the types of intelligence tests used to measure intelligence. We discussed earlier intelligence researchers such as Galton and Binet, who suggested that we could measure intelligence. Galton suggested that we could measure variability in intelligence, and he began to show this was true through tests of sensory discrimination and motor coordination. Binet, meanwhile, was developing intelligence tests among children. His test, the Binet-Simon scale, used many of the techniques that we see in modern-day intelligence tests – items presented in an order of difficulty, varying techniques to assess intelligence and standardised scorings to determine IQ. Later we see work by Terman and Yerkes among US adults; this research introduced the idea of mass testing, deviation IQ and consideration of culture and culture-free specific tests. Later, Spearman's introduction of the notion of general intelligence ('g') led to the introduction of the Weschler tests and Raven's Progressive Matrices. With the theoretical work of Cattell, Horn and Carroll we see the development of Woodcock-Johnson Psychoeducational Battery-Revised: Tests of Cognitive Ability.

There are many intelligence tests in use today that reflect this theoretical and empirical growth in the understanding of intelligence and IQ. The Stanford-Binet test that we described in the last chapter is now in its fifth edition (Roid, 2003), and is used among people aged from 2 to 90 plus years. It still can be used not only to compute an overall measure of IQ but also to assess fluid reasoning, knowledge, quantitative reasoning, visual-spatial processing, and working memory as well as the ability to compare verbal and non-verbal performance. The Wechsler tests are still in use today, and comprise the Wechsler Preschool and Primary Scale of Intelligence (WPPSI) for use among 3- to 7-year-olds, the Wechsler Intelligence Scale for Children (WISC) for use among 7- to 16-year-olds and the Wechsler Adult Intelligence Scale (WAIS) for use among people who are 16 years and over. The scale contains measures of verbal and performance intelligence. The Woodcock-Johnson III Tests of Cognitive Abilities are used among people aged from 2 to 90+ years and also give an overall score of general intelligence (IQ score), as well as looking at working memory and executive function skills.

The distinction between the psychometric and the cognitive psychology approaches to intelligence testing

The aforementioned tests (and those covered in the last chapter) have become known to represent the **psychometric** approach towards intelligence. This is because they are based on the findings of factor-analytic studies that have looked at the various psychometric properties of intelligence scales.

However, there is another set of intelligence tests that reflect a slightly different approach in intelligence testing, called the **cognitive psychology** approach. One notable feature of intelligence tests that fall within the cognitive psychology approach is that they highlight biological and physiological processes and aspects to intelligence. We are going to introduce you to some of these cognitive tests; but first, we need to give you to a historical context to such tests, notably the history of measuring biological and physiological aspects to intelligence.

Simple biological and physiological measures of intelligence

Our story of biological and physiological measures of intelligence begins with the observations that intelligence can be linked to biological and physiological factors. There is evidence that relatively simple biological and physiological measures of intelligence might be very good indicators of intelligence. We will illustrate two areas: brain size and a series of tests called elementary cognitive tasks (ECTs), evoked potentials (EPs) and response times (RTs).

Brain size and intelligence

One area of research is the idea that intelligent people have bigger brains. As far back as 1836, German anatomist and physiologist Frederick Tiedmann (Tiedmann, 1836) suggested that there is an indisputable connection between the size of a person's brain and their mental energy. Modern studies that have used magnetic resonance imaging (MRI) have allowed such an idea to be examined. MRI is a method of creating images of the inside of organs in living organisms, such as the brain. Researchers have been able to take images of the size of participants' brains and compare them to their overall intelligence score. Studies have shown that there is a relationship between brain size and IQ. Willerman et al. (1991) examined brain size and IQ among 40 US university students and reported a correlation of $r = .35$. Raz et al. (1993) reported a correlation of $r = .43$ between brain size and general intelligence among 29 adults aged between 18 and 78 years of age. In a meta-analysis of 37 samples across 1,530 people (McDaniel, 2005), US psychologist Michael McDaniel estimated the correlation between brain size and overall intelligence was 0.33. The correlation was higher for females than males and higher for adults than children. However, in all age and sex groups, it was clear that brain volume is positively correlated with intelligence.

Elementary cognitive tasks and intelligence

One of the main advocates of more biological examination is Arthur Jensen, an American educational psychologist. In his book, *The g Factor: The Science of Mental Ability* (Jensen, 1998), he argues the case for using biological measures of intelligence. He calls these measures elementary cognitive tasks.

Elementary cognitive tasks (ECTs) are simple tasks used to measure different cognitive processes such as understanding stimulus, stimuli discrimination, choice, visual search and retrieval of information from both the short-term and long-term memory. All elementary cognitive tasks are designed to be simple, so that every person in the study can perform them easily, and performance must be measured in terms of response time. Consequently, an individual's intelligence, as measured through elementary cognitive tasks, is based on their response times to different tasks that involve understanding and identifying stimulus, being able to discriminate between stimuli, searching visual stimuli and being able to memorise things. You will see researchers who use elementary cognitive tasks measuring response time in different ways, including these:

- **Reaction time** – This is a participant's median reaction time, representing the average response time over a number of trials.
- **Standard deviation of reaction time (RTSD)** – This task is a measure of variability; that is, to what extent do a participant's responses vary over a number of trials? For example, are response times all roughly the same (low standard deviation), or do the subject's response times vary enormously (high standard deviation)? Due to the variability of response times, the RTSD is sometimes recorded so researchers can present a fuller consideration as to how much each individual varies in elementary cognitive skills.
- **Inspection time (IT)/Evoked potential** (EP) – These response time measures indicate the sheer speed of perceptual discrimination (visual or auditory) and the time people take to process information. Participants are linked to an electroencephalogram (EEG) machine, which measures brain waves. The participant is then presented with either visual (a flash) or auditory (a loud click) stimuli. On the EEG machine, after the participant receives this stimulus, a spike appears in the brain waves. This spike is what has been 'evoked' by the stimulus. The time between the stimulus and the spike is thought to be a measure of intelligence, with a shorter gap between stimulus and response representing higher intelligence.

Measures of response times to elementary cognitive tasks are correlated with more traditional measures of intelligence. There is some debate about to what extent these tasks are related to intelligence tests. Jensen himself suggests that the correlations range from about $r = .10$ to $r = .50$, with the correlations averaging about $r = .35$. However, overall scores based on the use of various elementary cognitive tasks with different measures of response times typically are found to correlate with scores on general intelligence tests of between $r = .50$ and $r = .70$.

Jensen argues that elementary cognitive tasks can be used to measure general intelligence more accurately and analytically than with conventional intelligence tests. This, he claims, is because many of the items in those intelligence tests are based on knowledge, reasoning and problem solving – all of which combine several relatively complex cognitive processes. For Jensen, elementary cognitive tasks are useful because they involve no past learned information, or if they do, the content is so well known that it is familiar to all people doing the elementary cognitive task (e.g., responding to pictures of a cat or a dog). Jensen concedes that the physiological properties of the brain that might account for the speed-of-processing aspects of intelligence are not yet known completely; but he suggests that this way of measuring intelligence taps into several different cognitive functions that compare differences in neurological intelligence among individuals.

Alexander Romanovich Luria

The inspiration for cognitive measures of intelligence begins with the work of Soviet psychologist Alexander Romanovich Luria, who is best known for his work in neuropsychology but also contributed to cross-cultural psychology. He gained his degree in 1921 at the age of 19, after entering university at the age of 16.

Luria's earliest research involved devising methods for assessing Freudian ideas about abnormalities of thought and mental processes. A lot of Luria's work was concerned with measuring thought processes, but he was also concerned with making diagnoses based on them. For example, one of the first tests Luria developed was a 'combined motor method' (Luria, 1932). This method was used for diagnosing the thought processes of individual subjects who were asked to carry out three tasks simultaneously. Participants were asked to hold one hand steady while using the other to repeatedly press a key or squeeze a rubber ball and to respond verbally to experimenters' questions.

However, Luria's major contributions occurred starting in 1924, when he worked with Lev Semyonovich Vygotsky and Alexei Nikolaivitch Leontiev. Vygotsky was a Russian psychologist who had already made a huge contribution to conceptualising intelligence. Vygotsky influenced modern constructivist thinking, which is an area of psychology that emphasises knowledge as a value-laden, subjective construction rather than a passive acquisition of objective facts and features. That is, social meaning is an important influence on human thought and intelligence. Vygotsky also argued that unlike animals, who react only to their environment, human beings are able to extensively alter the environment for their own purposes. Vygotsky's approach to intelligence emphasises it as a process of activity rather than a solid aspect that never changes. Within this work Luria, Vygotsky and Leontiev developed a psychological approach that accounted for how physical development and sensory mechanisms intertwine with culture to produce psychological processes and function in adults, including intelligence. The approach of Vygotsky and his colleagues encompassed aspects of 'cultural', 'historical' and 'instrumental' psychology. These researchers emphasised that these three aspects are important in understanding psychological functioning and intelligence, they also greatly emphasised the role of culture, the social environment and particularly language in influencing human thoughts, feelings and action.

From this work Luria sought to elaborate this cultural-historical-instrumental psychology. Luria was particularly interested in developing a comprehensive theory of brain and behaviour and focused on neurological connections. One of Luria's main contributions to psychology was to question the early assumption that all the processing of visual information, perception and visual imagery occurred within the right cerebral hemisphere of the brain and that the processing of auditory information, verbal expression and propositional thinking occurred in the left hemisphere of the brain (see Figure 12.1 for a breakdown of the processes of the brain).

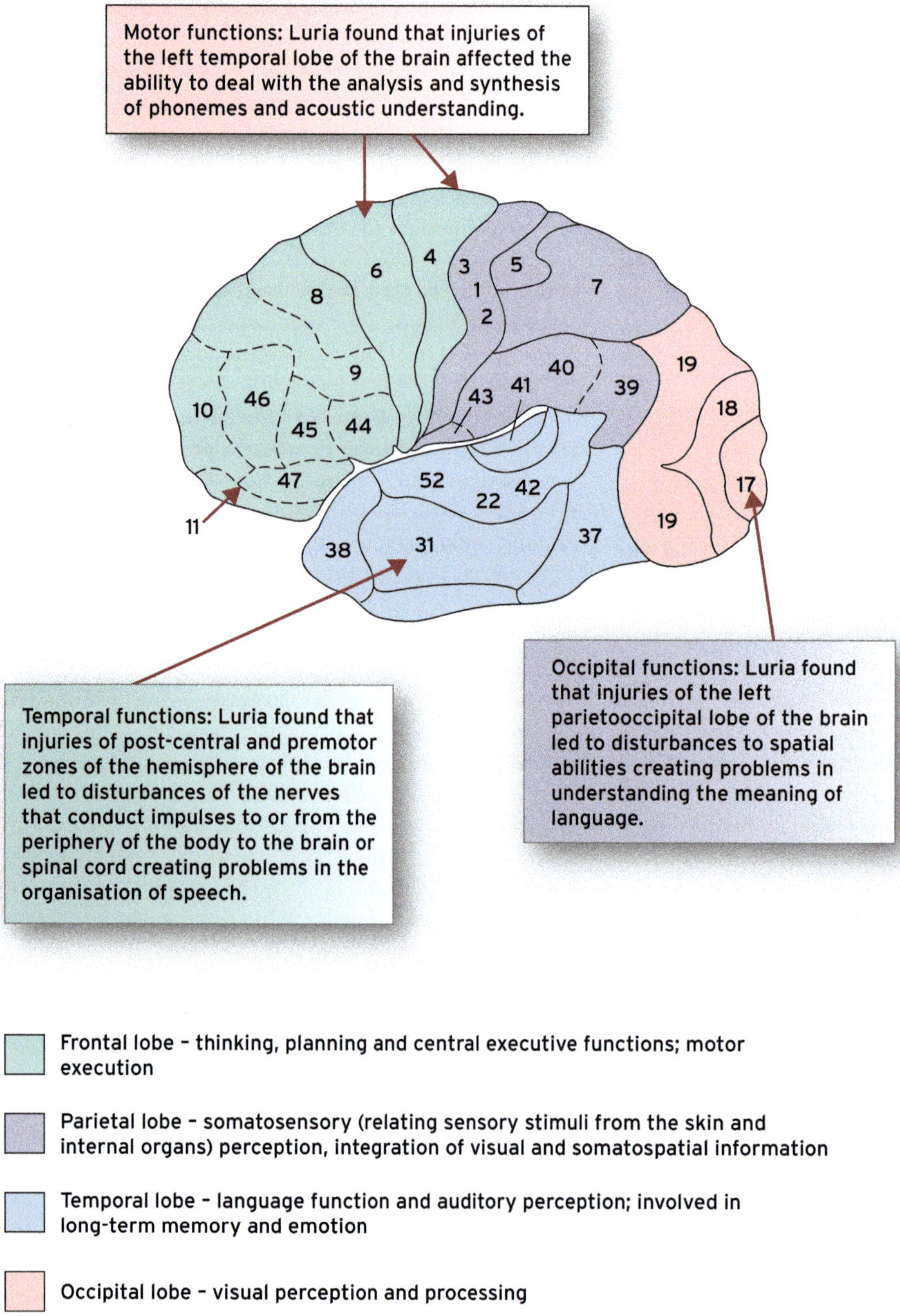

Figure 12.1 Summary of Luria's findings using Brodmann's definitions of areas of the brain.

Luria (1973) was one of the first academics who questioned this distinction and thought it too simplistic. He suggested that the left hemisphere of the brain contains greater cognitive power and viewed it as a source of conscious control of behaviour, with the right hemisphere of the brain responsible for automatic and subconscious aspects of behaviour not under the conscious control of the brain. Luria also distinguished between simultaneous (processing that happens all at once) and successive (characterised by a series or sequence of events) cognitive processing. **Simultaneous processing** is cognitive processing that allows individuals to explore and discover relationships between components of information and to integrate this information, leading to spatial awareness. For example, this is the sort of thinking would allow you to gather information for an essay from several texts and then put it together into a new essay. **Successive processing** enables individuals to put information into a serial order. For example, to learn how to perform a statistical test on a computer, you must do it in a particular order to get the result. Luria thought successive processing occurred in the fronto-temporal regions of the brain and simultaneous processing occurred in the occipital-parietal region of the brain.

During the 1930s Luria investigated perception, problem solving and memory and specialised in the study of brain injuries to the higher cortical parts of the brain (those areas of the brain that deal with complex brain functions such as language or reading). With this approach, he compared and examined patients with brain injuries, using the results to understand how brain functions and higher functions such as language were intrinsically linked together. By studying these results, Luria was able to to single out basic neuropsychological factors underlying speech. He was able to identify the following links:

- Injuries of the left temporal lobe of the brain affect the ability to deal with the analysis and synthesis of phonemes (the smallest sounds in a language capable of conveying a distinction in meaning, i.e., the 'm' in 'mum') and acoustic understanding (indicated by the red temporal functions box in Figure 12.1).
- Injuries of post-central and premotor zones of the left hemisphere of the brain lead to disturbances of the nerves that conduct impulses to or from the periphery of the body to the brain or spinal cord and create problems in the organisation of speech (indicated by the yellow motor functions box in Figure 12.1).
- Injuries of the left parietooccipital lobe of the brain lead to disturbances to spatial abilities, creating problems in understanding the meaning of language (indicated by the blue occipital functions box in Figure 12.1).

If all these aspects of intelligence can be affected by neurological functions, you can then see why it is important to acknowledge that these functions and their development are important to intelligence.

What was important in Luria's work was that he didn't seek just to diagnose these neurological malfunctions, but to remedy them. Luria produced a variety of methodological approaches; but he never produced a test, because he believed that each patient was different, and the tests he used would need to be adapted for each patient. Luria published two case studies, both published a few years before his death. One study describes a man with an excellent but idiosyncratic (temperamental) memory, and the other describes a man with a traumatic brain injury (Luria, 1968, 1972). In both cases, Luria showed how it was possible to combine classical diagnostic methods with methods that sought to remedy neurological problems to improve the consequences of the brain injury.

It is Luria's emphasis on neurological functioning, his distinction between simultaneous and sequential processing and his emphasis on using tests to both diagnose the problem and improve performance, centred on the individual, that have influenced the work of current-day researchers, who have developed cognitive psychology intelligence tests. We will now outline two modern-day cognitive psychology intelligence tests that have been influenced by the biological and physiological work of Luria:

- J. P. Das and Jack Naglieri's Cognitive Assessment System;
- Alan and Naneen Kaufman's ability tests.

Das and Naglieri's Cognitive Assessment System and the Kaufmans' ability test

Both Das and Naglieri and the Kaufmans have developed models and tests of IQ. These tests are based on biological and psychophysiological models of intelligence.

Das and Naglieri's Cognitive Assessment System (CAS)

In 1979, J. P. Das and colleagues (Das, Kirby & Jarman, 1979) developed a successive-simultaneous test based on Luria's theory and validated the model with several studies of children. Within this test, Das used the simultaneous-sequential distinction made by Luria. It was this distinction, and this test, that became the basis of the Cognitive Assessment System (Naglieri & Das, 1997).

The **Cognitive Assessment System** (CAS) is an IQ test designed to measure cognitive processing, integrating theoretical and applied areas of psychological knowledge, thereby assessing how knowledge is organised and accessed in the memory system as well as assessing how various intellectual tasks are achieved. The model that Naglieri and Das devised to measure IQ is the PASS system (PASS stands for Planning, Attention, Simultaneous and Successive).

Naglieri and Das define each aspect of the PASS model as follows:

- **Planning** – This is a set of decisions or strategies that an individual not only uses but adapts to solve a problem and/or reach a goal. Within the CAS, planning is measured by presenting the participant with a task and asking them to develop some approach to complete the task efficiently and effectively.
- **Attention** – In the CAS, this refers to alertness or awareness of stimuli and is seen as important and a prerequisite for learning and memory. Attention tasks in the CAS require the individual to select one aspect and ignore the other aspect of a two-dimensional stimulus.
- **Simultaneous processes** – In Luria's theory, simultaneous processes reflect a person's ability or facility to see associations and integrate single and separate pieces of information. Simultaneous tasks in the CAS require the individual to put together different parts of a particular item in a meaningful way (i.e., complete a pattern) to arrive at the correct answer.
- **Successive processes** – In Luria's theory, successive processes represent the ability to place and maintain things in a particular order. Successive tasks in the CAS require the participants to order or reproduce a particular sequence of events or answer some questions that require correct interpretation of the order of the events.

The Cognitive Assessment System is used among children and adolescents between the ages of 5 and 17 years. The test not only predicts achievement and looks for discrepancies between ability and achievement, but uses the measures of planning and attention employed in the evaluation of attention deficits and hyperactivity disorders, learning disabilities, giftedness and brain injuries. The Cognitive Assessment System helps practitioners and teachers to choose interventions for children with learning problems and to work with them to address those problems.

The Kaufmans' ability tests

Alan and Naneen Kaufman have developed a number of ability tests, including the Kaufman Assessment Battery for Children (K-ABC), Kaufman Brief Intelligence Test (K-BIT) and the Kaufman Adolescent and Adult Intelligence Test (KAIT). These tests are based again on research and theory in cognition and neuropsychology, although the Kaufmans' draw not only on Luria's neuropsychological model but also on the Cattell-Horn-Carroll (CHC) approach (discussed in Chapter 11). One major aim of the Kaufmans' work is to address the number of children who are referred for evaluation with learning problems. The Kaufmans suggest that one reason for this increase is that a lot of school-based tasks are measures of verbal intelligence

Profile Alan S. Kaufman

Alan S. Kaufman, PhD, is Professor of Psychology at the Yale University School of Medicine, Child Study Center. Dr Kaufman was born in Brooklyn, New York, in April 1944. He earned his undergraduate degree from the University of Pennsylvania in 1965, his MA in Educational Psychology from Columbia University in 1967 and his PhD from Columbia University in 1970, where he studied under Robert L. Thorndike.

In 1968, Kaufman went to work as Assistant Director at The Psychological Corporation. There, he worked with David Wechsler on a revision of the Wechsler Intelligence Scale for Children. He worked at the University of Georgia in 1974 and at the University of Alabama starting in 1984 before taking his current position at Yale in 1995.

Kaufman is best known for his development of the Kaufman Assessment Battery for Children, which has been translated, adapted for and standardized in more than fifteen countries. He has also developed a variety of other psychological and educational tests including the Kaufman Brief Intelligence Test (K-BIT), the Kaufman Adolescent and Adult Intelligence Test (KAIT), the Kaufman Short Neuropsychological Assessment Procedure (K-SNAP) and the Kaufman Functional Academic Skills Test (K-FAST).

During his career he has published around twenty books and more than two hundred journal articles. His books include the well-cited *Assessing Adolescent and Adult Intelligence* (1990), which was turned into a second edition with Liz Lichtenberger in 2002. He was a co-editor of the journal *Research in the Schools* from 1992 to 2004 and has been on the editorial board of five professional journals.

Sequential processing/short-term memory

'Say the numbers just as I do.'

2 – 9

6 – 4 – 3 – 1

8 – 10 – 5 – 2 – 6 – 4 – 3 – 9 – 1

a) **Number recall:** The child says a series of numbers in the same sequence as the examiner recites them. The length of sequence increases from two to nine digits

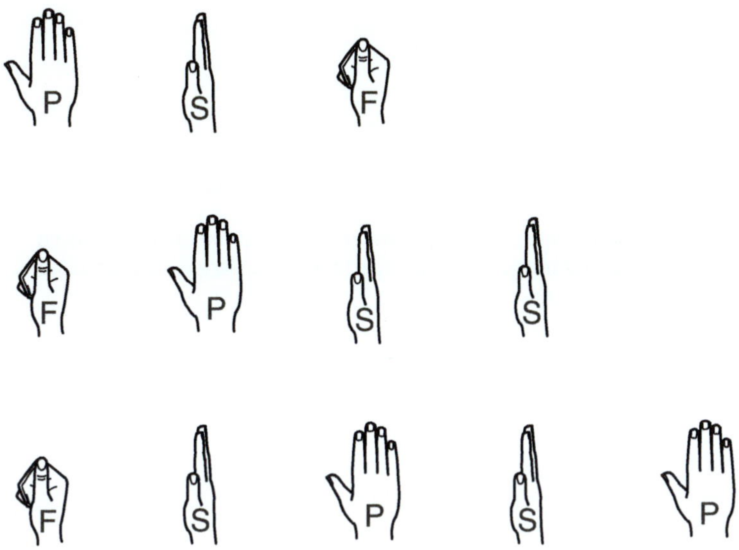

b) **Hand movements:** The responses to this test are non-verbal. The child performs a series of hand movements in the same sequence as the examiners shows him or her

c) **Word order:** This subtest ask each child to respond by touching silhouettes of common objects after the examiner repeats their names in sequence

Figure 12.2 Examples of the Kaufman's tests, including items measuring Simultaneous and Sequential processing. Both the Kaufman and Cognitive Assessment System have both been influenced by the biological and physiological work of Luria and measure simultaneous and successive/sequential processing.
Source: From the *Kaufman Assessment Battery for Children for Children,* Second Edition (KABC-II). Copyright © 2004 AGS Publishing. Reprinted with permission of Pearson Assessments, a business of Pearson Education.

Simultaneous/visual processing

d) **Conceptual thinking:** This test for children ages 3-6 requires the examinee to look at a group of 4-5 pictures and identify the one that is not like the others.

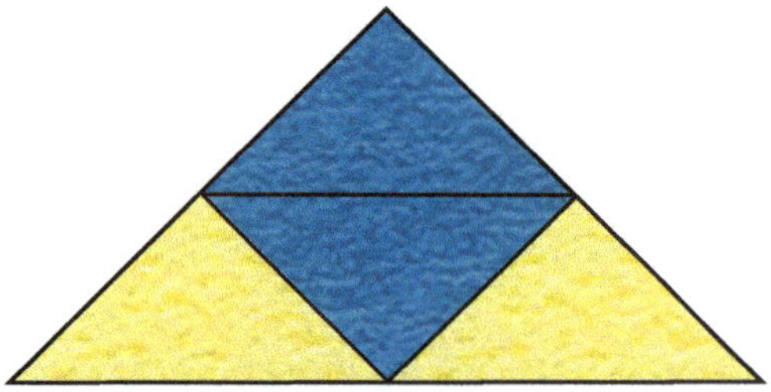

e) **Triangles:** Children are asked to copy or build designs using coloured triangles or plastic shapes or different sizes of colours.

f) **Rover:** This subtest asks children to move a dog toward a bone through a checkerboard-like grid that includes obstacles. It requires the child to picture different possible routes and then select the shortest.

g) **Block counting:** Shown a picture of a stack of blocks (some of which are hidden), the child must visualise the unseen blocks and determine how may there in the stack.

h) **Gestalt closure:** This subtest uses incomplete pictures to measure a child's ability to fill in gaps to identify an image.

Stop and Think

The British Ability Scales

Also worth noting alongside the IQ tests are the British Ability Scales. The British Ability Scales, now in their second edition, were developed by Colin Elliott (Elliot, 1983, 1996). The British Ability Scales are an individually administered cognitive battery for children, combining both the psychometric and cognitive approaches that we have outlined so far. The British Ability Scales are organised as follows:

- **Core and achievement scales** - block building; verbal comprehension; picture similarities; naming vocabulary, early number concepts; copying; block design; recall of designs; word definitions; matrices; similarities; quantitative reasoning, basic number skills; spelling and word reading
- **Diagnostic scales** - matching letter-like forms; recall of digits; digits backwards; recall of objects; recognition of pictures; speed of information processing

(vocabulary, general knowledge, oral arithmetic), and a lot of the children who are referred for help for learning problems are bilingual or bicultural. Using their test approach, the authors believe they can make meaningful school-based recommendations for children based on cognitive processes rather than cultural knowledge.

The Kaufman tests (see Figure 12.2) typically measure three aspects of intelligence:

- **Achievement** – This test measures acquired knowledge, including reading and arithmetic skills.
- **Simultaneous processing** – This test involves spatial or analogic tasks that ask the participant to simultaneously integrate and synthesise information.
- **Sequential processing scale** – In this test, the participant typically solves tasks by arranging the stimuli in sequential or serial order.

Features, uses and problems surrounding intelligence tests

In the last section we described different types of intelligence tests. In the following sections we are going to consider the features, uses and problems found in intelligence tests.

Typical features of intelligence tests

Let us establish some of the important aspects that are essential to good intelligence tests. Sattler (2002) establishes three main aspects that tend to be typical in all good intelligence tests.

A variety of tasks are involved in intelligence tests

To assess a full range of abilities, a good intelligence test needs to contain a number of tasks. For example, tests such as the Wechsler Adult Intelligence Scale will contain various measures including ability tests of general knowledge, digit span, vocabulary, arithmetic, comprehension, similarities, picture completion, picture arrangement, block design, digit symbol and object assembly. Such 'subtests' used together provide a fuller understanding of the overall intelligence of the person as well as their particular strengths.

Standardisation of administration

The aim of standardising administration is to provide a controlled environment in which the test is taken to allow comparisons among children (though note that different test authors differ in the emphasis they place on the importance of making comparisons *among* children). For example, if conditions differed during the test administration, such as the wording of questions or the exact time given for the test, then differences in intelligence between children might be (at least partly) attributed to the differences in administration conditions rather than to differences in their intelligence. The administration of any intelligence test is standardised, from instructions for completing the test, to the location of the test, to which and how many people should be present. Two further important aspects to this standardisation are the length of administration of the test and the conditions under which it is taken.

- As typically intelligence tests are administered to schoolchildren, the length of time children can take on a task will vary with the age of the child. For example,

Source: Tina Manley/Alamy

How do you think IQ tests have changed since WWI?

younger children will tend to be able to concentrate less over longer periods of time than older children will, and they will want to spend less time on more complicated tasks. Researchers will seek to standardise the length of time of the test depending on the age of the child.

- There is a need for the actual test to be done in comfortable conditions and to be administered by a qualified test administrator. If you have ever taken an intelligence test at school, you will probably recall that it was administered by a trained staff member. This qualified person ensures the quality of administration of the test. This person ensures that test-takers are comfortable, and particularly where children are concerned, the administrator might seek to develop a rapport with the students, responding to needs as they arise (i.e., when a student is in distress, making sure respondents aren't rushed into starting the test). You can see that without being provided with this type of approach, individuals might feel that their performance on the test wasn't only due to their intelligence, but to the conditions under which it was taken.

Norm referencing

This is another form of standardisation. The aim of making an intelligence test norm-referenced is to allow comparisons to be made with other children. There is no point in determining the IQ score of a person as being 140, unless you have something to compare it with. As we saw in the previous chapter with the work of Terman, all tests will have to be administered to a large group of people around the same age (or at the same age among children) and of similar demographics (sex, race, area of residence, occupational status) to allow accurate comparisons to be made. The standard example is to use 100 to describe an average score and then compare all scores around that number. Some authors of intelligence tests play down the need to make comparisons on this basis among children because the tests are designed for individual assessment. However, even these intelligence tests will provide some norm-referenced material, so that the person using the intelligence test may have a context for understanding individual scores.

The uses of intelligence tests

Intelligence tests are used for all sorts of purposes, but mainly for the following three: selection, diagnosis and evaluation.

You may first come across intelligence tests in schools. Here intelligence tests might be used for selection purposes, streaming children into high-ability and low-ability classes, or conceivably might be used by school selectors to ensure they only take on high-ability children. Intelligence tests might be used for diagnostic purposes, to help teachers determine whether there are problems in children with low ability and specifically where these problems might exist so children might be helped. They would also be used for evaluating the child's ability and could help teachers decide which students might be capable of performing better in national examinations.

Similar ideas apply to intelligence tests when they are used in higher education and the workplace, with colleges, universities and employers using them to select candidates. You can easily see how an applicant who scores well in general knowledge, vocabulary, arithmetic and comprehension (all specific intelligence abilities) might be more likely to get a vacancy over someone who does not achieve a high score in these abilities.

This application of tests is not without good reason. People who suggest and support the use of intelligence tests would argue that IQ tests are valid and useful as they show a positive correlation with school achievement and job performance.

As regards school achievement, research has looked at various indices including examination ability, specific abilities in a particular topic (for example, Mathematics, English) and whether students stay on in school. Overall reviews by US psychologists Alan Kaufman and Elizabeth Lichtenberger (Kaufman, 1990; Kaufman & Lichtenberger, 2005) provide a review of key papers that have looked at the correlation between general intelligence and school attainment and achievement. They conclude that the average correlation between general intelligence (IQ) and a number of school indicators is around $r = .50$, suggesting intelligence does predict achievement at school.

Two strong examples of this predictive power of intelligence tests can also be found in the workplace. In 1984 two US psychologists, John E. Hunter and R. F. Hunter (Hunter & Hunter, 1984), did a meta-analysis (a **meta-analysis** is a technique that combines the results of several studies) and put together the results of studies that examined various predictors at the start of a job with eventual job performance. In all, the authors looked at results for over 32,000 workers. They found that the correlation between general intelligence (IQ) and job performance was $r = .54$ (a medium-sized correlation) and had a much larger association with job performance than with the curriculum vitae of the candidate ($r = .37$), previous experience of the candidate ($r = .18$), job interviews ($r = .14$) and education of the candidate ($r = .10$).

The first ever meta-analysis of this type was repeated in the United Kingdom by UK psychologist Cristina Bertua, Dutch psychologist Neil Anderson and Spanish psychologist Jesús F. Salgado, who looked at over 280 samples, comparing 13,262 people's scores on different intelligence tests and their later job performance (Bertua, Anderson & Sagado, 2005). In this study the researchers examined several different types of jobs, including clerical, engineering, professional, management and sales and ranging from low-skilled jobs to higher-skilled professional jobs. Bertua and her colleagues found that both general intelligence and specific ability tests were good predictors of job performance, with correlations being similar to those reported by Hunter and Hunter (1984) of between $r = .5$ and $r = .6$.

However, the potential usefulness of intelligence tests does not stop there. Some psychologists have shown that general intelligence in childhood can predict variables across the life span. In 1931 the Mental Survey Committee in Scotland met and decided (due to there being no reliable way of getting a representative sample) to measure general intelligence and obtain IQ scores for everyone in Scotland. So on Wednesday, 1 June 1932, nearly every child attending school in Scotland who was born in 1921 took the same intelligence test ($n = 89{,}498$). This exercise was repeated in 1947, testing almost all people born in 1936 ($n = 70{,}805$).

A group of psychologists from Scotland – Ian Deary, Martha Whiteman, John Starr, Lawrence Whalley and Helen Fox (2004) – have pointed out that in intelligence testing history, this sample is very unusual. Scotland remains the only nation with mental test data for an entire birth cohort, never mind two. In their study, the authors look at a number of factors in old age and their relationship to the test-takers' IQ scores from the 1932 and 1947 cohorts. Some of their main findings are summarised in Table 12.1. In this table we have taken some of the information from Deary et al.'s paper regarding the 1947 cohort in terms of those who were found by to have died, those who had been diagnosed with cancer and those who had been diagnosed with a cardiovascular (involving the heart and the blood vessels) disease by the time of Deary et al.'s study.

What you can see from this table is that people who were reported to have died and those having been diagnosed with cardiovascular disease had scored significantly lower on IQ in 1947 than those who had neither died nor been diagnosed with cardiovascular disease. However, note that no significant difference was found in the IQs of people who were later diagnosed with cancer. This finding suggests, at the very least, that IQ has some level of predictive strength very much later in life.

The relationship between general intelligence and other factors is the focus of debate in the next chapter. However, it is worth noting that, like the health variables just discussed, it is proposed that general intelligence predicts poverty, the likelihood of being in prison, divorced and unemployed (Gottfredson, 1997). All in all, the evidence suggests that general intelligence – particularly IQ test scores – is not only related to, but may be a relatively important predictor of, many aspects of our lives.

Problem and issues with intelligence tests

However, intelligence tests are not without their criticisms. There are three main considerations of IQ tests that you will commonly find in the intelligence literature. These considerations are based on:

- the reliability of intelligence tests;
- the validity of intelligence tests;
- whether the usefulness of intelligence tests is overemphasised.

Table 12.1 The relationship between general intelligence (IQ) scores and a number of health outcomes in later life.

Outcome	Number of people suffering from the outcome	Number of people not suffering from the outcome	Mean IQ of people suffering from the outcome	Mean IQ of people not suffering from the outcome	Significance
People dying	125	783	97.7	104.6	$p < .001$
People being diagnosed with cancer	78	830	101.3	103.9	$p > .05$
People being diagnosed with cardiovascular disease	98	810	100.1	104.1	$p < .05$

Source: Statistics from Deary et al. (2004).

Reliability of intelligence tests

The reliability of any test refers to two aspects:

- **Internal reliability** – Any measure of intelligence with good internal reliability will have a number of items that correlate positively with one another, this suggests they are measuring the same construct.
- **Test-retest reliability (reliability of the test over time)** – A good intelligence test will show a good level of reliability over time. Your general intelligence is thought to be relatively stable over time. Therefore you would expect that if you took an intelligence test on one occasion (and got an IQ score) and you took the same intelligence test three months later (and got an IQ score), you would expect your IQ scores to be very similar.

If you want to read more about reliability, you can refer to the supplementary material in Chapter 24.

The internal reliability of intelligence scales is often well established in the research programmes that accompany the development of intelligence tests. Tests such as the Stanford-Binet Intelligence Scales and the Wechsler Intelligence Scales will provide information in their test manuals that shows the items that make up the different subscales, and the subscales that are used to compute an overall IQ score are positively related to one another. However, as established intelligence items and intelligence scales would be largely developed on the basis that they should be correlated with one another (i.e., if one item or subscale is not correlated, then test developers would omit it from the test), the concern surrounding the internal reliability of established intelligence tests is not a major issue in intelligence. However, the issues surrounding the stability of intelligence test scores over time present a much more important consideration.

People who question whether intelligence tests are reliable over time point to the fact that general intelligence (IQ) scores fluctuate. That is, if you took an intelligence test today and took the same one a week later, your IQ score computed from taking that test would probably be different. Some researchers have estimated that this fluctuation may be as much as 15 IQ points (Benson, 2003). Furthermore, individual performances on intelligence tests may fluctuate between administrations because the individual may perform differently while taking the test (they may be having a particularly good day or a particularly bad day). This fluctuation is further compounded because test-takers are not meant to take the same intelligence test twice, as they will have learnt some of the answers or the techniques involved in the test and consequently would perform better. The point is that once you have taken one general intelligence test, you will be assigned an IQ score. It is not possible to take the test again, because your later scores will be influenced by your taking the test before. Furthermore, given that IQ test scores fluctuate between administrations, how can you be sure that your first (and only) IQ score is not just a fluctuation from your real intelligence? You can see that if we are to assign people IQ scores and compare people's IQ scores based on their performance on a single administration of an intelligence test, these fluctuations of IQ scores may present a concern about the accuracy of IQ tests.

This concern of IQ scores fluctuating has been a long-term consideration of intelligence researchers, and it has spawned a whole area of research to consider these fluctuations over time. Findings suggest that though intelligence test scores do fluctuate, they do remain relatively stable over time. We will now outline some of this research.

US developmental psychologists Constance J. Jones and Nancy Bayley (1941) set up what is now known as the Berkley Growth Study. This study was started in the late 1920s and represents data from people born in Berkeley, California, between 1928 and 1929. These researchers tested a sample of children annually throughout childhood and adolescence on a number of measures, including intelligence, and calculated their IQ scores. Jones and Bayley found that IQ scores of children at 18 years were positively correlated with their IQ scores at 12 years ($r = .89$) and 6 years ($r = .77$).

It is important to remember here what is meant by stable IQ in childhood (Neisser et al., 1996). You will remember that IQ scores are based around a mean of 100 and are calculated by comparing the individual's score with other individuals at that age. An average IQ score for a typical 7-year-old would be stable if the same person, at age 18, showed the same average IQ score. A lack of variation in IQ score between age 7 and age 18 does not mean that their IQ has stayed the same, because individual knowledge, critical thinking, vocabulary and ability to reason will increase with age. Rather, it means that their score stays the same to relative to other people. A 7-year-old with an IQ score of 100 is at the mean IQ of 7-year-olds, while an 18-year-old with an IQ score of 100 is at the mean of 18-year-olds.

The findings of Jones and Bayley are supported by more recent studies. The longest follow-up study of intelligence and relationship between IQ scores used the Mental Survey Committee in Scotland that had measured intelligence in Scottish children born in 1921 and attending school on June 1, 1932 ($N = 87.498$). Scottish psychologists Ian Deary, Lawrence Whalley, Helen Lemmon, J. R. Crawford and John Starr (2000) followed up 101 people at the age of 77 years. They found that the correlation between the two occasions was $r = .63$ (which was adjusted to $r = .73$ when corrected for fine details regarding ability range within the 77-year-olds). This finding shows substantial stability from childhood to late life of IQ scores on tests.

The correlations between intelligence scores across these age ranges are impressive. However, they are not perfect; and though we would not expect them to show perfect correlations, you can see that if there are fluctuations between IQ scores on administrations, you can also see why people might be concerned or cautious when assigning a child a particular IQ score.

Profile Nancy Bayley

Nancy Bayley was born in Oregon in 1899. As a child she was rather ill, and this prevented her from attending school until the age of 8. Not deterred by this late start in her education, she went to the University of Washington with the intention of becoming an English teacher. However, Bayley quickly changed to psychology and earned her undergraduate degree in 1922 and her master's degree in 1924. During the study of her master's degree, she worked as a research assistant for the Gatzert Foundation for Child Welfare and devised performance tests for children under the age of 5. She gained her doctoral degree in 1926 from the State University of Iowa; for her thesis, she measured electrical skin responses to fear in children.

This type of research was to remain a focus of Bayley's research for the rest of her career. In 1928, she went to the Institute of Child Welfare at the University of California at Berkeley. She resided there for most of her career while holding research positions in Psychology and Anatomy at Stanford University at the same time.

At the Institute of Child Welfare, Bayley began a major study of normal and handicapped infant development. This became the now famous Berkeley Growth Study, which represents data from people born in Berkeley, California, between 1928 and 1929. Her first publications – *The California First-year Mental Scale* (1933), *Mental Growth During the First Three Years* (1933) and *The California Infant Scale of Motor Development* (1936) – introduced new methodologies for assessing developments in infants and are seen as significant milestones in developmental psychology. In the end Bayley published over two hundred publications while also helping to design the National Collaborative Perinatal Project for the study of cerebral palsy, mental retardation and other neurological and psychological disorders.

Bayley was a fellow of the APA and of the American Association for the Advancement of Science. Her work was recognized by her contemporaries: She earned the G. Stanley Hall Award of the APA's Division of Developmental Psychology in 1971. She received the Gold Medal Award of the American Psychological Foundation in 1982. She earned the distinguished contribution award from the Society for Research in Child Development.

During her career, Nancy Bayley came to be recognised as a pioneer in the field of human development. Her career was dedicated to measuring and researching intellectual abilities in infants, children and adults. Bayley died of respiratory failure in 1994.

Validity of intelligence tests

Validity of tests refers to the question of whether the test measures what it claims to measure (for more information, see Chapter 24). In the context of intelligence tests we can ask, do intelligence tests measure intelligence?

Well, within one context they do; if we answer the question, 'Do intelligence tests measure what they *claim* to measure?' If you consider an intelligence test, like the Wechsler Adult Intelligence Scale for example, then there is little doubt that the subtests of this intelligence test are measuring the different specific intelligence abilities that they have been designed to measure. Again, intelligence test developers set about establishing validity for all aspects of their intelligence test when developing them. If an intelligence test, or a particular intelligence subtest, did not show validity in development, then test developers would seek to improve that measure of intelligence. You can also see that on the face of it (sometimes called **face validity**), an intelligence test that involves solving problems using mental arithmetic probably measures, to a greater degree, mental arithmetic intelligence. Similarly, a subtest that requires a number of simple jigsaws to be completed probably measures intelligence in object assembly.

Furthermore, intelligence tests show **concurrent validity** due to their relationship with other measures of intelligence. Neisser and the rest of the Intelligence Task Force (Neisser et al., 1996) argue that is generally accepted that individuals perform equally as well or poorly on different intelligence tests, suggesting that intelligence tests tend to correlate with other intelligence tests – though there is evidence to suggest that when IQ is calculated from different intelligence tests, scores can also fluctuate by up to 15 IQ points (Benson, 2003). Also, as we have just seen, intelligence tests have been used to predict 'real-world' measures of intelligence or achievement, for example, school achievement and job performance (this is known as **predictive validity**). All these findings suggest evidence for the general validity of intelligence tests measuring what they claim to measure – general intelligence (as defined by an IQ score) that is worked out by adding together the performance on several subtests of specific abilities (e.g., arithmetic, object assembly, comprehension).

However, the discussion takes a turn when we consider the general question of validity in a slightly different way: 'Do intelligence tests measure *intelligence*?'

Some critics argue that the main problem with intelligence tests is that they assume, particularly when they produce an overall IQ score, that there is an idea of general intelligence when in fact there is no agreement on whether such a global mental capacity exists (Benson, 2003). We saw in Chapter 11 that though some theorists and researchers suggest there is a general factor of intelligence (e.g., Spearman), some theorists and researchers have questioned the idea that there is a general intelligence. For example, psychologists such as Howard Gardner identified nine intelligences that comprise his multiple intelligence theory (Gardner, 1993, 1995), and Robert Sternberg devised the triarchic theory of intelligence (Sternberg, 1985b, 1988) that comprises three aspects of intelligence (componential, contextual and experiential). In this chapter we saw that cognitive intelligence tests (such as the Kaufmans') emphasise sequential and simultaneous cognitive processes as well as more traditional achievement abilities.

What is crucial about these different approaches is that some critics of intelligence tests emphasise that intelligence is probably much more than what can be measured by intelligence tests; rather, intelligence is the result of the individual engaging in a variety of skills and information within their cultural context. For example, we have seen in Chapter 10 of this book how everyday theories that surround intelligence differ between Eastern and Western cultures, and how those theories change within cultures due to changing perceptions of intelligence with age or across different disciplines (for example, business and philosophy).

Consequently, the concern is that many intelligence tests cannot be valid, as no single intelligence test covers the many different theoretical interpretations and cultural considerations that need to be made when accurately measuring intelligence.

Modern-day intelligence researchers continually wrestle with these types of considerations and distinctions. However, it is timely to remember that early intelligence researchers strived to develop intelligence tests that allowed and considered cultural differences. Both Yerkes' Army Beta test and Raven's Progressive Matrices were developed around theories of intelligence that emphasised general intelligence and IQ scores but sought their tests to be free of influences of literacy and the English language. The Wechsler Intelligence Scale for Children (WISC) and the Stanford-Binet Intelligence Scale have been recently changed so they better reflect the abilities of test-takers from diverse cultural and linguistic backgrounds.

Nonetheless, one of the big distinctions regarding the validity of intelligence tests is the exact question we ask when questioning their validity. If we ask whether intelligence tests measure what they claim to measure, then they probably do. If we ask whether intelligence tests measure intelligence, then the answer is much less certain; it depends on what your definition of intelligence is.

Is the usefulness of intelligence tests overemphasised?

Another criticism of intelligence tests is that their capacity to predict intellectual performance in different walks of life is overplayed, overstated or overemphasised (Benson,

2003). We have seen how intelligence tests have been known to predict, quite strongly, both academic achievement and job performance. In the latter case of job performance, the predictive strength of intelligence tests is greater than that of interviews, curriculum vitae and previous experience. You can see why people would put emphasis on intelligence testing as it is such a strong predictor of job performance.

However, critics of intelligence testing note that there are fluctuations in the predictive strength of intelligence tests. For instance, time has a great effect on the ability of the intelligence test to predict performance. That is, the longer the time between the administration of the test and the measurement of the performance, the weaker the relationship. Furthermore, the predictive strength of intelligence tests fluctuates when other variables are considered, for example when different demographics are considered (such as age, race, sex) or situations or tasks change.

Benson (2003) notes that one area where these concerns are apparent is that of special education, which is concerned with people with learning disabilities. This concern arises from the use of IQ tests to classify learning disabilities using the 'IQ-achievement discrepancy model'. The IQ-achievement discrepancy model was based on comparing children's achievement to their IQ score. Where children's achievement scores are a standard deviation or more below their IQ scores, they are identified as learning disabled. Benson (2003) suggests that identifying students using the IQ-achievement discrepancy model does little to help teachers understand what they need to do practically to help the student to learn, and it holds no clue to the educational programme that child may need to undertake to improve themselves. Therefore other assessments of children's needs, for example, the child's behaviour at school and home, might be a better indicator. Indeed, problems with the use of intelligence tests in this area have been recognised by the US government. On 3 October 2001, President George Bush established a Commission on Excellence in Special Education to collect information and study issues related to federal, state and local special education programmes with the goal of recommending policies for improving the education performance of students with disabilities. The President's Commission on Excellence in Special Education (PCESE) delivered its report to President Bush on 1 July 2002. One recommendation of this report was to suggest that the use of intelligence tests to diagnose learning disabilities should be discontinued.

Benson suggests that supporters of intelligence tests would readily accept the possible flaws in this application of intelligence testing within an IQ-achievement discrepancy model. Researchers in the area of intelligence have been thinking about such problems for a long time. For example, Kaufman and Kaufman (2001) were suggesting, before the President's Commission on Excellence in Special Education, that intelligence tests should not be administered by anonymous research scientists in schools, but by specially trained educational practitioners or teachers with an expertise in child learning. These administrators wouldn't just total an IQ score, but look at the child, work with the child more and make special recommendations. Kaufman and Kaufman (2001) suggest that in this context there is no reason to get rid of intelligence tests altogether. Rather, intelligence testing should be used with a number of educational tools to arrive at as good an assessment as possible of the child.

The intelligent use of intelligence tests

All this debate and concern about intelligence tests has led to one recommendation. If intelligence tests are to be used, they should be used intelligently (Benson, 2003).

A point made by Kaufman (Benson, 2003; Kaufman & Kaufman, 2001) is that there is a huge difference today in the way that intelligence tests are used and viewed – and in the theories and tests that have been developed around them. He suggests that critics of intelligence tests are generally using evidence and arguments that may have been accurate 20 or more years ago, but it is less so today.

Stop and Think

Alternatives to intelligence testing

Former APA President Dr Diane F. Halpern of Claremont McKenna College once said, 'Critics of intelligence testing often fail to consider that most of the alternatives are even more prone to problems of fairness and validity than the measures that are currently used.'

- What argument do you think Dr Halpern is trying to put forward?
- What alternatives do you think there are to intelligence testing?

However, Kaufman argues that this misconception may be the result of some practitioners using the tests in more traditional ways. Kaufman and Kaufman have insisted that while academic researchers and theorists are using more and more advanced methods of design and interpretation, if intelligence tests are still being administered en masse and IQ test scores are simply churned out to make comparisons today, then such an application is a long way behind modern-day thinking measurement and application.

Moreover, authors such as Naglieri suggest that rather than abandoning intelligence testing, given its firm basis, it needs to be pushed further (Benson, 2003; Naglieri, 1998). Naglieri has suggested that today intelligence practitioners want not only to test children's intelligence but also to follow it up with interventions designed to improve the child's learning in the areas where they have shown weakness. These authors suggest that such a dynamic approach will not only more accurately determine a child's intelligence but also automatically consider the differing abilities of children from different linguistic and cultural backgrounds.

Some concluding comments

It would be rash to simply dismiss intelligence tests. There is a lot of evidence for their reliability, their validity and their usefulness. However, the shortcomings of intelligence tests should not be ignored or underemphasised. Fluctuations within and between intelligence tests are hard to ignore simply because the application of intelligence tests, particularly IQ scores, represents high stakes for individuals. When you are a child, intelligence tests can used to classify your future at school. When you are an adult, they can be used to classify your access to the workplace.

That said, intelligence testing has begun to move on from a more traditional view. Intelligence test developers and researchers are the most aware of such shortcomings. Consequently, test developers are always working on new, more sophisticated ways of creating items for intelligence tests, administering intelligence tests and interpreting the scores obtained on intelligence tests. This is why you see continually updated versions of the Standford-Binet Scales,

Stop and Think

Mozart and the rats

Listening to Mozart boosts your intelligence . . . or does it? In 1993 physicist Gordon Shaw and Frances Rauscher, a former concert cellist and an expert on cognitive development from the University of California, studied the effects on college students of listening to the first 10 minutes of the Mozart *Sonata for Two Pianos in D Major* (Rauscher, Shaw & Ky, 1993). The researchers found a temporary enhancement of spatial-temporal reasoning (ordering objects in space and time) by 8 or 9 points, lasting for 10-15 minutes, as measured by the Stanford-Binet IQ test. Writing later on the topic, Dr Alfred A. Tomatis coined the term 'Mozart effect', which is the suggested increase in brain development that occurs in children when they listen to the music of Wolfgang Amadeus Mozart. The original Mozart effect researchers based their rationale on earlier findings by Leng and Shaw (1991) that neural firing patterns occur in the cerebal cortex (a part of the brain that helps with motor control, speech, memory and auditory reception) when subjects are listening to music and performing spatial tasks. The cerebral cortex is a part of the brain that helps with, among other things, motor control, speech, memory and auditory reception. Rauscher and Shaw (1998) hypothesized that listening to certain types of complex music may 'warm up' neural transmitters inside the cerebral cortex and thereby improve spatial performance. This find caused a great amount of media attention, and the Mozart effect has been put forward as an educational tool (for example, some schools suggested playing Mozart during lesson times). Shaw (2001) reports that the Mozart effect has been seen to be useful in enhancing the visual-spatial task performance of Alzheimer's disease/dementia patients and for reducing seizures in epileptic patients.

Clearly this finding attracted a lot of attention from the media as discussions of how music could raise intelligence in early childhood took hold. This interest also led to Shaw and Rauscher creating their own institute: The Music Intelligence Neural Development (MIND) Institute.

However, no sooner had such findings been reported and caused an interest than researchers were questioning their findings. In 1999, Christopher Chabris of Harvard University in the United States presented a meta-analysis of 17 studies. Chabris (1999) noted that the first Mozart effect publication showed participants' spatial intelligence scores improved by 8-9 points, by far the largest increase reported in the literature.

Across the other studies that measured changes in spatial intelligence, these studies showed a less-dramatic increase of 2.1 IQ points. The change could not be considered significant, and Chabris concluded that the Mozart effect is less than what would arise by chance. Some authors, like US psychologist Kenneth M. Steele (2000), have suggested that the Mozart effect might just be a phenomena in testing in which the music arouses the participant or changes their mood to make them ready for doing well at the task, particularly if the person likes Mozart.

Rauscher and Shaw (1998) had already suggested that failures in replicating their findings were due to inappropriate procedures or inappropriate spatial reasoning measures. Shaw and Fancher have defended such criticisms by continuing their research and emphasizing that they only noted a brief shift in spatial IQ performance in their original study. They argue that what they have shown, rather than that listening to Mozart passively raises your intelligence, is that patterns of neurons in pre-existing sites in the brain fire in sequences that respond to certain frequencies. Rauscher and Shaw have suggested that researchers should instead concentrate on the idea that the major transfer effects of music are likely to come from active involvement and playing of music and in continual music education experiences. For example, Rasucher, Shaw and their colleagues (Rauscher et al., 1997) conducted an experiment with three groups of under 5-year-olds. One group received private piano lessons, a second group received private computer lessons and a third group received no additional lessons over a period of 6 months. Those children who received piano/keyboard training performed 34 per cent higher on tests of spatial-temporal ability than the others did. These findings indicate that music uniquely enhances preschool children's spatial-temporal reasoning.

One interesting finding also put forward as evidence of the Mozart effect was a study by Rauscher and colleagues (Rauscher, Robinson & Jens, 1998). In these experiments rats were exposed in utero (before birth in the uterus), plus 60 days post-partum (the period shortly after childbirth) to either complex music (a Mozart sonata), a minimalist music composition (by Philip Glass; your parents will know who he is) or white noise or silence. The rats were tested for 5 days, 3 trials per day, in a multiple T-maze. By day 3, the experimenters reported that rats exposed to the Mozart completed the maze more rapidly and with fewer errors than did the rats assigned to the other groups, and that this difference increased in magnitude through day 5. The authors suggested that this repeated exposure to complex music induces improved spatial-temporal learning in rats, supporting those results found in human beings.

Kenneth M. Steele (2003) has, however, thrown doubts on these findings. First, Steele makes the point that the music in the uterus would have been ineffective in the experiment because rats are born deaf. Secondly, Steele points out that human beings and rats hear at different frequencies and that the range of hearing for rats is at a higher frequency than that of human beings. In his analysis of Mozart's sonata, Steele suggests that rats were deaf to much of the hypothesized effects of the music because more than half of the notes in the sonata were not in the frequency range of rats, and therefore they wouldn't have heard them.

Whatever the effect of Mozart on human beings and rats, the findings of Rasucher and Shaw provide both intrigue and controversy in equal amounts.

the Wechsler Intelligence Scales, the Raven's Matrices and the Woodcock-Johnson Psychoeducational Battery-Revised, along with papers in the psychological literature comparing and establishing both the reliability and validity of intelligence tests.

The Flynn effect

In the last section we talked about the features, uses and problems surrounding the use of intelligence tests. One thing we noted was that scores on intelligence tests, and particularly IQ scores, have a tendency to fluctuate. However, we have dedicated the second half of this chapter to a consideration of one of the most well-known fluctuations in intelligence testing history, the discovery of continued year-on-year rise of intelligence test scores in all parts of the world. This rise, known as the **Flynn effect**, was named after the person who discovered it – James R. Flynn, now an Emeritus Professor of Political Studies at the University of Otago in Dunedin, New Zealand.

How was the Flynn effect discovered?

In 1981 Flynn had begun to survey the test manuals of well-known tests, such as the Wechsler and Stanford-Binet manuals (Flynn, 1999). Whenever a new IQ test had been published, one thing that was done to help establish the validity of the new test was to compare scores of the same people on the old version and the new version. Part of this process involves restandardising the norms for the test, so that subjects are not scored against norms that were established with the old version of the test, which might cause problems when comparing scores between different samples and populations. As hoped for by the test publishers, norms were established; and there was always a high correlation between both versions of the test, suggesting validity for the new test.

However, Flynn noted something else in the manuals. He noticed that whenever a sample of test-takers were given both the new test and an older test, they always got higher scores on the newer test. To illustrate, Flynn has looked at the Wechsler Intelligence Scale for Children, for which norms among a representative sample of white US residents had been established between 1947 and 1948, and its revision, the Wechsler Intelligence Scale for Children – Revised, for which norms were established in 1972. Flynn found that if a group of participants averaged an IQ of 100 on the Wechsler Intelligence Scale for Children – Revised (1972), they averaged 108 on the Wechsler Intelligence Scale for Children (1947/1948). This meant that these samples were setting higher standards for average IQ scores over time. That is, you had to be more intelligent to score an average IQ of 100 on the new Wechsler Intelligence Scale for Children – Revised than you did to score an average IQ of 100 on the previous version of the Wechsler Intelligence Scale for Children. Flynn suggested from this finding that between 1948 and 1972 (a period of 24 years – a generation), among a sample representative of US residents, Americans had gained 8 IQ points.

Spurred on by this finding Flynn (Flynn, 1984) looked at 73 studies (covering 7,500 US white participants aged between 2 and 48 years) in which each group of participants had taken two (or more) versions of either the Wechsler or Stanford-Binet IQ tests between 1932 and 1978. His analyses showed that during this time, white Americans had gained 14 IQ points, an average of 0.30 IQ points per year.

Then Flynn became interested to discover whether this was a phenomenon only in the United States, or whether it could be found in other cultures. Also at that time, Flynn engaged in several personal communications with Arthur Jensen. Jensen noted to Flynn that Wechsler and Stanford-Binet tests may measure intelligence partially through items taught at school (e.g., vocabulary, general knowledge) and therefore rises in IQ that Flynn had noted might reflect better schooling (Flynn, 1999). Jensen suggested it would be important to look not only at intelligence tests like the Wechsler and Stanford-Binet tests but also at tests like the Raven's Matrices, because these were purely non-verbal tests purporting to be a measure of general intelligence, and they would not be as open to cultural effects such as school. It is also important to note that this distinction between verbal and non-verbal intelligence tests is sometimes best represented by Cattell's theoretical distinction between fluid (primary reasoning ability, including the ability to solve abstract relational problems free of cultural influences) and crystallised intelligence (acquired knowledge and skills, such as factual knowledge, generally related to a person's stored information and their cultural influences; see Chapter 11 for more details).

Flynn published what has become a seminal paper in the intelligence literature (Flynn, 1987). Flynn published data from 14 countries (he later updated this to 20 in 1994; Flynn, 1994). We have adapted the table from his 1987 data to show the country, the test and type of test (verbal or non-verbal or both) administered, the growth in IQ points across many of the samples and a figure of average growth in IQ per year (see Table 12.2).

Flynn had some reservations about some of the data. For example, he noted that some of the data sets, particularly from Germany and Japan, may have been more unreliable or speculative. He also warned that the data covered different time periods. He suggested caution in comparing nations using this data. However, he did come to the conclusion that IQ scores were rising yearly across a number of nations.

Moreover, Flynn found the highest rises in IQ occurred in the non-verbal tests (fluid intelligence) and the lowest gains were in verbal tests (crystallised intelligence). Medium gains were seen in mixed verbal and non-verbal tests, such as the Wechsler tests.

Following his finding, the so-called Flynn effect was confirmed by numerous studies. In 1994, Flynn presented more evidence and considered this growth of IQ within generations (30 years) of populations across 20 countries for which data were available. He concluded that non-verbal tests (IQ tests of fluid intelligence) on average tended to show an increase of about 15 points per generation (ranging from 5 to 25 points), while verbal tests (IQ tests of crystallised intelligence) have been more moderate, with an average of about 9 points per generation.

What is particularly intriguing about this finding for the two different intelligences is that this it not what was suggested by Flynn and Jensen's discussion after Flynn's earlier findings – that rises in IQ scores on the Weschler and Stanford-Binet tests might simply be the result of better schooling. If this was the case, then it would be the verbal/crystallised intelligence tests of IQ that would rise, rather than the non-verbal/fluid intelligence tests. Consequently the reasons for, or the explanations of, the rise in IQ test scores over generations became Flynn's next concern.

Explanations of the Flynn effect

There are a number of explanations for the Flynn effect. These range from Flynn's first considerations of the reasons for the effect to a series of questions about the possible genetic and cultural effects. We will concentrate on some initial explanations of the Flynn effect, which we will see have themselves spawned areas of research. We will then show you how these areas have developed into a major

Table 12.2 Country, the test and type of test (verbal or non-verbal or both) administered, the growth in IQ points across many of the samples and a figure of average growth in IQ per year.

Location	Test	Type of IQ test (verbal or non-verbal)	Period of study	Rise in IQ points over the period	Rate
Leipzig, East Germany	Raven's	non-verbal	1968-1978	10.00-15.00	1.250
France	Raven's	non-verbal	1949-1974	25.12	1.005
Japan	Wechsler	non-verbal/verbal	1951-1975	20.03	0.835
Vienna, Austria	Wechsler	non-verbal/verbal	1962-1979	12.00-16.00	0.824
Belgium	Raven's	non-verbal	1958-1967	7.15	0.794
West Germany	Wechsler	non-verbal/verbal	1954-1981	20.00	0.741
Belgium	Shapes	non-verbal	1958-1967	6.45	0.716
Netherlands	Raven's	non-verbal	1952-1982	20.00	0.667
Zurich, Switzerland	Wechsler	non-verbal/verbal	1954-1977	10.00-20.00	0.652
Norway	Matrices	non-verbal	1954-1968	8.80	0.629
Saskatchewan, Canada	Otis	verbal	1958-1978	12.55	0.628
West Germany	Horn-Raven's	non-verbal	1961-1978	10.00	0.588
Norway	Verbal-Math Test	verbal	1954-1968	8.15	0.582
Edmonton, Alberta, Canada	California Test of Mental Maturity	non-verbal/verbal	1956-1977	11.03	0.525
Australia	Jenkins	non-verbal	1949-1981	15.67	0.490
Belgium	Verbal-Math Test	verbal	1958-1967	3.67	0.408
Edmonton, Alberta, Canada	Raven's	non-verbal	1956-1977	8.44	0.402
France	Wechsler	non-verbal/verbal	1955-1979	9.12	0.380
France	Verbal-Math	verbal	1949-1974	9.35	0.374
Saskatchewan, Canada	Otis	verbal	1958-1978	6.95	0.348
Australia	Raven's	non-verbal	1950-1976	8.76	0.337
United States	Wechsler-Binet	non-verbal/verbal	1932-1972	12.00	0.300
United States	Wechsler	non-verbal/verbal	1954-1978	5.95	0.243
New Zealand	Otis	verbal	1936-1968	7.73	0.242
Norway	Matrices	non-verbal	1968-1980	2.60	0.217
United Kingdom	Raven's	non-verbal	1938-1979	7.75	0.189
Solothurn, Switzerland	Wechsler	non-verbal/verbal	1977-1984	1.30	0.186
United Kingdom	Raven's	non-verbal	1940-1979	7.07	0.181
Norway	Verbal-Math	verbal	1968-1980	−1.60	−0.133

Source: Statistics from Flynn (1987).

division in the intelligence research literature – the nutrition versus the cognitive stimulation effect.

Flynn began by considering some hypotheses (Flynn, 1987, 1994). The first was that generations are getting more and more intelligent. The idea that later generations are more intelligent than previous generations is one element that Flynn rules out. For this to be true, we would expect to find a lot more geniuses in the world (Flynn estimated 20 times as many, based on his statistics), and we would be undergoing some sort of intelligence revolution. Instead, he proposed that the results suggested that intelligence tests do not measure intelligence but rather correlate with intelligence. He suggested that what had risen through generations was not intelligence itself, but some kind of 'abstract problem-solving ability'. Flynn (1994, 1999) favoured environmental explanations for the increase in these test scores. This was because these gains are far too rapid to result from genetic changes. The possible environmental influences were best summarised in a book edited by Ulrich Neisser in 1998 (Neisser, 1998). Remember, the Flynn effect does not only concentrate on rises in IQ scores but also notes a greater rise for fluid (non-verbal) intelligence than for crystallised (verbal) intelligence. Neisser considers five main environmental areas to explain the Flynn effect:

- schooling
- test-taking sophistication
- parental rearing styles
- visual and technical environment
- nutrition.

Length of schooling

Intelligence test scores might be rising because people are attending school for more years than their parents and their grandparents did (Neisser, 1988). Two academics of the Hebrew University in Jerusalem, Sorel Cahan and Nora Cohen (1989), compared the effects of a year of school (controlling for age) with those of a year of age on a number of verbal (e.g., verbal and numerical skills) and non-verbal (abstract and reasoning tests, including the Raven's Matrices) IQ tests. Length of schooling was important in predicting, and mattered more than age, the scores for all the verbal tests. Length of schooling, however, made a contribution (although a smaller contribution) to some of the non-verbal tests, including the items from the Raven's Matrices.

Though the findings suggest that length of schooling influences intelligence score, Neisser notes that this trend (schooling predicts larger rises in verbal tests and lower rises in non-verbal tests) is very different from the trend established by Flynn's data (generations have larger rises in non-verbal tests and lower rises in verbal tests). You will also note that this observation is consistent with Jensen's original proposal as outlined earlier. Neisser notes that schooling is not a good explanation of the secular rise in IQ test scores through the generations.

Test-taking sophistication

Is there just a culture, or knowledge of taking IQ tests in modern life, that wasn't around when intelligence tests were first introduced? It would be true today that before you even did this course, or did psychology, you knew what an intelligence test was. If at school you were given an intelligence test, a great amount of time would be taken by the school to explain to you and your parents what the IQ tests were for. Neisser (1998) also suggests that teaching today is increasingly geared to, or at least combines, certain kinds of achievement tests. If you think about it, even though verbal ability and mathematical ability contributed to schooling at the start of the twentieth century, advanced ideas about spatial reasoning contribute to classroom teaching today. Such ideas might not have been recognised, or even thought of, in the early twentieth century.

Certainly, then, it is likely that knowledge of intelligence tests by those taking it, and by parents and schools, might be related to increases in intelligence. However, would such knowledge explain the Flynn effect's emphasis on non-verbal rather than verbal aspects of intelligence? Furthermore, Neisser notes that children who take the very same test twice usually only gain 5 or 6 IQ points, so increased familiarity with tests cannot fully explain the Flynn effect.

Child-rearing practices and Head Start

Ever wondered what the Teletubbies were all about – well, us, too. For those of you who don't know, the *Teletubbies* is a children's programme (though a lot of adults seem to know more about the programme than they should) that involves Dipsy, Tinky Winky, Laa-Laa and Po, a multi-coloured band of . . . er, Teletubbies, who are shaped like dumplings, run about excitedly, bump their tummies together, fall over and giggle. Well, that is what it seems to we ordinary adults, but to the makers of the programme, Dipsy, Tinky Winky, Laa-Laa and Po are designed to engage children to enhance their learning experience and cognitive abilities. Let us also go down to *Sesame Street*, a multi-award-winning programme whose principal purpose was to provide early mental stimulation to raise children's awareness and intelligence. *Sesame Street* is now recognised as historically changing children's educational television, particularly in encouraging the development of children's understanding and abilities (Palmer, 2003).

Neisser raises the issue that all parents today are more interested in their children's intellectual development and are probably doing more and more to develop it.

One example of such early interventions has not been shown to have 'lasting' effects on intelligence. A well-cited example is the Head Start programme in the United States. Established in the 1960s by President Lyndon Johnson, Head Start was designed to give America's poorest children a head start in preparing them for school in order to break the cycle of poverty. The programme, which still runs today, aims to narrow the gap between disadvantaged children and all other children in vocabulary, numeracy and writing skills. Here are some statistics regarding children in the Head Start programme today:

- Almost half of Head Start parents make less than $12,000 a year.

Stop and Think

What other issues and evidence surround Head Start?

Despite a lack of evidence for a permanent rise of IQ test scores among children attending the Head Start scheme, debate still exists around its usefulness. Professor Michael J. A. Howe, writing an article in the British Psychological Society magazine *The Psychologist* (Howe, 1998) on whether an individual's IQ score is fixed, draws attention to a number of studies noting that there have been large gains in IQ scores as the result of the Head Start programme. Howe's point is that it may be foolish to disregard these findings simply because they are not long-term changes. Howe suggests that lots of abilities would decline if not given further opportunity to develop. For example, you may have learnt a musical instrument as a child but given it up after a few years. Now if you tried to pay the same musical instrument, you wouldn't be as good as you once were. Therefore, in the case of Head Start, Howe suggests that the very conditions that led to the children being in Head Start - poverty, unemployment, poor housing - are still there when the children leave the programme, and therefore the children return to these conditions and the advantages fade.

Furthermore, the people who run Head Start stress that IQ test scores are not the only thing measured in the programme, and they can show that Head Start has obtained lasting educational benefits (McKey et al., 1985). In McKey's meta-analysis of Head Start schemes, the evidence is clear that Head Start produces immediate gains for children and families by linking families with services available in the community. Furthermore, children in Head Start make substantial progress in word knowledge, letter recognition, mathematics skills and writing skills relative to national averages. These findings suggest that children receive a much-needed boost and that, in terms of education achievement, compared to similar disadvantaged peers, Head Start children are less likely to repeat a grade, less likely to need special education services and more likely to graduate from high school.

- About 1 in 5 children are reported to have been exposed to community or domestic violence in their lives.
- Almost 1 in every 6 Head Start children have one or more disabilities – generally a speech or language impairment, and half of all children's disabilities are identified after the child enters Head Start.

Very quickly, evidence was provided to assess the usefulness of such a programme. US Individual Differences psychologist Charles Locurta (Locurta, 1991) provides a review of this evidence. In 1969 Arthur Jensen suggested that Head Start had failed. The reason for Jensen's pronouncement was that though children attending the programme had shown an initial increase in IQ points (sometimes as much 7–8 points on IQ tests), after 2 or 3 years, these higher IQ points were lost (Locurota, 1991). There has been a lot of debate about the effectiveness of Head Start (see Stop and Think: What other issues and evidence surround Head Start?). In terms of IQ gains however, perhaps a final word goes to the Advisory Committee on Head Start Quality and Expansion, which published a final report in 1999. In 1981, the Advisory Committee undertook to synthesise all the early research on Head Start, both published and unpublished. More than 200 reports were studied, and 76 of these became part of the meta-analysis by McKey et al. (1985), who reported on the IQ effects of the Head Start programme on children. In regard to scores on intelligence tests, McKey et al. (1985) reported that children enrolled in Head Start enjoy significant immediate gains in IQ test scores; but in the longer term (3–4 years), the IQ scores of Head Start students do not remain superior to disadvantaged children who did not attend Head Start.

With such evidence, Neisser (1998) suggests that early childhood experience and intellectual promotion in early childhood cannot explain the Flynn effect.

The technological age and the cognitive stimulation hypothesis

Neisser (1998) suggests that we have to look at the visual and technical environment that surrounds us today. The most obvious change in the late twentieth century was our increasing use of and exposure to visual media. During the twentieth century, we have seen the growth of movies, video and then DVD; televisions in almost all homes; and the use of home computers. Because of such growth we may have become much more visually aware. Even with something as simple as television adverts, we are asked to extract meaning from many in which the message is obscured. Adverts have changed compared with many years ago, when their messages were more straightforward.

Children spend more time now learning through this medium, rather than just simply concentrating on material in a classroom setting presented by the teacher. At the same time, we adults are more used to processing complicated visual information.

It is this visual revolution that Neisser (1998) argues might account for growth in fluid intelligence. Remember that tests like the Raven's Matrices rely on only visual material. Therefore, recent generations' exposure to complex visual media has produced genuine increases in a significant form of intelligence, which Neisser (1998) calls visual analysis. Non-verbal intelligence tests such as Raven's Matrices may show the larger Flynn effect gains because they measure this visual analysis directly. Neisser, however, notes that little direct evidence exists for the visual-analysis hypothesis.

Nutrition and IQ

Nutrition is the study of food, and specifically the relationship between diet and states of health and disease. Richard Lynn, Professor at the University of Ulster (1990), has proposed that nutrition and health care improvements are among the main causal factors of the Flynn effect.

Lynn starts by drawing attention to gains in human height over the last century (approximately 1.2 cm per decade). These gains are being attributed to nutrition, such as growth in the consumption of milk and dairy products (300%), fruit (100%), vegetables (50%) and fish (20%). Lynn poses the question: If this is true of height, why not of something also biological, the brain and its functioning (i.e., intelligence) particularly as nutrition has been linked to larger brain sizes, and malnutrition has been linked to poor brain development? Lynn's hypothesis is that better-nourished brains would allow subjects to perform better on IQ tests as well as in everyday activities.

The conclusion that nutritional sources can aid aspects of IQ as measured by intelligence tests is a common finding. Austrialian nutritionist Wendy H. Oddy and her colleagues (Oddy et al., 2004) examined over two thousand Australian children and followed them from before birth until the age of 8 years. Oddy and her colleagues found that stopping breast feeding early (at 6 months or less) was associated with reduced verbal intelligence, while children who were fully breast fed for more than 6 months scored between 3 and 6 points higher on a vocabulary test than did those who were never breast fed.

Similarly, another study conducted by US health psychologist Melanie Smith and her colleagues (Smith, Durkin, Hinton, Bellinger & Kuhn, 2003) examined 439 school-age, low-birth-weight children born in the United States. These authors found differences in intelligence test scores between breast-fed children and those who did not receive any breast milk. The researchers found that breast-fed children scored 3.6 IQ points higher for overall intellectual functioning and 2.3 IQ points higher for verbal ability than children who were not breast fed.

Chinese nutritionist Ming Qian and his colleagues (Qian et al., 2005) looked at the effects of iodine on intelligence in children. Iodine was one of the first minerals to be recognised as crucial for good health. It is still considered one of the most important minerals. In the human body, it forms an essential component of the main hormone produced by the thyroid gland, which controls the basic metabolism and oxygen consumption of tissues, regulates the rate of energy production and body weight and promotes proper growth. It is also thought to improve mental ability. Qian et al. (2005), as part of a meta-analysis of 37 reported studies (for a total of 12,291 children), compared those children living in severely iodine-deficient areas (they had received iodine supplements during their mothers' pregnancy and after their birth as part of a health programme) with those children living in severely iodine-deficient areas (they had received no supplements). Each group was matched on a number of social and economic demographic variables, and each group was compared and matched with a control group of children living in iodine-sufficient areas. Those children receiving iodine supplementation before and after birth scored 8.7 IQ points higher than the group who didn't receive supplements. The IQ score rose to between 12 IQ points on a non-verbal measure of intelligence (the Raven's Matrices) and 17.25 IQ points on a non-verbal and verbal measure of intelligence (the Standford-Binet) three and a half years after the iodine supplementation health programme was introduced.

So, there is some data supporting a general hypothesis that nutrition increases intelligence. But what about the idea that nutrition accounts for the Flynn effect (more dramatic rises in fluid/non-verbal intelligence than in crystallised/verbal intelligence)? Testing Lynn's hypothesis is hard because he has formulated his ideas by looking at trends and changes in IQ scores over several decades, and today any studies will be of relatively well-nourished children, particularly in the Western cultures where the effect was observed. However, researchers have tried to test Lynn's theory in relation to the Flynn effect.

A well-known study in this area was carried out by two Welsh psychologists, David Benton and Gwilym Roberts (Benton & Roberts, 1988), who published a study in the British medical journal, *The Lancet*. Benton and Roberts had completed an experiment on 90 children. Thirty of the children were given a supplement containing a number of vitamins and minerals, including riboflavin; vitamins A, B_{12}, C, D, E and K; magnesium and iron. Thirty were given

Stop and Think

Nutrition advertising

The Observer, on Sunday 18 September 2005 (Briffa, 2005), carried a report of the UK Advertising Standards Authority's decision regarding the claims of a particular breakfast cereal by its makers. The advert, like some others for breakfast cereal, suggested that eating a bowl of cereal in the morning can help children's concentration in school. Following these adverts, the Advertising Standards Authority (ASA) in the United Kingdom received complaints that Cereal Partners UK had claimed in one of their adverts, for the breakfast cereal Shreddies, that 'studies show a breakfast like Shreddies helps give kids the mental energy they need to stay involved at school'. When the ASA asked the company to substantiate such claims, it could offer evidence from one small study that tested the effects of its cereal in this respect. However, some of this evidence involved a comparison between eating any breakfast and eating nothing at all; therefore, any effect could not be the result of eating Shreddies, but of eating breakfast. Consequently, the ASA judged that the advert made potentially misleading claims for the effects of Shreddies on children's concentration at school and banned the advert.

Imagine you were employed by Cereal Partners UK to help relaunch the campaign. Given the evidence just described, what recommendations would you make to them regarding the claims and the approach they could take in any advert?

a placebo. The last group of 30 took no capsules. After 8 months, there was no significant difference between the groups on verbal intelligence scores. However, only the supplemented group increased in non-verbal (fluid) intelligence – from 111 to 120 IQ points – while the placebo group scores remained relatively unchanged, with these groups gaining no more than 4 IQ points. This sort of finding is consistent with Lynn's hypothesis.

This study caused great interest and controversy. In England the findings were reported in a special television programme, and by the following week, health shops had sold out of vitamin or mineral supplements for children. The findings generated commentary among the medical and nutritional communities, including criticisms of the study's methodology. *The Lancet*, where the study report originally appeared, published 7 letters from a total of 11 nutritional scientists, 2 statisticians and 3 others who were all deeply critical of the study.

Benton and Roberts' study also led to further studies trying to replicate the findings. However, these studies have confused rather than clarified the situation. Some authors have replicated the findings but only with certain children and certain supplements. For example, US psychologist Stephen J. Schoenthaler, professor of Criminal Justice at California State University, and his colleagues conducted randomised trials in which children were given placebos or low-dose vitamin-mineral tablets designed to raise nutrient intake to the equivalent of a well-balanced diet (Schoenthaler, Bier, Young, Nichols, & Jansenns, 2000). The authors reported significantly greater gains in non-verbal intelligence (around 2 to 3 points) among some groups of children who were given vitamin-mineral tablets, but these were children who were poorly nourished. The authors suggest that lack of a greater rise was due to the fact that most Western schoolchildren were already adequately nourished. However, other studies, such as that carried out by Ian K. Crombie and his colleagues (Crombie et al., 1990), reported a small, non-significant difference between the control and supplementation groups in non-verbal intelligence; this finding thus provided no support of Benton and Roberts' findings.

Overviews of these types of studies (e.g., Benton, 1991) have drawn the following conclusion: in the majority of studies there is a positive effect on IQ as the result of vitamin-mineral supplements, in at least some of the children, on non-verbal measures of intelligence. Benton, like many commentators, suggests that more work needs to be done in this area – concentrating on a wide range of ages, dietary styles and different economic and social backgrounds – and that more work needs to be done in looking at what supplements affect what children, on what intelligence tests.

Lynn's hypothesis holds some weight. As Neisser (1998) has pointed out, it is difficult to demonstrate a relationship between diet and intelligence because malnutrition or vitamin and mineral deficiency in childhood almost certainly produces negative cognitive effects. But this also happens with other forms of deprivation, such as aspects of poverty, schooling, parenting styles and visual and technological environment (all mentioned earlier). That makes those effects difficult to analyse.

Source: Dennis MacDonald/Alamy

Reasons given for the Flynn effect include that we are becoming more technology minded.

The nutrition hypothesis versus the cognitive stimulation hypothesis

However, the debate doesn't stop with Neisser's commentary. The argument put forward by Neisser has evolved in modern intelligence research into setting up the comparison of a nutrition hypothesis versus a cognitive stimulation hypothesis in order to explain the Flynn effect. Lynn (1990) originally set up two opposing hypotheses that have been developed by Flynn (2003). This comparison is based on comparing the nutrition hypothesis with a cognitive stimulation hypothesis.

The nutrition hypothesis, as noted before, sees nutrition as part of a package in which increased intelligence is part of a nurturing environment that includes increased height and life span, improved health, decreased rate of infant disease and better vitamin and mineral nutrition.

Stop and Think

An end to the Flynn effect?

Two recent studies in Europe have speculated that the Flynn effect may be at an end, or in reverse. In 2004, Norwegians Jon Martin Sundet, Dag G. Barlaug and Tore M. Torjussen (Sundet et al., 2004) published a study reporting trends for scores on a language and mathematics intelligence test (verbal/crystallised intelligence) and a Raven-like IQ (non-verbal/fluid intelligence) test among Norwegian male conscripts tested from the mid-1950s to 2002. Sundet and his colleagues, similarly to the findings of Flynn, found that IQ on a non-verbal measure of intelligence increased from the mid-1950s to the late 1990s by about 16-17 IQ points, and smaller gains were found for the two verbal tests measuring crystallised intelligence. However, the authors report that for the non-verbal intelligence test, IQ ceased to increase after the mid to late 1990s. The authors suggest that this finding indicates the Flynn effect may have come to an end in Norway.

A year later, Danish psychologist Thomas W. Teasdale and US psychologist David R. Owen replicated Sundet et al.'s findings. Teasdale and Owen (2005) analysed the data for over 500,000 young Danish men, tested between 1959 and 2004, and found that performance peaked in the late 1990s and has since declined moderately to pre-1991 levels, suggesting the Flynn effect might be in decline.

Both groups of authors are noting a trend in these Scandinavian countries, but suggest that the gains seem to be caused mainly by a decreasing prevalence of low scorers. That is, the rise in IQ scores was a result of there being fewer and fewer low scorers who were dragging the average IQ score down. Eventually, in the 1990s, the prevalence of low scorers perhaps levelled out, and this has led to the levelling out of IQ test scores. However, as with the Flynn effect, no one knows the reason. However, it is tempting to attribute it to some factors that have been previously suggested. For example, if low nutrition among a number of people was a factor in the mid-1950s contributing to low IQ scores, then improving nutrition during the following decades would have slowly removed the number of people with low scores on IQ tests. What psychologists like Sundet are suggesting is that poor nutrition may no longer be a problem in the 1990s, and therefore the slow removal of people with low IQ scores on intelligence tests due to poor nutrition has ceased.

It will be interesting to see whether the factors discussed in this chapter, such as education, parental rearing, test-taking sophistication, technology, nutrition, or the nutrition versus cognitive stimulation hypotheses are seen to be important in explaining any levelling out of the Flynn effect.

The cognitive stimulation hypothesis largely draws on the work of Flynn and Neisser, as mentioned earlier. It suggests that higher intelligence scores are derived from improvements in cognitive stimulation. This concept arises not only from Neisser's 'visual analysis' intelligence but also from ideas about improved schooling, about different parental rearing styles, that parents are better educated, that families are smaller (so parents spend more time with each child) and about the greater availability of educational toys.

Researchers have used this distinction in trying to build some understanding for the Flynn effect. The suggestion has been that if the cognitive stimulation hypothesis holds true, we should see a rise of intelligence test scores across generations at all levels of IQ (Flynn, 2003; Lynn, 1990). On the other hand, if the nutrition hypothesis holds true, intelligence gains will predominantly occur at the lower end of the distribution of IQ test scores where nutritional deprivation is most severe (Flynn, 2003).

In 2005, Spanish psychologists Roberto Colom, Josep M. Luis-Font and Antonio Andrés-Pueyo (Colom, Luis-Font & Andrés-Pueyo, 2005) presented data supporting the nutrition hypothesis. Two large samples of Spanish children (459 boys tested in 1970 and 275 boys tested in 1999) were assessed with a 30-year gap in a measure of fluid/non-verbal intelligence. Comparison of the IQ scores distribution indicated that the mean IQ had increased by 9.7 IQ points, suggesting the Flynn effect; but the gains, which were concentrated in the lower half of the distribution, gradually but steadily decreased from low to high IQ. At the lowest level of IQ scores (lowest percentile) the difference was greatest, with the change in raw scores (not IQ points, but scores on the measure) on the fluid/non-verbal IQ test being around 9 IQ points. With average scores in IQ the increase in scores was 4–5 IQ points; and at the high level of IQ scores, the top percentile, the increase in scores was only around 1 IQ point. The authors claim their findings suggest that intelligence gains are mainly (although not exclusively) concentrated among lower intelligence levels and would support the nutritional hypothesis.

Colom and his colleagues point to two previous studies that also support their conclusions. First, Teasdale and Owen (1989) studied a Danish representative sample of 30,804 males. The gains in fluid/non-verbal intelligence were observed among lower IQ test score levels, with the authors finding no evidence of IQ gains in the top half of the distribution of IQ scores. Secondly, Lynn and Hampson (1986) – in a study of US, Japanese and British IQ test scores across several generations – reported a greater rise in the lower half of individuals' IQ scores on measures of fluid/non-verbal intelligence than in the top half of individuals' IQ scores among a British sample.

Such findings are new, and interesting, but in need of further examination. An important point to remember regarding research like this is that, by looking closely at trends in intelligence test scores, by revisiting and developing ideas, researchers are being inventive in examining whether rises in intelligence (whether in fluid/non-verbal or crystallised/verbal intelligences) can be attributed largely to one set of factors over another.

Final comments

Our last word on the preceding topic perhaps goes to the comments of French psychologist France Bellisle, writing in the *British Journal of Nutrition* (Bellisle, 2004). As we ourselves have seen in this chapter, Bellisle writes that nutrition can affect intelligence, but the secret is that good regular dietary habits are the best way to ensure optimal mental performance at all times. These sentiments can be carried to other dimensions discussed in this chapter. Underlying each dimension are attempts to understand, to measure more effectively and to attain the optimal outcome for all people. From the uses of IQ tests to the problems and attempts to address these criticisms, to attempts to understand the Flynn effect, there is always an effort to imaginatively and thoroughly advance our understanding of intelligence. We would like you to leave this chapter on a positive note, particularly as there are some much darker debates to come in the next chapter.

Summary

- Many intelligence tests in use today reflect this theoretical and empirical growth in the understanding of intelligence.
- There is a distinction between psychometric and cognitive intelligence tests.
- Psychometric intelligence tests are based on factor-analytic studies.
- Cognitive psychology tests of intelligence are based on biological and psychophysiological models of intelligence.

- There is a history of biological and psychophysiological theory and research in intelligence testing. Areas of research include brain size, ECTs (elementary cognitive tasks), EPs (evoked potentials) and RTs (response times).
- The inspiration for some modern measures of intelligence was the work of Luria. It is Luria's emphasis on neurological functioning, his distinction between simultaneous and sequential processing and his emphasis on using tests to both diagnose and improve performance centred on the individual that influences Das and Naglieri's Cognitive Assessment System (CAS) and the Kaufmans' ability tests.
- Sattler (2002) establishes three main aspects in all good intelligence tests: the variety of tasks involved, standardisation of administration and norm referencing. Intelligence tests are used for all sorts of purposes, but mainly for these three: selection, diagnosis and evaluation.
- IQ test scores are important in predicting school and work performance. The average correlation between intelligence and a number of school indicators is around $r = .50$, suggesting that intelligence does predict performance at school. The correlation between intelligence (cognitive ability) and job performance is also around $r = .5$.
- Some psychologists have shown that intelligence in childhood can predict variables across the life span; these include death by a certain age and people being diagnosed with certain illnesses, but not all health-related matters.
- At one level the criticisms of and issues with intelligence tests are rather easy to identify. The issues are of reliability, validity and whether the importance of intelligence tests is overemphasised.
- There is a huge difference between the way that intelligence tests are used and viewed and the modern-day theories and intelligence tests that have been developed in the past 20 years. Naglieri has suggested that today, intelligence practitioners want not only to test childrens' intelligence, but to follow it up with interventions that are designed to improve the child's learning in the areas where they have shown weakness.
- The Flynn effect is the continued year-on-year rise of intelligence test scores in all parts of the world, with these rises being larger with fluid/non-verbal intelligence than with crystallised/verbal intelligence.
- Explanations for the Flynn effect include schooling, test-taking sophistication, parental rearing styles, the visual and technical environment and nutrition. Later theorists have suggested that these explanations subsume two hypotheses: the nutrition hypothesis and the cognitive stimulation hypothesis.

Connecting Up

This chapter should be read after Chapter 11 (Theories and Measurement of Intelligence) in this part of the book. Many of these issues surrounding the cognitive stimulation hypothesis and the nutritional hypothesis are expanded on in Chapter 13.

Critical Thinking

When discussing intelligence, you really need to think not only about how all these ideas fit around the idea of the 'usefulness' of intelligence tests but also about the issues they raise and the role they play in society.

Discussion questions

- Are people more intelligent today?
- Are intelligence tests valid measures of intelligence?

- Discuss the various merits of the nutrition and cognitive stimulation hypotheses.
- What do you think is the cause of the Flynn effect?

Essay questions

- Critically examine the uses, advantages and problems that surround intelligence testing.
- Critically examine the role of physiological and biological factors in intelligence testing.
- Critically discuss how the nutrition hypothesis and the cognitive stimulation hypothesis contribute to our understanding of the Flynn effect.
- Discuss the view that nutrition can affect an individual's intelligence.
- Critically examine the view that rises in intelligence are due to cognitive stimulation.

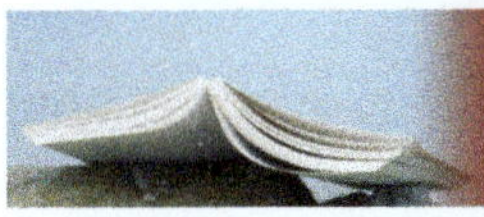

Going Further

Books

- Flynn, J. R. (1984). *The mean IQ of Americans: Massive gains from 1932 to 1978*. New York: Harper & Row.
- Neisser, U. (Ed.). (1998). *The rising curve*. Washington, DC: American Psychological Association.

Journals

These articles are recommended reading regarding modern uses of intelligence tests and evidences and issues around the Flynn effect.

- Flynn, J. R. (1987). Massive IQ gains in 14 nations: What IQ tests really measure. *Psychological Bulletin, 101*, 171-191. *Psychological Bulletin* is published by American Psychological Association. Available online via PsycARTICLES.
- Flynn, J. R. (1999). Searching for justice: The discovery of IQ gains over time. *American Psychologist, 54*, 5-20. *American Psychologist* is published by American Psychological Association. Available online via PsycARTICLES.
- Naglieri, J. A. (1998). A closer look at new kinds of intelligence tests. *American Psychologist, 53*, 1158-1159. Published by American Psychological Association. Available online via PsycARTICLES.
- In this chapter we looked at the notion of whether IQ and intelligence can change. A good article that summarises the main issues is Howe, J. A. (1998). Can IQ change? *The Psychologist, 11*, 69-72. This article is freely available online. You can find *The Psychologist* on the British Psychological Society website **(http://www.bps.org.uk/).**

Articles on the main intelligence issues discussed in these chapters are often found in these journals.

- **Intelligence: A Multidisciplinary Journal.** Published by Elsevier Science. Available online via Science Direct.
- **Personality and Individual Differences**. Published by Elsevier Science. Available online via Science Direct.
- **American Psychologist**. Published by American Psychological Society. Available online via Psych-Articles.

Web resources

- **Head Start** is an Information and Publication Center that supports the innovative early childhood development program, and is sponsored by the US federal government **(http://www2.acf.dhhs.gov/programs/hsb/).**

Film and Literature

- **Good Will Hunting** (1997; directed by Gus Van Sant). A janitor at a prestigious university, Will Hunting is gifted in mathematics that can take him beyond his blue-collar job and roots. The film provides you with an analysis on how natural intelligence can come into conflict with socioeconomic variables.
- **Dangerous Minds** (1996; directed by John N. Smith). This is another film that shows how natural intelligence can come into conflict with socioeconomic variables. In this film, a US high school teacher starts teaching a class and slowly realises that the students in her class are highly intelligent but have social problems.
- **Discovering Psychology video** (1990; Educational Resource Film). Topics on intelligence, creativity and the self, limitations of testing and measuring the brain. WGBH/Annenberg-PCB-Project/CS.

Chapter 13

Heritability and Socially Defined Race Differences in Intelligence

Key Themes

- Genetic heritability of intelligence
- Genetic and environmental influences on intelligence
- The bell curve
- Socially defined race differences in intelligence
- Eugenics in intelligence research

Learning Outcomes

By the end of this chapter you should:

- Understand what is meant by genetic heritability in intelligence
- Be able to outline the different dimensions of genetic and environmental influences that are thought to affect intelligence
- Be familiar with the main points of Herrnstein and Murray's bell curve analysis
- Be aware of some criticisms of Herrnstein and Murray's bell curve analysis

Introduction

Source: Photodisc/Getty Images

In 1994 Arthur Jensen, a prominent IQ psychologist, wrote:

> Consideration of the book's actual content is being displaced by the rhetoric of denial: name calling ("neo-Nazi," "pseudo-scientific," "racism"), sidetracks ("but does IQ really measure intelligence?"), non sequiturs ("specific genes for IQ have not been identified, so we can claim nothing about its heritability"), red herrings ("Hitler misused genetics"), falsehoods ("all the tests are biased"), hyperbole ("throwing gasoline on a fire"), and insults ("creepy", "indecent," "ugly").
>
> (Jensen, 1994, p. 48)

What book created these descriptions, and why did Jensen feel it necessary to defend such a book? In this chapter we address the history, theory and debate that surround the examination of race differences in intelligence, and explore the debates and consequences of some of the conclusions that are drawn from this research. It is not a pretty side of psychology. Assertions and evidence presented are not always palatable to many. Group differences in intelligence are an interesting area of debate, but it is not without its dark side. And as part of this chapter, we are going to explore the actual content of the aforementioned book.

This chapter is slightly longer than many others in the book. In this chapter we deal with some controversial and sensitive issues in the psychology of intelligence. We argue that many areas need to be explained and fully explored. Additionally, we introduce a number of concepts that you have come across in previous chapters, so rather than suggest you spend your time going backwards and forwards through the book, we have spent a little time restating the main issues and findings from other discussions, to make it clear how these issues apply to the debates in this chapter. Consequently, you should find some of this material easier going because you have been introduced to a lot of the arguments in previous chapters.

However, we realise that there is slightly more material here, so we have split the chapter into two main sections. Please remember, however, that these two areas are intrinsically linked.

➔

- **Section A - Intelligence: The nature versus nurture debate.** In this section we will outline what has become known as the nature versus nurture debate, in which we compare and consider genetic versus environmental effects on intelligence. Key themes in this debate include heritability of intelligence and genetic and environmental influences on intelligence.
- **Section B - The bell curve: Race differences in intelligence.** In this section we will outline what has become known as the bell curve debate. We consider evidence and arguments regarding race differences in intelligence. Key themes in this debate include an outline and consideration of a bell curve, group differences, most notably race differences in intelligence, and the role of eugenics in intelligence research.

Section A
The Heritability of Intelligence

Intelligence: the nature versus nurture debate

Here we will outline what has become known as the nature versus nurture debate. We will compare and consider genetic versus environmental effects on intelligence.

Galton

In 1865, Sir Francis Galton began to study the heritability of intelligence, following his reading of his cousin Charles Darwin's publication *Origin of Species*, which dealt with the idea that all species gradually evolve through the process of natural selection. In following this work, Galton soon became interested in studying the variations in human ability, and particularly intelligence. In his book *Hereditary Genius* (Galton, 1869), he began investigating why higher intelligence seemed to run in families. He suggested that man's natural abilities are inherited under the same conditions as physical features of the animal world described by Darwin. Galton suggested that children inherit their intelligence from their parents.

To support such an assertion, Galton started analysing the obituaries of the *Times* newspaper so that he could identify the ancestry of eminent men. What Galton did was to compare different degrees of relationship between individuals in terms of being biological relatives (i.e., parents, siblings, cousins) and the eminence of each of these individuals. First-degree relatives are relatives with whom an individual shares an estimated average of 50 per cent (half) of their genes (though note this is an estimated average percentage; you will learn more about why this is an estimated average in this chapter). First-degree relatives include your parents, brothers and sisters and children. A second-degree relative is a relative with whom an individual shares an estimated average of 25 per cent (a quarter) of their genes, that is, grandparents, grandchildren, aunts, uncles, nephews, nieces. A third-degree relative is a relative with whom an individual shares an estimated average of 12.5 per cent (one-eighth) of their genes. Third-degree relatives include your great-grandparents, great-aunts, great-uncles and first cousins. Galton found that the number of eminent relatives of an eminent person was greater for first-degree relatives than for second-degree relatives; and again, the number was greater for second-degree relatives than for third-degree relatives. This result suggested to Galton that there is evidence for the heritability of intelligence.

However, Galton quickly became concerned with whether intelligence was simply heritable, or whether it was also influenced by the environment. It was here that Galton was the first psychologist to make the distinction between 'nature' and 'nurture' (and he was the first to use this now-common phrase). To examine this idea, he surveyed 190 Fellows of the Royal Society, of which Galton was a member (Galton, 1874). The Royal Society is a highly prestigious scientific society dedicated to establishing the truth of scientific matters through experiment. It has had several famous scientists as members, including Robert Boyle, Sir Christopher Wren and Issac Newton. Galton asked his fellow members of the society several questions regarding their birth order and the occupation and race of their parents. He wanted to find out whether members of the society's achievements and interest in science were due to their natural makeup (nature) or to their environment, for example, the encouragement of their talents by others (nurture).

You have to remember that many of Galton's speculations arose before we knew as much about genetics as we do today. That is why many recognise him as a truly great scientist. Galton himself recognised the inherent problems of such studies (Galton, 1875). For example, he speculated about the confounding effects of the environment and realised that eminent people might not have arisen to their current status alone, but with the help of relatives. Galton believed that the question of whether nature or nurture influences intelligence could be examined more carefully by comparing twins. He suggested that comparisons of

Source: Stuart Atkins/Rex Features

Galton felt that there was some value in studying eminent families as an indicator of the heritability of intelligence. How well would such an approach work today?

twins who were similar at birth but had grown up in different environments, and comparisons of dissimilar twins who had grown up in similar environments, might hold the key to examining the nature-nurture debate surrounding intelligence. He also proposed that adoption studies might be useful to analyse the different effects of heredity and environment. His speculations about twins and adoption studies laid the groundwork for modern attempts to examine the nature-nurture debate in intelligence.

Heritability of intelligence

Within the nature versus nurture consideration of intelligence, we find ourselves concentrating on behavioural genetic principles (you will have come across many of these ideas if you have read Chapter 8). One area of behavioural genetics concentrates on the relationships between genes and environment, to compare the similarities and differences between individuals within a particular population and assess the relative influence of genes and the environment on any behaviour. In this case, the behaviour we are looking at is intelligence.

What do we mean by heritability of intelligence?

Behavioural geneticists such as Robert Plomin have written extensively about behavioural genetics (Plomin, 2004; Plomin, DeFries, McClearn, & McGuffin, 2000). The start of the heritability of intelligence begins with the fact that genes are biologically transmitted from biological parents to the child. Children inherit 50 per cent of their father's genes and 50 per cent of their mother's genes. We can use this information as a starting point to explore how genes influence intelligence.

The assessment of the extent to which any phenotype (any outward manifestation of the individual – physical attractiveness, behaviour, intelligence) is passed on from parents to children, from the results of their genes, is termed as **genetic heritability**. The genetic heritability of any phenotype is assessed in terms of variability (i.e., how much they differ) between the parents and the child. This variability is often assessed within the *proportion of shared variance* of that behaviour between the parent and child. Proportion of shared variance is presented as a percentage (i.e., out of 100 per cent). When a parent and child are very similar in a particular characteristic, there is thought to be a low variability between parent and child, and the proportion of shared variance of that behaviour is high (nearer 100 per cent). In other words, the parent and child are not very different in this characteristic. Conversely, when a parent and child are quite different in a particular characteristic, there is thought to be a high variability between parent and child, and the proportion of shared variance of that behaviour is low (nearer 0 per cent).

The heritability of a human physical characteristic, such as having a nose, is entirely genetic and not in any way influenced by factors such as the environment. In fact the environment is seen as having zero variability, or a proportion of shared variance of 100 per cent. However, some aspects of human behaviour (including intelligence), in which the environment is thought to have an influence, have greater amounts of heritable variability and lower shared variance. For example, choosing which football team to support would be heavily determined by environmental factors such as where you are born, your parents' football team, your friends, and the first football team you see. Choosing a favourite football team has high variability between parent and child, but the proportion of shared variance of favourite football team due to genetic heritability would be zero (0 per cent).

In behavioural genetics of intelligence, researchers are primarily interested in *estimating* the extent of genetic heritability of intelligence across a population, and stating the genetic heritability of that behaviour in terms of shared variance. This estimated average of genetic heritability is known as h^2. Therefore, h^2 is the *average estimate* of the proportion of variance for intelligence thought to be accounted for by genetic factors across a population.

You may have noticed we emphasised *estimating*, *estimate* ('estimate' meaning to calculate approximately) and *average*. This is because, for a long time in psychology, for any phenotype (characteristic or behaviour) the estimates of the strength of genetics factors were done and interpreted within a process called the *additive assumption*.

This additive assumption suggests that there are only two dimensions that determine heritability of any behaviour (in our case, intelligence): (1) the genetic part, which we've just outlined, and (2) the environment. Consequently, overall, heritability of intelligence is estimated in terms of the relative strength of both (e.g., nature versus nurture). Therefore, the influence of genetic (G) and environmental (E) components, in this theory, will always add together to account for 100 per cent of the variance of intelligence. On the basis of this assumption, the heritability coefficient (h^2) can be subtracted from 100% to calculate the environmental contribution to intelligence. If researchers computed, for example, that genetics accounted for an average of 25 per cent of the variance for intelligence, we would estimate that the environmental factors account for an average of 75 per cent of the variance of intelligence. However, it is important to note that the additive assumption is now considered a starting point for calculating heritability of intelligence and for estimating the amount of genes that people are expected to share (e.g., brothers and sisters are expected to share 50 per cent). We will see later in this chapter that this view of assessing heritability has changed a lot. The idea of determining the relative strength of genetics and environmental factors by simply adding together genetic and environmental factors is more complicated than once thought, and psychologists really do emphasise the words 'estimate' and 'average' when referring to heritability.

Methods for assessing genetic heritability of intelligence

So, how might we assess genetic influences on intelligence? Well, as Galton himself mentioned, the relationship between genes and intelligence has traditionally been studied by concentrating on the similarities and differences between populations of individuals to assess the relative influence of their shared genes in intelligence.

Plomin (2004) identifies three main types of studies that use this technique: family studies, twin studies and adoption studies. As children share an estimated average of 50 per cent of their genes with each of their parents, and they also share genes with their brothers and sisters, it is of interest to behavioural genetics researchers to examine possible associations between parents' and children's behaviours within a family. This leads to the first type of study, family studies. However, these studies on their own potentially tell us very little because all children share an estimated average of 50 per cent of their genes with each of their parents and with their brothers and sisters. As well as this, using observation, interview or questionnaire measures also presents a problem because similarities between personalities might be due to environmental influence (i.e., an intelligent daughter might be like her extraverted mother because she copies her behaviour). These are real concerns until we consider the occasions when families don't typically share genes in this way. There are two main examples: twin studies and adoption studies.

Twin studies provide an interesting area of research, as there is a possibility of comparing different types of genetic makeup so as to compare genetic influences. The term 'twin' refers to two individuals who have shared the same uterus (the uterus or womb is the major female reproductive organ). Identical twins (or monozygotic) occur when a single egg is fertilised to form one zygote, but the zygote then divides into two separate embryos. The two embryos develop into fetuses sharing the same womb. Identical twins are always of the same sex and have the same arrangement of genes and chromosomes (which contain the hereditary information necessary for cell life). These twins share 100 per cent of genes with each other. Fraternal twins (non-identical twins, or dizygotic) usually occur when two fertilised eggs are implanted in the uterine wall at the same time. The two eggs form two zygotes (hence they are dizygotic). These twins share an estimated average of 50 per cent of their genetic makeup. Consequently, some researchers compare behaviours across non-twins, identical and fraternal twins to examine the relative influence of genetics.

The influence of the environment and genetics is often compared in adoption studies. Intelligence can be compared between parents and adopted children, as there is no genetic heritability. Variables are often compared between siblings, or twins, reared apart to examine the extent of genetic and environmental effects. For example, if two twins show similar behaviours, despite being raised in different environments, this suggests that genes may be important in that behaviour.

Once you consider all these types of studies together, in which intelligence is compared between parents and children, and siblings that share 0–100 per cent genetic similarity, you can begin to make assessments of the extent of genetic heritability across a population.

It is important to remember that there is no physiological procedure in these sorts of studies. Behaviour geneticists do not have the ability to assess the genetic heritability of intelligence using advanced biological measures, or a complex scientific genetic analysis (well, not yet). Rather, researchers look for similarities and differences in intelligence among individual people by using observation, interview or questionnaire measures. They look for similarities between parents' and children's intelligence (using intelligence measures) to determine the extent of genetic influence on intelligence. What is also important to remember is that, when we deal with heritability estimates, we don't talk about heritability estimates for particular individuals; rather, researchers estimate the average heritability among certain populations of people – monozygotic (MZ, identical) twins, dizygotic (DZ, fraternal) twins, family members, parents and children. So an heritability estimate of 50 per cent for intelligence does not mean that we all inherit 50 per cent of that intelligence trait from our genes; it means that across the population, the genetic heritability of intelligence has been estimated at an average of 50 per cent.

Heritability estimates of intelligence

What is the heritability of intelligence from these types of studies? Well, some studies have estimated the heritability of intelligence based on family, twin and adoption studies.

For example, there have been a number of findings from Bouchard's Minnesota Study of Twins Reared Apart (overseen by US behavioural geneticist Thomas Bouchard). This research involves not only the medical and psychological assessment of identical (monozygotic) and fraternal (dizygotic) twins separated early in life and reared apart, on which figures are given, but also their intelligence. A well-cited documentation of these studies was recently provided by behavioural geneticist journalist Matt Ridley (Ridley, 1999). Ridley put together all the modern family, twin and adoption studies, which mainly included the findings of Bouchard and McGues' meta-analysis of 111 studies (Bouchard & McGue, 1981). The following analysis by Ridley is the concordance rate of IQ (the presence of the same intelligence level between two individuals) from all these studies (in parentheses are concordance rate given by Bouchard and McGue's meta-analysis; see also Figure 13.1):

- 100%: Perfect Concordance Rate;
- 87%: Same person tested twice;
- 86%: Identical twins reared together (86%);
- 76%: Identical twins reared apart (72%);
- 55%: Fraternal twins reared together (60%);
- 47%: Biological siblings reared together (47%);
- 40%: Parents and children living together (42%);
- 31%: Parents and children living apart (22%);
- 24%: Biological siblings reared apart (24%);
- 15%: Cousins (Bouchard & McGue only);
- 00%: Adopted children living together;
- 00%: Unrelated people living apart.

Evidence such as this, coming from studies throughout the century, was consistent, and researchers were able to make estimates on the level of genetic heritability of intelligence. You can see from evidence like this how people would tend to estimate the influence of genetics on intelligence as

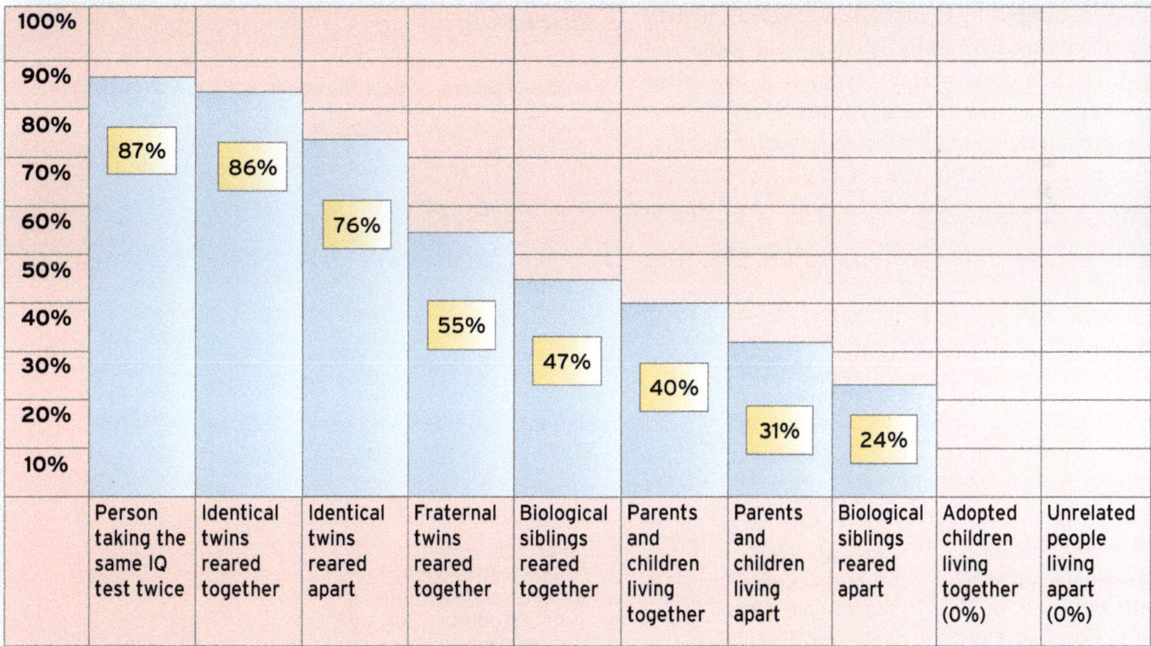

Figure 13.1 Concordance rates of intelligence.

Source: From Ridley, M. (1999). *Genome: the autobiography of a species in 23 chapters.* London: Fourth Estate. Copyright © M. Ridley 1999. Reprinted with permission of HarperCollins Publishers Ltd.

in some instances relatively high, because the evidence for heritability, in some instances, is over 80 per cent. For example, Professor Hans Eysenck (Eysenck, 1979) used this sort of evidence to suggest that the estimation of heritability of intelligence was around 69 per cent in the general population. Later, Herrnstein and Murray (1994), whose work we will discuss at greater length later, estimated heritability in the general population at 74 per cent.

However, we know a lot more about the influences of genetics on intelligence today. We outlined some of these influences in Chapter 8, but we are going to outline them fully here so you can see their relevance to the literature on intelligence as well as how the estimates of the genetic influence on intelligence might be lower than previously estimated.

Considerations within behavioural genetics and intelligence

The idea of how genes and the environment are viewed, and used, to predict the heritability of intelligence has changed over recent years.

Authors such as US psychologist E. E. Maccoby (2000) and Robert Plomin (2004) suggest the additive principle of determining heritability of intelligence (or any phenotype) is not applicable any more. The validity of the additive assumption in computing the relative strength of genetics and environment in determining behaviour has been widely challenged. The first problem is that estimating the environment is usually done without utilising any direct measures of environmental factors. For example, researchers often compute genetic heritability and then subtract that from 100 per cent. Obviously, if the estimates of heritability are indeterminate, or prone to error, so are the estimates of E derived by subtracting heritability from 100 per cent. A further problem with the additive assumption of computing heritability is that when genetic heritability is large, it assumes that all environmental factors associated with that behaviour must be small. Therefore, it is better to see human intelligence as a joint result of an interaction between a person's genes and environmental factors. Intelligence should not be seen as the result of 'genetics + environment' but rather of 'genetics × environment'. For example, it is better to view the relative influences of genes and environment on intelligence as the result of a long-term interaction, with environmental factors triggering certain genetic behaviours. and the effects of the environment differing between individuals because of their genetic makeup.

What is important for you to note is that these changes and developments in research and thinking have been suggested, encouraged and developed by both theorists and researchers, many of whom we have already mentioned, who support and criticise the idea of genetic heritability in intelligence. So, what has brought about, and resulted from, such a general shift in thinking, from the additive principle of 'genetics + environment' to the later, more integrative idea of 'genetics × environment'? Well, four considerations surrounding modern-day thinking in behavioural genetics are important when considering any phenotype, particularly intelligence (see Figure 13.2):

- conceptions of heritability and the environment;
- different types of genetic variance;
- the representativeness of twin and adoption studies;
- assortative mating.

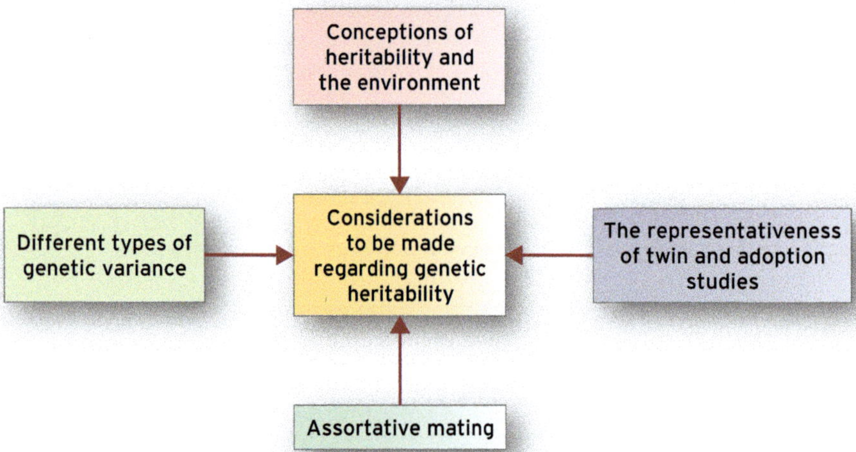

Figure 13.2
Considerations to be made regarding genetic heritability.

Conceptions of genetic heritability and the environment

Gregory Carey (2002) suggests that there are two important contexts within which to consider heritability and environmental influences on intelligence:

- **Abstract concepts** – These are generally theoretical (not applied or practical) concepts. As Carey explains, whatever the numerical estimates of either genetic or environmental influences, they provide us with little information about the specific genes, or specific environmental variables, that influence intelligence.
- **Population concepts** – All of these estimates refer to any group of people considered as a population, but they tell us very little about any single individual. For example, just because intelligence may have a genetic heritability of around 60 per cent, it does not mean, for any one individual, that 60 per cent of their intelligence is due to genes and 40 per cent of their intelligence is due to the environment. Rather, it is estimated across the population that genetic heritability of intelligence is at an average of around 40 per cent, and individuals will vary around that estimate.

Different types of genetic variance

So far, in this chapter, we have treated genetic influence on intelligence only as a single entity, namely, the influence of your genes on your intelligence. However, behavioural genetics researchers such as Thomas Bouchard and M. McGue (Bouchard & McGue, 1981) note that genetic influence does not simply comprise one aspect, but in fact three aspects: (1) additive genetic variance, (2) dominant genetic variance and (3) epistatic genetic variance.

Additive genetic variation is the genetic variance that we have previously described in this chapter, which is genetic variation in behaviour that is the total of the individual's genes inherited from their parents.

However, the two other types of genetic variation are known as non-additive genetic variance.

First, **dominant genetic variance** is part of a process by which certain genes are expressed (dominant genes) and other genes are not expressed (recessive genes). Every one of us has two copies of every gene, one inherited from our mother and one from our father. Sometimes the two genes, which determine a particular trait (for example, eye colour) will actually code for two types of characteristics (for example, blue eyes and brown eyes). If one of these genes is dominant, then only its character is expressed and not that of the other gene. For example, if blue eyes were a dominant gene, and your mother had brown eyes and your father had blue eyes, you would inherit blue eyes.

Secondly, **epistatic genetic variance** (known as interactive genetic variance) refers to a process by which genes interact. It is now known that several different genes not only influence physical characteristics and behaviour on their own, but work and interact together. Unlike dominant genetic variance, which just applies to one gene replacing another, epistatic genetic variance is the result of the way certain genes that we inherit determine whether other genes we inherit will be expressed or suppressed (this process is called **epistasis**).

It is difficult to measure dominant genetic variance and epistatic genetic variance when it comes to intelligence. However, it is now accepted that these three aspects – additive genetic variance, dominance genetic variance and epistatic genetic variance – are thought to make up **total genetic variance** of intelligence.

You can see the genetic side of things is a lot more complicated than just viewing genes as a single entity, as genes interact and suppress other genes. You will see, in the literature, behavioural geneticists referring to terms such as 'narrow heritability' and 'broad heritability'. Narrow heritability is just additive genetic variance. Broad heritability is all three aspects of genetic heritability (additive genetic variance + dominant genetic variance + epistatic genetic variance).

Consequently, authors such as Thomas Bouchard and M. McGue (1981) and US psychologists Heather Chipeur, Michael Rovine and Robert Plomin, (1990) have suggested that original estimates of the average percentage of parental genes that children inherit, and siblings share, may have been previously oversimplified. For example, these authors suggest that genetic variations in heritability of any phenotype (including intelligence) should be made in the following terms:

- identical (monozygotic; MZ) twins = additive genetic variance + non-additive genetic variance (where previously it was presumed to be just additive genetic variance);
- fraternal (dizygotic; DZ) twins = 0.5 of additive genetic variance + 0.25 of non-additive genetic variance (rather than just 0.5 of additive genetic variance).

As you can see, computing the level of genetic variance may be more complicated than previously thought. Today, behavioural geneticists take these factors into account when suggesting the strength of heritability estimates of intelligence.

Problems with the representativeness of twin and adoption studies

One of the considerations put forward by psychologists such as Maccoby and by Leon Kamin and Arthur Goldberger (2002) concerns adoption and twin studies. A significant portion of studies examining heritability effects is devoted to twin and adoption studies. Twin studies are important because they allow the comparison of different types of twins to compare genetic influences; monozygotic (MZ, identical) twins who share 100 per cent of their genes, and dizygotic (DZ, fraternal) twins who share 50 per cent of their genes. Adoption studies are important because they include two sets of factors that may account for differences in behaviour: biological parents and environmental parents. Therefore, it is argued that these families aren't necessarily representative of the normal populations. This natural bias in sampling may underestimate or overestimate heritability estimates across the general population because genetic influences in these samples may not be representative of the whole population.

This issue is particularly important when considering research that assesses heritability of intelligence using twin and adoption studies. Leon Kamin and Arthur Goldberger (2002) estimate that twin studies might overestimate the role of genetics, particularly because identical twins have more similar environments than do same-sex fraternal twins. Also, research shows identical twins are treated more similarly by their parents, spend more time together and more often have the same friends. Their environmental experience comprises a greater proportion of each other's social environment than does that of fraternal siblings. Consequently, if genetic heritability estimates are usually larger in twin studies than in adoption studies, then some of the estimated similarity that is attributed to genetic influence might not be correct. Stoolmiller (1998) has also suggested that adoption studies lead to a similar restriction of the measurement of environmental factors. Stoolmiller argues that the placement strategies of adoption agencies might influence heritability estimates. For example, adoption agencies might always place children in affluent or middle- to high-income families; thus the effects of economic status are never fully explored in these studies, because an adopted child would rarely be placed into a household suffering from poverty.

Assortative mating

Nicholas Mackintosh (Mackintosh, 1998), animal-learning theorist at the University of Cambridge, raises the issue that assortative mating can have an effect on genetic variance and, therefore, on estimates of genetic heritability of intelligence. **Assortative mating** is a complicated name for the simple concept that, when couples mate, they either have several traits in common or contrast wildly in their traits. A lot of the understanding of genetic variation is based on the assumption that two individuals mate quite randomly with random people and, therefore, that any genetic similarity between them is by chance. But we know this is not true. We know that people mate with people who they perceive are similar to themselves. For example, we tend to see people mating with people who are of a similar size, or similar in their 'good-lookingness'. This is called positive assortative mating. Although, equally, we find people mating who are completely the opposite. This is called negative assortative mating. Therefore, in much the same way, the assortative mating principle can be applied to intelligence. That is, individuals may seek to mate with people who are of a similar intelligence. Think about your parents; do they have a similar educational background to each other?

Stop and Think

Cyril L. Burt

For many lecturers and students across the psychology discipline, Cyril Burt is psychology's equivalent of the bogeyman. Like parents who tell children who are naughty that the bogeyman will come and get them, lecturers inform students who are naughty and make up their data that they will be branded with the Cyril Burt label. No one knows the truth about Cyril Burt; but stories of acts done, a long time ago, are told through generations of lecturers. Your lecturers were told by their lecturers about Cyril Burt, and though many stories about him may be untrue, academics today still argue and swap conspiracy, and counterconspiracy, stories surrounding Cyril Burt.

Cyril L. Burt was born on 3 March 1893 and died 10 October 1971. He was a British educational psychologist. He studied at Oxford in the United Kingdom, and in Germany. Between 1908 and 1971, he worked at the University of Liverpool and had a chair of Psychology at University College, London. He also worked as Chief Psychologist at London County Council. He was President of the British Psychological Society (in 1942), was editor and co-editor of the *British Journal of Statistical Psychology* (between 1947 and 1963) and was the first psychologist to be knighted (in 1946). He founded the field of Educational Psychology in the United Kingdom and helped to establish Eleven-Plus testing in Great Britain.

In his academic work, Burt published nine books and more than three hundred articles, lectures and book chapters. Much of his work investigated differences in intelligence among social classes, gender and race, and examined heritability among intelligence of identical twins reared apart. It was this work that was to create the controversy.

During the 1970s Leon Kamin, who was opposed to the idea of genetic heritability, and Arthur Jensen, who was in favour of genetic heritability, both spotted something in Burt's reports on correlations for IQ test scores of identical twins (Jensen, 1973; Kamin, 1974). Burt's original results were published in 1943 for 15 pairs of twins. In 1955 he had results for 21 pairs of twins (including the 15 original pairs of twins), and by 1966 he reported the results for a total of 53 pairs of twins. What Kamin and Jensen noted was that the correlation coefficients between the IQ scores were similar across the samples. In his studies, Burt reported the following coefficients: $r = .770$ (1943); $r = .771$ (1955); and $r = .771$ (1966). Kamin and Jensen suggested that they would expect to see greater variability among the correlations when more sets of twins were added, and that it was very unusual that the correlations had stayed the same.

On 24 October 1976, an article, 'Crucial data was faked by eminent psychologist', was published by Dr Oliver Gillies in the UK newspaper *Sunday Times*. In this article, Gillies not only pointed to the problems with the correlational data but also claimed that Burt had invented his co-authors, Miss Margaret Howard and Miss J. Conway (who Burt claimed helped him update the twin data), as they could not be traced. Gillies also pointed out that Howard and Conway did appear to have written book reviews praising Burt's work for the *Journal of Statistical Psychology* - but only during the time that Burt was editor. Later, US psychologist William H. Tucker picked up on accusations that Burt would have been unlikely to find so many sets of monozygotic twins reared apart. Tucker (1997) examined the numbers of participants involved in twin studies with similar criteria used by Burt between 1922 and 1990 and found that the combination of all the twins together did not total the number of participants Burt had obtained.

With this, Cyril Burt seemed to be forever denounced as a fraud. However, people have reviewed this evidence. For example, UK psychologist Ronald Fletcher, (1991) set out to locate the missing research assistants. He found proof of their existence. One of the assistants, Miss J. Conway, worked in child care for London County Council. Miss M. A. Howard is listed as a member of the British Psychological Society in 1924. In addition, Fletcher reported that other individuals stepped forward and said they remembered Burt's assistants. Fletcher suggests that this repeated accusation against Burt may be the result of poor investigatory journalism rather than imagined helpers.

This is not the only accusation against the media. Some authors such as Fletcher, Robert Joynson (1989), and J. Phillipe Rushton (1994) have suggested that Burt's reported correlation coefficients indicated a strong relationship between genetics and intelligence - and they point out this was not, and still isn't, a popular finding. This is because such findings have strong implications where differences in intelligence are sexually or racially based. Often, there is the inference that certain groups of people (based on sex or race differences) are genetically inferior in intelligence. We will explore such ideas in full later in the chapter. However, these ideas are surrounded by controversy, and Fletcher and Rushton point out that, if Burt's findings can be discredited, then it seems to some that the case for the genetic heritability of intelligence is discredited. Therefore, Fletcher and Rushton argue that people who disagree with the genetic heritability of intelligence will be more likely to conspire in the media and in academia to discredit Burt's work.

Rushton points to possible conspiratorial behaviour. He suggests that not only the media sought to discredit Burt's findings too quickly, but other academics did, too. He cites the example of Burt's papers being destroyed by his housekeeper immediately after his death - on the advice of Professor Liam Hudson, an educational psychologist at Edinburgh University, an ardent opponent of Burt who had rushed to Burt's flat after learning he had died.

Rushton also points out that new evidence from studies of twins raised apart (as we see from the summary of Ridley earlier in this chapter) indicates results similar to Burt's high heritability estimate. Therefore, the accusations that he simply made up all the data to exaggerate the effects of genetics are somewhat weakened.

Authors like Ronald Fletcher and Robert Joynson suggest that the case of fraud by Burt is not proven. Whatever the truth, and the lessons to be learnt from Cyril Burt, we hope that whatever judgements you make, you understand the importance of giving the full facts before you pass on the story . . . and *never* make up your data.

Modern estimates of the genetic heritability of intelligence

In light of the considerations just outlined, different researchers have tried to estimate the overall heritability of intelligence across the general population. These estimates tend to be broad estimates of genetic variance (additive and nonadditive genetic variance) in intelligence. They break down by what percentage of intelligence is determined by genetics and what percentage can be attributed to the environment. As we have already mentioned, higher estimates of heritability have come from authors like Hans Eysenck (1971, 1991), who once estimated it at 69 per cent. There is no evidence to suggest that this is wrong; however,

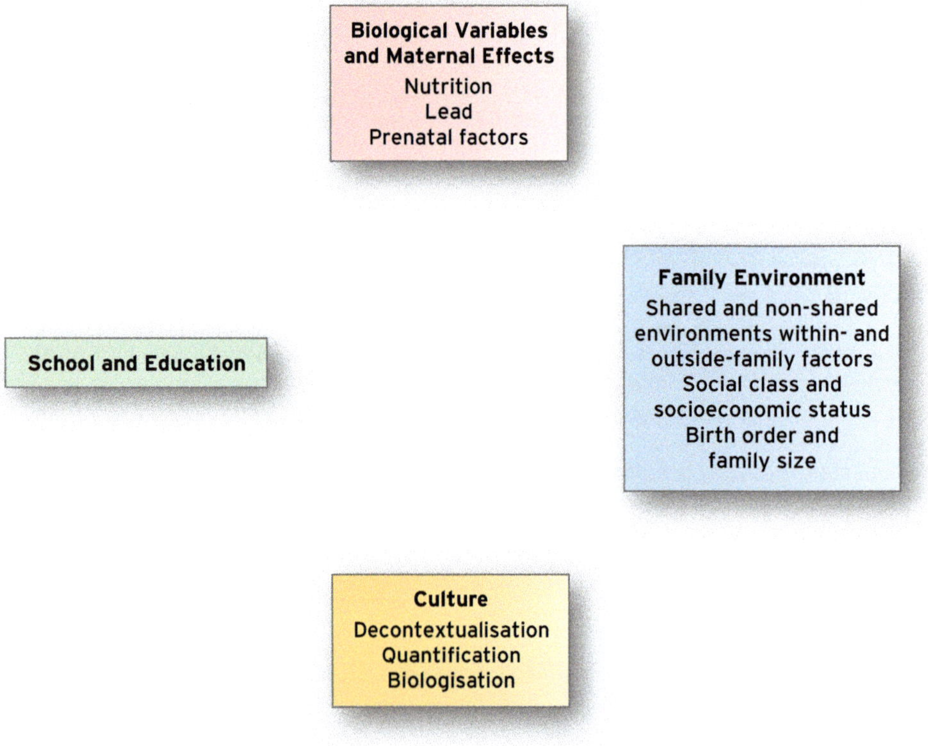

Figure 13.3 Environmental effects on intelligence.

modern-day commentators, given the preceding issues relating to heritability estimates, are more conservative; that suggests heritability falls into a range. The American Psychological Association task force (that we mentioned in Chapter 10), headed by Ulric Neisser, estimates the heritability of intelligence ranges from 40 to 80 per cent (Neisser et al., 1996), while Nicolas Mackintosh (1998) suggests a range of 30 to 75 per cent. If you are looking for a more exact figure, Chipeur et al. (1990) have suggested the genetic heritability of intelligence at 50 per cent which is a commonly – but not always – accepted viewpoint.

All this discussion, and we haven't even considered the extent of environmental effects on intelligence yet!

Environmental influences on intelligence

The list of possible environmental effects on intelligence could be endless. It could range from the effects on intelligence of long-term poverty (for example, never getting the opportunities to develop skills at home, at school and consequently in a career), through to one conversation with one teacher who suggests that the person will never amount to much. Thomas Bouchard and Nancy Segal (1985) list 21 factors that are related to intelligence, including malnutrition, weight at birth, height, years in school, father's economic status, father's and mother's education and influence, average TV viewing, self-confidence, criminality and emotional adaptation. However, the American Psychological Association task force (Neisser et al., 1996) identified four main areas of environmental effects on intelligence which can be deemed as the most important. This information allows us to concentrate the debate. Some of these environmental effects you will have come across before (for example, nutrition, schooling and occupation) in the last chapter, but we will revisit them so that you can see how they apply directly to the issues of the nature versus nurture debate on intelligence. These four areas are (1) biological variables, (2) family, (3) school and education and (4) culture (see Figure 13.3).

Biological variables and maternal effects

It is well acknowledged by the APA task force (Neisser et al., 1996) that a number of biological factors influence intelligence. These include nutrition, before- and after-birth factors and substances like alcohol and lead poisoning.

Nutrition

We introduced much of the nutrition hypothesis in the last chapter. Nutrition is the study of food; specifically, the relationship between diet and states of health and disease. You will remember from the last chapter that Lynn (1990) has proposed that nutrition and health care improvements are among the main factors of the Flynn effect. However, outside Lynn's hypothesis there are findings that nutritional sources can aid aspects of intelligence.

Australian nutritionist Wendy H. Oddy and her colleagues (Oddy et al., 2004) examined over two thousand Australian children and followed them from birth until the age of 8 years. Oddy and her colleagues found that stopping breast feeding early (at 6 months or less) was associated with reduced verbal intelligence, while children who were fully breast-fed for more than 6 months scored between 3 and 6 IQ points higher on a vocabulary intelligence test than did those children who were never breast-fed. Similarly, another study conducted by US health psychologist Melaine Smith and her colleagues (Smith, Durkin, Hinton, Bellinger & Kuhn, 2003) examined 439 school-age, low-birth-weight children born in the United States. These authors found differences in IQ test scores between breast-fed children and those who did not receive any breast milk. These were 3.6 IQ points for overall intellectual functioning and 2.3 IQ points for verbal ability. You will also remember the debate in Chapter 12 surrounding the study carried out by two Welsh psychologists, David Benton and Gwilym Roberts (Benton & Roberts, 1988), who found that children given a vitamin-mineral supplement containing several vitamins and minerals were found to show increased IQ scores.

Regardless of the controversy surrounding this work, findings do suggest that nutrition has a positive effect on intelligence. It is important to remember, though, that a number of socioeconomic conditions are often associated with nutrition. You may also remember the words of Lynn (1990), who we discussed in the last chapter: the nutrition hypothesis sees nutrition as a package (or nurturing environment) in which increased intelligence is part of a nurturing environment that includes increased height and life span, improved health, decreased rate of infant disease and better vitamin and mineral nutrition. Where those things do not occur – where there is poverty, malnutrition and low economic and social opportunities – there might be lower intelligence scores.

Lead

However, while nutrition is seen as having a positive effect, there are occasions when other biological factors can have a negative effect on IQ. Neisser et al. (1996) highlight research concentrating on the effect that exposure to lead can have on intelligence.

The most comprehensive study was carried out in a place called Port Pirie in Australia. In 1986, Australian psychologist Anthony J. McMichael and four colleagues (McMichael, Vimpani, Robertson, Baghurst & Clark, 1986) examined the possible relationship between body lead burden and pregnancy outcome among 749 pregnant women in, and around, the largest lead smelting facilities in Australia. Among these women, premature deliveries were statistically significantly associated with higher levels of maternal blood lead concentration at delivery. What followed the initial findings was a series of studies in Port Pirie, which looked at the association between environmental exposure to lead and children's intelligence at 2 years (McMichael et al., 1988), 4 years and 7 years (Baghurst et al., 1992) and 11 and 13 years (Tong, Baghurst, McMichael, Sawyer & Mudge, 1996). The Port Pirie cohort study started in 1979 and involved 723 children, though 375 took part in the final study. IQ scores were made on the Bailey IQ scales at 2 years of age, the McCarthy IQ scale at 4 years of age and the Wechsler IQ scale for children at 7 years, 11 years and 13 years of age. At all these ages, IQ scores were significantly associated with lead concentration in people's bodies, even when socioeconomic status, home environment and maternal intelligence were controlled for. This study suggests that there is an association between early exposure to environmental lead and intelligence, and it persists into later childhood.

Prenatal factors

Finally, there are prenatal factors. You are well aware that pregnant women are expected to stop drinking and smoking. According to many health councils, avoiding smoking and alcohol consumption in pregnancy is crucial. Smoking nearly doubles a woman's risk of having a premature or low-birth-weight baby who faces an increased risk of serious health problems. Further, many conditions can arise from the mother's alcohol consumption when she is pregnant; the most common condition is foetal alcohol syndrome (FAS), which is characterised by a pattern of facial abnormalities, growth retardation and brain damage.

Neisser et al. (1996) point to these types of consumption by mothers during pregnancy as having an effect on intelligence. Low-birth-weight babies, as well as babies suffering from FAS, show reduced intelligence. Danish scientist Erik Lykke Mortensen and colleagues at the University of Copenhagen (Mortensen, Michaelsen, Sanders & Reinisch, 2005) examined maternal smoking and subsequent IQ scores among 3,044 males aged between 18 and 19 years. The study found that regardless of factors such as parental social status and education, single-mother status, mother's height and age, number of pregnancies, the women who smoked 20 or more cigarettes daily late in their pregnancy were likely to have sons who performed less well on standardised IQ tests at age 18 or 19. Evidence also suggests that FAS is related to a number of cognitive functions.

US psychologist Sarah Mattson and colleagues at San Diego State University (Mattson & Riley, 1998; Mattson, Riley, Delis, Stern & Jones, 1996;) have found that children prenatally exposed to alcohol exhibit a variety of problems with memory (when they found that children with FAS aged 5 years to 16 years had learned fewer words than children of comparable ages) and demonstrate attention problems. Uecker and Nadel (1996) found that children of mothers who drank heavily during pregnancy performed badly in learning spatial relationships among objects. Furthermore, South African psychologist Piyadasa Kodituwakku and her colleagues (Kodituwakku, Handmaker, Cutler, Weathersby & Handmaker, 1995) have shown that children with FAS show deficits in activities that require abstract thinking, such as planning and organising information.

However, research is by no means conclusive. Other research suggests that the links between factors such as smoking, or alcohol consumption, in pregnancy and intelligence might be moderated, disappear or be highlighted by other factors. US psychologists S. W. Jacobson J. L. Jacobson, R. J. Sokol, L. M. Chiodo and R. Corobana (2004) found, among 337 inner-city African American children, that prenatal alcohol exposure was not related to IQ scores on the Weschler Intelligence Test. However, they found that among children who had older mothers, prenatal alcohol was related to IQ scores on the Wechsler Intelligence Test. Bailey et al. (2004) examined alcohol use among mothers at a prenatal visit, and then IQ among children at 7 years, among 500 black children. Again, no relationship was found between prenatal alcohol exposure and intelligence, though mothers who binge drink when pregnant were 1.7 times more likely to have children who had IQ scores in the mentally retarded range.

These findings suggest that age and excess drinking are further factors in the relationship between prenatal drinking and offspring intelligence. But overall, the findings suggest that smoking and alcohol consumption are factors that, to a greater or lesser extent, are connected with IQ.

Maternal effects model

Today, factors such as prenatal nutrition and alcohol consumption are combined into the maternal effects model. US psychiatrist Dr. Bernie Devlin and US statistician Michael Daniels (Devlin, Daniels & Roeder, 1997) showed that prenatal conditions may have substantial effects on the concordance of subsequent scores on IQ for identical twins. Previously, maternal effects had usually been assumed to be small, or non-existent, in terms of affecting genetic variance of intelligence between twins. However, a meta-analysis of 212 studies suggests 20 per cent of genetic variance between twins and 5 per cent between siblings. These authors suggest that broad heritability estimates when including maternal effect (additive and non-additive genetic variance) might have to be reduced from about 60 to 48 per cent. This suggestion indicates that the environmental effects on intelligence may extend to interactions with biological factors.

Family environment

The second environmental factor identified by Neisser et al. (1996) is the family environment. There are three sources of related research and evidence that we will concentrate on in this discussion:

- shared and non-shared environments – within- and outside-family factors;
- the social and economic status of the family and the intelligence of the child;
- birth order, family size and child intelligence.

Shared and non-shared environments

We saw in the last discussion that the conception of genetics as a single dimension has developed over time. The same could be said of environmental factors. Within behavioural genetics, the conception of how the environment influences intelligence is through two sets of experiences: shared and non-shared. When growing up, siblings (brothers and sisters) are thought to experience both shared and unique environments. **Shared environments** are environments that are shared between two individuals, whilst **non-shared environments** are environments that are *not* shared between two individuals who share genes. Siblings growing up within the same family will share many environments. These environments may range from minor experiences to more significant ones. Therefore, two siblings having the same parents, living within the same house, going to the same school and experiencing particular times together (e.g., same family relatives, home environment, chaotic mornings before school, dad's awful jokes) have shared environments. A unique environment is an environment that has not been shared by siblings. Again, these environments may range from minor experiences to significant ones. Examples of unique environments might be when two siblings have been raised by different families. However, siblings raised in the same family might also have unique environments from each other. Siblings may have different sets of friends, may go to different schools, may have different types of relationships with their parents and have different interactions with teachers.

What is important in this area is that the theory and research around the differences between environment influences on intelligence has grown in complexity. To begin with, researchers tend to concentrate on comparing how shared and non-shared environmental factors influence on intelligence. Early consideration by reviewers such as Bouchard (1994) and Eysenck (1990b) suggested that the environmental influences shared by siblings or twins contribute only marginally to intelligence differences. However, one interesting point to emerge from the literature, carried out by such researchers as US behaviour geneticists Braungart, Plomin, DeFries and Fulker (1992a), is that those environmental factors that are unique (non-shared) to family members are influential over *shared* environmental factors. Therefore, non-shared environmental factors, such as different peer friendships, are important mechanisms that explain why members of the same family may differ in their intelligence. This idea is supported by two pieces of research suggesting that the extent of differences in the experiences during childhood among siblings have been found to be related to intelligence differences in adulthood (Baker & Daniels, 1990; Plomin & Daniels, 1987).

Such a finding has led to the development of whole areas of research that have emphasised how important non-shared environmental factors are to intelligence. Most of the research in this area considers how non-shared environmental factors develop (1) within the family and (2) outside the family.

Within-family factors

US behavioural geneticist David Reiss (1997) identifies three ways in which inherited genes form phenotypes (behaviours) based on the family environment (see Figure 13.4):

- the passive model
- the child-effects model
- the parent-effects model.

First is the **passive model.** This model suggests that intelligence is generally explained by the 50 per cent overlap between a child and their parent. Therefore, intelligence may occur in the child because the child and parent share the same genes that influence a particular type of behaviour.

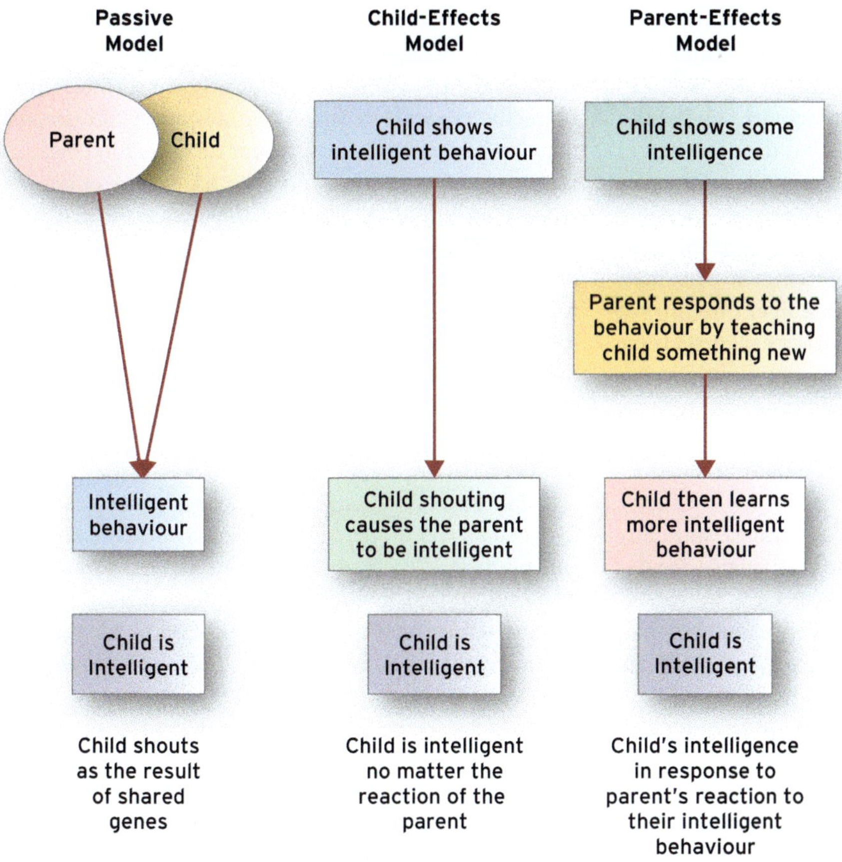

Figure 13.4 Reiss three models of genetic transmission.

For example, if a child is highly intelligent due to genetic influences, they are so because one of their biological parents had the genes that cause this high intelligence. The model, very much, just assumes a general genetic overlap and inheritance of behaviour without considering other possible factors and interactions within the family. This is why it is called the passive model. The other two models very much emphasise other dynamic occurrences.

In the **child-effects model**, the genes cause intelligence in the child, which in turn causes the same or similar behaviour in the parent. Within this model, the parent does not matter in the development of the behaviour, as the child's development of intelligence is the result of genes. An example of this is that the shared genes cause the child to be intelligent (due to their genetic makeup), which in turn causes the parent to act intelligently back to the child (due to their genetic makeup). The parent's own intelligence does not matter in the development of the behaviour, as the child's intelligence is a consequence of genetic makeup of the child rather than the parent.

US psychologist Judith Harris (1995) has expanded this viewpoint to **child-driven effects**, which influence family circumstances that in turn influence the child's intelligence. Harris documents studies showing that adults do not behave in the same way to a child who shows different tendencies. They will treat an attractive child differently to one of their children who is less attractive; they will react differently to the one child who shows bad behaviour than to the one who is well behaved. This behaviour will also apply to intelligence. For example, imagine a family with twin children, one of them intelligent and the other not as intelligent. These differences in the children will cause different reactions in the parents. The parents will begin to treat their children differently. The intelligent one may be encouraged to engage in more intelligent activities, while the one perceived to be less intelligent might not be encouraged to do these activities. Harris suggests these reactions by parents to their children's natural intelligence tendencies can be viewed in two ways: *positive feedback loops* and *negative feedback loops*. Positive feedback loops arise from parents reinforcing children's natural tendencies, as in the example described earlier, where children's natural intelligence abilities are encouraged and any differences between children in their intelligence are developed (the intelligent child is encouraged to be intelligent, while the 'unintelligent' child is encouraged and allowed to engage in other activities). Negative feedback loops occur when children are stopped from behaving in ways consistent with their natural tendencies. Therefore, an intelligent child might be encouraged to stop engaging in merely intelligence-stimulating activities, and an 'unintelligent' child might be encouraged to spend more time engaging in such activities.

In the **parent-effects model**, the behaviour of the child is responded to by the parent, which in turn brings out behaviour in the child (see Figure 13.4). Within this model, how the parent responds does affect the development of the child's behaviour. For example, a child may begin showing intelligence; this then leads the parent to show intelligence with the child (as it is part of their genetic makeup). This in turn causes the child to become even more intelligent (as it is part of their genetic makeup). Within this model, the parent's behaviour leads to the development of intelligence, which then leads to the development of intelligent behaviour in the child.

Again, Harris extends this idea to within-family situations. In these situations, children might be treated in a particular way by parents, not because of that child's own characteristics, but because of the parents' own beliefs or the characteristics of a child's siblings (brothers or sisters). Let us first look at the example of how the parents' own beliefs shape natural tendencies of children. Again, take our family with the one intelligent twin and the one 'less-intelligent' twin. Our parents of the family may have certain beliefs about behaviour, such as 'children should know the limits of their knowledge and never contradict their parents'. Therefore, the children will be encouraged and directed to behave in such ways. So, in our case of the intelligent and less-intelligent twin, the intelligent child who is likely to contradict their parents will be encouraged not to show their intelligence, and the unintelligent child will be encouraged to gain some knowledge up to their 'limits'. Both children will have had their new behaviour (knowing their limits and not contradicting their parents) driven by their parents' behaviour. Secondly, let us look at how parents might influence children's behaviours in terms of a child's siblings. Harris notes research suggesting that parents who consider their first child to be 'difficult' tend to label their second-born as 'easy'. We can also see how less-intelligent children might be asked, or encouraged, to be more like their intelligent sibling. Equally, the intelligent sibling might be encouraged to spend less time in intelligence-promoting activities and play more like their brother or sister.

What Reiss' and Harris' commentaries do is to suggest that *within-family effects* pose problems when considering genetic heritability. That is, child effects and parent effects can lead to overestimations and underestimations of heritability. Remember, behavioural geneticists looking at intelligence are only looking at the concordance between sets of children based on their scores on an intelligence test at some point. However, let us return to our family with the one intelligent twin and one less-intelligent twin. Let us imagine that the parents of these twin children have been engaged in a negative feedback loop. They have been trying to encourage both children to be similar, that is, somewhat intelligent.

Therefore, the intelligent child has been discouraged from being intelligent all the time, and the less-intelligent child is being discouraged from being too unintelligent. If we then compared these two children, we would find that these twin children have similar intelligence; but this is, in fact, not due to genetic tendencies at all. It is simply because the parents are trying to encourage similar behaviour in both children (i.e., not too active or not too quiet). Therefore, any estimation of similarities in intelligence being due to genetic heritability of the twins would be an overestimation. However, if the same pair of twins had been reared differently and both had been in a positive feedback loop – the intelligent child had been encouraged to be more and more intelligent and the less-intelligent child had been encouraged to be more and more unintelligent – then any estimation of the similarities in intelligence being due to genetic heritability would be an underestimation because the differences have been exaggerated due to parents encouraging the twins to be more and more like themselves. Therefore, as Harris concludes, children's within-family situations not only play an important role in shaping their intelligence but also are an important consideration in estimating the genetic heritability of intelligence.

Outside-family factors

However, Harris (1995) has suggested that non-shared factors outside the family may in fact be more important in developing people's intelligence. Harris presents the group socialisation theory to explain the importance of non-shared environmental factors in determining intelligence.

Group socialisation theory is based largely on the ideas surrounding social identity theory and social categorisation (Tajfel & Turner, 1986). Social psychologists have provided a lot of theoretical and empirical research work that has looked at how individuals perceive their social world as comprising in-groups and out-groups and suggesting that these groups help us form our social identity. Social psychologists argue that one mechanism humans use for understanding the complex social world is social categorisation. In social categorisation, individuals are thought to place other individuals into social groups on the basis of their similarities and differences to the individual. Put simply, individuals who are viewed as similar to the person tend to be placed within their in-group. Individuals who are viewed as different to the person tend to be placed within an out-group. This is a process by which we come to understand our world. As a consequence, the individual's identity (social identity) is based on and derived from the groups they feel they belong to and their understanding of their similarities and differences to different social groups. Social groups can be anything, but common groups could be sex group, ethnic group, your religion, your peers, your interests, your educational status and so on. As such, your identity is based, to greater or lesser extent, on how much you identify with different social groups. What is also important to our identity is that when we attach ourselves to certain groups, we also try to fit in with those groups; therefore, our intelligence might begin to reflect the characteristics of a certain group (i.e., you might make friends with people who are highly intelligent; you may then do more intellectual activities than you used to, and you may become more intelligent).

Harris uses this theoretical basis to show how social groups can influence people's intelligence and points out how these non-shared environments that occur in children of the same family can have a huge effect on intelligence. As part of this theory, Harris lists five aspects that are important to consider in how non-shared characteristics might influence our intelligence (we go into greater depth on each of these issues in Chapter 8 if you want to read more).

- **Context-specific socialisation** – This aspect refers to the fact that children learn intelligence abilities not only at home but also outside the home. As children get older, they become less influenced by their family life and more influenced by their life outside the family home.
- **Outside-the-home socialisation** – In this aspect Harris makes the point that children may identify with a number of social groups, based on people's age, gender, ethnicity, abilities, interests, personality, intelligence etc. In other words, we have a range of groups that we identify with and share norms with (attitudes, interests, intelligence), and these groups have different influences on our intelligence.
- **Transmission of culture via group processes** – In this aspect Harris makes two points about the transmission of culture via group processes, which establish norms in our social world that influence our intelligence. First, the shared norms that might influence a child's intelligence aren't necessarily the result of parents sharing them with their children; they are really the result of shared norms among the parents' peers and social groups being passed on to the children. That is, your parents' values, abilities, personality and intelligence are not the result of their parents' norms, but rather of their own social identity, their identification with their own social groups. The second point considers that individual norms, which we have developed from our family, are shared with other people only if they are accepted. For example, an individual might be intelligent and like reading books. However, unless their friends approve of this behaviour, they may be unlikely to carry on this pastime.
- **Group processes that widen differences between social groups** – It is important to note that with your

intelligence, norms are based not just on how you identify with your in-group but also on whether you identify with or reject the out-groups. For example, consider sex roles; your intelligence as a male or female isn't just based on your identification with people of your own sex, but on your rejection of characteristics of the opposite sex. For example, some young women at school believe that subjects such as science and mathematics are men's subjects; consequently, these women become interested in what they perceive to be women's subjects, such as English. This behaviour might have an effect on intelligence.

- **Group processes that widen differences among individuals within the group** – So far, we have assumed that all the groups that we are involved in basically share the same structure. However, we know that within all our social circles we play different roles that might influence, or bring out, different aspects of our intelligence. In our family, as a child, we take a less-senior role; however, with our friends we might be allowed to be more like ourselves. However, the opposite may be true, and we might not feel we lead a group of friends, but tend to do what others say. It may even be possible that among one group of friends you feel more comfortable than others. Harris' point is that our position in groups changes, and that our intelligence – and influences on our intelligence – change due to the hierarchies within a group. For example, if you are in a group of friends and they all look up to you, your intelligence will be influenced because you might think there is an expectation to come up with ideas for things to do or to solve problems within the group.

What is important to consider in both within-family and outside-family factors is that these aspects can influence intelligence of children to a much greater extent than previously thought. It is not Harris' point that behavioural genetics is wrong and that environmental factors are more important, but rather that behavioural geneticists may sometimes have oversimplified family influences. By ignoring these variables, behavioural geneticists might be underestimating or overestimating heritability effects of either genetics or the environment on intelligence.

Socioeconomic status of the family

A family's socioeconomic status is based on its income, parental education level, parental occupation and status in the community. Socioeconomic status is related to various factors, including number of children in the family, opportunities for success in employment, health and area of residence. These factors all might influence intelligence.

Often socioeconomic status is ranked in many countries. For example, in the United Kingdom, one way in which socioeconomic status is measured is by the grading of parents' occupations into five categories:

- Class I: Professional occupations;
- Class II: Managerial and technical occupations;
- Class III: Skilled occupations: Manual (M) and unmanual (U);
- Class IV: Partly skilled occupations;
- Class V: Unskilled occupations.

Socioeconomic status is related to intelligence. Authors such Linda Gottfredson (Gottfredson, 1986), Arthur Jensen (Jensen, 1993a), Richard Herrnstein and Charles Murray (Herrnstein & Murray, 1994) and J. Phillipe Rushton and C. D. Ankney (Rushton & Ankney, 1996) estimate that in Europe, North America and Japan, socioeconomic status is significantly correlated with scores on standard IQ between $r = .3$ and $r = .4$, and that there are 45 IQ points between members of the professional occupations (Class I) and those of unskilled occupations (Class V).

In addition, Nicolas Mackintosh (1998) and Nicholas Mascie-Taylor (1984) presented evidence linking socioeconomic status to intelligence using the British National Child Development Study (NCDS) data. The NCDS examined social and obstetric (care of women during and after pregnancy) factors associated with stillbirth and infant mortality among over 17,000 babies born in Britain in 1958. Surviving members of this birth cohort have been surveyed on five further occasions in order to monitor their changing health, education, social and economic circumstances, including IQ, in 1965 (age 7), 1969 (age 11), 1974 (age 16), 1981 (age 23) and 1991 (age 33). Mackintosh (1998) and Mascie-Taylor (1984) present evidence that even when aspects such as financial hardship, birth weight, size of family, overcrowding, type of accommodation and residence area are taken into account, children who had fathers in Class I (professional occupations) scored 10 IQ points higher than did children who had fathers in Class V (unskilled occupations).

Research also suggests that improved socioeconomic status can improve intelligence. Canadian behavioural geneticist Douglas Wahlsten (Wahlsten, 1997) points to a series of adoption studies in France, in which an infant is moved from a family having low socioeconomic status to a home where parents have high socioeconomic status, and the child's IQ score improves by 12 to 16 points. Wahlsten also points to studies in the United States that have demonstrated improvements in children's IQ by the same margin, achieved by improving the lives of infants in families with low educational and financial resources and providing them with additional educational day care outside the home, every weekday from the age of 3 months to the start of school.

These types of findings turn our attention to the research that has examined the conditions arising in certain families and how those conditions have influenced intelligence. One interesting and extensive debate has arisen from studies examining the influence on intelligence of birth order and family size.

Birth order, family size and intelligence

In 1973 Dutch psychologists Lillian Belmont and Francis Marolla (Belmont & Marolla, 1973) published a study looking at the birth order of the child, the size of family to which the child belonged and the child's overall IQ score on the Raven Progressive Matrices, among 386 ninteen-year-old Dutch men. What Belmont and Marolla (1973) found was that even when social class was controlled for, children from larger families had a lower IQ. Furthermore, the authors found that within each family size, the first-born child always had a better IQ; and to some extent there were declining scores with rising birth order, so that the first-born children scored better than second-born children, second-born children scored better than third-born children and so on. These authors also found that these two factors interacted, and as family size increased and birth order position increased, IQ scores became lower. So for example, a second-born child from a family with three children would score higher than would a second-born child from a family containing four children.

Clearly, birth order, family size and intelligence are of interest to parents, politicians and researchers. Furthermore, if such findings are correct, they would have implications for optimum family size and parental choice regarding children's education. Since then, hundreds of research articles have addressed the relationship between family size, birth order and intelligence, and the proposed relationships between family size, birth order and IQ have been found among many cross-section studies. For example, Russian psychologist T. A. Dumitrashku (Dumitrashku, 1996) found that family size and birth order affected intelligence among Russian schoolchildren.

However, this wouldn't be a section about intelligence if debate didn't fiercely surround these findings. The debate, today, on family size, birth order and intelligence centres on the explanation of why, and whether, such effects occur.

Family size and intelligence

In the research area of family size and intelligence, Joseph Lee Rodgers and his colleagues (Rodgers, Cleveland, van den Oord & Rowe, 2000) published a seminal paper that looked at data from the United States. The National Longitudinal Survey of Youth (NLSY) followed 11,406 young people at yearly intervals from ages 14 to 22 years, and then children born to the original female respondents were surveyed every other year. Rodgers et al. found no direct relationship between family size and intelligence. They suggested that previous research has been inaccurate because it combined 'across-family' measures (family size) with 'within-family' (birth order) measures and treated them in the same way. That, is previous authors had treated family size as a within-family effect.

Let us explain what the authors mean. What the authors are highlighting, here, is a statistical fallacy (see Chapter 22 on academic argument) that occurs when comparing populations of people. Say, for example, that a statistical agency released figures for death rates of the UK Army during the recent Iraq War and for death rates in London (the capital of the United Kingdom). The agency found that among the army, death rates were 13 per thousand, while deaths in London were 26 per thousand. You perhaps also would not be surprised to find that on the announcement of these figures by the statistical agency that their figures caught the attention of the media. You might even find a national newspaper running a headline story suggesting that people were safer in the army in Iraq than they were living in London. However, the problem with this sort of statement is that you are comparing two different populations. In the army population you have men and women who are healthy, and most of them are young. In the second population, London, you have a full age range of people – including those people with high mortality rates, such as old people, and people who are terminally ill. The issue is that you are comparing two populations for which a number of different factors determine death rates.

This fallacy applies to the current debate. Rodgers et al. illustrate the fallacy with this example. They suggest comparing the intelligence of three children, but these children are:

- a first-born child in a large middle-class white family in Michigan;
- a second-born child in a medium-sized affluent black family in Atlanta;
- a third-born child in a small low-income Hispanic family in California.

If differences are observed in these children's intelligence, Rodgers et al. suggest it is impossible to tell whether the differences are down to birth order, family size, socioeconomic status, region of the country or any other variables related to these dimensions.

Birth order and intelligence

In the area of birth order and intelligence, research still generally supports Belmont and Marolla's findings. However, other authors have sought to explain that this relationship may be an artefact of another relationship rather than a real relationship. There are three models explaining why birth order may be linked to intelligence: the admixture hypothesis, the confluence model and the resource dilution model.

The first is the **admixture hypothesis**. E. P. Page and G. Grandon (1979) and more recently Joseph Rodgers (2001) suggested an 'admixture hypothesis' that explains the relationship between birth order and IQ. What this hypothesis suggests is that parental intelligence, or socioeconomic status, are additional factors to consider in the relationship between birth order and IQ scores, coupled with the fact that parents with lower IQ scores tend to have more children. This has made findings in previous studies look as if higher birth order causes lower intelligence, when in fact lower intelligence results because parents with lower socioeconomic status and IQ scores tend to have more children. For example, a parent with five children is likely to have a lower IQ score and a lower socioeconomic status. Parents with higher IQ scores and higher socioeconomic status tend to have fewer children. Consequently, any calculation of the relationship between birth order and intelligence is problematic because parents with higher IQ scores and higher socioeconomic status do not tend to have as many children. Thus there cannot be equal measurement of the number of children across the population.

The second model is the **resource dilution model**. This model was proposed by Judith Blake (Blake, 1981) and elaborated by Douglas Downey (Downey, 2001), but its ideas were first presented by Galton (1874). The resource dilution model of birth order and intelligence test scores suggests that parental resources (time, energy and financial resources) are finite and that, as the number of children in the family increases, the resources (time, energy and financial) that can be gained by any single child decreases. Therefore, the first child will get 100 per cent of available resources from their parents, the second child will only ever get 50 per cent, the third child will only ever get 33 per cent and a fourth child will only ever get 25 per cent. This model also feeds into the idea that children in larger families have lower intelligence test scores because, as that family grows, the resources that can be accessed also diminish.

Third is the **confluence model**, which was originally proposed by US psychologist Robert B. Zajonc (Zajonc, 1976; Zajonc & Markus, 1975) – though, again, Galton (1874) proposed some of these ideas. The confluence model suggests that intellectual development, and therefore intelligence, must be understood within the context of the family, and there is an ever-changing intellectual environment within the family. Zajonc suggests the following factors might influence the relationship between birth order and intelligence:

- First-borns have the advantage of some time in which they do not have to share their parents' attention with any of their siblings.
- Any additional birth automatically limits the amount of attention any of the siblings get, including the first-born.
- First-borns and older siblings have to look after and care for younger siblings to some degree. This means that they undertake some amount of responsibility and may have to explain things to their younger siblings. Zajonc believed that this sort of tutoring helps the older children to develop intelligence abilities, as they have to explain ideas and processes to other people.
- First-born children are exposed to a greater proportion of adult language and ideas from their parents. Those children born later are exposed to less-mature speech and ideas because they listen not only to their parents, but to their other siblings. This means they spend a lower proportion of their time listening to adult language and ideas and a greater proportion of time listening to other children's language and ideas.

These last two findings also feed into the idea that children in larger families have lower IQ scores because, as that family grows, the agenda and the context of the family focuses more and more on the children.

Education and intelligence

We mentioned education and its relationship to intelligence in the last chapter. However, we will remind you of some of the findings and extend your view on this area in this chapter.

Neisser et al. (1996) found that education is both an independent and dependent variable in terms of its relationship to intelligence. Going to school is likely to increase your abilities, particularly those that comprise intelligence (intelligence is a dependent variable), and intelligence is likely to influence your attendance at school and your length of schooling (i.e., whether you end up going to university) and the quality of school you attend (intelligence is an independent variable here). Consequently, intelligence and education are intrinsically linked.

You will remember evidence from the last chapter. Overall, reviews by US psychologists Alan Kaufman and Elizabeth Lichtenberger (Kaufman, 1990; Kaufman & Lichtenberger, 2005) provide a review of key papers that have looked at the correlation between general intelligence and school attainment and achievement. They conclude that the average correlation between IQ scores and a number of school indicators is around $r = .50$, suggesting that intelligence does predict performance at school. Also, two academics of the Hebrew University in Jerusalem, Sorel Cahan and Nora Cohen (1989), compared the effects of a year of school (controlling for age) with those of a year of age on a number of verbal (e.g., verbal and numerical skills) and non-verbal (abstract and reasoning tests, including the Raven's Matrices) intelligence tests. Length of schooling was important in predicting performance, and mattered more than age, for all the verbal tests. Length of schooling, however, made a contribution – but a smaller contribution – to performance on some of the nonverbal tests, including the items from the Raven's Matrices.

Other key evidence you need to know when considering education as an environmental factor on intelligence is found in the well-cited papers of US child development psychologist Stephen Ceci (1990, 1991). Ceci did a meta-analysis of studies, and his findings suggest that there are many effects of education on intelligence test scores. The data presented by Ceci includes the overall finding that children who attend school regularly score higher on intelligence tests than do those who attend less regularly, intelligence test scores among pupils decrease over the long summer holidays and there is a rise of 2.7 IQ points for each year of schooling (see also Winship & Korenman, 1997). Douglas Wahlsten (1997) notes that studies have shown that delays in starting school cause intelligence tests scores to drop by 5 IQ points a year (i.e., Winship & Korenman, 1997).

Also, it is worth reminding you of Head Start and other similar programmes that have explored the relationship between education and intelligence. You remember that Head Start, which we mentioned in the last chapter, was started in the 1960s by President Lyndon Johnson and was designed to give America's poorest children a head start in preparing them for school and to start to break the cycle of poverty. Evidence was provided to assess the usefulness of such a programme. US individual differences psychologist Charles Locurta (Locurta, 1991) provides a review of this evidence. In 1969, Arthur Jensen suggested that Head Start had failed. The reason for Jensen's pronouncement was that, although children attending the programme showed an initial increase in IQ points – sometimes as much 7–8 points on IQ tests – after 2 or 3 years these higher IQ points were lost (Locurta, 1991). There has been a lot of debate about the effectiveness of Head Start, but in terms of IQ gains, McKey et al. (1995) reported that children enrolled in Head Start had significant immediate gains in IQ scores. However, in the longer term (3–4 years), the IQ test scores of Head Start students did not remain superior to disadvantaged children who did not attend Head Start.

Finally, there is evidence to suggest that ideas that we covered in the last discussion regarding socioeconomic status are related to education variables, which together are related to intelligence. Socioeconomic status might influence aspects of education, and then intelligence, in a number of ways:

- Families with a high socioeconomic status often are able to prepare their children for school because they have access to resources (e.g., child care, books and toys) and information (what are the best schools? what aspects are taught to children?) that enhance children's social, emotional and cognitive development and help parents to better prepare their young children for school (Demarest, Reisner, Anderson, Humphrey, Farquhar & Stein, 1993).
- Families of a low economic status face hard challenges when it comes to providing optimal care and education for their children. When basic necessities such as money and time are missing, housing, food, clothing and health care come first. Educational toys and books, and time searching out the best schools, are luxuries that parents may not have the time or money to pursue (Ramey & Ramey, 1994).
- Parents from poor socioeconomic backgrounds often grew up in poor socioeconomic conditions themselves. Consequently, parents may have inadequate reading skills or may lack knowledge about childhood nutrition (or not be able to afford it), and these benefits aren't passed on to the children before school (Zill, Collins, West & Hausken, 1995).

Culture and intelligence

The final environmental area that Neisser et al. (1996) suggest is important to influencing intelligence is the cultural environment people live in. 'Culture' refers to people's individual values, and the values of their society. Nessier et al. suggest culture can have an effect not only on intelligence but also on the type of intelligence that might develop.

You remember that in Chapter 10 of this book, we outlined implicit theories of intelligence. Those theories showed how the definition of what constitutes intelligence shifts across cultures, particularly when you compare Western and Eastern cultures, and how conceptions of intelligence shift across age and through different disciplines. Well, clearly that discussion of implicit theories of intelligence is relevant here (you may want to reread some of that chapter).

However, in addition to implicit theories of intelligence, Serpell (2001) identifies three concepts that explain how intelligence in Western societies is set apart from other cultures in the world. These three concepts are decontextualisation, quantification and biologisation.

Decontextualisation

A lot of Western thinking is inherited from three thousand years of classical Greek philosophy. Socrates, Plato and Aristotle were all Greek philosophers who have had a profound impact on the way we think in our culture. In Western culture there is a tendency to emphasise mathematics, the scientific method and language. We make clear distinctions between what is right and wrong, what constitutes justice, the need to follow a logical progression and the idea that there are higher and lower planes of ideas and activities – and perhaps a universal truth. **Decontextualisation** is the ability to disconnect, or detach oneself, from a particular situation and think abstractly, and then generalise about it. Serpell (2001) argues that the ability to think abstractly and generalise about things has gained importance in Western society because of industrialisation. With the growth of capitalism there is a need for efficiency, some level of bureaucracy and functionality (the ability to come up with abstract principles) to help govern Western life, including the markets (financial, housing, consumer), industry and education. These needs become increasingly important. Serpell questions the need to always view decontextualisation as a sign of intelligence, and a failure to decontextualise as a sign of unintelligence.

Quantification

Quantification is the act of discovering, or expressing, the quantity of something. Serpell suggests that the study of intelligence is surrounded by quantification in three ways:

- First is the way the intelligence theory and research is designed to quantify intelligence. That is, when we ask 'what is intelligence?' we are trying to encapsulate a number of meanings and ideas into one word, 'intelligence'.
- Second is a concept called reification (see also Gould, 1981). Reification is the tendency to regard an abstract idea as if it had concrete or material existence. We see intelligence as something that is located in the brain, but we do not know where it is located. Intelligence isn't just about certain processes; but it encapsulates things that are not measurable, such as beauty or sophistication. For many, the invention of the steam engine, or the wheel, are highly intelligent acts; but they are also acts of beauty to some, and they are certainly of sophistication to many.
- Third is a tendency to quantify intelligence in terms of numbers. We give people intelligence tests, which contain an optimum number of items that should be completed within a certain amount of time. These items have been selected in accordance with studies that have used statistical procedures to determine what aspects of intelligence are out there. The test that is given is determined by the person's age. When participants have finished, they are given scores for their performance, and these scores are then transformed into IQ scores. These IQ scores can then be compared against standardised scores for the tests of people of the same age.

Serpell suggests that consideration of these three points indicates that our understanding of intelligence is surrounded by quantification. All this is not to say that quantification is not a good process to understand intelligence. To produce meaning and conceptual understanding of words; to try to define, measure and locate concepts; and to use numbers as objective criteria are excellent methods by which to ensure the progress and understanding of intelligence. However, Serpell suggests that when we are dealing with something like intelligence, we must be sure that we do not seek to over-quantify this concept.

Biologisation

Serpell (2001) raises our awareness that biological and evolutionary theories have grown in prominence in late twentieth century and early twenty-first century thinking (**biologisation**). You will be aware that, in our psychophysiological and evolutionary chapters (Chapters 8 and 9), we outlined the dramatic developments in the understanding of genes, and that evolutionary psychologists are able to link the evolution of the human species to animals who lived billions of years ago. Many of the arguments put forward by biological and evolutionary psychology are convincing, and inspiring, in the understanding of why we behave the way we do. However, Serpell suggests some caution in overemphasising these models. It must be remembered that many of these models talk about developments over millions of years, and our advanced study of ourselves is relatively new. Therefore, we must be careful to ensure that our understanding of genetics, evolutions over a long course of history, and genetic variation are not used to explain intelligence within a relatively short period of history.

Final comments on genetic heritability and environmental influences on intelligence

Perhaps the last word in this section goes to Bouchard and Loehlin (2001), who suggest a framework for observing sources of population variance in psychological traits (see Figure 13.5). We presented this framework in Chapter 8 and think that it is applicable to intelligence.

To assess population variations in intelligence, Bouchard and Loehlin's framework is not only a good overview of the debate but also sets some prudent criteria in terms of assessing elements such as genetic effects and environmental effects on intelligence. So, in all, we must consider:

- **Genetic influences** – including questions about what gene is involved and what type of genetic variation (for example, additive or non-additive). Is there a sex limitation (e.g., brain size)?

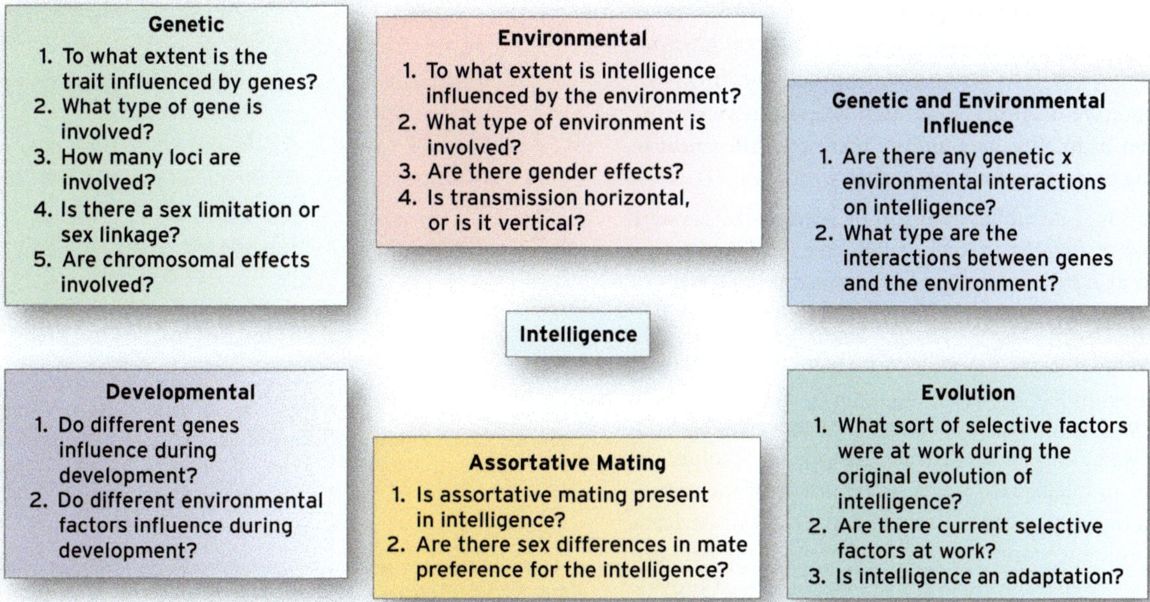

Figure 13.5 Framework and questions regarding sources of population variance in intelligence.
Source: Bouchard and Loehlin (2001).

- **Environmental influences** – including, to what extent does environment influence the genes, what types of environments are involved (e.g., education, culture) and are there gender effects?
- **Interaction between genetic and environmental influence** – including what type are the interactions between genes and the environment (e.g., nutrition, prenatal causes)?

Stop and Think

Smoking and IQ scores

In 2005, Lawrence Whalley of the University of Aberdeen and his colleagues (Whalley, Fox, Deary, & Starr, 2005) investigated smoking as a possible risk for intelligence decline from age 11 to 64. In 1931, the Mental Survey Committee in Scotland met and decided (due to there being no reliable way of getting a representative sample) to measure IQ scores for everyone in Scotland. So, on Wednesday, 1 June 1932, nearly every child attending school in Scotland who was born in 1921 took the same intelligence test (n = 89,498); this exercise was repeated in 1947, testing almost all people born in 1936 (n = 70,805). Whalley et al. analysed a subsample of these respondents between 2000 and 2002, looking not only at smoking and IQ scores but also at childhood IQ scores, occupational status, level of education, presence of heart disease, hypertension and lung function. Whalley et al., found that current smokers and non-smokers had significantly different IQ scores at age 64 and that differences remained after accounting for childhood IQ score. All in all, smoking appeared to predict a drop in IQ by just under 1 per cent.

What do you think are possible explanations for smoking contributing to a fall in IQ scores?

- **Developmental influences** – including do different genes influence during development, and do different environmental factors influence during development?
- **Assortative mating** – including is assortative mating present in intelligence, and are there sex differences in mating preference for intelligence?
- **Evolution** – including what sort of selective factors were at work during the original evolution of intelligence (e.g., different need for intelligences across different areas of the world)? Are there current selective factors at work?

Clearly, when it comes to intelligence, some of these areas are easier to identify or consider than others. For example, no one has discovered whether there is a gene for intelligence; nor can we be certain about what the different evolutional demands on intelligence are. However, many of the areas – assessing the level of genetic influence, the types of environmental influence, and the possible interactions between genes and the environment – are known, or at least provide sources of evidence which provide evidence for a debate. Applying Bouchard and Loehlin's model to intelligence provides a focus to an area that debates the relative influences of (1) genes, (2) the environment and (3) the interactions between genes and the environment on intelligence.

Section B
The Bell Curve: Race Differences in Intelligence

In this section we will outline what has become known as the bell curve debate. Here, we consider evidence and arguments concerning race differences in intelligence.

The Bell Curve

We have deliberately held back on discussing this material until now, although it covers some of the topics we have discussed in this and other chapters, because we wanted you to be prepared for this discussion. In psychology, the discussion of differences in intelligence, particularly race differences, raises a lot of emotions and debate. We will, later in this chapter, highlight this area of psychology further, in the area of eugenics. We would like to think that your reading of this material also raises emotions, not only as a psychologist but also as a human being. However, we would also like to think that you can see past some of your emotions, pick out the argument and debate that exist here, and use argument, rather than emotion, to decide on the relative merits that are put forward (if you're worried about seeing this distinction, read more about academic argument and fallacies in Chapter 22 of this book).

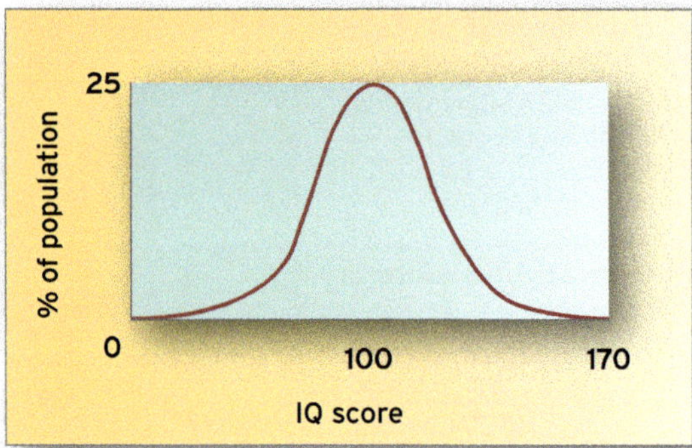

Figure 13.6 The distribution of IQ scores: A bell curve.

The Bell Curve: Intelligence and Class Structure in American Life

In 1994 two authors from the United States, Richard J. Herrnstein and Charles Murray, published a book called *The Bell Curve: Intelligence and Class Structure in American Life* (Herrnstein & Murray, 1994). The book is an analysis of IQ test scores in the United States. The term 'bell curve' refers to the shape of the distribution of a large number of IQ scores in the United States – it looks like a bell (see Figure 13.6).

The book caused huge debate because it reported many things about intelligence, particularly the extent to which intelligence is genetically inherited. It claimed to describe the rise of a 'cognitive elite' in the United States – a social group of persons with high intelligence, with an increasingly good chance of succeeding in life. This book noted several cultural differences in intelligence, but its authors also made some suggestions regarding the intellectual inferiority of certain cultural groups. Such work was perceived by many as difficult for US society. The authors' findings were seen as having implications for social and public policy as well as pointing to potential sources of inequality in the United States. We will now briefly describe the main arguments put forward by Herrnstein and Murray.

Herrnstein and Murray's main arguments are built on six premises (or as they present them, conclusions) about intelligence. We have used Herrnstein and Murray's original words here, but have put simpler wording in parentheses:

1. 'There is such a thing as a general *factor* of cognitive ability on which human beings differ.' (*There exists a general factor of intelligence, and individuals differ in their intelligence; i.e., high, low, average intelligence.*)

Profiles

Richard Herrnstein and Charles Murray

Richard Herrnstein (1930-1994) was a prominent researcher in comparative psychology. He was Charles Sanders Pierce Professor of Psychology at Harvard University. During his career, he worked with B. F. Skinner (advocate of behaviourism, which seeks to understand behaviour as a function of environmental histories of reinforcement) in the Harvard pigeon lab, where he did research on choice and other topics in behavioural psychology.

In the 1960s, as part of this work on pigeon intelligence, Herrnstein formulated the 'matching law', which outlined how reinforcement and behaviour are linked. The matching law addresses the idea of choice. It views choice not as a single event or an internal process of the person, but as a rate of observable external events over time. Some have suggested that the matching law is an important explanatory account of choice behaviour, and its applications spread from psychology into other fields, notably economics.

Charles Murray was born in 1943 in Newton, Iowa, in the United States. He studied for his undergraduate degree in history at Harvard. In 1965 he immediately joined the Peace Corps for five years in rural Thailand (Peace Corps volunteers travel overseas and work with people there). By 1974 Murray had returned to the United States, where he completed his PhD in political science at the Massachusetts Institute of Technology. He has written extensively on economics, crime and poverty and has become one of the nation's most influential thinkers. His book *Losing Ground: American Social Policy*, 1950-1980 (Murray, 1984), was used by President Ronald Reagan in developing his domestic policy. Murray has been the subject of articles in *Newsweek*, *The New York Times Magazine* and *The Los Angeles Times Magazine*.

2. 'All standardised tests of *academic* aptitude, or achievement, measure this general factor to some degree, but *IQ* tests, expressly designed for that purpose, measure it most accurately.' (*There are many tests of academic aptitude or achievement, but IQ tests, which are specifically designed to measure intelligence, measure intelligence most accurately*).
3. 'IQ scores match, to a first degree, whatever it is that people mean when they use the word *intelligent or smart* in ordinary language.' (*IQ scores reflect whatever most people mean by the word intelligent.*)
4. 'IQ scores are stable, although not perfectly so, over much of a person's life.' (*Throughout an individual's life, their IQ score remains relatively stable.*)
5. 'Properly administered IQ tests are not demonstrably biased against social, economic, ethnic, or racial groups.' (*IQ tests, when they are properly administered, are not biased against any social, economic, ethnic or racial groups.*)
6. 'Cognitive ability is substantially heritable, apparently no less than 40 percent and no more than 80 percent.' (*Genetic heritability of intelligence is between 40 and 80 per cent.*)

Herrnstein and Murray then go on to discuss four main ideas in their book: (1) the cognitive elite, (2) socioeconomic variables and IQ scores, (3) the relationship between race and intelligence and (4) the implications for social policy.

The cognitive elite: looking at the higher end of the bell curve

In their book, Herrnstein and Murray begin by looking at the high end of the bell curve – that is, at those who score higher on intelligence tests – and examine the relationship between intelligence and education. Herrnstein and Murray analysed IQ scores and admissions to universities and colleges over 50 years, and they found that the most important factor in college attendance was the intelligence of the students, not social class or wealth. It is this fact, Herrnstein and Murray maintain, that places the most intelligent people in US society in the same place – university and colleges.

Herrnstein and Murray argue that the next stage of this process is the relationship between university and colleges and the workplace. University and college graduates are often placed within a select few occupations, reserved for those obtaining college and university degrees including teaching, engineering, law, research, medicine and accounting.

The authors then draw on studies showing that intelligence is related to efficient and proficient (advanced degree of competence) employees. You may remember the finding of two US psychologists, John E. Hunter and R. F. Hunter (1984), who did a meta-analysis (a meta-analysis is a technique that combines the results of several studies) that put together the results of studies examining various predictors at the start of a job with eventual job performance. They found that the correlation between intelligence and job performance was much larger than job performance and the individual's curriculum vitae, their previous experience, the job interview and education (r = .10). With findings like this, Herrnstein and Murray conclude that intelligence is the single most powerful predictor of job success and workplace productivity.

Herrnstein and Murray suggest that there is the emergence in the United States of the cognitive elite, based on a separation of society through education (university and colleges) and the workplace (certain professions such as teaching, research, law and medicine), in which the central factor is intelligence. Consequently, Herrnstein and Murray predict that intelligence will soon become the basis of the American class system, and people with higher intelligence will be at the top of this class system.

IQ scores and social and economic problems: looking at the lower end of the bell curve

Next, Herrnstein and Murray turn their attention to the lower end of the bell curve – that is, people with low scores on intelligence tests. What Herrnstein and Murray do is to look at several factors in the context of IQ scores; these factors include poverty, schooling, unemployment, family life, welfare dependency and crime.

An example of the type of analysis they performed is given in Table 13.1. This table is adapted from Linda Gottfredson (1997), who summarised Herrnstein and Murray's (1994) analysis, and we have picked out just a few of their findings to illustrate their analysis. The first row of the table shows the percentage of people who fall within the range of standardised IQ scores (remember that IQ scores are transformed to a mean of 100). This standardisation into a normal distribution is consistent with the practice of standardising scores into a mean of 100 and a standard deviation of 15 (there is more on this process in Chapter 11 if you need to refresh your memory). Therefore, the greater percentages of people are concentrated in the middle, with lower percentages at either end of the curve. As shown in the first row of numbers in Table 13.1, 50 per cent of people fall within the middle category of 90–110 IQ points range, with 20 per cent of individuals falling within the 75–90 and 110–125 IQ points range, and 5 per cent of people scoring less than 75 and greater than 125 IQ points.

Herrnstein and Murray examined each sample (i.e., number of people in poverty, number of people in prison) in terms of their IQ scores distribution and expressed this as a percentage of the overall population (i.e., less than 75; between 90 and 110 points). As you can see, larger percentages of people (expressed in terms of the overall population) in each of the social and economic subsamples are

Table 13.1 Social and economic indicators broken down by sample, and divided in terms of IQ score category and expressed as a percentage of the overall population.

	IQ				
Social and economic indicators	Less than 75	75-90	90-110	110-125	Greater than 125
US population distribution	5%	20%	50%	20%	5%
Men who are unemployed for more than 1 month out of year	12%	10%	7%	7%	2%
People who are divorced within 5 years of marriage	21%	22%	23%	15%	9%
Mothers with children with IQ less than 75	39%	17%	6%	7%	0%
Lives in poverty	30%	16%	6%	3%	2%
Ever been in prison	7%	7%	3%	1%	0%
Mothers in receipt of long-term welfare support	31%	17%	8%	2%	0%
Dropping out from high school (secondary education)	55%	35%	6%	0.4%	0%

Source: Reprinted from Gottfredson, L.S. (1997). Why g matters: the complexity of everyday life. *Intelligence*, Vol. 24, pp. 79-132. Copyright © 1997, reproduced with permission from Elsevier.

concentrated towards the lower end of the IQ curve, that is, less than 75 IQ points and 75–90 IQ points.

Herrnstein and Murray used these statistics to develop their argument. For Herrnstein and Murray the statistics on poverty, schooling, unemployment and crime clearly show that intelligence underlies many of these social and economic problems. They suggest that low IQ scores are a strong precursor to poverty, more so than any socioeconomic conditions. With schooling, low IQ scores predict whether people are likely to drop out of high school (secondary education) and decrease the likelihood of a person gaining a degree. The authors point out that the figures suggest that a person with a high IQ score is likely to finish high school regardless of their social or economic circumstances. Herrnstein and Murray find that low IQ scores are related to unemployment and are seen in people who are injured more often or who have given up work. They find that the best predictor of unemployment among men is not socioeconomic status or education, but IQ scores. The authors conclude that low IQ scores are associated with higher rates of divorce, lower rates of marriage and higher rates of illegitimate births. They also find that IQ scores are related to family structure, with families comprising a nuclear or traditional structure (2 parents, 2 children) scoring higher on intelligence tests than did families with extended members living in the family home. They suggest that the disappearance of the traditional nuclear family in the United States was a result of low intelligence. Additionally, Herrnstein and Murray point to the fact that the average US criminal has an IQ score about 8 IQ points lower than that of the average US citizen, suggesting intelligence is linked to a propensity for crime in the United States.

In other areas, Herrnstein and Murray are less certain, but also suggest that long-term welfare dependency and parenting are related to IQ scores. They argue that low intelligence is the primary factor in predicting people's first use of welfare, but then a culture of dependency (learnt from childhood experiences of parents and relatives being on welfare) may emerge that leads to individuals using welfare in the long term. Finally, Herrnstein and Murray point out that low IQ scores among mothers correlate with their children's poor motor skills and with social development and behavioural problems from 4 years and upwards. Herrnstein and Murray point out that although being of lower intelligence does not prevent individuals from being good parents, family environments where damage is done to a child's intellectual development occur when parents are on the lower end of the intelligence distribution.

In considering the relationships between these factors and intelligence, Herrnstein and Murray build an argument where they suggest that an individual's intelligence is more important than their socioeconomic status in predicting their eventual economic and social welfare.

The relationship between race and IQ: implications for social policy

Herrnstein and Murray next turn their attention to the differences that occur between various ethnic groups. They examine the different fertility patterns of groups on the intelligence distribution, but generally they adopt the position that intelligence is largely genetically heritable.

Herrnstein and Murray compared IQ test scores by ethnicity. For example, they found that individuals of Asian and Asian American ethnic origin scored on average around 5 IQ points higher than white Americans, particularly on measures of crystallised (verbal) intelligence. However, it is in the comparison between white Americans and black Americans that larger differences emerge.

On the Wechsler Intelligence test (remember this is a measure of verbal and non-verbal [crystallised/fluid] intelligence), Herrnstein and Murray reported that white Americans score 15 IQ points higher than black Americans. On the Stanford-Binet test (remember this is also a measure of verbal/non-verbal intelligence), Herrnstein and Murray reported that white Americans scored 18 IQ points higher than black Americans. Therefore, on both intelligence tests, the gap between the two races is almost 1 standard deviation (15 IQ points). In terms of normed IQ scores, white Americans averaged 102 IQ points, while black Americans averaged 87 IQ points. Herrnstein and Murray also note that the average IQ scores of immigrants coming into the United States were 95 IQ points, lower than the national IQ average (see Figure 13.7).

It is here that Herrnstein and Murray move towards the most controversial part of the book. They say the evidence suggests that certain social factors in the United States are pushing down its citizens' intelligence. These factors include the number of children produced, which is greater for women who have lower IQ scores than for those with higher IQ scores; consequently, the United States is producing more and more children born into lower-intelligence environments. They suggest that as more and more immigrants come into the country, they show lower levels of intelligence. They suggest, then, that these factors are causing a downward pressure on intelligence in the United States; and as the average intelligence of the nation falls, social problems such as poverty, unemployment and crime will increase as these social problems are associated with people with low intelligence scores. Additionally inherent in Herrnstein and Murray's argument is that, at least by implication, those groups of people in the country with lower intelligence (for example, immigrants, African Americans), are potentially part of these social problems.

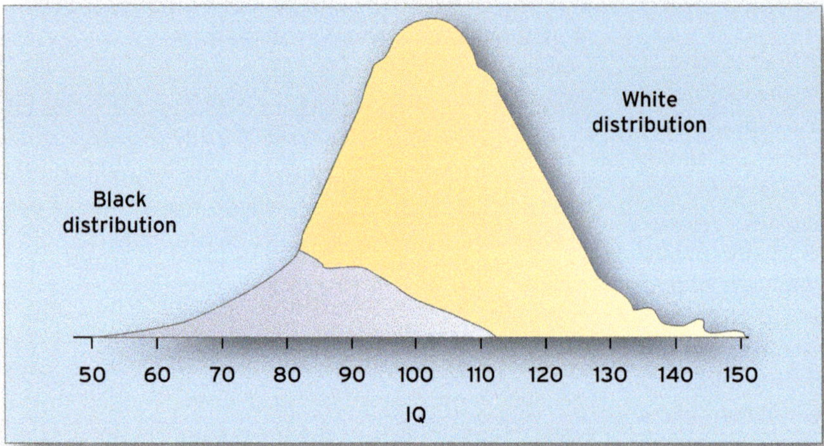

Figure 13.7 Distribution of IQ scores for white Americans (average 102) and black Americans (average 87 IQ points).

Source: Adapted from Herrnstein, R.J. & Murray, C. (1994). *The bell curve: intelligence and structure in American life.* New York: The Free Press.

Moreover, Herrnstein and Murray suggest that the way forward is not to address social problems by trying to compensate for individual differences in intelligence through supporting and increasing these people's intelligence. They point to previous attempts to raise intelligence, such as nutrition (as mentioned earlier and in the last chapter) or preschool programs (such as Head Start) that have not been successful in permanently raising intelligence. They also suggest that as intelligence has a 40 to 80 per cent genetic heritability, there should be little expectation that intelligence should rise in these situations.

Furthermore, they argue against affirmative action programmes in the United States. Affirmative action (or positive discrimination) is a policy providing advantages for people of a minority group who are seen to have traditionally been discriminated against; the aim of such policy is to create a more equal society. Herrnstein and Murray suggest that preferential access to education or employment for African Americans and immigration groups (where institutions increase the selection and promotion of candidates from these ethnic minority groups in the United States) has also failed. The authors argue that such approaches have not only led to a decrease of intelligence in education and the workplace (leading to further downward pressure on intelligence in US society and, therefore, increasing the potential of social problems) but also caused racial tension in education and the workplace. This tension arises from resentment between ethnic groups due to lower levels of student attainment – or more dropping out in education – and poorer job performance in the workplace as a result of people with lower intelligence undertaking study or jobs to which they are not suited.

Herrnstein and Murray's position is that American education and the workplace have been 'dumbed down' as they take on people with lower intelligence. The authors suggest that while US education and work institutions have been good in helping the underprivileged, this success has been at the expense of gifted students. Thus, by being ignored, gifted students have not been able to develop their true potential. Herrnstein and Murray argue that their aim is to point to places of inequality; they observe that pretending inequality does not exist has not been sensible. Instead, they suggest, we should try living with inequality; doing so is preferable because it is reality.

Herrnstein and Murray suggest that the money for education should be shifted from supporting disadvantaged programmes for those with a low intelligence (where there is a predominance of African Americans and other ethnic minorities) to programmes that support those with a high intelligence (where there is a predominance of white Americans and Asians). They argue that it is in promoting and further valuing the gifted, and in raising the intelligence of the nation, that the future of the United States lies. An educational system that aids the gifted will value and raise intelligence throughout society, particularly the workplace; and social problems such as poverty, unemployment and crime will be reduced.

Criticisms of *The Bell Curve: Intelligence and Class Structure in American Life*

When first published, the *The Bell Curve* received a great deal of positive publicity, including cover stories in *Newsweek* and articles in *Time, The New York Times* and the *Wall Street Journal.* But there was a large amount of negative response, particularly in the scientific community, suggesting the book was oversimplified and had flawed analysis. Much of this commentary was in response to the authors' discussion of race differences in intelligence. In reaction to this publicity and controversy surrounding *The Bell Curve*, the American Psychological Association (the largest and most influential psychological society in the world) established a special task force to publish an investigative report on the research presented in the book as well as an analysis of what is known and unknown about intelligence. This task force was headed by Ulric Neisser, then at Emory University in the United States. After an extended consultative process, Neisser chose a range of academics representing a broad range of expertise and opinion in the literature of intelligence, including Thomas J. Bouchard Jr, Stephen J. Ceci, Diane F. Halpern, John C. Loehlin and Robert J. Sternberg (who are all mentioned in these chapters). After analysing Herrnstein and Murray's conclusions regarding race and intelligence, the task force agreed that, while large differences exist between the average IQ scores of African Americans and white Americans, there is no definite evidence suggesting these differences are genetic; they may, in fact, be cultural.

More extensive critical considerations of Herrnstein and Murray's book can be found in the literature. However, in the following discussion, we are going to highlight some of the critiques that appeared at the time of *The Bell Curve* so that you can develop a critical analysis of the arguments contained within Herrnstein and Murray's analysis.

There are three main areas of criticism of Herrnstein and Murray's book that we will now outline:

- analysis of the assumptions used by Herrnstein and Murray in their analysis (led by comments by Stephen Jay Gould);
- statistical and evidence-based problems in Herrnstein and Murray's analysis (led by comments by Leon J. Kamin);
- a darker side of psychology related to Herrnstein and Murray's analysis (led by comments by Stephen Jay Gould and Leon J. Kamin).

Analysis of the assumptions used by Herrnstein and Murray

Stephen Jay Gould (Gould, 1995), an academic at Harvard, starts to dismantle some of the premises within Herrnstein and Murray's book to attack their arguments regarding what should happen in the United States (for example, that money for education be shifted from supporting disadvantaged programmes for those with a low intelligence to programmes that support those with a high intelligence).

Premises are the foundation of any argument. You can read Chapter 22 in this book for more details on the importance of premises in arguments (though Gould used the term 'assumption', in this example they can be treated to mean the same thing). For example, imagine you criticise a particular person as useless (your argument about them) because they haven't done a job you asked them to, and you assume they have not done the job because they are lazy (your premise). If you find out later that they haven't done the job because they had hurt themselves,

Profile Stephen Jay Gould

Stephen Jay Gould (1941-2002) was born and raised in New York. He obtained his PhD at Columbia and served as a member of the faculty at Harvard beginning in 1967. Gould's expertise was varied; he was a paleontologist (a person who studies the forms of life existing in prehistoric or geologic times), evolutionary biologist and historian of science. At the end of his career he was the Alexander Agassiz Professor of Zoology at Harvard.

In 1972 he worked with Niles Eldridge to develop the evolutionary theory of punctuated equilibrium. In this theory, Eldridge and Gould suggested that evolution does not always represent long, drawn-out evolutionary processes; instead, evolutionary change may sometimes work in fits and starts and can happen relatively rapidly, particularly in times of environmental stress.

then this makes your argument invalid (that they are useless) because the premises that form your argument (that the person is lazy) are wrong.

Well, in the same way, Gould begins to dismantle some of the premises informing the arguments that Herrnstein and Murray develop in their book about what should happen in the United States. We will now look at each of the premises that Herrnstein and Murray use – and Gould seeks to attack (though we have supplemented them with evidence and argument from more recent considerations so as to bring the debate up to date).

Assumption 1: 'There is such a thing as a general *factor* of cognitive ability on which human beings differ.'

In Chapter 11 we outlined Spearman's theory of a general factor of intelligence ('g'). However, we know from our discussion of intelligence in Chapters 11 and 12, that there are difficulties in assuming that there is a general factor of intelligence (g). These difficulties reflect the work of theorists and researchers who:

- Use factor analysis to identify general factors of intelligence and suggest intelligence is better understood as comprised in a hierarchy of intelligence abilities. For example, see Carroll (intelligence in three stratums) or Cattell (intelligence comprised of two related but distinct components, crystallised intelligence and fluid intelligence) (Chapter 11).
- Challenge, entirely, the notion of a general intelligence, and suggest it is best represented by a number of different, and separate intelligences. For example, see Sternberg's triarchic theory and Gardner's multiple intelligence theory (Chapter 11).
- Emphasise cognitive psychology processes and argue that intelligence is about not only general factors of abilities but also cognitive processes. For example, see the Kaufman's ability tests and Das and Naglieri's Cognitive Assessment System (Chapter 12).

As we can see, the assumption that there is a general factor of cognitive ability (intelligence) on which human beings differ is open to debate.

Assumption 2: 'All standardised tests of *academic* aptitude or achievement measure this general factor to some degree, but *IQ* tests expressly designed for that purpose measure it most accurately.'

If we accept the previous counterargument, that a general factor of cognitive ability (intelligence) on which human beings differ is 'open to debate', then the assumption that the intelligence tests expressly designed for measuring IQ can measure intelligence most accurately is also open to debate, as such tests cannot measure the many different definitions of intelligence proposed by the different theorists.

We have seen that, even with established general intelligence (IQ) tests (described in Chapters 11 and 12), there are distinctions between psychometric-based intelligence tests that measure verbal and non-verbal general intelligence (e.g., the Wechsler tests and the Stanford-Binet IQ), psychometric based non-verbal intelligence (e.g., the Raven's Matrices) and cognitive-based intelligence tests that measure intelligence abilities and intelligence processes (Kaufman's abilities tests and the Cognitive Assessment System). Therefore, we can see that this assumption is open to debate, and may be particularly important because Herrnstein and Murray rely heavily on psychometric IQ test scores to build their arguments.

Assumption 3: 'IQ scores match, to a first degree, whatever it is that people mean when they use the word *intelligent* or *smart* in ordinary language.'

There is a problem with this assumption if we consider implicit (or everyday) theories of intelligence (which we covered in Chapter 10). Implicit theories of intelligence specifically address what people mean when they use the word 'intelligent' in ordinary language.

The first point to emerge from studies looking at implicit theories of intelligence is the difference between Western and Eastern cultures of intelligence. You will remember that intelligence in Western cultures suggests an emphasis on the speed of mental processing and the ability to gather, assimilate, and sort information quickly and efficiently. In Eastern cultures, these ideas do not fully apply; instead, intelligence extends to social, historical and spiritual aspects of everyday interactions, knowledge and problem solving. It would be unfair to extend this observation to debate Herrnstein and Murray's *Bell Curve* assumption as they were talking about only one Western culture, the United States. Nonetheless, they did build some of their arguments on the fact that immigrants coming into the United States are scoring lower than the national IQ score average and exerting a downward pressure on the intelligence of the United States. Might it be that these immigrants are coming from other countries where different types of intelligence are emphasised?

Other findings with studies of implicit theories of intelligence do extend directly to Herrnstein and Murray's argument. For example, our conceptions of intelligence do change across the age range, or across academic disciplines, in Western cultures. Remember the study mentioned in Chapter 11 by Canadian psychologist Prem Fry (Fry, 1984) who found that intelligence at the three main stages of educational development – primary school (5- to 11-year-olds), secondary school (11- to 18-year-olds), and tertiary (college and university) levels (18+-year-olds) – differed strongly. Also remember Sternberg's study examining implicit theories of intelligence among art, business, philosophy and physics professors (Sternberg, 1985). He found that conceptions of intelligence across these experts differed greatly.

Therefore, Herrnstein and Murray's assumption that intelligence test scores match, to a first degree, whatever it is that people mean when they use the word 'intelligent' in ordinary language, is widely open to debate.

Assumption 4: 'IQ (intelligence test) scores are stable, although not perfectly so, over much of a person's life.'

The assumption rests on whether intelligence can substantially change over a person's life. This is still a major debate in the intelligence literature, it is referred to as the fixed versus malleable intelligence debate. There are two areas to consider in examining this assumption.

First is the view that intelligence does not substantially change during one's lifetime (that is, it remains fixed). As you will remember from Chapter 12, some authors have reported that IQ scores remain stable over long periods of time; these findings support the view that intelligence is generally fixed. Jones and Bayley (Jones & Bayley, 1941) found that IQ scores of children at 18 years were positively correlated with their IQ scores at 12 years ($r = .89$) and 6 years ($r = .77$). Deary, Whalley, Lemmon, Crawford and Starr (2000) found that over a period of 60 years, IQ scores were correlated high (at least $r = .63$). Also, evidence that educational schemes such as Head Start among disadvantaged children (outlined in this chapter and Chapter 12), in which initial gains in IQ scores were *not* sustained, supports the view that intelligence is fixed.

However, the second area to consider points to evidence suggesting that intelligence is malleable (does or can change). We described, in this chapter, Ceci's (1990, 1991) meta-analysis of hundreds of studies. His results suggest that there are many effects of schooling and education on IQ scores, including the findings that children who attend school regularly score higher on IQ tests (a rise of 2.7 IQ points) and that delays in starting school cause intelligence scores to drop (by 5 IQ points per year missed). We also described Wahlsten's (1997) mention of adoption studies in France: an infant is moved from a family with a low socioeconomic status to a family with a high socioeconomic status, and the child's IQ score improves by 12 to 16 points. Finally, you will remember our discussion of the role of nutrition in intelligence, particularly the role of vitamin supplements on IQ scores among children. Reviews of these studies suggest that in the majority of cases, there is a positive effect on intelligence as the result of vitamin and mineral supplements in at least some of the children on non-verbal (fluid) measures of intelligence (Benton, 1991).

The question of whether intelligence is fixed or malleable is open to debate. Consequently, there is some evidence in this area to question the assumption that IQ scores are stable, although not perfectly so, over much of a person's life.

Assumption 5: 'Properly administered intelligence (IQ) tests are not demonstrably biased against social, economic, ethnic, or racial groups.'

The first thing to acknowledge in this area is that it was agreed by the APA task force (Neisser et al., 1996) that properly administered intelligence tests are not demonstrably biased against social, economic, ethnic, or racial groups. The argument that they are biased, however, is often put forward by opponents. However, this view that intelligence tests, themselves, are biased against such groups may be misguided. Rather, a more sensible position to adopt at this stage is not that intelligence tests are biased against such groups, but that the theory from which they are developed may be biased. For example, there is a general factor of intelligence, or the view that intelligence comprises *only* speed of mental processing and the ability to gather, assimilate and sort information quickly and efficiently, that is strongly emphasised in Western culture.

Assumption 6: 'Cognitive ability is substantially heritable, apparently no less than 40 per cent and no more than 80 per cent.'

As we noted earlier in this chapter, a number of sources, including the APA task force (Neisser et al., 1996) agree that cognitive ability is substantially heritable – apparently no less than 40 per cent and no more than 80 per cent. As you already know, there is some convincing evidence that intelligence, to some extent, is genetically inherited. However, it is worth noting that this margin, of 40 to 80 per cent, is quite large.

However, Gould's issue with this assumption is that heritability can then be used to explain differences for intelligence scores between ethnic groups. You remember that earlier we outlined a fallacy in comparing populations and gave the example of comparing death rates among a population of army recruits and the death rates for the population of a capital city from the same general population. We noted that you have to be aware of several different factors determining death rates between these two different populations.

Well, this fallacy also exists in Herrnstein and Murray's application of genetic heritability to explain differences between black and white Americans (though Herrnstein and Murray do acknowledge this problem in their work). However, Gould argues that substantial heritability of intelligence within a population group (e.g., white or black Americans) cannot be used to explain average differences between groups (white Americans versus black Americans).

To extend this argument, evidence from geneticists could even ask whether race is a valid distinction to make between populations. In terms of understanding differences in intelligence between populations, such as race, one important context to consider in genetic influence is the amount of variance that is accounted for by race in the first place. We all know the saying that the colour of one's skin is only skin deep. Well, as we also know, this is a scientific fact. Typically, people looking at race differences make those distinctions based on what they can see; this is called **socially defined race**. As R. S. Cooper and his colleagues note, researchers tend to define race within broad concepts of white, African, Asian, Chinese or Hispanic (Cooper et al., 2000). However, these distinctions generalise across a huge number of different cultures and languages. For example, are white Americans the same as white individuals from the United Kingdom, Italy and Australia?

Due to advanced techniques in understanding our physiology, our understanding of race differences have dramatically changed. Authors such as US evolutionary biologists Masatosi Nei and Arun Roychoudhury (Nei & Roychoudhury, 1982, 1993) and Joseph Graves (Graves, 2001) note that the genetic variance within a population is around 10 times greater than genetic variance between races. In fact, two people who are closely related in terms of their 'race' may differ many more times in their genetic makeup than will two people of two separate 'races'. Today, biologists suggest the criteria by which we determine race, which is mainly based on skin colour, does not make sense in genetic terms. There are virtually no expressed genes (where the gene's information is converted into a living cell) that can be found in all the members of one race.

In fact Mei also suggests that within genetic research, most of the genes that influence appearance are not known. However, biologists have used the similarities between our common proteins to map human populations. Proteins are essential to the structure and function of all living cells and viruses, and play structural and mechanical roles in our genetic makeup. When scientists do this mapping, they get a different genetic picture of the world to socially defined race. For example, when geneticists have mapped the human population in terms of our blood types (remember, there are A, B, AB and O blood types), they find that the English, Spaniards, Eskimos and Norwegians cluster together; the Australians, Aborigines and Sicilians cluster together; the Icelanders and Japanese cluster together and the Swedes and the Ethiopians cluster together.

In all, these considerations suggest that the validity of the arguments that Herrnstein and Murray develop from intelligence having some genetic heritability, and from race differences in IQ scores, is seriously questionable.

Gould's analysis, in which we are asked to consider the strength of Herrnstein and Murray's premises, begins to undermine some of their arguments. Though none of the assumptions are entirely wrong, there clearly exists debate around four or five of them. This suggests that the premises on which Herrnstein and Murray base their arguments and recommendations are less secure than originally presented.

If you want to see the two arguments presented in the final form, go to Stop and Think: The arguments of Herrnstein and Murray and Gould. (It will help you to read Chapter 22, Academic Argument and Thinking.)

Statistical and evidence-based problems in *The Bell Curve* arguments

Leon J. Kamin (a professor of psychology at Northeastern University in the United States) questions some of the statistical thinking and research evidence used by Herrnstein and Murray (Kamin, 1995).

You may remember this statement from your first statistical classes in psychology: 'Correlation does not mean causation'. It is important to remember, when reporting any sort of correlation, not to immediately infer that one variable *causes* another. Therefore, if we found a relationship between optimism and depression, it would usually be the case that we would not infer causation. Often you will hear it is likely that the two variables influence each other (you can read more on this in Chapter 22). It is this criterion that Kamin applies to much of the evidence used by Herrnstein and Murray. Kamin suggests that Herrnstein and Murray, in a lot of their work, ignore that principle in interpreting correlations.

He also suggests that in Herrnstein and Murray's pursuit of determining what factors may cause differences in intelligence, and what factors are caused by differences in intelligence, they begin to blur the fact that they are just using correlational data. They end up ignoring the 'correlation, not causation' rule. Kamin uses as an example Herrnstein and Murray's analysis of the relationship between socioeconomic status and intelligence, which is central to many of their arguments. In exploring this relationship, Herrnstein and Murray use data from the National Longitudinal Survey of Labor Market Experience of Youth, in which over 12,000 children provided data on a number of variables, including their socioeconomic status and their intelligence. As part of their analysis, Herrnstein and Murray conclude that the intelligence of a person is more important than their

Stop and Think

The arguments of Herrnstein and Murray and Gould

Let us take you through the two major arguments presented around Herrnstein and Murray's theories. Also remember that when we use the term 'true' here, we actually mean that 'a majority of evidence suggests', because in psychology we deal with probability estimates of findings. We cannot ever say anything is completely true, proved or disproved (see Chapter 22 if you want a full explanation of academic argument).

Argument 1: Herrnstein and Murray's argument

Major Premises

- If it is true there is such a thing as a general factor of cognitive ability on which human beings differ;
- And it is true that all standardised tests of academic aptitude or achievement measure this general factor to some degree, but IQ tests expressly designed for that purpose measure it most accurately;
- And it is true that IQ scores match, to a first degree, whatever it is that people mean when they use the word;
- And it is true that IQ scores are stable, although not perfectly so, over much of a person's life;
- And it is true that properly administered IQ tests are not demonstrably biased against social, economic, ethnic or racial groups;
- And it is true that cognitive ability is substantially heritable, apparently no less than 40 per cent and no more than 80 per cent;

Minor Premises

- And if it is also true that one population group identified by their ethnicity had an average IQ score lower than another population group identified by their ethnicity;

Conclusion

- Therefore, it must be true that the population group who had the lower average IQ score must be less intelligent than the population group who had the higher average IQ score.

Argument 2: The counter argument based on Gould's analysis

Major Premises

- *It is not neccesarily true* there is such a thing as a general factor of cognitive ability on which human beings differ (because of multifactor theories of intelligence);
- *It is not neccesarily true* that all standardised tests of academic aptitude or achievement measure this general factor to some degree, but IQ tests expressly designed for that purpose measure it most accurately (because general intelligence tests are very different today and there is a real distinction between psychometric and cognitive ability tests);
- *It is not neccesarily true* that IQ scores match, to a first degree, whatever it is that people mean when they use the word (because implicit theories of intelligence suggest conceptions of intelligence vary between and within cultures);
- *It is not neccesarily true* that IQ scores are stable, although not perfectly so, over much of a person's life (because there is evidence that suggests intelligence does or can change substantially);
- It is true that properly administered IQ tests are not demonstrably biased against social, economic, ethnic or racial groups (mainly due to the conclusion drawn by the APA Task Force);
- It is true that cognitive ability is substantially heritable, apparently no less than 40 per cent and no more than 80 per cent:

Minor Premises

- And if it is also true that one population group identified by their ethnicity had an average IQ score lower than another population group identified by their ethnicity;

Conclusion

- Therefore, it can't be necessarily true (due to faults with four of the major premises) that the population group who had the lower IQ score must be less intelligent than the population group who had the higher IQ score.

Which argument would you support?

socioeconomic status in predicting their eventual economic and social welfare. However, as we know from discussions in this chapter and Chapter 12, socioeconomic status is bound up in a number of factors – including nutrition, educational success and poverty – that are related to intelligence. Kamin's problem with Herrnstein and Murray's analysis is that they force causal relationships on the variables when this approach is not appropriate. They do so by treating both IQ test scores and socioeconomic status as causal variables of eventual economic and social welfare. They then remove socioeconomic status as a factor, as it is not as powerful as intelligence in predicting eventual economic and social welfare. This hides the fact that intelligence and socioeconomic status are intrinsically linked not only with each other, but with economic and social welfare success. Kamin argues that this type of analysis is not valid.

Kamin also raises some questions regarding the research basis of Herrnstein and Murray's arguments. His first concern is with the validity of some of the measures used by Herrnstein and Murray to assess key variables. One of these is the variable mentioned earlier – socioeconomic status data from the National Longitudinal Survey of Labor Market Experience of Youth. The measurement of socioeconomic status was achieved by getting students' self-report of their socioeconomic status. No check was made in this study on whether students were accurate in their reporting of socioeconomic status (for example, by asking their parents). Kamin suggests that while such reports are not completely unreliable, they do cast doubts on the reliability of Herrnstein and Murray's building of arguments and analyses based on this data.

Kamin also suggests that there are problems with some of the research studies used to support some of Herrnstein and Murray's arguments. Kamin suggests that Herrnstein and Murray rely too heavily on the work of certain academics in the world of intelligence, particularly that of Arthur Jensen and Richard Lynn. Kamin argues that there are problems with Jensen's and Lynn's work. One such piece of work is Herrnstein and Murray's reliance on a review paper by Lynn in which he examines the evidence for the evolution of race differences in intelligence and discusses the genetic components of intelligence as explaining differences between ethnic groups (Lynn, 1991). In his review paper, Lynn describes a publication by Ken Owen (who is with the Human Sciences Research Council, Pretoria, in South Africa) as the best single study of racial differences in intelligence (Owen, 1989). The study compared white, Indian and black pupils (including pupils from a Zulu tribe) on an intelligence measure called the Junior Aptitude Tests. In this study Owen did not assign IQ scores to any of the groups he tested; he merely reported test-score differences between groups. Owen also noted that the lower scores of black children (which there were) would be due to the poor knowledge of English among the black participants. Also, Owen reported that the tests used figures of items such as electrical appliances and microscopes, which were unknown to Zulus. However, Kamin notes that despite these reservations by Owen about his data, Lynn constructed IQ scores from the data and based many of his conclusions in this review on apparent differences between white, Indian and black children in the study.

Kamin points to other questions that surround Lynn's (1991) review paper and are then reported by Herrnstein and Murray. Lynn also refers to a finding by A. L. Pons, who tested 1,011 Zambian copper miners on the Raven's Matrices (Pons, 1974). Pons presented his data orally at the 1974 26th Congress of the South African Psychological Association. However, later D. H. Crawford-Nutt reported this finding alongside some other data, when reporting on test and item bias in the use of the Junior Aptitude Test as a suitable measure of IQ among white, Indian and black pupils (Crawford-Nutt, 1976). Pons had found that the copper miners performed poorly on the Raven's Matrices, and Lynn used this finding in his review paper to support racial differences in intelligence. Yet, Kamin points out that in his paper, Crawford-Nutt also presented data among 228 black high school students in Soweto, South Africa, who had scored slightly higher on the Raven's Matrices when compared to the norms for the test for white students of the same age in the country. Yet, Lynn ignores this finding in his review paper.

Kamin also points to problems owing to Herrnstein and Murray's citing some of Jensen's work (Jensen, 1993b) regarding race differences in reaction time (an indicator of IQ). In this work, Jensen had tested black and white reaction responses to stimuli. As you may remember, there are different ways of measuring reaction time. Simply, reaction time measures how quickly a participant responds to any particularly stimulus. However, Jensen had also developed a measure of 'choice reaction time', a more complex task, which required participants to react to various stimuli presented in a random order. Jensen found that black participants did better than white participants (suggesting they have higher intelligence), but the result was reported as an inconsistency.

For Kamin, the fact that Herrnstein and Murray have used problematic research evidence, as well as faulty statistical thinking, to build their arguments, casts doubts on the validity of their final arguments.

A darker side of psychology related to Herrnstein and Murray's analysis

Gould referred to the 'ghosts' of *The Bell Curve*. We noted at the beginning of this chapter that Jensen referred to a number of comments about Herrnstein and Murray's book, including it being described as 'neo-Nazi'. What are these authors referring to? Why did *The Bell Curve* book attract such comments? The answer is that many thought *The Bell Curve* was raising issues regarding eugenics.

Eugenics

To say the role of eugenics in psychology is a controversial one is an understatement. It is something that is rarely talked about in psychology undergraduate classes, but psychology has a dark history.

Eugenics refers to a selection process within human reproduction with the intent to create children with desirable traits. Generally, eugenics policies are divided into two aspects: positive and negative eugenics. *Positive eugenics* refers to the practice of encouraging increased reproduction in those who are seen as having superior traits (for example, higher intelligence). *Negative eugenics* refers to the practice of discouraging or eliminating reproduction in those perceived to have poor hereditary traits (for example, lower intelligence).

To look at one of the first developments of eugenics, we must go back to where we first began in this chapter, with Francis Galton. Galton, you will remember, became interested in studying the variations in intelligence after reading Charles Darwin's *Origin of the Species*, which described how all species evolve through a process of natural selection and survival of the fittest. In 1865, Galton outlined eugenics principles (Galton, 1865). He felt that human society sought to protect the weak, and that these principles were at odds with the process of natural selection that suggested the survival of the fittest.

As Galton felt that intelligence was something that was inherited through the genes, he argued that one could use artificial selection to increase intelligence among humans. He argued that such selection was needed as the less-intelligent people were reproducing more than the intelligent people, and this was causing the human race to become weaker.

Galton's theories were adopted by other psychologists. One notable supporter was Lewis Terman (whom we mention in Chapter 11), at one time a president of the American Psychological Association, who had used the Binet-Simon test among California schoolchildren and later adapted it into the Stanford-Binet test. However, Terman continued Galton's ideas. In *Genetic Studies of Genius* (Terman, 1925; Terman & Oden, 1947, 1959), he argued that low intelligence was often found in Spanish-Indian, African American and Mexican families, and such low intelligence was inherited. He argued that such groups should be segregated into special classes and could only ever be trained to be efficient workers. He also expressed concerns that these families seemed to breed more than white Americans did, and from a eugenics point of view (the selection of certain traits), this presented a problem as it was necessary to preserve the United States from low intelligence.

By then, eugenics views had made their way into social policy, politics and the law. By 1922 the process by which human selection was to be initiated was being made abundantly clear: sterilisation (the act of making a person infertile, unable to reproduce). A member of the US House of Representatives Committee on Immigration and Naturalization, H. H. Laughlin, published the Model Eugenical Sterilization Law. This bill formed the basis of state sterilisation laws, and in it Laughlin listed the types of people who were to be subjected to mandatory sterilisation. He included the feebleminded (low intelligence), the insane, the criminal, the epileptic, the blind, deformed and the dependent (e.g., orphans, homeless).

In 1927, the US Supreme Court ruled in the case of *Buck v. Bell* and supported a new legislative law in the state of Virginia. The law concerned a 17-year-old woman named Carrie Buck, who was a resident at the Virginia Colony for the Epileptic and Feebleminded – an asylum home for epileptics, the mentally retarded and the severely disabled. Carrie had the IQ score of a 9-year-old, and her mother, who also resided at the colony, had a mental age of less than 8. Carrie Buck had given birth to a daughter who, at 1 year old, was given an infant IQ test and was found to be less than normal. In response to this, the state of Virginia wanted to have the child sterilised against her will. The US Supreme Court ruled in favour of the enforced sterilisation; and in writing up the decision, Justice Oliver Wendell Holmes wrote, 'three generations of imbeciles are enough'. By that part of the twentieth century, 29 US states had laws allowing the compulsory sterilisation of individuals thought to be mentally retarded, alcoholic or 'having a criminal nature'. In 1945, information from the *Journal of the American Medical Association* suggested that over 42,000 people were sterilised in the United States between 1941 and 1943.

But the United States was not alone. During the twentieth century, Canada, Sweden, Australia, Norway, Finland, Denmark and Switzerland all had various types of eugenics programmes. These included promoting different birth rates among populations, compulsory sterilisation, marriage restrictions, birth control and immigration control. However, it was in Germany that eugenics became a central focus, with Hitler, the Nazi Socialist Party and the Second World War.

In 1925, Adolf Hitler had published *Mein Kampf* (the book outlines Hitler's major ideas, including violent anti-Semitism) in which he identified the 'mentally unworthy' among the African race and suggested that they mustn't be allowed to perpetuate their race. In 1933, Adolf Hitler and the Nazi Socialist Party set up the sterilisation law, which was directly based on the Model Eugenical Sterilization Law introduced by H. H. Laughlin in 1922. In Germany, before the Second World War and between 1933 and 1939, over

Source: Getty Images

The defeat of Hitler and the Nazi part in the Second World War led to a number of countries putting an end to their eugenic practices.

20,000 people were sterilised for being feebleminded. Then the Holocaust occurred. The Holocaust was the attempt to eradicate entirely particular target groups. By that time, sterilisation of target groups such as the mentally retarded had extended to the extermination of whole groups of people and races including the Jews, the Poles, Russians, Communists, homosexuals, the mentally ill, the disabled, intelligentsia and political activists, Catholic and Protestant clergy, some Africans and common criminals. During the Second World War, Germany occupied a number of countries, including France and part of the Soviet Union. In 1939, seven million Jews were killed in central and eastern Europe, 3 million in Poland and over 1 million in the Soviet Union.

Following the Second World War, and the experience of Nazi Germany and Hitler with his aspirations for the perfect race, eugenics fell into disrepute. The Nuremberg Trials were trials of Nazis involved in World War II and the Holocaust, and these trials revealed to the world the Nazis' genocidal practices. Clearly, governments couldn't condone those policies that had been advocated by Hitler, and many re-examined their eugenics-based policies. In 1948, and in response to this gross abuse, the United Nations affirmed that men and women of full age, without any limitation due to race, nationality or religion, have the right to marry and to found a family.

Eugenics and *The Bell Curve*

However, what has eugenics got to do with *The Bell Curve*? Well, critics of the book, such as Gould, felt that some of the issues raised by Herrnstein and Murray echoed eugenics thoughts and practices. Their emphasis on singling out people with low intelligence and segregating aspects of society, their emphasis on genetic influence on intelligence and their concerns about immigration brought up some issues that surround eugenics. These sorts of concerns about Herrnstein and Murray's work were not helped, as Kamin points out, by the fact that one main advocate of eugenics in modern intelligence research is an academic on whose evidence Herrnstein and Murray largely relied – Richard Lynn.

Richard Lynn, known for his work on race and a firm supporter of the genetic heritability of intelligence, wrote a book on dysgenics (the biological study of the factors

Stop and Think

To tell the truth, the whole truth and nothing but the truth

Consider the following story. It is part of an obituary written about Richard Herrnstein in 1994, after his death, by Charles Murray (Murray, 1994). Think about this statement in regards to reporting group differences in intelligence.

> About four years ago, shortly after Dick (Richard Herrnstein) and I had begun to collaborate on a new book about intelligence and social policy (*The Bell Curve*), we were talking over a late-evening Scotch at his home in Belmont, Mass(achusetts). We had been musing about the warning shots the prospective book had already drawn and the heavy fire that was sure to come. The conversation began to depress me, and I said, 'Why the hell are we doing this, anyway?' Dick recalled the day when, as a young man, he had been awarded tenure. It was his dream fulfilled - a place in the university he so loved, the chance to follow his research wherever it took him, economic security. For Dick, being a tenured professor at Harvard was not just the perfect job, but also the perfect way to live his life. It was too good to be true; there had to be a catch. What's my part of the bargain? He had asked himself. 'And I figured it out,' he said, looking at me with that benign, gentle half-smile of his. 'You have to tell the truth.' (Murray, 1994, p. 22)

producing degeneration of genes in offspring, especially of a particular race or species), which argued that eugenicists were right in their belief that modern populations have been deteriorating genetically in respect to their intelligence (Lynn, 1996). In a second book (Lynn, 2001), he considers what measures could be taken to rectify the effects of dysgenics and argues that genetic improvement is likely to evolve when women use in vitro fertilisation (IVF; fertilisation of an egg in the laboratory) to grow a number of embryos, then have them genetically assessed and before selecting those with genetically desirable qualities. However, it is important to note that Lynn does not condone Hitler's actions of genocide. Instead, he sees eugenics as purely a scientific pursuit to establish what is known about genetic inheritance and that the aims and objectives of eugenics should be open to scientific scrutiny.

It is also crucial to note that at no point do Herrnstein and Murray discuss eugenics research or policy. However, it is the discussion of a number of issues in Herrnstein and Murray's work that have been previously linked to eugenics (low intelligence, genetic inheritability of intelligence, race differences, their concerns about immigration past) that Gould is pointing to when he mentions the ghosts of *The Bell Curve*'s past.

Final comments

Phew! What a debate! That certainly may have got your blood boiling, but please remember when discussing such things in class and in essays that the arguments arising from the discussion must generally be academically based, not personally based (to read more on fallacies, go to Chapter 22). Notwithstanding the discussion, you should now be able to outline:

- what is meant by genetic heritability in intelligence;
- the different dimensions of genetic and environmental influences that are thought to impact on intelligence;
- the main points of Herrnstein and Murray's *Bell Curve* analysis;
- some criticisms of Herrnstein and Murray's *Bell Curve* analysis.

Summary

- Sir Francis Galton suggested that man's natural abilities are inherited under the same conditions as physical features of the animal world that had been described by Darwin. Galton suggested that intelligence is passed down to children through heredity.
- Heritability of intelligence is the estimated assessment of the extent to which intelligence is passed down from parents to children through their genes on average across the population.
- There are largely three types of study that you will regularly see in the heritability of intelligence: family studies, twin studies and adoption studies.
- Heritability estimates of intelligence vary greatly, ranging from an average of 40 per cent to an average of 80 per cent.
- There are four general issues surrounding genetic heritability estimates: conceptions of heritability and the environment, different types of genetic variance, the representativeness of twin and adoption studies and assortative mating.
- We identify five main areas in which to consider environmental effects on intelligence.
- The first area is biological variables (nutrition, lead and prenatal factors) and the maternal-effects model.
- The second area is the consideration of family environment and shared and non-shared factors. Non-shared environments consider within-family factors and outside-family factors, including context-specific socialisation, outside the home socialisation, transmission of culture via group processes, group processes that widen differences between social groups and group processes that widen differences among individuals within the group.
- The third area is socioeconomic status variables that also include consideration of birth order, family size and intelligence.
- The fourth and fifth areas are education and culture, respectively, the latter comprising consideration of factors such as decontextualisation, quantification and biologisation.
- In 1994 two US authors, Richard J. Herrnstein and Charles Murray, published a book called *The Bell Curve: Intelligence and Class Structure in American Life* (Herrnstein & Murray, 1994). The

→

term 'bell curve' refers to the distribution of a large number of IQ test results in the United States.

- Herrnstein and Murray analyse the distribution of scores, comparing the high end and low end of the distribution of IQ scores and discussing the emergence of the cognitive elite, social and economic problems and the relationship between race and IQ.
- There are huge criticisms of the arguments presented by Herrnstein and Murray. First, these criticisms centre on analysing some of the premises used in the argument, including whether (1) there is such a thing as a general factor of intelligence, (2) all standardised tests of IQ measure intelligence accurately, (3) IQ scores match what people mean by intelligence and (4) IQ scores are stable, although not perfectly so, over much of a person's life.
- Other criticisms of *The Bell Curve* focus on the consideration of the use of statistics and research ethics and its perceived link with eugenics ideas.

Connecting Up

- This chapter should be read after Chapters 11 and 12.
- There are also some links to Chapter 8 (Biological Basis of Personality I: Genetic Heritability of Personality and Biological and Physiological Models of Personality), which outlines to a greater extent some of the issues surrounding heritability estimates.
- Also, Chapter 22 may need to be read in order to gain better insight into some of the elements of academic argument.

Critical Thinking

Discussion questions

- Discuss the relative importance of genes and the environment in determining IQ.
- Do differences in average IQ scores have any relationship to, or infer anything about, the race of an individual?
- Discuss the view that without Herrnstein and Murray's work, the public today would know a lot less about what factors influence intelligence.
- Critically examine the implications for schooling and work, assuming that intelligence consists of one general ability and is inherited.

Essay questions

- Critically assess the view that genetics are more important than the environment in determining intelligence.
- How do narrow and broad definitions of IQ heritability differ? How has our understanding of genetics informed the nature versus nurture debate on intelligence?
- To what extent do racial group differences in intelligence exist? Identify some important considerations relating to these findings.
- The main problem with Herrnstein and Murray's bell curve is that there are major flaws in the premises of the argument they present. Critically discuss.

Going Further

Books

- Herrnstein, R. J., & Murray, C. (1994). *The bell curve*. New York: Free Press.
- Jacoby, R., & Glauberman, N. (Eds.). *The bell curve debate*. New York: Times/Random House.
- Plomin, R. (2004). *Nature and nurture: An introduction to human behavioral genetics*. London: Wadsworth.
- Plomin, R., DeFries, J. C., McClearn, G. E., & McGuffin, P. (2000). *Behavioral genetics: A primer*. London: Freeman.

Journals

- Zyphur, M. J. (2006). On the complexity of race. *American Psychologist, 61*, 179-180. In this chapter we explained that the analyses of race within mainstream psychology usually relies on simple social categories, but we also argued that there are problems with this method as it bears little resemblance to those methods used in the genetic analysis of race. If you want to read more about this issue, then a good short starting point is this article. *American Psychologist* is published by American Psychological Association. Available online via PsycARTICLES.
- In this chapter and the last, we looked at the notion of whether IQ and intelligence can change. A good article summarising the main issues is Howe, J. A. (1998). Can IQ change? *The Psychologist, 11, 69-72*. This is freely available online. You can find *The Psychologist* on the British Psychological Society Website **(http://www.bps.org.uk/).**
- Maccoby, E. E. (2000). Parenting and its effects on children: On reading and misreading behavior genetics. *Annual Review of Psychology, 51*, 1-27. *Annual Review of Psychology* is published by Annual Reviews, Palo Alto, California. Available online via Business Source Premier.
- Baker, L. D., & Daniels, D. (1990). Nonshared environmental influences and personality differences in adult twins. *Journal of Personality and Social Psychology, 58*, 103-110. Published by the American Psychological Association. Available online via PsycARTICLES.
- Bouchard, T. J. Jr, & Loehlin, J. C. (2001). Genes, personality, and evolution. *Behavioural Genetics, 31*, 243-273. Published by Kluwer Academic Publishers. Available online via Kluwer or SwetsWise.
- Harris, J. R. (1995). Where is the child's environment? A group socialization theory of development. *Psychological Review, 102*, 458-489. Published by the American Psychological Association. Available online via PsycARTICLES.

Articles on the intelligence issues discussed in these chapters are often found in these journals.

- **Intelligence: A multidisciplinary journal.** Published by Elsevier Science. Available online via Science Direct.
- **American Psychologist.** This journal has a number of articles relating to the heritability of intelligence. Published by the American Psychological Association. Available online via PsycARTICLES.

Web resources

- In this chapter we have covered a number of topics including heritability of intelligence, the bell curve and birth order. Some of these topics are controversial and evoke a lot of emotions, and therefore there are a lot of websites that discuss these issues; but the evidence they use is not appropriate. We would suggest that when it comes to topics like these it is best to adhere to academic books and journals. However, if you want to search the web, then the place to start is the Hot Topics section of the Human Intelligence website **(http://www.indiana.edu/~intell/).**

Film and Literature

- **David Copperfield**, by Charles Dickens (1869) and **Under the Greenwood Tree**, by Thomas Hardy (1872). Our first discussion of intelligence in this chapter was to do with Galton's view of intelligence and the reasons underlying it at the beginning of the twentieth century. Galton looked to members of the Royal Society and saw eminence as an indicator of intelligence. However, the argument of what surrounds intelligence was demonstrated in many novels of the time. The writing of Charles Dickens (for example, *David Copperfield*) and Thomas Hardy (*Under the Greenwood Tree*) used intelligence to distinguish the main characters. In both books, there is a contrast made between the small village family, whose members are intelligent in terms of the countryside around them and have inherited wisdom passed through generations of their family, and the city family, whose members are eminent, rich and own businesses but are actually portrayed as incredibly unwise compared to the village families. This treatment contrasts greatly with Galton's assumptions about the study of eminent people living in London as reflecting intelligence.
- **Gattaca** (1997; directed by Andrew Niccol). Vincent (played by Ethan Hawke) is one of the last 'natural' babies born into a sterile, genetically enhanced world, where a person's life expectancy and the likelihood of disease are ascertained at birth. Born with a heart defect and due to die at 30, Vincent has no chance of a career in a society that now discriminates against your genes, instead of your gender, race or religion. This film suggests a natural progression of eugenics, and raises some issues about what happens to those who fall afoul of the perfect genetic world.
- **The Intelligent Man** (1984; Educational Resources Film). This video looks at the sometimes controversial work of Sir Cyril Burt and his work with intelligence tests and theory. The filmmaker looks at the experiments and findings of the work carried out by Cyril Burt and contrasts intelligence theories. BBC Videos for Education and Training.

CHAPTER

6 GENETICS

Read the Chapter on mysearchlab.com

"What a piece of work is man! How noble in reason! How infinite in faculty! In form and moving how express and admirable! In action how like an angel! In apprehension how like a god! The beauty of the world! The paragon of animals!"
William Shakespeare, Hamlet, *Act II, scene ii*

Do these words sound familiar to you? Of course they do, but do you recall the few lines preceding these classic words?

I have of late—but wherefore I know not—lost all my mirth.

And earlier in Act I, scene ii:

O, that this too, too solid flesh would melt,
Thaw, and resolve itself into a dew!
Or, that the Everlasting had not fix'd
His canon 'gainst self-slaughter! O God! God!
How weary, stale, flat and unprofitable,
Seem to me all the uses of this world!

Hamlet is depressed. Of course, he has good reason to be, with his father recently dead, his uncle trying to take over the kingdom, and his mother remarrying too soon. What makes a person depressed? Is depression caused by a genetic predisposition, such that some people are doomed to be depressed? Or is depression caused by experiences that are so devastating that *anybody* would be depressed by them?

For years, psychologists wondered what caused clinical depression: a debilitating combination of profound sadness, loss of interest in formerly pleasurable activities, lack of energy, hopelessness, feelings of worthlessness, and even thoughts of suicide. Although life events such as death of a parent, job loss, or stress no doubt cause people to be sad, what causes this devastating condition?

Because some psychologists had noticed that depression ran in families—or at least in some families—researchers tried to find a genetic mechanism of depression. Consider a study by Haeffel et al. (2008). They identified a sample of adolescent boys who were ordered by the courts to attend a residential juvenile delinquent detention facility in the Arkhangelsk region of northern Russia. The sample was not very diverse—about 98% of the sample was of Russian ancestry—but perfect for investigating possible genetic causes of depression.

The researchers looked for genetic and environmental differences between the youths who were depressed and those who were not. The amazing thing is that they found—nothing! That is, they found no impact of either genes or environment on rates of depression.

But, when they looked closer and divided up the sample depending on which of three specific gene combinations—called **genotypes**—a participant had, the results were startling, as Figure 6.1 shows. If a youth had both a stressful environment (as measured by maternal rejection in this study) and Genotype 3, there was a good chance that he was depressed. However, if a youth had any of the three genotypes without maternal rejection or maternal rejection with either Genotype 1 or Genotype 2 he was not as likely to develop clinical depression. Further, this combination of environment (maternal rejection) and genotype predicted related outcomes such as suicide ideation and depressive symptoms but not *un*related psychological problems such as an anxiety disorder. This suggests that there is something magical (perhaps alarming is a better word) about this particular interaction of *these* genes with *this* environment.

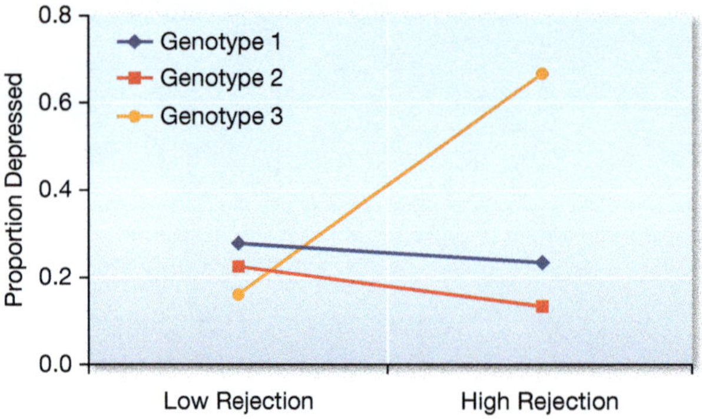

Figure 6.1 Incidence of clinical depression as a function of genotype and maternal rejection. *Source:* From Haeffel et al. (2008, Figure 1, p. 66), Haeffel, G. J., Getchell, M., Koposov, R. A., Yrigollen, C. M., DeYoung, C. G., af Klinteberg, B., et al. (2008), "Association between polymorphisms in the dopaminetransporter gene and depression," *Psychological Science,* 19(1), 62–69. Reprinted by permission of Blackwell Publishing.

Like Haeffel et al. (2008), other researchers have found it notoriously difficult to find main effects of genes on personality traits (Krueger & Johnson, 2008). This highlights an important theme of this chapter: The interesting question is not whether genes *or* environment affect our personalities, for surely both do. The real question is *how* do genes and environment *work together* to make us the kind of people we are? To answer this question we need to explore some basics of **behavioral genetics**, which is the study of the genetic and environmental contributions to individual differences in personality and behavior (DiLalla, 2004). (To get you thinking about these issues, you may want to try the self-assessment exercise in Table 6.1).

The goal of this chapter is not to present a catalog of personality characteristics that have a genetic component, for the list would be too long! Neither will we explore the molecular mechanism of specific genes important for personality development, for the research evidence is piling up too quickly for a textbook to keep up with. Instead, we will focus on understanding how genetic principles work in explaining differences in personality. Armed with this broad understanding as your groundwork, you will be able to understand the genetics behind any personality characteristic you encounter in this book and to understand the newest breakthroughs in genetics research that you may hear about in the news.

Table 6.1 How Much Do Genes and Environment Contribute to Personality?

Instructions: Identify four family members or friends who differ in their blood-relation to you and in whether you grew up in the same environment by using the following descriptions for Person 1, Person 2, and so on and filling in their names at the top of each of the four columns in the chart.

Person 1 = Genetic parent (of same sex as you, if possible).

Person 2 = Genetic sibling (of same sex as you, if possible). If you are an only child, use a cousin or other relative.

Person 3 = Unrelated person (or less related to you than Person 2) living in your household while you were growing up.

Person 4 = Unrelated person, not living in your household while you were growing up (e.g., best friend, peer, roommate).

If you are unable to identify any of Persons 1 to 3, then use people who lived in your household, even if you were not related to them, and compare them with unrelated people who did not live in your household while growing up.

Next, rate how similar you are to each of these people using the following scale:

1	2	3	4	5	6
Completely different	Different	More different than Similar	More similar than Different	Similar	Very similar, almost the same

	Person 1	Person 2	Person 3	Person 4
Name of person:				
Characteristic:				
1. Height				
2. Sense of humor				
3. Weight				
4. Political views				
5. Adventurousness				
6. Taste in music				
7. Extraversion				
8. Anxiousness				
9. Individualistic				
10. Tech-savy				

Based on your responses, can you venture a guess as to which has a greater influence on the development of each characteristic, genes or environment? Finally, do you think that each characteristic is caused more by genes and environment working separately, working together, or by influencing each other?

"Environmental factors always contribute to individual differences in human behavior. . . . Genes contribute to individual differences in almost every dimension of human behavior that has been studied thus far."
Carey (2003, pp. 3–4)

Nature and Nurture as Allies

Imagine that you are taking a standardized test and the following item appears in your test book:

Lemonade is

a. lemon juice.
b. water.
c. sugar.

How would you answer this question? Would you start to panic and wonder if this was a trick question? After all, *everybody* knows that lemonade is made up of all of these! In fact, we might say that lemonade is a compound solution entirely different from its constituent parts. So, this question, obviously, makes no sense. But consider this equally nonsensical question:

Extraversion is

a. genetic.
b. cultural.
c. familial.
d. due to all your idiosyncratic learning experiences.

When it comes to understanding human behavior, this question makes no sense either. That is, human behavior—and personality in particular—is an inextricable combination of both genetics and environment. In fact, taking sides in the nature–nurture debate is a massive "scientific mistake" (Krueger & Johnson, 2008, p. 287). So, if you are wondering *whether* genes determine your personality, stop right there: Personality is lemonade! (This fantastic example comes from Carey, 2003, pp. 2–3.)

The best characterization of the nature–nurture issue is that nature and nurture *transact*. That is, genes and environment can work separately, together, or they may influence one another (Canli, 2008, p. 299). When we talk about heritability and environmentality separately, we are assuming that genes and environment each have a unique contribution to the whole personality. That is, genes and environment may operate separately but in parallel (i.e., at the same time) to influence our personalities. You can think of genes and environment as co-actors (Cardno & McGuffin, 2002). This is the simplest case, as we shall soon see, and may not, in fact, be the way most aspects of personality develop.

A more interesting case is that genes and environment may interact with each other, such that they change aspects of human personality by acting together on a person. You know that saying *the whole is greater than the sum of its parts?* Well, it is possible that certain

Genes and environment as co-actors: Physically and psychologically, we are the result of an inextricable combination of both genetics and environment.

environments have different effects on people depending on their specific genetic makeup. We call this combination of nature and nurture a *genotype–environment interaction.* With more sophisticated ways of exploring the human genome, especially at the molecular level, this is the most exciting, and potentially groundbreaking kind of research that personality researchers are conducting. This is partially what we meant by lemonade in the discussion that opened this chapter: sugar, lemon, and water, when mixed in the right proportions, combine to make something fundamentally different (and better!) than each separate ingredient.

Yet another possibility is that it may be impossible to separate the effect of genes from the effect of the environment. What if people change environments and environments change people, so that we really can't separate the impact of genes on environment? This is called a *genotype–environment correlation.* This is yet another sense in which personality is lemonade: There is no way to separate out the ingredients, as they are inextricably combined.

In fact, some researchers advocate an even more complicated equation for understanding the manifestation of complex human traits—a concept known as **phenotype** (Cardno & McGuffin, 2002, p. 40):

$$\text{Phenotype} = \text{Genotype} + \text{Environment} + \text{Gene–environment correlation}$$
$$+ \text{Gene–environment interaction.}$$

We will consider each part of this equation in turn.

Genes and Environment as Co-actors

When we say that a characteristic is due to both genetics and environment, how do we know? Scientists are able to estimate how much of the differences among people on a given characteristic are because of their genes. For example, consider the students in your personality class. No doubt there are wide variations of height, with some taller people and some shorter people and lots of people of average height. The question is, how much of this observed height difference among people in your class is due to their differing genetic makeup? In this section we examine the concepts of *heritability* and *environmentality.*

Heritability

"Everything is heritable."
Turkheimer (2004, p. 161)

Heritability (h^2) is the amount of observed individual differences in some characteristic that can be accounted for by genetic differences (Carey, 2003). Heritability refers to differences across a group or population of people—not to a specific person. It is impossible to say how much of *your* height is due to *your* genes. But, considering a sample of people, like your personality class, we can estimate that about 80% of the observed differences in height is due to differing genetic makeup of your classmates and 20% is due to differing environments your classmates were raised in, plus some percentage of measurement error (because nothing, especially not our measurement instruments, is perfect).

To illustrate, imagine that you and your friends like to bake (and eat!) chocolate chip cookies, and each time you make them, they come out slightly different. Why might this be? Different brands of chocolate chips? Different types of flour? Is it possible that different bakers produce different cookies? You can readily see that the differences among batches could be due to differences in any of these factors. But suppose I asked you, which is more important to the flavor of *this particular cookie:* the flour or the eggs? Well, obviously we need both in order to have a good cookie! The question makes no sense. The same principle applies to understanding heritability: We cannot know what contributes more to the personality of a particular person, but we can know how much genetics and environment each account for differences in a particular personality characteristic of this particular sample of people.

THINK ABOUT IT

What environmental factors could account for differences in height among a group of people?

Heritability, therefore, refers to the inheritance of *a particular trait in a particular population at a particular time,* so sometimes heritability estimates differ depending on the exact

Heritability: Just as the variation among batches of cookies is due to variations in ingredients, the variation of a particular trait in a particular population at a particular time is due to differences in their genetic makeup.

sample and methods used by researchers (Plomin, DeFries, McClearn, & McGuffin, 2008, p. 86). To understand this, let's continue discussing height, a characteristic with a fairly large genetic component. The heritability of height is 80% or higher in the United States but it is only 65% in China and western Africa. And in Australia, one study estimated height heritability as 87% for men and 71% for women (Silvetoinen et al., 2003)! This is because of genetic variations among ethnic groups and because of the distinct environments they face. For example, Americans, Chinese, and Africans vary in native climates, lifestyle, and dietary habits, as do men and women in many cultures (Lai, 2006). This is why heritability is considered an estimate that refers to a specific population: Estimates vary between samples.

Environmentality

It's unlikely that genetics account for 100% of the variance in *any* personality variable, so what accounts for the rest of the variation? The environment, of course! We use the term **environmentality** (e^2) for that. Environmentality estimates the extent to which observed individual differences can be traced in any way to individual differences in environments (Carey, 2003). Together, heritability, environmentality, and measurement error account for all the differences we see among people on a given characteristic.

By now, it must be getting clearer to you that environment and genetics work together to impact human behavior so that it doesn't make sense to pit nature *against* nurture. As a general rule, the greater the heritability of a characteristic the less the environmentality. And the greater the environmentality, the less the heritability. Whereas height does have a large genetic component, the environmentality of height is fairly strong too, somewhere in the neighborhood of 20 to 40%. What kinds of environmental factors influence height? The biggest influence is childhood nutrition, especially protein, but also calcium, vitamin A, and vitamin D. In particular, childhood *mal*nutrition is particularly detrimental to adult height. Childhood diseases can also limit adult height, and by the same token human growth hormones can counteract some of these detrimental effects (Lai, 2006). This is how genetically similar populations may show differing heritability estimates: environmentality.

SEE FOR YOURSELF

Consider your extended family of great-grandparents, grandparents, aunts, uncles, and cousins. Can you identify particular environmental factors that may account for height differences, especially between generations in your family?

We see higher heritability estimates in equalizing environments (i.e., environments that are the same for everybody, and lower estimates in more variable environments; Plomin et al., 2008). This is because when everybody has access to resources in rich environments there is little variance in the effect the environment can have. For example, there's a limit to how much meat will increase height. Once all or nearly all of the people in a society have access to good health care, high levels of protein, and enriched foods, then we will see a very strong effect of genetics. Essentially, the only thing left to vary at this point *is* genetics. This is why heritability estimates for height are the greatest in developed countries such as the United States, and lower in less developed countries. In fact, average height in the United States has plateaued, meaning that as a nation we've gotten about as tall as we're going to get due to environmental effects (Lai, 2006).

Shared and Nonshared Environments

Traditionally, environment referred only to any part of the phenotype not accounted for by genes. However, these days researchers are trying to zero in on, and specifically identify, the exact aspects of an environment that account for differences in personality among a group of people. One way of thinking about environmental influences on characteristics such as height or personality is to identify aspects of the environment that are shared and unshared among relatives living together in a household.

Shared environment includes aspects of the family environment that are generally the same for all the children in the household (Krueger & Johnson, 2008) including physical, psychological, and social aspects (Carey, 2003). Physical aspects of a household may be the type of dwelling (e.g., apartment vs. house) and its layout, the number of computers or books in the home, or the presence of a video gaming system. Psychological aspects might include home atmosphere, parenting practices, the quality of sibling interactions, or psychopathology (e.g., alcoholism, drug use, depression) in the home. Social variables include socioeconomic status, family structure, educational attainment of the parents, an urban or a rural setting, and religion. In the broadest sense, *anything* not accounted for by genetics that makes relatives similar has been considered part of the shared environment (Carey, 2003).

SEE FOR YOURSELF

What are some aspects of your physical, psychological, and social environment shared among you and your parents or you and your siblings?

In contrast, the **nonshared environment** includes experiences that relatives have which make them different from one another (Carey, 2003; Krueger & Johnson, 2008; Plomin, Asbury, & Dunn, 2001). These may include unique experiences within the family (e.g., being the eldest, being the only boy, spacing of siblings, differential parental treatment), or outside the family (e.g., peers, teachers, sports, hobbies). When it comes to personality, most of the environmental influence ends up being of the nonshared variety (Krueger & Johnson, 2008; Plomin & Caspi, 1999; Turkheimer & Waldron, 2000). The big surprise to researchers has been that when family members resemble one another it is more often due to heredity than to shared environment (Krueger & Johnson, 2008; Plomin & Caspi, 1999). That is, children growing up in the same family are not any more similar to one another than children growing up in different families. Even when children experience the same event, like a divorce, it may be experienced differently by each of the children depending on their individual personalities or ages (e.g., a relief, the end of the world; Hetherington & Clingempeel, 1992). Certainly environment is important; however, the important aspects of the environment for personality development do not appear to be shared by family members.

SEE FOR YOURSELF

What are some aspects of your physical, psychological, and social environment *not* shared among you and your parents or you and your siblings that are unique to you?

It may be that family environment makes children *different* from one another (e.g., "Jerry is the adventurous one; Tony is the thoughtful one") or it may be that researchers are looking too broadly and have not identified specific aspects of the environment that are shared (e.g., sense of humor, openness to ideas, cultural and aesthetic values). Also, parents may handle children differently depending on their personality, creating a unique environment for each child. For all of these reasons, researchers have had a difficult time identifying the precise shared and nonshared aspects of the child's environment that, along with genetics, account for differences in personality.

For example, although we know that teachers and peers have a big impact on children's development (e.g., Shaffer, 2009), is this part of the shared or the nonshared environment? In most behavioral genetic research the effect of schools, neighborhoods, and communities gets labeled as shared family experiences when they might not even be shared by siblings and they don't involve family! To untangle familial experiences from nonfamilial experiences one study employed an unusual control group.

Richard Rose and colleagues (Rose & Dick, 2004/2005; Rose et al., 2003) studied a sample of identical twins and nonidentical twins along with kids who were from the same neighborhood, school, and even classroom as each of the twins. The study took place in Finland, which at the time required parents to send their children to the closest neighborhood school. In this way, the researchers could estimate the separate effects of genetics (by comparing identical twins with nonidentical twins), familial environments (comparing twins with their matched control classmates), nonfamilial environments (comparing control kids from the same classes to one another), and personal environments (comparing kids from different neighborhoods to one another).

The twins were part of a longitudinal study known as the Finn Twin studies (Rose & Dick, 2004/2005). Only same-sex twins were used, and each member of the twin pair was matched to a child of the same sex from the same school, and in about 90% of the cases, they were from the same classroom. In all, there were 333 identical twins, 298 nonidentical twins, and 1,262 matched classmates for a total of 2,524 11- and 12-year-olds (Rose et al., 2003).

The participants were asked a series of yes-or-no questions about their smoking, drinking, and church activities (Rose & Dick, 2004/2005; Rose et al., 2003). From their responses, the researchers were able to estimate the amount of variance in the kids' self-reported behaviors that was due to genetics, familial environment, school environment, or personal environment.

Which source of variance was the most important? That depended on the behavior. In no case did genetics explain *all* of the variance in participants' self-reports. For some variables, notably smoking cigarettes, saying prayers, and seeing adults drunk, there was a greater effect of shared environment (i.e., the household) than shared genes. This makes sense because these are the kind of behaviors that parents model in front of their children. For alcohol use, both shared environment and shared genes had an impact.

SEE FOR YOURSELF

In what ways are you more similar to your friends than to your siblings? Why might this be?

When it came to drinking with peers without parents around, the neighborhood was more important than the household, as you might expect. After all, kids typically engage in these sorts of behaviors with their friends and do so far away from parental surveillance.

Finally, unique, unshared environment—what we might think of as a kid's personal environment—was more important for participation in church activities. You can see that even though the parents might encourage certain behaviors in the family such as saying prayers, it appears that kids themselves are choosing to get involved or not in church activities beyond Sunday services. And, indeed, the influence of family was the largest and genetics the smallest for having prayers in the home while growing up.

This study illustrates how the relative importance of genetics and environments varies depending on the question. Research designed to take account of various sources of social influence can shed light on shared and nonshared environments in accounting for personality and behavior.

One method of studying genetic influence is to compare personality traits in identical twins and in nontwin siblings.

Estimating Heritability

By now you must be wondering how researchers are able to measure heritability. We estimate the heritability of a characteristic by seeing if people who have similar genes show similar characteristics. If a characteristic has a strong genetic component, then we would expect identical twins, who share 100% of their genes, to be more similar than strangers in that characteristic. We can see this more clearly in physical characteristics, but it is harder to see the effects of genes and environment in personality, which is why so far in this chapter we've been looking at tangible things such as height.

Consider twins. As you know, there are two kinds of twins: identical and fraternal. Identical twins, called **monozygotic (MZ) twins**, are exact genetic duplicates of each other. This happens when a fertilized egg, the zygote, splits into two (or sometimes more) identical parts that each go on

Identical twins, called monozygotic (MZ) twins, are exact genetic duplicates of each other.

to develop into a fetus. Identical twins are quite rare in the population, occurring just over 32 times in 1,000 births in the United States.

In contrast, fraternal twins occur when two zygotes develop in utero at the same time. We call these kinds of twins **dizygotic (DZ) twins.** DZ twins result from the fertilization of two different eggs by two different sperm cells, hence they are genetically distinct. Essentially fraternal twins are no more alike than ordinary siblings, sharing about 50% of their genes (Carey, 2003). Although twins may look alike, the only way to be sure if they are identical (MZ) or fraternal (DZ) is to conduct a genetic test (of course, if the twins are of different sexes, then we know that they must be fraternal twins). Because of increased use of fertility drugs and in vitro fertilization the incidence of fraternal twins has been steadily increasing since the early 1980s (Plomin et al., 2008).

One measure of heritability, then, is to calculate the correlation (r) between twins on a given trait and compare the correlation between MZ twins and DZ twins (Plomin et al., 2008). The exact formula is to double the difference between these correlations or

$$h^2 = 2(r_{mz} - r_{dz})$$

A second way of estimating heritability is to compare identical twins who have been raised in separate environments (Plomin ct al., 2008). We call these kinds of twins **MZA twins** (monozygotic twins raised apart). If such twins score similarly in a trait such as Extraversion, then we know that Extraversion has a strong genetic component. Studies of MZA twins are particularly powerful in disentangling the effects of genes and environment because they have identical genes but different environments. Here is a second formula for estimating heritability:

$$h^2 = r_{MZA}$$

We'll consider the logic behind adoption studies and twin studies in the Research Methods Illustrated section, in a moment. For now, note that both of these

Nonidentical twins, called dizygotic (DZ) twins, are no more alike than siblings, having about 50% of their genetic makeup in common.

estimates of heritability have limitations, and researchers may use more sophisticated formulas to account for these potential problems. The double-the-difference method assumes that twins were reared under equal environments (Cardno & McGuffin, 2002; Carey, 2003; DiLalla, 2004; Plomin et al., 2008). That is, it assumes that people have not treated MZ twins more alike than DZ twins. Whereas certainly *twins* are often treated differently than nontwins, the question is, are identical twins treated more similarly than are fraternal twins? If MZ twins are treated more alike, then they may score more similarly on a particular trait, artificially inflating the heritability estimate (you can see this for yourself by looking at our first formula). Essentially, what is really an environmental effect (similar treatment) gets mislabeled as a genetic effect (similar personality).

THINK ABOUT IT

Do people treat identical twins differently from non-identical twins?

This **equal environments assumption** applies only to similar treatment that is related to the specific characteristic under study. For example, people often dress their twins alike in identical sailor suits or matching dresses. This probably happens more often to MZ twins than to DZ twins. If we were studying something like fashion sense, then this would violate our equal environments assumption. But unless wearing matching outfits affects a specific personality characteristic like shyness, then this assumption still holds (Carey, 2003).

You'll see that researchers often test this assumption by asking research participants (or their parents) to describe how they were treated while growing up. Indeed, such studies have concluded that for the most part, parents of MZ twins don't treat their twins any more alike than parents of DZ twins so that this equal environments assumption is a fair assumption (Cardno & McGuffin, 2002; Carey, 2003; Plomin et al., 2008).

THINK ABOUT IT

Does being a twin affect one's personality more so than having a sibling close to your own age would?

The double-the-difference formula also assumes that twins are typical of the population. We call this the **assumption of representativeness** (Plomin et al., 2008). For example, twins are often premature and have a lower birthrate than single births. Twins, therefore, may not be representative of the general population on variables that are affected by prematurity or low birth weight. Again, this is something researchers may test for, and for the most part this assumption holds as well (Carey, 2003; Plomin et al., 2008).

The r_{MZA} method of estimating heritability also has its limitations. Here, researchers assume that the adopted families of each twin are different from each other. If the identical twins are placed in similar environments this may increase the similarity between the twins, artificially inflating our heritability estimate. That is, twins may be more alike on a certain characteristic due to **selective placement** during the adoption process and not to their genetics. Selective placement makes it impossible to see the effect of genetics apart from the effect of environment because it confounds the two (Plomin, DeFries, & Loehlin, 1977; Plomin et al., 2008).

Adoption studies of MZA twins also assume that families who adopt are the same as families who do not adopt. Again, if there is something special about adoptive families, then this environmental effect will get improperly labeled as a genetic effect. For example, prospective adoptive families often go through an interview to rule out extreme poverty, criminal behavior, drug abuse, and other factors that affect the ability of the family to provide a safe and secure environment for a child. We might wonder how representative adoptive families are. Although the mean income of adoptive families and the general population are not much different, there are fewer families in extreme poverty among adoptive families (Carey, 2003). This suggests a potential problem of range restriction among adoptive families, making it harder to detect a significant effect of environment. Again, whereas this might be a problem for some variables (e.g., antisocial behavior) it may not be a problem when it comes to personality traits (Carey, 2003). Both of these assumptions, selective placement and representativeness of adoptive families, have been tested by researchers and are not a problem for most studies (Plomin et al., 1977, 2008).

Research Methods Illustrated: Correlational Designs I: The Logic of Adoption and Twin Studies

What do we mean when we say that a certain trait "runs in families"? For example, families often share inside jokes and find the same sorts of things amusing. Does sense of humor run in families? If so, why might this be? When we say that a trait runs in families, is this because of shared genetics among family members? Or, is it because family members all live in the same environment, where they might watch the same TV programs, tell amusing stories around the dinner table, and laugh at one another's jokes, for example? The trouble is, under ordinary conditions we can't tell the two apart.

Sure, we could design a kind of science-fiction experiment: Imagine a set of MZ twins who are identical in their genetic makeup. For about 9 months, let's say they share identical conditions inside their mother's womb (although in reality MZ twins grow in their own subenvironment of the womb). Then we would take these twins, separate them at birth, and randomly place them in contrasting environments. When they grow to adulthood we see what kinds of cartoons they think are funny and then see if this is more similar to their birth family's sense of humor or to their adopted family's sense of humor. This would be the way to design a true experimental test, but obviously such an experiment is completely unethical and impossible to do.

However, such natural experiments do happen in the world. Babies—both twins and nontwins—are adopted and raised in families that provide a nurturing environment but no genetic material. Similarly, twins—both genetically identical and not—are raised in the same environment. Thus adoption studies and twin studies go a long way to helping researchers understand both the genetic and environmental impact on human behavior, including personality.

Recall that a true experiment allows a researcher to infer causality between the presence or absence of a variable and some outcome measure. This is because the researcher is able to manipulate the independent variable and to randomly assign participants to various levels of that independent variable. Therefore, any difference in the outcome between the groups must be due to differences in what the experimenter manipulated. Of course, this assumes everything else was exactly the same for each and every participant. These two requirements—experimental control and random assignment to conditions—are the defining qualities of a true experiment.

However, there are times when one or both of these requirements are impossible. Like in our little sci-fi experiment, you can't randomly assign children to parents! That violates the random assignment to condition requirement. Similarly, you can't control whether children get raised in families with a dry sense of humor or into families with a corny sense of humor, violating the control of the independent variable requirement. So, sometimes it's unethical to conduct a true experiment and sometimes it's just impossible. Often, it's just impractical or inconvenient, due to limited time or resources.

As an alternative to a true experiment, researchers turn to correlational designs. In a correlational design the experimenter doesn't attempt to manipulate the presence or absence of the independent variable, but instead measures it along with some outcome measure. Because the independent variable is not under the experimenter's control, if we see a difference between participants in the outcome of the dependent variable, we can't assume that the independent variable is what *caused* the difference. In this case, the best we can say is that the two variables—our independent variable and our dependent variable—are related.

Although it is very rare to find identical twins who were separated at birth, studying such twins is a good way to understand the effects of genetics and environment on personality. For example, Bob and Bob first met as adults and discovered they had many similarities, including their name and occupation.

Recall that when two variables are related, there are always at least three possible explanations for the findings. First, it's possible that one variable causes the other, like being around the same people all the time causes people to develop a similar sense of humor. Second, it's also possible that the second variable causes the first one, like people who have a similar sense of humor spend more time hanging around each other. Finally, it's also possible that some third variable—like genetics—causes people to hang around each other (i.e., family) and to find the same jokes funny.

The beauty of twin and adoption studies is that they are able to rule out some of these explanations. For example, if adopted children are more similar to their birth parents than to their adoptive parents (or adopted siblings, even), then we can assume that the trait in question has a stronger genetic component. However, if adopted children are more similar to their adoptive parents than to their birth parents, then the trait in question must have a stronger environmental component.

An especially strong case for the relative contribution of genetics and environment may be made if we can study twins who were separated at birth. In these cases, we have two people with identical genetic makeup who have been exposed to different environments. If they respond similarly then we can conclude that genetics must have caused the similarity; if they respond differently then we can conclude that the environment must have caused the difference.

Take a look at Table 6.2 which shows the correlations between various family members in Extraversion and Neuroticism. Recall that positive correlations between two variables mean that the two variables are similar: as one variable increases (or decreases), the other variable increases (or decreases) too. Where are the correlations the highest? The lowest? As you can see, the more genetically similar two people are—for example, identical twins—the more similar they are in both of these characteristics. Being raised apart lessens the similarity, but being raised together without a genetic predisposition does little to make people similar on these traits. You can readily see how twin and adoption studies help us sort out the relative effects of genes and environment.

SEE FOR YOURSELF

Is your sense of humor more similar to your family's or your friends'? Why might this be?

With all of this background on adoption studies, twin studies, and how to interpret correlations, we can now address our question: Does sense of humor run in families? And if so, why might this be? Using a sample of MZ and DZ female twin pairs, researchers had each twin rate how funny they found a series of five *Far Side* cartoons by Gary Larson (Johnson, Vernon, & Feiler, 2008). The researchers were careful to have the women rate the cartoons in separate rooms so they couldn't hear or see their twin's reaction.

How similar were the twins in their ratings of the cartoons? Overall, the ratings of each twin were pretty similar for each of the five cartoons. For one of the cartoons, for example, the correlation between ratings of one MZ with her twin was .50 and for DZ twins it was .41. This suggests that there is a medium, positive relationship between humor ratings of this cartoon in twins.

Take a closer look at these two correlations. Do you think that these correlations are different enough to suggest a genetic component to sense of humor? The researchers tested this idea using

Table 6.2 Twin, Family, and Adoption Correlations for Neuroticism and Extraversion

Type of Relative	Neuroticism	Extraversion
Identical twins reared together	.43	.52
Fraternal twins reared together	.19	.18
Identical twins reared apart	.31	.42
Fraternal twins reared apart	.23	.08
Nonadoptive parents and offspring	.14	.18
Adoptive parents and offspring	.05	.06
Nonadoptive siblings	.18	.19
Adoptive siblings	.12	−.05

Note: Based on a meta-analysis of 145 studies.

Source: From Johnson et al. (2008).

advanced statistical techniques and found that there was no significant impact of genetics on the ratings of these cartoons. However, they estimated that about 49% of the differences between twin pairs was due to differences in shared environment whereas 51% was due to nonshared environment. This suggests that sense of humor, at least for these kind of cerebral off-the-wall cartoons, is something that is partly learned at home and partly picked up from friends, and other aspects of a individual's unique environment.

Note that in this study the researchers did not randomly assign participants to be MZ twins or DZ twins, nor did they manipulate people to share 50 or 100% of the genes. And yet, we are able to estimate the relative contribution of genes, shared environment, and unique environment on people's sense of humor. Such is the value of correlational designs, adoption studies, and twin studies.

Heritability of Common Personality Characteristics

A solid finding in the research—one that has been well replicated across many samples and for both self-report and other report—is that virtually all individual differences in human behavior including cognitive abilities, personality, social attitudes, psychological interests, and psychopathology are moderately heritable (Bouchard & McGue, 2003). In the words of one researcher, "some degree of heritability is practically inevitable" (Turkheimer, 2004, p. 162).

"Quantitative genetics is hardly needed any longer merely to ask whether and how much genetic factors influence behavioral traits because the answers are 'yes' and 'a lot,' respectively, for nearly all traits that have been studied, including personality and cognitive abilities"

(Plomin, Happé, & Caspi, 2002, p. 88).

The heritability of personality traits ranges from .40 to .60, and is the same for both men and women (Carey, 2003; Johnson et al., 2008; Krueger & Johnson, 2008; Plomin & Caspi, 1999; Plomin & Daniels, 1987; Plomin et al., 2008). In fact, one researcher went so far as to say that this is true for all known human differences (Turkheimer, 2000). In addition, shared environment typically accounts for very little variation (Johnson et al., 2008; Krueger & Johnson, 2008; Turkheimer, 2000), whereas nonshared environment accounts for a great deal (Johnson et al., 2008; Krueger & Johnson, 2008; Turkheimer, 2000). The variance in personality traits typically breaks down like this (Krueger & Johnson, 2008):

$$\text{Observed differences in personality traits} = 40\%\ \text{Genetics} + 0\%\ \text{Shared environment} + 40\%\ \text{Nonshared environment} + 20\%\ \text{Error.}$$

So even after we account for the 40 to 60% of variation in most personality traits that comes from genetics (Plomin et al., 2002), there is still plenty of variance left to be explained (Turkheimer, 2004)!

To illustrate this model, let's take a closer look at the heritability of the five-factor model (FFM) of traits. According to this model, human personality can be described using five broad categories of traits: Neuroticism, Extraversion, Openness, Agreeableness, and Conscientiousness (McCrae & Costa, 2008) (we learned about these factors in earlier chapters). Table 6.3 presents a summary of results based on 85,640 pairs of MZ twins, 106,644 pairs of DZ twins, and 46,215 nontwin kinships from 145 studies published from 1955 to 2006 (Johnson et al., 2008). As you can see, identical twins are very similar in the five-factor traits, even if they are raised apart, indicating a moderately strong genetic component to these traits. Indeed, the heritability of all five factors is in the .41 to .50 range, indicating that about 41 to 50% of the variation in these traits is due to genetic factors.

SEE FOR YOURSELF

How similar are you and your siblings or parents in how emotional you are (Neuroticism)? In aesthetic sense such as appreciation for art and classical music (Openness)?

But look closely: Identical twins who were raised together have the highest correlations and indeed, even fraternal twins who are raised together look a bit like each other even though fraternal twins share only about 50% of their genes on average. This suggests that there is a moderate effect of the environment too. Indeed, the environment—both shared and nonshared—accounts for about 47 to 53% of the variance in these traits. Finally, the shared environment accounts for only about 8 to 17% of the variation in these traits. Other researchers have found similar results when looking at the individual facet traits that make up each of the five factors (Jang, McCrae, Angleitner, Riemann, & Livesley, 1998).

Table 6.3 Kinship Correlations, Heritability Estimates, and Environmentality Estimates for Traits of the Five-Factor Model

Type of Relative	N	E	O	A	C
Identical twins reared together	.43	.52	.48	.42	.47
Fraternal twins reared together	.19	.18	.24	.23	.22
Identical twins reared apart	.31	.42	.34	.19	.33
Fraternal twins reared apart	.23	.08	.14	.03	.09
Heritability	.41	.50	.46	.43	.49
Environmentality	.53	.47	.47	.49	.48
Shared environment	.08	.08	.12	.17	.11

Note: Based on a meta-analysis of 145 studies. N = Neuroticism, E = Extraversion, O = Openness, A = Agreeableness, and C = Conscientiousness.

A similar picture emerges from a study of 660 MZ and 200 DZ twins from Germany and Poland (Riemann, Angleitner, & Strelau, 1997). Each twin and two friends of that twin filled out questionnaires to measure the twin's personality on the five personality factors. The peer's ratings correlated .61 with one another and .55 with the twin's own rating indicating considerable agreement among the three raters in what the twin was like.

As you can see in Figure 6.2, although each of the five factors has moderate heritability—genetics accounted for about 35 to 60% of the variance in self-reported traits—there was a greater effect of nonshared environment on these traits (Plomin & Caspi, 1999). In fact, shared environment accounted for the smallest amount of variance in both self-reports and peer reports.

Here is a puzzle for you to think about. Notice that there is a strong genetic component to the peer ratings. Does this mean that we "inherit" the opinions of our friends? If not, then what might cause this correlation? It's easy to see how our genetic makeup would account for our own ratings, but why would our genetic makeup correlate with our friends' ratings? Stay tuned to find out!

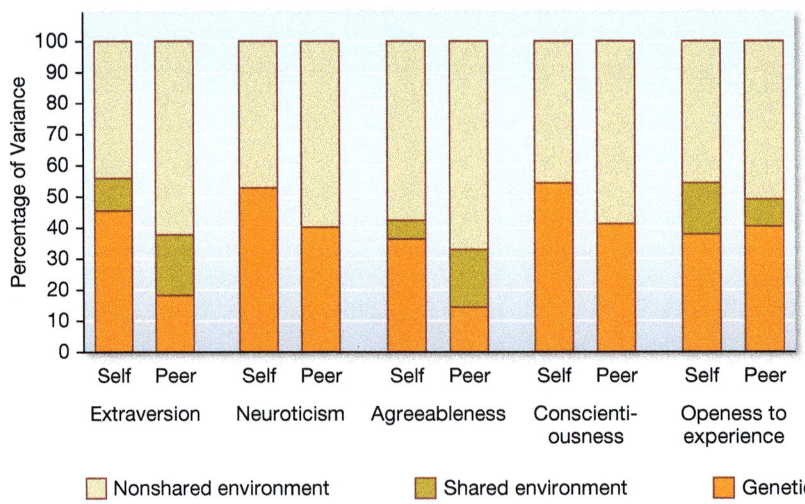

Figure 6.2 Genetic and environmental influences for self-reports of Big Five personality traits. *Source:* From Plomin and Caspi (1999, Figure 9.1, p. 252). From L. A. Pervin & O. P. John, eds., *Handbook of Personality: Theory and Research* (2nd ed., p. 251–276). New York, NY: Guilford Press. Copyright © 1999 Guilford Press. Reprinted with permission.

Then and Now: The Science of Genetics

"When all the human genes are truly known, scientists will have produced a Periodic Table of Life."

Peltonen and McKusick (2001, p. 1224)

To think the whole field of genetics started with a simple Augustinian friar named Gregor Johann Mendel (1822–1884), who was born and lived in what is now the Czech Republic, is mind-boggling. The son of a tenant farmer, he worked on the farm and learned about the grafting of fruit trees from his father. Mendel and his family recognized that he was too smart to simply follow in his father's footsteps working land that he could never own, so he joined the monastery and attended the University of Vienna to earn the credentials he needed to teach high school science. It was there that this farmboy "began to turn himself into one of the greatest experimental biologists of all time" (Mawer, 2006, p. 38). The friars of the Abbey of St. Thomas in Brno were unusual in their desire to practice public ministry, getting involved in political causes of the day (Mendel may have taken part in protests against the Austrian Empire as a student) and fostering intellectual pursuits. Although some brothers were philosophers and others were accomplished composers, the stout, amiable, shy, introverted, sensitive, and nearsighted Mendel spent his free time conducting experiments in the monastery gardens:

> *Throughout each spring and summer the man spent hours and hours tending his plants, pollinating, scoring, labeling, harvesting, drying, putting seeds away for the next year, peering at the world through his gold-rimmed spectacles, puzzling and pondering, counting, and tallying, explaining to anyone who would listen what was going on. Visitors were in the presence of a man inspired—a Beethoven or a Goethe—and all they saw was a dumpy little friar with a sense of irony introducing them to his "children."* (Mawer, 2006, p. 63).

His children were, of course, pea plants—over 28,000 of them! He studied the variation in plants and noticed that sometimes characteristics of plants seemed to skip a generation. He meticulously planted and recorded details of his pea plants and counted their offspring instead of merely generalizing the results as earlier researchers had done (Plomin et al., 2008). In particular, the nearly obsessive Mendel followed seven "characters" of plants over successive generations by crossing one kind of plant with another. These characteristics included smooth or wrinkled peas, yellow or green seeds, white seed coat with white flowers or gray seed coat with purple flowers, smooth or constricted peapods, green or yellow peapods, flowers at the top of the plant or all along the stem, and tall or dwarf plants (Mawer, 2006).

At the time, people believed that inherited characteristics—of people and plants—were blended. That is, the offspring of a pea plant with wrinkled peas and a plant with smooth peas would have moderately wrinkled peas. But that is not what Mendel found. Instead, he found that the next generation was all smooth. What happened to the genetic information for wrinkly peas? Mendel reasoned that the trait must still be present in the genotype even though it was not expressed in the phenotype. If this was true, then the genotype ought to be passed on to the next generation. Indeed, about 75% of the plants in the *next* generation were smooth and 25% were wrinkled. How can it be that each generation can seem so different? From such observations, Mendel developed two hypotheses, part of what we now consider his first law of inheritance (Plomin et al., 2008).

First, each parent plant passes on one form of the gene (Mendel used the word *element*) for a given characteristic to its offspring, who get two forms of the gene, one from each parent (note that different forms of the same gene are called **alleles**). These two alleles can either be the same or different. When the alleles are different, one characteristic will be dominant over the other. However, both alleles will be passed on to the next generation.

For example, say a pea plant with wrinkled peas breeds with a plant that has smooth peas. The next generation will each get some combination of alleles for smooth and wrinkly peas. If smoothness is the dominant characteristic, then the peas will look smooth, but the plants will still carry and pass on the recessive wrinkly pea trait to the next generation (see Figure 6.3). When a trait is recessive, the trait will appear only when a plant receives *two* alleles for the recessive trait—in this case wrinkly peas.

This concept of dominance explains the pattern of seeds Mendel observed in successive generations. In fact, such inheritance patterns where one trait dominates over another is called **Mendelian inheritance** and Mendel is now known as the founder of modern genetics (Mawer, 2006).

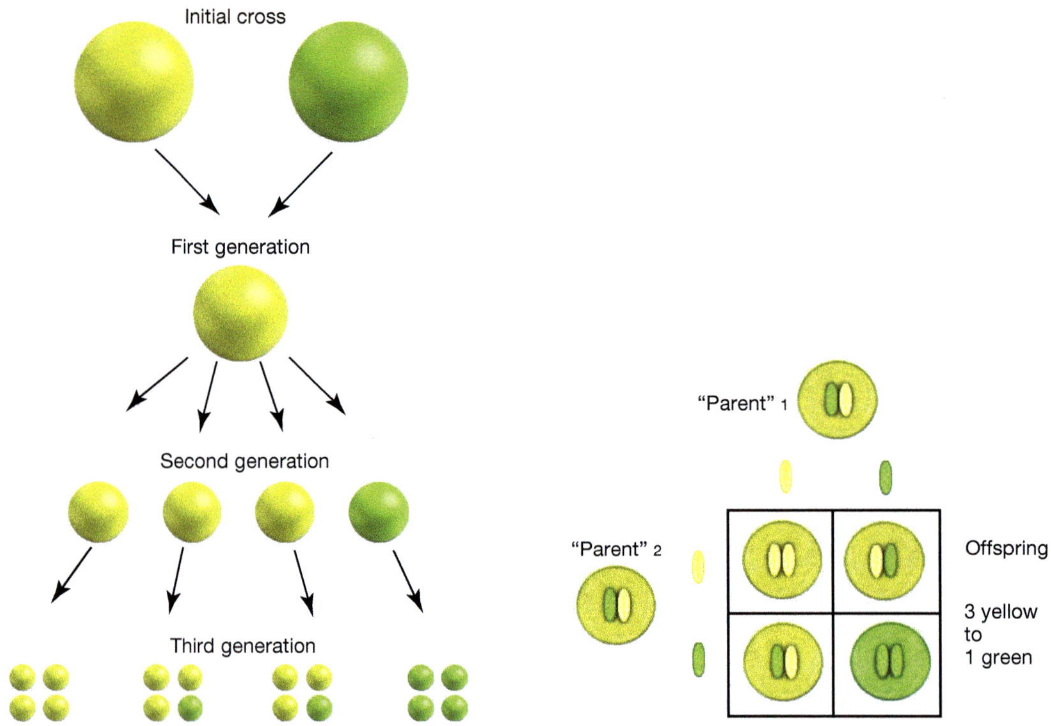

Figure 6.3 Summary of Mendel's experiments with peas. *Source:* From Mawer (2006, p. 54). Gregor Mendel: Planting the seeds of genetics. New York, NY: Abrams.

Fast-forward almost 150 years to the present day. Instead of inheritance of smooth or wrinkled peas, scientists are trying to understand what causes any number of human characteristics: physical diseases, psychological disorders, and even personality traits. Since the start of the century, a collaborative of international scientists have identified the 20,000 to 25,000 genes that make up the human genome (Mawer, 2006; Venter et al., 2001). Whereas about 99.9% of the human DNA sequence is the same for each and every one of us, it's that .1% that does differ that makes us unique individuals (Plomin, DeFries, Craig, & McGuffin, 2003).

Have researchers discovered a genetic, yet noninheritable means by which the environment fundamentally changes human functioning? Apparently so. This exciting new area of genetics research is called **epigenetics**. We know that a **gene** is a sequence of DNA that codes for a specific trait. Genes are composed of coding regions called **exons** and noncoding regions called **introns**. Of the 3.3 billion base pairs of DNA in the human genome, only about 2 to 3% are functioning genes. The remainder of the DNA—nearly 2 meters of it—was once thought to do nothing because it occurs outside genes (Mawer, 2006). This so-called junk DNA is actually turning out to be more interesting than the coding genes themselves. Some of this "junk" appears to orchestrate—alter its regulation to underexpress or overexpress—a nearby gene (Plomin et al., 2003). In fact, some of these noncoding sequences end up changing how the genes function in *direct response to the environment.*

What might this look like? Cole et al. (2007) identified a sample of older American adults, with a median age of 55 years, who scored in the top 15% of the UCLA Loneliness Scale. They were matched to adults of the same sex, age, ethnicity, and socioeconomic status who scored in the bottom 15% of the scale.

Previous research had established that people who are socially isolated are vulnerable to a host of cardiovascular and infectious diseases due to increased levels of the stress hormone cortisol. In the Cole et al. (2007) study both the lonely group and the socially connected group

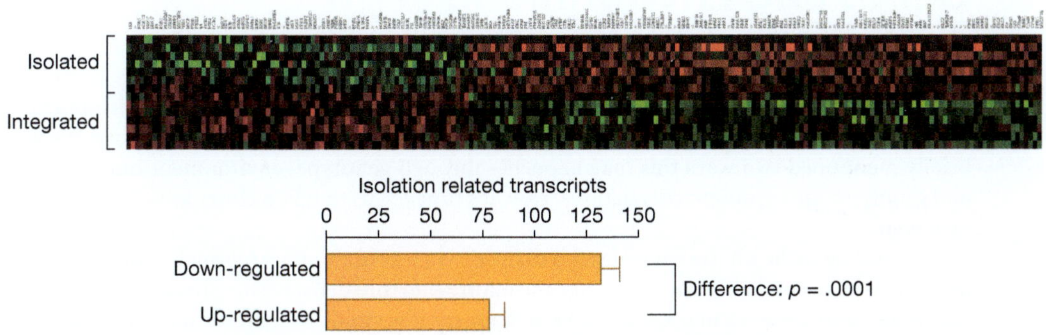

Figure 6.4 Gene expression as a function of loneliness status. The top strip indicates how the genes are functioning in isolated individuals, the bottom strip in connected individuals. Horizontal location indicates function of gene: Those on the left increase disease, those on the right prevent disease. Color indicates activity of genes: Green indicates overexpression (up-regulated) and red indicates underexpression (down-regulated). Here, the genes that code for disease are overexpressed in lonely people (green cells on the left) and underexpressed in socially connected people (red cells on the left). However, the genes that code for disease prevention are underactivated in lonely people (red cells on the right) and overexpressed in socially connected people (green cells on the right). Lonely individuals have significantly more underexpressed genes (red) than socially connected people. *Source:* From Cole et al. (2007, Figure 1, p. R189.4). Cole, S.W., Hawkley, L.C., Arevalo, J.M., Sung, C.Y., Rose, R.M., & Cacioppo, J.T. (2007). Social regulation of gene expression in human leukocytes. *Genome Biology,* 8, R189 (doi:10.1186/gb-2007-8-9-r189)

gave samples of blood for genetic analysis to identify problems in the coding of glucocorticoid response genes that regulate how the body responds to stress hormones.

Figure 6.4 vividly shows the differences between these two groups in gene expression as a function of their feelings of isolation or connection. Significantly more genes that regulate immune functioning were turned down (not expressed at the same levels) in the lonely group than in the socially supported group. Specifically, those cells that protect against disease were turned down (red), whereas genes that increased disease were turned up (green). These results suggest that loneliness directly impacts immune functioning by regulating the specific genes that control immune functioning.

This is how epigenetics works for just one human behavior. As we learn more about genes involved in disorders and about the noncoding sequences of DNA that may turn out to regulate the genes, researchers may develop amazing new ways of treating diseases, both physical and psychological, perhaps in your lifetime. Scientists are searching for similar environmental effects behind diseases including (Carey, 2003) breast cancer, diabetes, high cholesterol, atherosclerosis, Alzheimer's disease, and also schizophrenia (Gottesman, 1991) and bipolar disorder (McGuffin, 2004).

For example, if a disease was inherited, once we have identified the exact gene involved in a disorder we can diagnose or screen who has the gene. Researchers then will be able to use this information to replace faulty genetic code with new and improved code that has been cloned to match as precisely as possible the recipient's genetics (McGuffin, 2004). This is called **positional cloning**.

In the words of one researcher:

> *It is now possible for behavior genetics to move beyond statistical analyses of differences between identical and nonidentical twins and identify individual genes that are related to behavioral outcomes.* (Turkheimer, 2000, p. 163).

This is where the cutting-edge research is happening in behavioral genetics and the results are very exciting. We are finding that often the environment affects people differently depending on a specific genotype. We'll talk about some of these genotype–environmental interactions and the specific genes involved in the next section.

Genes and Environment: A Dialectical Synthesis

So far in this chapter we've been looking at the separate effects of genes and environment. But when it comes to personality, often genes and environment influence each other. We've briefly mentioned two ways this may happen—through genotype–environment interactions and genotype–environment correlations. Now it's time for us to take a closer look at these two processes.

THINK ABOUT IT

Can you think of another example of a dialectic?

According to the philosopher Hegel, a **dialectic** is a way of thinking in which contradictions are seen to be part of a higher truth. Take the nature–nurture debate. This phrase suggests that nature and nurture work in opposition. What happens if we think of "nature" and "nurture" not as opposing forces, but as forces that can be combined or synthesized in some fashion? What if genes and environment worked together as allies instead of working against each other as foes?

Recall our formula from the beginning of the chapter in which the amount of variance in an observed characteristic can be due to genetics, environment, and some combination of the two (Cardno & McGuffin, 2002, p. 40):

$$\text{Phenotype} = \text{Genotype} + \text{Environment} + \text{Gene–environment correlation} \\ + \text{Gene–environment interaction.}$$

Until the 1980s, researchers had been considering genes and environment only as separate factors influencing phenotype. Plomin et al. (1977) suggested that researchers can increase the accuracy of their results—and detect new effects—by specifically testing for two ways in which genes and environment influence each other: a **genotype–environment interaction** and a **genotype–environment correlation.** A genotype–environment interaction occurs when a genotype *responds* differently to an environment; a genotype–environment correlation occurs when a genotype is *exposed* differently to an environment (Loehlin, 1992). These two effects are really examples of how nature and nurture work together and lead us to a higher truth. In this way, nature–nurture is more of a dialectic than a debate.

Two caveats are in order here. First, whereas we may be unable to see the joint effects of genes and environment in a single individual (remember lemonade?) we can explore only genotype–environment interactions and genotype–environment correlations within a population (Plomin et al., 1977). Although we will illustrate these concepts using individual examples, in practice we can really only gauge the genotype–environment effects in a group of people in which we are able to estimate key aspects of their genetic makeup and of their environment.

Second, Plomin et al. (1977) noted that in practice it is sometimes difficult to distinguish genotype–environment interactions from genotype–environment correlations. Researchers must be careful to define and measure aspects of both personality and the environment to truly see which kind of effect is occurring, ideally through a study that looks at these variables over time (Carey, 2003; Plomin et al., 1977). That is, it often comes down to sophisticated statistical tests to determine which effect—an interaction or a correlation—accounts for the data. Next we will define genotype–environment interactions and genotype–environment correlations in more detail and take a closer look at some interesting research findings that illustrate both kinds of effects.

Genotype–Environment Interactions

One way that genetics and environment work on each other is through a genotype–environment interaction. This is when people respond differently to the same environment because of their differing genetic makeup. That is, the environment has a different impact *depending* on a person's genotype (Plomin et al., 1977).

To illustrate how this works, let's go back to the study that opened the chapter. Recall that in a sample of juvenile delinquents in Russia even though many of the boys experienced maternal rejection in their lives (e.g., physical punishment, lack of respect for their point of view, public criticism), only those with a certain genotype experienced clinical depression (Haeffel et al., 2008).

As you can see now, this is an example of genotype–environment interaction. The same environment—maternal rejection—led to clinical depression only in boys with one specific genotype (look back to Figure 6.1). In case you were wondering, maternal rejection was not correlated with clinical depression, so these really are separate effects.

To identify the specific genotype related to depression, researchers took blood samples from the participants. They then analyzed the samples to find out if the young men carried one of the three variations of a gene suspected to be related to depression. This gene (DAT1 or SLC6A3) is an important regulator of the neurotransmitter dopamine. Evidence suggests that prolonged exposure to dopamine may lead to depression.

Despite knowing which genes are related to dopamine functioning, scientists have been unable to prove that these genes cause depression. That is, no genetic difference has been found between depressed and nondepressed people. Recall that in this study researchers initially found no effect of genes alone or environment alone on clinical depression. But when they looked at the combination of a specific genotype with an environment of maternal rejection, that's when they found a significant genotype–environment interaction. In this case, genes and environment interacted with each other to cause a psychological outcome. We might well wonder what other genotype–environment interactions researchers may have missed out on by looking separately at genes and environment!

In fact, remember our earlier discussion of how shared environment effects on the development of personality traits have been difficult to find? Well, Lahey (2009) pointed out that shared environments may impact the personality trait of Neuroticism through genotype–environment interactions. By not considering interactive effects of environment on genes, researchers may have accidentally overestimated genetic effects and underestimated the impact of shared environments.

A second potential genetic risk factor for depression, anxiety, and other mood disorders involves a certain region of the serotonin transporter gene. The thinking here is that depression may be caused by a lack of the neurotransmitter serotonin in the spaces between the neurons. In fact, many popular antidepressant drugs, called selective serotonin reuptake inhibitors (SSRIs), work by blocking the cells that process serotonin so that it stays in the system a bit longer. People actually get two versions of the gene that regulates serotonin one from each parent. This leads to three different variations of the gene depending on which allele a person gets from his or her parents: *ss*, *sl*, and *ll*. These letters stand for the "short" (*s*) and "long" (*l*) versions of the gene. People with the short version (*ss* or *sl*), especially two short alleles (*ss*), are less efficient at regulating serotonin so they are at risk for depression, whereas people with two long alleles (*ll*) may have a measure of protection from depression.

Early research on the link between the short version of the gene and depression was, in the words of one group of researchers, "inconclusive" (Caspi, Sugden, et al., 2003, p. 387). These researchers wondered if there might be an interaction between life stressors and genotype. Using a longitudinal sample of 1,037 men and women in New Zealand who were studied extensively from ages 3 to 26, they were able to divide the sample into three groups depending on their genotype of the serotonin transporter promoter gene: *ss*, *sl*, and *ll*. In addition, participants noted if any of 14 major life events occurred to them between the ages of 21 and 26. These events included things such as a major change in employment, housing, finances, health, and relationships. Finally, participants were asked if they experienced any symptoms of depression, thoughts of suicide, suicide attempts, or a depressive episode in the past year. Interestingly, there were no differences in number of life stressors among the three genotype groups suggesting that genes did not cause people to experience more life stressors.

As you can see in Figure 6.5, for all of the outcomes studied, participants with the *ss* genotype were the most at risk whereas participants with the *ll* genotype were the least at risk for depression or symptoms of depression (Caspi, Sugden, et al., 2003). Participants with the *sl* genotype fell somewhere in between. In all cases, the environment—that is, having more life stressors—put a person at greater risk for symptoms of depression or a full-blown depressive episode, but there was little impact of genotype on symptoms or incidence of depression. However, when a person with a specific genotype—*ss*—encountered stressful life events, the person was particularly likely to develop depression or depressive symptoms. Thus the interaction between genes and environment was statistically significant in every instance (Caspi, Sugden, et al., 2003). No wonder early research was inconsistent; apparently it takes both the environment and a special genotype for a person to experience depression in his or her lifetime (see Monroe & Reid, 2008, for a review and Munafò & Flint, 2009, for a criticism of this work).

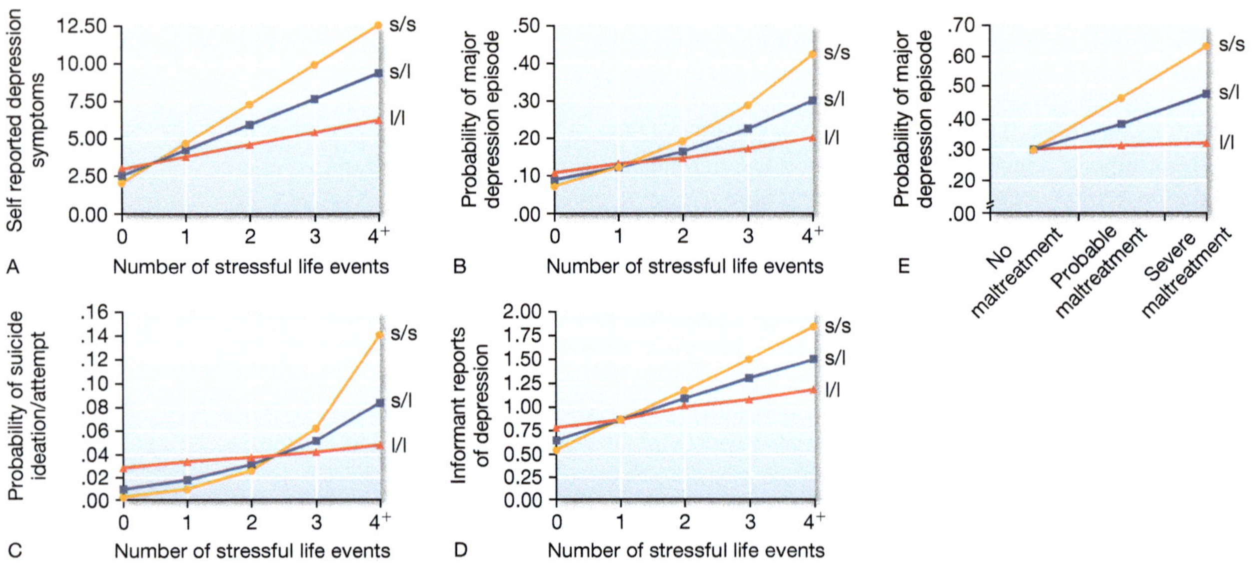

Figure 6.5 Incidence of clinical depression symptoms as a function of genotype and life stressors. *Source:* From Caspi, Sugden, et al. (2003, Figures 1 and 2, p. 388). From Caspi, A., Sugden, K., Moffitt, T. E., Taylor, A., Craig, I. W., Harrington, H., et al. (2003). Influence of life stress on depression: Moderation by a polymorphism in the 5-HTT gene. Science, 301(5631), 386–389. Reprinted by permission of the American Association for the Advancement of Science.

THINK ABOUT IT

What does it mean to say that there is a genotype–environment interaction between negative life events and Neuroticism? What kinds of people are more vulnerable to negative events?

These are just two examples of an increasing trend in personality where researchers look for genotype–environment interactions. One group of researchers suggested that such interactions probably occur more often than we realize, especially for psychopathology (Krueger, Markon, & Bouchard, 2003). Interactions between genes and environment have been found to account for religious upbringing lessening the impulsiveness of high sensation seekers (Boomsma, de Geus, van Baal, & Koopmans, 1999), parental bonding and family functioning decreasing emotional instability (Jang, Dick, Wolf, Livesley, & Paris, 2005), a monoamine oxidase A (MAOA) promoter gene and parental harshness increasing adolescent antisocial behavior (Krueger et al., 2003), the DRD2 gene and stress increasing alcoholism (Madrid, MacMurray, Lee, Anderson, & Comings, 2001), and negative life events increasing Neuroticism (Lahey, 2009).

Genotype–Environment Correlations

"We propose that development is indeed the result of nature *and* nurture but that genes drive experience. Genes are components in a system that organizes the organism to experience its world."

Scarr and McCartney (1983, p. 425)

It seems easy enough to think about the effects of genes and environment. However, researchers soon discovered a curious finding: Measures of environments showed evidence of genetic influence (Plomin et al., 2002). In other words, measures of environmental effects, such as parenting styles on, or peer ratings of, a child, for example, were not strictly environmental. That is, people's personalities affected the environments they found themselves in and also how they described those environments on questionnaires. This puzzle soon led to a breakthrough in personality research which led to many interesting findings (Plomin et al., 2002). Perhaps you can see now how this accounts for the genetic component of peer ratings in the twin study of the five-factor model of personality study discussed earlier (Riemann et al., 1997). Did you figure it out?

The answer to this puzzle is that people construct their environments. That is, we select, modify, create, and re-create in our memory (and on questionnaires administered by researchers!) our experiences (Plomin et al., 2002). When people's experiences are related to—that is, are correlated with—their genetic inclinations we call this a genotype–environment correlation. A genotype–environment correlation occurs when people with a gene for a specific characteristic find themselves in an environment that fosters—or discourages—the expression of that characteristic (Carey, 2003). Or, to think of it another way, people with different genotypes are exposed to different environments *depending on that genotype* (Plomin et al., 1977). Because both the genes and the environment occur together, we can't be sure which is causing the manifestation of that characteristic.

Table 6.4 Three Types of Genotype–Environment Correlations

Type	Description	Pertinent Environment
Passive	Children are given genotypes linked to their environment	Natural parents and siblings
Reactive	Children are reacted to on the basis of their genotype	Anybody
Active	Children seek an environment conductive to their genotype	Anytime

Source: From Plomin et al. (1977, Table 1, p. 311). Plomin, R., DeFries, J. C., & Loehlin, J. C. (1977). Genotype-environment interaction and correlation in the analysis of human behavior. *Psychological Bulletin*, 84(2), 309–322.

Another way to think about genotype–environment correlations goes back to our definition of what a correlation is. In this case, a genotype–environment correlation occurs when people with high "genetic values" (i.e., a strong genetic predisposition for a specific characteristic) find themselves in environments with high values (i.e., environments that push for that characteristic; Carey, 2003). Similarly, a genotype–environment correlation also occurs when people with low genetic values (i.e., no particular inclination for a characteristic) find themselves in environments with low values (i.e., environments with no particular demand for that characteristic). The interesting question is *why* people with certain genotypes find themselves in certain environments. There are three possible explanations, which lead to three types of correlations: passive, reactive, and active (Plomin et al., 1977; see Table 6.4).

Types of Genotype–Environment Correlations. When parents provide both the genes and an environment that is favorable (or unfavorable) to the development of those genes, we observe a **passive genotype–environment correlation** (Plomin et al., 1977). For example, imagine parents who have very high verbal skills—gifted even—who not only pass on these fabulous genes to their children but also provide a home filled with books and games and other activities that are likely to help their children develop good verbal skills (Plomin et al., 1977). Because the children did nothing to cause the environment to provide these resources—and in fact, such resources may have been in place long before children were even on the scene—the genotype–environment correlation is passive.

SEE FOR YOURSELF

Can you identify a characteristic you may have developed due to a passive genetic–environment correlation between your genes and the environment your parents created for you?

But consider the same highly verbal parents who see that their baby is babbling constantly and often seems as if she is trying to communicate to them. These parents may purposely try to engage the baby in conversation (e.g., "Who's Mama's precious little baby?") or encourage the baby to talk ("Say Dada!"). Because the parents are responding to something in the child, we call this kind of relationship a **reactive genotype–environment correlation** (Plomin et al., 1977). Just as with the passive genotype–environment correlation, we can't be sure if the child's genetics or environment caused him or her to be so verbal because the two co-occur.

Genotype–environment correlations occur when people are exposed to different environments depending on their genotype. Genotype–environment correlations can be passive, reactive, or active. This young boy is already an accomplished ballet dancer. Do you think this is an example of a passive or active genotype–environment correlation?

SEE FOR YOURSELF

Can you identify a characteristic you may have developed due to a reactive genotype–environment correlation between your genes and the environment your parents created for you?

SEE FOR YOURSELF

Can you identify a characteristic you may have developed due to an active genotype–environment correlation between your genes and the environment your parents created for you?

SEE FOR YOURSELF

Can you identify a characteristic you may have failed to develop due to a passive, reactive, or active genotype–environment correlation between your genes and the environment your parents created for you?

Now imagine that this child of highly verbal parents is spending the weekend with grandparents (with whom the child shares about 25% of her genes, on average). Suppose the baby babbles to both grandparents, but because Grandma is in the middle of cooking dinner, Grandpa investigates the noises coming from the crib. "Are you trying to talk, little baby?" he says while laughing. "Go on, tell me all about it." For the rest of the weekend, the baby crawls to Grandpa whereever he is and continues to babble at him. This would be an example of an **active genotype–environment correlation**. Here, the parents (or grandparents, in this case) have provided both the genes and the environment. The baby can either interact with Grandma or Grandpa, but she chooses to "talk" with, and indeed seeks out, the more responsive one, Grandpa. Here, her high verbal ability comes from both her genetics and the environment, but she is the one who specifically seeks out the environment.

Genotype–environment correlations can be either positive or negative. The previous examples illustrated **positive genotype–environment correlations**, where conditions were favorable for developing a certain characteristic. In this case, verbal behavior was encouraged in the child either by an environment that just happens to encourage verbal ability (passive), responded to the child (reactive), or which the child sought out (active). But we could easily imagine scenarios where verbal behavior was discouraged or where the child found herself in an environment that was unfavorable for developing verbal ability because the TV was on all the time (passive), where there was an older sibling who talked at the baby and interrupted her babbling (reactive), or where the baby preferred the company of a quiet relative to a talkative relative (active). These would be examples of **negative genotype–environment correlations.**

In the case of a negative genotype–environment correlation, people with high genetic values for a characteristic find themselves in environments with low values for that characteristic. Often, the result is that the environment discourages the expression of that characteristic. The inverse is also possible, where people with low genetic values for a characteristic find themselves in environments with high values for that characteristic. They may end up developing some of their less pronounced characteristics.

Keep in mind that whether a genotype–environment correlation is positive or negative does *not* depend on the ultimate outcome—the development or lack of development of a characteristic—but on the relative levels of the genotype and the environment (see Table 6.5). Often positive genotype–environment correlations encourage a specific characteristic whereas negative genotype–environment correlations discourage a specific characteristic, but this is not necessarily the case. For example, Scarr and McCartney (1983) described a negative passive genotype–environment correlation where parents might be highly skilled readers and have a child who is not reading so well. They may decide to enhance the environment for this child—because they are good at reading and not because of anything about the child—more than they might for a child who is already reading well or more than parents who are not highly skilled readers would do if they had such a child.

For personality characteristics, Raymond Cattell suggested that negative genotype–environment correlations were probably more common than positive correlations (Plomin et al., 1977). For example, a person who is too domineering will probably be put in her place by her peers, indicating a negative reactive genotype–environment correlation (Plomin et al., 1977). Although it may seem odd that people would seek out environments that work

Table 6.5 Positive and Negative Genotype–Environment Correlations

Type of Correlation	Genotype	Environment
Positive	High	High
Positive	Low	Low
Negative	High	Low
Negative	Low	High

Note: High or low indicates the amount of the characteristic present in the genes or in the environment.

against their natural inclinations, as is the case with negative active genotype–environment correlations, you could imagine a person who is anxious and easily upset seeking out stable and reassuring friends to calm him down (Plomin et al., 1977). What would a negative passive genotype–environment correlation look like? Imagine parents who are emotionally reactive and get angry easily and yet have a child who is similar to them in this regard. They are very likely to squelch any unseemly reaction in their child (Plomin et al., 1977).

According to Scarr and McCartney (1983):

> *People seek out environments they find compatible and stimulating. We all select from the surrounding environment some aspects to which to respond, learn about, or ignore. Our selections are correlated with motivational, personality, and intellectual aspects of our genotypes. The active genotype → environment effect, we argue, is the most powerful connection between people and environments and the most direct expression of the genotype in experience. (p. 427)*

Note that these three types of correlations differ in terms of what constitutes the environment. For passive, the environment is the child's immediate environment: parents, siblings, and other members of the household that he or she is born into. For reactive, the environment is any person who interacts with or responds to the child. For example, peers may reciprocate the affection of a sociable child or teachers may provide an enriched environment for a student who shows special aptitude. Finally, for active, the environment can be other people or indeed, the physical environment itself. For example, a musical child can rush to play the piano at Grandma's house, gravitate to the music store at the mall, or even bang on pots and pans in the kitchen to make music. Further, the relative importance of these environments—and hence the type of genotype–environment correlation that is operating—shifts over the life span. For example, passive genotype–environment influences may decrease from infancy to adolescence whereas active genotype–environment influences increase as the child experiences more of the world away from home.

What's the Evidence? Researching Genotype–Environment Correlations. What evidence is there for this idea that social experiences are evoked by one's genotype? One way to find a reactive genotype–environment correlation is to look at twin studies over time, where we might be able to see changes in a child's behavior and if these changes correlate with changes in the environment. For example, comparing MZ twins and DZ twins, Narusyte, Andershed, Neiderhiser, and Lichtenstein (2007) found that childhood aggression was related to parental criticism that was related, in turn, to self-reported antisocial behavior in adolescence. The researchers suggested that this is an example of a reactive genotype–environment correlation: Children at risk for antisocial behavior are indeed more aggressive than children not at risk, and they are also more likely to elicit negative reactions in their parents.

A similar reactive genotype–environment correlation was found in an adoption study, where teens' antisocial behavior was correlated with both their biological parent's substance abuse or antisocial personality (genotype) and with the harsh or inconsistent disciplinary practices of their adoptive mothers and fathers (environment; Ge et al., 1996).

Another way to investigate a reactive genotype–environment correlation is to create one in the laboratory, something researchers have only begun to explore. Burt conducted an experiment in which undergraduate men were put in a controlled situation to see how they interacted with others (Burt, 2008, 2009). Would they elicit certain reactions from their peers as a function of their genotype? If they did, then this would demonstrate a reactive genotype–environment correlation in an experimental situation.

In this unusual experiment, Burt identified men who had either a G-allele or an A-allele for a certain serotonin receptor gene (5-HTR2A) and had them interact in small groups on two tasks. In previous research, the G-allele was associated with an increased response to selective serotonin reuptake inhibitors (SSRIs). When normal volunteers are given SSRIs they act friendlier (indeed, recall that the administration of SSRIs has been shown to reduce clinical depression). Burt hypothesized that participants with the G-allele would be more likely than

Can one person's gene code for other people's responses? A reactive genotype–environmental correlation occurs when our genes, as expressed in our personalities, influence the environment around us.

those with the A-allele to be friendly, smile, and socialize with others, eventually becoming one of the most popular members of the group.

The groups were charged with two sets of tasks: answering brainteasers and planning two parties, one with a strict budget and the other with unlimited funds and the instructions to "be creative and have fun." Afterward the participants rated how much they liked each person in their group. The researchers created a composite of group ratings for each participant indicating how likable each participant was perceived to be by the others in the group. In addition, observers took note of how often a participant joked, supported, or suggested, that the group break rules either during the planning of their party or as part of the entertainment at the party. For example, some participants suggested that they somehow steal money to supplement their limited budget, or, in the case of the creative second party, provide alcohol (even though all participants were under the legal drinking age), marijuana, other drugs, or even prostitutes. An overall composite measure of rule-breaking was created from these observer ratings along with self-reports. Burt reasoned that among young people, particularly men, rule-breaking is a way of establishing status and popularity.

As predicted, men with the G-allele were more likely to suggest or encourage rule-breaking and were, in fact, rated as more popular by their group-mates compared to men with the A-allele (Burt, 2008, 2009). As Burt explained, the funny thing is that it is biologically impossible for a person's gene to code for *another* person's response. It seems that this particular gene codes for behaviors like rule-breaking that then lead people to be perceived as more likable. Burt's results suggested that genes code for a particular behavior (e.g., rule-breaking) and for the social consequences of that behavior (e.g., popularity). This is an example of a positive reactive genotype–environment correlation, where genes cause behavior to which the environment, in this case other people, then responds.

Burt (2009) recognized that rule-breaking is just one aspect of popularity. He suggested that researchers explore other aspects of personality that are known to affect liking such as social dominance, extraversion, physical attractiveness, and perceived athletic ability, or specific gestures that affect first impressions such as eye contact and smiling, to see if these might help explain the correlation between genotype and popularity.

There are many examples of gene–environment correlations, especially in developmental psychology. Correlations between genes and environment have been found for adolescents' perceptions of parental warmth or conflict (Johnson & Krueger, 2006), physical punishment and misbehavior (Jaffee et al., 2004), parental harshness and antisocial behavior (Krueger et al., 2003), memories of childhood environment (Krueger et al., 2003), and family bonding and neuroticism (Jang et al., 2005).

The movie *Gattaca* portrays a futuristic world where parents select the exact genetic makeup of their offspring. As individuals and society we need to decide what to do with the results of genetic research.

The Personality of Everyday Life

What can genetics research do for us?

If the concept of cloning or prenatal genetic testing makes you nervous, you are not alone. Keep in mind that genetics is a tool, not a goal, so that understanding the human genome is really only the beginning (Carey, 2003). As a tool, genetics is value-neutral. The real moral question is, what do we do with the findings from genetic research? To make these kinds of decisions it is imperative that informed citizens understand what genetics can and can't do so that we can be involved in the issues and not leave the debate solely to the scientists or lawmakers.

One way that findings from genetics have been misused in the past includes the eugenics movement, which claimed the moral superiority of one group over another (witness the so-called Final Solution of the Nazis) and even went so far as to control who gets to reproduce or not (for example, the United States for a time instituted forced sterilization of people with supposedly lower IQs as part of a eugenics program; Mawer, 2006). Another questionable use of genetics is cloning, although some say human cloning may be nearly impossible (Smith, 2005).

Although gene therapy involving the cloning of the common cold virus has successfully cured some diseases, such as severe combined immune deficiency syndrome (SCIDS; Smith, 2005), sometimes the risk of this type of therapy is too great (Collins & Vedantam, 1999). The biggest fear may be that genetic testing will be used to modify or even select for traits that are not disease related such as gender, intelligence, eye color, physical strength, or sociability—a brave new world indeed!

And yet, the knowledge gleaned from genetics can be used for a world of good. Some possible goals currently under investigation by geneticists include identification of genetic risk indicators (Plomin et al., 2008), medical treatments individually tailored to our DNA (Plomin et al., 2008), the conservation of endangered animal and plant species (Mawer, 2006), a better understanding of evolution (Carey, 2003), identification of our common ancestors (Mawer, 2006), increased use of forensic evidence (Reilly, 2006), cures for cancers and other diseases (Reilly, 2006; Smith, 2005), improvement of crop production (Reilly, 2006), prevention of famine (Reilly, 2006), solutions to historical puzzles (Reilly, 2006), and a better use of the limited resources of our planet (Reilly, 2006).

We must not forget our discussion from the beginning of this chapter: Personality is lemonade. For personality psychologists, knowing that even when a personality trait

"[I]f you really want to engineer your child's IQ, stick to the old ways. Send them to Eton. And if governments want to improve the nations' intelligence, the best value for money would be to double teachers' salaries."

Geneticist Steve Jones as cited in Smith (2005, p. 188)

"There is no gene for the human spirit."
Tagline from the 1997 movie *Gattaca,* written and directed by Andrew Niccol

is genetic the environment still has a big impact suggests that mental health may be a public health issue (e.g., Lahey, 2009). Problems such as depression and antisocial behavior (Carey, 2003) may be preventable whereas increasing intelligence, cooperation, and a host of other prosocial traits may be possible. With genes as an early warning system (Plomin et al., 2003), behavioral and environmental engineering will work with genetic engineering (Plomin et al., 2008). It all starts with an understanding of the genetic—and environmental—influences on human behavior and personality (e.g., Moffitt, Caspi, & Rutter, 2006).

Chapter Summary

Study and **Review** on **mysearchlab.com**
Go online for more resources to help you review.

How does genetics make us who we are? Basically, we develop the personalities we do, as a result of the following:

1. Inheritance of specific genes (e.g., Gregor Mendel and his pea plants).
2. Genes and environment working together as co-actors (e.g., heritability, environmentality).
3. Genes and environment working together as a dialectic (e.g., genotype–environment interactions, genotype–environment correlations).
4. Environmental toxins, stressors, social situations (both nurturing and neglecting) that affect the regulation of specific genes (e.g., turning them up or turning them down). Environmental effects can not only trigger negative outcomes in a genetically vulnerable person, but can also offset genetic vulnerabilities for maladaptive outcomes.

Researchers often study twins (both MZ twins and DZ twins) to estimate the heritability of personality traits. Because it would be impossible to conduct a true experiment, researchers have relied on correlational designs (e.g., family studies, twin studies, adoption studies) to study genetics and personality.

We discovered that there are two ways of estimating heritability (double the difference in correlations between MZ twins and DZ twins; the correlation between MZ twins raised apart), and that heritability refers to a particular trait in a particular population at a particular time. Further, a phenotype (the observed manifestation of a gene) is a function of a person's genotype, environment (including shared and nonshared aspects), the interaction of both, the correlation of both, and measurement error.

"It was a self-evident truth to the signers of the American Declaration of Independence that all men are created equal. . . . The founding fathers of America were not so naïve as to think that all people are created identical. The essence of a democracy is that all people should have legal equality despite their genetic differences."
Plomin et al. (2008, p. 91)

When it comes to personality, just about every individual difference characteristic you can think of (e.g., Neuroticism, Extraversion, Openness, Agreeableness, Conscientiousness) has a substantial genetic component (about 40% of the variance in a trait is due to genetics) and a substantial environmental component. Further, the important part of the environment appears to be the part that is unique to us and not shared with siblings raised in the same environment (also about 40%).

Where once psychologists who studied the genetics of personality concerned themselves with the heritability of personality characteristics, they now think in terms of epigenetics, or how genes are regulated by events or experiences in the environment. In fact, researchers believe that most aspects of personality including mental and physical illness are controlled by complex genetics (e.g., involving many genes, interacting with the environment, and even regulated by environmental conditions). One day we may be able to treat disorders with drugs or behavioral interventions that operate at the level of gene regulation. With the foundation of this chapter you will be able to understand both the ethical issues and the implications of research breakthroughs that will no doubt emerge in your lifetime in this most exciting area of personality research. In sum: "This ain't your parents' genetics!"

Review Questions

1. If the real question is not whether genes or environment affect personality, what is the right question to ask? What does it mean to say that nature and nurture transact?
2. What is heritability? What is environmentality? What is shared environment? What is nonshared environment?
3. What are the two common ways of estimating heritability? What assumptions does each of these formulas depend on?
4. What is the logic behind adoption and twin studies? What makes a correlational design different from a true experiment? Based on research with twins, does sense of humor run in families? Why might this be?
5. What can we say about the heritability of the traits of Neuroticism, Extraversion, Openness, Agreeableness, and Conscientiousness? Which is more important for developing these traits, shared or nonshared environment?
6. How do noncoding sequences of DNA change how genes function in direct response to the environment? Explain using the example of loneliness and immune functioning.
7. What does it mean to say that genes and environment are a dialectic? What is a dialectic? What is a genotype–environment interaction? Describe how genotype and life stressors interact to cause clinical depression according to research by Caspi, Sugden, et al. (2003).
8. What is a genotype–environment correlation? What is a positive genotype–environment correlation? What is a negative genotype–environment correlation? What are passive, reactive, and active genotype–environment correlations?
9. What are some uses genetic research may be put to in the near future?

"Genetic diversity is the essence of life."
Plomin et al. (2008, p. 91)

Key Terms

Genotype
Behavioral genetics
Phenotype
Heritability
Environmentality
Shared environment
Nonshared environment
Monozygotic (MZ) twins
Dizygotic (DZ) twins
MZA twins
Equal environments assumption
Assumption of representativeness
Selective placement
Alleles
Mendelian inheritance
Epigenetics
Genes
Exon
Intron
Positional cloning
Dialectic
Genotype–environment interaction
Genotype–environment correlation
Passive genotype–environment correlation
Reactive genotype–environment correlation
Active genotype–environment correlation
Positive genotype–environment correlation
Negative genotype–environment correlation

A complex blend of genetic and environmental influences leads members of this three-generation Inupiat family of western Alaska to be both alike and different in physical characteristics and behavior.

© LAWRENCE MIGDALE/STOCK BOSTON, LLC

2

Biological and Environmental Foundations

"It's a girl," announces the doctor, who holds up the squalling little creature while her new parents gaze with amazement at their miraculous creation.

"A girl! We've named her Sarah!" exclaims the proud father to eager relatives waiting by the telephone for word about their new family member.

As we join these parents in thinking about how this wondrous being came into existence and imagining her future, we are struck by many questions. How could this baby, equipped with everything necessary for life outside the womb, have developed from the union of two tiny cells? What ensures that Sarah will, in due time, roll over, reach for objects, walk, talk, make friends, learn, imagine, and create—just like every other normal child born before her? Why is she a girl and not a boy, dark-haired rather than blond, calm and cuddly instead of wiry and energetic? What difference will it make that Sarah is given a name and place in one family, community, nation, and culture rather than another?

To answer these questions, this chapter takes a close look at the foundations of development: heredity and environment. Because nature has prepared us for survival, all humans have features in common. Yet each human being is also unique. Take a moment to jot down the most obvious similarities and differences in physical characteristics and behavior for several of your friends and their parents. Did you find that one person shows combined features of both parents, another resembles just one parent, whereas a third is not like either parent? These directly observable characteristics are called **phenotypes.** They depend in part on the individual's **genotype**—the complex blend of genetic information that determines our species and influences all our unique characteristics. Yet throughout life, phenotypes are also affected by the person's history of experiences in the environment.

We begin our discussion of development at the moment of conception, an event that establishes the hereditary makeup of the new individual. In the first section of this chapter, we review basic genetic principles that help explain similarities and differences between us in appearance and behavior. Next, we turn to aspects of the environment that play powerful roles throughout the lifespan. In the final section of this chapter, we take up the question of how nature and nurture *work together* to shape the course of development.

Genetic Foundations

Each of us is made up of trillions of separate units called *cells.* Inside every cell is a control center, or *nucleus,* that contains rodlike structures called **chromosomes,** which store and transmit genetic information. Human chromosomes come in 23 matching pairs (an exception is the XY pair in males, which we will discuss shortly). Each pair member corresponds to the other in size, shape, and genetic functions. One is inherited from the mother and one from the father (see Figure 2.1).

The Genetic Code

Chromosomes are made up of a chemical substance called **deoxyribonucleic acid, or DNA.** As Figure 2.2 shows, DNA is a long, double-stranded molecule that looks like a twisted ladder. Each rung of the ladder consists of a specific pair of chemical substances called *bases,* joined together between the two sides. It is this sequence of bases that provides genetic instructions. A **gene** is a segment of DNA along the length of the chromosome. Genes can be of different lengths—perhaps 100 to several thousand ladder rungs long. An estimated 30,000 genes lie along the human chromosomes.

We share some of our genetic makeup with even the simplest organisms, such as bacteria and molds, and most of it with other mammals, especially primates. Between 98 and 99 percent of chimpanzee and human DNA is identical. This means that only a small portion of our heredity is responsible

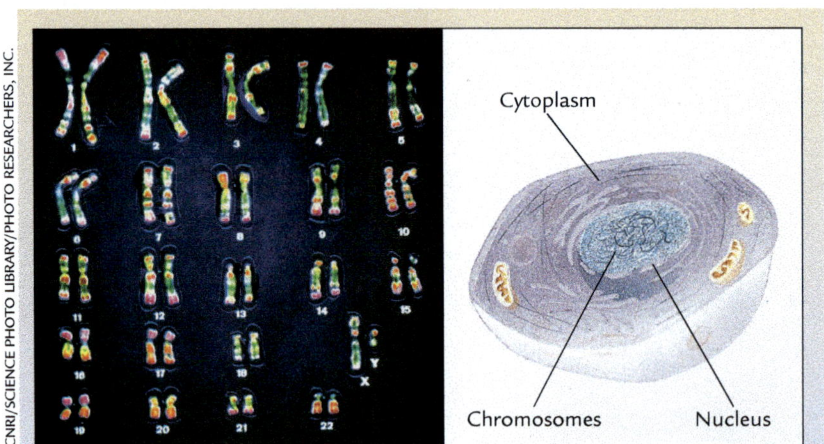

■ FIGURE 2.1 **A karyotype, or photograph, of human chromosomes.** The 46 chromosomes on the left were isolated from a body cell (shown on the right), stained, greatly magnified, and arranged in pairs according to decreasing size of the upper "arm" of each chromosome. Note the twenty-third pair, XY. The cell donor is a male. In a female, the twenty-third pair would be XX.

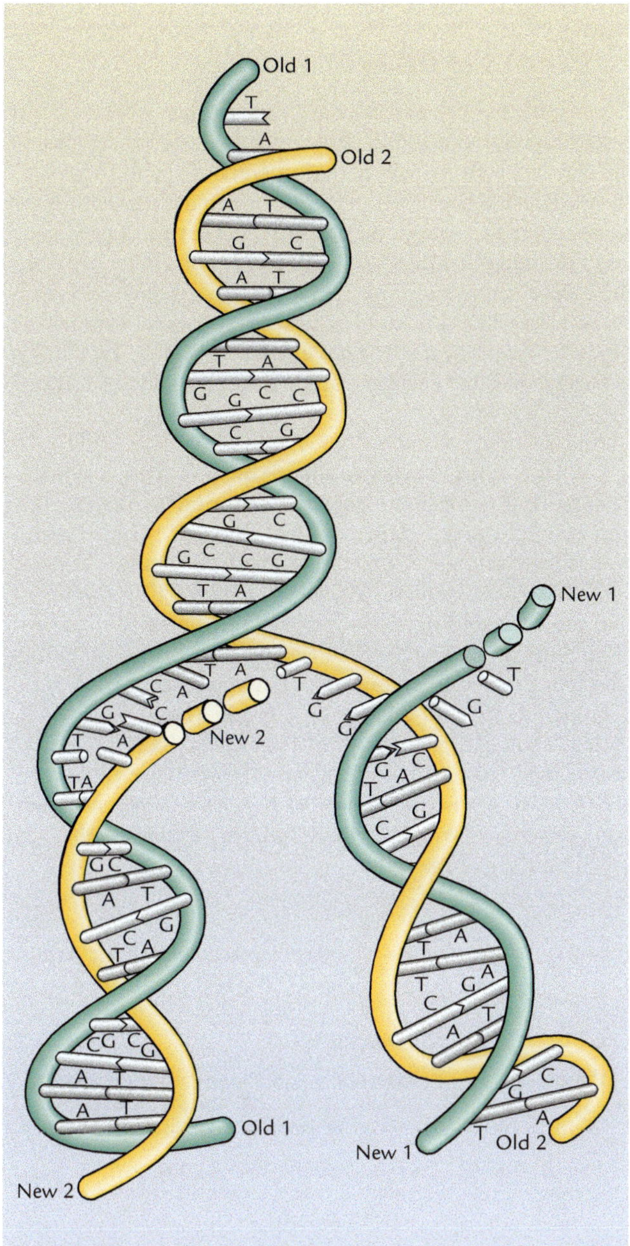

■ **FIGURE 2.2 DNA's ladderlike structure.** This figure shows that the pairings of bases across the rungs of the ladder are very specific: adenine (A) always appears with thymine (T), and cytosine (C) always appears with guanine (G). Here, the DNA ladder duplicates by splitting down the middle of its ladder rungs. Each free base picks up a new complementary partner from the area surrounding the cell nucleus.

for the traits that make us human, from our upright gait to our extraordinary language and cognitive capacities. And the genetic variation from one human to the next is even less! Individuals around the world are about 99.1 percent genetically identical (Gibbons, 1998). Only a tiny quantity of DNA contributes to human variation in traits and capacities.

A unique feature of DNA is that it can duplicate itself through a process called **mitosis.** This special ability permits the one-celled fertilized ovum to develop into a complex human being composed of a great many cells. Refer again to Figure 2.2, and you will see that during mitosis, the chromosomes copy themselves. As a result, each new body cell contains the same number of chromosomes and identical genetic information.

Genes accomplish their task by sending instructions for making a rich assortment of proteins to the *cytoplasm,* the area surrounding the cell nucleus. Proteins, which trigger chemical reactions throughout the body, are the biological foundation on which our characteristics are built. How do humans, with far fewer genes than scientists once thought (only twice as many as the worm or fly), manage to develop into such complex beings? The answer lies in the proteins our genes make, which break up and reassemble in staggering variety—about 10 to 20 million altogether. In simpler species, the number of proteins is far more limited. Furthermore, the communication system between the cell nucleus and cytoplasm, which fine-tunes gene activity, is more intricate in humans than in simpler organisms. Within the cell, a wide range of environmental factors modify gene expression (Davies, Howell, & Gardner, 2001). So even at this microscopic level, biological events are the result of *both* genetic and nongenetic forces.

The Sex Cells

New individuals are created when two special cells called **gametes,** or sex cells—the sperm and ovum—combine. A gamete contains only 23 chromosomes, half as many as a regular body cell. Gametes are formed through a cell division process called **meiosis,** which ensures that a constant quantity of genetic material is transmitted from one generation to the next. When sperm and ovum unite at conception, the cell that results, called a **zygote,** will again have 46 chromosomes.

In *meiosis,* the chromosomes pair up and exchange segments, so that genes from one are replaced by genes from another. Then chance determines which member of each pair will gather with others and end up in the same gamete. These events make the likelihood of nontwin offspring of the same two parents being genetically the same extremely slim—about 1 in 700 trillion (Gould & Keeton, 1997). Therefore, meiosis helps us understand why siblings differ from each other, even though they have features in common because their genotypes come from the same pool of parental genes.

In the male, four sperm are produced when meiosis is complete. Also, the cells from which sperm arise are produced continuously throughout life. For this reason, a healthy man can father a child at any age after sexual maturity. In the female, gamete production results in just one ovum. In addition, the female is born with all her ova already present in her ovaries, and she can bear children for only 3 to 4 decades. Still, there are plenty of female sex cells. About 1 to 2 million are present at birth, 40,000 remain at adolescence, and approximately 350 to 450 will mature during a woman's childbearing years (Moore & Persaud, 1998).

Male or Female?

Return to Figure 2.1, and note that 22 of the 23 pairs of chromosomes are matching pairs, called **autosomes.** The twenty-third pair consists of **sex chromosomes.** In females, this pair is called XX; in males, it is called XY. The X is a relatively long chromosome, whereas the Y is short and carries little genetic material. When gametes are formed in males, the X and Y chromosomes separate into different sperm cells. In females, all gametes carry an X chromosome. Therefore, the sex of the new organism is determined by whether an X-bearing or a Y-bearing sperm fertilizes the ovum.

Multiple Births

Ruth and Peter, a couple I know well, tried for several years to have a child, without success. When Ruth reached age 33, her doctor prescribed a fertility drug, and twins—Jeannie and Jason—were born. Jeannie and Jason are **fraternal,** or **dizygotic, twins,** the most common type of multiple birth, resulting from the release and fertilization of two ova. Therefore, Jeannie and Jason are genetically no more alike than ordinary siblings. Older maternal age (up to 35 to 39 years) and fertility drugs are major causes of multiple births—factors responsible for the dramatic rise in twinning since the 1970s (Bortolus et al., 1999). As Table 2.1 shows, other genetic and environmental factors are also involved.

Twins can be created in another way. Sometimes a zygote that has started to duplicate separates into two clusters of cells that develop into two individuals. These are called **identical,** or **monozygotic, twins** because they have the same genetic makeup. The frequency of identical twins is unrelated to the factors listed in Table 2.1. It is about the same around the world—about 3 of every 1,000 births (Tong, Caddy, & Short, 1997). Animal research has uncovered a variety of environmental influences that prompt this type of twinning, including temperature changes, variation in oxygen levels, and late fertilization of the ovum.

During their early years, children of single births are often healthier and develop more rapidly than twins (Mogford-Bevan, 1999). Jeannie and Jason were born early (as are most twins)—3 weeks before Ruth's due date. As we will see in Chapter 3, like other premature infants, they required special care after birth. When the twins came home from the hospital, Ruth and Peter had to divide time between them. Perhaps because neither baby got quite as much attention as the average single infant, Jeannie and Jason walked and talked several months later than other children their age, although both caught up in development by middle childhood (Lytton & Gallagher, 2002).

Patterns of Genetic Inheritance

Jeannie has her parents' dark, straight hair, whereas Jason is curly-haired and blond. Patterns of genetic inheritance—the way genes from each parent interact—explain these outcomes. Recall that except for the XY pair in males, all chromosomes come in corresponding pairs. Two forms of each gene occur at the same place on the autosomes, one inherited from the mother and one from the father. If the genes from both parents are alike, the child is **homozygous** and will display the inherited trait. If the genes are different, then the child is **heterozygous,** and relationships between the genes determine the trait that will appear.

● **Dominant–Recessive Inheritance.** In many heterozygous pairings, **dominant–recessive inheritance** occurs: Only one gene affects the child's characteristics. It is called *dominant;* the second gene, which has no effect, is called *recessive.* Hair color is an example. The gene for dark hair is dominant (we can represent it with a capital *D*), whereas the one for blond hair is recessive (symbolized by a lowercase *b*). A child who inherits a homozygous pair of dominant genes *(DD)* and a child who inherits a heterozygous pair *(Db)* will be dark-haired, even though their genotypes differ. Blond hair (like Jason's) can result only from having two recessive genes *(bb).* Still, heterozygous individuals with just one recessive gene *(Db)* can pass that trait to their children. Therefore, they are called **carriers** of the trait.

Table 2.1 Maternal Factors Linked to Fraternal Twinning

Factor	Description
Ethnicity	Occurs in 4 per 1,000 births among Asians, 8 per 1,000 births among whites, 12 to 16 per 1,000 births among blacks[a]
Family history of twinning	Occurs more often among women whose mothers and sisters gave birth to fraternal twins
Age	Rises with maternal age, peaking between 35 and 39 years, and then rapidly falls
Nutrition	Occurs less often among women with poor diets; occurs more often among women who are tall and overweight or of normal weight as opposed to slight body build
Number of births	Is more likely with each additional birth
Fertility drugs and in vitro fertilization	Is more likely with fertility hormones and in vitro fertilization (see page 54), which also increase the chances of triplets to quintuplets

[a]Worldwide rates, not including multiple births resulting from use of fertility drugs.

Source: Bortolus et al., 1999; Mange & Mange, 1998.

■ These identical, or monozygotic, twins were created when a duplicating zygote separated into two clusters of cells, and two individuals with the same genetic makeup developed. Identical twins look alike, and as we will see later in this chapter, tend to resemble each other in a variety of psychological characteristics.

Some human characteristics that follow the rules of dominant–recessive inheritance are given in Table 2.2 on the right and Table 2.3 on page 48. As you can see, many disabilities and diseases are the product of recessive genes. One of the most frequently occurring recessive disorders is *phenylketonuria,* or *PKU.* It affects the way the body breaks down proteins contained in many foods. Infants born with two recessive genes lack an enzyme that converts one of the basic amino acids that make up proteins (phenylalanine) into a by-product essential for body functioning (tyrosine). Without this enzyme, phenylalanine quickly builds to toxic levels that damage the central nervous system. By 1 year, infants with PKU are permanently retarded.

Despite its potentially damaging effects, PKU provides an excellent illustration of the fact that inheriting unfavorable genes does not always lead to an untreatable condition. All U.S. states and Canadian provinces require that each newborn be given a blood test for PKU. If the disease is found, doctors place the baby on a diet low in phenylalanine. Children who receive this treatment show delayed development of higher-order cognitive skills, such as planning and problem solving, in infancy and childhood because even small amounts of phenylalanine interfere with brain functioning. But as long as dietary treatment begins early and continues, children with PKU usually attain an average level of intelligence and have a normal lifespan (Pietz et al., 1998; Smith, Klim, & Hanley, 2000).

In dominant–recessive inheritance, if we know the genetic makeup of the parents, we can predict the percentage of children in a family who are likely to display or carry a trait. Figure 2.3 (see page 49) illustrates this for PKU. Notice that for a child to inherit the condition, each parent must carry a recessive gene.

Only rarely are serious diseases due to dominant genes. Think about why this is so. Children who inherit the dominant gene always develop the disorder. They seldom live long enough to reproduce, and the harmful dominant gene is eliminated from the family's heredity in a single generation. Some dominant disorders, however, do persist. One of them is *Huntington disease,* a condition in which the central nervous system degenerates. Why has this disease endured? Its symptoms usually do not appear until age 35 or later, after the person has passed the dominant gene to his or her children.

● **Codominance.** In some heterozygous circumstances, the dominant–recessive relationship does not hold completely. Instead, we see **codominance,** a pattern of inheritance in which both genes influence the person's characteristics.

The *sickle cell trait,* a heterozygous condition present in many black Africans, provides an example. *Sickle cell anemia* (see Table 2.3) occurs in full form when a child inherits two recessive genes. They cause the usually round red blood cells to become sickle (or crescent-moon) shaped, especially under low-oxygen conditions. The sickled cells clog the blood vessels and block the flow of blood. Individuals who have the disorder suffer severe attacks involving intense pain, swelling, and tissue damage. They generally die in the first 20 years of life; few live past age 40. Heterozygous individuals are protected from the disease under most circumstances. However, when

Table 2.2 Examples of Dominant and Recessive Characteristics

Dominant	Recessive
Dark hair	Blond hair
Normal hair	Pattern baldness
Curly hair	Straight hair
Nonred hair	Red hair
Facial dimples	No dimples
Normal hearing	Some forms of deafness
Normal vision	Nearsightedness
Farsightedness	Normal vision
Normal vision	Congenital eye cataracts
Normally pigmented skin	Albinism
Double-jointedness	Normal joints
Type A blood	Type O blood
Type B blood	Type O blood
Rh-positive blood	Rh-negative blood

Note: Many normal characteristics that were previously thought to be due to dominant–recessive inheritance, such as eye color, are now regarded as due to multiple genes. For the characteristics listed here, there still seems to be general agreement that the simple dominant–recessive relationship holds.

Source: McKusick, 1998.

Table 2.3 Examples of Dominant and Recessive Diseases

Disease	Description	Mode of Inheritance	Incidence	Treatment
Autosomal Diseases				
Cooley's anemia	Pale appearance, retarded physical growth, and lethargic behavior begin in infancy.	Recessive	1 in 500 births to parents of Mediterranean descent	Frequent blood transfusion; death from complications usually occurs by adolescence.
Cystic fibrosis	Lungs, liver, and pancreas secrete large amounts of thick mucus, leading to breathing and digestive difficulties.	Recessive	1 in 2,000 to 2,500 Caucasian births; 1 in 16,000 births to North Americans of African descent	Bronchial drainage, prompt treatment of respiratory infection, dietary management. Advances in medical care allow survival with good life quality into adulthood.
Phenylketonuria (PKU)	Inability to metabolize the amino acid phenylalanine, contained in many proteins, causes severe central nervous system damage in the first year of life.	Recessive	1 in 8,000 births	Placing the child on a special diet results in average intelligence and normal lifespan. Subtle difficulties with planning and problem-solving are often present.
Sickle cell anemia	Abnormal sickling of red blood cells causes oxygen deprivation, pain, swelling, and tissue damage. Anemia and susceptibility to infections, especially pneumonia, occur.	Recessive	1 in 500 births to North Americans of African descent	Blood transformations, painkillers, prompt treat-ment of infection. No known cure; 50 percent die by age 20.
Tay-Sachs disease	Central nervous system degeneration, with onset at about 6 months, leads to poor muscle tone, blindness, deafness, and convulsions.	Recessive	1 in 3,600 births to Jews of European descent and to French Canadians	None. Death by 3 to 4 years of age.
Huntington disease	Central nervous system degeneration leads to muscular coordination difficulties, mental deterioration, and personality changes. Symptoms usually do not appear until age 35 or later.	Dominant	1 in 18,000 to 25,000 births	None. Death occurs 10 to 20 years after symptom onset.
Marfan syndrome	Tall, slender build; thin, elongated arms and legs. Heart defects and eye abnormalities, especially of the lens. Excessive lengthening of the body results in a variety of skeletal defects.	Dominant	1 in 20,000 births	Correction of heart and eye defects sometimes possible. Death from heart failure in young adulthood is common.
X-Linked Diseases				
Duchenne muscular dystrophy	Degenerative muscle disease. Abnormal gait, loss of ability to walk between 7 and 13 years of age.	Recessive	1 in 3,000 to 5,000 male births	None. Death from respiratory infection or weakening of the heart muscle usually occurs in adolescence.
Hemophilia	Blood fails to clot normally. Can lead to severe internal bleeding and tissue damage.	Recessive	1 in 4,000 to 7,000 male births	Blood transfusions. Safety precautions to prevent injury.
Diabetes insipidus	Insufficient production of the hormone vasopressin results in excessive thirst and urination. Dehydration can cause central nervous system damage.	Recessive	1 in 2,500 male births	Hormone replacement.

Note: For recessive disorders listed, carrier status can be detected in prospective parents through a blood test or genetic analyses. For all disorders listed, prenatal diagnosis is available (see page 53).
Sources: Behrman, Kliegman, & Arvin, 1996; Chodirker et al., 2001; Gott, 1998; Grody, 1999; Knoers et al., 1993; McKusick, 1998; Schulman & Black, 1997.

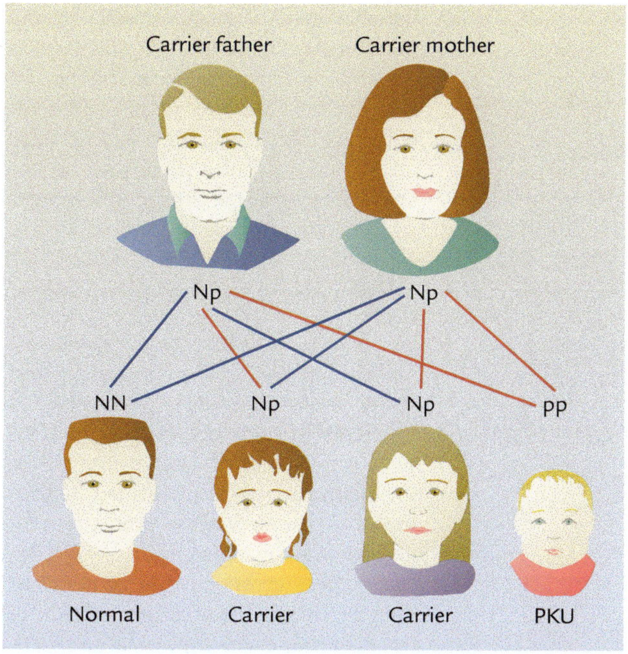

FIGURE 2.3 Dominant–recessive mode of inheritance, as illustrated by PKU. When both parents are heterozygous carriers of the recessive gene (*p*), we can predict that 25 percent of their offspring are likely to be normal (*NN*), 50 percent are likely to be carriers (*Np*), and 25 percent are likely to inherit the disorder (*pp*). Notice that the PKU-affected child, in contrast to his siblings, has light hair. The recessive gene for PKU affects more than one trait. It also leads to fair coloring.

they experience oxygen deprivation—for example, at high altitudes or after intense physical exercise—the single recessive gene asserts itself, and a temporary, mild form of the illness occurs.

The sickle cell gene is common among black Africans for a special reason. Carriers of it are more resistant to malaria than are individuals with two genes for normal red blood cells. In Africa, where malaria is common, these carriers survived and reproduced more frequently than others, leading the gene to be maintained in the black population.

X-Linked Inheritance. Males and females have an equal chance of inheriting recessive disorders carried on the autosomes, such as PKU and sickle cell anemia. But when a harmful recessive gene is carried on the X chromosome, **X-linked inheritance** applies. Males are more likely to be affected because their sex chromosomes do not match. In females, any recessive gene on one X chromosome has a good chance of being suppressed by a dominant gene on the other X. But the Y chromosome is only about one-third as long and therefore lacks many corresponding genes to override those on the X. A well-known example is *hemophilia,* a disease in which the blood fails to clot normally. Figure 2.4 on page 50 shows its greater likelihood of inheritance by male children whose mothers carry the abnormal gene.

Besides X-linked disorders, many sex differences reveal the male to be at a disadvantage. Rates of miscarriage, infant and childhood deaths, birth defects, learning disabilities, behavior disorders, and mental retardation are greater for boys (Halpern, 1997). It is possible that these sex differences can be traced to the genetic code. The female, with two X chromosomes, benefits from a greater variety of genes. Nature, however, seems to have adjusted for the male's disadvantage. Worldwide, about 106 boys are born for every 100 girls, and judging from miscarriage and abortion statistics, an even greater number of males are conceived (Pyeritz, 1998).

Nevertheless, in recent decades the proportion of male births has declined in many industrialized countries, including Canada, Denmark, Germany, Finland, the Netherlands, Norway, and the United States (Jongbloet et al., 2001). Some researchers blame increased occupational and community exposure to pesticides for a reduction in sperm counts overall, especially Y-bearing sperm. But the precise cause is unknown.

Genetic Imprinting. More than 1,000 human characteristics follow the rules of dominant–recessive and codominant inheritance (McKusick, 1998). In these cases, whichever parent contributes a gene to the new individual, the gene responds in the same way. Geneticists, however, have identified some exceptions. In **genetic imprinting,** genes are *imprinted,* or chemically marked, in such a way that one member of the pair (either the mother's or the father's) is activated, regardless of its makeup. The imprint is often temporary: It may be erased in the next generation, and it may not occur in all individuals (Everman & Cassidy, 2000).

Imprinting helps us understand certain puzzling genetic patterns. For example, children are more likely to develop diabetes if their father, rather than their mother, suffers from it. And people with asthma or hay fever tend to have mothers, not fathers, with the illness. Imprinting may also explain why Huntington disease, when inherited from the father, tends to emerge at an earlier age and to progress more rapidly (Navarrete, Martinez, & Salamanca, 1994).

Genetic imprinting can also operate on the sex chromosomes, as *fragile X syndrome* reveals. In this disorder, an abnormal repetition of a sequence of DNA bases occurs on the X chromosome, damaging a particular gene. Fragile X syndrome is the most common inherited cause of mild to moderate mental retardation. It has also been linked to 2 to 3 percent of cases of autism, a serious emotional disorder of early childhood involving bizarre, self-stimulating behavior and delayed or absent language and communication. Research reveals that the defective gene at the fragile site is expressed only when it is passed from mother to child (Ashley-Koch et al., 1998).

Mutation. How are harmful genes created in the first place? The answer is **mutation,** a sudden but permanent change in a segment of DNA. A mutation may affect only one or two genes, or it may involve many genes, as in the chromosomal disorders we will discuss shortly. Some mutations occur

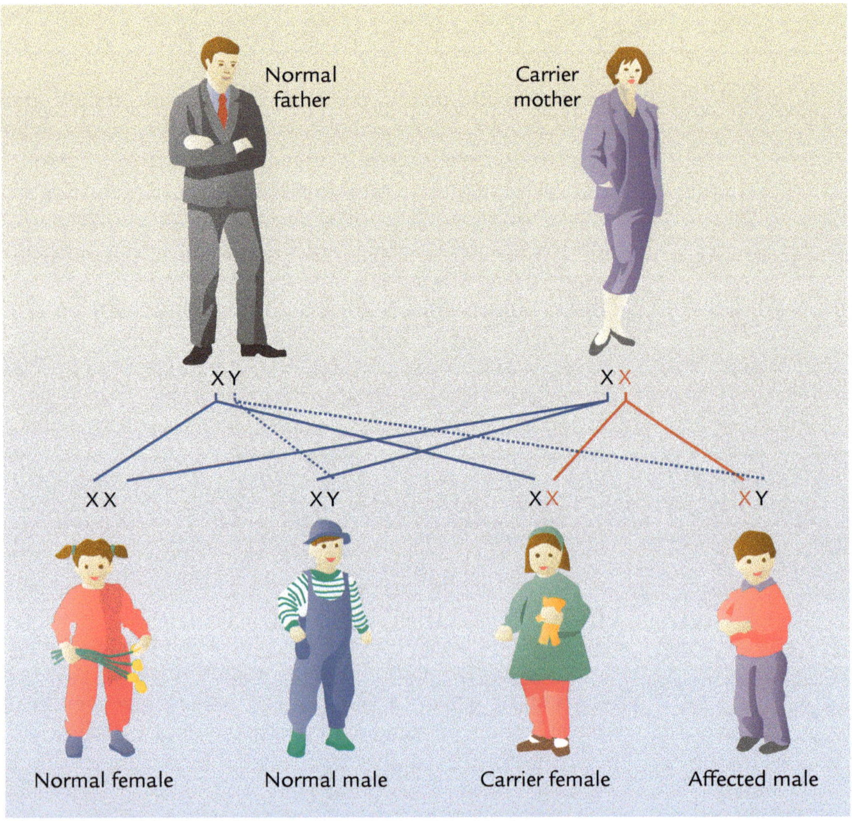

FIGURE 2.4 X-linked inheritance. In the example shown here, the gene on the father's X chromosome is normal. The mother has one normal and one abnormal recessive gene on her X chromosomes. By looking at the possible combinations of the parents' genes, we can predict that 50 percent of male children are likely to have the disorder and 50 percent of female children are likely to be carriers of it.

spontaneously, simply by chance. Others are caused by hazardous environmental agents in our food supply or the air we breathe.

Although nonionizing forms of radiation—electromagnetic waves and microwaves—have no demonstrated impact on DNA, ionizing (high-energy) radiation is an established cause of mutation. Women who receive repeated doses before conception are more likely to miscarry or give birth to children with hereditary defects. Genetic abnormalities, such as physical malformations and childhood cancer, are also higher when fathers are exposed to radiation in their occupations (Brent, 1999). However, infrequent and mild exposure to radiation does not cause genetic damage. Instead, high doses over a long period impair DNA.

Polygenic Inheritance. So far, we have discussed patterns of inheritance in which people either display a particular trait or do not. These cut-and-dried individual differences are much easier to trace to their genetic origins than are characteristics that vary continuously among people, such as height, weight, intelligence, and personality. These traits are due to **polygenic inheritance,** in which many genes determine the characteristic in question. Polygenic inheritance is complex, and much about it is still unknown. In the final section of this chapter, we will discuss how researchers infer the influence of heredity on human attributes when they do not know the precise patterns of inheritance.

Chromosomal Abnormalities

Besides harmful recessive genes, abnormalities of the chromosomes are a major cause of serious developmental problems. Most chromosomal defects result from mistakes during meiosis, when the ovum and sperm are formed. A chromosome pair does not separate properly, or part of a chromosome breaks off. Because these errors involve more DNA than problems due to single genes, they usually produce many physical and mental symptoms.

Down Syndrome. The most common chromosomal disorder, occurring in 1 out of every 800 live births, is *Down syndrome.* In 95 percent of cases, it results from a failure of the twenty-first pair of chromosomes to separate during meiosis, so the new individual inherits three of these chromosomes rather than the normal two. In other less frequent forms, an extra broken piece of a twenty-first chromosome is present. Or an error occurs during the early stages of mitosis, causing some but not all body cells to have the defective chromosomal makeup (called a *mosaic* pattern). In these instances, because less genetic material is involved, symptoms of the disorder are less extreme (Hodapp, 1996).

The consequences of Down syndrome include mental retardation, memory and speech problems, limited vocabulary, and slow motor development (Chapman & Hesketh, 2000). Affected individuals also have distinct physical features—a short, stocky build, a flattened face, a protruding tongue, almond-shaped eyes, and an unusual crease running across the palm of the hand. In addition, infants with Down syndrome are often born with eye cataracts and heart and intestinal defects. Three decades ago, most died by early adulthood. Today, because of medical advances, many survive into their sixties and beyond (Selikowitz, 1997).

Infants with Down syndrome smile less readily, show poor eye-to-eye contact, and explore objects less persistently. But when parents encourage them to engage with their surroundings, Down syndrome children develop more favorably (Sigman, 1999). They also benefit from infant and preschool

■ The facial features of the 9-year-old boy on the left are typical of Down syndrome. Although his intellectual development is impaired, this child is doing well because he is growing up in a stimulating home where his special needs are met and he is loved and accepted. Here he collaborates with his normally developing 4-year-old brother in making won ton dumplings.

intervention programs, although emotional, social, and motor skills improve more than intellectual performance (Hines & Bennett, 1996). Thus, environmental factors affect how well children with Down syndrome fare.

The risk of Down syndrome rises dramatically with maternal age, from 1 in 1,900 births at age 20, to 1 in 300 at age 35, to 1 in 30 at age 45 (Halliday et al., 1995; Meyers et al., 1997). Why is this so? Geneticists believe that the ova, present in the woman's body since her own prenatal period, weaken over time. As a result, chromosomes do not separate properly as they complete the process of meiosis at conception. In about 5 to 10 percent of cases, the extra genetic material originates with the father. However, Down syndrome and other chromosomal abnormalities are not related to advanced paternal age (Muller et al., 2000; Savage et al., 1998). In these instances, the mutation occurs for other unknown reasons.

● **Abnormalities of the Sex Chromosomes.** Disorders of the autosomes other than Down syndrome usually disrupt development so severely that miscarriage occurs. When such babies are born, they rarely survive beyond early childhood. In contrast, abnormalities of the sex chromosomes usually lead to fewer problems. In fact, sex chromosome disorders often are not recognized until adolescence when, in some of the deviations, puberty is delayed. The most common problems involve the presence of an extra chromosome (either X or Y) or the absence of one X in females.

A variety of myths exist about individuals with sex chromosome disorders. For example, males with *XYY syndrome* are not necessarily more aggressive and antisocial than XY males. And most children with sex chromosome disorders do not suffer from mental retardation. Instead, their intellectual problems are usually very specific. Verbal difficulties—for example, with reading and vocabulary—are common among girls with *triple X syndrome (XXX)* and boys with *Klinefelter syndrome (XXY)*, both of whom inherit an extra X chromosome. In contrast, girls with *Turner syndrome (XO)*, who are missing an X, have trouble with spatial relationships—for example, drawing pictures, telling right from left, following travel directions, and noticing changes in facial expressions (Geschwind et al., 2000; Money, 1993; Ross, Zinn, & McCauley, 2000). These findings tell us that adding to or subtracting from the usual number of X chromosomes results in particular intellectual deficits. At present, geneticists do not know why.

Ask Yourself

REVIEW

Explain the genetic origins of PKU and Down syndrome. Cite evidence that both heredity and environment contribute to the development of individuals with these disorders.

APPLY

Gilbert's genetic makeup is homozygous for dark hair. Jan's is homozygous for blond hair. What color is Gilbert's hair? How about Jan's? What proportion of their children are likely to be dark-haired? Explain.

CONNECT

Referring to ecological systems theory (Chapter 1, pages 24–25), explain why parents of children with genetic disorders often experience increased stress. What factors, within and beyond the family, can help these parents support their children's development?

www.

Reproductive Choices

Two years after they were married, Ted and Marianne gave birth to their first child. Kendra appeared to be a healthy infant, but by 4 months her growth slowed. Diagnosed as having Tay-Sachs disease (see Table 2.3), Kendra died at 2 years of age. Ted and Marianne were devastated by

Kendra's death. Although they did not want to bring another infant into the world who would endure such suffering, they badly wanted to have a child. They began to avoid family get-togethers, where little nieces and nephews were constant reminders of the void in their lives.

In the past, many couples with genetic disorders in their families chose not to bear a child at all rather than risk the birth of an abnormal baby. Today, genetic counseling and prenatal diagnosis help people make informed decisions about conceiving, carrying a pregnancy to term, or adopting a child.

Genetic Counseling

Genetic counseling is a communication process designed to help couples assess their chances of giving birth to a baby with a hereditary disorder and choose the best course of action in view of risks and family goals (Shiloh, 1996). Individuals likely to seek counseling are those who have had difficulties bearing children, such as repeated miscarriages, or who know that genetic problems exist in their families. In addition, women who delay childbearing past age 35 are candidates for genetic counseling. After this time, the overall rate of chromosomal abnormalities rises sharply, from 1 in every 190 to as many as 1 in every 10 pregnancies at age 48 (Meyers et al., 1997).

If a family history of mental retardation, physical defects, or inherited diseases exists, the genetic counselor interviews the couple and prepares a *pedigree,* a picture of the family tree in which affected relatives are identified. The pedigree is used to estimate the likelihood that parents will have an abnormal child, using the same genetic principles discussed earlier in this chapter. In the case of many disorders, blood tests or genetic analyses can reveal whether the parent is a carrier of the harmful gene. Carrier detection is possible for all of the recessive diseases listed in Table 2.3, as well as others, and for fragile X syndrome.

When all the relevant information is in, the genetic counselor helps people consider appropriate options. These include "taking a chance" and conceiving, choosing from among a variety of reproductive technologies (see the Social Issues box on pages 54–55), or adopting a child.

Prenatal Diagnosis and Fetal Medicine

If couples who might bear an abnormal child decide to conceive, several **prenatal diagnostic methods**—medical procedures that permit detection of problems before birth—are available (see Table 2.4). Women of advanced maternal age are prime candidates for *amniocentesis* or *chorionic villus sampling* (see Figure 2.5). Except for *ultrasound* and *maternal blood analysis,* prenatal diagnostic methods should not be used routinely, as they have some chance of injuring the developing organism.

Prenatal diagnosis has led to advances in fetal medicine. For example, by inserting a needle into the uterus, doctors can

Table 2.4 Prenatal Diagnostic Methods

Method	Description
Amniocentesis	The most widely used technique. A hollow needle is inserted through the abdominal wall to obtain a sample of fluid in the uterus. Cells are examined for genetic defects. Can be performed by 11 to 14 weeks after conception but safest after 15 weeks; 1 to 2 more weeks are required for test results. Small risk of miscarriage.
Chorionic villus sampling	A procedure that can be used if results are desired or needed very early in pregnancy. A thin tube is inserted into the uterus through the vagina, or a hollow needle is inserted through the abdominal wall. A small plug of tissue is removed from the end of one or more chorionic villi, the hairlike projections on the membrane surrounding the developing organism. Cells are examined for genetic defects. Can be performed at 6 to 8 weeks after conception, and results are available within 24 hours. Entails a slightly greater risk of miscarriage than does amniocentesis. Also associated with a small risk of limb deformities, which increases the earlier the procedure is performed.
Fetoscopy	A small tube with a light source at one end is inserted into the uterus to inspect the fetus for defects of the limbs and face. Also allows a sample of fetal blood to be obtained, permitting diagnosis of such disorders as hemophilia and sickle cell anemia as well as neural defects (see below). Usually performed between 15 and 18 weeks after conception, but can be done as early as 5 weeks. Entails some risk of miscarriage.
Ultrasound	High-frequency sound waves are beamed at the uterus; their reflection is translated into a picture on a videoscreen that reveals the size, shape, and placement of the fetus. By itself, permits assessment of fetal age, detection of multiple pregnancies, and identification of gross physical defects. Also used to guide amniocentesis, chorionic villus sampling, and fetoscopy. When used five or more times, may increase the chances of low birth weight.
Maternal blood analysis	By the second month of pregnancy, some of the developing organism's cells enter the maternal bloodstream. An elevated level of alpha-fetoprotein may indicate kidney disease, abnormal closure of the esophagus, or neural tube defects, such as anencephaly (absence of most of the brain) and spina bifida (bulging of the spinal cord from the spinal column). Isolated cells can be examined for genetic defects, such as Down syndrome.
Preimplantation genetic diagnosis	After in vitro fertilization and duplication of the zygote into a cluster of about eight to ten cells, one or two cells are removed and examined for hereditary defects. Only if that sample is free of detectable genetic disorders is the fertilized ovum implanted in the woman's uterus.

Sources: Eiben et al., 1997; Lissens & Sermon, 1997; Moore & Persaud, 1998; Newnham et al., 1993; Quintero, Puder, & Cotton, 1993; Sutcliffe, 2002; Wapner, 1997; Willner, 1998.

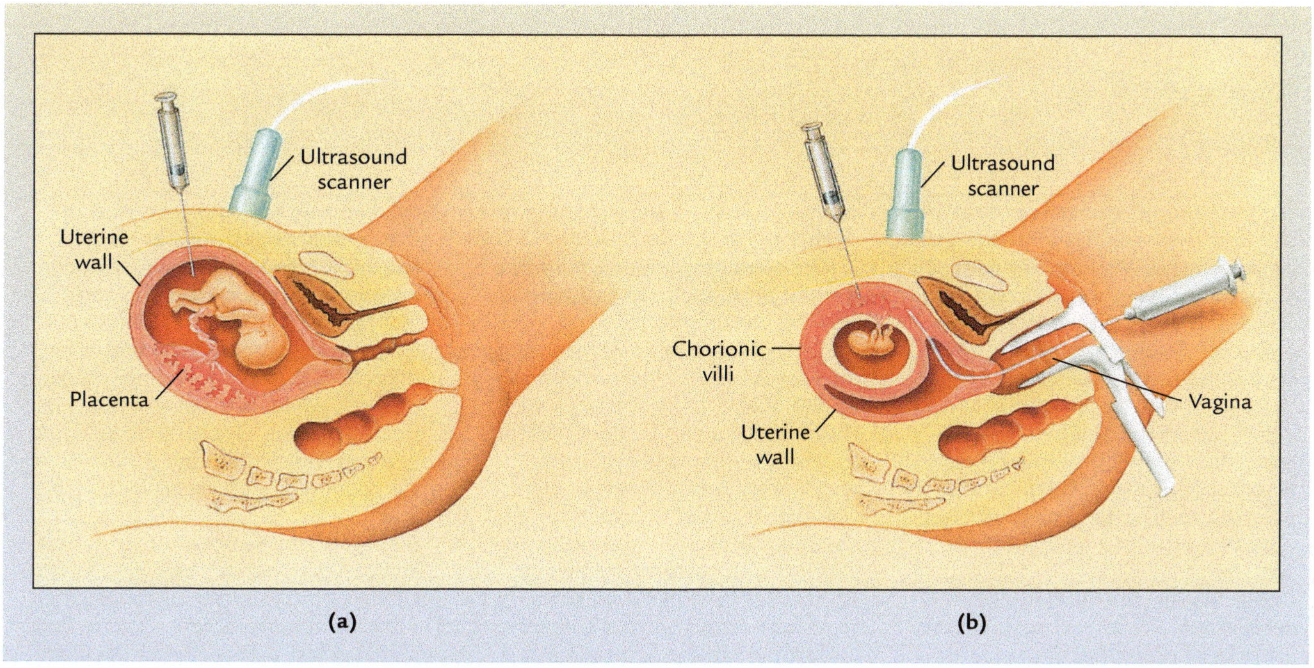

■ **FIGURE 2.5 Amniocentesis and chorionic villus sampling.** Today, more than 250 defects and diseases can be detected before birth using these two procedures. (a) In amniocentesis, a hollow needle is inserted through the abdominal wall into the uterus. Fluid is withdrawn and fetal cells are cultured, a process that takes about 3 weeks. (b) Chorionic villus sampling can be performed much earlier in pregnancy, at 6 to 8 weeks after conception, and results are available within 24 hours. Two approaches to obtaining a sample of chorionic villus are shown: inserting a thin tube through the vagina into the uterus and inserting a needle through the abdominal wall. In both amniocentesis and chorionic villus sampling, an ultrasound scanner is used for guidance. (From K. L. Moore & T. V. N. Persaud, 1998, *Before We Are Born,* 5th ed., Philadelphia: Saunders, p. 115. Adapted by permission of the publisher and author.)

administer drugs to the fetus. Surgery has been performed to repair such problems as heart and lung malformations, urinary tract obstructions, and neural defects. A fetus with a hereditary immune deficiency received a bone marrow transplant from his father that succeeded in creating a normally functioning immune system (Flake et al., 1996).

These techniques frequently result in complications, the most common being premature labor and miscarriage (James, 1998). Yet parents may be willing to try almost any option, even if there is only a slim chance of success. Currently, the medical profession is struggling with how to help parents make informed decisions about fetal surgery. One suggestion is that the advice of an independent counselor be provided—a doctor or nurse who understands the risks but is not involved in doing research on or performing the procedure.

Advances in *genetic engineering* also offer hope for correcting hereditary defects. As part of the Human Genome Project—an ambitious, international research program aimed at deciphering the chemical makeup of human genetic material (genome)—researchers have mapped the sequence of all human DNA base pairs. Using that information, they are "annotating" the genome—identifying all its genes and their functions, including their protein products and what they do. A major goal is to understand the estimated 4,000 human disorders, those due to single genes and those resulting from a complex interplay of multiple genes and environmental factors.

Already, thousands of genes have been identified, including those involved in hundreds of diseases, such as cystic fibrosis, Huntington disease, Duchenne muscular dystrophy, Marfan syndrome, and some forms of cancer (Jimeniz-Sanchez, Childs, & Valle, 2001). As a result, new treatments are being explored, such as *gene therapy*—delivering DNA carrying a functional

■ The Human Genome Project is leading to new gene-based treatments for hereditary disorders such as Alzheimer's disease. When the daughter and granddaughter of this Alzheimer's victim reach late adulthood, they may be spared this devastating illness.

Social Issues

The Pros and Cons of Reproductive Technologies

Some couples decide not to risk pregnancy because of a history of genetic disease. Many others—in fact, one-sixth of all couples who try to conceive—discover that they are sterile. And some never-married adults and gay and lesbian partners want to bear children. Today, increasing numbers of individuals are turning to alternative methods of conception—technologies that, although they fulfill the wish of parenthood, have become the subject of heated debate.

Donor Insemination and In Vitro Fertilization. For several decades, *donor insemination*—injection of sperm from an anonymous man into a woman—has been used to overcome male reproductive difficulties. In recent years, it has also permitted women without a heterosexual partner to become pregnant. Donor insemination is 70 to 80 percent successful, resulting in 30,000 to 50,000 births in North America each year (Cooper & Glazer, 1999).

In vitro fertilization is another reproductive technology that has become increasingly common. Since the first "test tube" baby was born in England in 1978, 1 percent of all children in developed countries—about 39,000 babies in the United States and 3,500 babies in Canada—have been conceived through this technique annually (Sutcliffe, 2002). With in vitro fertilization, hormones are given to a woman, stimulating ripening of several ova. These are removed surgically and placed in a dish of nutrients, to which sperm are added. Usually, in vitro fertilization is used to treat women whose fallopian tubes are permanently damaged. But a recently developed technique permits a single sperm to be injected directly into an ovum, thereby overcoming most male fertility problems. And a new "sex sorter" method helps ensure that couples who carry X-linked diseases (which usually affect males) have a daughter. Once an ovum is fertilized and begins to duplicate into several cells, it is injected into the mother's uterus.

The overall success rate of in vitro fertilization is about 25 to 30 percent. However, success declines steadily with age, from 37 percent in women younger than age 35 to 3 percent in women age 43 and older (U.S. Department of Health and Human Services, 1999a). By mixing and matching gametes, pregnancies can be brought about when either or both partners have a reproductive problem. Fertilized ova and sperm can even be frozen and stored in embryo banks for use at some future time, thereby guaranteeing healthy zygotes should age or illness lead to fertility problems.

Children conceived through these methods may be genetically unrelated to one or both of their parents. In addition, most parents who have used in vitro fertilization do not tell their children about their origins, although health professionals now encourage them to do so. Does lack of genetic ties or secrecy surrounding these techniques interfere with parent-child relationships? Perhaps because of a strong desire for parenthood, caregiving is actually somewhat warmer for young children conceived through in vitro fertilization or donor insemination. And in vitro infants are as securely attached to their parents, and children and adolescents as well adjusted, as their counterparts who were naturally conceived (Chan, Raboy, & Patterson, 1998; Gibson et al., 2000; Golombok, MacCallum, & Goodman, 2001).

Although donor insemination and in vitro fertilization have many benefits, serious questions have arisen about their use. Most U.S. states and Canadian provinces have no legal guidelines for these procedures. As a result, donors are not always screened for genetic or sexually transmitted diseases. Furthermore, in many countries (including the United States and Canada), doctors are not required to keep records of donor characteristics. Yet the resulting children may someday want to know their genetic background or need to know it for medical reasons. Also, critics worry that the in vitro "sex sorter" method will lead to parental sex selection, thereby eroding the moral value that children of both sexes are equally precious. And finally, in some instances, frozen embryos have been stolen—that is, taken and sold without permission of the couple owning them (Blum, 2000).

Surrogate Motherhood. An even more controversial form of medically assisted conception is *surrogate motherhood.* Typically in this procedure, sperm from a man whose wife is infertile are used to inseminate a woman, called a surrogate, who is paid a fee for her childbearing services. In return, the surrogate agrees to turn the baby over to the man (who is the natural father). The child is then adopted by his wife.

Although most of these arrangements proceed smoothly, those that end up in court highlight serious risks for all concerned. In one case, both parties rejected the infant with severe disabilities that resulted from the pregnancy. In others, the surrogate mother wanted to keep the baby or the couple changed their mind during the pregnancy. These children came into the world in the midst of conflict that threatened to last for years.

Because surrogacy favors the wealthy as contractors for infants and the less economically advantaged as surrogates, it may promote exploitation of financially needy women (Sureau, 1997). In addition, most surrogates already have children of their own who may be deeply affected by the pregnancy. Knowledge that their mother would give away a baby for profit may cause these youngsters to worry about the security of their own family circumstances.

New Reproductive Frontiers. Reproductive technologies are evolving faster than societies can weigh the ethics of these procedures. Doctors have used donor ova from younger women in combination with in vitro fertilization to help postmenopausal women become pregnant. Most recipients are in their 40s, but a 62-year-old has given birth in Italy and a 63-year-old in the United States. Even though candidates for postmenopausal-assisted childbirth are selected on the basis of good health, serious questions arise about bringing children into the world whose parents may not live to see them reach adulthood. Based on U.S. life expectancy data, 1 in 3 mothers and 1 in 2 fathers having a baby at age 55 will die before their child enters college (U.S. Bureau of the Census, 2002c).

Currently, experts are debating other reproductive options. In one instance, a woman with a busy stage career who could have become pregnant naturally chose to combine in vitro fertilization (using her own ova and her husband's sperm) and surrogate motherhood. This permitted the woman to continue her career while the surrogate carried her biological child (Wood, 2001). At donor banks, customers can select ova or sperm on the basis of physical characteristics and even IQ. Some worry that this practice is a dangerous step toward selective breeding through "designer babies"—controlling offspring characteristics by manipulating the genetic makeup of fertilized ova.

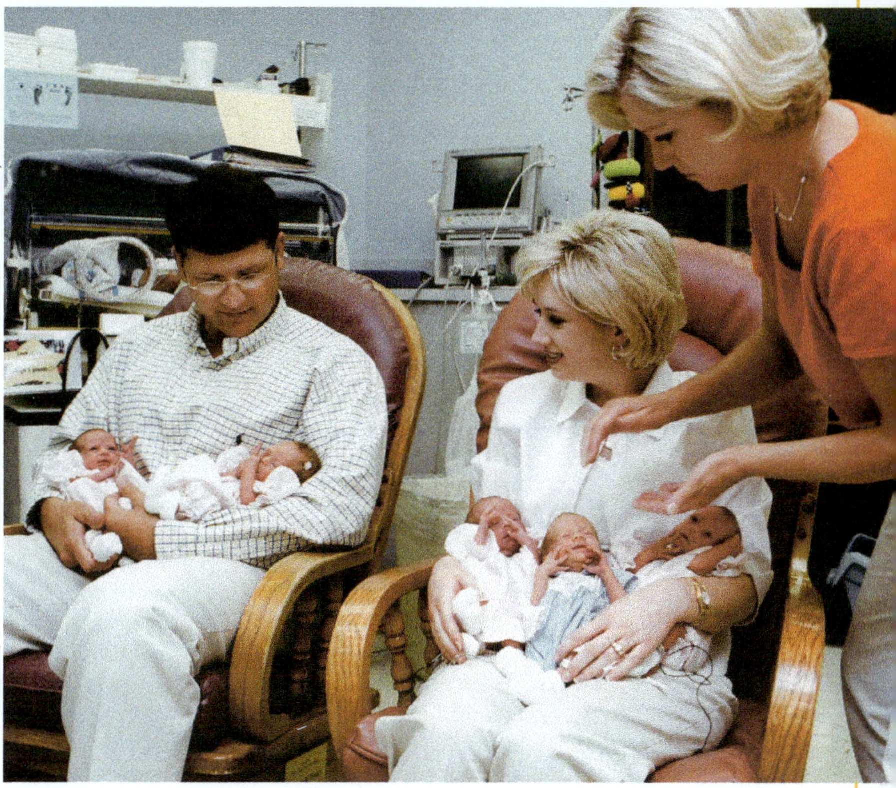

■ Although reproductive technologies permit many barren couples to have healthy newborns, they can pose grave ethical dilemmas. Fertility drugs and in vitro fertilization often lead to multiple fetuses. When three or more fill the uterus, pregnancy complications are often so severe that doctors recommend aborting one or more to save the others. These 3-week-old babies, being held by their parents in the intensive care nursery, are the only documented quintuplets to have all been born alive in Mississippi.

Finally, scientists have successfully cloned (made multiple copies of) fertilized ova in sheep, cattle, and monkeys, and they are working on effective ways to do so in humans. By providing extra ova for injection, cloning might improve the success rate of in vitro fertilization. But it also opens the possibility of mass-producing genetically identical people. Therefore, it is widely condemned (Fasouliotis & Schenker, 2000).

Although new reproductive technologies permit many barren couples to rear healthy newborn babies, laws are needed to regulate such practices. In Australia, New Zealand, and Sweden, individuals conceived with donated gametes have a right to information about their genetic origins (Hunter, Salter-Ling, & Glover, 2000). Pressure from those working in the field of assisted reproduction may soon lead to similar policies in the United States and Canada.

In the case of paying surrogate mothers to bear another's child, Australia, Canada, many European nations, and some U.S. states have banned the practice, arguing that the status of a baby should not be a matter of commercial arrangement and that a part of the body should not be rented or sold (McGee, 1997). England, France, and Italy have prohibited in vitro fertilization for women past menopause (Andrews & Elster, 2000). At present, nothing is known about the long-term health and psychological consequences of being a product of these procedures. Research on how such children grow up, including later-appearing medical conditions and knowledge and feelings about their origins, is important for weighing the pros and cons of these techniques.

Caregiving Concerns

Steps Before Conception to Increase the Chances of Having a Healthy Baby

SUGGESTION	RATIONALE
Arrange for a physical exam.	A physical exam before conception permits detection of diseases and other medical problems that might reduce fertility, be difficult to treat after the onset of pregnancy, or affect the developing organism.
Reduce or eliminate toxins under your control.	Because the developing organism is highly sensitive to damaging environmental agents during the early weeks of pregnancy (see Chapter 3), drugs, alcohol, cigarette smoke, radiation, pollution, chemical substances in the home and workplace, and infectious diseases should be avoided while trying to conceive. Furthermore, ionizing radiation and some industrial chemicals are known to cause mutations.
Consider your genetic makeup.	Find out if anyone in your family has had a child with a genetic disease or disability. If so, seek genetic counseling before conception.
Consult your doctor after 12 months of unsuccessful efforts at conception.	Long periods of infertility may be due to undiagnosed spontaneous abortions, which can be caused by genetic defects in either partner. If a physical exam reveals a healthy reproductive system, seek genetic counseling.

gene to the cells, thereby correcting a genetic abnormality. In recent experiments, gene therapy relieved symptoms in hemophilia patients and patients with severe immune system dysfunction (Cavazzana-Calvo et al., 2000; Kay et al., 2000). Another approach is *proteomics,* modifying gene-specified proteins involved in biological aging and disease (Blumenthal, 2001).

Genetic treatments, however, seem some distance away for most single-gene defects—and far off for diseases involving multiple genes that combine in complex ways with each other and the environment (Collins & McKusick, 2001). The Caregiving Concerns table above summarizes steps that prospective parents can take before conception to protect the genetic health of their child.

Genetic Testing

Fortunately, over 90 percent of pregnancies in the United States result in the birth of healthy infants with a good chance of a life free of genetic disease. For those who harbor genes that might lead to later-emerging disorders, a few predictive tests exist, such as those for breast and colon cancer. Scientists predict that by the year 2010 many more such tests will be available, permitting people to find out about their genetic risks and, hopefully, take steps to reduce them—through medical monitoring, lifestyle changes, or drug therapy (Druker & Lydon, 2000).

Although its potential benefits are great, at present genetic testing raises serious social, ethical, and legal concerns. A major controversy involves testing children and adults who are at risk but who do not yet show disease symptoms. Delay between the availability of predictive tests and effective interventions means that people must live with the knowledge that they might become seriously ill. A related concern is the need for greater knowledge of genetics, by both health professionals and the general public. Without this understanding, doctors and patients may misinterpret genetic risk. For example, genes associated with breast cancer were first identified in families with a high incidence of the disease. In those families, 85 percent of individuals harboring the genes developed cancer. But in the general population, the risk is reduced to 35 to 50 percent (Burke, Atkins, & Gwinn, 2002). Furthermore, some people whose tests revealed abnormal genes have encountered discrimination in the workplace, where they have lost their health insurance and even their jobs.

Experts in medical ethics recommend that genetic testing be offered only to high-risk individuals who undergo extensive education and counseling and agree to close medical and psychological follow-up if they test positive (Haddad et al., 1999). And procedures have been devised in the United States and Canada to ensure the privacy of genetic information and to prohibit mandatory genetic testing by employers (Privacy Commissioner of Canada, 2002; Yang, Flake, & Adzick, 1999). As the Human Genome Project continues to make invaluable contributions to human health, scientists are debating the best ways to protect the public interest while reaping the project's monumental rewards.

Adoption

Adults who cannot bear children, who are likely to pass along a genetic disorder, or who are older and single but want a family are turning to adoption in increasing numbers. Adoption agencies usually try to find parents of the same ethnic and religious background as the child. Where possible, they also try to choose parents who are the same age as most natural parents. Because the availability of healthy babies has declined (fewer young unwed mothers give up their babies today than in the past), more people are adopting from other countries or taking children who are older or who have developmental problems.

Adopted children and adolescents—whether born in another country or in the country of their adoptive parents—have more learning and emotional difficulties than other children, a difference that increases with the child's age at time of adoption (Levy-Shiff, 2001; Miller et al., 2000; Sharma, McCue, & Benson, 1998). There are many possible reasons for adoptees' more problematic childhoods. The biological mother may have been unable to care for the child because of emotional problems believed to be partly genetic, such as alcoholism or severe depression. She may have passed this tendency to her offspring. Or perhaps she experienced stress, poor diet, or inadequate medical care during pregnancy—factors that can affect the child (as we will see in Chapter 3). Furthermore, children adopted after infancy are more likely than their nonadopted peers to have a history of conflict-ridden family relationships, lack of parental affection, and neglect and abuse. Finally, adoptive parents and children, who are genetically unrelated, are less alike in intelligence and personality than biological relatives—differences that may threaten family harmony.

But despite these risks, most adopted children fare surprisingly well. In a Swedish study, researchers followed over 600 infant candidates for adoption into adolescence. Some were adopted shortly after birth; some were reared in foster homes; and some were reared by their biological mothers, who changed their minds about giving them up. As Figure 2.6 shows, adoptees developed much more favorably than children reared in foster families or returned to their birth mothers (Bohman & Sigvardsson, 1990). And in a study of internationally adopted children in the Netherlands, sensitive maternal care and secure attachment in infancy predicted cognitive and social competence at age 7 (Stams, Juffer, & van IJzendoorn, 2002). So even when children are not genetically related to their parents, an early warm, trusting parent–child relationship fosters development. Older-placed adoptive children with troubled family histories also develop feelings of trust and affection for their adoptive parents as they come to feel loved and supported in their new families (Sherrill & Pinderhughes, 1999).

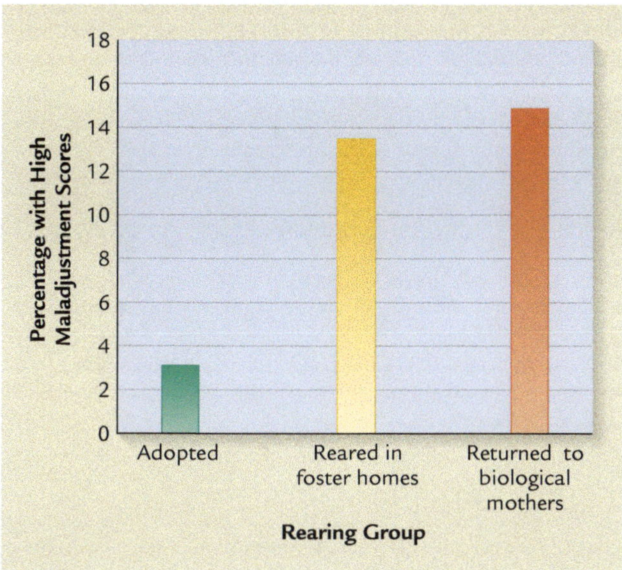

FIGURE 2.6 Relationship of type of rearing to maladjustment among a sample of Swedish adolescents who had been candidates for adoption at birth. Compared with the other two groups, adopted young people were rated by teachers as having far fewer problems, including anxiety, withdrawal, aggression, inability to concentrate, peer difficulties, and poor school motivation. (Adapted from Bohman & Sigvardsson, 1990.)

By adolescence, adoptees' lives are often complicated by unresolved curiosity about their roots. Some have difficulty accepting the possibility that they may never know their birth parents. Others worry about what they would do if their birth parents suddenly reappeared (Grotevant & Kohler, 1999). Nevertheless, the decision to search for birth parents is usually postponed until early adulthood, when marriage and childbirth may trigger it (Schaffer & Kral, 1988). Despite concerns about their origins, most adoptees appear well adjusted as adults. And as long as their parents took steps to help them learn about their heritage in childhood, transracially or transculturally adopted young people generally develop identities that are healthy blends of their birth and rearing backgrounds (Brooks & Barth, 1999).

As we conclude our discussion of reproductive choices, perhaps you are wondering how things turned out for Ted and Marianne. Through genetic counseling, Marianne discovered a history of Tay-Sachs disease on her mother's side of the family. Ted had a distant cousin who died of the disorder. The genetic counselor explained that the chances of giving birth to another affected baby were 1 in 4. Ted and Marianne took the risk. Their son Douglas is now 12 years old. Although Douglas is a carrier of the recessive allele, he is a normal, healthy boy. In a few years, Ted and Marianne will tell Douglas about his genetic history and explain the importance of genetic counseling and testing before he has children of his own.

Ask Yourself

REVIEW

Why is genetic counseling called a *communication process*? Who should seek it?

REVIEW

Describe the ethical pros and cons of fetal surgery, surrogate motherhood, and postmenopausal-assisted childbearing.

CONNECT

How does research on adoption reveal resiliency? Which of the factors related to resiliency (see Chapter 1, pages 10–11) is central in positive outcomes for adoptees?

www.

Environmental Contexts for Development

Just as complex as the genetic inheritance that sets the stage for development is the surrounding environment—a many-layered set of influences that combine to help or hinder physical and psychological well-being. Take a moment to reflect on your own childhood, and jot down a brief description of events and people that you regard as having had a significant impact on your development. Next, do the same for your adult life. When I ask my students to do this, most items they list involve their families. This emphasis is not surprising, since the family is the first and longest-lasting context for development. But other settings turn out to be important as well. Friends, neighbors, school, workplace, community organizations, and church, synagogue, or mosque generally make the top ten.

Think back to Bronfenbrenner's ecological systems theory, discussed in Chapter 1. It emphasizes that the environments extending beyond the *microsystem,* or the immediate settings just mentioned, powerfully affect development. Indeed, my students rarely mention one very important context. Its impact is so pervasive that we seldom stop to think about it in our daily lives. This is the *macrosystem,* or broad social climate of society—its values and programs that support and protect human development. All people need help with the demands of each phase of the lifespan—through well-designed housing, safe neighborhoods, good schools, well-equipped recreational facilities, affordable health services, and high-quality child care and other services that permit them to meet both work and family responsibilities. And some people, because of poverty or special tragedies, need considerably more help than others.

In the following sections, we take up these contexts for development. Because they affect every age and aspect of change, we will return to them in later chapters. For now, our discussion emphasizes that besides heredity, environments can enhance or create risks for development. And when a vulnerable child or adult—an individual with physical or psychological problems—is exposed to unfavorable contexts, development is seriously threatened.

The Family

In power and breadth of influence, no context equals the family. The family creates bonds between people that are unique. Attachments to parents and siblings usually last a lifetime and serve as models for relationships in the wider world of neighborhood, school, and community. Within the family, children learn the language, skills, and social and moral values of their culture. And at all ages, people turn to family members for information, assistance, and interesting and pleasurable interaction. Warm, gratifying family ties predict physical and psychological health throughout development. In contrast, isolation or alienation from the family is often associated with developmental problems (Parke & Buriel, 1998).

Contemporary researchers view the family as a network of interdependent relationships. Recall from ecological systems theory that *bidirectional influences* exist in which the behaviors of each family member affect those of others (Bronfenbrenner, 1989, 1995). Indeed, the very term *system* implies that the responses of all family members are related. These system influences operate both directly and indirectly.

Direct Influences. The next time you have a chance to observe family members interacting, watch carefully. You are likely to see that kind, patient communication evokes cooperative, harmonious responses, whereas harshness and impatience engender angry, resistive behavior. Each of these reactions, in turn, forges a new link in the interactive chain. In the first instance, a positive message tends to follow; in the second, a negative or avoidant one tends to occur.

These observations fit with a wealth of research on the family system. For example, many studies show that when parents' requests are accompanied by warmth and affection, children tend to cooperate. And when children willingly comply, their parents are likely to be warm and gentle in the future. In contrast, parents who discipline with harshness and impatience have children who refuse and rebel. And because children's misbehavior is stressful for parents, they may increase their use of punishment, leading to more unruliness by the child (Dodge, Pettit, & Bates, 1994; Stormshak et al., 2000). This principle applies to other two-person family relationships, such as brother and sister, husband and wife, and

© PETER SANDERS/HAGA/THE IMAGE WORKS

The family is a complex social system in which each person's behavior influences the behavior of others, in both direct and indirect ways. The positive mealtime atmosphere in this Saudi Arabian family is a product of many sources, including parents who respond to children with warmth and patience, aunts and uncles who support parents in their child-rearing roles, and children who have developed cooperative dispositions.

parent and adult child. In each case, the behavior of one family member helps sustain a form of interaction in the other that either promotes or undermines psychological well-being.

● **Indirect Influences.** The impact of family relationships on development becomes even more complicated when we consider that interaction between any two members is affected by others present in the setting. Bronfenbrenner calls these indirect influences the effect of *third parties.*

Third parties can serve as supports for development. For example, when parents' marital relationship is warm and considerate, mothers and fathers praise and stimulate their children more and nag and scold them less. In contrast, when a marriage is tense and hostile, parents tend to be less responsive to their children's needs and to criticize, express anger, and punish (Cox, Paley, & Harter, 2001; Erel & Burman, 1995). Similarly, children can affect their parents' relationship in powerful ways. For example, as we will see in Chapter 10, some children show lasting emotional problems when their parents divorce. But longitudinal research reveals that long before the marital breakup, some children of divorcing couples were impulsive and defiant. These behaviors may have contributed to as well as been caused by their parents' marital problems (Amato & Booth, 1996; Hetherington, 1999).

Yet even when family relationships are strained by third parties, other members may help restore effective interaction. Grandparents are a case in point. They can promote children's development in many ways—both directly, by responding warmly to the child, and indirectly, by providing parents with child-rearing advice, models of child-rearing skill, and even financial assistance. Of course, like any indirect influence, grandparents can sometimes be harmful. When quarrelsome relations exist between grandparents and parents, parent–child communication may suffer.

● **Adapting to Change.** Think back to the *chronosystem* in Bronfenbrenner's theory (see page 25). The interplay of forces within the family is dynamic and ever-changing. Important events, such as the birth of a baby, a change of jobs, or an elderly parent joining the household due to declining health, create challenges that modify existing relationships. The way such events affect family interaction depends on the support provided by other family members as well as on the developmental status of each participant. For example, the arrival of a new baby prompts very different reactions in a toddler than in a school-age child. And caring for an ill elderly parent is more stressful for a middle-aged adult still rearing young children than for an adult of the same age without child-rearing responsibilities.

Historical time period also contributes to a dynamic family system. In recent decades, a declining birth rate, a high divorce rate, and expansion of women's roles have led to a smaller family size. This, combined with a longer lifespan, means that more generations are alive with fewer members in the youngest ones, leading to a "top-heavy" family structure. Consequently, young people today are more likely to have older relatives than at any time in history—a circumstance that can be enriching as well as a source of tension. In sum, as this complex intergenerational system moves through time, relationships are constantly revised as members adjust to their own and others' development as well as to external pressures.

Despite these variations, some general patterns in family functioning do exist. In the United States, Canada, and other Western nations, one important source of these consistencies is socioeconomic status.

Socioeconomic Status and Family Functioning

People in industrialized nations are stratified on the basis of what they do at work and how much they earn for doing it—factors that determine their social position and economic well-being. Researchers assess a family's standing on this continuum through an index called **socioeconomic status (SES).** It combines three interrelated, but not completely overlapping, variables: (1) years of education and (2) the prestige of and skill required by one's job, both of which measure social status, and (3) income, which measures economic status. As socioeconomic status rises and falls, people face changing circumstances that profoundly affect family functioning.

SES affects the timing and duration of phases of the family life cycle. People who work in skilled and semiskilled manual occupations (for example, machinists, truck drivers, and custodians) tend to marry and have children earlier as well as give birth to more children than people in white-collar and professional occupations. The two groups also differ in values and expectations. For example, when asked about personal qualities they desire for their children, lower-SES parents tend to emphasize external characteristics, such as obedience, politeness, neatness, and cleanliness. In contrast, higher-SES parents emphasize psychological traits, such as curiosity, happiness, self-direction, and cognitive and social maturity (Hoff, Laursen, & Tardiff, 2002; Tudge et al., 2000). In addition, fathers in higher-SES families tend to be more involved in child rearing and household responsibilities. Lower-SES fathers, partly because of their gender-stereotyped beliefs and partly because of economic necessity, focus more on their provider role (Rank, 2000).

These differences are reflected in family interaction. Parents higher in SES talk to and stimulate their infants and preschoolers more and grant them greater freedom to explore. When their children are older, higher-SES parents use more warmth, explanations, and verbal praise. Commands, such as "You do that because I told you to," as well as criticism and physical punishment occur more often in low-SES households (Hoff, Laursen, & Tardiff, 2002).

The life conditions of families help explain these findings. Lower-SES adults often feel a sense of powerlessness and lack of influence in their relationships beyond the home. For example, at work, they must obey the rules of others in positions of power and authority. When they get home, their parent–child interaction seems to duplicate these experiences, with them in the authority role. Higher levels of stress combined with a stronger belief in the value of physical punishment contribute to low-SES parents' greater use of coercive discipline (Pinderhughes et al., 2000). Higher-SES parents, in contrast, have more control over their own lives. At work, they are used to making independent decisions and convincing others of their point of view. At home, they teach these skills to their children (Greenberger, O'Neil, & Nagel, 1994).

Education also contributes to SES differences in family interaction. Higher-SES parents' interest in providing verbal stimulation and nurturing inner traits is supported by years of schooling, during which they learned to think about abstract, subjective ideas (Uribe, LeVine, & LeVine, 1994). Furthermore, the greater economic security of higher-SES families permits them to devote more time, energy, and material resources to nurturing their children's psychological characteristics.

As early as the second year of life, SES is positively correlated with cognitive and language development. Throughout childhood and adolescence, higher-SES youngsters do better in school (Brody, 1997b; Walker et al., 1994). And they attain higher levels of education, which greatly enhances their opportunities for a prosperous adult life. Researchers believe that differences in family functioning have much to do with these outcomes.

The Impact of Poverty

When families slip into poverty, development is seriously threatened. Consider the case of Zinnia Mae, who grew up in Trackton, a close-knit black community located in a small southeastern American city (Heath, 1990). As unemployment struck Trackton in the 1980s and citizens moved away, 16-year-old Zinnia Mae caught a ride to Atlanta. Two years later, Zinnia Mae was the mother of three children—a daughter and twin boys. She had moved into high-rise public housing.

Each of Zinnia Mae's days was much the same. She watched TV and talked with girlfriends on the phone. The children had only one set meal (breakfast) and otherwise ate whenever they were hungry or bored. Their play space was limited to the living room sofa and a mattress on the floor. Toys consisted of scraps of a blanket, spoons and food cartons, a small rubber ball, a few plastic cars, and a roller skate abandoned in the building. Zinnia Mae's most frequent words were "I'm so tired." She worried about where to find baby-sitters so she could go to the laundry or grocery, and about what she would do if she located the twins' father, who had stopped sending money.

Over the past 30 years, economic changes in the United States and Canada have caused the poverty rate to climb substantially; in recent years, it has dropped and then risen again. Today, nearly 12 percent of the population in the United States and Canada are affected. Those hit hardest are parents under age 25 with young children and elderly people who live alone. Poverty is also magnified among ethnic minorities and women. For example, 17 percent of American and Canadian children are poor, a rate that climbs to 32 percent for Native American children, 34 percent for African-American and Hispanic children, and 60 percent for Canadian Aboriginal children. (Aboriginal peoples in Canada include First Nations, Inuit, and Métis.) For single mothers with preschool children and elderly women on their own, the poverty rate in both countries is nearly 50 percent (Canadian National Council of Welfare, 2002; U.S. Bureau of the Census, 2002c).

Joblessness, a high divorce rate, a lower remarriage rate among women than men, widowhood, and (as we will see later) inadequate government programs to meet family needs are responsible for these disheartening statistics. The child poverty rate is higher than that of any age group. And of all Western nations, the United States has a higher percentage of extremely poor children. These circumstances are particularly worrisome because the earlier poverty begins, the deeper it is, and the longer it lasts, the more devastating its effects on physical and mental health and school achievement (Children's Defense Fund, 2003; Zigler & Hall, 2000).

The constant stresses that accompany poverty gradually weaken the family system. Poor families have many daily hassles—bills to pay, the car breaking down, loss of welfare and unemployment payments, something stolen from the house, to name just a few. When daily crises arise, family members become depressed, irritable, and distracted, and hostile interactions increase (McLoyd, 1998). These outcomes are especially severe in families that must live in poor housing and dangerous neighborhoods—conditions that make everyday existence even more difficult, while reducing social supports that help people cope with economic hardship (Brooks-Gunn & Duncan, 1997).

Besides poverty, another problem—one uncommon 25 years ago—has reduced the life chances of many children and adults. On any given night, approximately 35,000 people in Canada and 350,000 people in the United States have no place

■ Homelessness in the United States and Canada has risen over the past 2 decades. Families like this one travel from place to place in search of employment and a safe and secure place to live. Because of constant stress and few social supports, homeless children are usually behind in development, have health problems, and show poor psychological adjustment.

© TONY FREEMAN/PHOTOEDIT

to live (Pohl, 2001; Wright, 1999). The majority are adults on their own, many of whom suffer from serious mental illness. But nearly 29 percent of the homeless in Canada and 40 percent in the United States are families with children. The rise in homelessness is due to a number of factors, the most important of which is a decline in the availability of government-supported low-cost housing and the release of large numbers of mentally ill people from hospitals and institutions, without an increase in community treatment programs aimed at helping them adjust to ordinary life and get better.

Most homeless families consist of women with children under age 5. Besides health problems (which affect most homeless people), homeless children suffer from developmental delays and serious emotional stress (Bratt, 2002). An estimated 25 to 30 percent of those who are old enough do not go to school. Those who do enroll achieve less well than other poverty-stricken children due to poor attendance and health and emotional difficulties (Vostanis, Grattan, & Cumella, 1997).

© ROBERT BRENNER/PHOTOEDIT

■ The resources neighborhoods offer are important for development and well-being at all ages. Here, adults and children participate in a barn raising for a needy family living in their neighborhood.

Beyond the Family: Neighborhoods, Towns, and Cities

In ecological systems theory, the mesosystem and exosystem underscore that ties between family and community are vital for psychological well-being throughout the lifespan. From our discussion of poverty, perhaps you can see why. In poverty-stricken urban areas, community life is usually disrupted. Families move often, parks and playgrounds are in disarray, and community centers providing organized leisure time activities do not exist. Family violence and child abuse and neglect are greatest in neighborhoods where residents are dissatisfied with their community, describing it as a socially isolated place to live. In contrast, when family ties to the community are strong—as indicated by regular church attendance and frequent contact with friends and relatives—family stress and adjustment problems are reduced (Garbarino & Kostelny, 1993; Magnuson & Duncan, 2002).

● **Neighborhoods.** Let's look closely at the functions of communities in the lives of children and adults by beginning with the neighborhood. What were your childhood experiences like in the yards, streets, and parks surrounding your home? How did you spend your time, whom did you get to know, and how important were these moments to you?

The resources and social ties offered by neighborhoods play an important part in children's development. In several studies, low-SES families were randomly assigned vouchers to move out of public housing into neighborhoods varying widely in affluence. Compared with their peers who remained in poverty-stricken areas, children and youths who moved into low-poverty neighborhoods showed substantially better physical and mental health and school achievement (Goering, 2003; Rubinowitz & Rosenbaum, 2000).

Neighborhood resources have a greater impact on economically disadvantaged than well-to-do young people (McLeod & Shanahan, 1996). Affluent families are not as dependent on their immediate surroundings for social support, education, and leisure pursuits. They can afford to reach beyond the streets near their homes, transporting their children to lessons and entertainment and, if necessary, to better-quality schools in distant parts of the community (Elliott et al., 1996). In low-income neighborhoods, after-school programs that substitute for lack of resources by providing enrichment activities are associated with improved school performance and psychological adjustment in middle childhood (Posner & Vandell, 1994; Vandell & Posner, 1999). Neighborhood organizations and informal social activities predict favorable development in adolescence, including increased self-confidence, school achievement, and educational aspirations (Gonzales et al., 1996).

Neighborhoods also affect adults' well-being. For example, an employed parent who can rely on a neighbor to assist her school-age child in her absence and who lives in an area safe for walking to and from school gains the peace of mind essential for productive work. During late adulthood, neighborhoods become increasingly important because elders spend more time in their homes. Despite the availability of planned housing for older people, about 90 percent remain in regular housing, usually in the same neighborhood where they lived during their working lives (Parmelee & Lawton, 1990; U.S. Bureau of the Census, 2002c). Proximity to relatives and friends is a significant factor in the decision to move or stay put late in life. In the absence of nearby family members, the elderly mention neighbors and nearby friends as resources they rely on most for physical and social support (Hooyman & Kiyak, 2002).

● **Towns and Cities.** Neighborhoods are embedded in towns and cities, which also mold children's and adults' daily lives. A well-known study examined the kinds of community settings children entered and the roles they played in a Midwestern town with a population of 700 (Barker, 1955). Many settings existed, and children were granted important responsibilities—stocking shelves at Kane's Grocery Store, playing in the town band, and operating the snow plow when help was short. They did so alongside adults, who taught them skills needed to become responsible members of the community. Compared with large urban areas, small towns offer stronger connections between settings that influence children's lives. For example, since most citizens know each other and schools serve as centers of community life, contact between teachers and parents occurs often—an important factor in promoting children's academic achievement (Eccles & Harold, 1996).

Like children, adults in small towns penetrate more settings and are more likely to occupy positions of leadership because a greater proportion of residents are needed to meet community needs—for example, by serving on the town council, on the school board, or in other civic roles. In late adulthood, people residing in small towns and suburbs have neighbors who are more willing to provide assistance. As a result, they develop a greater number of warm relationships with nonrelatives (Lawton, 1980). As one 99-year-old resident of a small Midwestern community, living alone and leading an active life, commented, "I don't think I could get along if I didn't have good neighbors." The family next door helps him with grocery shopping, checks each night to make sure his basement light is off (the signal that he is out of the shower and into bed), and looks out in the morning to see that his garage door is raised (the signal that he is up and okay) (Fergus, 1995).

Of course, children and adults in small towns cannot visit museums, go to professional baseball games, or attend orchestra concerts on a regular basis. The variety of settings is reduced compared to large cities. In small towns, however, active involvement in the community is likely to be greater throughout the lifespan. Also, public places in small towns are relatively safe and secure. Responsible adults are present in almost all settings to keep an eye on children. And the elderly feel safer—a strong contributor to how satisfied they are with their place of residence (Parmelee & Lawton, 1990). These conditions are hard to match in today's urban environments.

Think back to the case of Zinnia Mae and her three young children described on page 60. It reveals that community life is especially undermined in high-rise urban housing projects, which are heavily populated by young single mothers who are separated from family and friends by the cost and inconvenience of cross-town transportation. They report intense feelings of loneliness in the small, cramped apartments. Zinnia Mae agreed to tape-record her family interactions over a 2-year period (Heath, 1990). In 500 hours of tape, Zinnia Mae started a conversation with her daughter and twin sons only 18 times. Cut off from community ties and overwhelmed by financial worries and feelings of helplessness, she found herself unable to join in activities with her children. The result was a barren, understimulating environment—one very different from the home and community in which Zinnia Mae herself had grown up.

The Cultural Context

Our discussion in Chapter 1 emphasized that human development can be fully understood only when viewed in its larger cultural context. In the following sections, we expand on this important theme by taking up the macrosystem's role in development. First, we discuss ways that cultural values and practices affect environmental contexts for development. Second, we consider how healthy development depends on laws and government programs that shield people from harm and foster their well-being.

Cultural Values and Practices. Cultures shape family interaction and community settings beyond the home—in short, all aspects of daily life. Many of us remain blind to aspects of our own cultural heritage until we see them in relation to the practices of others.

Each semester, I ask my students to think about the question: Who should be responsible for rearing young children? Here are some typical answers: "If parents decide to have a baby, then they should be ready to care for it." "Most people are not happy about others intruding into family life." These statements reflect a widely held opinion in the United States—that the care and rearing of children, and paying for that care, are the duty of parents, and only parents (Rickel & Becker, 1997; Scarr, 1996). This autonomous view has a long history—one in which independence, self-reliance, and the privacy of family life emerged as central North American values. It is one reason, among others, that the public has been slow to accept the idea of government-supported benefits for all families, such as high-quality child care. This strong emphasis on individualism has also contributed to the large number of American and Canadian families that remain poor, despite the fact that their members are gainfully employed (Pohl, 2002; Zigler & Hall, 2000).

Although many people value independence and privacy, not all citizens share the same values. Some are part of **subcultures**—groups of people with beliefs and customs that differ from those of the larger culture. Many ethnic minority groups in the United States and Canada have cooperative family structures, which help protect their members from the harmful effects of poverty. As the Cultural Influences box on the following page indicates, the African-American tradition of **extended family households,** in which three or more generations live together, is a vital feature of black family life that has enabled its members to survive, despite a long history of prejudice and economic deprivation. Within the extended family, grandparents play meaningful roles in guiding younger generations; adults with employment, marital, or child-rearing difficulties receive assistance and emotional support; and caregiving is enhanced for children and the elderly. Active and involved extended families also characterize other minorities, such as Asian, Native American, Hispanic, and Canadian Aboriginal subcultures (Harrison et al., 1994).

Consider our discussion so far, and you will see that it reflects a broad dimension on which cultures and subcultures

Cultural Influences

The African-American Extended Family

The African-American extended family can be traced to the African heritage of most black Americans. In many African societies, newly married couples do not start their own households. Instead, they live with a large extended family, which assists its members with all aspects of daily life. This tradition of maintaining a broad network of kin ties traveled to the United States during the period of slavery. Since then, it has served as a protective shield against the destructive impact of poverty and racial prejudice on African-American family life. Today, more black than white adults have relatives other than their own children living in the same household. African-American parents also live closer to kin, often establish familylike relationships with friends and neighbors, see more relatives during the week, and perceive them as more important figures in their lives (Wilson et al., 1995).

■ Strong bonds with extended-family members have helped protect many African-American children growing up under conditions of poverty and single parenthood. This extended family gathers to celebrate the eighty-fifth birthday of their oldest member.

By providing emotional support and sharing income and essential resources, the African-American extended family helps reduce the stress of poverty and single parenthood. In addition, extended-family members often help with child rearing. Furthermore, black adolescent mothers living in extended families are more likely to complete high school and get a job and less likely to be on welfare than are mothers living on their own—factors that in turn benefit children's well-being (Trent & Harlan, 1994).

For single mothers who were very young at the time of their child's birth, extended-family living continues to be associated with more positive adult–child interaction during the preschool years. Otherwise, establishing an independent household with the help of nearby relatives is related to improved child rearing. Perhaps this arrangement permits the more mature mother who has developed effective parenting skills to implement them (Chase-Lansdale, Brooks-Gunn, & Zamsky, 1994). In families rearing adolescents, kinship support increases the likelihood of effective parenting, which is related to adolescents' self-reliance, emotional well-being, and reduced delinquency (Taylor & Roberts, 1995).

Finally, the extended family plays an important role in transmitting African-American culture. Compared with nuclear-family households (which include only parents and their children), extended-family arrangements place more emphasis on cooperation and moral and religious values. And older black adults, such as grandparents and great-grandparents, regard educating children about their African heritage as especially important (Taylor, 2000). These influences strengthen family bonds, protect children's development, and increase the chances that the extended-family lifestyle will carry over to the next generation.

differ: the extent to which *collectivism versus individualism* is emphasized. In **collectivist societies,** people define themselves as part of a group and stress group goals over individual goals. In **individualistic societies,** people think of themselves as separate entities and are largely concerned with their own personal needs (Triandis, 1995). Although individualism tends to increase as cultures become more complex, cross-national differences remain. The United States is strongly individualistic, and Canada falls between the United States and most Western European countries. As we will see in the next section, collectivist versus individualistic values have a powerful impact on a nation's approach to protecting human development and well-being.

● **Public Policies and Lifespan Development.** When widespread social problems arise, such as poverty, homelessness, hunger, and disease, nations attempt to solve them by developing **public policies**—laws and government programs designed to improve current conditions. For example, when poverty increases and families become homeless, a country might decide to build more low-cost housing, raise the minimum wage, and increase welfare benefits. When reports indicate that many children are not achieving well in school, federal and state governments might grant more tax money to school districts and make sure that help reaches pupils who need it most. And when senior citizens have difficulty making ends meet because of inflation, a nation might increase its social security benefits.

Nevertheless, American and Canadian public policies safeguarding children and youths have lagged behind policies for the elderly. And both sets of policies have been especially slow to emerge in the United States.

Policies for Children, Youths, and Families. We have already seen in previous sections that although many North American children fare well, a large number grow up in environments that threaten their development. As Table 2.5 reveals, the United States does not rank well on any key measure of children's health and well-being. Canada fares better, devoting considerably more of its resources to education and health. For example, it grants all its citizens government-funded health care.

The problems of children and youths extend beyond the indicators in the table. For example, approximately 14 percent of American children have no health insurance, making them the largest segment of the U.S. uninsured population (Children's Defense Fund, 2002). Furthermore, the United States and Canada have been slow to move toward national standards and funding for child care. In both countries, much child care is substandard in quality (Goelman et al., 2000; NICHD Early Child Care Research Network, 2000a). In families affected by divorce, weak enforcement of child support payments heightens poverty in mother-headed families. By the time they finish high school, many North-American non-college-bound young people do not have the vocational preparation they need to contribute fully to society. And about 11 percent of U.S. and Canadian adolescents leave high school without a diploma. Those who do not finish their education are at risk for lifelong poverty (Children's Defense Fund, 2002; Statistics Canada, 2002o).

Why have attempts to help children and youths been especially difficult to realize in the United States and, to a lesser extent, in Canada? A complex set of political and economic forces is involved. North American values of self-reliance and privacy have made government hesitant to become involved in family matters. Furthermore, good social programs are expensive, and they must compete for a fair share of a country's economic resources. Children can easily remain unrecognized in this process because they cannot vote or speak out to protect their own interests, as adult citizens do (Zigler & Finn-Stevenson, 1999). Instead, they must rely on the goodwill of others to become an important government priority.

Policies for the Elderly. Until well into the twentieth century, the United States had few policies in place to protect its aging population. For example, social security benefits, which address the income needs of retired citizens who contributed to society through prior employment, were not awarded until the late 1930s. Yet most Western nations had social security systems in place a decade or more earlier; Canada's began in 1927 (DiNitto, 2002). In the 1960s, U.S. federal spending on programs for the elderly rapidly expanded. Medicare, a national health insurance program for older people that pays partial health care costs, was initiated. Canadian elders, like other residents of Canada, benefit from government-supported full health coverage, a system initiated in the 1950s (also called Medicare).

Table 2.5 How Do the United States and Canada Compare to Other Nations on Indicators of Children's Health and Well-Being?

Indicator	U.S. Rank[a]	Canadian Rank[a]	Some Countries the United States and Canada Trail
Childhood poverty[b] (among 23 industrialized nations considered)	19th	19th	Australia, Czech Republic, Germany, Norway, Sweden, Spain
Infant deaths in the first year of life (worldwide)	24th	15th	Hong Kong, Ireland, Singapore, Spain
Teenage pregnancy rate (among 45 industrialized nations considered)	45th	25th	Albania, Australia, Czech Republic, Denmark, Poland, Netherlands
Expenditures on education as percentage of gross domestic product (among 22 industrialized nations considered)	10th	6th	*For Canada:* Israel, Sweden *For the U.S.:* Australia, France, New Zealand, Sweden
Expenditures on health as a percentage of gross domestic product[c] (among 22 industrialized nations considered)	16th	4th	*For Canada:* Iceland, Switzerland, France *For the U.S.:* Austria, Australia, Hungary, New Zealand

[a]1 = highest rank

[b]The U.S. and Canadian childhood poverty rates of 17 percent greatly exceed those of any of these nations. For example, the rate is 12 percent in Australia, 6 percent in the Czech Republic, 4 percent in Norway, and 2.5 percent in Sweden.

[c]Gross domestic product is the value of all goods and services produced by a nation during a specified time period. It provides an overall measure of a nation's wealth.

Sources: Perie et al., 2000; Singh & Darroch, 2000; United Nations Children's Fund, 2000; United Nations Development Programme, 2002; U.S. Bureau of the Census, 2002b.

© LAIMA DRUSKIS/STOCK BOSTON, LLC

■ Overall, senior citizens in the United States are better off economically than are children. Nevertheless, many older adults—especially women and ethnic minorities—are poverty stricken. American elders are less well off than Canadian elders, who benefit from Canada's more generous income supplements and full health-care coverage.

Social security and Medicare consume 96 percent of the U.S. federal budget for the elderly; only 4 percent is devoted to other programs. Consequently, U.S. programs for the elderly have been criticized for neglecting social services (Hooyman & Kiyak, 2002). To meet this need, a national network for planning, coordinating, and delivering assistance to the aged has been established. Approximately 700 Area Agencies on Aging operate at regional and local levels, assessing community needs and offering communal and home-delivered meals, self-care education, elder abuse prevention, and a wide range of other social services. However, limited funding means that the Area Agencies help far too few people in need.

As noted earlier, many senior citizens—especially women, ethnic minorities, and those living alone—remain in dire economic straits. Those who had interrupted employment histories, held jobs without benefits, or suffered lifelong poverty are not eligible for social security. Although all Americans age 65 and older are guaranteed a minimum income, it is less than the poverty line—the amount judged necessary for bare subsistence by the federal government. Furthermore, social security benefits are rarely enough to serve as a sole source of retirement income; they must be supplemented through other pensions and family savings. But a substantial percentage of U.S. aging citizens do not have access to these resources. Therefore, they are more likely to be among the "near poor" than are other age groups (Koff & Park, 1999). Because of Canada's more generous income supplements as part of its Old Age Security Program, far fewer Canadian than U.S. elders are poverty stricken.

Nevertheless, the U.S. aging population is financially much better off now than in the past. Today, the elderly are a large, powerful, well-organized constituency, far more likely than children or low-income families to attract the support of politicians. As a result, the number of aging poor has declined from 1 out of 3 people in 1960 to 1 out of 10 in the early twenty-first century (U.S. Bureau of the Census, 2002c). And senior citizens are healthier and more independent than ever before. Still, as Figure 2.7 shows, the elderly in the United States are not as well off as those in other Western nations.

● **Looking Toward the Future.** Despite the worrisome state of many children, families, and aging citizens, progress is being made in improving their condition. Throughout this book, we will discuss many successful programs that could be expanded. Also, growing awareness of the gap between what we know and what we do to better people's lives has led experts in human development to join with concerned citizens as advocates for more effective policies. As a result, several influential interest groups with the well-being of children or the elderly as their central purpose have emerged. Among the most vigorous in the United States are the Children's Defense Fund and the American Association of Retired Persons.

A private, nonprofit organization founded by Marion Wright Edelman in 1973, the *Children's Defense Fund* engages in research, public education, legal action, drafting of legislation, congressional testimony, and community organizing. Each year, it publishes *The State of America's Children,* which provides a comprehensive analysis of the current condition of children, government-sponsored programs serving them, and proposals for improving child and family programs.

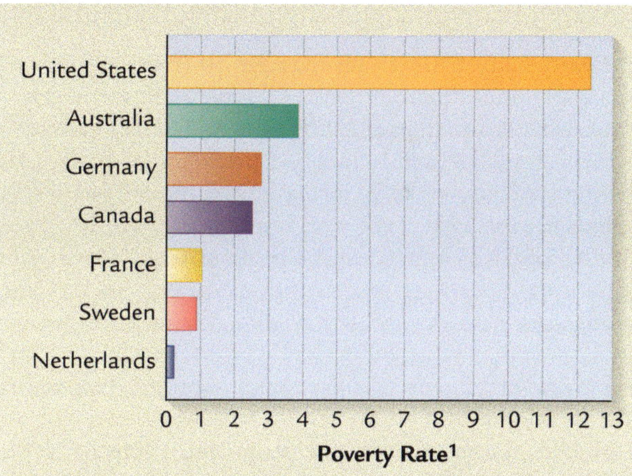

[1] Percentage of citizens age 65 and older earning 40 percent or less of the country's median income, adjusted for number of persons in household.

■ FIGURE 2.7 **Percentage of citizens age 65 and older living in poverty in seven industrialized nations.** Among countries listed, public expenditures on social security and other income guarantees for senior citizens are highest in the Netherlands, lowest in the United States (United Nations Development Programme, 2002). Consequently, poverty among the elderly is virtually nonexistent in the Netherlands but greatly exceeds that of other nations in the United States.

© WESTENBERGER/GETTY IMAGES

In 1973, Marion Wright Edelman founded the Children's Defense Fund, a private, nonprofit organization that provides a strong, effective voice for American children, who cannot vote, lobby, or speak for themselves. Edelman continues to serve as president of the Children's Defense Fund today.

Nearly half of Americans over age 50 (both retired and employed)—more than 35 million people—are members of the *American Association of Retired Persons (AARP).* Founded by Ethel Percy Andrus in 1958, AARP has a large and energetic lobbying staff that works for increased government benefits of all kinds for the aged. Each year, it releases the *AARP Public Policy Agenda,* which forms the basis for advocacy activities in diverse areas, including income, health care, social services, housing, and personal and legal rights. Among AARP's programs is an effort to mobilize elderly voters, an initiative that keeps lawmakers highly sensitive to policy proposals affecting older Americans.

Besides strong advocacy, the design and implementation of public policies that enhance human development depend on policy-relevant research that documents needs and evaluates programs to spark improvements. Today, more researchers are collaborating with community and government agencies to enhance the social relevance of their investigations. They are also doing a better job of disseminating their findings to the public, through television documentaries, newspaper stories, magazine articles, and direct reports to government officials (Denner et al., 1999). As a result, they are helping to create a sense of immediacy about the condition of children, families, and the aged that is necessary to spur a society into action.

Ask Yourself

REVIEW

Links between family and community foster development throughout the lifespan. Cite examples and research findings from our discussion that support this idea.

APPLY

On one of your trips to the local shopping center, you see a father getting very angry at his young son. Using ecological systems theory, list as many factors as you can that might account for the father's behavior.

APPLY

Check your local newspaper and one or two national news magazines to see how often articles appear on the condition of children, families, and the aged. Why is it important for researchers to communicate with the general public about the well-being of these sectors of the population?

CONNECT

How does poverty affect the functioning of the family system, thereby placing all domains of development at risk?

www.

Understanding the Relationship Between Heredity and Environment

So far in this chapter, we have discussed a wide variety of hereditary and environmental influences, each of which has the power to alter the course of development. Yet people who are born into the same family (and who therefore share genes and environments) often are quite different in characteristics. We also know that some individuals are affected more than others by their homes, neighborhoods, and communities. Cases exist in which a person provided with all the advantages in life does poorly, whereas another exposed to the worst of rearing conditions does well. How do scientists explain the impact of heredity and environment when they seem to work in so many different ways?

All contemporary researchers agree that both heredity and environment are involved in every aspect of development. But for polygenic traits (due to many genes) such as intelligence and personality, scientists are a long way from knowing the precise hereditary influences involved. They must study the impact of genes on these complex characteristics indirectly.

Some believe that it is useful and possible to answer the question of *how much* each factor contributes to differences among people. A growing consensus, however, regards that question as unanswerable. These investigators view genetic and environmental influences as inseparable. The important question, they maintain, is how nature and nurture work together. Let's consider each position in turn.

The Question, "How Much?"

Two methods—heritability estimates and concordance rates—are used to infer the role of heredity in complex human characteristics. Let's look closely at the information these procedures yield, along with their limitations.

Heritability. **Heritability estimates** measure the extent to which individual differences in complex traits, such as intelligence and personality, in a specific population are due to genetic factors. Researchers have obtained heritabilities for intelligence and a variety of personality characteristics. We will take a brief look at their findings here and return to them in later chapters, when we consider these topics in greater detail. Heritability estimates are obtained from **kinship studies,** which compare the characteristics of family members. The most common type of kinship study compares identical twins, who share all their genes, with fraternal twins, who share only some. If people who are genetically more alike are also more similar in intelligence and personality, then the researcher assumes that heredity plays an important role.

Kinship studies of intelligence provide some of the most controversial findings in the field of human development. Some experts claim a strong genetic influence, whereas others believe that heredity is barely involved. Currently, most kinship findings support a moderate role for heredity. When many twin studies are examined, correlations between the scores of identical twins are consistently higher than those of fraternal twins. In a summary of more than 13,000 twin pairs, the correlation for intelligence was .86 for identical twins and .55 for fraternal twins (Scarr, 1997).

Researchers use a complex statistical procedure to compare these correlations, arriving at a heritability estimate ranging from 0 to 1.00. The value for intelligence is about .50 for child and adolescent twin samples in Western industrialized nations. This indicates that differences in genetic makeup can explain half the variation in intelligence (Plomin, 1994b). However, heritability increases in adulthood, with some estimates as high as .80. As we will see later, one explanation is that adults exert greater control over their intellectual experiences than do children (McClearn et al., 1997; McGue & Christensen, 2002). The intelligence of adopted children is more strongly related to the scores of their biological parents than to those of their adoptive parents, offering further support for the role of heredity (Horn, 1983; Scarr & Weinberg, 1983).

Heritability research also reveals that genetic factors are important in temperament and personality. For frequently studied traits, such as sociability, emotional expressiveness, and activity level, heritability estimates obtained on child, adolescent, and young adult twins are moderate, at .40 to .50 (Rothbart & Bates, 1998). Unlike intelligence, however, heritability of personality does not increase over the lifespan (Brody, 1997).

© T. K. WANSTALL/THE IMAGE WORKS

Identical twins Bob and Bob were separated by adoption shortly after birth and not reunited until adulthood. The two Bobs discovered they were alike in many ways. Both hold bachelor's degrees in engineering, are married to teachers named Brenda, wear glasses, have mustaches, smoke pipes, and are volunteer firemen. The study of identical twins reared apart reveals that heredity contributes to many psychological characteristics. Nevertheless, not all separated twins match up as well as this pair, and generalizing from twin evidence to the population is controversial.

Concordance. A second measure used to infer the contribution of heredity to complex characteristics is the **concordance rate.** It refers to the percentage of instances in which both twins show a trait when it is present in one twin. Researchers typically use concordance to study the contribution of heredity to emotional and behavior disorders, which can be judged as either present or absent.

A concordance rate ranges from 0 to 100 percent. A score of 0 indicates that if one twin has the trait, the other one never has it. A score of 100 means that if one twin has the trait, the other one always has it. When a concordance rate is much higher for identical twins than for fraternal twins, heredity is believed to play a major role. Twin studies of schizophrenia (a disorder involving delusions and hallucinations, difficulty distinguishing fantasy from reality, and irrational and inappropriate behaviors) and severe depression show this pattern of findings. In the case of schizophrenia, the concordance rate for identical twins is 50 percent, that for fraternal twins only 18 percent. For severe depression, the figures are 69 percent and 25 percent (Gottesman, 1991; McGuffin & Sargeant, 1991). Once again, adoption studies support these results. Biological relatives of schizophrenic and depressed adoptees are more likely than adoptive relatives to share the same disorder (Bock & Goode, 1996; Loehlin, Willerman, & Horn, 1988).

Taken together, concordance and adoption research suggests that the tendency for schizophrenia and depression to run in families is partly due to genetic factors. However, we also know that environment is involved, since the concordance rate for identical twins would have to be 100 percent for heredity to be the only influence.

Limitations of Heritability and Concordance. Serious questions have been raised about the accuracy of heritability estimates and concordance rates. First, each value refers only to the particular population studied and its unique range of genetic and environmental influences. For example, imagine a country in which people's home, school, and community experiences are very similar. Under these conditions, individual differences in intelligence and personality would be largely genetic, and heritability estimates would be close to 1.00. Conversely, the more environments vary, the greater their opportunity to account for individual differences, and the lower heritability estimates are likely to be (Plomin, 1994a).

Second, the accuracy of heritability estimates and concordance rates depends on the extent to which the twin pairs used reflect genetic and environmental variation in the population. Yet most twins studied are reared together under highly similar conditions. Even when separated twins are available, social service agencies often place them in advantaged homes that are alike in many ways (Eisenberg, 1998). Because the environments of most twin pairs are less diverse than those of the general population, heritability estimates are likely to exaggerate the role of heredity.

Heritability estimates are controversial because they can easily be misapplied. For example, high heritabilities have been used to suggest that ethnic differences in intelligence, such as the poorer performance of black children compared to white children, have a genetic basis (Jensen, 1969, 1985, 1998). Yet this line of reasoning is widely regarded as incorrect. Heritabilities computed on mostly white twin samples do not tell us what is responsible for test score differences between ethnic groups. We have already seen that large economic and cultural differences are involved. In Chapter 9, we will discuss research indicating that when black children are adopted into economically advantaged homes at an early age, their scores are well above average and substantially higher than those of children growing up in impoverished families.

Perhaps the most serious criticism of heritability estimates and concordance rates has to do with their usefulness. Although they are interesting statistics, they give us no precise information about how intelligence and personality develop or how individuals might respond to environments designed to help them develop as far as possible (Bronfenbrenner & Ceci, 1994; Wachs, 1999). Indeed, the heritability of intelligence is higher in advantaged homes and communities, which permit children to actualize their genetic endowment. In disadvantaged environments, children are prevented from realizing their potential. Consequently, enhancing their experiences through interventions—such as parent education and high-quality preschool or child care—has a greater impact on development (Bronfenbrenner & Morris, 1998).

According to one group of experts, heritability estimates have too many problems to yield any firm conclusions about the relative strength of nature and nurture (Collins et al., 2000). Although these statistics confirm that heredity contributes to complex traits, they do not tell us how environment can modify genetic influences.

The Question, "How?"

Today, most researchers view development as the result of a dynamic interplay between heredity and environment. How do nature and nurture work together? Several concepts shed light on this question.

Reaction Range. The first of these ideas is **range of reaction,** or each person's unique, genetically determined response to the environment (Gottesman, 1963). Let's explore this idea in Figure 2.8. Reaction range can apply to any characteristic; here it is illustrated for intelligence. Notice that when environments vary from extremely unstimulating to highly enriched, Ben's intelligence increases steadily, Linda's rises sharply and then falls off, and Ron's begins to increase only after the environment becomes modestly stimulating.

Reaction range highlights two important points. First, it shows that because each of us has a unique genetic makeup, we respond differently to the same environment. Note in Figure 2.8 how a poor environment results in similarly low scores for all three individuals. But Linda is by far the best-performing child when environments provide an intermediate level of stimulation. And when environments are highly enriched, Ben does best, followed by Ron, both of whom now outperform

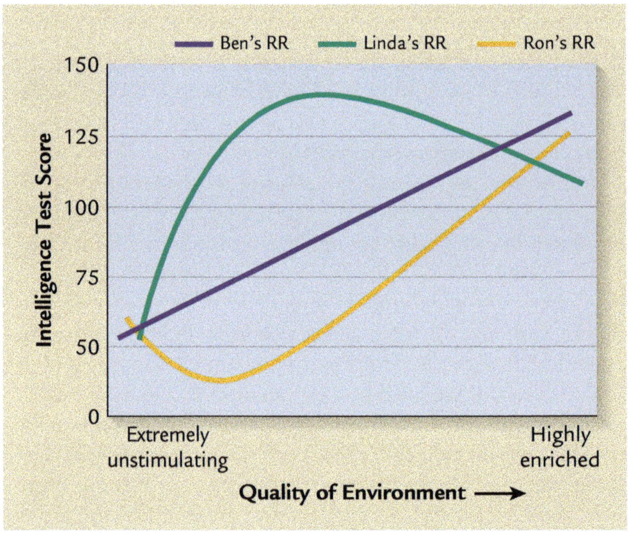

FIGURE 2.8 Intellectual ranges of reaction (RR) for three children in environments that vary from extremely unstimulating to highly enriched. Each child, due to his or her genetic makeup, responds differently as quality of the environment changes. Ben's intelligence increases steadily, Linda's rises sharply and then falls off, and Ron's begins to increase only after the environment becomes modestly stimulating. (Adapted from Wahlsten, 1994.)

Linda. Second, sometimes different genetic–environmental combinations can make two people look the same! For example, if Linda is reared in a minimally stimulating environment, her score will be about 100—average for people in general. Ben and Ron can also obtain this score, but to do so, they must grow up in a fairly enriched home. In sum, range of reaction reveals that unique blends of heredity and environment lead to both similarities and differences in behavior (Wahlsten, 1994).

● **Canalization.** The concept of canalization provides another way of understanding how heredity and environment combine. **Canalization** is the tendency of heredity to restrict the development of some characteristics to just one or a few outcomes. A behavior that is strongly canalized follows a genetically set growth plan, and only powerful environmental forces can change it (Waddington, 1957). For example, infant perceptual and motor development seems to be strongly canalized because all normal human babies eventually roll over, reach for objects, sit up, crawl, and walk. It takes extreme conditions to modify these behaviors. In contrast, intelligence and personality are less strongly canalized, since they vary much more with changes in the environment.

When we look at the behaviors constrained by heredity, we can see that canalization is highly adaptive. Through it, nature ensures that children will develop certain species-typical skills under a wide range of rearing conditions, thereby promoting survival.

● **Genetic–Environmental Correlation.** Nature and nurture work together in still another way. Several investigators point out that a major problem in trying to separate heredity and environment is that they are often correlated (Plomin, 1994b; Scarr & McCartney, 1983). According to the concept of **genetic–environmental correlation,** our genes influence the environments to which we are exposed. The way this happens changes with age.

Passive and Evocative Correlation. At younger ages, two types of genetic–environmental correlation are common. The first is called *passive* correlation because the child has no control over it. Early on, parents provide environments influenced by their own heredity. For example, parents who are good athletes emphasize outdoor activities and enroll their children in swimming and gymnastics. Besides getting exposed to an "athletic environment," the children may have inherited their parents' athletic ability. As a result, they are likely to become good athletes for both genetic and environmental reasons.

The second type of genetic–environmental correlation is *evocative.* Children evoke responses that are influenced by the child's heredity, and these responses strengthen the child's original style. For example, an active, friendly baby is likely to receive more social stimulation than a passive, quiet infant. And a cooperative, attentive child probably receives more patient and sensitive interactions from parents than an inattentive, distractible child.

©MITCH WOJNAROWICZ/THE IMAGE WORKS

■ This mother is an accomplished skier who exposes her children to skiing. In addition, the children may have inherited their mother's athletic talent. When heredity and environment are correlated, they jointly foster the same capacities, and the influence of one cannot be separated from the influence of the other.

Active Correlation. At older ages, *active* genetic–environmental correlation becomes common. As children extend their experiences beyond the immediate family and are given the freedom to make more choices, they actively seek environments that fit with their genetic tendencies. The well-coordinated, muscular child spends more time at after-school sports, the musically talented youngster joins the school orchestra and practices his violin, and the intellectually curious child is a familiar patron at her local library.

This tendency to actively choose environments that complement our heredity is called **niche-picking** (Scarr & McCartney, 1983). Infants and young children cannot do much niche-picking because adults select environments for them. In contrast, older children, adolescents, and adults are much more in charge of their environments. The niche-picking idea explains why pairs of identical twins reared apart during childhood and later reunited may find, to their great surprise, that they have similar hobbies, food preferences, and vocations—a trend that is especially marked when twins' environmental opportunities are similar (Bouchard et al., 1990; Plomin, 1994b). Niche-picking also helps us understand longitudinal findings that identical twins become somewhat more alike, and fraternal twins and adopted siblings less alike, in intelligence with age (Loehlin, Horn, & Willerman, 1997; McGue & Bouchard, 1998). The influence of heredity and environment is not constant but changes over time. With age, genetic factors may become more important in determining the environments we experience and choose for ourselves.

Biology & Environment

Uncoupling Genetic–Environmental Correlations for Mental Illness and Antisocial Behavior

Diagnosed with schizophrenia, Lars's and Sven's biological mothers had such difficulty functioning in everyday life that each gave up her infant son for adoption. Lars had the misfortune of being placed with adoptive parents who, like his biological mother, were mentally ill. His home life was chaotic, and his parents were punitive and neglectful. Sven's adoptive parents, in contrast, were psychologically healthy and reared him with love, patience, and consistency.

Lars displays a commonly observed genetic–environmental correlation: a predisposition for schizophrenia coupled with maladaptive parenting. Will he be more likely than Sven, whose adoption *uncoupled* this adverse genotype–environment link, to develop mental illness? In a large Finnish adoption study, nearly 200 adopted children of schizophrenic mothers were followed into adulthood (Tienari et al., 1994). Those (like Sven) who were reared by healthy adoptive parents showed little mental illness—no more than a control group with healthy biological and adoptive parents. In contrast, psychological impairments piled up in adoptees (like Lars) with both disturbed biological and adoptive parents. These children were considerably more likely to develop mental illness than were controls whose biological parents were healthy but who were being reared by severely disturbed adoptive parents.

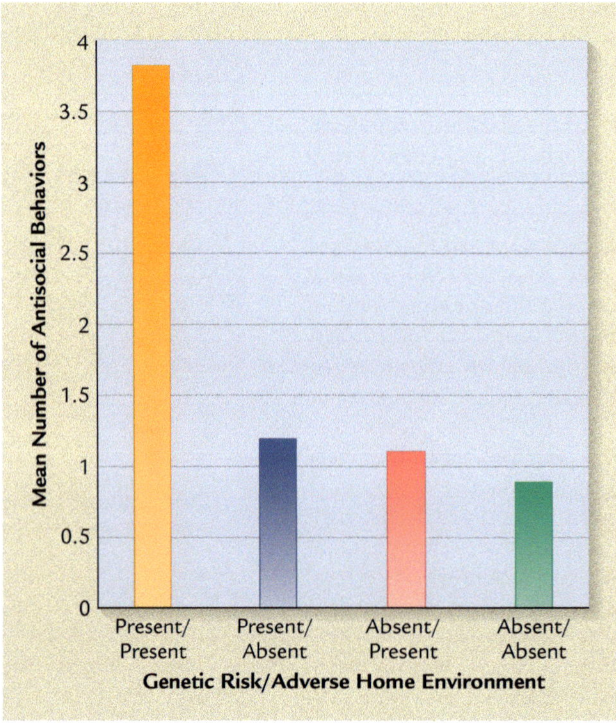

■ FIGURE 2.9 **Antisocial behavior of adoptees varying in genetic and home-environment risk for criminality.** Adolescent adoptees at genetic risk for criminality displayed a high rate of antisocial behavior only when reared in unfavorable homes. When reared in favorable homes, they did not differ from adoptees at no genetic risk. (Adapted from Cadoret, Cain, & Crowe, 1983.)

Similar findings emerged in several American and Swedish adoption studies addressing genetic and environmental contributions to antisocial behavior (Bohman, 1996; Yates, Cadoret, & Troughton, 1999). As Figure 2.9 shows, adopted infants whose biological mothers were imprisoned criminal offenders displayed a high rate of antisocial behavior in adolescence only when reared in unfavorable homes, as indicated by adoptive parents or siblings with severe adjustment problems. In families free of psychological disturbance, adoptees with a predisposition to criminality did not differ from those without this genetic background.

In sum, the chances that genes for psychological disorder will be expressed are far greater when child rearing is maladaptive. Healthy-functioning families seem to promote healthy development in children, despite a genetic risk associated with mental illness or criminality in a biological parent.

• **Environmental Influences on Gene Expression.** Notice how, in the concepts just considered, heredity is granted priority. In range of reaction, it *limits* responsiveness to varying environments. In canalization, it *restricts* the development of certain behaviors. Similarly, some theorists regard genetic–environmental correlation as entirely driven by genetics (Harris, 1998; Rowe, 1994). They believe that children's genetic makeup causes them to receive, evoke, or seek experiences that realize their inborn tendencies. Others argue that heredity does not dictate children's experiences or development in a rigid way. For example, as the Biology and Environment box above illustrates, parents and other caring adults can *uncouple* unfavorable genetic–environmental correlations. They often provide children with experiences that modify the expression of heredity, yielding favorable outcomes.

Accumulating evidence reveals that the relationship between heredity and environment is not a one-way street, from genes to environment to behavior. Instead, like other system

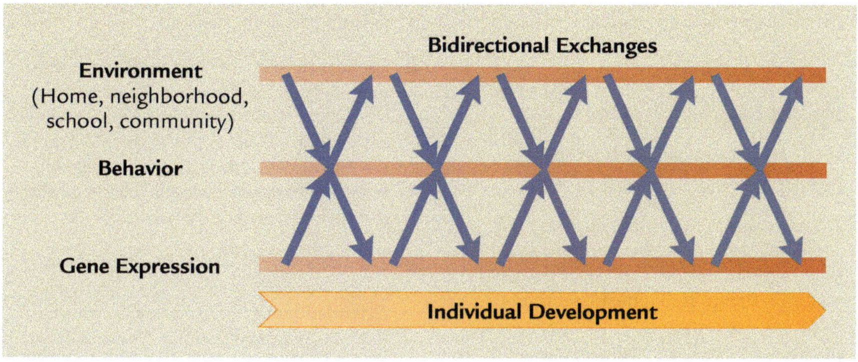

FIGURE 2.10 The epigenetic framework. Development takes place through ongoing, bidirectional exchanges between heredity and all levels of the environment. Genes affect behavior and experiences. Experiences and behavior also affect gene expression. (Adapted from Gottlieb, 2000.)

influences considered in this and the previous chapter, it is bidirectional: Genes affect people's behavior and experiences, but their experiences and behavior also affect gene expression (Gottlieb, 2000). Stimulation—both internal to the person (activity within the cytoplasm of the cell) and external to the person (home, neighborhood, school, and community)—triggers gene activity.

Researchers call this view of the relationship between heredity and environment the *epigenetic framework* (Gottlieb, 1998, 2002). It is depicted in Figure 2.10. **Epigenesis** means development resulting from ongoing, bidirectional exchanges between heredity and all levels of the environment. To illustrate, granting a baby a healthy diet increases brain growth, leading to new connections between nerve cells, which transform gene expression. This opens the door to new gene–environment exchanges—for example, advanced exploration of objects and interaction with caregivers, which further enhance brain growth and gene expression. These ongoing, bidirectional influences foster cognitive and social development. In contrast, harmful environments can dampen gene expression, at times so profoundly that later experiences can do little to change characteristics (such as intelligence) that were flexible to begin with.

A major reason that researchers are interested in the nature–nurture issue is that they want to improve environments so people can develop as far as possible. The concept of epigenesis reminds us that development is best understood as a series of complex exchanges between nature and nurture. Although people cannot be changed in any way we might desire, environments can modify genetic influences. The success of any attempt to improve development depends on the characteristics we want to change, the genetic makeup of the individual, and the type and timing of our intervention.

Ask Yourself

REVIEW

What is epigenesis, and how does it differ from range of reaction and genetic–environmental correlation? Provide an example of epigenesis.

APPLY

Bianca's parents are accomplished musicians. At age 4, Bianca began taking piano lessons. By age 10, she was accompanying the school choir. At age 14, she asked if she could attend a special music high school. Explain how genetic–environmental correlation promoted Bianca's talent.

CONNECT

One possible reason for the increase in heritability of intelligence from childhood to adulthood is that compared with children, adults exert more control over their own intellectual experiences (see page 68). What type of genetic–environmental correlation is involved? What light does this explanation shed on whether heritability estimates yield "pure" measures of genetic influences on human traits?

www.

Summary

Genetic Foundations

What are genes, and how are they transmitted from one generation to the next?

- Each individual's **phenotype,** or directly observable characteristics, is a product of both **genotype** and environment.

Chromosomes, rodlike structures within the cell nucleus, contain our hereditary endowment. Along their length are **genes,** segments of **DNA** that send instructions for making a rich assortment of proteins to the cytoplasm of the cell—a process that makes us distinctly human and influences our development and characteristics. We share most of our genetic makeup with other mammals, especially primates.

- **Gametes,** or sex cells, are produced by the process of cell division known as **meiosis.** Because each individual receives a unique set of genes from each parent, meiosis ensures that children will be genetically different. Once sperm and ovum unite, the resulting **zygote** starts to develop into a complex human being through cell duplication, or **mitosis.**

- If the fertilizing sperm carries an X chromosome, the child will be a girl; if it contains a Y chromosome, a boy will be born. **Fraternal,** or **dizygotic, twins** result when two ova are released from the mother's ovaries and each is fertilized. In contrast, **identical,** or **monozygotic,** twins develop when a zygote divides in two during the early stages of cell duplication.

Describe various patterns of genetic inheritance.

- **Dominant–recessive** and **codominant** relationships are patterns of inheritance that apply to traits controlled by single genes. In dominant–recessive inheritance, **heterozygous** individuals with one recessive gene are **carriers** of the recessive trait.

- When recessive disorders are **X-linked** (carried on the X chromosome), males are more likely to be affected. **Genetic imprinting** is a newly discovered pattern of inheritance in which one parent's gene is activated, regardless of its makeup.

- Unfavorable genes arise from **mutations,** which can occur spontaneously or be induced by hazardous environmental agents.

- Human traits that vary continuously, such as intelligence and personality, are **polygenic,** or influenced by many genes. Because the genetic principles involved are unknown, scientists must study the influence of heredity on these characteristics indirectly.

Describe major chromosomal abnormalities, and explain how they occur.

- Most chromosomal abnormalities are due to errors in meiosis. The most common chromosomal disorder is Down syndrome, which results in physical defects and mental retardation. Disorders of the **sex chromosomes** are generally milder than defects of the **autosomes.** Contrary to popular belief, males with XYY syndrome are not prone to aggression. Studies of children with triple X, Klinefelter, and Turner syndromes reveal that adding to or subtracting from the usual number of X chromosomes leads to specific intellectual problems.

Reproductive Choices

What procedures can assist prospective parents in having healthy children?

- **Genetic counseling** helps couples at risk for giving birth to children with genetic abnormalities decide whether or not to conceive. **Prenatal diagnostic methods** make early detection of genetic problems possible. Although reproductive technologies, such as donor insemination, in vitro fertilization, surrogate motherhood, and postmenopausal-assisted childbirth, permit many individuals to become parents who otherwise would not, they raise serious legal and ethical concerns.

- Many parents who cannot conceive or who have a high likelihood of transmitting a genetic disorder decide to adopt. Adopted children have more learning and emotional problems than children in general. However, warm, sensitive parenting predicts favorable development, and in the long run most adopted children fare well.

Environmental Contexts For Development

Describe the social systems perspective on family functioning, along with aspects of the environment that support family well-being and development.

- Just as complex as heredity are the environments in which human development takes place. The family is the first and foremost context for development. Ecological systems theory emphasizes that the behaviors of each family member affect those of others. The family system is also dynamic, constantly adjusting to new events, to developmental changes in its members, and to societal change.

- Despite these variations, one source of consistency in family functioning is **socioeconomic status (SES).** Higher-SES families tend to be smaller, to place greater emphasis on nurturing psychological traits, and to promote warm, verbally stimulating interaction with children. Lower-SES families often stress external characteristics and engage in more restrictive child rearing. Development is seriously undermined by poverty and homelessness.

- Supportive ties to the surrounding environment foster well-being throughout the lifespan. Communities that encourage constructive leisure activities, warm interactions among residents, connections between settings, and children and adults' active participation enhance development.

- The values and practices of cultures and **subcultures** affect all aspects of daily life. **Extended family households,** in which three or more generations live together, are common among ethnic minorities. They protect development under conditions of high life stress.

- In the complex world in which we live, favorable development depends on **public policies.** Effective social programs are influenced by many factors, including cultural values that stress **collectivism** over **individualism,** a nation's economic resources, and organizations and individuals that work for an improved quality of life. American and Canadian policies safeguarding children and their families are not as well developed as those safeguarding the elderly.

Understanding the Relationship Between Heredity and Environment

Explain the various ways heredity and environment may combine to influence complex traits.

- Some researchers believe it is useful and possible to determine "how much" heredity and environment contribute to individual differences. These investigators compute **heritability estimates** and **concordance rates** from **kinship studies.** Although these measures show that genetic factors influence such traits as intelligence and personality, their accuracy and usefulness have been challenged.

- Most researchers view development as the result of a dynamic interplay between nature and nurture and ask "how" heredity and environment work together. The concepts of **range of reaction, canalization, genetic–environmental correlation, niche-picking,** and **epigenesis** remind us that development is best understood as a series of complex exchanges between nature and nurture that change over the lifespan.

60 Molecular genetics I – fundamental principles

Deoxyribonucleic acid (DNA) is the genetic material of all cellular organisms. Its structure is outlined in Chapter 53.

***KEY POINT** The sequence of the bases A, G, T and C carries the genetic information of the organism. A section of DNA that encodes the information for a single polypeptide or protein is referred to as a gene, while the entire genetic information of an organism is called the genome.*

The amount of DNA in the genome is usually expressed in terms of base pairs (bp), rather than M_r, and its size depends on the complexity of the organism: for example, the human papilloma virus has a genome of 8×10^3 base pairs (8 kbp), that of *Escherichia coli* is 4×10^6 base pairs (4 Mbp), while the human haploid genome is very large, comprising 3×10^9 base pairs (3000 Mbp). The human genome contains about 23 000 genes (distributed on 23 pairs of chromosomes), which represent only about 1 per cent of the total amount of genomic DNA (i.e. 99 per cent of human DNA is non-coding). Organisms with smaller genomes have smaller amounts of non-coding DNA: some viral genomes have 'overlapping' genes, where the same base sequences carry information for more than one protein.

Definition

Units of nucleic acid size (length) – Kilobase pair (kbp) = 10^3 base pairs
Megabase pair (Mbp) = 10^6 base pairs

The size of each individual gene varies considerably: the largest ones may exceed 10 Mbp. Chromosomes represent the largest organisational units of DNA: in eukaryotes, they are usually linear molecules, complexed with protein and RNA, varying in length from tens to hundreds of Mbp. The unit used to denote physical distance between genes (base pairs) differs from that used to describe genetic distance (centimorgan, cM), which is based on recombination frequency (p. 416). In humans, 1 cM ≈ 1 Mbp, though this relationship varies widely depending on recombination frequency within particular regions of a chromosome.

Each template for the synthesis of RNA (transcription) begins at a promoter site upstream of the coding sequence and terminates at a specific site at the end of the gene. The base sequence of this RNA is complementary to the 'template strand' and equivalent to the 'coding strand' of the DNA. In eukaryotic cells, transcription occurs in the nucleus, where the newly synthesised RNA, or primary transcript, is also subject to processing, or 'splicing', in which non-coding regions within the gene (introns) are excised, joining the coding regions (exons) together into a continuous sequence. Further processing results in the addition of a polyadenyl 'tail' at the 3′ end and a 7-methylguanosine 'cap' at the 5′ end of what is now mature eukaryotic messenger RNA (mRNA). The mRNA then migrates from the nucleus to the cytoplasm, where it acts as a template for protein synthesis (translation) at the ribosome: the translated portion of mRNA is read in coding units, termed codons, consisting of three bases.

Each codon corresponds to a specific amino acid, including a codon for the initiation of protein synthesis (Table 60.1). Individual amino acids are brought to the ribosome by specific transfer RNA (tRNA) molecules that recognise particular codons. The amino acids are incorporated into the growing polypeptide chain in the order dictated by the sequence of codons until a termination codon is recognised, after which the protein is released from the ribosome.

Table 60.1 The Genetic Code – combinations of nucleotide bases coding for individual amino acids

	2nd Base				
1st Base	***U***	***C***	***A***	***G***	3rd Base
U	F	S	Y	C	***U***
	F	S	Y	C	***C***
	L	S	*	*	***A***
	L	S	*	W	***G***
C	L	P	H	R	***U***
	L	P	H	R	***C***
	L	P	Q	R	***A***
	L	P	Q	R	***G***
A	I	T	N	S	***U***
	I	T	N	S	***C***
	I	T	K	R	***A***
	M	T	K	R	***G***
G	V	A	D	G	***U***
	V	A	D	G	***C***
	V	A	E	G	***A***
	V	A	E	G	***G***

* = termination codons.
Standard abbreviations for the above amino acids are as given in Table 50.1.
Note that AUG (=M) is the initiation codon.
The above codons are given for mRNA – the coding strand of DNA would have T in place of U, while the template strand would have complementary bases to those given above.

Good practice in molecular genetics *– this includes:*

- *accurate pipetting down to 1 μl, or less;*
- *steadiness of hand in sample loading;*
- *keeping enzyme solutions cold during use and frozen during storage;*
- *using sterile plasticware;*
- *using double-distilled ultrapure water;*
- *wearing disposable gloves to avoid contamination.*

The techniques described in this and subsequent chapters are used widely in many aspects of molecular biology, including the identification and characterisation of genes, gene cloning and genetic engineering, medical genetics and genetic fingerprinting.

KEY POINT An important characteristic of nucleic acids is their ability to hybridise: two single strands with complementary base pairs will hydrogen bond (anneal) to produce a duplex, as in conventional double stranded (ds)DNA. This duplex can be converted to single stranded (ss)DNA (i.e. 'melted') by conditions that disrupt hydrogen bonding, e.g. raising the temperature or addition of salt, and then reannealed by lowering the temperature or by removal of salt.

DNA can be easily purified and assayed (Chapter 53), and it is relatively stable in its pure form. Most of the problems of working with such a large biomolecule have been overcome by the following:

Using restriction digests of viral genomes *– the controlled fragmentation pattern obtained when a phage or plasmid is cut with a specific restriction enzyme can be used to create a 'DNA ladder' – a set of DNA fragments of known length that can be used as reference standards in gel electrophoresis (p. 431).*

- using restriction enzymes (see below) to cut DNA precisely and reproducibly: mammalian DNA may yield millions of fragments, with sizes ranging from a few hundred base pairs to tens of kbp, while small viral genomes may give only a few fragments;
- electrophoretic methods for the separation of DNA fragments on the basis of their sizes (p. 431);
- segments of DNA can be detected by 'probes' that specifically hybridise with the DNA of interest (p. 433);
- once separated, specific segments of DNA can be obtained in almost unlimited quantities by insertion into vectors and multiplication within suitable host cells (DNA cloning, Chapter 62);
- methods are now available for rapidly determining the base sequence of DNA segments (p. 436), together with strategies for combining information from several adjacent segments to give contiguous sequences ('contigs') representing entire genomes in well-studied organisms (Chapter 11);
- specific target sequences of DNA within a genome can be amplified by more than a billion-fold by the polymerase chain reaction (PCR, see Chapter 61).

Example ClustalW software can be used for multiple sequence alignment – it can be downloaded from the European Bioinformatics Institute website at: http://www.ebi.ac.uk/clustalw/

Producing DNA fragments

Using restriction enzymes in genetic engineering *– those enzymes that cleave DNA to give single stranded 'sticky ends' are particularly useful in gene cloning (Chapter 62). Two different molecules of DNA cut with the same restriction enzyme will have complementary single stranded regions, allowing them to anneal as a result of hydrogen bonding between individual bases within these regions.*

Fragments of DNA can be produced by mechanical shearing or ultrasonication (p. 245), producing a random array of fragment sizes. Reproducible cleavage can be achieved using type II restriction endonucleases (commonly called restriction enzymes) which recognise and cleave at a specific palindromic sequence of double stranded DNA (usually four or six base pairs), known as the restriction site. Each enzyme is given a code name derived from the name of the organism from which it is isolated, e.g. *Hin* dIII was the third restriction enzyme to be obtained from *Haemophilus influenzae* strain Rd (Fig. 60.1). Most restriction enzymes will cut each DNA strand at a slightly different position within the restriction site to produce short, single stranded regions known as cohesive ends, or 'sticky ends', as shown in Figure 60.1. A few restriction enzymes cleave DNA to give blunt-ended fragments (e.g. *Hin* dII or *Sma* I).

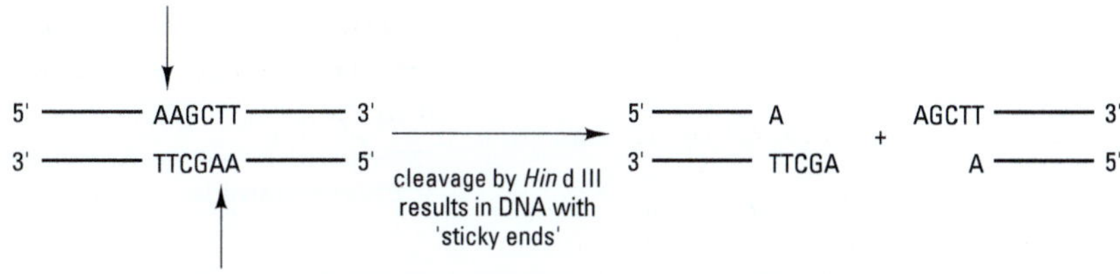

Fig. 60.1 Recognition base sequence and cleavage site for the restriction enzyme *Hin* dIII. This is the conventional representation of double-stranded DNA, showing the individual bases, where A is adenine, C cytosine, G guanine and T thymine. The cleavage site on each strand is shown by an arrow.

Maximising recovery of DNA *– these large molecules are easily damaged by mechanical forces, e.g. vigorous shaking or stirring during extraction. In addition, all glassware must be scrupulously cleaned and gloves must be worn, to prevent deoxyribonuclease contamination of solutions.*

Working with small volumes in molecular biology *– use a pipettor of appropriate size (e.g. P2 or P20 Gilson Pipetman) with a fine tip. For very small volumes, pre-wet the tip before delivering the required volume.*

SAFETY NOTE Using an electrophoresis tank – always ensure that the top cover is in position, to prevent evaporation of buffer solution and to reduce the possibility of electric shock.

Separation of nucleic acids using gel electrophoresis

Separation of DNA by agarose and polyacrylamide gel electrophoresis

Electrophoresis is the term used to describe the movement of ions in an applied electrical field. DNA molecules are negatively charged, migrating through an agarose gel towards the anode at a rate which is dependent upon molecular size – smaller, compact DNA molecules can pass through the sieve-like agarose matrix more easily than large, extended fragments. Electrophoresis of plasmid DNA is usually carried out using a submerged agarose gel (Fig. 60.2). The amount of agarose is adjusted, depending on the size of the DNA molecules to be separated, e.g. 0.3% w/v agarose is used for large fragments (>20 000 bp) while 0.8% is used for smaller fragments. Very small fragments are best separated using a polyacrylamide gel (Table 60.2). Note the following:

- Individual samples are added to pre-formed wells using a pipettor. The volume of sample added to each well is usually less than 25 μl so a steady hand and careful dispensing are needed to pipette each sample.
- The density of the samples is usually increased by adding a small amount of glycerol or sucrose, so that each sample is retained within the appropriate well.
- A water-soluble anionic tracking dye (e.g. bromophenol blue or xylene cyanol) is also added to each sample, so that migration can be followed visually.

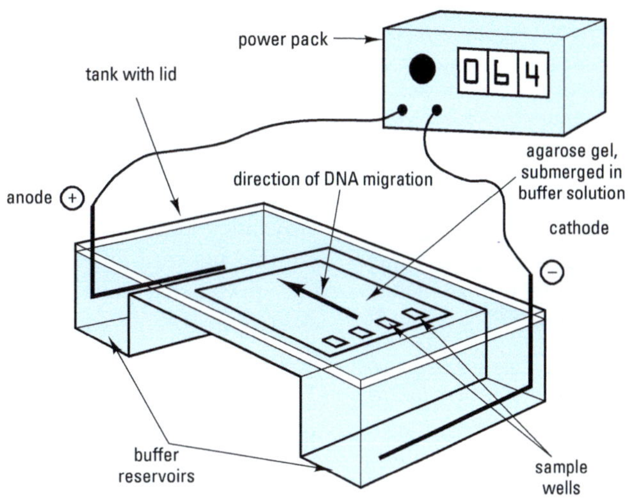

Fig. 60.2 Agarose gel electrophoresis of DNA.

Table 60.2 Gel concentrations for the separation of DNA of various sizes

Type of gel	% (w/v)	Range of resolution of DNA (bp)
Polyacrylamide	20.0	5–100
	15.0	20–150
	5.0	75–500
	3.5	100–1000
Agarose	2.0	100–5000
	1.2	200–8000
	0.8	400–20 000
	0.3	1000–70 000

Using DNA fragment size markers *– for accurate determination of fragment size (length) your standards must have the same conformation as the DNA in your sample, i.e. linear DNA standards for linear (restriction) fragments and closed circular standards for plasmid DNA.*

SAFETY NOTE Handling ethidium bromide – ethidium bromide is carcinogenic so always use gloves when handling stained gels and make sure you do not spill any staining solution, or use a safer alternative, such as SYBR Safe.

SAFETY NOTE Working with a UV radiation source – always wear suitable UV-filtering plastic safety glasses or goggles to protect your eyes.

Assaying nucleic acids in solution *– double stranded DNA at 50 μg ml^{-1} has an A_{260} of 1, and the same absorbance is obtained for single stranded DNA at 33 μg ml^{-1} and (single stranded) RNA at 40 μg ml^{-1}. These values can be used to convert the absorbance of a test solution to a concentration of nucleic acid.*

- DNA fragment size markers ('molecular weight' standards) are added to one or more wells. After electrophoresis, the relative positions of bands of known molecular weight can be used to prepare a calibration curve (usually by plotting $\log_{10}$ of the size (length) of each band against the distance travelled).
- The gel should be run until the bromophenol blue tracking dye has migrated across 80% of the gel (see manufacturer's instructions for appropriate voltages/times).
- After electrophoresis, the bands of DNA can be visualised by soaking the gel for around 5 min in 0.1–0.5 mg l^{-1} ethidium bromide (Fig. 53.4), which binds to DNA by intercalation between the paired nucleotides of the double helix.
- Under UV light, bands of DNA are visible due to the intense fluorescence of the ethidium bromide. The limit of detection using this method is around 10 ng DNA per band. The migration of each band from the well can be measured using a ruler. Alternatively, a photograph can be taken, using a digital camera and adaptor, or a dedicated system, e.g. GelDoc from BioRad.
- If a particular band is required for further study (e.g. a plasmid), the piece of gel containing that band is cut from the gel using a clean scalpel. The DNA can be separated from the agarose by solubilising the gel slice and then binding the DNA to an anion exchange resin, followed by elution in water or buffer (e.g. TE buffer, containing 10 mmol l^{-1} TRIS/HCl at pH 8.0 plus 1 mmol l^{-1} EDTA). Various commercial kits based on this approach are also available, e.g. from Qiagen.

Electrophoretic separation of RNA

Total cellular RNA or purified mRNA can be separated on the basis of size by electrophoretic separations similar to those used for DNA fragments. However, under the conditions used to separate dsDNA, RNA molecules tend to develop a secondary structure, and this leads to anomalous mobilities. To eliminate RNA secondary structure, samples are pretreated by heating in dilute formamide or glyoxal, and electrophoresis is carried out in 'denaturing gels' which include buffers containing formaldehyde.

Pulsed field gel electrophoresis (PFGE)

If structural information is to be gained about large stretches of genomic DNA, then the order of the relatively short DNA segments (generated by

> **Definition**
>
> **Chromosome walking** – a method for analysing areas of interest in DNA, in which the end of a segment of DNA is used as a probe to locate other segments that overlap the first segment: long stretches of DNA can be analysed by subsequent use of probes made from the ends of successive overlapping segments.

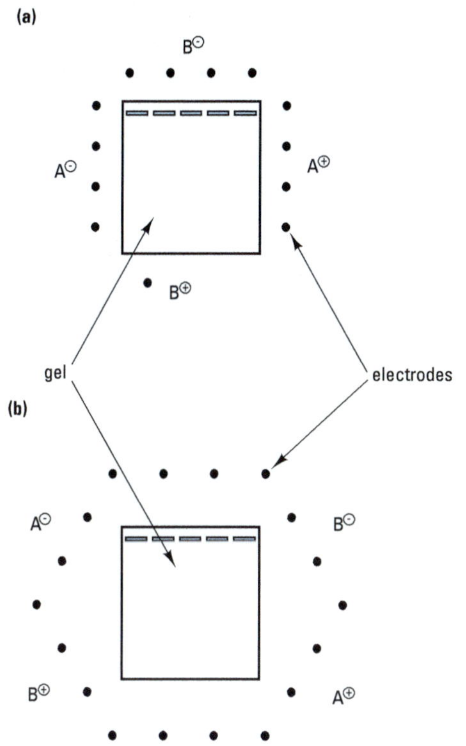

Fig. 60.3 The configuration of electrodes for conventional PFGE (a) and CHEF/PACE (b).

the restriction enzymes described above) needs to be established. This is technically possible by techniques such as 'chromosome walking', but is time-consuming and potentially difficult, especially when dealing with large chromosomes such as those from yeast (a few Mbp) and humans (50–100 Mb), in contrast to the smaller genomes of bacteria and viruses. The technique of PFGE allows separation of DNA fragments of up to ≈12 Mb.

Very large DNA fragments (>100 kbp) can be generated from chromosomal DNA by the use of certain restriction enzymes that recognise base sequences that are present at relatively low frequency, e.g. the enzyme *Not* I, which recognises a sequence of 8 bp rather than 4–6 bp. These enzymes are sometimes called 'rare cutters'. Genomic DNA prepared in the normal way is not suitable for digestion by these enzymes, as shearing during extraction fragments the DNA. Therefore, genomic DNA for analysis by PFGE is prepared as follows:

- cells are embedded in an agarose block;
- the block is incubated in solutions containing detergent, RNase and proteinase K, lysing the cells and hydrolysing RNA and proteins. The products of RNase and proteinase digestion diffuse away, leaving behind genomic DNA molecules exceeding several thousand kbp;
- the block is incubated *in situ* in a buffered solution containing an appropriate 'rare cutter': restriction fragments are produced, of up to ≈800 kbp.

PFGE differs from conventional electrophoresis in that it uses two or more alternating electric fields. An explanation for the effectivess of the technique is that large DNA fragments will be distorted by the voltage gradient, tending to elongate in the direction of the electric field and 'snaking' through pores in the gel. If the original electric field (Fig. 60.3a), is removed, and a second is applied at an angle to the first (Fig. 60.3b), the DNA must reorientate before it can migrate in the new direction. Larger (longer) DNA molecules will take more time to reorientate than smaller molecules, resulting in size-dependent separations.

The original configuration of electrodes used in PFGE is shown in Fig. 60.3a; this tends to produce 'bent' lanes that make lane-to-lane comparisons difficult. This can be overcome by using one of the many variants of the technique, one of which employs contour clamped homogeneous electric fields (CHEF). Here, multiple electrodes are arranged in a hexagonal array around the gel (Fig. 60.3b) and these are used to generate homogeneous electric fields with reorientation angles of up to 120°. A further development of CHEF involves programmable, autonomously controlled electrodes (PACE), which allows virtually unlimited variation of field and pulsing configurations, and can fractionate DNA molecules from 100 bp to 6 Mbp.

Identification of specific nucleic acid molecules using blotting and hybridisation techniques

Southern blotting

After separation by conventional agarose gel electrophoresis (p. 431), the fragments of DNA can be denatured and immobilised on a filter membrane using a technique named after its inventor, E.M. Southern.

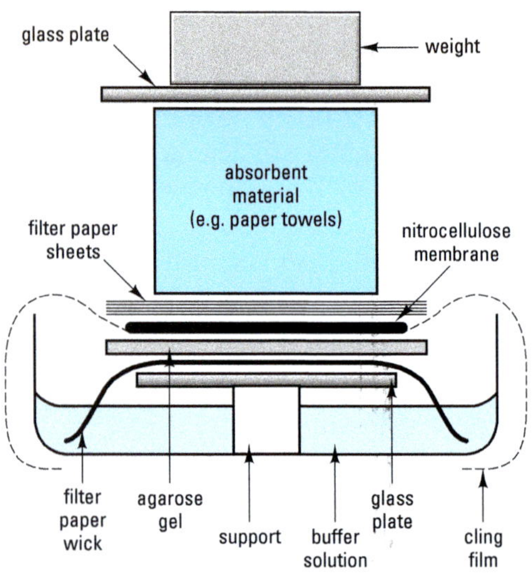

Fig. 60.4 Components of Southern blotting apparatus.

The main features of the conventional apparatus for Southern blotting are shown in Figure 60.4. The principal stages in the procedure are:

1. To ensure efficient transfer, the gel is first soaked in HCl, leading to random cleavage of the DNA into smaller fragments.
2. The gel is subsequently soaked in alkali to denature the dsDNA to ssDNA, then neutralised: this is necessary to allow hybridisation with probe DNA after blotting.
3. A nitrocellulose or nylon membrane is then placed directly on the gel, followed by several layers of absorbent paper. The DNA is 'blotted' onto the filter as the buffer solution soaks into the paper by capillary action.
4. The filter is baked in a vacuum oven at 80 °C for 3–5 h or exposed to UV light, in order to 'fix' the DNA.
5. Specific DNA fragments are identified by incubation (6–24 h) with complementary labelled probes of ssDNA, which will hybridise with a particular sequence, followed by visualisation, often using an enzyme-based system. If radiolabelled probes are used (see below), the desired fragments are located by autoradiography (p. 271).

Modifications of the method use either a vacuum apparatus, an electric field ('electroblotting') or positive pressure to transfer the DNA fragments from the gel to the membrane. These modifications reduce the time for transfer by around 10-fold.

Northern blotting

This process is virtually identical to Southern blotting, but RNA is the molecule that is separated and probed.

Dot blotting or slot blotting

Biomedical applications of dot blotting – *these include the detection of specific pathogenic microbes in samples and the identification of particular genetic markers, e.g. in inherited genetic disorders and forensic science.*

Here, samples containing denatured DNA or RNA samples are applied directly to the nitrocellulose membrane (*via* small individual round or slot-like templated holes) without prior digestion with restriction enzymes or electrophoretic separation. The 'blot' is then probed in a similar manner to that described for Southern blotting. This allows detection of a particular nucleic acid sequence in a sample.

Definition

Probe – a labelled DNA or RNA sequence used to detect the presence of a complementary sequence (by molecular hybridisation) in a mixture of DNA or RNA fragments.

Types of probe

The probes used in blotting and DNA hybridisation can be obtained from a variety of sources including:

- cDNA (complementary or copy DNA) which is produced from isolated mRNA using reverse transcriptase. This retroviral enzyme catalyses RNA-directed DNA synthesis (rather than the normal transcription of DNA to RNA). After the mRNA has been reverse transcribed, it is degraded by the addition of alkali or ribonuclease, leaving the ssDNA copy. This is then used as a template for a DNA polymerase, which directs the synthesis of the second complementary DNA strand to form dsDNA. This is denatured to ssDNA before use.
- Oligonucleotide probes (15–30 nucleotides) can be produced if the amino acid sequence of the gene product is known. Since the genetic code is degenerate, i.e. some amino acids are coded for by more than one codon (see Table 60.1) it may be necessary to synthesise a mixture of oligonucleotides to detect a particular DNA sequence: this mixture of oligonucleotides is termed a 'degenerate probe'.

Example For a simple tripeptide containing methionine, aspartate and phenylalanine, the synthetic oligonucleotide probes would include combinations of the following codons:
1st codon (met): ATG
2nd codon (asp): GAT, GAC
3rd codon (phe): TTT, TTC

- Specific genomic DNA sequences, where the gene has been characterised.
- PCR-generated fragments (Chapter 61).
- Heterologous probes, i.e. sequences for the same gene, or its equivalent, in another organism.

Labelling of probes

Detection of very low concentrations of target DNA sequences requires probes that can be detected with high sensitivity. This is achieved by radiolabelling, e.g. using ^{33}P, or by using enzyme-linked methods, which are often available in kit form:

Using commercial kits *– do not blindly follow the protocol given by the manufacturer without making sure you understand the principles of the method and the reasons for the procedure. This will help you to recognise when things go wrong and what you might be able to do about it.*

- Radiolabelled probes can be made by several methods, including the nick-translation technique. This uses DNA polymerase I from *E. coli*, which has (i) an exonuclease activity that 'nicks' dsDNA and removes a nucleotide, and (ii) a polymerase activity that can replace this with a labelled deoxyribonucleotide. After several cycles of nick-translation, the labelled DNA is denatured to ssDNA for use as probes. Newer approaches include random priming of single stranded template DNA, followed by the synthesis of radiolabelled DNA fragments complementary to the template using a DNA polymerase and a radiolabelled deoxynucleoside triphosphate (dNTP). Probe hybridisation to a target sequence is detected by autoradiography. Oligonucleotide probes cannot be labelled using the above methods and require 'end labelling', where a kinase is used to replace the 5′ terminal phosphate group with a radiolabelled group.
- Enzyme-linked methods involve incorporating a modified nucleotide precursor, such as biotinylated dTTP, into the DNA by nick-translation or random priming. When the probe hybridises with the target sequence, it can be detected by addition of an enzyme (e.g. horse radish peroxidase) coupled to streptavidin. The streptavidin binds specifically to the biotin attached to the probe and the addition of a suitable fluorogenic or chromogenic substrate for the enzyme allows the probe to be located.

Using labelled probes *– an alternative approach is the chemiluminescent system based on dioxygenin-labelled nucleotides.*

Hybridisation of probes

The stability of the duplex formed between the probe and its target is directly proportional to the number and type of complementary base pairs that can be formed between them: stability increases with the amount of G + C, since these bases form three hydrogen bonds per base pair, rather than two (p. 369). Duplex stability is also influenced by temperature, ionic strength and pH of the hybridisation buffer, and these can be varied to suit the stringency of hybridisation required:

Example Low stringency hybridisation can be useful when using a heterologous probe, i.e. from another species.

- In 'low stringency' hybridisation, duplex formation with less than perfect complementarity is promoted, either by lowering the temperature, or increasing ionic strength.
- 'Stringent' hybridisation conditions usually involve high temperatures, or decreased ionic strength, and will sustain only perfectly matched duplexes.

Example High stringency conditions can be used for detecting a single base change in a mutant gene using a dot-blot hybridisation procedure with a specific oligonucleotide probe.

DNA sequencing

By fragmenting target DNA with several restriction enzymes and then sequencing the overlapping fragments, it is possible to determine the nucleotide sequences of very large stretches of DNA, including entire

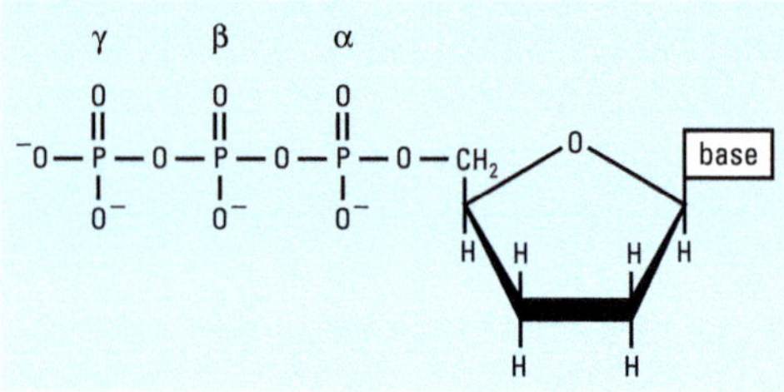

Fig. 60.5 A 2′,3′-dideoxynucleoside triphosphate.

genomes. Sequencing methods rely on polyacrylamide gel electrophoresis (p. 323). The Sanger, or chain termination, method is the most widely used in DNA sequencing. This makes use of dideoxynucleotides (Fig. 60.5), which have no –OH group at either the C-2 or C-3 of ribose. A dideoxynucleoside triphosphate (ddNTP) can be added to a growing DNA chain, but since it lacks an –OH group at the C-3 position it cannot form a phosphodiester bond with the incoming dNTP of the growing chain. Therefore a dideoxynucleotide acts as a terminator at the site it occupies. Details of theSanger sequencing method are given in Box 60.1 and Figure 60.6.

Box 60.1 DNA sequencing using the chain termination (Sanger) method

The DNA to be sequenced must first be obtained as single-stranded fragments, typically around 200 bp, e.g. using a denatured plasmid. Sequencing is often performed using a commercial kit and the principal stages are as follows:

1. **Set up the strand synthesis reaction**: four separate tubes are required, each containing a small amount of one of the dideoxynucleoside triphosphates. Each tube contains all of the other components required for DNA synthesis, i.e. (i) the DNA selected for analysis (template DNA), e.g. denatured plasmid, (ii) a DNA polymerase (e.g. thermostable *Taq* polymerase), (iii) a [^{35}S] oligonucleotide primer of known sequence, to allow synthesis of the complementary DNA strand, (iv) dGTP, dATP, dCTP, dTTP (in excess) together with (v) one type of ddNTP (i.e. ddGTP, ddATP, ddCTP or ddTTP) in limited concentration. New DNA strands are synthesised by addition of dNTPs to the primer, guided by the template DNA until a ddNTP is added. As an example of the principle of the method, consider the ddTTP tube. When T is required to pair with A on the template DNA strand, the dTTP will be competing with the ddTTP, but because the dTTP is in excess this will normally be added to the chain at the appropriate position. However on occasions a ddTTP will be inserted at a given site and this will terminate DNA synthesis on the template strand. Thus, synthesis will be halted at all possible sites where ddT has substituted for dT and several strands of different length will be formed in the reaction mixture, each ending with ddT.

2. **Terminate the strand synthesis reaction**: after 5–10 min at 37 °C add a 'stop' solution containing formamide to disrupt hydrogen bonding between complementary bases and incubate at 80 °C for 15 min, to produce ssDNA.

3. **Separate the fragments using polyacrylamide gel electrophoresis**: 4–6% (w/v) denaturing acrylamide gels are used, containing urea (46% w/v) as the denaturing agent. Thin gels (0.35 mm thickness) are used, typically 20 cm wide by 50 cm long. The products in each of the four tubes are placed in four lanes side by side on the same gel and are separated by electrophoresis at 35–40 W (up to 32 mA, 1.5 kV) for 2.5 h. The high voltage raises the gel temperature to ≈50 °C, helping denaturation. A single gel can separate DNA fragments that differ in length by a single nucleotide.

4. **Locate the positions of individual bands by autoradiography**: the gel is fixed for 15 min with 10% (v/v) acetic acid, covered with Whatman 3MM paper and Saran wrap, then vacuum-dried, to avoid quenching the radioisotope signal (p. 270) and to prevent it from sticking to the X-ray film. The gel is unwrapped and placed next to an X-ray film for 24 h.

5. **Read the gel**: the nucleotide sequence can be read directly from the band positions that represent the newly made DNA segments of varying lengths (Fig. 60.6). The smallest segment is represented by the band at the bottom, since it travels furthest in the gel. The nucleotide sequence of the template strand can be deduced directly from that of the new strand, since the base on the template strand will be represented by an incomplete chain that terminates with the complementary dd nucleotide, i.e. template A with ddT, G with ddC, T with ddA, and C with ddG (Fig. 60.6).

Troubleshooting and other points to note: streaking can be due to damage to wells, air bubbles in wells/gel, or contamination by dirt/dust; faint and fuzzy gels may be due to insufficient template DNA, primer and/or dNTPs, due to poor annealing of primer and template, or to errors in preparing or running the gel; bands in more than one lane can indicate contamination of the template DNA, more than one primer site on the template, or secondary structure of DNA, giving 'ghost' banding.

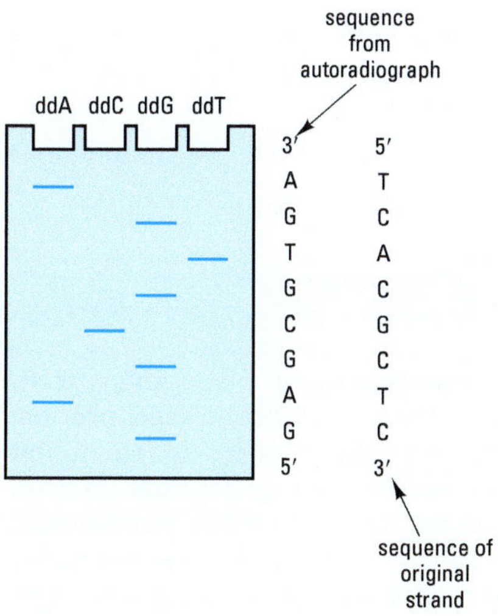

Fig. 60.6 Sanger sequencing gel, showing how the banding pattern is converted into a sequence of nucleotide bases.

***Using PCR (p. 439) for sequencing** – with the four ddNTPs tagged using different fluorophores, the products can be run in the same lane and detected by laser excitation at the end of the gel, with the sequence of fluorophores giving the base sequence.*

***DNA microarrays and bioinformatics** – interpretation of DNA microarray data is a growing area of bioinformatics, requiring dedicated software, e.g. the TM_4 microarray analysis freeware programs available from the Institute of Genomic Research, at: http://www.tm4.org/*

The alternative approach to sequencing is based on chemical degradation (the Maxam and Gilbert method), using different reagents to break the target DNA sequence into fragments which are then separated by polyacrylamide gel electrophoresis. The Maxam and Gilbert method is more involved than the Sanger technique, and is reserved for specialised applications, e.g. for studying the interaction between DNA and proteins.

Automated DNA sequencing

The development of automated DNA sequencing machines (so-called 'DNA sequenators') has enabled sequencing to be performed several orders of magnitude faster than with manual methods. Base-specificity is achieved by using primers labelled with fluorophores with different fluorescence characteristics in each of the four reaction tubes (Box 60.1). After the reactions are separately completed, the four sets of products can be pooled and fractionated by electrophoresis in a single lane. The fluorophore-labelled fragments are detected as they pass a scanning laser detector and the DNA sequence is determined by using both the specific wavelength emitted by the fragment (indicating the base) and by the migration time (indicating the fragment size, which corresponds to the base location in the DNA sequence). Nowadays, automated DNA sequencing tends to be performed by capillary electrophoresis (p. 331) rather than polyacrylamide gel electrophoresis.

DNA microarrays

This area has seen rapid, recent development. DNA microarrays ('gene chips') support the quantitative analysis of many different genes/sequences at the same time. This involves synthesising and fixing single-stranded probes for a large number (>1000) of different nucleotide sequences onto specific sites on a glass, quartz or silicon wafer. When single-stranded labelled nucleic acid is added, it will hybridise only with probes having a complementary sequence and these can be determined by the presence of an attached label, e.g. a fluorescent dye, detected using a scanning laser. One application involves the detection of labelled cDNA produced from the mRNA in an organism by using an 'expression' microchip, which contains probes for all of the expressed genes in an organism, enabling the relative expression of each gene to be determined from the fluorescence signal at each location on the microarray. Other applications include the use of single nucleotide polymorphism (SNP) microarrays to identify mutations and genetic variation, e.g. in screening for genetic diseases and in forensic DNA analysis. A commercial example is the Affymetrix GeneChip system.

Sources for further study

Anon. *NCBI Microarray Factsheet*. Available: http://www.ncbi.nlm.nih.gov/About/primer/microarrays.html Last accessed: 01/04/07.
[A basic guide to the principles of DNA microarrays]

Brown, T.A. (2002) *Essential Molecular Biology: A Practical Approach*, Vols 1 and 2, 2nd edn. Oxford University Press, Oxford.

Clark, M. (2003) *In Situ Hybridization: Laboratory Companion*. Wiley-VCH, Mannheim.

Darby, I.A. and Hewitson, T.D. (2003) *In Situ Hybridization Protocols*. Humana Press, New Jersey.

Hames, B.D. and Higgins, S.J. (1995) *Gene Probes: A Practical Approach*. Oxford University Press, Oxford.

Monaco, A.P. (1995) *Pulsed Field Gel Electrophoresis: A Practical Approach.* IRL Press, Oxford.

Nuber, U. (2005) *DNA Microarrays.* Bios (Advanced Methods Series). Taylor & Francis, Abingdon.

Sambrook, J. and Russell, D.W. (2001) *Molecular Cloning: A Laboratory Manual*, 3rd edn. Cold Spring Harbor Lab, Cold Spring Harbor.

Study exercises

60.1 Practise the calculations involved in working with nucleic acids. Imagine that you have been supplied with a freeze-dried sample of a single stranded DNA probe 24 bases in length, which you reconstitute in 1 ml of buffer (reconstituted probe). You take 5 µl, add it to 495 µl of water and determine the A_{260} as 0.14.

(a) What is the mass concentration of the probe in this solution, in $\mu g\ ml^{-1}$?

(b) Assuming the average M_r of a nucleotide is 325, what is the concentration of the probe in the solution, expressed in micromolar terms (i.e. as $\mu mol\ l^{-1}$)?

(c) The concentration of probe required in a blotting procedure is $10\ pmol\ ml^{-1}$ and a total of 10 ml of this solution is required. You have been asked to prepare 5 ml of a stock solution of the DNA probe at 100× the concentration required in the blotting procedure, so that 0.100 ml can be diluted to 10 ml for the final blotting procedure, while the rest will be stored at −20 °C, for subsequent experiments. How would you prepare the 100× stock solution?

Express all answers to three significant figures.

60.2 Select an electrophoretic technique for separating DNA fragments of different sizes. Which technique would you use to separate DNA fragments in the following ranges: (a) 1–70 kbp; (b) 75–500 bp; (c) 100–6 Mbp.

60.3 Test your understanding of the term 'stringency' in relation to nucleic acid probes. What does the term 'stringency' mean in the context of molecular biology? What factors cause increased stability between a nucleic acid probe and its target sequence? Give examples of when you might use 'low stringency' and 'high stringency' hybridisation.

60.4 Interpret the results of a Sanger sequencing gel. The figure represents a typical gel from a dideoxynucleotide sequencing procedure. Determine the sequence of the original DNA strand.

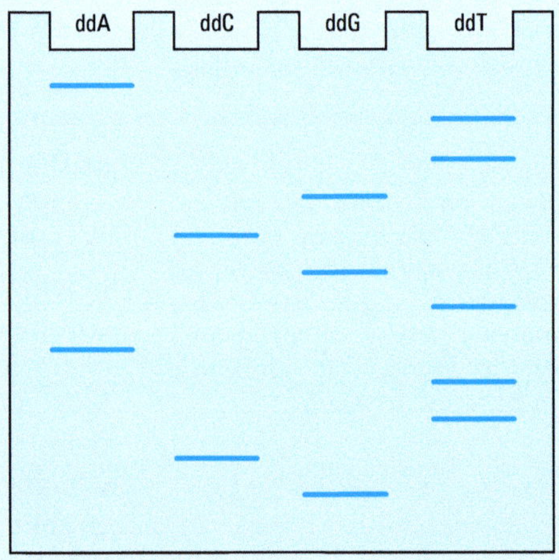

61 Molecular genetics II – PCR and related applications

The polymerase chain reaction (PCR) is a rapid, inexpensive and simple means of producing μg amounts of DNA from minute quantities of template.

***Applications of PCR** – these include:*

- *diagnosis and screening of genetic diseases and cancer;*
- *rapid detection of slowly growing microorganisms (e.g. mycobacteria) and viruses (e.g. HIV);*
- *HLA typing in transplantation;*
- *analysis of DNA in archival material;*
- *DNA fingerprinting in forensic science;*
- *preparation of nucleic acid probes;*
- *clone screening, mapping and sub-cloning (p. 446).*

***KEY POINT** PCR offers an alternative approach to gene cloning (Chapter 62) for the production of many copies of an identical sequence of DNA. The starting material may be genomic DNA (e.g. from a single cell), RNA, DNA from archival specimens, cloned DNA or forensic samples.*

***Understanding the terminology of PCR** – cloned (amplified) DNA sequences produced using PCR techniques are often termed amplicons.*

The technique uses *in vitro* enzyme-catalysed DNA synthesis to create millions of identical copies of DNA. If the base sequence of the adjacent regions of the DNA to be amplified is known, this enables synthetic oligonucleotide primers to be constructed that are complementary to these so-called 'flanking regions'. Initiation of the PCR occurs when these primers are allowed to hybridise (anneal) to the component single strands of the target DNA, followed by enzymatic extension of the primers (from their 3′ ends) using a thermostable DNA polymerase. A single PCR cycle consists of three distinct steps, carried out at different temperatures (Fig. 61.1), as follows:

1. Denaturation of dsDNA by heating to 94–98 °C separating the individual strands of the target DNA.
2. Annealing of the primers, which occurs when the temperature is reduced to 37–65 °C.
3. Extension of the primers by a thermostable DNA polymerase (e.g. *Taq* polymerase, isolated from *Thermus aquaticus*) at 72 °C; this step should last long enough to generate the PCR product: approximately 1 min of reaction time is required per kbp of sequence.

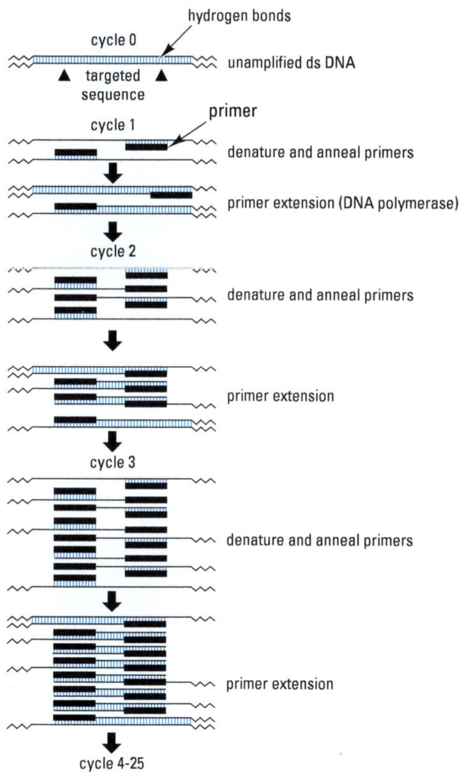

Fig. 61.1 The polymerase chain reaction (PCR).

In the first cycle, the product from one primer is extended beyond the region of complementarity of the other primer, so each newly synthesised strand can be used as a template for the primers in the second cycle (Fig. 61.1). Successive cycles will thus generate an exponentially increasing number of DNA fragments, the termini of which are bounded by the 5′ ends of the primers (length of each fragment = length of primers + length of target sequence). Since the amount of DNA produced doubles in each cycle, the amount of DNA produced = 2^n, where n is the number of cycles. Up to 1 μg of amplified target DNA can be produced in 25–30 cycles from a single-copy sequence within 50 ng of genomic DNA, assuming close to 100% efficiency during the cycling process. After electrophoresis, the PCR product is normally present in sufficient quantity to be visualised directly, for example with ethidium bromide or SYBR Safe.

The temperature changes in PCR are normally achieved using a thermal cycler, which is simply a purpose-built incubator block that can be programmed to vary temperatures, incubation times and cycle numbers.

***KEY POINT** PCR is so sensitive that one of the main problems associated with the technique is contamination with 'foreign' DNA. Great care is required to avoid sample contamination during* in vitro *amplification (Box 61.1).*

PCR components and conditions

These are readily available in kit form from commercial suppliers; they include a thermostable DNA polymerase, such as *Taq* polymerase, dNTPs, buffer, a detergent (e.g. Triton), KCl, $MgCl_2$ or $MgSO_4$, and primers. Protocols for PCR vary considerably for particular applications – a typical procedure is given in Box 61.1. However, if you are trying to develop your own PCR procedure, the following information may be useful:

***Storing primers for PCR** – primers are best stored in ammonia solution, which remains liquid at −20°C, avoiding the need for repeated freezing and thawing when dispensed. Before use, aliquots of stock solution should be heated in a fume cupboard, to drive off the ammonia.*

- Primers need to be at least 18 nucleotides long (primers longer than 18 nucleotides should be unique, even in a large eukaryotic genome); both primers should have similar annealing temperatures, T_m, p. 372), with a minimal degree of self-complementarity (to avoid formation of secondary structures), and no complementarity to each other (so that primer dimers are not formed).
- For most applications, the final concentration of each primer should be 0.1–0.5 μmol l^{-1}, which gives an excess of primers of about 10^7 with respect to the template, e.g. target genomic DNA at a concentration of 50 ng per 10 µl reaction mixture.
- Annealing temperatures are based around T_m, the temperature at which 50% of the primers are annealed to their target sequence (Fig. 53.7). For primers of <20 bases, T_m can be roughly calculated in °C from the equation:

$$T_m = 4(G + C) + 2(A + T) \quad [61.1]$$

  where G, C, A and T are the number of bases in the primer. Using this as a starting point, the optimum annealing temperature can be determined by trial and error. The T_m values of the two primers should be within 5 °C of each other (and, therefore, be ideally identical in G + C content). The annealing temperature is then set 5 °C below the lowest T_m of the primer pair.

***Using dNTP solutions** – make up stock solutions, pool in small volumes (50–100 µl of each dNTP) and store separately at −20°C.*

- The last two bases at the 3′ end (where elongation is initiated) should be either G or C (3 hydrogen bonds, giving strong annealing), rather than either A or T (only 2 hydrogen bonds).
- dNTPs should be used at equal concentrations of 200 μmol l^{-1}, which should provide the initial excess required for incorporation into DNA.
- One of the key variables in PCR is the Mg^{2+} concentration; Mg^{2+} is required as a cofactor for the thermostable DNA polymerase (Anon., 2002). Excess Mg^{2+} stabilises dsDNA and may prevent complete denaturation of product at each cycle; it also promotes spurious annealing of primers, leading to the formation of undesired products. However, very low Mg^{2+} concentration impairs polymerisation. The purpose of gelatin and Triton X-100 is to stabilise the DNA polymerase during thermal cycling.

***Establishing the optimum concentration of Mg^{2+}** – this can be determined by trial and error, and can be a useful starting point for any new PCR; try a range of different Mg^{2+} concentrations and select the one giving the strongest intensity of the target band following gel electrophoresis.*

- The most frequently used thermostable DNA polymerase is *Taq* polymerase, which extends primers at a rate of 2–4 kbp per min at 72 °C. It should be used at a concentration of ⩾1 nmol l^{-1} (⩾0.1 U per 5 µl reaction mixture). A disadvantage of *Taq* polymerase is that it has a relatively high rate of misincorporation of bases (one aberrant nucleotide per 100 000 nucleotides per cycle). Other polymerases are available (e.g. *Pfu* polymerase from *Pyrococcus furiosus*, KOD polymerase from *Thermococcus kodakarensis* or genetically modified forms of *Taq* polymerase), which have lower misincorporation rates.

***Understanding codes for primers and probes** – oligomeric nucleotides are often referred to by the number of bases, e.g. a 20-mer primer will contain 20 nucleotide bases.*

Box 61.1 How to carry out the polymerase chain reaction (PCR)

The protocol given below is typical for a standard PCR. Note that temperatures, incubation times and the number of cycles will vary with the particular application, as discussed in the text.

1. **Make sure you have the required apparatus and reagents to hand**, including: (i) a thermal cycler; (ii) template thermostable DNA ($\geqslant$50 ng/μl); (iii) stock solution of all dNTPs (5 mmol l^{-1} for each dNTP); (iv) a DNA polymerase (at 5 U/μl); (v) primers at e.g. 30 μmol l^{-1}; (vi) stock buffer solution, e.g. containing 100 mmol l^{-1} TRIS (pH 8.4), 500 mmol l^{-1} KCl, 15 mmol l^{-1} $MgCl_2$, 1% (w/v) gelatin, 1% (v/v) Triton X-100 (this stock is often termed '10x PCR buffer stock').

2. **Prepare a reaction mixture**: for example, a mixture containing: 1.0 μl target DNA; 2.5 μl stock buffer solution; 1.0 μl primer 1; 1.0 μl primer 2; 1.0 μl of each of the stock solutions of dNTPs, 0.1 μl *Taq* polymerase; 15.4 μl distilled deionised water, to give a total volume of 25.0 μl.

3. **Use appropriate positive and negative controls**: a positive control is a PCR template that is known to work under the conditions used in the laboratory, e.g. a plasmid, with appropriate primers, known to amplify at the annealing temperature to be used. A commonly used negative control is the PCR mixture minus the template DNA, though negative controls can be set up lacking any one of the reaction components.

4. **Cycle in the thermal cycler**: for example, an initial period of 5 min at 94 °C, followed by 30 cycles of 94 °C for 1 min (denaturation), then 50 °C for 1 min (primer annealing; temperature depends upon G + C and A + T content, Eqn [61.1] p. 440), then 72 °C for 1 min (chain extension).

5. **Assess the effectiveness of the PCR**: for example, by gel electrophoresis and ethidium bromide staining.

Troubleshooting

- If no PCR product is detected, repeat the procedure, checking carefully that all components are added to the reaction mixture. If there is still no product, check that the annealing temperature is not too high, or the denaturing temperature is not too low.
- If too many bands are present, this may indicate that (i) the primers may not be specific, (ii) the annealing temperature is too low, or (iii) there is an excess of Mg^{2+}, dNTPs, primers or enzyme.
- Bands corresponding to primer-dimers indicate that (i) the 3′ ends of the primers show partial complementarity, (ii) the annealing temperature is not high enough, or (iii) the concentration of primers is too high.

Avoiding contamination in diagnostic PCR

The sensitivity of PCR is also the major drawback, since the technique is susceptible to contamination, particularly from DNA from the skin and hair of the operator, from previous PCR products, from airborne microbes and from positive control plasmids. A number of routine precautions can be taken to avoid such contamination:

- use a laminar flow cabinet (p. 205) dedicated to PCR use and located in a separate lab from that used to store PCR products or prepare clones;
- keep separate supplies of pipettors, tips, microfuge tubes and reagents – these should be exclusive to the PCR, with separate sets for sample preparation, reagents and product analysis;
- autoclave all buffers, distilled deionised water, pipette tips and tubes;
- wear disposable gloves at all times and change them frequently: protective coverings for the face and hair are also advisable;
- avoid contamination due to carry-over by including dUTP in the PCR mixture instead of dTTP. Thus copies will contain U rather than T. Before the template denaturing step, treat the mixture with uracil-N-glycosylase (UNG, available commercially as AmpEase): this will destroy any strands containing U, i.e. any strands carried over from a previous reaction, or any contaminating material from another PCR. The target DNA will contain T, rather than U and will not be degraded by UNG. At the first heating step, the UNG will be denatured, so any newly synthesised U-containing copies will remain intact.
- for very sensitive work, use a strong UVC light (p. 276) inside the PCR workstation for 20–30 minutes before starting your work, to degrade any contaminating DNA.

SAFETY NOTE *Note that you must not expose your skin or eyes to such a UVC source.*

PCR variations

Nested PCR

This can be used when the target sequence is known, but the number of DNA copies is very small (e.g. a single DNA molecule from a microbial genome), or if the sample is degraded (e.g. a forensic sample). The process involves two consecutive 'rounds' of PCR. The first PCR uses so-called 'external' primers, and the second PCR uses two 'internal' (or 'nested') primers that anneal to sequences within the product of the first PCR. This increases the likelihood of amplification of the target sequences by selecting for it using different primers during each round. Thus, nested PCR also increases the specificity of the reaction, since a single set of primers used in isolation may give a reasonable yield but several bands, while the use of a second set of primers ensures that a unique sequence is amplified, e.g. in microbial diagnostics.

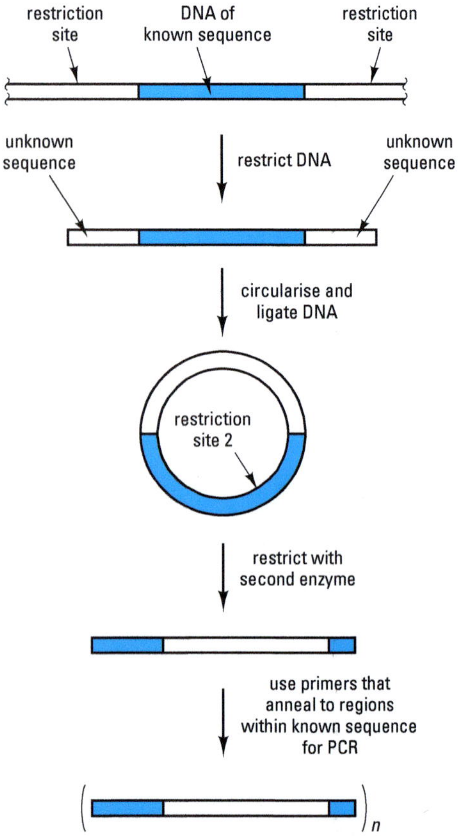

Fig. 61.2 Inverse PCR – basic principles.

Inverse PCR

This is a useful technique for amplifying a DNA sequence flanking a region of known base sequence (Fig. 61.2), e.g. to provide material for characterising an unknown region of DNA. The DNA is cut with a restriction enzyme so that both the region of known sequence and the flanking regions are included. This restriction fragment is then circularised and cut with a second restriction enzyme with specificity for a region in the known sequence. The now linear DNA will have part of the known sequence at each terminus, and by using primers that anneal to these parts of the known sequence, the unknown region can be amplified by conventional PCR. The product can then be sequenced and characterised (Chapter 60).

Reverse transcriptase-PCR (RT-PCR)

This technique is useful for detecting cell-specific gene expression (as evident by the presence of specific mRNA) when the amount of biological material is limited. Using either an oligo-dT primer to anneal to the 3′ polyadenyl 'tail' of the mRNA, or random hexamer primers, together with reverse transcriptase, cDNA is produced which is then amplified by PCR. RT-PCR is often a useful method of generating a probe, the identity of which can be confirmed by sequencing (p. 436).

Amplification fragment length polymorphism (AFLP)

This term refers to several closely related techniques in which a single oligonucleotide primer of arbitrary sequence is used in a PCR reaction under conditions of low stringency, so that the primer is able to anneal to a large number of different sites within the target DNA. Some of the multiple amplification products will be polymorphic (e.g. the presence or absence of a particular annealing site will result in presence or absence of a particular band on the gel, after PCR and electrophoresis). Such polymorphisms can be used to detect differences between dissimilar DNA sequences.

Example Random amplification of polymorphic DNA (RAPD-PCR) can be used as a form of 'molecular typing' (p. 219), to identify a particular strain of an organism, e.g. in tracing the route of transmission of a pathogenic microbe.

PCR and DNA fingerprinting techniques

Genetic mapping and sequencing studies have led to the discovery of highly variable regions in the non-coding regions of DNA between different individuals. These hypervariable regions, often termed 'minisatellite DNA', are found at many sites throughout the genome.

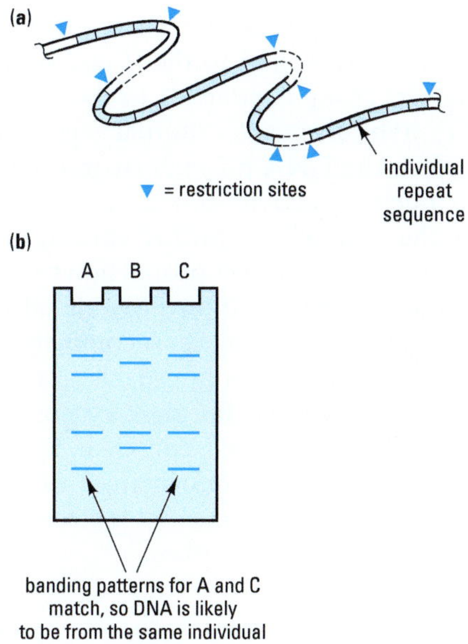

Fig. 61.3 Simplified representation of DNA fingerprinting: (a) tandem repeat sequences within DNA are cut using a restriction enzyme to yield fragments of different size; (b) these fragments are then separated by agarose gel electrophoresis on the basis of their size (M_r), giving a banding pattern that is a characteristic of the DNA used.

Each minisatellite contains a defined sequence of nucleotides which is repeated a number of times in a tandem fashion (Fig. 61.3); the greater the number of repeats, the longer the minisatellite. The number of tandem repeats in any particular minisatellite varies from one person to another (i.e. they have a variable number of tandem repeats or VNTRs). This is exploited in identifying individuals on the basis of their DNA profile, by carrying out the following steps:

1. Extraction of DNA from cells of the individual (e.g. leukocytes, buccal cells, spermatozoa).
2. Digestion of the DNA with a restriction enzyme that cuts at sites other than those within the minisatellite, to produce a series of fragments of different M_r.
3. Electrophoresis and Southern blotting of the restriction fragments using probes that are specific to the particular minisatellite.

The size of the fragments identified will depend on the number of minisatellites that each fragment contains, and the pattern obtained in the Southern blot is characteristic of the individual being profiled (Fig. 61.3).

PCR is widely used in DNA profiling in circumstances where there is a limited amount of starting material. By selecting suitable primers, highly variable regions can be amplified from very small amounts of DNA, and the information from several such regions is used to decide, with a very low chance of error, whether any two samples of DNA are from the same individual or not, e.g. in forensic science (see Kirby, 2002).

Real-time PCR

Conventional PCR techniques rely on end-point detection of amplified product, e.g. by electrophoretic separation and staining (p. 431). However, such methods are time-consuming and are only semi-quantitative, since they are based predominantly on the detection of an amplified fragment (band) in a sample, rather than being designed to give exact information on its abundance (copy number). Quantitative analysis is only feasible during the early stages of PCR, where reagents are in excess and where the amount of amplified product is small, thereby avoiding the problems of product hybridisation, which would compete with primer binding. Real-time PCR enables the simultaneous amplification and quantification of template DNA in a sample by establishing the number of copies present by working in the exponential (early) phase of amplification. Currently, while several different formats are available for real-time PCR, all rely on the generation of a fluorescent signal.

Dye fluorescence

This is the simplest and least expensive approach. A fluorescent dye such as SYBR Green is included in the PCR mixture and the level of fluorescence is monitored as the reaction proceeds; since SYBR Green binds strongly to dsDNA, showing an enhancement in fluorescence of over 100-fold, any increase in fluorescence is directly proportional to the amount of dsDNA produced. Calibration is achieved by running a series of standards containing known amounts of dsDNA. This approach works well for optimised single PCR product reactions where non-specific reactions are minimised.

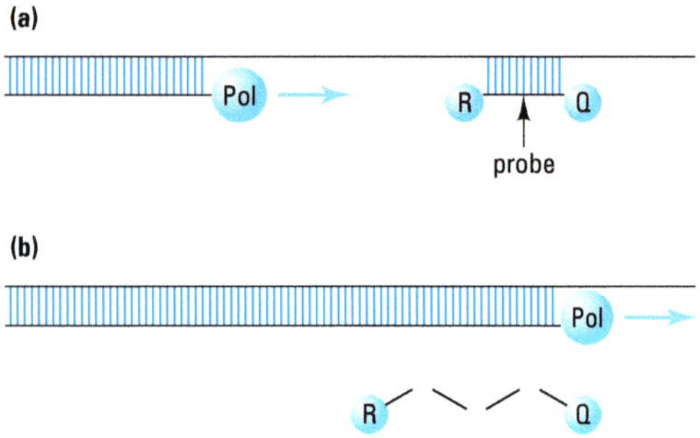

Fig. 61.4 Real-time PCR using a fluorescent reporter probe. In (a) the probe is bound to the target sequence while in (b) the 5′ nuclease activity of the DNA polymerase (Pol) has cleaved the reporter dye (R) and quencher (Q), resulting in fluorescence.

Fluorescent reporter probes

Here a fluorescent reporter dye is covalently bound to the 5′ end of an oligonucleotide probe while a 'quencher' group is attached to the 3′ end (Fig. 61.4). The probe is designed to hybridise to an internal region of the target sequence. During PCR, when the DNA polymerase molecule reaches the hybridised probe, the 5′ nuclease activity of the polymerase will cleave the reporter dye from the rest of the probe, causing an increase in fluorescence with each cycle that is in direct proportion to the amount of PCR product being formed, which is itself directly related to the original number of copies of the target DNA sequence. A commercial example is the TaqMan series of probes – while this approach is more accurate and reliable than dye fluorescence, it is also far more expensive, since a specific reporter probe must be synthesised for each target sequence. Other variants rely on changes in 3D conformation of the probe when it binds to the target sequence, causing an increase in fluorescence, e.g. Molecular Beacons and Scorpion probes.

***KEY POINT** You should note that the PCR technique is continually being updated, with subtle new variations being produced on a regular basis – novel approaches and novel acronyms are very likely to be reported within the lifetime of this book.*

Text references

Anon. *PCR Optimization*. Available: http://www.promega.com/paguide/chap1.htm Last accessed: 01/04/07. [Details of how to optimise Mg^{2+} and polymerase concentration, etc.]

Kirby, L.T. (2002) *DNA Fingerprinting: An Introduction. Breakthroughs in Molecular Biology*. Oxford University Press, Oxford.

Sources for further study

Altshuler, M.L. (2006) *PCR Troubleshooting: the Essential Guide*. Caister Academic Press, Wymondham.

Diffenback, C.W. and Dveksler, G.S. (2003) *PCR Primer: a Laboratory Manual*, 2nd edn. Cold Spring Harbor Laboratory, Cold Spring Harbor.

Dorak, M.T. (2006) *Real-Time PCR*. Taylor & Francis, Abingdon.

McPherson, M.J. and Moller, S.G. (2006) *PCR Basics*. Taylor & Francis, Abingdon.

Study exercises

61.1 Investigate the role of magnesium ions in PCR. Find out why optimising the Mg^{2+} concentration is important for successful amplification of target DNA in PCR.

61.2 Check your knowledge of primer design. List the principal factors that should be taken into account when designing primers for PCR.

61.3 Carry out a T_m calculation for a primer. For the following primer, what would be the temperature at which 50% of the molecules are annealed to their target sequence (i.e. T_m)?

5′-TGCATGGCTGGATTAGCG-3′

Study exercises (continued)

61.4 Consider how the risk of contamination can be reduced in PCR. List the most important practical steps that can be taken to reduce the possibility of contamination.

61.5 Select appropriate primers for a specific PCR amplification. The sequence in the box below represents a region of DNA that is to be amplified by PCR.

Which of the following three pairs of primers is most suited to amplify a PCR product from the above sequence?

(a) 5′-TCGCTGAAGGACATGTCG-3′ and 5′-CGATCTAGGCGACATGTCC-3′

(b) 5′-TCGCTGAAGGACATGTCG-3′ and 5′-TCCTTAGGTCTCGACCGTA-3′

(c) 5′-TCGCTGAAGGACATGTCG-3′ and 5′-GTCTCGACCGTAGCTAGCATC-3′

61.6 Find out what types of DNA analysis might be suitable for forensic examination of degraded DNA samples. In 1918 Tsar Nicholas of Russia, his wife Tsarina Alexandra, and their five children were executed and buried in a shallow grave in Yekaterinberg, Russia. Samples from the bones of the family were analysed by the UK Forensic Science Service (FSS). What types of DNA-based tests would you expect to have been carried out to confirm that a family group was present in the grave?

```
5′-TCGCTGAAGGACATGTCGATGCTAGCTACGGTCGAGACGTAAGGACATGTCGGCTAGATCGC-3′
3′-AGCGACTTCCTGTACAGCTACGATCGATGCCAGCTCTGCATTCCTGTACAGCCGATCTAGCG-5′
```

Genetically engineered *Caenorhabditis elegans* roundworms that have turned blue in response to an environmental stress, such as toxins or heat.

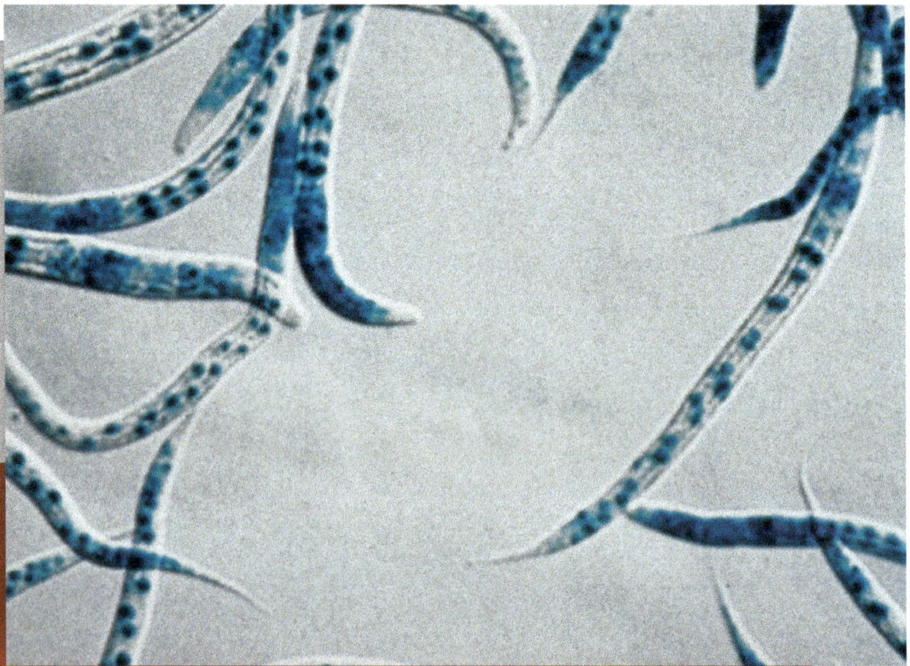

24

Genetics of Behavior

CHAPTER CONCEPTS

- Behavior is a complex response to stimuli that is mediated both by genes and by the environment.
- The behavior-first approach is used to establish that behavioral traits are heritable. If so, genetic crosses are used to identify the number and chromosomal location of genes contributing to the trait.
- The gene-first approach utilizes mutagenesis to establish strains carrying single-gene mutations that contribute to a behavioral response. Subsequent comparisons of the normal and mutant alleles provide insight into the underlying mechanism controlling a behavioral response.
- The behavior-first and gene-first approaches have been successfully used to dissect behavioral responses in *Drosophila,* making it a useful model organism for the study of nervous system function and the mechanisms that underlie human behavioral disorders.
- Many human behavioral disorders are complex responses to stimuli. These responses are mediated by genes, environmental factors, and interactions among genes and the environment. More recently, newly developed genomic techniques are being used to study the role of genes in human behavior.

Behavior is generally defined as a reaction to stimuli, whether internal or external, that alter an organism's response to its environment. Animals run, remain still, or counterattack in the presence of a predator; birds build complex and distinctive nests in response to a combination of internal and external signals; plants bend toward light; and humans behave in both simple and complex ways guided by their intellect, emotions, and culture.

Efforts to study the role of heredity in behavior began in the nineteenth century with Francis Galton, who systematically studied behavior and heredity. In one of his early studies, he examined his own family (he was a cousin of Charles Darwin) trying to find a pattern of inheritance associated with intelligence. By the early 1900s, clear-cut cases of genetic influence on behavior had been identified, but at the time, behavior was primarily of interest to psychologists, who were concerned with learned or conditioned behavior. Such behaviors were thought to reflect the influence of the environment to the exclusion of the genotype. The difference between these two approaches to studying behavior was the starting point for what has been called the nature versus nurture debate. In this simplistic (and false) dichotomy, behavior is controlled entirely either by genes or by the environment.

This controversy presented a distorted view of the nature of behavioral responses. After all, any behavior must rely on the expression of an individual's genotype, which takes place within a hierarchy of environmental settings (that is, gene expression depends on interactions within the cell, the tissue, the organ, the organism, and finally the population and surrounding environment). Without genes and their environments, there could be no behavior. Nevertheless, the nature–nurture controversy flourished well into the 1950s. By then, it became clear that behavioral patterns were the result of the interaction of genetic and environmental factors. Because the nervous system senses the environment, processes the information, and initiates the response that we perceive as behavior, much of the study of behavior in genetics and molecular biology focuses on the development, structure, and function of the nervous system. Since about 1950, research into genetic components of behavior has intensified, and appreciation for the importance of genetics in understanding behavior has increased.

With this brief history in mind, here are some of the basic questions we will answer in this chapter.

- How do we define behavior?
- What evidence is there that behavior has a biological or a genetic basis?
- How is behavior genetics studied?
- How does a gene influence or control a specific behavior?
- How do genes interact with the environment to produce a behavioral response?
- What is the pathway from a gene to a behavioral phenotype?

The definition of behavior presented at the beginning of this chapter, based on observable changes in the relationship of a cell or an organism to its environment as the result of some stimulus, broadly identifies the phenotype that geneticists use as a starting point for investigating the biological basis of behavior. Evidence that some behaviors have a genetic basis comes from several sources: observable species-specific behaviors, such as courtship rituals, and artificial selection, which draws upon individual variations in behavior among organisms in populations that can be used to establish strains with heritable differences in behavior. In humans, twin studies and adoption studies have provided evidence for the role of heredity in behavioral responses.

Two different approaches have been used to study the genetic control of behavior, to define the interactions between genotype and environmental factors, and to dissect the pathways leading from genes to a behavioral phenotype. One of these approaches is a top-down, or *behavior-first,* method in which a specific behavior is identified in an organism, and then, genetic crosses are used to produce strains that bred true for either a high level or a low level of this behavioral response. Once these strains are established, further crosses identify and analyze the genetic components of the behavior. The second approach is a bottom-up, or *gene-first,* approach in which mutagenesis followed by screening is used to identify single-gene mutations associated with variant or abnormal behaviors. Analysis of the molecular mechanism of gene action in these mutant strains often provided a direct explanation of the behavior. Each approach has its advantages and shortcomings, but in spite of their differences, both share the same goals: to establish the inherited nature of a specific behavior, to identify and enumerate the genes or gene systems involved in the behavior being studied, to map these genes or gene systems to specific chromosomes, and to elucidate the molecular mechanisms by which these genes influence a behavioral response. A recently developed third approach to studying the genetics of behavior is based on methods that allow entire genomes to be scanned to identify genes and markers for genes and genome variations related to specific behaviors.

The prevailing view today is that most behaviors are complex traits involving a number of genes, as well as interactions between and among these genes and environmental influences. In this scenario, the genotype provides the biological underpinnings or mental ability (or both) required to execute a behavior and further determines the limitations of environmental influences. In this chapter, we will examine the three approaches to studying the genetic basis of behavior, evaluate the strengths and weaknesses of each, and consider what we have learned about human behavior from these methods and the use of model organisms.

24.1 The Behavior-First Approach Can Establish Genetic Strains with Behavioral Differences

The behavior-first approach begins by selecting organisms exhibiting a specific behavior from members of a genetically heterogeneous population. If genetic strains can be established that uniformly express this behavior, and if the trait can be transferred by genetic crosses to another strain that initially does not exhibit the behavior under study, genetic involvement in the behavior is confirmed. Often, selection is used to establish two strains: one showing high levels and one showing low levels of the behavior under investigation. This bidirectional selection creates two lines with progressively greater differences in behavior. If the genetic background of the strains remains constant, this method maximizes differences in genes that control the trait of interest, and can minimize differences in all other genes. The study of emotional behavior in mice and geotaxis in *Drosophila* will be used to illustrate this approach.

Mapping Genes for Anxiety in Mice

To identify and map genes controlling emotional behavior in mice, Jonathon Flint and colleagues have used quantitative trait loci (QTL) mapping (see Chapter 23 for a discussion of QTLs). In one experiment, heterozygotes from crosses between C57BL/6J (a nonemotional, low-anxiety strain) and BALB/cJ (an emotional, high-anxiety strain) were intercrossed, and the progeny were selected over multiple generations for extremes of high (H1a) or low (L1a) anxiety. These inbred strains were subjected to several different behavioral tests of anxiety, including the open field, the elevated plus maze (Figure 24–1), and a test called the light–dark box. In this last-named test, mice are placed in an environment in which there is a dark, enclosed box, from which they can emerge into a brightly lit area. Fearful animals prefer to remain in the box and do not explore the lighted areas of the environment. The phenotypically most extreme progeny recovered from these anxiety tests were analyzed for 84 microsatellite markers and four different measures of emotionality. A QTL on chromosome 1 was identified and localized to a small region of the chromosome spanning 66 Mb. Analysis of over 1600 mice in replicated

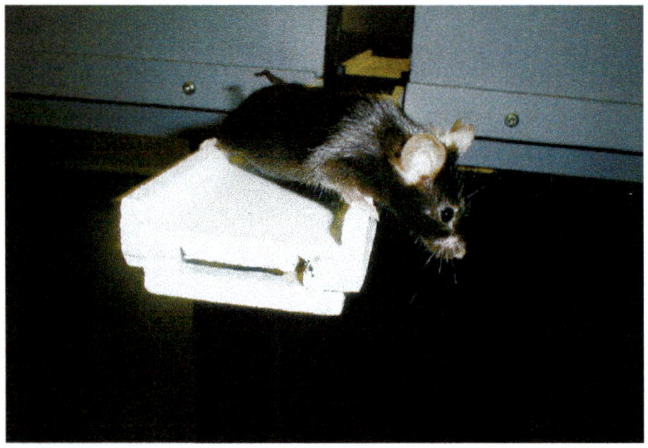

FIGURE 24–1 A mouse explores a new environment from the open arm of an elevated plus maze, a standard device for measuring fear in mice. This experiment was one of a series designed to identify genes involved in fear and anxiety in mice.

populations consistently gave the same results. Similar experiments using microsatellite markers have shown that QTLs controlling other aspects of behavior are distributed on all mouse chromosomes (Figure 24–2).

To advance beyond the mapping of a QTL region, which may contain dozens of genes, and to identify the specific loci involved in emotional behavior requires the combined use of genetics and genomics. Genes in the chromosome 1 QTL region identified as having a behavioral phenotype are being tested in genetic complementation assays to detect interactions among these loci. DNA sequencing of these regions is being used to identify and clone these genes. Once identified, the mechanisms of action of these behavioral loci and their relevance to human behavior remain to be assessed.

Selection for Geotaxis in *Drosophila*

A **taxis** (pronounced *tak sis*) is a movement toward or away from an external stimulus. The response may be positive (moving toward the stimulus) or negative (away from it). Many types of

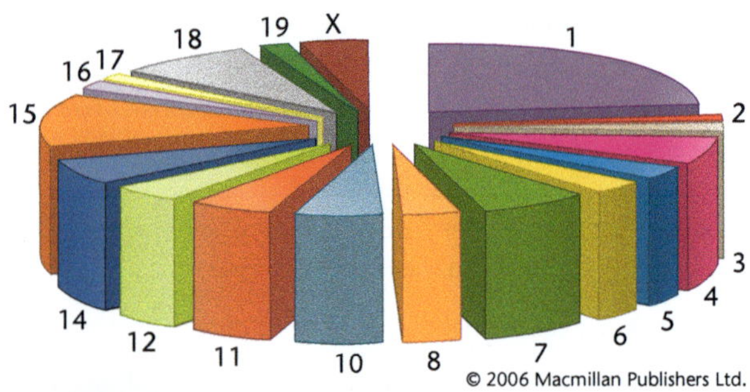

FIGURE 24–2 Loci for genes controlling fear and other forms of emotional behavior are distributed on 17 of 19 autosomes in the mouse genome. Significant numbers of these genes are located on chromosomes 1, 15, and 18.

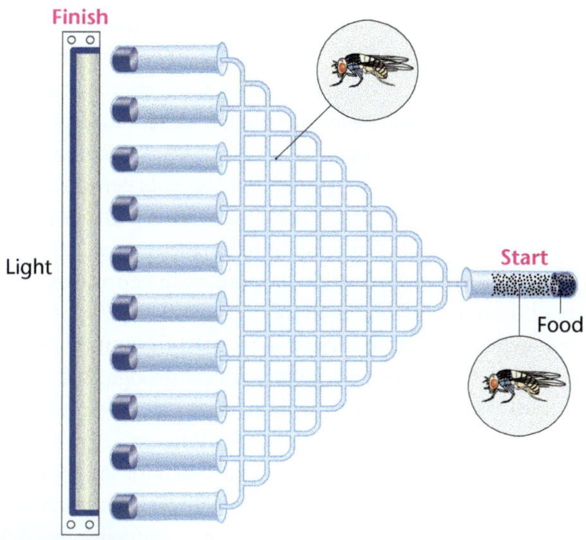

FIGURE 24-3 Schematic drawing of a maze used to study geotaxis in *Drosophila*.

stimuli elicit this form of behavior, including chemicals (chemotaxis), gravity (geotaxis), and light (phototaxis).

To investigate geotaxis in *Drosophila,* Jerry Hirsch and his colleagues designed a maze that tests about 200 flies per trial, as shown in Figure 24–3. Once in the maze, flies are repeatedly required to choose between moving up or down. Flies that turn up at each intersection will collect in tubes at the top of the maze; those that always turn down will collect in tubes at the bottom; and those making both "up" and "down" decisions will end up somewhere in between. Flies can be selected both for positive (going up in the maze) and for negative geotaxis (going down in the maze), establishing the existence of a genetic influence on this behavioral response. As shown in Figure 24–4, mean

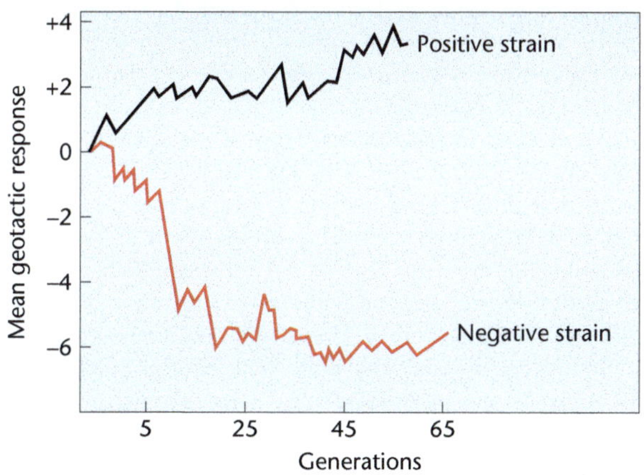

FIGURE 24-4 Selection for positive and negative geotaxis in *Drosophila* over many generations. The scores represent the sum of upward (+) or downward (−) turns in the maze.

scores of flies in this maze vary from about +4 to −6, indicating that selection is stronger for negative geotaxis than for positive geotaxis.

The two lines have undergone selection for almost 40 years, encompassing over 1000 generations and the testing of more than 80,000 flies. Throughout the experiment, clear-cut, but fluctuating, differences have been observed. These results indicate that this complex behavior in *Drosophila* is genetically controlled and is a polygenic trait. Using the lines selected for positive and negative geotaxis, Hirsch and his colleagues analyzed the relative contribution of genes on different chromosomes to this behavior. The effects of chromosomes X, 2, and 3 on geotaxis were identified in an ingenious way. Figure 24–5 shows how this

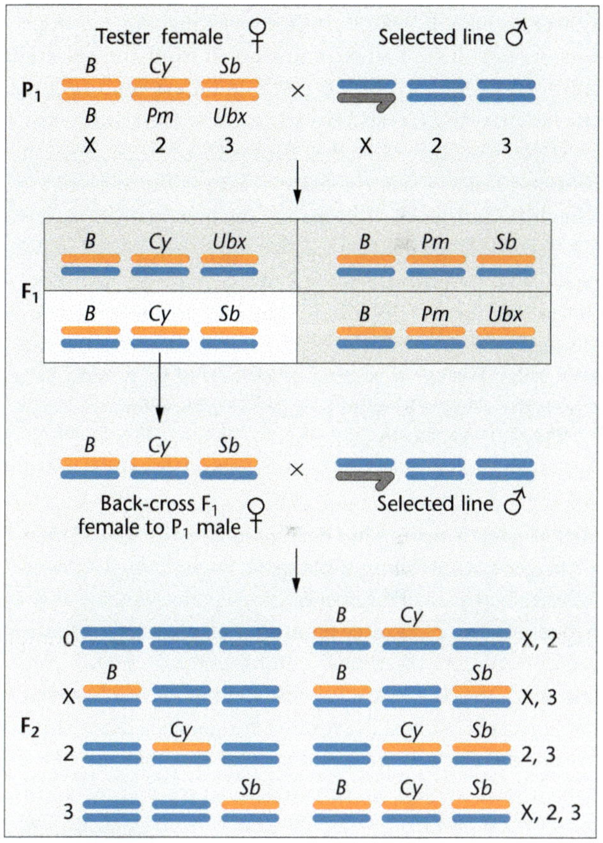

FIGURE 24-5 In this mating scheme in *Drosophila,* the effect of genes located on specific chromosomes that contribute to geotaxis can be assessed. The progeny produced by backcrossing the female contain all combinations of chromosomes. Examining the presence or absence of dominant marker phenotypes in these flies makes it possible to determine which chromosomes from the selected strain are present. Subsequent testing for geotaxis is then performed. (*B* = *Bar eyes; Cy* = *Curly wing; Sb* = *Stubble bristles; Pm* = *Plum eye color; Ubx* = *ultrabithorax*) The designations alongside each genotype in the F_2 generation (e.g., X, 2, and 3) indicate which chromosomes are heterozygous.

is accomplished. A male from a selected line is crossed to a "tester" female, whose chromosomes are each marked with a dominant mutation (these chromosomes are called **balancer chromosomes**). Each balancer chromosome carries one or more inversions to suppress the recovery of any crossover products. An F_1 female will be heterozygous for each chromosome and is backcrossed to a male from the original line. In the F_2, female offspring contain all combinations of the marker chromosomes and the chromosomes from the selected strain. The dominant mutations carried by the marker chromosomes make it possible to recognize which chromosomes from the selected lines are present in homozygous or heterozygous configurations. Flies with genotypes 0 and X (Figure 24–5) are homozygous and heterozygous, respectively, for the X chromosome from the selected strain. Similarly, flies with genotypes 0 and 2 are homozygous and heterozygous, respectively, for chromosome 2 from the selected strain, and flies with genotypes 0 and 3 are homozygous and heterozygous, respectively, for chromosome 3 from the selected strain. By testing flies with all these chromosome combinations in the maze, it is possible to assess the behavioral influence of genes on any given chromosome. For negatively geotaxic flies (the ones that go up in the maze), genes on chromosome 2 make the largest contribution to the phenotype, followed by loci on chromosome 3 and the X chromosome (a gradient of chromosome effects $2 > 3 > X$). For the positive line (flies that go down in the maze), the reverse gradient ($X > 3 > 2$) is seen.

Overall, the results indicate that geotaxis is under polygenic control and that the loci controlling this trait are distributed on all three major chromosomes of *Drosophila.* Further genetic testing has been used to estimate the number of genes controlling geotaxis in *Drosophila.* This work indicates that a small number of genes, perhaps as few as two to four loci, are responsible for most of the geotactic response in *Drosophila.* As ingenious as this work is, it is also arduous, and illustrates one of the limitations of the behavior-first approach. Although selection for geotaxis showed that this behavior is genetically controlled and that loci on all major chromosomes are involved, it is very difficult to use this method to identify specific genes involved in this behavior. This is partly because the behavior is polygenically controlled, and many of these genes may make only a small contribution to the phenotype.

Genomic technology including microarray analysis (described in Chapters 21 and 22) offers a way to identify specific genes that influence complex polygenic traits, including behavior. Microarrays are one example of the high-throughput experimental methods that are revolutionizing genetics and molecular biology. Instead of measuring changes in expression one gene at a time, microarrays make it possible to measure changes in hundreds or thousands of genes in a single experiment. Genes to be used in microarray analysis can be selected on the basis of their expression patterns in specific tissues, in specific cells, or in whole genome scans.

To study geotaxis genes in *Drosophila,* researchers used a two-step process. First, cDNA microarrays containing about one-third of the genes in the *Drosophila* genome were used to analyze mRNA levels from the strains with the highest (*Hi5*) and lowest (*Lo*) geotaxis behavior. A small number of genes showed reproducible differences in expression and were chosen for further analysis. To narrow the list of candidate genes further, the researchers used mutant alleles of these genes that were associated with neurological defects. Ten lines, including several control lines, were selected for the second step in this gene-identification strategy: analysis of geotaxis behavior. The geotactic behavior and mRNA levels of three genes in the mutant flies showed a correlation between levels of mRNA expression and behavior in *Hi5* and *Lo* flies. Individually, each of these genes made small, incremental contributions to geotaxis, as would be expected for a polygenically controlled trait. The mechanism by which these three genes, *cryptochrome* (*cry*), *Pendulin* (*Pen*), and *Pigment-dispersing-factor* (*Pdf*), are involved in geotaxis is unknown. However, all three are involved in the development and function of the brain and nervous system, and their role in geotaxis is currently being investigated, but whether they are the primary genes involved or are downstream targets of other, unidentified genes is not known. However, the use of this two-step strategy is significant because it illustrates the successful integration of classical genetics with genomics to identify genes involved in a polygenic trait.

NOW SOLVE THIS

24–1 Certain inbred strains of mice (i.e., C57BL and C3H/2) appear to exhibit a preference for alcohol in free-choice consumption experiments, and a variety of techniques have been applied to assess underlying genetic predispositions. Presumably, these strains differ from each other in the alleles they carry at specific loci. How might the analysis of such inbred strains provide insight into molecular mechanisms that drive such a behavior? Tarantino et al. (1998) applied QTL analysis to alcohol preference in mice using microsatellite markers. They found three significant QTLs on chromosomes 1, 4, and 9 and three suggestive QTLs on chromosomes 2, 3, and 10. How might QTL analysis lead to an understanding of alcohol preference in mice? Summarize the strengths and weaknesses of each approach.

■ HINT: *This problem involves an understanding of what information can be obtained by studying strain-specific behaviors and knowledge of what QTLs are, and the key to its solution depends on knowing how QTLs are mapped using chromosome-specific markers.*

24.2

The Gene-First Approach Analyzes Mutant Alleles to Study Mechanisms That Underlie Behavior

Although we discussed geotaxis in *Drosophila* as an example of the behavior-first approach, much has also been learned using this organism for gene-first studies of behavior. Although *Drosophila* and humans separated from a common ancestor millions of years ago, molecular aspects of cellular function in the nervous system overlap considerably in these two organisms. As a result, work with mutant strains of *Drosophila* has provided insight into the fundamental mechanisms that govern nerve impulse transmission. As the name implies, the gene-first approach to studying behavior first isolates mutant strains with a behavioral abnormality and then investigates the structural and/or functional abnormalities that underlie this altered behavior.

The gene-first approach has several advantages over the behavior-first approach. Using this approach allows researchers to quantify the impact of single genes on a complex behavioral response. Use of this method must take into account the polygenic nature of behavior and the interaction of contributing genes. In this context, the gene-first approach can in theory, be used to identify, map, clone, and sequence all genes contributing to a behavior. This approach is simplified in *Drosophila,* because researchers have developed an extensive and sophisticated set of genetic tools, especially marker chromosomes and collections of strains with deleted and duplicated chromosome regions, as well as mutants with cytological markers for mosaic analysis.

In the following sections, we will explore the use of mutant analysis in dissecting mechanisms of nerve impulses and their direct application to human disorders, and then we will discuss one form of complex behavior, learning, to further illustrate how *Drosophila* serves as a model organism for studying the molecular aspects of behavior.

Genes Involved in Transmission of Nerve Impulses

Figure 24–6 shows a neuron (nerve cell) in which impulses are generated at one end (on a dendrite) and move along the cell to the other end (the axon), which transmits the impulse to adjacent neurons. During this process, the impulse is propagated by the transport of sodium and potassium ions across the plasma membrane of the neuron. The movement of these charged ions can be monitored by measuring changes in the electrical potential of the membrane.

To screen for genes that control the generation and transmission of nerve impulses, Barry Ganetzky and his colleagues screened behavioral mutants of *Drosophila* to identify those with electrophysiological abnormalities in the generation and propagation of nerve impulses. Two general classes of such mutants have been isolated: those with defects in the movement of sodium and those with defects in potassium transport (Table 24.1). One mutant identified in the screening procedure is a temperature-sensitive allele of the *paralytic* gene. Flies homozygous for this mutant

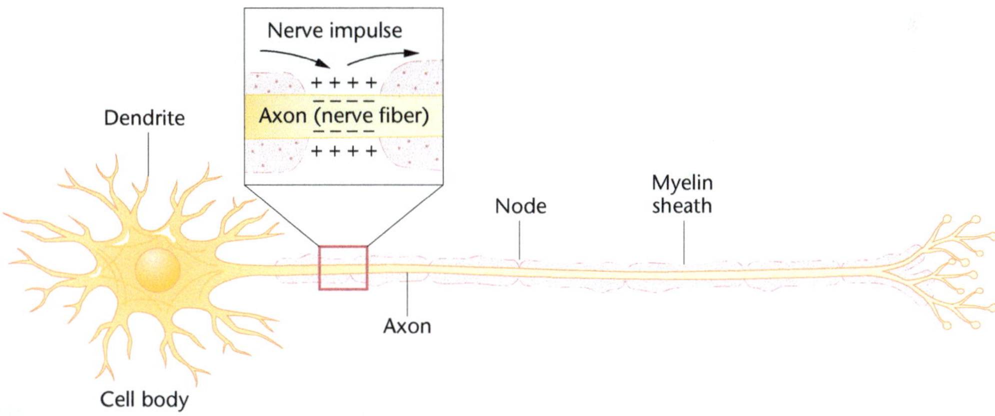

FIGURE 24–6 A nerve cell (neuron) has extensions called dendrites that carry impulses toward the cell body and also has one or more axons that carry impulses away from the cell body. The axon is encased in a sheath of myelin, except at nodes spaced at intervals along the axon. Nerve impulses are accelerated by jumping from node to node. Electrodes placed on either side of the neuron's plasma membrane can record the electric potential across the membrane. When the neuron is at rest, there is more sodium outside the cell and more potassium inside the cell. When a nerve impulse is generated, sodium moves into the cell, and potassium moves out, altering the electric potential. As the impulse moves away, ions are pumped across the membrane to restore the original electric potential.

TABLE 24.1

Behavioral Mutants of *Drosophila* in Which Nerve Impulse Transmission Is Affected

Mutation	Map Location	Ion Channel Affected	Phenotype
nap^{ts}	2-56.2	Sodium	Adults and larvae paralyzed at 37.5°C; reversible at 25°C
para^{ts}	1-53.9	Sodium	Adults paralyzed at 29°C, larvae at 37°C; reversible at 25°C
Tip-E	3-13.5	Sodium	Adults and larvae paralyzed at 39–40°C; reversible at 25°C
sei^{ts}	2-10.6	Sodium	Adults paralyzed at 38°C, larvae unaffected; adults recover at 25°C
Sh	1-57.7	Potassium	Aberrant leg shaking in adults exposed to ether
eag	1-50.0	Potassium	Aberrant leg shaking in adults exposed to ether
Hk	1-30.0	Potassium	Ether-induced leg shaking
sio	3-85.0	Potassium	At 22°C, adults are weak fliers; at 38°C, adults are weak, uncoordinated

allele become paralyzed when exposed to temperatures at or above 29°C, but recover rapidly when the temperature is lowered to 25°C. Electrophysiological studies showed that mutant flies have defective sodium transport associated with the conduction of nerve impulses.

Subsequently, Ganetzky and his colleagues mapped, isolated, and cloned the *paralytic* gene. This locus encodes a sodium channel protein, which controls the movement of sodium across the membrane of nerve cells in many different organisms, from flies to humans. These same researchers found that another mutant allele, called *Shaker* (originally isolated over 40 years ago as a behavioral mutant), encodes a potassium channel protein. This gene has also been cloned and characterized. Because the mechanism of nerve impulse conduction has been highly conserved during animal evolution, the cloned *Drosophila* genes were used as probes to isolate the equivalent human ion channel genes. Study of the human genes is providing new insights into the molecular basis of neuronal activity. The sodium channel gene is defective in a heritable form of cardiac arrhythmia. The identification and cloning of the human gene now make it possible to screen for family members at risk for this potentially fatal condition.

NOW SOLVE THIS

24–2 Assume that you discovered a fruit fly that walked with a limp and was continually off balance as it moved. Describe how you would determine whether this behavior was due to an injury (induced in the environment) or to an inherited trait. Assuming that it was inherited, what are the various ways a gene might lead to this trait? Describe how you would determine the mechanism of gene expression experimentally if the gene were X-linked.

■ HINT: *This problem involves an understanding of how traits are inherited and transmitted to offspring in Mendelian crosses and the expected outcome of crosses involving recessive, dominant, and X-linked genes. The key to its solution is to first determine whether your analysis will use the behavior-first or the gene-first method.*

Drosophila Can Learn and Remember

Researchers gain a great advantage when they can study the genetics of a complex behavior, such as learning, in a model organism that is as convenient to manipulate as *Drosophila.* However, this is possible only if the model organism can perform the complex behavior the researchers are interested in studying. Thus, before using *Drosophila* to study learning, researchers needed to know whether *Drosophila* could learn. Seymour Benzer's lab was one of the first to identify genes that control learning and memory in *Drosophila.* To do so, Benzer's group used an olfactory-based shock-avoidance learning system in which flies are presented with a pair of odors, one of which is associated with an electric shock. Flies quickly learn to avoid the odor associated with the shock. For several reasons, this response is thought to be learned. First, performance is associated with the pairing of a stimulus or response with reinforcement. Second, the response is reversible: Flies can be trained to select an odor they previously avoided. Third, flies exhibit short-term memory for the training they have received.

The demonstration that *Drosophila* can learn opened the way to selecting mutants that are defective in learning and memory (Table 24.2). To accomplish this, males from an inbred wild-type strain were treated with mutagens and mated to females from the same strain. Their progeny were recovered and mated to produce strains that carried a mutagenized X chromosome. Mutations that affected learning were selected by testing for responses in the olfactory shock apparatus. A number of learning-deficient mutants, including *dunce, turnip, rutabaga,* and *cabbage,* were isolated in this way. In addition, a memory-deficient mutant, *amnesia,* which learns normally, but forgets four times faster than normal, was recovered. Each of these mutations represents a single gene defect that affects a specific form of behavior. Because of the method used to recover them, all

TABLE 24.2

Some *Drosophila* Mutations That Affect Learning and Memory

Behavior Genes	Molecular Function	Behavior Phenotype, Function
dunce (dnc)	cAMP-specific phosphodiesterase	Locomotor rhythms, ethanol tolerance
rutabaga (rut)	Adenylate cyclase	Courtship learning, ethanol tolerance, grooming
amnesiac (amn); cheapdate (chpd)	Neuropeptide	Ethanol tolerance
latheo (lat)	DNA-replication factor	Larval feeding
Shaker (Sh)	Voltage-sensitive potassium channel	Courtship suppression, gestation defect, ether sensitivity
G proteins 60 A	Heterotrimeric G protein	Visual behavior, cocaine sensitivity
DCO; cAMP-dependent protein kinase I (Pka-C1)	Protein Ser/Thr kinase	Locomotor rhythms, ethanol tolerance
cAMP-response-element-binding protein B at 17A	Transcription factor	Locomotor rhythms *(CrebB17A); dCREB*
Calcium/calmodulin-dependent protein kinase II (CaMKII)	Protein Ser/Thr kinase	Courtship suppression
Neurofibromatosis 1 (Nf1)	Ras GTPase activator	Embryonic, nervous system defects

Source: Adapted by permission from Macmillan Publishers Ltd: *Nature Reviews Genetics*, "Drosophila: Genetics Meets Behavior," by M.B. Sokolowski. *Nature Reviews Genetics* 2:879–890, table 1, p. 882. Copyright 2001, www.nature.com/nrg.

the mutants found so far are X-linked genes. Using other methods, autosomal genes that control learning and memory have been identified.

Dissecting the Mechanisms and Neural Pathways in Learning

Screening for learning and memory-defective *Drosophila* was successful in identifying a number of single genes involved in these behaviors. Some of these mutants acted in different stages of the same biochemical pathway, leading to the identification of neural mechanisms and pathways involved in learning and memory. For example, one group of *Drosophila* learning mutations is defective in a signal transduction system that plays an important role in learning.

In cells of the nervous system and many other cell types, cyclic adenosine monophosphate (cAMP) is produced from adenosine triphosphate (ATP) in the cytoplasm in response to signals received at the cell surface (see Figure 24–7). Once produced, cyclic AMP (cAMP) activates protein kinases, which, in turn, phosphorylate proteins, transfer the signal to the nucleus, and initiate a cascade of changes in gene expression.

Behavioral mutants of *Drosophila* were among the first to show the link between cAMP metabolism and learning. The *rutabaga* (*rut*) locus encodes adenylyl cyclase, the enzyme that synthesizes cAMP from ATP. In a mutant allele of *rutabaga*, a missense mutation destroys the catalytic activity of adenylyl cyclase, leading to learning deficiency in homozygous flies. The *dunce* (*dnc*) locus encodes the structural gene for the enzyme cAMP phosphodiesterase, which degrades adenylyl cyclase. Mutant alleles of *dunce* also lead to learning deficiencies. The *turnip* (*tur*) mutation occurs in a gene encoding a G protein, a class of molecules that bind guanosine-triphosphate (GTP) and, in turn, activate adenylyl cyclase. Analysis of these mutations also identified parts of the nervous system where sensory information is processed and where both short-term and long-term memory are formed.

Cells in the *Drosophila* brain, called mushroom body neurons (Figure 24–8), integrate and process sensory input from olfactory stimuli and from electric shocks. When both stimuli arrive at a mushroom body simultaneously, adenylyl

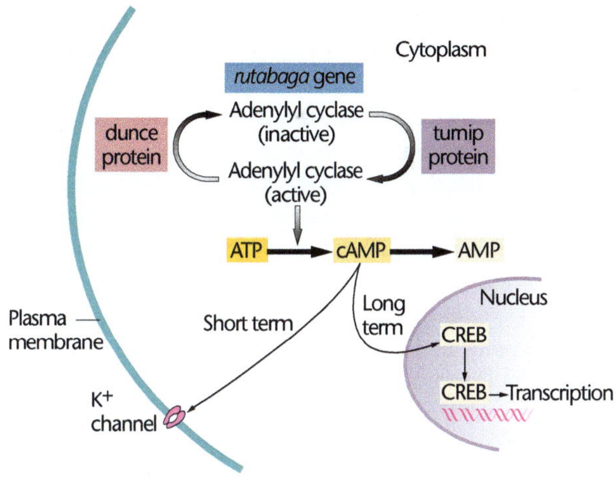

FIGURE 24–7 The pathway for cyclic AMP (cAMP) synthesis and degradation. ATP is converted into cAMP by the enzyme adenylyl cyclase; cAMP affects short-term memory via the potassium channel in the plasma membrane and affects long-term memory by regulating the transcription factor CREB. In *Drosophila,* the *rutabaga* gene encodes adenylyl cyclase. When produced, the enzyme is inactive; it is converted to its active form by a protein encoded by the *turnip* gene. The enzyme is inactivated by a protein encoded by the *dunce* gene. Mutations in any of these genes affect learning and memory in *Drosophila.*

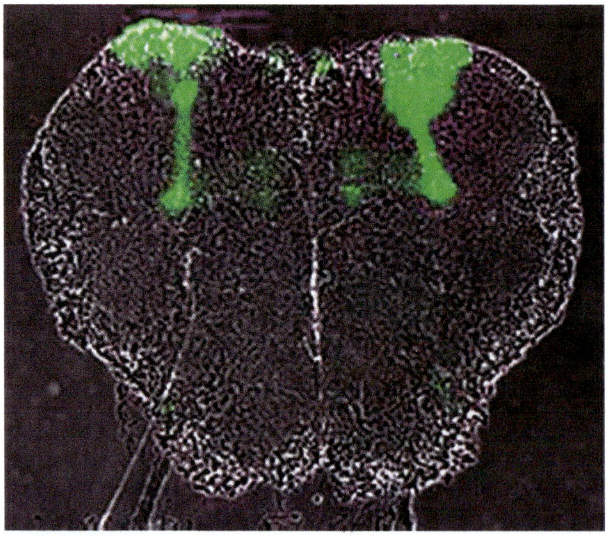

FIGURE 24-8 Green fluorescent protein (GFP) labeling of the neurons in the mushroom body of the *Drosophila* brain. Cells in this region are important in learning and memory.

cyclase is stimulated and activates a G-protein-linked receptor, which leads to elevated cAMP levels. The increase in cAMP leads to changes in the excitability of the mushroom body neuron. Elevated levels of cAMP upregulate expression of a protein kinase, which enhances short-term and long-term memory. Short-term memory is mediated by changes in potassium channels. Long-term memory is associated with changes in gene expression within mushroom body neurons, which is controlled by a transcriptional activator, CREB (cAMP response element binding protein). CREB binds to elements upstream of cAMP inducible genes and changes the pattern of gene expression, encoding memory.

The biochemical pathways that control learning and memory in *Drosophila* are similar to those in other organisms, including mice and humans. The mammalian homologs of the *Drosophila* genes are active in parts of the mouse brain involved in learning and memory. New genetic screening methods in both mice and flies are being used to identify new genes and other biochemical pathways involved in learning.

24.3 Human Behavior Has Genetic Components

The genetic control of behavior has proven more difficult to characterize in humans than in other organisms, partly because the types of responses considered to be the most interesting forms of human behavior, including aspects of *intelligence, language, personality,* and *emotion,* are difficult to study. Two problems arise in studying such behaviors. First, these traits are difficult to define objectively and to measure quantitatively. Second, they are affected by environmental factors and there is a wide range of individual variation in the responses to these factors. In each case, the environment is extremely important in shaping, limiting, or facilitating the final phenotype.

Historically, the study of human behavior genetics has been hampered for other reasons as well. Many early studies of human behavior were conducted by psychologists with limited training in genetics. Second, traits involving intelligence, personality, and emotion have great social and political significance. Consequently, research findings concerning these traits are likely to be distorted by sensationalism when reported to the public. In fact, because the study of these traits often comes close to infringing upon individual liberties, such as the right to privacy, the studies themselves, much less their conclusions, very frequently stir up controversy.

In lamenting the gulf between psychology and genetics in the study of human behavior, C. C. Darlington wrote in 1963, "Human behavior has thus become a happy hunting ground for literary amateurs. And the reason is that psychology and genetics, whose business it is to explain behavior, have failed to face the task together." Since 1963, some progress has been made in bridging this gap, but the genetics of human behavior remains somewhat controversial.

Here we will consider three approaches to the study of human behavior genetics: analysis of single genes with behavioral components, the use of animal models, and genomic methods. Like other areas of behavioral genetics, the study of human behavior depends on the analysis of single genes, as well as on the investigation of complex, multigenic traits with environmental components.

Single Genes and Behavior: Huntington Disease

Neurodegenerative disorders affect millions of people in the United States and across the world. These diseases are associated with the progressive accumulation of misfolded proteins in intra- and extracellular spaces, leading to the death of brain cells, with behavioral consequences. Some of these, such as familial Alzheimer disease (AD), Parkinson's disease, amyotrophic lateral sclerosis (ALS), and **Huntington disease (HD),** can be caused by mutations in single genes.

HD is inherited as an autosomal dominant disorder that affects about 1 in 10,000 people, causing cell death in selected brain cells. Symptoms usually appear in the fifth decade of life as a gradual loss of motor function and coordination. As structural degeneration of the brain progresses, personality changes occur. The symptoms are caused by brain-cell death in specific brain regions, including the cerebral cortex and the striatum. Most victims die within 10 to 15 years after the onset of the disease.

The symptoms of HD usually appear between the ages of 35 and 45, generally after someone has had children, who then must live with the knowledge that they face a 50 percent probability of developing the disorder (affected individuals are usually heterozygotes). The *HD* gene, on chromosome 4, was one of the first genes to be located by using restriction fragment length polymorphism (RFLP) analysis. The gene encodes a large protein (350 kDa) called huntingtin (Htt) that is essential for the survival of certain neurons in adult brains. Mutant HD alleles have an expanded number of cytosine-adenine-guanine (CAG) trinucleotide repeats in exon 1 (see Chapter 15 for a discussion of trinucleotide repeats). Normal alleles of the *HD* gene carry 7 to 34 CAG repeats, which specify insertion of multiple copies of the amino acid glutamine near the amino terminus of the huntingtin protein. In mutant alleles, expansion of the CAG repeats places additional glutamine residues in the encoded protein. The addition of more than 40 CAG repeats and the additional glutamine residues cause Htt to become toxic and cause cell death in certain regions of the brain, leading to behavioral abnormalities.

Transgenic animal models of neurodegenerative diseases caused by single-gene mutations, including AD, ALS, and HD, have been developed. These model systems are used to study the molecular events of synthesis, processing, and aggregation of mutant proteins, and the links between protein accumulation, cell death, and behavioral changes.

A Transgenic Mouse Model of Huntington Disease

Several animal models of HD have been developed to study the normal function of huntingtin, to model the disease process and study its effects at the molecular level, and to develop drugs that slow or stop the degeneration and death of brain cells. To study the relation between CAG repeat length and disease progression, Danilo Tagle and his colleagues constructed transgenic mice carrying a human *HD* gene with 16, 48, or 89 copies of the CAG repeat. In the vector used for gene transfer, the *HD* gene was placed adjacent to a promoter and an enhancer to ensure high levels of expression (see Chapter 22 for a discussion of transgenic organisms). Mice carrying the transgene were monitored from birth to death to determine the age of onset and progression of abnormal behavioral phenotypes. Animals carrying 48- or 89-repeat *HD* genes showed behavioral abnormalities as early as 8 weeks, and by 20 weeks, these mice showed both behavioral and motor-coordination abnormalities compared with the control animals and mice carrying human *HD* genes with 16 CAG repeats.

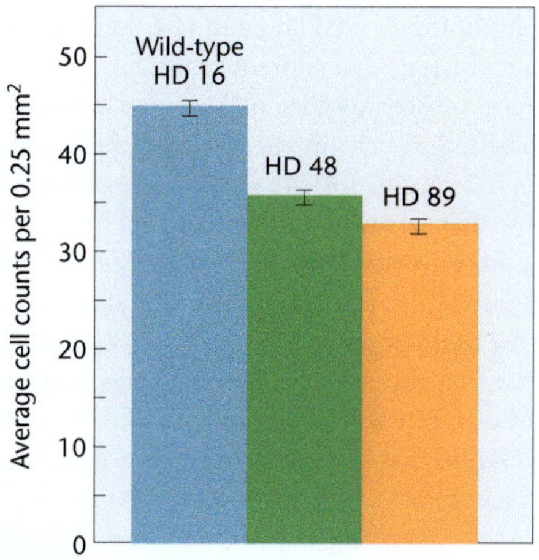

FIGURE 24–9 Relative levels of neuronal loss in HD transgenic mice. Cell counts show a significant reduction of certain neurons (small-medium neurons) in the corpus striatum of the brains of HD48 mutants (middle column) and HD89 mutants (right column) compared to wild-type (left column) mice. Cell loss in this brain tissue is also found in humans with HD, making these transgenic mice valuable models to study the course of this disease.

At various ages, brains of wild-type mice and of transgenic animals carrying mutant alleles with 16, 48, and 89 copies of the CAG repeat were examined for changes in structure. Degenerating neurons and cell loss were evident in mice carrying 48 and 89 repeats, but no changes were seen in brains of wild-type mice or of those carrying a 16-repeat transgene (Figure 24–9).

The behavioral changes and the degeneration in specific brain regions in the transgenic mice parallel the progression of HD in humans. These mice are now used to study early changes in brain structure that occur before the onset of early symptoms, and in the development of experimental treatments to slow or reverse cell loss. Having a mouse model for the disease allows researchers to administer treatment at specific times in disease progression and to evaluate the outcome of treatments in the presymptomatic stages of HD.

Mechanisms of Huntington Disease

Although the *HD* gene was mapped, isolated, and characterized over 25 years ago, the mechanism by which mutant forms of the Htt protein (mHtt) cause HD is still unknown. Htt is expressed in all cells of the body, with highest levels in the brain and testes. The mutant form of Htt causes cell death initially in striatal cells in the brain. Several mechanisms have been proposed to explain the region-specific pattern of cell death, including abnormal mitochondrial metabolism, increased activity of proteases associated with cell death (apoptosis), misfolding of Htt, and the formation of nuclear inclusions that contain Htt fragments.

The recent discovery that mHtt binds to Rhes, a small protein localized to cells in the brain's striatal region may explain the cell-specific toxicity of the mHtt protein. Experiments show that when bound to Rhes, mHtt is chemically modified and converted to a form that causes cell death. Low levels of Rhes are also present in the cerebral cortex, another region of the brain in which Htt causes cell death. This finding suggests that the development of drugs that block the interaction of mHtt with Rhes may be valuable in treating HD. However, as discussed below, Htt is a multifunctional protein that interacts with more than 100 other proteins, including those involved with transcription, cell signaling, and intracellular transport, offering other avenues for treatment. Recent work has focused on the role of mHtt in the disruption of transcriptional regulation.

In affected individuals, onset of HD is associated with decreases in mRNA levels for genes encoding certain neurotransmitter receptors. In a transgenic HD mouse model, researchers used cDNA arrays to screen nearly 6000 mRNAs from striatal cells. They found lower levels of mRNA from a small set of genes involved in signaling pathways that are critical to striatal cell function. Similar results were found in another transgenic HD mouse model and are consistent with findings from HD patients, implicating aberrant gene expression as one of the underlying causes of HD. The mutant form of Htt interacts with and binds to several transcription factors and may alter patterns of gene expression by making these proteins unavailable. Some proteins that interact with Htt have histone-modifying activity and are found in Htt protein aggregates in brains of transgenic HD mice and patients with HD.

Using transgenic HD mice, several groups showed that drugs which alter histone modification increased survival and reduced cell death. Similar drugs are now being used in human clinical trials on HD patients, and other drugs are being screened in mouse models for therapeutic effects.

Complex Behavioral Traits: Schizophrenia

Although genomic techniques have been used successfully to identify mutant alleles associated with single-gene behavioral disorders (such as *HD*), other behaviors are polygenic with strong environmental components, making their genetics more difficult to dissect. For example, schizophrenia is a brain disorder affecting about 1 percent of the population and is an example of a complex genetic disease. **Schizophrenia** is a collection of mental disorders characterized by avoidance of social contact and by bizarre and sometimes delusional behavior. Those affected by the condition are unable to lead normal lives and are periodically disabled by its symptoms. It is clearly a familial disorder, with relatives of schizophrenics having a much higher incidence of the condition than the general population (Figure 24–10). Furthermore, the closer the genetic or biological relationship to an affected individual, the greater is a person's probability of developing the disorder. Twin studies have helped establish a genetic link to schizophrenia. If both twins express a trait, they are said to be concordant for that trait; if one expresses the trait, but the other does not, they are discordant for that trait. In studies of monozygotic and dizygotic twins for schizophrenia, concordance is higher in monozygotic twins than in dizygotic twins. Although these results suggest that a genetic component exists, they do not reveal the precise genetic basis of schizophrenia. Other studies emphasize the importance of the effects of pleiotropy, epistasis, as well as shared environmental factors, in the development of this disorder. The current view is that schizophrenia is a genetically mediated but not genetically determined neurodevelopmental disorder. The genetic contributions to schizophrenia have been difficult to identify. Simple monohybrid inheritance, dihybrid inheritance, and multiple-gene control have been discounted as causes of schizophrenia. It does not seem

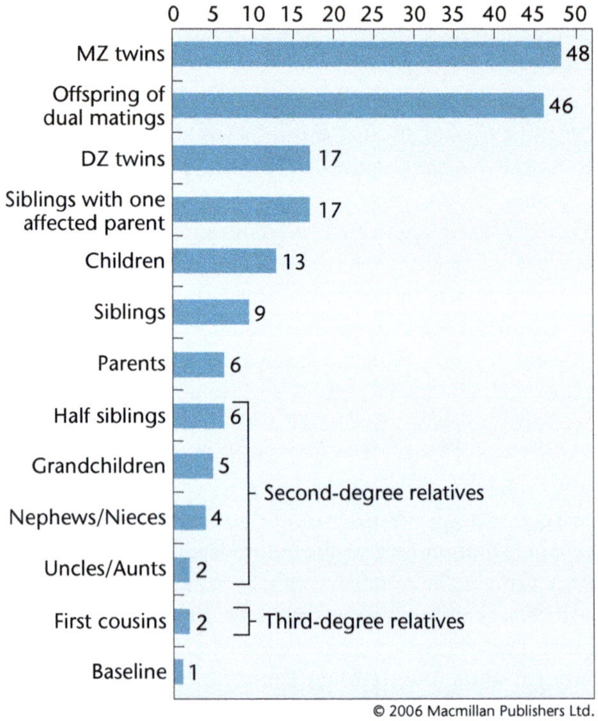

FIGURE 24–10 Relative lifetime risk of schizophrenia for nonrelated individuals and for relatives of a schizophrenic proband.

likely that only one or two loci are involved, nor is it likely that the disorder is strictly quantitative, as in polygenic inheritance. Schizophrenia is currently regarded as a multifactorial and quantitative trait, influenced by genes, by the environment, and by interactions between the genotype and environmental factors.

The search for the role of genes in schizophrenia parallels the development of technologies that allow new ways of searching for genes associated with complex traits. Beginning in the late 1980s, linkage studies with RFLP markers identified chromosome regions that segregated in families with affected members. By 2000, a small number of candidate genes had been identified on chromosomes 6, 8, and 13. The role of some of the encoded proteins in nerve impulse transmission supports the idea that these genes may play a role in schizophrenia, although there is some controversy about their importance in the disease process.

New experimental methods developed during and after the Human Genome Project have used haplotype mapping and high-throughput sequencing approaches to study schizophrenia. Foremost among these are genome-wide association studies (GWAS) that utilize some of the more than 10 million single-nucleotide polymorphisms (SNPs) present in the human genome (SNPs are discussed in Chapter 21). Subsets of 300,000 to 500,000 SNPs organized in closely linked clusters called **haplotypes** spread across the genome are used with sequencing platforms to survey thousands of genomes, looking for an association between haplotypes and a trait, in this case, schizophrenia (Figure 24–11). The haplotypes are markers that identify

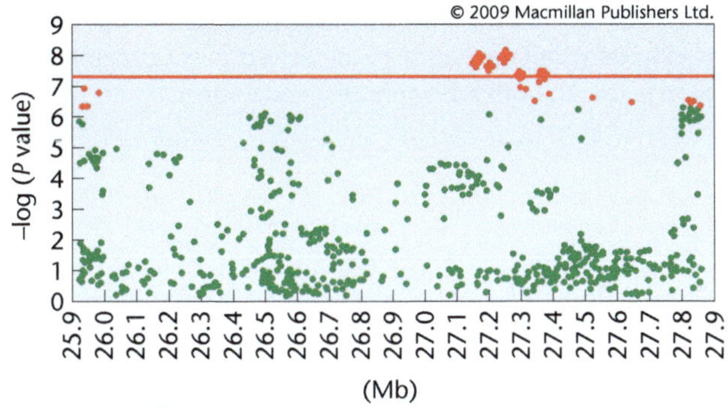

FIGURE 24–11 The results of a genome-wide association study for the association of SNPs and schizophrenia on chromosome 6p22.1. SNPs above the statistical threshold for association (the red line) are shown as red diamonds. Seven SNPs spanning 209 kb of DNA show significance. Red circles represent SNPs at the threshold of statistical significance, and green circles indicate SNPs with no association. The X axis marks the location of the SNPs in million-base pairs (Mb) within the 6p22.1 region.

chromosome regions that may contain genes associated with schizophrenia.

The evidence from GWAS on schizophrenia indicates that no single gene or allele makes a significant contribution to this disorder. Instead, the results point to the involvement of hundreds of genes that each contributes only a small amount to schizophrenia. GWAS are based on the assumption that common gene variants (present in more than 5 percent of the population) contribute to disease risk (the common disease/common variant hypothesis, abbreviated as CDCV). In this case, common variants identified by GWAS contribute only about 4 to 30 percent of the risk for schizophrenia.

The failure of GWAS to identify the majority of genes that are risk factors for schizophrenia and other disorders has generated a debate among human geneticists. Some argue that by greatly increasing the number of genomes scanned, GWAS will be able to identify many low-effect genes for a specific disorder. Others point out that there is no way to know the sample size needed to identify all genes that contribute to any disorder and in fact, GWAS may be the wrong strategy. In this view, it is thought that searching for rare allele variants that may underlie relative common disorders (the common disease/rare variant (CDRV) hypothesis) may be the best strategy to identify alleles responsible for many complex disorders. Large-scale whole-genome resequencing to identify allelic variants associated with gene–phenotype associations are proposed as a means of identifying these variants. Still others argue that other mechanisms, such as gene–gene interactions, protein–protein interactions, epigenetic alterations, or copy number variations (CNVs), may be important in schizophrenia and other psychiatric disorders.

A recent study showed that *de novo* CNVs representing both deletions and duplications were three to four times more frequent in cases of schizophrenia than in normal individuals. Many genes in these CNVs are involved in brain development, providing clues to the cellular basis of schizophrenia. Following this study, other work showed that CNVs distributed in other regions of the genome are disproportionately represented in schizophrenia; this finding emphasizes the need for the use of several techniques in dissecting this and other complex behavioral disorders.

Schizophrenia and Autism Are Related Neurodevelopmental Disorders

Like schizophrenia, family studies and twin studies show that autism spectrum disorders (ASD) are complex, multifactorial diseases with a genetic component. It is estimated that ASD affects about 3.4 per 1000 children between the ages of 3 and 10 years. These disorders are characterized by severe and pervasive deficits in (1) thinking, (2) language skills, (3) feelings, and (4) social interaction. These disorders range from a severe form called autism through several intermediates to a mild form called Asperger's syndrome.

Some rare mutations and chromosomal rearrangements are associated with ASD, but taken together, account for only about 5 to 15 percent of all cases. GWAS results have identified SNPs associated with susceptibility to ASD. Some of these SNPs are also risk factors for schizophrenia, indicating that these disorders may be related. Other studies reveal the existence of rare copy number variants (CNVs) associated with the development of both disorders.

CNVs covering seven genomic regions have been linked to both schizophrenia and ASD (Table 24.3). In two of these regions, deletions are associated with an increased risk of autism, and duplications are associated with an increased risk of schizophrenia (16p11.2, 22q13.3). In two others (1q21.1, 22.q11.21), deletions increase the risk of schizophrenia, and duplications are associated with ASD. The region at 16p13.1 supports a model of overlap between the two conditions.

Further work has shown that genes in these chromosomal regions play important roles in the development of brain cells, the maturation of synapses, and the interconnection of neurons. These genes have been mapped into functional pathways using methods of systems biology, and reveal interconnected nodes of gene interaction that are important in the formation and function of parts of the nervous system.

Expression profiles show that schizophrenia and ASD are disorders that represent opposite sides of the same coin. ASD is associated with increased activity in these developmental pathways leading to cellular overgrowth and increased brain and head size, while schizophrenia is characterized by a reduced activity in these pathways, resulting in developmental undergrowth and reduced brain and head size. Mapping of other genes in these chromosomal regions into functional networks should advance our knowledge of normal brain development and the nature of the defects in gene regulation associated with both schizophrenia and autism.

TABLE 24.3

Frequencies of CNV deletions or duplications associated with autism or schizophrenia

CNV Locus	Condition	Deletion Cases	Duplication Cases
1q21.1	Autism	**2**	**10**
	Schizophrenia	**15**	4
15q13.3	Autism	3	2
	Schizophrenia	**10**	4
16p11.2	Autism	**14**	5
	Schizophrenia	5	**24**
16p13.1	Autism	0	**3**
	Schizophrenia	8	**23**
17p12	Autism	4	1
	Schizophrenia	**8**	0
22q11.21	Autism	1	**8**
	Schizophrenia	**16**	1
22q13.3	Autism	**5**	0
	Schizophrenia	0	**4**

Entries in bold indicate that the CNV is statistically documented as a risk factor for the condition specified.
From: Crespi, B, et al., 2010. Comparative genomics of autism and schizophrenia. Proc. Nat. Acad. Sci. 107: 1736–1741; their Table 1, page 1737.
Contact: crespi@sfu.ca

CASE STUDY | Primate models for human disorders

Huntington disease (HD) is a dominantly inherited, adult-onset neurodegenerative disorder that affects about 1 in 10,000 people. Onset is around 50 years of age, there is no treatment, and the disorder inevitably causes dementia and loss of motor control, and is fatal. To study the cellular and molecular mechanisms associated with HD, animal models, including mice and *Drosophila*, have been created by transferring mutant human *HD* genes into these organisms. However, some of the behavioral changes seen in HD mice and fruit flies are difficult to correlate with those seen in affected humans. To more closely replicate the cognitive and motor changes in HD, researchers have created a primate model using rhesus macaques, which are one of our closest relatives and share many similarities with humans, including life span, cellular metabolism, as well as endocrine and reproductive functions. However, their use raises several important questions.

1. What are the ethical concerns related to research with primate models of human disease?
2. Does it seem likely that results from using rhesus macaques will translate directly to an understanding of the disease process in humans and lead to treatment?
3. If the primate HD model is successful, should it be used for other human behavioral disorders such as Alzheimer or Parkinson disease?

EXPLORING GENOMICS

HomoloGene: Searching for Behavioral Genes

MG™ *Study Area: Exploring Genomics*

This chapter discussed some of the complexities of understanding behavior—in humans and other species—as a product of both genes and environment. In this exercise, we will explore the NCBI database **HomoloGene** to search for genes implicated in behavioral conditions. HomoloGene is a database of homologs from several eukaryotic species, and it contains genes that have been implicated in behavioral conditions both in animal models and in humans. Some of these are mutant genes, which, on the basis of single-nucleotide polymorphisms or linkage mapping, are thought to contribute to a behavioral phenotype. Keep in mind that correlation of a gene with a particular behavioral condition does not necessarily mean that the gene is the cause of the condition. Nor does it mean that the gene is the only one involved in the behavioral condition or that the condition is entirely due to genetics. Nonetheless, exploring HomoloGene is an interesting way to search for putative behavioral genes and learn more about them.

Exercise I – HomoloGene

1. Access **HomoloGene** from the ENTREZ site at http://www.ncbi.nlm.nih.gov/gquery/ gquery.fcgi.
2. Search HomoloGene using the following list of terms related to behavioral conditions in humans. What human genes are listed in the top two categories of gene homologs that result from the HomoloGene search for each condition? Name these genes and identify their chromosomal loci. Notice the list of other species thought to share homologs of each gene.
   a. alcoholism
   b. depression
   c. nicotine addiction
   d. seasonal affective disorder
   e. intelligence
3. For each of the top two categories of homologs, click on the category title to open a report on those genes. Then use the links for individual genes to learn more about the functions of those genes. In addition to other good resources, the "Additional Links" category at the bottom of each gene report page will provide you with access to the Online Mendelian Inheritance in Man (OMIM) site that we have used for other exercises.
4. Search HomoloGene for any behavioral conditions you are interested in to see if the database contains genes that may be implicated in those conditions.

Summary Points

MG™ *For activities, animations, and review quizzes, go to the study area at www.masteringgenetics.com*

1. Behavior is a multifactorial trait controlled by genes, environmental factors, and interactions among these genes and the environment.
2. The behavior-first approach can generate strains that exhibit specific behaviors but cannot be used to identify genes associated with those behaviors.
3. The gene-first approach can be used to analyze the effect of single genes on complex behaviors that are controlled by multiple genes, but is difficult to use in the study of naturally-occurring variation.
4. Because of the large number of genetic resources available, *Drosophila* and other organisms are useful or the study of behavioral disorders in humans.
5. Genomic technology has opened new avenues of investigation into the development of the human nervous system and the mechanisms of behavioral disorders.

INSIGHTS AND SOLUTIONS

1. Bipolar disorder is a mental illness associated with pervasive and wide mood swings. It is estimated that 1 in 100 individuals has or will suffer from this disorder at least once in his or her lifetime. Genetic studies indicate that bipolar disorder is familial and that mutations in several genes are involved. In an attempt to identify genes associated with bipolar disorder (this condition was formerly called manic depression), researchers began by using conventional genetic analysis. In 1987, two separate studies using pedigree analysis, RFLP analysis, and a variety of other genetic markers reported a linkage between manic depression and, in one report, markers on the X chromosome and, in the other report, markers on the short arm of chromosome 11. At the time, these reports were hailed as landmark discoveries. It was thought that genes controlling this behavioral disorder could be identified, mapped, and sequenced in much the same way as genes for cystic fibrosis, neurofibromatosis, and other disorders. It was hoped that this discovery would open the way to the development of therapeutic strategies based on knowledge of the nature of the gene product and its mechanism of action. One of the challenges of human genetics results from the fact that some disorders show variable times of onset, and the bipolar studies provide an example of this. Following the original analysis identifying markers, some of the controls (unaffected individuals) who did not carry the markers subsequently developed bipolar disorder. This outcome weakened the evidence for linkage. These findings do not exclude the role of major genes on the X chromosome and chromosome 11 in bipolar disorder, but they do exclude linkage to the markers used in the original reports. This setback not only caused embarrassment and confusion, but also forced a reexamination of the validity of the newly developed recombinant DNA-based methods used in mapping other human genes and of the analysis of data from linkage studies involving complex behavioral traits. Several factors have been proposed to explain the flawed conclusions reported in the original studies. What do you suppose some of these factors were?

Solution: Although some of the criticisms were directed at the choice of markers, most of the factors at work in this situation appear to be related to the phenotype of manic depression. At least three confounding factors have been identified. One factor relates to the diagnosis of bipolar disorder itself. The phenotype is complex and not as easily quantified as height or weight. In addition, mood swings are a universal part of everyday life, and it is not always easy to distinguish transient mood alterations and the role of environmental factors from disorders having a biological or genetic basis (or both). A second confounding factor is that, in the populations studied, there may in fact be more than one major X-linked gene and more than one major autosomal gene that trigger bipolar disorder. A third factor is age of onset. There is a positive correlation between age and the appearance of the symptoms of bipolar disorder. Therefore, at the time of a pedigree study, younger individuals who will be affected later in life may not show any signs of bipolar disorder. Taken together, these factors illustrate the difficulty in researching the genetic basis of complex behavioral traits. Individually or in combinations, the factors described might skew the results enough so that the guidelines for proof that are adequate for other traits are not stringent enough for behavioral traits with complex phenotypes and complex underlying causes.

Problems and Discussion Questions

MG™ *For instructor-assigned tutorials and problems, go to www.masteringgenetics.com*

HOW DO WE KNOW?

1. In this chapter we focused on how genes that control the development, structure, and function of the nervous system and interactions with environmental factors produce behavior. At the same time, we found many opportunities to consider the methods and reasoning by which much of this information was acquired. From the explanations given in the chapter, what answers would you propose to the following fundamental questions:
(a) How do we know there is genetic variation for a specific behavior that is present in strains of a species?
(b) How do we know that geotaxis in *Drosophila* is under genetic control?
(c) How do we know that *Drosophila* can learn and remember?
(d) How do we know how the mutant gene product in Huntington disease functions?
(e) How do we know that schizophrenia has genetic components?
2. Contrast the two principal approaches used in studying behavioral genetics. What are the advantages and disadvantages of each method with respect to the type of information gained?
3. In humans, the chemical phenylthiocarbamide (PTC) is either tasted or not. When the offspring of various combinations of taster and nontaster parents are examined, the following data are obtained:

Parents	Offspring
Both tasters	All tasters
Both tasters	1/2 tasters 1/2 nontasters
Both tasters	3/4 tasters 1/4 nontasters
One taster and One nontaster	All tasters
One taster One nontaster	1/2 tasters 1/2 nontasters
Both nontasters	All nontasters

Based on these data, how is PTC tasting behavior inherited?

4. Jerry Hirsch and colleagues have used the behavior-first approach to study the genes responsible for geotaxis in *Drosophila*. Their elegant genetic analysis has shown that this behavior is under genetic control, and they estimate the number of genes responsible for geotactic behavior. Although the approach has been successful, what are the limitations of the behavior-first approach as used here? What steps did Hirsch and his colleagues take to overcome those limitations? Has this approach been successful?
5. Various approaches have been applied to study the genetics of problem and pathological gambling (PG), and within-family vulnerability has been well documented. However, family studies, while showing clusters within blood relatives, cannot separate genetic from environmental influences. Eisen (2001) applied "twin studies" using 3359 twin pairs from the Vietnam-era Twin Registry and found that a substantial portion of the variance associated with PG can be attributed to inherited factors. How might twin studies be used to distinguish environmental from genetic factors in complex behavioral traits such as PG?
6. *Caenorhabditis elegans* has become a valuable model organism for the study of development and genetics for a variety of reasons. The developmental fate of each cell (1031 in males and 959 in hermaphrodites) has been mapped. *C. elegans* has only 302 neurons whose pattern of connectivity is known, and it displays a variety of interesting behaviors including chemotaxis, thermotaxis, and mating behavior, to name a few. In addition, isogenic lines have been established. What advantage would the use of *C. elegans* have over other model organisms in the study of animal behavior? What are likely disadvantages?
7. Using the behavioral phenotypes of a series of 18 mutants falling into five phenotypic classes, Thomas (1990) described the genetic program that controls the cyclic defecation motor program in *Caenorhabditis elegans*. The first step in each cycle is contraction of the posterior body muscles, followed by contraction of the anterior body muscles. Finally, anal muscles open and expel the intestinal contents. Below is a list of selected mutants (simplified) that cause defects in defecation.

Gene	Phenotype
exp	failure to open the anus and expel intestinal contents
unc	failure to contract anterior body muscles
pbo	failure to contract posterior body muscles
aex	failure to open the anus and expel intestinal contents and failure to contract anterior body muscles
cha	alteration of cycle periodicity, all other components being completely functional

Present a simple schematic that illustrates genetic involvement in *C. elegans* defecation. Account for the action of the *aex* gene and speculate on the involvement and placement of the *cha* gene.
8. Discuss why the study of human behavior genetics has lagged behind that of other organisms.
9. J. P. Scott and J. L. Fuller studied 50 traits in five pure breeds of dogs. Almost all the traits varied significantly in the five breeds, but very few bred true in crosses. What can you conclude with respect to the genetic control of these behavioral traits?

Extra-Spicy Problems

For instructor-assigned tutorials and problems, go to www.masteringgenetics.com

10. Although not discussed in this chapter, *C. elegans* is a model system whose life cycle makes it an excellent choice for the genetic dissection of many biological processes. *C. elegans* has two natural sexes: hermaphrodite and male. The hermaphrodite is essentially a female that can generate sperm as well as oocytes, so reproduction can occur by hermaphrodite self-fertilization or hermaphrodite–male mating. In the context of studying mutations in the nervous system, what is the advantage of hermaphrodite self-fertilization with respect to the identification of recessive mutations and the propagation of mutant strains?
11. Hypothetical data concerning the genetic effect of *Drosophila* chromosomes on geotaxis are shown here:

	Chromosome		
	X	*2*	*3*
Positive geotaxis	+0.2	+0.1	+3.0
Unselected	+0.1	−0.2	+1.0
Negative geotaxis	−0.1	−2.6	+0.1

What conclusions can you draw?
12. In July 2006, a population of flies, *Drosophila melanogaster*, rode the space shuttle *Discovery* to the International Space Station (ISS) where a number of graviperception experiments and observations were conducted over a nine-generation period. Frozen specimens were collected by astronauts and returned to Earth. Researchers correlated behavioral and physiological responses to microgravity with changes in gene activity by analyzing RNA and protein profiles. The title of the project is "*Drosophila* Behavior and Gene Expression in Microgravity." If you were in a position to conduct three experiments on the behavioral aspects of these flies, what would they be? How would you go about assaying changes in gene expression in response to microgravity? Given that humans share over half of the genome and proteins of *Drosophila*, how would you justify the expense of such a project in terms of improving human health?
13. Of a variety of investigational approaches that have been applied to the study of schizophrenia, two separate approaches, twin studies and genomic analysis, have provided strong support for a genetic component.
(a) Provide a summary of the contribution that each has played in understanding schizophrenia.
(b) Speculate on the value that genomic analysis using samples from monozygotic and dizygotic twins might have for enhancing research on schizophrenia.
14. Describe the use of single-nucleotide polymorphisms (SNPs) in the study of genetic causes of schizophrenia.
15. Autism, a relatively common complex of human disorders, can range from severe to mild. What evidence indicates a possible link between genetics and autism?

16. An interesting and controversial finding by Wedekind and colleagues (1995) suggested that a sense of smell, flavored with various HLA (Human Leukocyte Antigen) haplotypes, plays a role in mate selection in humans. Women preferred T-shirts from men with HLA haplotypes unlike their own. The HLA haplotypes are components of the Major Histocompatibility Complex (MHC) and are known to have significant immunological functions. In addition to humans, mice and fish also condition mate preference on MHC constitution. The three-spined stickleback (*Gasterosteus aculeatus*) has recently been studied to determine whether females use an MHC odor-based system to select males as mates. Examine the following data (modified from Milinski et al., 2005) and provide a summary conclusion. Why might organisms evolve a mate selection scheme for assessing and optimizing MHC diversity?

	Male with optimal MHC	**Male with nonoptimal MHC**
Gravid female time spent (seconds)	350	250
Number spawning females	11	3

The table compares odor-based choices made by gravid females for males with optimal MHC alleles and males with nonoptimal MHC alleles. Gravid females chose different amounts of time (seconds) for exposure to males with optimal MHC alleles versus those with nonoptimal MHC alleles. The number of females spawning when exposed to different males with different MHC complements is also presented in the table.

SPECIAL TOPICS IN MODERN GENETICS

Genomics and Personalized Medicine

Physicians have always practiced personalized medicine in order to make effective treatment decisions for their patients. Doctors take into account a patient's symptoms, family history, lifestyle, and data derived from many types of medical tests. However, within the last 20 years, personalized medicine has taken a new and potentially powerful direction based on genetics and genomics. Today, the phrase *personalized medicine* is used to describe the application of information from a patient's unique genetic profile in order to select effective treatments that have minimal side-effects and to detect disease susceptibility prior to development of the disease.

Despite the immense quantities of medical information and pharmaceuticals that are available, the diagnosis and treatment of human disease remains an imperfect process. It is sometimes difficult or impossible to accurately diagnose some conditions. In addition, some patients do not respond to treatments, while others may develop side-effects that can be annoying or even life-threatening. As much of the basis for disease susceptibility and the variation that patients exhibit toward drug treatments are genetically determined, progress in genetics, genomics, and molecular biology has the potential to significantly advance medical diagnosis and treatment.

In the near future, personalized medicine will allow physicians to predict which diseases you will develop, which therapeutics will work for you, and which drug dosages are appropriate.

The sequencing of the human genome, the cataloging of genetic sequence variants, and the linking of sequence variants with disease susceptibility form the basis of the newly emerging field of personalized medicine. By 2009, the number of diseases detectable by genetic tests rose to approximately 2000. In addition, a rapidly growing list of genetic tests help physicians determine whether a patient will have an adverse drug reaction and whether a particular pharmaceutical will be effective for that patient.

Although much of the promise of personalized medicine remains in the future, significant progress is underway. As genome technologies advance and the cost of sequencing personal genomes declines, it is becoming easier to examine a patient's unique genomic profile in order to diagnose diseases and prescribe treatments. Proponents of personalized medicine foresee a future in which each person will have his or her genome sequence determined at birth and will have the sequence stored in a digital form within a personal computerized medical file. Medical practitioners will use automated methods to scan the sequence information within these files for clues to disease susceptibility and reactions to drugs. In the near future, genomic profiling and personalized medicine will allow physicians to predict which diseases you will develop, which therapeutics will work for you, and which drug dosages are appropriate.

In this Special Topics chapter, we will outline the current uses of genetic and genomic-based personalized medicine in disease diagnosis and drug selection. In addition, we will outline the future directions for personalized medicine, as well as some ethical and technical challenges associated with it.

Personalized Medicine and Pharmacogenomics

At present, the most developed aspect of the new personalized medicine is in the field of pharmacogenomics. **Pharmacogenomics** is the study of how an individual's entire genetic makeup determines the body's response to drugs. The term *pharmacogenomics* is used interchangeably with *pharmacogenetics,* which refers to the study of how sequence variation within specific candidate genes affects an individual's drug responses.

In pharmacogenomics, scientists take into account many aspects of drug metabolism and how genetic traits affect these aspects. When a drug enters the body, it interacts with various proteins including carriers, cell-surface receptors, transporters, and metabolizing enzymes. These proteins affect a drug's target site of action, absorption, pharmacological response, breakdown, and excretion. Because there are so many interactions that occur between a drug and proteins within the patient, many genes and many different genetic polymorphisms can affect a person's response to a drug.

In this subsection, we examine two ways in which genomics and personalized medicine are changing the field of pharmacogenomics: by optimizing drug therapies and by reducing adverse drug reactions.

Optimizing Drug Therapies

When it comes to drug therapy, it is clear that "one size does not fit all." On average, a drug will be effective in only about 50 percent of patients who take it (ST Figure 2–1). This situation means that physicians often must switch their patients from one drug to another until they find one that is effective. Not only does this waste time and resources, but also it may be dangerous to the patient who is exposed to a variety

Drug type		
Anti-depressants (SSRIs)	38%	
Asthma drugs	40%	
Diabetes drugs	43%	
Arthritis drugs	50%	
Alzheimer's drugs	70%	
Cancer drugs	75%	

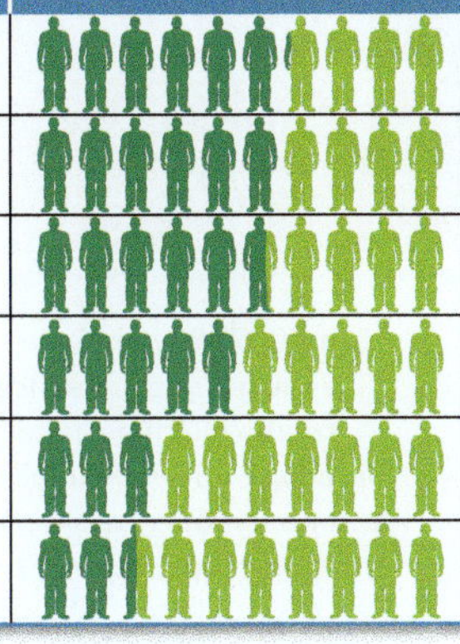

ST FIGURE 2–1 **Variations in patient response to drugs. This figure gives a general summary of the percentages of patients for which a particular class of drugs is effective.**

of different pharmaceuticals and who may not receive appropriate treatment in time to combat a progressive illness.

Pharmacogenomics increases the efficacy of drugs by targeting those drugs to subpopulations of patients who will benefit. One of the most common current applications of personalized pharmacogenomics is in the diagnosis and treatment of cancers. Large-scale sequencing studies show that each tumor is genetically unique, even though it may fall into a broad category based on cytological analysis or knowledge of its tissue origin. Given this genomic variability, it is important to understand each patient's mutation profile to select an appropriate treatment—particularly those newer treatments based on the molecular characteristics of tumors (Box 1).

One of the first success stories in personalized medicine was that of the ***HER-2*** gene and the use of the drug **Herceptin®** in breast cancer. The human epidermal growth factor receptor 2 (*HER-2*) gene is located on chromosome 17 and codes for a transmembrane tyrosine kinase receptor protein called HER-2. These receptors are located within the cell membranes of normal breast epithelial cells and are responsible for sending signals to the cell nucleus that result in the transcription of genes involved in cell growth and division. In a normal situation, an extracellular growth factor (ligand) binds to a HER-2 protein, which then dimerizes with another HER family receptor and phosphorylates tyrosine residues on specific target proteins within the cell. These phosphorylated proteins are then activated and phosphorylate a series of other proteins, in a process known as **signal transduction**. The end result of this cascade of signal transduction is that transcription factors in the nucleus stimulate the transcription of genes whose products regulate cell proliferation.

BOX 1

The Story of Pfizer's Crizotinib

In 2007, Beverly Sotir was diagnosed with advanced non-small-cell lung cancer (NSCLC). Beverly, a 68-year-old grandmother and nonsmoker, received standard chemotherapy, but her cancer continued to proliferate. She was given six months to live. At this same time, an apparently unrelated scientific study was underway by the pharmaceutical company, Pfizer. Pfizer had developed a compound called crizotinib, which was designed to inhibit the activity of MET, a tyrosine kinase that is abnormal in a number of tumors. Although crizotinib also inhibited another kinase called ALK (anaplastic lymphoma kinase), scientists did not consider it significant. After clinical trials for crizotinib began, an article was published* describing a chromosomal translocation found in a small number of NSCLCs. This translocation fused the *ALK* gene to another gene called *EML4,* leading to production of a fusion protein that stimulated cancer cell growth. Pfizer immediately changed its clinical trial to include NSCLC patients. Beverly's doctors at the Dana-Farber Cancer Institute in Boston tested her tumors, discovered that they contained the *ALK/EML4* fusion gene, and enrolled Beverly in the trials. The results were dramatic. Within six months, Beverly's tumors shrunk by more than 50 percent and some disappeared entirely. As of September 2010, Beverly continued to do well.

Results of the Phase I and II clinical trials for crizotinib showed that tumors shrunk or stabilized in 90 percent of the 82 patients whose tumors contained the *ALK* fusion gene. Those patients who responded well to treatment had positive responses for up to 15 months. Scientists report that the *ALK* fusion gene tends to occur most frequently in young NSCLC patients who have never smoked. Approximately 4 percent of patients with NSCLC have this translocation in their tumor cells. Although this appears a small percentage of people who might benefit from crizotinib, this means that about 45,000 people a year, worldwide, may be eligible for this treatment. Crizotinib is now in Phase III clinical trials.

*Choi, S.M., et al. 2007. Identification of the transforming EML4-ALK fusion gene in non-small-cell lung cancer. *Nature* 448: 561–566.

In about 25 percent of invasive breast cancers, the *HER-2* gene is amplified and the protein is overexpressed on the cell surface. In some breast cancers, the *HER-2* gene is present in as many as 100 copies per cell. The presence of *HER-2* gene amplification is associated with increased tumor invasiveness, metastasis, and cell proliferation, as well as a poorer patient prognosis.

Using recombinant DNA technology, Genentech Corporation in California developed a monoclonal antibody known as trastuzumab (or Herceptin®) that is designed to bind specifically to the extracellular region of the HER-2 receptor. When bound to the receptor, Herceptin® appears to inhibit the signaling capability of HER-2 and may also flag the HER-2-expressing cell for destruction by the patient's immune system. In cancer cells that overexpress HER-2, Herceptin treatment causes cell-cycle arrest, and in some cases, death of the cancer cells.

Because Herceptin will only act on breast cancer cells that have amplified *HER-2* genes, it is important to know the HER-2 phenotype of each cancer. In addition, Herceptin has potentially serious side-effects. Hence, its use must be limited to those who could benefit from the treatment. A number of molecular assays have been developed to determine the gene and protein status of breast cancer cells. Two of the most commonly used tests are based on **immunohistochemistry (IHC)** and **fluorescence *in situ* hybridization (FISH)**. In IHC assays, an antibody that binds to HER-2 protein molecules is added to fixed tissue on a slide. The antibody is bound to another molecule that reacts to produce a visual stain. After washing and staining, the tissues are observed under a microscope. The level of HER-2 staining is assessed from "0" (fewer than 20,000 HER-2 molecules per cell) to "+3" (approximately 2 million molecules per cell) (ST Figure 2–2(a)). In FISH, DNA or RNA molecules with sequence complementarity to the *HER-2* gene sequence are added to the fixed tissue on the slide. These DNA or RNA probes are labeled with a fluorescent tag molecule. After hybridizing the probes to the tissue and washing off excess probe, the location and intensity of the probe are determined by observing the tissue under a fluorescence microscope. The number of *HER-2* genes is assessed by comparing the fluorescence signal of the *HER-2* probe with a control signal from another gene that is not amplified in the cells (ST Figure 2–2(b)).

Herceptin has had a major effect on the treatment of HER-2 positive breast cancers. When Herceptin is used in combination with chemotherapy, there is a 25 to 50 percent increase in survival, compared with the use of chemotherapy alone. Herceptin is now one of the biggest selling biotechnology products in the world, generating more than $5 billion in annual sales.

There are now dozens of drugs whose prescription and use depend on the genetic status of the target cells. Approximately 10 percent of FDA-approved drugs have labels that include pharmacogenomic information (ST Table 2.1). For example, about 40 percent of colon cancer patients respond

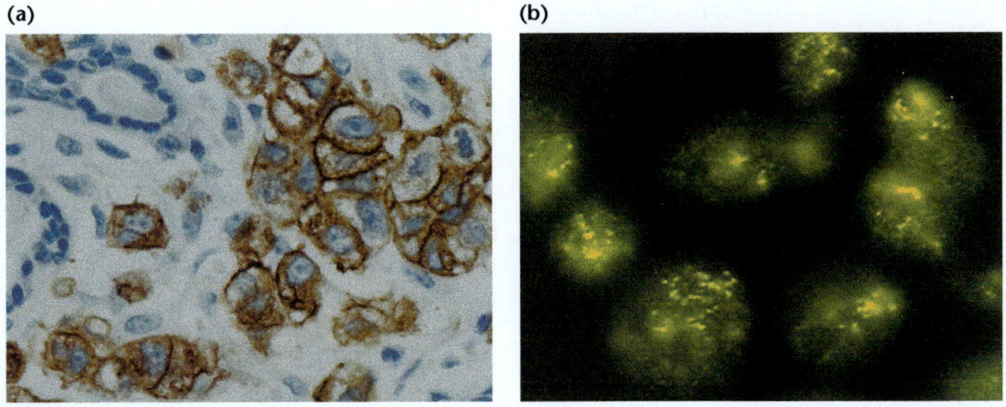

ST FIGURE 2-2 ***HER-2* gene and protein assays.** (a) Normal and breast cancer cells within a biopsy sample, stained by HER-2 immunohistochemistry. Cell nuclei are stained blue. Cancer cells that overexpress HER-2 protein stain brown. (b) Cancer cells from the same tumor assayed in (a), assayed for *HER-2* gene copy number by fluorescence *in situ* hybridization. Cancer cell nuclei appear green under the fluorescence microscope and the *HER-2* gene DNA appears bright yellow. Large clumps of yellow stain indicate *HER-2* gene amplification (more than 20 copies per nucleus).

Source: The Case for Personalized Medicine, Figure 1, Page 5. © 2009 Personalized Medicine coalition. Used by permission.

to the drugs **Erbitux®** (cetuximab) and **Vectibix®** (panitumab). These two drugs are monoclonal antibodies that bind to **epidermal growth factor receptors (EGFRs)** on the surface of cells and inhibit the EGFR signal transduction pathway. In order to work, cancer cells must express EGFR on their surfaces and must also have a wild-type *K-RAS* gene. The ***K-RAS*** gene encodes a small signaling protein that is part of the EGFR pathway. Mutations in *K-RAS* codons 12, 13, and 61 are common in colorectal cancers, and the presence of these mutations makes treatment with these drugs ineffective. Prior to treatment with Erbitux or Vectibix, tumor cells from patients are screened for the presence of EGFR and a wild-type *K-RAS* gene. The EGFR is detected with an immunohistochemistry test, as described for HER-2. *K-RAS* mutations are detected using an assay based on the polymerase chain reaction (PCR). The PCR method was described previously in Chapter 20. The *K-RAS* assay is based on the observation that the *Taq* DNA polymerase can distinguish between a perfect primer match and a one-nucleotide mismatch at the 3′ end of the primer. By including primers that hybridize perfectly with only the mutations in codons 12, 13, or 61, only the mutated *K-RAS* genes will be amplified by PCR. The primers are labeled with a fluorescing molecule, and the presence of a PCR product is visualized by automated equipment.

Another example of treatment decisions being informed by genetic tests is that of the **Oncotype DX®** Assay (Genomic Health Inc.). This assay analyzes the expression (amount of mRNA) from 21 genes in breast cancer samples, in order to help physicians select appropriate treatments and

ST TABLE 2.1

Examples of Personalized Medicine Drugs and Diagnostics

Therapy	Gene Test	Description
Herceptin® (trastuzumab)	*HER-2* amplification	Breast cancer test to accompany herceptin use
Erbitux® (cetuximab)	*EGFR* expression, *K-RAS* mutations	Protein and mutation analysis prior to treatment
Gleevec® (imatinib)	*BCR/ABL* fusion	Gleevec used in treatment of Philadelphia chromosome$^+$ chronic myelogenous leukemia
Gleevec® (imatinib)	*C-KIT*	Gleevec used in stomach cancers expressing mutated *C-KIT*
Tarceva® (erlotinib)	*EGFR* expression	Lung cancer for EGFR$^+$ tumors
Drugs/surgery	MLH1, MSH2, MSH6	Gene mutations related to colon cancers
Hormone/chemotherapies	**Oncotype DX® test**	Selection of breast cancer patients for chemotherapy
Chemotherapies	**Aviara Cancer TYPE ID®**	Classifies 39 tumor types using gene-expression assays
Rituximab	**PGx Predict®** (*FcRIIIa*)	Detects CD-20 variants that predict response to rituximab in Non-Hodgkin's lymphoma

predict the course of the disease. These genes were chosen because their levels of gene expression correlate with breast cancer recurrence after initial treatment. To perform the assay, scientists extract nucleic acids from tumor tissue and remove the DNA by treating the sample with the enzyme DNase I. They then convert the mRNA molecules to single-stranded DNA molecules (cDNA) using reverse transcriptase. The cDNA is amplified in PCR reactions using primers that are specific for each of the 21 genes. This technique, known as reverse transcription PCR (RT-PCR), is described in detail in Chapter 20. The level of amplification of each cDNA during the PCR reaction reflects its concentration. Based on the mRNA expression levels revealed in the assay results, scientists calculate a "Recurrence Score," estimating the likelihood that the cancer will recur within a ten-year period. Those patients with a low-risk rating would likely not benefit by adding chemotherapy to their treatment regimens and so can be treated with hormones alone. Those with higher risk scores would likely benefit from more aggressive therapies.

Reducing Adverse Drug Reactions

Every year, about 2 million people in the United States have serious side-effects from pharmaceutical drugs, and approximately 100,000 people die. The costs associated with these **adverse drug reactions (ADRs)** are estimated to be $136 billion annually. Although some ADRs result from drug misuse, others result from a patient's inherent physiological reactions to a drug.

Sequence variations in a large number of genes can affect drug responsiveness (ST Table 2.2). Of particular significance are the genes that encode the cytochrome P450 families of enzymes. These family members are encoded by 57 different genes. The products of the *CYP2A6, CYP2B6, CYP2C9, CYP2C19, CYP2D6, CYP2E1,* and *CYP3A4* genes are responsible for metabolizing most clinically important pharmaceutical drugs. People with some gene variants metabolize and eliminate drugs slowly, which can lead to accumulations of the drug and overdose side-effects. In contrast, other people have variants that cause drugs to be eliminated quickly, leading to reduced effectiveness. An example of gene variants that affect drug responses is that of *CYP2D6*. This member of the cytochrome P450 family encodes the debrisoquine hydroxylase enzyme, which is involved in the metabolism of approximately 25 percent of all pharmaceutical drugs, including diazepam, acetaminophen, clozapine, beta blockers, tamoxifen, and codeine. There are more than 70 variant alleles of this gene. Some mutations reduce the activity of the enzyme, and others can increase it. Approximately 80 percent of people are homozygous or heterozygous for the wild-type *CYP2D6* gene and are known as extensive metabolizers (ST Figure 2–3). Approximately 10 to 15 percent of people are homozygous for alleles that decrease activity (poor metabolizers), and the remainder of the population have duplicated genes (ultra-rapid metabolizers). Poor metabolizers are at increased risk for ADRs, whereas ultra-rapid metabolizers may not receive sufficient dosages to have an effect on their conditions.

Another example of gene variants affecting drug metabolism is the enzyme **thiopurine S-methyltransferase (TPMT)**, encoded by the *TPMT* gene. This enzyme metabolizes a large number of drugs, including many psychoactive drugs and thiopurine drugs used to treat cancers. There are more than 28 variant alleles of this gene, most of which are **single-nucleotide polymorphisms (SNPs)** that create amino acid substitutions and reduced enzyme activity.

ST TABLE 2.2

Examples of Variant Gene Products that Affect Drug Responses

Gene Product	Variant Phenotype	Drugs Affected	Response
Acetyl transferase NAT2	Slow, rapid acetylators	Isoniazid, sulfamethazine, dapsone, paraminosalicylic acid, heterocyclic amines	Slow: toxic neuritis, lupus erythematosus, bladder cancer; Rapid: colorectal cancer
Thiopurine methyltransferase	Poor TPMT Methylators	6-mercaptopurine, 6-thioguanine, azathioprin	Bone marrow toxicity, liver damage
Catechol O-methyl transferase	High, low methylators	Levodopa, methyl dopa	Low or increased response
CYP2C19	Poor, extensive hydroxylators	Mephenytoin, hexobarbital, proguanil, etc.	Poor or increased toxicity, poor efficacy (proguanil)
β_2 Adrenoceptor	Enhanced receptor downregulation	Albuterol, ventolin	Poor asthma control
5-HT2A serotonergic receptor	Multiple polymorphisms	Clozapine	Variable drug efficiencies
Multiple drug resistance transporter	Overexpression in cancer	Vinblastin, doxorubicin, paclitaxel, etc.	Drug resistance

Source: Adapted from Table 1 of Mancinelli, L., et al. 2000. Pharmacogenomics: The promise of personalized medicine. *AAPS PharmSci* 2(1): Article 4.

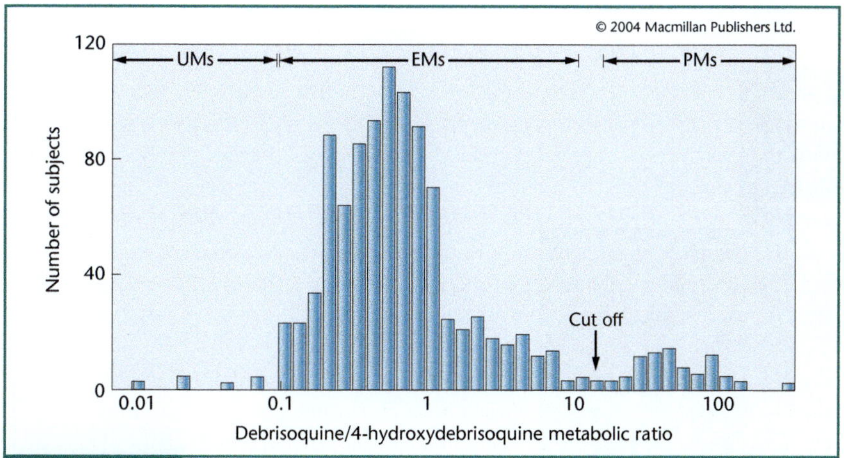

ST FIGURE 2–3 ***CYP2D6* pharmacogenetic profile in a Swedish population.** Individuals were tested for their ability to metabolize debrisoquine to 4-hydroxydebrisoquine, as an indication of the efficiency of debrisoquine hydroxylase enzyme activity. The population sample was divided into the categories UMs (ultra-rapid metabolizers), EMs (extensive metabolizers), and PMs (poor metabolizers). The "cut-off" label indicates the cut-off between extensive and poor metabolizers.

Genetic and enzymatic tests are now able to detect variations in TPMT activity, allowing tailoring of therapeutic doses to individual patients. TPMT variants and their effects are also discussed in Chapter 22.

In 2005, the FDA approved a microarray gene test called the **AmpliChip® CYP450** assay (Roche Diagnostics) that detects 29 genetic variants of two genes—*CYP2D6* and *CYP2C19.* This test detects SNPs as well as gene duplications and deletions. The AmpliChip CYP450 assay is an example of a genotyping microarray, such as those described in Chapter 22. To perform the assay, DNA is extracted from a patient's blood sample. The *CYP2D6* and *CYP2C19* genes are amplified from the DNA sample, using mixtures of gene-specific primers and PCR amplification. After PCR amplification, the amplification products are cleaved into short fragments (50–200 nucleotides) using limited digestion with the enzyme **DNase I**. The short fragments of amplified DNA are labeled at their 3′ ends with biotin. In the next step, the biotin-labeled fragments are hybridized onto the microarray. The microarray is a 20×20 μm glass surface that holds approximately 15,000 different synthetic oligonucleotides (called probes) in a specific grid pattern (ST Figure 2–4). Each probe location contains up to 10^7 copies of a specific probe. The sequences of the probes are complementary to known sequence variations in the two genes. The PCR amplified DNA fragments are hybridized to the microarray at temperatures that allow only perfect matches of probe and DNA fragment to anneal. After washing off the excess amplified DNA, the presence of hybridized amplification products is visualized by staining the microarray with a fluorescent stain that binds to biotin molecules. An automated scanner detects the location of stained DNA, and the stain intensity reflects the amount of hybridized DNA on each probe. After scanning, the data are analyzed by computer software, and the *CYP2D6/CYP2C19* genotype of the individual is generated.

Another example of pharmacogenomics in personalized medicine is that of the *CYP2C9* and *VKORC1* genes and the drug **warfarin.** Warfarin (also known as Coumadin) is an anticoagulant drug that is prescribed to prevent blood clots after surgery and to aid people with cardiovascular conditions who are prone to clots. Warfarin inhibits the vitamin K-dependent synthesis of several clotting factors. There is an approximately ten-fold variability between patients in the doses of warfarin that have a therapeutic response. In the past, physicians attempted to adjust the doses of warfarin through a trial-and-error process during the first year of treatment. If the dosage of warfarin is too high, the patient may experience serious hemorrhaging; if it is too low, the patient may develop life-threatening blood clots. It is estimated that 20 percent of patients are hospitalized during their first six months of treatment due to warfarin side-effects.

Variations in warfarin activity are affected by polymorphisms in several genes, particularly *CYP2C9* and *VKORC1.* Two single-nucleotide polymorphisms in *CYP2C9* lead to reduced elimination of warfarin and increased risk of hemorrhage. The first mutation is a C to T transition at codon 430, which leads to an arginine to cysteine amino acid substitution at amino acid 144 and a 30 percent lower activity of the *CYP2C9* gene product. The second mutation creates an isoleucine to leucine substitution at codon 359 and a 90 percent lower activity. About 25 percent of Caucasians are heterozygous for one of these polymorphisms, and 5 percent appear to be homozygous. About 5 percent of patients of Asian and African descent carry these variants. Patients who are heterozygous or homozygous for some alleles of *CYP2C9* require a 10 to 90 percent lower dose of warfarin. The *VKORCI* gene encodes **vitamin K epoxide reductase complex subunit 1,** a vitamin K-activating enzyme that is required for the formation of clotting factors. The activity of this enzyme is inhibited by warfarin. A common variant of *VKORC1* is a G to A transversion in the promoter region of the gene, leading to lower levels of VKORC1 and clotting factors. This mutation

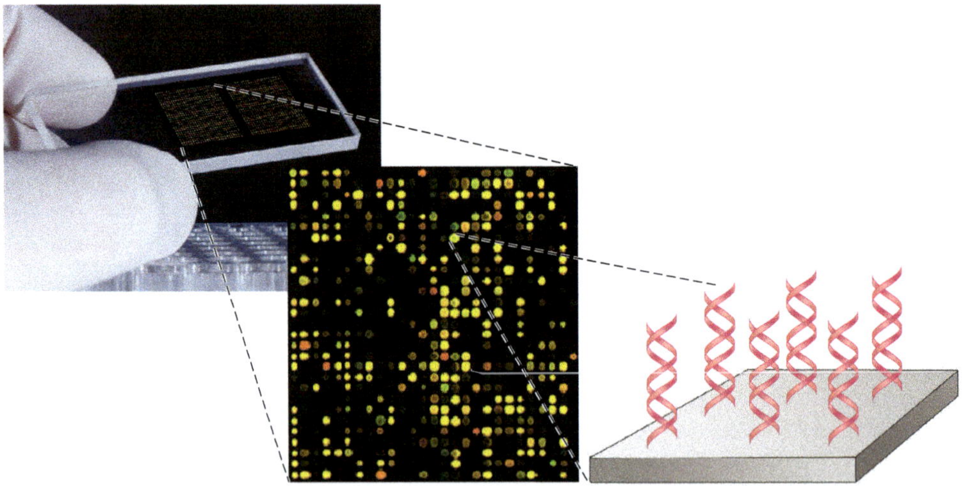

ST FIGURE 2–4 **Views of a DNA microarray.** The microarray cartridge is shown on the left, and a magnified version of the microarray is shown in the center. The 20-μm^2 microarray contains synthetic DNA oligonucletoide probes complementary to variants within genes such as *CYP2D6* and *CYP2C19*. Each probe type is located in a specific region of the microarray, called a probe cell. Within each probe cell, there are approximately 10^7 copies of the probe. After hybridization, washing, and staining, the microarray is scanned with a laser. The amount of light emitted by each fluorescent PCR amplification product is proportional to the amount of bound product on that probe cell.

leads to an increased sensitivity to warfarin, requiring lower doses of the drug. About 50 percent of Caucasians are heterozygous for this mutation and 14 percent are homozygous. Among Asians, about 18 percent are heterozygous and 80 percent are homozygous. Among African Americans, about 20 percent are heterozygous and fewer than 1 percent are homozygous.

Recently, the FDA recommended the use of *CYP2C9* and *VKORC1* genetic tests to predict the likelihood that a patient may have an adverse reaction to warfarin. Several companies now offer tests to detect the polymorphisms described earlier, using methods based on PCR amplification and allele-specific primers. It is estimated that the use of warfarin genetic tests could prevent 17,000 strokes and 85,000 serious hemorrhages per year. The savings in health care could reach $1.1 billion per year.

Pharmacogenomic tests and treatments, and the genetic information on which they are based, are rapidly advancing. A source of updated information on all aspects of pharmacogenomics can be found on the Pharmacogenomics Knowledge Base, which is described in Box 2.

Personalized Medicine and Disease Diagnosis

As of 2009, there were genetic tests for approximately 2000 different diseases (ST Figure 2–6). These tests are categorized according to their uses and can fall into one or more of the following groups: **Diagnostic tests** detect the presence or absence of gene variants linked to a suspected genetic disorder in a symptomatic patient; **predictive tests** detect a gene mutation in patients with a family history of having a known genetic disorder (for example, Huntington disease or BRCA-linked breast cancer); **carrier tests** help physicians identify patients who carry a gene mutation linked to a disorder that might be passed on to their offspring (for example Tay–Sachs or cystic fibrosis); **prenatal tests** detect potential genetic diseases in a fetus (for example, Down syndrome); and **preimplantation tests** are performed on early embryos in order to select embryos for implantation that do not carry a suspected disease. Most of these genetic tests

BOX 2

The Pharmacogenomics Knowledge Base (PharmGKB): Genes, Drugs, and Diseases on the Web

The Pharmacogenomics Knowledge Base (PharmGKB) is a publicly available Internet database and information source developed by Stanford University. It is funded by the National Institutes of Health (NIH) and forms part of the NIH Pharmacogenomics Research Network, a U.S. research consortium. The goal of PharmGKB is to provide researchers and the general public with information that will increase the understanding of how genetic variation contributes to an individual's reaction to drugs. On the PharmGKB Web site (see ST Figure 2-5), you may search for genes and more than 650 variants that affect drug reactions, information on a large number of drugs, diseases and their genetic links, pharmacogenomic pathways, gene tests, and relevant publications. Visit the PharmGKB Web site at http://www.pharmgkb.org

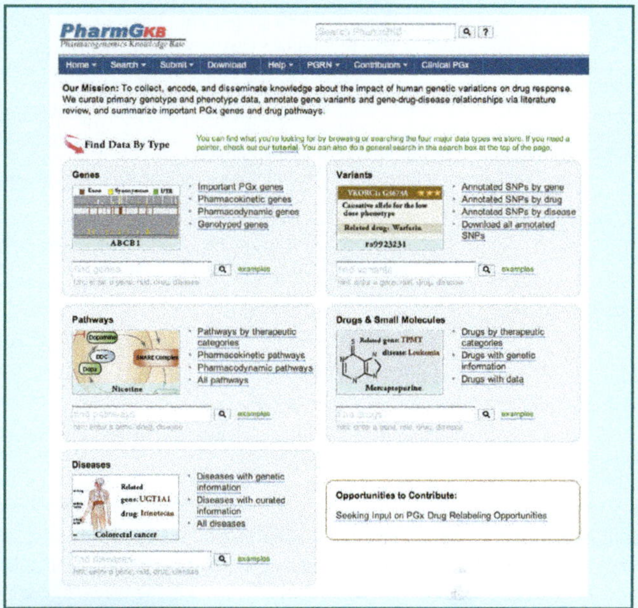

ST FIGURE 2-5 **The PharmGKB Web site home page.**

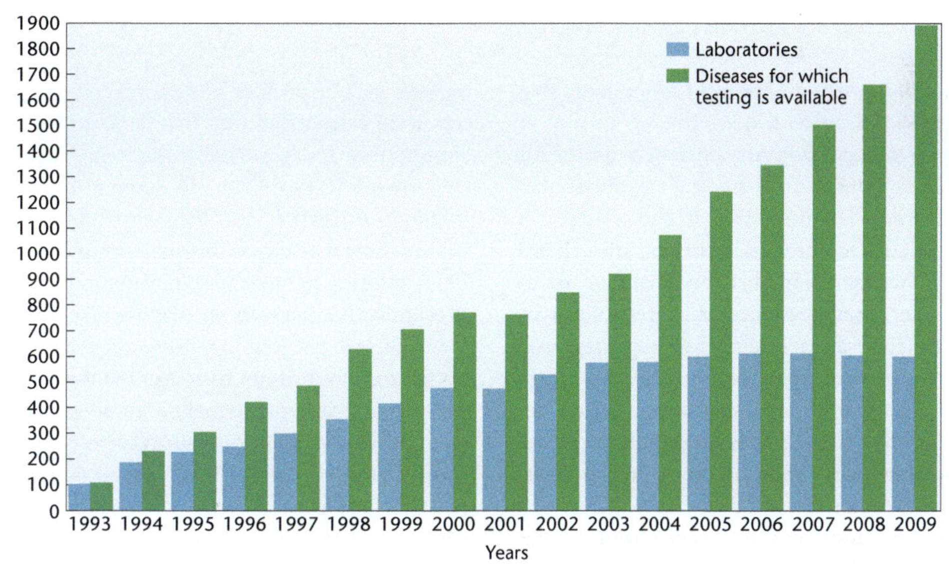

ST FIGURE 2-6 **Growth of gene tests and testing laboratories from 1993 to 2009.** From the GeneTests Web site at http://www.ncbi.nlm.nih.gov/projects/GeneTests/static/whatsnew/labdirgrowth.shtml.

ST TABLE 2.3

Some Single-Gene Defects for Which Genetic Tests Are Available

Disease	Gene Mutation	Description
Achondroplasia	*FGFR3* gene. 99% of patients have a G to A point mutation at nucleotide 1138 (G380R substitution)	Abnormal bone growth
Hereditary breast/ovarian cancer	*BRCA1* and *BRCA2* genes. Deletions, duplications, and point mutations	Predisposition to breast, ovarian, prostate, and other cancer
Duchenne muscular dystrophy	*DMD* gene. Point mutations, deletions, insertions, splicing mutations	Early-onset progressive muscular weakness, heart disease
Fragile-X syndrome	*FMR1* gene. Primarily expanded trinucleotide (CGG) repeats and loss of function	Mental retardation, developmental disorders
Friedrich's ataxia	*FXN* gene. 98% of cases have expanded trinucleotide (GAA) repeats in intron 1	Ataxia, muscle weakness, spasticity, heart and other organ dysfunctions
Hemophilia A	*F8* gene. Point mutations, insertions, deletions, inversions	Factor VIII blood-clotting defects, bleeding
Huntington disease	*HTT* (*HD*) gene. Trinucleotide (CAG) repeat expansions	Midlife onset of progressive motor and cognitive disorders
Lesch-Nyhan syndrome	*HPRT1* gene. Point mutations, deletions, duplications	Developmental, motor, and cognitive disorders
Marfan syndrome	*FBN1* gene. Point mutations, splicing mutations, deletions	Connective tissue disorders affecting numerous organs
Polycystic kidney disease, dominant	*PKD1* and *PKD2* genes. Sequence variants, partial or whole-gene deletions and duplications	Cysts in kidney, liver, and other organs, vascular abnormalities
Sickle cell disease	*HBB* gene. Point mutation leading to Glu to Val substitution at amino acid 6	Early-onset anemia

Source: GeneReviews at (http://www.ncbi.nlm.nih.gov/bookshelf/br.fcgi?book=gene).

SPECIAL TOPIC II

detect the presence of known mutations in single genes that are linked to a disease (ST Table 2.3).

Although these genetic tests are extremely useful for detecting some future diseases and guiding treatment, it is clear that most disorders are multifactorial and complex. It is likely that diseases such as diabetes, Alzheimer's, and heart disease are caused by interactions between many genes, as well as by factors contributed by epigenetic effects, lifestyle, and environment. These diseases tend to be chronic and have a significant burden on health-care systems.

Genome sequencing, SNP identification, and genome-wide association studies (GWAS) are beginning to reveal some of the DNA variants that may contribute to the risk of developing multifactorial diseases such as cancer, heart disease, and diabetes. For example, the Cancer Genome Atlas project (described in Chapter 19) is amassing data equivalent to 20,000 genome projects on normal and tumor DNA from patients with 20 different types of cancer. Such studies are revealing that cancers that were once classified broadly (such as "prostate cancer") are in fact many different diseases based on their genetic profiles. For example, in the past, blood cancers were categorized into two large groups: leukemias and lymphomas. Today, we know that each category can be broken down into more than 40 different types, based on gene mutation and expression characteristics. In addition, genome studies show that each individual tumor is unique genetically. This explosion in molecular information is now beginning to affect how these cancers are diagnosed and treated.

Although progress in genome science is accelerating, these studies have just begun to collect the vast amount of genetic data required in order to make accurate predictions and treatment choices for many diseases. As whole-genome sequencing becomes faster and more economical, scientists predict that genomics and personal genome sequencing will become a significant part of personalized diagnosis and treatment by 2015.

But what will genome-based personalized medicine look like in 2015? And how will we use it to our benefit? Also, are there ethical and social questions that we need to address as we enter the age of the new personalized medicine? The next sections will address these questions.

Analyzing One Personal Genome

In 2010, the journal *Lancet* published a report illustrating the type of information that we can currently obtain from a personal genome sequence.[1] The patient was a healthy 40-year-old male who had a family history of arthritis, aortic aneurysm, coronary artery disease, and sudden cardiac death. The researchers obtained his genomic DNA sequence using a rapid single-molecule sequencing method (Box 3). By comparing the patient's sequence with other human genome sequences in databases, a total of 2.6 million SNPs and 752 copy number variations were discovered. The researchers then sorted through the genome sequence data to determine which of these variants might have an effect on phenotype. This was accomplished by searching known SNPs in several large databases, manually creating their own disease-associated SNP database, and calculating likelihood ratios for various disease risks. The analysis required the combined efforts of more than two dozen scientists and clinicians over a period of about a year, and information gleaned from more than a dozen sequence databases, new and existing sequence analysis tools, and hundreds of individually accessed research papers.

To determine how this patient may respond to pharmaceutical drugs, the researchers searched the **PharmGKB database** (see Box 2) for the presence of known variants within pharmacogenomically important genes. The patient was found to have 63 clinically relevant SNPs within genes associated with drug reactions. In addition, his genome contained six previously unknown SNPs that could alter amino acid sequences in drug-response genes. For example, the genome sequence revealed that this patient was heterozygous for a null mutation in the *CYP2C19* gene. This mutation could make him sensitive to a range of drugs including those used to treat aspects of heart disease. He would also be more sensitive than normal to warfarin, based on SNPs within his *VKORC1* and *CYP4F2* genes. In contrast, the patient's sequence contained gene variants associated with good responses to statins; however, other gene variants suggested that he might require higher-than-normal statin dosages.

The search for mutations within genes that directly affect disease conditions revealed several potentially damaging variants. The patient was heterozygous for a SNP within the *CFTR* gene that would change a glycine to arginine at position 458. This mutation could lead to cystic fibrosis if it was passed on to a son or daughter who also inherited a defective *CFTR* gene from the other parent. Similarly, the patient was heterozygous for a recessive mutation in the hereditary haemochromatosis protein precursor gene (*HFE*), which is associated with the development of haemochromatosis, a serious condition leading to toxic accumulations of iron. Also, the patient was heterozygous for a recessive mutation in the solute carrier family 3 (*SLC3A1*) gene. This mutation is linked to cystinuria, an inherited disorder characterized by inadequate excretion of cysteine and development of kidney stones. The scientists discovered a heterozygous SNP within the parafibromin (*CDC73*) gene that would create a prematurely terminated protein. This gene is a tumor-suppressor gene linked to the development of hyperparathyroidism and parathyroid tumors. The presence of this SNP increased the risk that the patient might develop these types of tumors, if any of the patient's cells experienced a loss-of-heterozygosity mutation in the other copy of the gene.

The analysis of this patient's genome sequence for the purpose of predicting future development of multifactorial disease was more challenging. Genome-wide association studies have revealed large numbers of sequence variants that are associated with complex diseases; however, each of these variants most often contributes only a small part of the susceptibility to disease. Because not all variants have been discovered or characterized, it is difficult to establish a numerical risk score for each of these diseases based on the presence of one or more SNPs. As an example, the researchers discovered SNPs within three genes (*TMEM43*, *DSP*, and *MYBPC3*) that may be associated with sudden cardiac death. However, the exact effects of two of these SNPs are still unclear, and the other SNP had not previously been described. The patient had five SNPs in genes associated with an increased risk of developing myocardial infarction and two SNPs associated with a lower risk. Among the SNPs associated with increased risk, a variant in the apolipoprotein A precursor (*LPA*) gene is associated with a five-fold increased plasma lipoprotein(a) concentration and a two-fold increased risk of coronary artery disease. By taking into consideration the simultaneous potential effects of many different SNPs, as well as the patient's own environmental and personal lifestyle factors, the researchers concluded that the patient's genetics contributed to a significantly increased risk for eight conditions (such as type 2 diabetes, obesity, and coronary artery disease) and a decreased risk for seven conditions (such as Alzheimer's disease). The patient was offered the services of clinical geneticists, counselors, and clinical lab directors in order to help interpret the information generated from the genome sequence. Genetic counseling covered areas such as psychological and reproductive implications of genetic disease risk, the possibilities of discrimination based on genetic test results, and the uncertainties in risk assessments.

[1] Ashley, E.A., et al. 2010. Clinical assessment incorporating a personal genome. *Lancet* 375: 1525–1535.

SPECIAL TOPIC II

BOX 3

How to Sequence a Human Genome

The personal genome sequence described in this chapter was the first human genome to be sequenced using a method known as true single-molecule sequencing (tSMS™). Other methods such as the Sanger method and the second-generation high-throughput methods described in Chapter 21 require cloning or PCR amplification of template DNA prior to sequencing. In contrast, the tSMS method directly sequences individual DNA strands with minimum processing. The sequencing of this genome took about a week, was performed with one machine and the services of three people, and cost $48,000. The sequence was that of Dr. Stephen Quake, a Stanford University professor who developed the technology and headed the research group.

The sequencing machine used in this study is called a HeliScope™, a commercially available refrigerator-sized instrument that processes, visualizes and analyzes the sequence data. The HeliScope analyzes about 1 billion individual DNA molecules simultaneously per day as they are undergoing copying synthesis. The following is a brief summary of the tSMS method.

1. DNA is extracted from the patient's sample, fragmented into short pieces about 100 to 200 nucleotides long, and denatured into single strands.
2. PolyA tails are added to the 3′ ends of each single strand, and each strand is tagged with a fluorescent molecule. These are the template strands for DNA synthesis.
3. The template strands are hybridized to billions of oligo-T molecules immobilized on the surface of a flow cell.
4. The positions of each of these template-oligo-T molecules is visualized and located on the flow cell using the HeliScope's laser illumination and a high magnification camera.
5. The fluorescent tag molecules are cleaved from the templates and washed off.
6. Fluorescently labeled nucleotides (A, T, C, or G) along with a DNA polymerase are added, one nucleotide per reaction cycle, to the flow cell. If a template strand contains a complementary nucleotide next to the oligo-T primer sequence (let's say a G), then a fluorescent C will be incorporated during the C cycle (ST Figure 2–7).
7. After washing away the DNA polymerase and excess fluorescent C, those templates that contained a G at that position will fluoresce in the HeliScope and their location will be established (ST Figure 2–8).
8. After imaging the incorporation of the G, the fluorescent tag on the incorporated G nucleotides is cleaved off and washed away along with the DNA polymerase.
9. In the next cycle, DNA polymerase and another fluorescently tagged nucleotide (let's say T) are added to the flow cell. The T nucleotides will be incorporated into the growing complementary DNA strands if the template contains an A nucleotide next to the growing 3′ end.

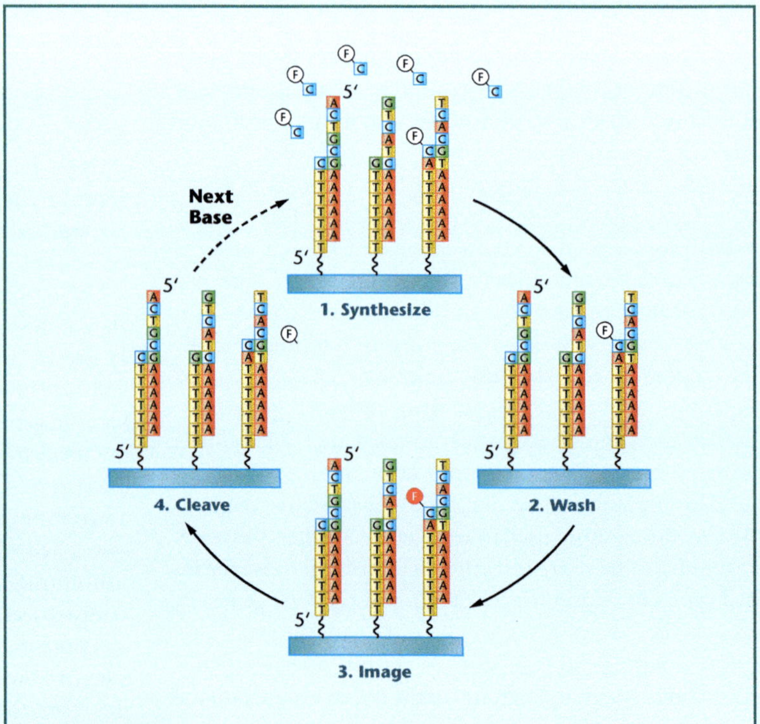

ST FIGURE 2–7 **Steps in true single-molecule sequencing (tSMS) technique. Oligo-T molecules, attached to a solid substrate, anneal to genomic DNA fragments. Step 1: A fluorescently labeled nucleotide (F-C) and DNA polymerase are added. F-C molecules are synthesized onto the oligo-T molecules, if a G residue is present in the genomic DNA. Steps 2 and 3: Excess F-C and DNA polymerase are washed off, and the presence of a labeled oligo-T molecule is imaged and the location of the label registered. Step 4: Fluorescent label (F) is cleaved from the incorporated F-C molecules. The steps are repeated with other fluorescently labeled nucleotides until synthesis reaches approximately 32 nucleotides.**

(Continued)

BOX 3

How to Sequence a Human Genome (*Continued*)

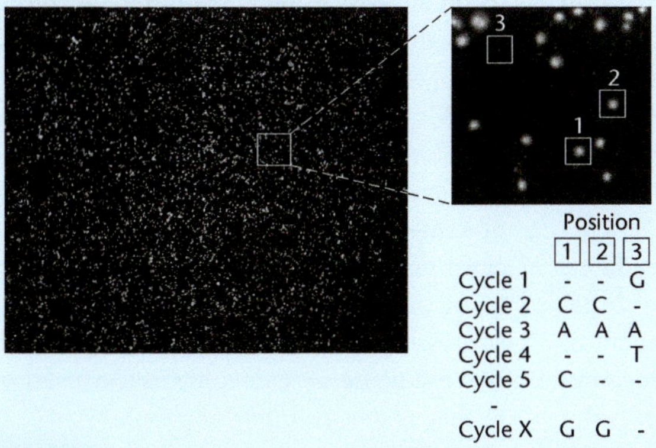

ST FIGURE 2-8 **Images taken by a HeliScope single-molecule sequencer.** A magnified view of a flow cell is shown on the left. On the right is a higher magnification of part of the flow cell, showing the position of individual molecules that have incorporated a fluorescent G (F-G) nucleotide during "Cycle X" of the most recent synthesis cycle. In this case, molecules 1 and 2 have incorporated an F-G, but molecule 3 has not.

10. The presence of a fluorescent T will be detected and mapped by the HeliScope, and the process is repeated through enough cycles to synthesize about 32 nucleotides of complementary DNA on each template.
11. The HeliScope determines the sequence of each of the template strands based on these cycles of synthesis and fluorescent imaging. It then performs sequence alignments of all the individual sequences in order to compile the entire genomic sequence.

The methods and analysis of tSMS are illustrated in a video available on the Helicos BioSciences Corporation Web site at: http://www.helicosbio.com/Technology/TrueSingleMoleculeSequencing/tabid/64/Default.aspx

Technical, Social, and Ethical Challenges

There are still many technical hurdles to overcome before personalized medicine will become a standard part of medical care. The technologies of genome sequencing and alignment, microarray analysis, and SNP detection need to be faster, more accurate, and cheaper. Scientists expect that these challenges will be overcome in the near future; however, personalized genome analysis needs to be used with caution until the technology becomes highly accurate and reliable. Even a low rate of error in genetic sequences or test results could lead to erroneous diagnoses and inappropriate treatments. Perhaps an even greater challenge lies in the ability of scientists to store and interpret the vast amount of emerging sequence data. Each personal genome generates the letter-equivalent of 200 large phone books, which must be stored in databases, mined for relevant sequence variants and meaning assigned to each SNP. To undertake these kinds of analyses, scientists need to analyze the results from large-scale population genotyping studies that will link sequence variants to phenotype, disease, or drug responses. Experts suggest that such studies will take the coordinated efforts of public and private research teams, and more than a decade to complete. Scientists will also need to develop efficient automated systems and algorithms to deal with this massive amount of information. Moreover, these data analyses will need to take into account the fact that genetic variants contribute only partially to personal phenotype. Personalized medicine will also need to integrate information about environmental, personal lifestyle, and epigenetic factors.

Another technical challenge for personalized medicine is the development of automated health information technologies. Health-care providers will need to use electronic health records to store, retrieve, and analyze each patient's genomic profile, as well as to compare this information with constantly advancing knowledge about genes and disease. Currently, fewer than 10 percent of hospitals and physicians in the United States have access to these types of information technologies.

Personalized medicine has a number of societal implications. To make personalized medicine available to everyone, the costs of genetic tests, as well as the genetic counseling that accompanies them, must be reimbursed by insurance companies, even in cases where there is no prior disease or symptoms. Regulatory changes are required to ensure that genetic tests and genomic sequencing are accurate and that the data generated are reliably stored in databases that guarantee the patient's privacy. At the present time, less than 1 percent of genetic tests are regulated by agencies such as the FDA.

Personalized medicine also requires changes to medical education. In the future, physicians will be expected to use genomics information as part of their patient management. For this to be possible, medical schools will need to train future physicians to interpret and explain genetic data. In addition, more genetic counselors and genomics specialists will be required. These specialists will need to understand genomics and disease, as well as to manipulate bioinformatic data. As of 2010, there were only about 2500 genetic counselors and 1100 clinical geneticists in North America.

The ethical aspects of the new personalized medicine are also diverse and challenging. For example, it is sometimes argued that the costs involved in the development of genomics and personalized medicine are a misallocation of limited resources. Some argue that science should solve larger problems facing humanity, such as the distribution of food and clean water, before embarking on personalized medicine. Similarly, some critics argue that such highly specialized and expensive medical care will not be available to everyone and represents a worsening of economic inequality. There are also concerns about how we will protect the privacy of genome information that is contained in databases and private health-care records. In addition, there needs to be effective ways to prevent discrimination in employment or insurance coverage, based on information derived from genomic analysis.

Most experts agree that we are at the beginning of a personalized medicine revolution. Information from genetics and genomics research is already increasing the effectiveness of drugs and enabling health-care providers to predict diseases prior to their occurrence. In the future, personalized medicine will touch almost every aspect of medical care. By addressing the upcoming challenges of the new personalized medicine, we can guide its use for the maximum benefit to the greatest number of people.

Selected Readings and Resources

Journal Articles

Ashley, E.A., et al. 2010. Clinical assessment incorporating a personal genome. *Lancet* 375: 1525–1535.

Collins, F. 2010. Has the revolution arrived? *Nature* 464: 674–675.

Hamburg, M.A., and Collins, F.S. 2010. The path to personalized medicine. *New England Journal of Medicine* 363: 301–304.

Manolio, T.A., et al. 2009. Finding the missing heritability of complex diseases. *Nature* 461: 747–753.

Ormond, K.E., et al. 2010. Challenges in the clinical application of whole-genome sequencing. *Lancet* 375: 1749–1751.

Pushkarev, D., et al. 2009. Single-molecule sequencing of an individual human genome. *Nature Biotech* 27: 847–850.

Ross, J.S. 2009. The HER-2 receptor and breast cancer: ten years of targeted anti-HER-2 therapy and personalized medicine. *The Oncologist* 14: 320–368.

Venter, J.C. 2010. Multiple personal genomes await. *Nature* 464: 676–677.

Weinshilboum, R., and Wang, L. 2004. Pharmacogenomics: Bench to bedside. *Nature Rev Drug Disc* 3: 739–748.

Web Sites

Personalized Medicine Coalition, 2009. The Case for Personalized Medicine. http://www.personalizedmedicinecoalition.org/sites/default/files/TheCaseforPersonalizedMedicine_5_5_09.pdf

University of Washington, 2010. GeneTests Web site: http://www.ncbi.nlm.nih.gov/sites/GeneTests/?db=GeneTests

U.S. Department of Energy Genome Program's Human Genome Project Information, 2008. Pharmacogenomics. http://www.ornl.gov/sci/techresources/Human_Genome/medicine/pharma.shtml

U.S. Food and Drug Administration, 2010. Table of Valid Genomic Biomarkers in the Context of Approved Drug Labels. http://www.fda.gov/Drugs/ScienceResearch/ResearchAreas/Pharmacogenetics/ucm083378.htm

SPECIAL TOPICS IN MODERN GENETICS

Epigenetics

The somatic cells of the human body contain 20,000 to 25,000 genes. Yet in any of these cells, only a relatively small percentage of all genes are active. In the more than 200 different cell types present in the body, different cell-specific gene sets are transcribed, while the rest of the genome is transcriptionally inactive. In addition, programs of gene expression become more and more restricted during development and differentiation as embryonic cells gradually become specialized adult cells with distinct phenotypes. The prevailing view has been that regulation of gene expression is coordinated by promoter, promoter–proximal, enhancer, and other *cis*-regulatory elements as well as DNA-binding proteins and transcription factors. This regulation can occur at any of the steps in gene expression. For example, steps in transcriptional regulation, as well as mRNA processing and other stages of posttranscriptional regulation, control the amount of gene product synthesized from a DNA template. However, as we learn more about genome organization and the regulation of gene expression, it is clear that classical genetic mechanisms cannot explain how some phenotypes arise. Monozygotic twins, for example, have identical genotypes but are not always phenotypically identical. Although for each gene, one allele is inherited maternally and one paternally, in some cases, only the maternal or paternal allele is expressed, while the other is transcriptionally silent.

The newly emerging field of epigenetics is providing us with a basis for understanding how heritable changes other than those in DNA sequence can influence phenotypic variation.

The newly emerging field of epigenetics is providing us with a basis for understanding how heritable changes other than those in DNA sequence can influence phenotypic variation. These advances greatly extend our understanding of the molecular basis of gene regulation and apply to wide-ranging areas including genetic disorders, cancer, and behavior.

An **epigenetic trait** is a stable, mitotically and meiotically heritable phenotype that results from changes in gene expression without alterations in the DNA sequence. **Epigenetics** is the study of the ways in which these changes alter cell- and tissue-specific patterns of gene expression. Epigenetic regulation of gene expression uses reversible modifications of DNA and chromatin structure to mediate the interaction of the genome with a variety of environmental factors and to generate changes in the patterns of gene expression in response to these factors. The **epigenome** refers to the epigenetic state of a cell. During its life span, an organism has one genome, but this genome can be modified in diverse cell types at different times to produce many epigenomes.

Current research efforts are focused on several aspects of epigenetics: how an epigenome arises in developing and differentiated cells, what mechanisms maintain these states, and how they are transmitted via mitosis and meiosis, making them heritable traits. In addition, because epigenetically controlled alterations to the genome are associated with cancer and some common diseases such as diabetes and asthma, efforts are also being directed at the development of drugs that can modify or reverse disease-associated epigenetic changes in cells.

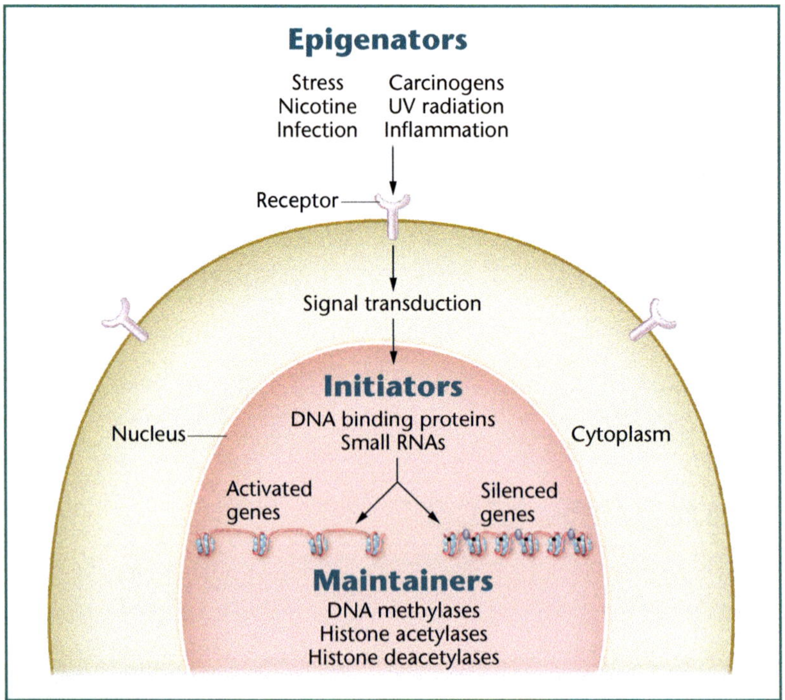

ST FIGURE 3–1 An epigenetic pathway involves the reception and processing of external signals resulting in alterations that change and maintain patterns of gene expression.

Several systems and pathways that result in the establishment, maintenance, and inheritance of the epigenetic state are recognized. These pathways are organized into three categories, but other mechanisms and categories undoubtedly remain to be elucidated. The first category includes environmental signals called *epigenators* that are received by the cell and that stimulate a response via an intracellular pathway. Responses to epigenator signals are called *epigenetic initiators.* Components of this second category produce epigenetic changes. These initiators include protein–protein signal transduction pathways, DNA-binding proteins, and noncoding RNAs. The actions of initiators define the location at which epigenetic changes in chromatin will take place. DNA sequence recognition is a necessary part of this response. Once the epigenetic modifications have occurred, they are maintained by molecular elements called *epigenetic maintainers.* Components of this third category conserve and sustain the epigenetic changes in the present and future generations. Epigenetic maintainers are not sequence-specific, they operate anywhere in the genome, and they depend on initiators to specify the loci at which chromatin modifications will take place. Epigenetic maintainers ensure that epigenetic modifications are transmitted by mitosis to daughter cells, or by meiosis to gametes and to subsequent generations. Maintainers include DNA methylation and histone modifications. ST Figure 3–1 shows these components of the epigenetic pathway along with examples. It should be noted that histone modifications are part of the general process of transcriptional activation; this means that some, but not all, histone modifications are epigenetic events.

Epigenetic modification of the genome provides a clear-cut response to environmental signals by mediating changes in gene expression that persist through several generations. Epigenetics has been implicated in many aspects of biology, including the progressive restriction of gene expression during development, allele-specific expression seen in gene imprinting, and environment–genome interactions during prenatal development that affect adult phenotypes. Abnormal regulation of the epigenome leads to human genetic disorders including Prader–Willi syndrome, Angelman syndrome, and Beckwith–Weidemann syndrome. The loss or alteration of other epigenetic states results in cancer.

Knowledge of the mechanisms of epigenetic modifications to the genome, how these modifications are maintained and transmitted, and their relationship to basic biological processes will be important for our understanding of development, disease processes, reproduction, and the evolution of adaptation to the environment.

Here we will focus on how epigenetic alterations impact some genetic diseases, cancer, and environment–genome interactions. Because epigenetic changes are potentially reversible, we will also examine how knowledge of molecular mechanisms of epigenetics is being used to develop drugs and treatments for human diseases.

BOX 1

The Beginning of Epigenetics

C.H. Waddington is credited with coining the term *epigenetics* in the 1940s to describe how environmental influences on developmental events can affect the phenotype of the adult. He showed that environmental alterations during development induced alternative phenotypes in organisms with identical genotypes. Using *Drosophila melanogaster,* Waddington found that wing vein patterns could be altered by administering heat shocks during pupal development. Adults with these environmentally induced changes were used to establish strains that showed the alternative phenotype without the need for continued environmental stimulus. He called this phenomenon "genetic assimilation." In other words, interactions between the environment and the genome during certain stages of development produce phenotypic effects that are heritable.

In the 1970s, Holliday and Pugh proposed that changes in programs of gene expression during development may depend on the methylation of specific bases in DNA, and that altering these patterns of methylation might affect the resulting phenotype. In addition, the progressive restriction of developmental pathways during differentiation may be explained by a program of methylation that silences gene sets at specific stages of embryogenesis. Several factors, including Waddington's work, the methylation model of Holliday and Pugh, and the discovery that expression of genes from both the maternal and paternal genomes is required for normal development, all helped set the stage for the birth of epigenetics and epigenomics as fields of scientific research.

Epigenetic Alterations to the Genome

Unlike the genome, which is identical in all cell types of an organism, the epigenome is cell-type specific and heritable. Like the genome, the epigenome can be transmitted to daughter cells by mitosis and to future generations by meiosis. Unlike genomic mutations, epigenetic modifications are reversible, opening the possibility for the development of drugs for treatment of conditions linked to dysfunction of epigenetic processes. In the following sections, we will examine mechanisms of epigenetics and their role in imprinting, cancer, and environment–genome interactions, providing a snapshot of the many roles played by this recently discovered mechanism of gene regulation.

There are three major epigenetic mechanisms: (1) reversible modification of DNA by the addition or removal of methyl groups; (2) modification of histones by the addition or removal of chemical groups; and (3) regulation of gene expression by small, noncoding RNA molecules.

Methylation

In mammals, methylation of DNA takes place after replication and involves the addition of a methyl group ($-CH_3$) to cytosine, a reaction catalyzed by methyltransferase enzymes. DNA methylation also occurs during the differentiation of adult cells. In both instances, methylation takes place almost exclusively on cytosine bases adjacent to a guanine, a combination called a CpG dinucleotide. Many of these dinucleotides are clustered in regions, called CpG islands, located in and near promoter sequences adjacent to genes (ST Figure 3–2). Islands adjacent to essential genes (housekeeping genes) and cell-specific genes are unmethylated, making these genes available for transcription. Other genes with adjacent methylated CpG islands are transcriptionally silenced. The methyl groups in CpG islands occupy the major groove of DNA, and block the binding of transcription factors necessary to form transcription complexes.

The bulk of methylated CpG dinucleotides are not adjacent to genes, but are found in repetitive DNA sequences located in heterochromatic regions of the genome, including the centromere. Methylation of these sequences contributes to silencing the transcription and replication of transposable elements such as LINE and SINE sequences (see Chapter 12), which constitute a major fraction of the human genome. Heterochromatic methylation also maintains chromosome stability by preventing translocation and other chromosomal abnormalities.

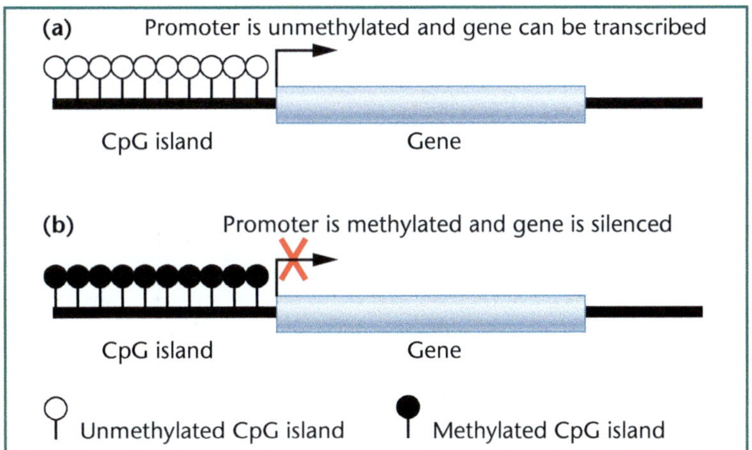

ST FIGURE 3–2 CpG islands are usually located upstream of promoter regions.

As part of dosage compensation, X chromosomes in mammalian females are inactivated by converting them to heterochromatin. These inactivated chromosomes have altered patterns of DNA methylation (see Chapter 7 for a detailed explanation of X inactivation). As mentioned above, CpG methylation in euchromatic regions causes a parent-specific pattern of gene transcription.

Histone Modification

In addition to DNA methylation, histone modification is an important epigenetic mechanism of gene regulation. Recall that chromatin is composed of DNA wound around an octamer core of histone proteins to form nucleosomes. Amino acids in the N-terminal region of these histones can be covalently modified in several ways, including acetylation, methylation, and phosphorylation (ST Figure 3–3). These modifications occur at conserved amino acid sequences in the N-terminal histone tails which protrude from the nucleosome. Chemical modification of histones alters the structure of chromatin, making genes accessible or inaccessible for transcription. Normally, when histones are modified by acetylation, a reaction catalyzed by the enzyme histone acetyltransferase (HAT), chromatin structure becomes "open," making genes on these modified nucleosomes available for transcription (ST Figure 3–4(a)). This modification is reversible, and acetyl groups can be removed by another enzyme, histone deacetylase (HDAC), changing the chromatin to a "closed" configuration, and silencing genes by making them unavailable for transcription (ST Figure 3–4(b)). However, the program of histone modification depends on other events, including the presence or absence of methyl groups on histones.

The program of amino acid modification is complex, and the same type of modification can often have opposite transcriptional outcomes. For example, methylation of lysine 4 or 27 on histone H3 causes transcriptional activation, while methylation of lysine 9 causes transcriptional silencing. We are learning that specific combinations of histone modifications control the transcriptional status of a chromatin region. For example, whether or not lysine 9 on histone H3 will be methylated is controlled by modifications made elsewhere on this protein. On one hand, if serine 10 is phosphorylated, methylation of lysine 9 is inhibited. On the other hand, if lysine 14 is deacetylated, methylation of lysine 9 is facilitated. The sum of the complex patterns and interactions of histone modifications that change chromatin organization and gene expression is called the **histone code**. The details of how this level of regulation works are beginning to emerge but are not yet fully understood.

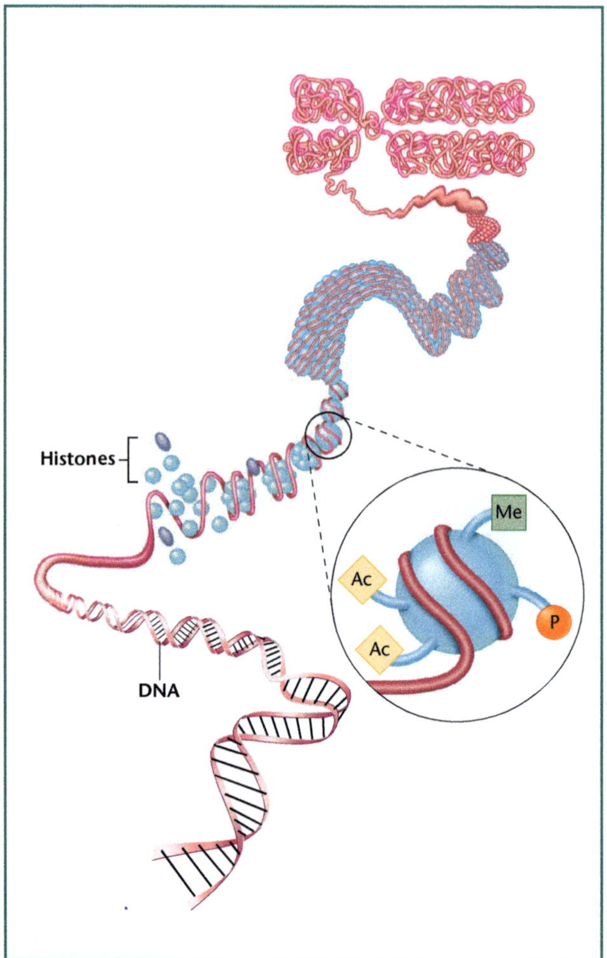

ST FIGURE 3–3 Clusters of histones, nucleosomes are the focus of epigenetic modifications. Ac = acetyl groups, Me = methyl groups, P = phosphate groups.

RNA Interference

In addition to DNA methylation and histone modification, small, noncoding RNA molecules (discussed in Chapter 17) also participate in epigenetic regulation of gene expression. After transcription, these small interfering RNA (siRNA) molecules associate with protein complexes to form RNA-Induced Silencing Complexes (RISCs). RISCs bind to mRNA molecules that carry sequences complementary to siRNA in the RISC. If the siRNA is not perfectly complementary to the mRNA, the binding interferes with translation, resulting in down-regulation of gene expression. If, however, the siRNA in the RISC *is* perfectly complementary to sequences in the mRNA, the mRNA is cleaved and destroyed, effectively silencing the gene.

Recently, it has been discovered that siRNAs can silence genes by directly interfering with transcription initiation. This does not involve any changes in existing epigenetic

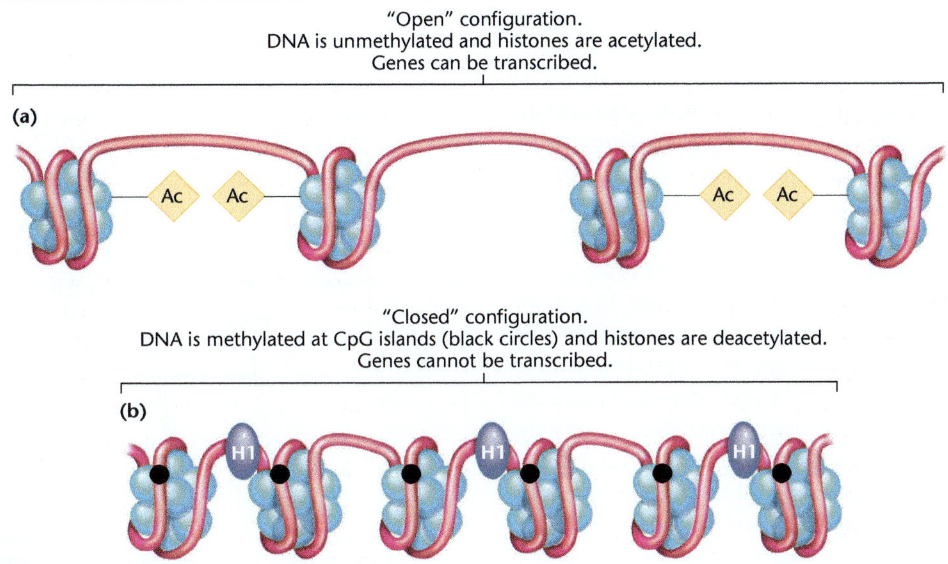

ST FIGURE 3–4 Epigenetic modifications to the genome.

promoter modifications, nor does it require new modifications. Instead, siRNAs complementary to promoter regions bind to a promoter. Binding blocks the assembly of the preinitiation complex by preventing binding of transcription factor TFIIB and RNA polymerase.

Short RNA molecules can also associate with protein complexes to form RNA-Induced Transcriptional Silencing (RITS) complexes. RITS complexes initiate formation of facultative heterochromatin that silences genes located within these newly created heterochromatic regions. Unlike the heterochromatin at telomeres and centromeres, which is constitutive, the heterochromatic state in facultative heterochromatin is reversible and can be converted to euchromatin, with genes in this region once again accessible for transcription.

In sum, epigenetic modifications alter chromatin structure by several mechanisms including DNA methylation, histone acetylation, and RNA interference, without changing the sequence of DNA. These epigenetic changes create an epigenome that in turn, can regulate normal development or generate responses to environmental signals.

Epigenetics and Imprinting

Mammals inherit a maternal and a paternal copy of each autosomal gene, and either or both copies of these genes can be expressed in the offspring. Imprinted genes show expression of only the maternal allele or the paternal allele. This parent-specific pattern of allele expression is laid down during gamete formation. Differential methylation of CpG-rich regions produce allele-specific imprinting and subsequent gene silencing.

In mice, fewer than 100 genes were thought to be imprinted, but recent work has identified more than 1300 imprinted genes. In humans, more than 150 candidate genes are thought to be imprinted, but the findings in mice suggest that many more imprinted genes remain to be identified in humans.

Once a gene has been methylated and imprinted, it remains transcriptionally silent during embryogenesis and development. Most imprinted genes direct aspects of growth during prenatal development. For example, in mice, genes on the maternal X chromosome are expressed in the placenta, while genes on the paternal X chromosome are silenced. At the level of individual genes, having only one functional allele makes these genes highly susceptible to the deleterious effects of mutations. Because imprinted genes are clustered, mutation in one gene can have an impact on the function of adjacent imprinted genes, amplifying its impact on the phenotype. Mutations in imprinted genes can arise by changes in the DNA sequence or by epigenetic changes, called **epimutations**, both of which are heritable changes in the activity of a gene.

The pattern of imprinting in mammals is reprogrammed every generation. For example, females receive a maternal and a paternal set of chromosomes. In somatic cells and in germ cells, the maternal chromosome set has female imprints, and the paternal set contains male imprints.

When gamete formation begins in female germ cells, both chromosome sets have their imprints erased and are each reprogrammed by changing the pattern of methylation to carry a female imprint pattern that is transmitted to the next generation through the egg (ST Figure 3–5). Similarly, in male germ cells, the paternal and maternal chromosome sets have their imprints erased and are reprogrammed by methylation to become a male imprinted set. Reprogramming occurs at two stages: in the parental germ cells and in the developing embryo just before implantation. In the first stage, erasure by demethylation and reprogramming by remethylation lay down a parent-specific imprinting pattern in germ cells of the parent. In the second stage, large-scale demethylation occurs in the embryo sometime before the 16-cell stage of development. After implantation, differential genomic remethylation recalibrates which maternal alleles and which paternal alleles will be inactivated. It is important to remember that once imprinted, alleles remain inactive in all cells, while genes silenced by epigenetic methylation can be reactivated by external signals during or after differentiation.

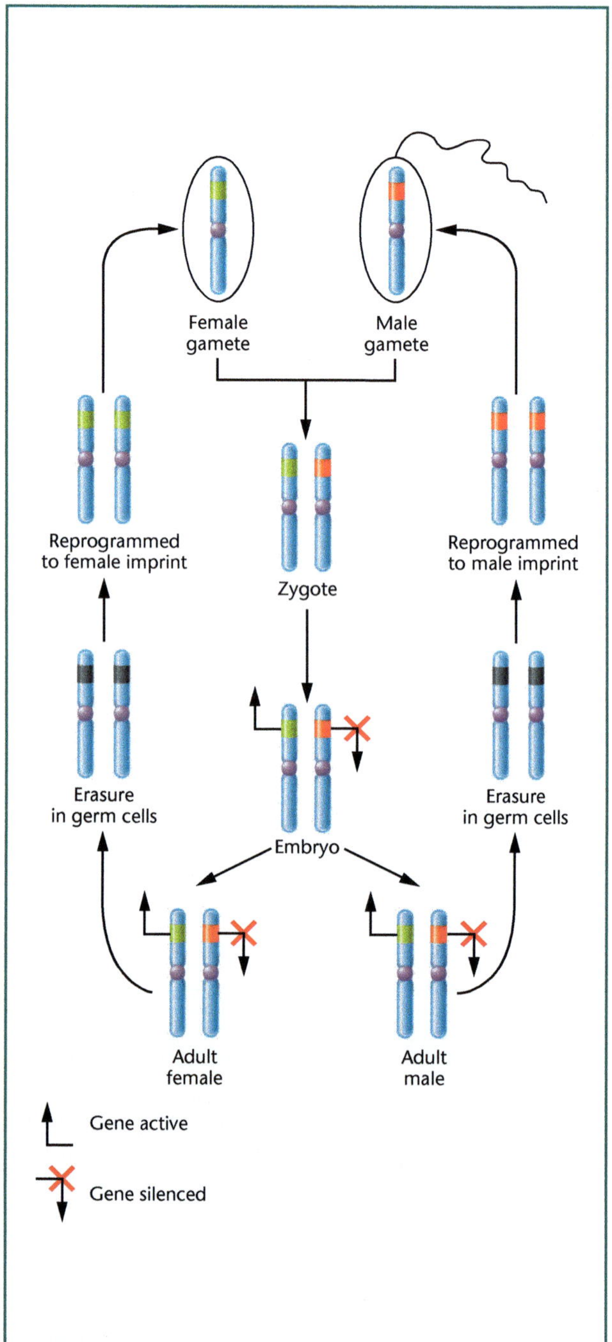

ST FIGURE 3–5 **Imprinting patterns are reprogrammed each generation.**

Most human disorders associated with imprinting have their origins during fetal growth and development. Imprinting defects cause Prader–Willi syndrome, Angelman syndrome, Beckwith–Wiedemann syndrome, and several other diseases (ST Table 3.1). However, given the number of candidate genes and the possibility that additional imprinted genes remain to be discovered, the overall number of imprinting-related genetic disorders may be much higher.

In humans, most known imprinted genes encode growth factors or other growth-regulating genes. Generally, maternally expressed alleles of imprinted genes suppress growth, and paternal alleles enhance growth. One autosomal dominant disorder of imprinting, Beckwith–Wiedemann syndrome (BWS), offers insight into how disruptions of epigenetically imprinted genes lead to an abnormal phenotype. BWS is a prenatal overgrowth disorder with abdominal wall defects, enlarged organs, large birth weight, and predisposition to cancer. BWS is not caused by mutation, nor is it associated with any chromosomal aberration. Instead it is a disorder of imprinting and is caused by abnormal methylation patterns.

Genes linked to BWS are located in a cluster of imprinted genes on the short arm of chromosome 11. This cluster contains more than a dozen imprinted genes, some of which are paternally expressed, while others are maternally expressed and all genes in this cluster regulate growth during prenatal development. The imprinted region is subdivided into two separately regulated domains, one of which contains the closely linked genes *IGF2* (insulin growth factor 2) and *H19*. Normally, the paternal allele of *IGF2* is expressed, and the allele on the maternal homolog is imprinted and silenced. In the case of *H19*, the situation is usually the reverse: The maternal allele is expressed, and the paternal allele is imprinted and silenced. The protein encoded by *IGF2* is a growth factor, and the product of the *H19* gene is a long, noncoding RNA that is a growth repressor. Expression of these genes is normally controlled by an imprinting control region (ICR) located within its chromosomal domain.

ST TABLE 3.1

Some Imprinting Disorders in Humans

Disorder	Locus
Albright hereditary osteodystrophy	20q13
Angelman syndrome	15q11-q15
Beckwith-Wiedemann syndrome	11p15
Prader-Willi syndrome	15q11-q15
Silver-Russell syndrome	Chromosome 7
Uniparental disomy 14	Chromosome 14

Abnormal maternal imprinting in one or both domains can lead to BWS, but many affected individuals have a loss of imprinting of the maternal *IGF2* allele. This causes both the maternal and paternal alleles to be transcriptionally active, resulting in the overgrowth of tissues characteristic of this disease.

The known number of imprinted genes represent only a small fraction of the genome, but they play major roles in controlling growth during embryonic and prenatal development. Because they act so early in life, external or internal factors that disturb the epigenetic pattern of imprinting or the expression of imprinted genes can have serious phenotypic consequences.

Following the introduction of *in vitro* fertilization (IVF) and embryo cloning in the production of farm animals, a high incidence of birth defects and neonatal deaths was noted. Studies showed that many of these problems were linked to abnormal epigenetic alterations during embryonic growth and development. These findings in animals raised the possibility that the use of IVF and other assisted reproductive technologies (ART) in humans may cause problems with imprinted genes.

Several studies have shown that children born after IVF are at risk for low or very low birth weight, a condition that may result from abnormal imprinting. The use of IVF and other ART procedures has also been associated with a three- to six-fold increased risk of Beckwith–Wiedemann syndrome (BWS). One study examined the epigenome of children with BWS who were born after a procedure called intracytoplasmic sperm injection (ICSI), where a single sperm is injected into the oocyte. The results showed that a majority of these children had specific changes in both imprinting and epigenetic patterns of methylation. Other studies have shown that more than 90 percent of children born with BWS after ART had imprinting defects. Because imprinting disorders are uncommon (BWS occurs with a frequency of about 1 in 15,000 births), large-scale and longitudinal studies will be needed to resolve a causal relationship among imprinting abnormalities, growth disorders, and ART.

Epigenetics and Cancer

Epidemiological studies investigate the role of environmental factors in normal phenotypic variation and as risk factors for disease. In many cases it is difficult to obtain quantitative measures of the effects of multidimensional environmental influences on an organism. For some complex diseases, there are strong links with environmental factors such as the association between smoking and lung cancer. The discovery that epigenetics mediates the process of changing patterns of gene expression in response to environmental signals offers a new and potentially more direct approach to understanding the interactions between the genome and the environment in diseases such as cancer.

Following the discovery of cancer-associated genes, including tumor-suppressor genes and proto-oncogenes, research into the genetic basis of cancer focused mainly on mutant alleles of genes involved in several cellular functions, including the cell cycle, differentiation, adhesion, and apoptosis. Until recently, the conventional view has been that cancer is clonal in origin and begins in a cell that has accumulated a suite of dominant and recessive mutations that allow it to escape control of the cell cycle. Subsequent mutations allow cells of the tumor to acquire metastatic properties, and the cancer spreads to other locations in the body where it establishes new malignant tumors. Converging lines of evidence are clarifying the role that epigenetic changes play in the initiation and maintenance of malignancy. These findings help explain properties of cancer cells that are difficult to explain by the action of mutant alleles alone. Evidence for the role of epigenetic changes in cancer now challenges the conventional paradigm for the origin of cancer and establishes epigenomic changes as a major pathway for the formation and spread of malignant cells.

The relationship between epigenetics and cancer was first noted in the 1980s by Feinberg and Vogelstein who observed that colon cancer cells had much lower levels of methylation than normal cells derived from the same tissue. Subsequent research by many investigators showed that global hypomethylation is a property of all cancers examined to date. In the ensuing years, it has become clear that the epigenetic states of normal cells are greatly altered in cancer cells and that other epigenetic changes, including selective hypermethylation and gene silencing, are also present in cancer cells. Cancer is now being viewed as a disease that involves both epigenetic *and* genetic changes that lead to alterations in gene expression (ST Figure 3–6).

DNA hypomethylation reverses the inactivation of genes, leading to unrestricted transcription of many gene sets including oncogenes. It also relaxes control over imprinted genes, causing cells to acquire new growth properties. Hypomethylation of repetitive DNA sequences in

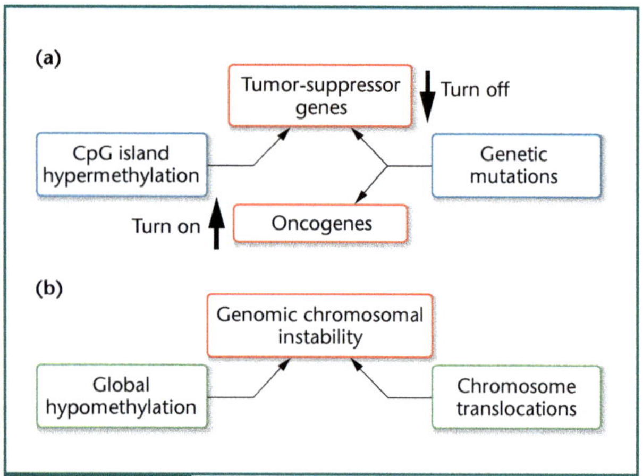

ST FIGURE 3–6 Cancer: epigenetic and mutational changes to the genome.

heterochromatic regions is associated with an increase in chromosome rearrangements and changes in chromosome number, both of which are characteristic of cancer cells. In addition, hypomethylation of repetitive sequences leads to transcriptional activation of transposable DNA sequences such as LINEs and SINEs, further increasing genomic instability.

While widespread hypomethylation is a hallmark of cancer cells, hypermethylation at CpG islands and inactivation of certain genes, including tumor-suppressor genes (ST Table 3.2), are also found in many cancers, often in a tumor-specific pattern. For example *BRCA1* is hypermethylated and inactivated in breast and ovarian cancer, and *MLH1* is hypermethylated in some forms of colon cancer. Inactivation of tumor-suppressor genes by hypermethylation is thought to play an important complementary role to mutational changes that accompany the transformation of normal cells into malignant cells. For example, in a bladder cancer cell line, one allele of the cell cycle control gene *CDKN2A* is mutated, and the other, normal allele is inactivated by hypermethylation of its CpG island. The inactivation of both alleles allows these cells to escape control of the cell cycle and divide continuously. In many clinical cases, the combination of mutation and hypermethylation occurs in familial forms of cancer.

ST TABLE 3.2

Some Cancer-Related Genes Inactivated by Hypermethylation in Human Cancers

Gene	Locus	Function	Related Cancers
BRCA1	17q21	DNA repair	Breast, ovarian
APC	5q21	Nucleo-cytoplasmic signaling	Colorectal, duodenal
MLH1	3p21	DNA repair	Colon, stomach
RB1	13q14	Cell-cycle control point	Retinoblastoma, osteosarcoma
AR	Xq11-12	Nuclear receptor for androgen; transcriptional activator	Prostate
ESR1	6q25	Nuclear receptor for estrogen; transcriptional activator	Breast, colorectal

However, genes other than tumor-suppressor genes are also hypermethylated in some cancer cells; these include genes that control or participate in DNA repair, differentiation, apoptosis, and drug resistance. In fact, the majority of hypermethylated genes in cancer cells are not tumor-suppressor genes, suggesting that the pattern of hypermethylation may result from a widespread deregulation of the methylation process rather than a targeted event.

In addition to altered patterns of methylation, many cancer cells also have disrupted histone modification profiles. In some cases, mutations in the genes encoding members of the histone-modifying proteins histone acetyltransferase (HAT) and histone deacetylase (HDAC) are linked to the development of cancer. For example, those affected with Rubenstein–Taybi syndrome inherit a germ-line mutation that produces a dysfunctional HAT and have a greater than 300-fold increased risk of cancer. In other cases, HDAC complexes are selectively recruited to tumor-suppressor genes by mutated, oncogenic DNA binding proteins. Action of the HDAC complexes at these genes converts the chromatin to a closed configuration and inhibits transcription, causing the cell to lose control of the cell cycle.

The mechanisms that cause epigenetic changes in cancer cells are not known, partly because they take place very early in the conversion of a normal cell to a cancerous one, and partly because by the time the cancer is detected, alterations in the methylation pattern have already occurred. The fact that such changes occur very early in the transformation process has led to the proposal that initiating epigenetic changes leading to cancer may occur in stem cells residing in normal tissue. Three lines of evidence support this idea. First, epigenetic mechanisms can replace mutations as a way of silencing individual tumor-suppressor genes or activating oncogenes. Second, global hypomethylation may cause genomic instability and the large-scale chromosomal changes that are a characteristic feature of cancer. Third, because epigenetic modifications can silence multiple genes, they are more effective than serial mutations of single genes in transforming normal cells into malignant cells. A model of cancer based on epigenetic changes in colon stem cells as

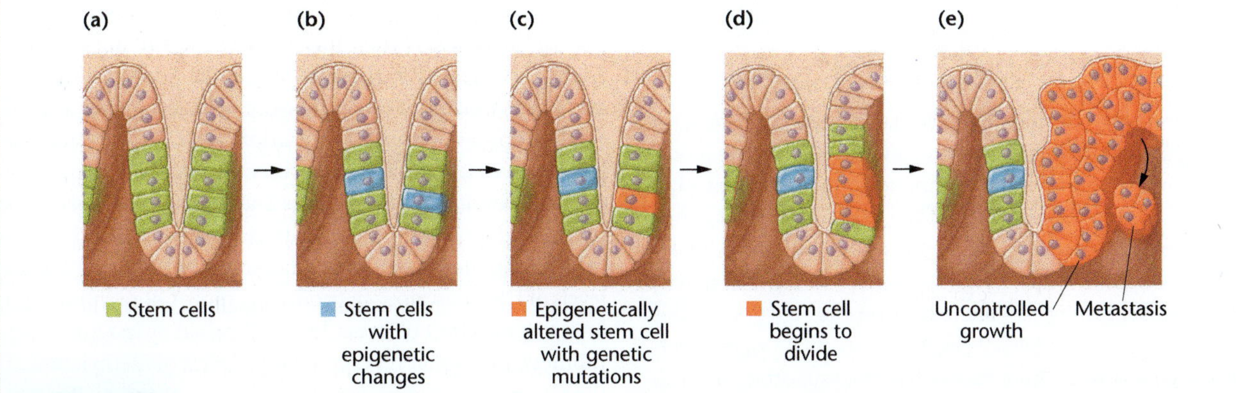

ST FIGURE 3–7 Epigenetic stem cell model proposes that both epigenetic changes and mutations are involved in the origins of cancer.

initiating events in carcinogenesis followed by mutational events is shown in ST Figure 3–7

In addition to changing ideas about the origins of cancer, the fact that epigenetic changes are potentially reversible makes the development of therapeutic drugs for cancer treatment a possible new approach to chemotherapy. The focus of epigenetic therapy is the reactivation of genes that have been silenced by methylation or histone modification, essentially reprogramming the pattern of gene expression in cancer cells. Several drugs for altering epigenetic genome modifications are in clinical trials, and one (decitabine, marketed as Vidaza) has been approved by the U.S. Food and Drug Administration for treatment of acute myeloid leukemia and myelodysplastic syndrome, a precursor to leukemia. This drug is an analog of cytidine and is incorporated into DNA during replication during the S phase of the cell cycle. Methylation enzymes (methyltransferases) bind irreversibly to decitabine, preventing methylation of DNA at many other sites, effectively reducing the amount of methylation in cancer cells. Other drugs that inhibit histone deacetylases (HDAC) are also being investigated for use in epigenetic therapy. Experiments with cancer cell lines indicate that inhibiting HDAC activity results in the reexpression of tumor-suppressor genes. One HDAC inhibitor now in clinical trials may be approved for the treatment of some forms of lymphoma. Further research into the mechanisms and locations of epigenetic genome modification in cancer cells will allow the design of more potent specific drugs to target epigenetic events as a form of cancer therapy.

BOX 2

What More We Need to Know about Epigenetics and Cancer

The discovery that epigenetic changes may be as important as genetic changes in the origin, maintenance, and metastasis of cancers has opened new avenues of cancer research. Key discoveries about epigenetic mechanisms include the finding of tumor-specific deregulation of genes by altered DNA methylation profiles and histone modifications, the discovery that epigenetic changes in histones or DNA methylation are interconnected, and the recognition that epigenetic changes can affect hundreds of genes in a single cancer cell. These advances were made in the span of a few years, and while it is clear that epigenetics plays a key role in cancer, many questions remain to be answered before we can draw conclusions about the relative contributions of genetics and epigenetics to the development of cancer. Some of these questions are as follows:

- Is global hypomethylation in cancer cells a cause or effect of the malignant condition?
- Do these changes arise primarily in stem cells or in differentiated cells?
- Once methylation alterations begin, what triggers hypermethylation in cancer cells?
- Is hypermethylation a process that targets certain gene classes, or is it a random event?
- Can we develop drugs that target cancer cells and reverse tumor-specific epigenetic changes?
- Can we target specific genes for reactivation, while leaving others inactive?

Epigenetics and Behavior

A growing body of evidence shows that epigenetic changes, including alterations in methylation patterns, and histone modification may be important components of behavioral phenotypes. In mice, two regions of the brain show preferential expression of parental genes. In one of these (the hypothalamus), sex-specific imprinting was more prominent in female offspring, suggesting parental effects on the function of this brain region in daughters. Altogether, parent-of-origin effects have been shown in more than 800 genes, supporting the idea that imprinting in different regions of the brain may represent a major form of epigenetic regulation.

In humans, epigenetic changes have been documented in the progression of neurodegenerative disorders and neuropsychiatric diseases with altered behavioral phenotypes. Epigenetic changes in the nervous system have been documented in cases of Alzheimer disease, Parkinson's disease, Huntington disease, and neuropsychiatric diseases including schizophrenia and bipolar disorder. Because the appearance of these disorders involves genetic predispositions, events in development, environmental effects, and the existence of transgenerational epigenetic effects, it has been difficult to define the precise role of epigenomic changes in neural disorders. In addition, different brain regions in unaffected individuals show different epigenetic profiles, adding a layer of complexity to the interpretation of results. Perhaps the most relevant problem is the difficulty of obtaining brain tissue for analysis. Most of the data on epigenetic alterations have been derived from samples obtained at autopsy, a situation that makes it impossible to directly correlate these alterations with the origin or progression of these disorders. However, in spite of these difficulties, there is enough evidence to suggest that in the future, epigenetics should be considered as part of the diagnosis and treatment of complex neural disorders.

One of the fastest-growing and perhaps most controversial theories related to epigenomics concerns the idea that epigenetic alterations linked to environmental signals during development or early in life influence behavior (and physical health) later in adult life. One of the first studies in behavioral epigenomics, published by Szyf and Meaney and their colleagues in 2004, showed that variations in rat maternal behavior act as epigenators, changing the way the way the pup's brain responds to stress during adulthood. Mice with nurturing mothers adapted better to stressful situations than mice that received little or no nurturing. In rats and humans, stress activates the hypothalamic-pituitary-adrenal (HPA) axis, which dampens the reaction to stress by increasing glucocorticoid levels in the blood.

In adult rats that experienced nurturing care early in life, expression of glucocorticoid receptors (GR) on cells in the hypothalamic region of the brain is increased. These receptors sense levels of glucocorticoids in the blood and are part of the feedback loop that reduces the amount of stress hormones released by the adrenal glands. Adult rats that received less nurturing care as newborns have a higher level of methylation and reduced transcription of the GR receptor gene. Lower levels of the GR receptor do not dampen the stress response in these rats. Rats that experienced high levels of care had 90 percent less methylation at a transcription factor binding site in the GR promoter region, allowing higher levels of GR transcription, producing more GR receptors and lowering the effect of stress. In adults raised by less nurturing mothers, drugs that reverse the high levels of methylation at the GR promoter allow enhanced GR transcription. This, in turn, reversed the effect of poor early-life nurturing and lowered the response to stress. Later work showed that female rats raised by more nurturing mothers are more attentive to their own pups, showing the role of epigenetic maintainers in transmitting these changes to offspring.

Following this research, other studies in rats and mice showed that environments experienced by pregnant animals or newborns affected the behavior and health of the offspring as adults. These experiments also showed that these behavioral changes were mediated by epigenetic methylation of DNA and modification of histones that alter chromatin configuration leading to altered levels of gene expression.

The question of whether these findings can be extrapolated to humans has become a source of some controversy. It has been established that adversity early in life, such as child abuse, increases the risk of depression and suicide. Can epigenetics be involved? In humans, there is little or no direct evidence that epigenetic changes in the brain early in life affect behavior later in life. For example, some studies show a correlation between low economic status (childhood poverty) and heart disease in adulthood. The question is whether epigenetic changes are involved in these and similar situations. Because it is not possible to obtain and analyze brain samples from individuals at intervals from infancy through adulthood, researchers have used other sources for material, including cord blood and white blood cells. Results using these cell types have been inconclusive at best. Whether epigenetic changes can be invoked as an explanation for the role of environmental conditions in adult behavior and disease will depend on results from work using the target human tissues, not by extrapolating findings from experimental animals or studies using surrogate cell types.

Epigenetics and the Environment

Environmental agents including nutrition, chemicals, and physical factors such as temperature can alter gene expression by affecting the epigenetic state of the genome. In humans it is difficult to determine the relative contributions of environmental or learned behavior as factors in changing the epigenome, but there is evidence that changes in nutrition and exposure to agents that affect the endocrine system can have effects on individuals in subsequent generations.

Women who were pregnant during the 1944–1945 famine in the Netherlands had children with increased risk of obesity, diabetes, and coronary heart disease, and members of the F2 generation also had abnormal patterns of weight gain and growth. In the United States, the drug diethylstilbestrol (DES) was prescribed for several decades to women in the belief that it would prevent complications of pregnancy and miscarriages. After it was discovered that girls and young women who were exposed to DES during prenatal development have a 40-fold increased risk of vaginal cancer, and are also at higher risk for breast cancer, use of the drug was discontinued. Males exposed to DES *in utero* have no identifiable physical problems or risk factors, but may have neurological and behavioral alterations. In addition, children of women who took DES have an increased risk of having children with birth defects, irregular menstrual periods, and a higher than normal frequency of infertility. Epigenetic modification of patterns of gene expression in embryogenesis can be invoked to explain the transgenerational transmission of these developmental problems. For the present, however, this is a questionable explanation because there is no direct evidence linking DES to epigenetic changes.

The clearest evidence for the role of environmental factors in epigenetic modifications comes from studies in experimental animals. A reduced protein diet fed to rats during pregnancy results in permanent changes in the expression of several genes in the F1 and F2 offspring. Increased expression of liver genes is associated with hypomethylation of their respective promoter regions, and other evidence indicates that epigenetic changes triggered by this diet modification were gene-specific.

In mice, coat color is controlled by the dominant allele *Agouti* (*A*). In homozygous *AA* mice, the allele is active only during a specific time during hair development, producing a yellow band on an otherwise black hair shaft, resulting in the agouti phenotype. A nonlethal mutant allele (A^{vy}) causes yellow pigment formation along the entire hair shaft, producing a yellow fur color. This allele is the result of the insertion of a transposable element near the transcription start site of the *Agouti* gene. A promoter element within the transposon is responsible for this change in gene expression. The degree of methylation in the transposon's promoter is related to the amount of yellow pigment deposited in the hair shaft and varies from individual to individual. The result is a wide variation in coat color in genetically identical mice (ST Figure 3–8), ranging from yellow (unmethylated) to pseudoagouti (highly methylated). In addition to a gradation in coat color, there is also a gradation in body weight. Yellow mice are more obese than the brown, pseudoagouti

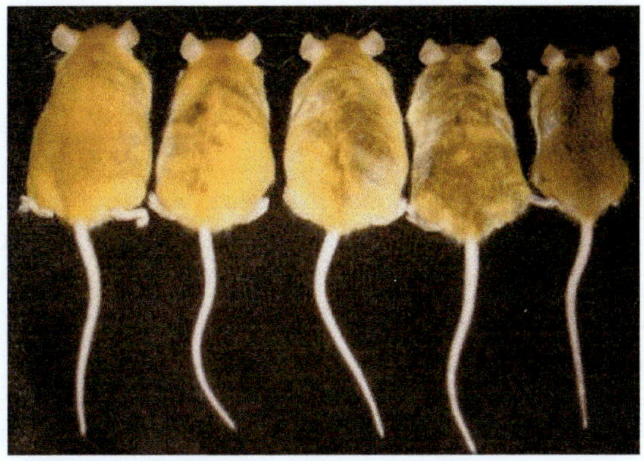

ST FIGURE 3–8 Variable expression of yellow phenotype in mice caused by diet-related epigenetic changes in the genome.

mice. Alleles such as A^{vy} that show variable expression from individual to individual in genetically identical strains caused by epigenetic modifications are called *metastable epialleles.* Metastable refers to the changeable nature of the epigenetic modifications, and epiallele refers to the heritability of the epigenetic status of the allele.

To evaluate the role of environmental factors in modifying the epigenome, the diet of pregnant mice was supplemented with methylation precursors, including folic acid, vitamin B_{12}, and choline. In the offspring, variation in coat color was reduced and shifted toward the pseudoagouti phenotype. The shift in coat color was accompanied by increased methylation of the transposon's promoter. Methylation profiles in the A^{vy} allele from tissues representing the three major cell types in the body (ectoderm, mesoderm, and endoderm) were also altered, showing that methylation at the A^{vy} allele occurred very early in embryonic development, before differentiation of the embryonic stem cells. These findings have applications to epigenetic diseases in humans. For example, the risk of colorectal cancer is linked directly to folate dietary deficiency and activity differences in enzymes leading to the synthesis of methyl donors.

Epigenome Projects

We conclude by discussing several projects that are underway to map the human epigenome, including the NIH Roadmap Epigenomics Project. This undertaking is based on the idea that many aspects of health and susceptibility to disease are related to epigenetic regulation or misregulation of gene activity. The program is focused on how epigenetic mechanisms controlling stem cell differentiation and organ formation generate biological responses to external and internal stimuli that result in disease. The Human Epigenome Atlas is one program of the NIH Roadmap Project. The atlas collects and catalogs data on a set of human epigenomes to serve as reference standards; it is being used to provide detailed information about epigenomic modifications at specific loci, cell types, physiological states, as well as genotypes. This atlas allows researchers to perform integrative and comparative analysis of epigenomic data across genomic regions or entire genomes.

Another project, called the Human Epigenome Project, is a multinational, public/private consortium established to identify, map, and establish the functional significance of all DNA methylation patterns in the human genome. Analysis of these methylation patterns may show that genetic responses to environmental cues mediated by epigenetic changes are a pathway to disease. Even as these projects are in their early stages of growth, the information already available strongly suggests that we are on the threshold of a new era in genetics, one in which we can study the impact of environmental factors on the genome at the molecular level. The results of these projects may help explain how environmental settings in early life can affect predisposition to adulthood diseases.

Selected Readings and Resources

Journal Articles

Burdge, G.C., and Lillicrop, K.A. 2010. Nutrition, epigenetics, and developmental plasticity: implications for understanding human disease. *Ann. Rev. Nutr.* 30: 315–339.

Butler, M.G. 2009. Genomic imprinting disorders in humans: a mini-review. *J. Assist. Reprod. Genet.* 20: 477–486.

Dulac, C. 2010. Brain function and chromatin plasticity. *Nature* 465: 728–735.

Iacobuzio-Donahue, C.A. 2009. Epigenetic changes in cancer. *Ann. Rev.* Pathol. Mech. Dis. 4: 229–249.

Petronis, A. 2010. Epigenetics as a unifying principle in the aetiology of complex traits and diseases. *Nature* 465: 721–727.

Relton, C.L., and Smith, G.D. 2010. Epigenetic epidemiology of common complex disease: prospects for prediction, prevention, and treatment. *PLoS Medicine* 7: (10) e1000356.

Web Sites

National Institutes of Health Roadmap for Epigenomics. http://www.nihroadmap.nih.gov/epigenomics/initiatives.asp

Human Epigenome Project. www.epigenome.org

Human Epigenome Atlas. http://www.genboree.org/epigenomeatlas/index.rhtml

Computational Epigenetics Group. http://www.computational-epigenetics.de